DATE DUE

A Companion to Post-War British Theatre

A COMPANION TO POST-WAR BRITISH THEATRE

Philip Barnes

BARNES & NOBLE BOOKS
Totowa, New Jersey

First published in the USA by
Barnes & Noble Books
81 Adams Drive
Totowa, New Jersey, 07512
Printed in Great Britain

Library of Congress Cataloging-in-Publication Data

Barnes, Philip.
A companion to post-war British theatre.

Includes index.
1. Theater — Great Britain — History — 20th century.
2. English drama — 20th century — History and criticism.
I. Title.
PN2595.B28 1986 792'.0941 86-17367
ISBN 0-389-20669-5

Contents

Introduction 3

A Companion to Post-War British Theatre 9

Title-Author Index 270

To Polly, Matthew and Tristan

It seems to me that while the politicians live
on the differences and hostilities of mankind,
the artists live on our common humanity, and
that may be why, in the cause of peace, money
spent on the theatre and on the arts is better
spent than money spent on all the machines for
mutual obliteration ever invented.

John Mortimer, *London Standard*,
Drama Awards Ceremony, 1983

A Companion to Post-War British Theatre

Introduction

Are we entering into another Elizabethan Age? There are indications of a glowing renaissance in Britain of culture and invention.

(Hannen Swaffer, 1944)[1]

The English Theatre possesses a long and inspiring tradition and has had many periods of historic grandeur. Perhaps no other moment has approached in splendour and achievement the glorious Restoration Period, when many notable talents and much vitality and enthusiasm were involved in the rebirth of our theatre. That is, no other moment until now.

(Laurence Olivier, 1946)[2]

Whilst such prophetic insights were very much a product of the joyous atmosphere of victory and the social and political hopes for the rebuilding of Britain after the Second World War, these two statements nevertheless anticipated the burgeoning of theatre in Britain in the post-war period remarkably accurately. There has indeed been a 'renaissance', a 'rebirth' of the theatre art comparable to those other two pulses in the rhythms of British culture, the Elizabethan and Restoration periods.[3] This is the major motivation behind the present compilation of a work of reference confined solely to the theatre in post-war Britain. Although many countries since the war have been close runners to the British achievement (France in particular), it remains artistically unique in the world.

There are many approaches to understanding and mapping the theatre history of the post-war years in Britain, some limiting themselves to the emergence of new writers and their plays, others emphasising experiments in the performance and staging of both old and new works, still others exploring the relationship of the new theatre to social and political change.

Two common arguments, the second countering the first, which have emerged in criticism and theatre history are worth mention. The first proposes that 'the event which marks "then" off decisively from "now" is the first performance of *Look Back in Anger* on 8th May 1956'.[4] It is a view which sees 1956 as an *annus mirabilis*,[5] a watershed, largely brought about through one sensational neo-naturalistic play (staged at the Royal Court Theatre by George Devine's English Stage Company) by a courageous playwright of the younger generation, John Osborne. From this point grows the *nouvelle vague* of socialist writers who were contemporaries of Osborne and were grouped together under the journalistic label of 'The Angry Young Men': Arnold Wesker, John Arden, Willis Hall, and a number of novelists and film-makers.

A second view tends to focus on the less sensational, and certainly less known or popular, experimental theatre which emerged in the years immediately following the war — thus providing a counter-argument to the focus on 1956. Here the emphasis is placed much more upon innovation in dramatic form and theatrical presentation and includes the influence of foreign drama on the British Theatre. Another avant-garde can be identified. The Group Theatre, which had explored the possibilities of bare staging in the years before the war and had presented experimental verse drama such as T.S. Eliot's *Sweeney Agonistes* (Westminster Theatre, October 1935, written 1926) and W.H. Auden and Christopher Isherwood's *The Dog Beneath the Skin* (Westminster, January 1936) and *The Ascent of F6* (Little Theatre,

April 1937), re-formed in 1950 for a further three years and presented, among other works, Jean Paul Sartre's *Les Mouches* in London.[6] Eliot continued his experiments in verse drama with three plays first performed at the Edinburgh Festival, and Christopher Fry wrote verse dramas. In the decade before *Look Back in Anger* the British Theatre also had its share of plays associated with a growing anti-naturalistic stance, the genre Martin Esslin was later to call the 'Theatre of the Absurd'.[7] In the second half of the 1940s the Arts Theatre, the Lyric (Hammersmith), and St Martin's Theatre all presented plays by Sartre and in 1955 the Arts Theatre presented Ionesco's *The Lesson* in March and Samuel Beckett's *Waiting for Godot* in August (in a production directed by Peter Hall). This largely French influence (Beckett wrote in French originally and translated into English, *Waiting for Godot* being first performed as *En Attendant Godot* in January 1953 in Paris) created an aesthetic which provided a different line of development from the socialist-naturalists in the second half of the 1950s. It was the line taken up by N.F. Simpson briefly but which also produced one of Britain's most distinguished playwrights, Harold Pinter, whose work, unlike Beckett's, manipulates the naturalistic *towards* the 'absurd'.

Yet other experiments with form and presentation were explored by Joan Littlewood, who had founded the Manchester Theatre of Action in 1933 and later the Theatre Union (with Ewan MacColl). She set up her Theatre Workshop company in Manchester in 1945 which (after British and foreign tours) moved to the Theatre Royal, Stratford East, London, in 1953. In addition to many adventurous productions of classics the company also staged the first British production of Bertolt Brecht's *Mother Courage and her Children* (Devon Festival, Barnstaple, June 1955, with Littlewood in the title-role). To these developments must be added the visit of the Berliner Ensemble to the Palace Theatre in August 1956 (with productions of Brecht's *Mother Courage, Trumpets and Drums* and *The Caucasian Chalk Circle*), Ann Jellicoe's founding of the Cockpit Theatre Club in 1951 to experiment with open stage productions, John Whiting's explorations of allegorical theatre in *Saint's Day* (Arts Theatre Club, September 1951) and *Marching Song* (St Martin's, April 1954), and Alan Simpson's founding of the Pike Theatre, Dublin, in 1953 where experiments in script evolution helped produce Behan's *The Quare Fellow* in November 1954,[8] later developed further by Theatre Workshop (Stratford East, May 1956).

These two maps of British theatre in the first decade after the war may at first seem to provide us with two sides of the same coin — content orientated and form-orientated emphases which taken together make a neat whole. However, cultural history never quite works in such a binary way, through a simple dialectical logic and synthesis of forces, but is more of a lattice-work of many and diverse forces at work simultaneously and as a product of what has gone before (culture, like language, being viewed both 'synchronically' and 'diachronically'[9]). All forms are mutable too, so that to 'fix' individual playwrights and their works, or modes of presentation into catalogues of like endeavour is to deny artistic growth and change, the very vitality of art, in that it must constantly ask questions about itself and break with established conventions and received ideas about what art may be. If one enjoys playing the game of 'influences' it is obvious that Osborne's second play *The Entertainer* (Royal Court, April 1957) is a less naturalistic play than *Look Back in Anger*, more of a popular entertainment (the music-hall elements are important structural components), and very much more akin to Brechtian theatre than its predecessor. John Arden's plays, Shelagh Delaney's *A Taste of Honey* (first performed by Theatre Workshop in 1958) and Theatre Workshop's *Oh! What a Lovely War* (1963) all show to some degree the growing influences of Brecht on British drama. This, together with Antonin Artaud's influence upon directors such as Peter Brook and Charles Marowitz, and the influences of Beckett and the French 'absurdists', tended to push the narrative structures of plays and their modes of presentation in many different directions as the new theatre developed.

Although *Look Back in Anger* remains very much a period-piece, a cultural record of a restless impatience with Establishment values in the early years of post-war Britain, and is a piece of theatrical history in itself because of the space it created for a more broadly-based, open and confident relationship between drama and society, there were, as I have briefly traced out, many other radical experiments, often relatively unnoticed at the time and occurring before 1956, which were pushing the aesthetic of the performed play beyond conventional practices.

It was, however, these very conventional practices (of the 'well-made play',[10] for example) which permitted playwrights such as Terence Rattigan and William Douglas Home to create popular plays that could fill theatres, and these too are as much a part of what we should understand as Post-War British Theatre as the 'new' drama. Another vital part of any theatre scene is the revival of classics and old plays in new interpretations. In this respect the work of many companies, such as the Old Vic Company in the early 1950s, must also be seen as an important dimension of the post-war theatre.[11]

There have been other developments which justify the limitation of the present book to Britain, the chief of which was the growth in Britain of a number of independent 'fringe' theatre groups towards the end of the 1960s and the beginning of the 1970s which produced a 'second wave' of dramatists, such as Howard Brenton, John McGrath, Howard Barker, David Hare and Trevor Griffiths, who evolved forms of politically committed drama which provided a fresh and radical energy for the theatre as well as a 'people's theatre'[12] as an alternative to the established theatres of the provinces and West End. Some of the most important of these companies, many of which are still in existence today, are the *Joint Stock Theatre Group*, the *Portable Theatre Company*, the *Pip Simmons Theatre Group* (disbanded 1974), *Ken Campbell's Roadshow, 7:84 Theatre Company (England and Scotland), The Belt and Braces Roadshow Company Ltd*, *Shared Experience* and *Welfare State.*[13] Some, like the last mentioned, have developed community events and happenings, whilst others such as the *Joint Stock Theatre Group* and *Shared Experience*, have developed original plays through collective improvisation in rehearsals. The 1960s and 1970s also saw the emergence of a number of uniquely individual playwrights of stature, including Robert Bolt, Joe Orton, Edward Bond, Tom Stoppard, Peter Shaffer, James Saunders, David Storey, Charles Wood and Peter Nichols, and there have been many playwrights who have written successfully for both stage and television, such as Alan Plater, David Mercer and Dennis Potter. Meanwhile Pinter, Wesker, Osborne and Arden have taken their writing in new directions.

In reading such maps many of the entries on playwrights for this compilation simply selected themselves but I also felt that the current debates about the extent to which performances of plays in the theatre should be dominated by the writer, actor or director ('playwrights' theatre', 'actors' theatre' or 'directors' theatre') ought to be reflected, however modestly, in my selection.[14] In the belief that actors and actresses are as much creative artists as the playwrights whose work they realise, and that beyond the final dress rehearsal they have a greater responsibility for the play than a director because it is they who perform the act of theatre itself,[15] I have placed my emphasis upon playwrights, actors and actresses. Nevertheless some of the directors who have most importantly influenced the development of theatre in post-war Britain, such as Peter Brook and Peter Hall, have been included. I also felt that students of the theatre, and many theatre-goers, would appreciate some entries on useful critical categories and on theatre terminology.

Compilers of reference works all have their nightmares over who and what should be selected for final inclusion. Beyond the sheer limitations of space my major difficulties have arisen in the choice of actors and actresses. Some, like the generation of Olivier, Gielgud, Richardson and Evans, appear by a process of natural selection, whilst others, such as those of McKellen, Rigg and Suzman's generation have been included on the basis of both an acclaimed reputation and the degree to which they have contributed to the theatre over a range of activities. Still others have been chosen because they are of the young rising generation of talent (Sher, Branagh, etc.) who have quickly made an impact on the public either originally through television or purely in the live theatre. Some, of all generations, have been included because they have become 'household names' through films, television, and the stage. Lastly, I have exercised the right to include some personal predilections. In all cases I have been guided by the principle that for the purpose of this project 'theatre' is taken to mean the live stage performance of plays (not ballet and opera) and that it is this species of drama that the book must serve. I have nevertheless included selective lists of film and television work.

I am only too conscious that every user of this book will find eccentricities of inclusion and omission. However, no such work can include everybody and everything. This compilation inevitably reflects one writer's view of post-war theatre in Britain. One of my chief reasons for writing it has been to update and bring together into one volume information which is diffused in reference works covering continental drama or world drama, all periods of the theatre or only part of the post-war period, or playwrights but not actors. I also wanted to provide simple introductory 'whetstones' (albeit selective in themselves) for more extensive study, and to this end I have supplied details of further reading (for which many of the books contain more extensive bibliographical information) at the end of most of the entries. Included within entries on playwrights are indications of the content and presentational form of the chief plays, and I have mixed published critical statement with my own. As far as possible I have also tried to include playwrights', actors' and directors' statements about their own craft. In order to provide greater detail than programme notes and many books covering the period, most entries give the venue and month, in addition to the year, of production.

No compiler of a book about this period of British theatre could do the job without a number of major sources from which to work. I have found the following particularly useful: the 17th edition of *Who's Who in the Theatre* (1981), Joseph Loney's *Twentieth Century Theatre* (1983), James Vinson's *Contemporary Dramatists* (1977 and 1982 edns), *Plays and Players* (an indispensable journal for anyone wishing to keep abreast of current events in British theatre or wishing to research the recent past), *The London Theatre Record* (issued fortnightly ever since 1981), Phyllis Hartnoll's *The Oxford Companion to the Theatre* (4th edn, 1983), *Theatre Quarterly, A Handbook of Contemporary Drama* (1972) by Michael Anderson *et al.*, and the *Directory of Playwrights, Directors and Designers 1* (1983), edited by Catherine Itzin.

Other useful but more general, historical or critical works include John Elsom, *Post-War British Theatre* (1976), Ronald Hayman, *British Theatre Since 1955: a Reassessment* (1979), Arnold Hinchliffe, *British Theatre 1950/70* (1974), John Russell Taylor, *Anger and After* (1962 and 1983) and *The Second Wave* (1971 and 1978), Charles Marowitz *et al.* (eds), *New Theatre Voices of the Fifties and Sixties* (1981) which contains selections from *Encore* magazine 1956-63, Simon Trussler (ed.), *New Theatre Voices of the Seventies* (1981) which is a selection of interviews from *Theatre Quarterly* 1970-80, Ronald Hayman, *Playback 1* and *Playback 2* (1973), Laurence Kitchin, *Mid-Century Drama* (1962) and *Drama in the Sixties* (1966), Harold Hobson, *Theatre in Britain* (1984), Katherine Worth, *Revolutions in Modern English Drama* (1973), Terry Browne, *Playwright's Theatre: The English Stage Company at the Royal Court* (1975), Peter Ansorge, *Disrupting the Spectacle: Five Years of Experimental and Fringe Theatre* (1975), Peter Roberts, *Theatre in Britain* (1975 edn), Michael Anderson, *Anger and Detachment* (1976), Frederick Lumley, *New Trends in Twentieth Century Drama* (1967), Oleg Kerensky, *The New British Drama: Fourteen Playwrights Since Osborne and Pinter* (1977), Benedict Nightingale, *An Introduction to Fifty Modern British Plays* (1982), John Russell Brown, *A Short Guide to Modern British Drama* (1982), Ronald Hayman, *Artaud and After* (1977), Judith Cook, *Directors' Theatre* (1974) and John Russell Brown (ed.), *Modern British Dramatists* (1968). One of the most stimulating essays on the period is Christopher Bigsby's 'The Language of Crisis in British Theatre: The Drama of Cultural Pathology', contained in the very useful collection of essays (edited by Bigsby) *Contemporary English Drama* (1981). Bigsby's analysis of the socio-economic backgrounds of contemporary playwrights and his discussion of the place of women writers in the theatre are both interesting and important.

For the more substantial quotations in the book I should like to acknowledge the permission of Brevet Publishing (UK) Ltd, St James Press, Professor J.C. Trewin, Methuen, London Ltd, A.D. Peters and Co. Ltd, Professor Laurence Kitchin, Hamish Hamilton Ltd, Phaidon Press Ltd, Pan Books Ltd, Manchester University Press, Penguin Books Ltd, Edward Arnold Ltd, and Basil Blackwell (Oxford). I could not possibly mention all those people who have given freely and generously of their time in order to help me in the writing of this book but I would be failing in my duty if I did not make special mention of Dr Frank Fricker, retired Head of the Department of English, Christ Church College, Canterbury, who diligently read the typescript and made invaluable corrections and suggestions to the extent that in places this book is almost as much his as it is mine, and Professor Harold Brooks, who not only read the typescript but also gave me the benefit of his memories, totally undiminished by his longevity, of productions he witnessed before I was born or was old enough to attend the adult theatre. I should also like to thank John Mortimer QC, Dr David Bradby of the University of Kent, Terence Wheeler, Bryan Podmore, John Miles-Brown, John Marshall and the Principal and Governors of Christ Church College, Canterbury, and my wife Polly who patiently typed the manuscript whilst maintaining her far more important philoprogenitive activities.

Notes

Bold type has been used for cross-referencing. Unless otherwise stated a date given in brackets following the title of a play refers to its first performance, not the date of publication.

1. Hannen Swaffer, *The Daily Herald*, October, 1944.
2. Laurence Olivier, 'Foreword' to Peter Noble, *British Theatre*, British Yearbooks, London, 1946.
3. Graham Greene wrote that we were heading for 'a world so new and changed it may well be that in the theatre it will seem as though Elizabeth were on the throne again', *Impressions of Literature*, 'Dramatists', 1944, earlier published in W.J. Turner's *Britain in Pictures* series of wartime volumes.
4. John Russell Taylor, *Anger and After*, 2nd (revised) edn, Methuen, London, 1983, p. 9.
5. See Arnold P. Hinchliffe, *British Theatre 1950-70*, Basil Blackwell, Oxford, 1974, Chapter 4; and Irving Wardle, 'Twenty-Five Years Back', *Drama*, Vol. 2, 2nd Quarter, 1981, pp. 5-7 for a useful discussion of this view.
6. See Michael Sidnell, *Dances of Death*, Faber and Faber, London, 1985 for a detailed account of the work of the Group Theatre.
7. Martin Esslin, *The Theatre of the Absurd* (1961), 3rd edn, Methuen, London, 1983.
8. In his 'Introduction' to *Behan: the Complete Plays*, Methuen, 1978, Alan Simpson gives a detailed account of the history of the variant texts which developed. He also comments: 'it will be remembered that this was two years before the arrival of the kitchen sink and the dustbin in respectable theatres round the world'.
9. See Ferdinand de Saussure, *Course in General Linguistics* (1915), trans. W. Baskin, Fontana/Collins, Glasgow, 1974.
10. See John Russell Taylor, *The Rise and Fall of the Well-Made Play*, Methuen, London, 1967.
11. As John Gielgud put it in 1959: 'The classics, it seems to me, have to be rediscovered every ten years or so ...

at each decade there is a sort of different note in the air. One must find it. When he has found it, he re-interprets the text.' See Ronald Hayman, *Playback*, Davis-pointer Ltd, London, 1973.

12. See David Bradby and John McCormick, *People's Theatre*, Croom Helm Ltd, London, 1978.

13. A full list of such companies can be found in Catherine Itzin (ed.), *The British Alternative Theatre Directory*, John Offord Publications, Eastbourne, published annually.

14. See Simon Trussler, 'Unfair to Actors?' *Royal Shakespeare Company 1982/83*, RSC Publications, Stratford-upon-Avon, 1983, pp. 6-7; and Simon Callow, *Being an Actor*, Methuen, London, 1984. In 'The Glory Boys', *Plays and Players*, August 1985, Al Senter stated: 'The spirit of self-help is in the air and the renaissance of the Actors' company at the National [McKellen and Petherbridge's company] may be echoed elsewhere. Actors are organising themselves, often in spite of their competitive spirit, the distinctions between the main elements of the theatrical process — actor, writer, designer — are increasingly blurred.'

15. Bill Gaskill writes, 'the first night is like *death* — it's like something that's just finished, which it never is for the actor', *Plays and Players*, August 1982, p. 13.

A

Absurd, Theatre of the

Martin Esslin's term used to describe a group of writers and plays achieving prominence in the 1950s and 1960s but also to describe a particular form of theatre. It could be seen as an extreme reaction to Realism in the theatre and historically has its roots in the work of Alfred Jarry (in such plays as *Ubu Roi*, 1896), Strindberg's Expressionist 'dream-plays' (such as *The Ghost Sonata*, 1924), Dada and Surrealism, Pirandello's *Six Characters in Search of an Author* (1921) and the works of a number of French Existentialist philosophers who flourished during and immediately after the Second World War, in particular Jean-Paul Sartre (*Being and Nothingness*, 1945) and Albert Camus (*The Myth of Sisyphus*, 1942) both of whom also wrote novels and plays.

The word 'absurd' in the context of Post-War Theatre does not mean precisely the same as it does in ordinary usage (where it is, for example, used for 'ridiculous', 'senseless' and 'incomprehensible') but refers to a concept (discussed by Camus in particular) concerned with man's existential relationship to the universe and nature. John Russell Taylor has usefully suggested that the 'absurd' involves 'humanity's plight as purposelessness in an existence out of harmony with its surroundings [absurd means literally out of harmony]. Awareness of this lack of purpose in all we do ... produces a state of metaphysical anguish which is the central theme of the writers in the Theatre of the Absurd.' It is not man who is 'absurd' and not the universe which is 'absurd' but man's *relationship* to the universe. It could be argued that the feelings of purposelessness, anxiety and abandonment by God engendered by thinking of man in this way were partly a product of the holocaust of the Second World War which was felt perhaps most keenly in France. It created a shock-wave of uncertainty and doubt which came through to dramatists as well as philosophers and political thinkers.

In France the major dramatists of the Absurd were Eugène Ionesco, Albert Camus, Jean-Paul Sartre, Jean Genet and Arthur Adamov. The central figure in post-war Britain and in France has been Samuel **Beckett** and the play generally regarded as the most representative of the Theatre of the Absurd is Beckett's *Waiting For Godot* (Paris, January 1953 and London, August 1955). Esslin has suggested that in this play man is 'stripped of the accidental circumstances of social position or historical context, confronted with basic choices, the basic situations of his existence'. It is a play which regards post-war twentieth-century man as having lost his bearings spiritually, as living in doubts and uncertainties, yet facing with some dignity, pride, humour and the capacity for endurance, the metaphysical horror that surrounding human existence there may be a vast cosmic 'Nothingness' with apparently no purpose.

The most important British-based dramatist of this group is Harold **Pinter**, whose plays possess a fascinating blend of realistic setting and ordinary language with incongruous behaviour and ambiguities produced through lack of communication between his characters. Pinter's characters activate uncertainties, mysteries and insecurity in his audiences in much the same way (Pinter himself has remarked) as in ordinary life meeting some stranger for the first time might do. His best plays are probably the one-acter *The Dumb Waiter* (1960) and the full-length plays *The Caretaker* (1960) and *No Man's Land* (1975). There have been other British dramatists influenced by

Absurd Theatre, such as N.F. **Simpson** (perhaps also influenced by *The Goons* radio show) and some of the plays of Tom **Stoppard**, in particular his *Rosencrantz and Guildenstern Are Dead* (1966), *After Magritte* (1970) and *Jumpers* (1972) which, with their relentless explorations of philosophical logic (through their characters' thoughts and actions), seem to manifest in a paradoxical way John Russell Taylor's general observation that in Theatre of the Absurd 'the ideas are allowed to shape the form as well as the content: all semblance of logical construction, of the rational linking of idea with idea in an intellectually viable argument, is abandoned, and instead the irrationality of experience is transferred to the stage'. With Stoppard the irrational is often created by an overt exploration of the rational and supposedly 'logical'.

To a degree the Absurd also influenced Peter **Brook**'s production of *King Lear* (1962) through his reading of Jan Kott's *Shakespeare Our Contemporary* (1967) which contains a chapter on Beckett and *King Lear*.

Though the main energies of Theatre of the Absurd seem to have been spent its influences still remain and probably will for a considerable time, if only because of its fundamental probing into the essence of the human condition and the state of post-war mankind: as Arnold Hinchliffe put it: 'Such a theatre, then, presents anxiety and despair, a sense of loss at the disappearance of solutions, illusions, and purposefulness. Facing up to this loss means that we face up to *reality itself*: thus Absurd drama becomes a kind of modern mystical experience.'

Further Reading

Martin Esslin, *The Theatre of the Absurd* (1961), 3rd edn, Penguin Books, Harmondsworth, 1983.
Arnold P. Hinchliffe, *The Absurd*, 'The Critical Idiom', Methuen, London, 1972.

Acting Area

The space on the stage where the action takes place. It includes stage furniture but excludes scenery. In **Proscenium** theatres it is divided into the following nine areas seen from the point of view of the actor looking at the audience: right, left, centre, down-stage right and left, upstage right and left, downstage centre and upstage centre (SR, SL, C, DSR, DSL, USR, USL, DSC, USC). *See also* **PS** and **OP**.

Actors' Company

See **McKellen, Ian**.

Ad Lib

Extempore speech used either deliberately as an improvisatory part of a play or because an actor needs to disguise the fact that he has forgotten his lines or that another member of the cast has missed his entrance.

Agitprop

A term widely used for any drama which attemps to change the audience's ideological viewpoint by propaganda and theatrical 'agitation'. Though the term is used loosely and most often in connection with left-wing alternative theatre groups and touring companies its actual derivation is from the Department of Agitation and Propaganda set up in 1920 as part of the Central Committee secretariat of the Communist Party in the Soviet Union. *See* **Alternative Theatre**.

Alderton, John

Born in Gainsborough, Lincolnshire, on 27 November 1940. He attended Kingston High School in Hull and made his first stage appearance in repertory at the Theatre Royal, York, in August 1961. His first London appearance was as Harold Crompton in *Spring and Port Wine* (**Mermaid** Theatre, November 1965, and later at the Apollo). In March 1969 he played Eric Hoyden in the **Royal Shakespeare Company**'s (**RSC**) production of *Dutch Uncle* and in July of the same year Jimmy Cooper in *The Night I Chased the Woman with an Eel* (Comedy Theatre). In October 1973 he was Stanley in *Punch and Judy Stories* (Howff) and played him again in *Judies* at the Comedy Theatre (January 1974). In January 1975 he took the part of Stanley in **Pinter**'s *The Birthday Party* (Shaw Theatre) and the next year played four parts in **Ayckbourn**'s *Confusions* (Apollo, May 1976). He was in *Rattle of a Simple Man* at the Savoy in 1980.

John Alderton has appeared many times in television plays and comedy series, notably the extremely popular *Please Sir* and *My Wife Next Door.* He is a member of Ray **Cooney**'s 'Theatre of Comedy' company.

Allen, Patrick

Born in Malawi on 17 March 1927, his post-war stage appearances include Jesse Bard in *The Desperate Hours* (Hippodrome, April 1955), Captain O'Keefe in *The Rough and Ready Lot* (Lyric, Hammersmith, June 1959). In 1961 he joined the **RSC** for a season at the Aldwych, playing Auguste in *Ondine* (January) and Jean d'Armagnac in John **Whiting**'s *The Devils* (February). In October 1962 he took the part of Achilles in *Troilus and Cressida* and in August 1967 Theo in *The Flip Side.* In the 1970s his work included Colin in *The Sandboy* (Greenwich, September 1971), Arthur in John **Arden**'s *The Island of the Mighty* (RSC at Aldwych, December 1972), Garry Essendine in *Present Laughter* (Thorndike, Leatherhead, April 1973), Kurt in *Play Strindberg* (Hampstead, July 1973) and the Captain in Strindberg's *The Father* (Greenwich, November 1977). He was one of the first television-series heroes of the post-war period in the title-role of *Crane* and has appeared in numerous films, notably *1984* (1955), *High Tide at Noon* (1957), *Dunkirk* (1958), *I Was Monty's Double* (1958), *The Traitors* (1962), and *The Night of the Generals* (1966). Recent television appearances have been in *The Troubleshooters* and *Brett.* Patrick Allen is also a well-known contributor to the advertising profession.

Alternative Theatre

A term used for a type of theatre generally associated with 'fringe' theatre or 'theatre collectives' which provide alternatives to the establishment or 'mainstream' theatres of London's **West End** and the provinces. The term 'fringe' theatre probably derives from the **Edinburgh Festival** where small theatre groups perform in a variety of makeshift venues which have little or no connection with the main productions and theatres during the festival. These theatre groups usually provide a variety of radical drama (ranging from student shows and satirical reviews to new plays by professional companies) which is mainly controversial, experimental, or committed to a particular ideology (most often political).

Alternative Theatre grew in Britain towards the end of the 1960s and beginning of the 1970s partly in response to the political and cultural upheavals in France in 1968, and partly as a reaction to the domination of British Theatre by commercial and heavily-subsidised theatres, and began to create a successful independent theatre movement. This consisted of the founding of a number of touring companies which presented new, mostly left-wing, plays often developed through collective improvisation. Some of the best known of these companies are the *Pip Simmons Theatre Group* founded by Pip Simmons in 1968 (disbanded 1974), *Inter-Action* formed by Ed Berman in 1968, *Hull Truck Company* founded by Mike Bradwell in 1971, *John Bull Puncture Repair Kit* established by Michael Bank and others in 1968, *The Freehold* formed by members of Wherehouse La Mama in London, 1969, *The Red Ladder Theatre* (formerly *Agit-Prop Theatre*) established in 1968, *Portable Theatre* founded by David **Hare** and Tony Bicat in 1968, *7:84 Theatre Company (England and Scotland)* founded by John **McGrath** in 1971, the *Ken Campbell Roadshow* formed by Ken Campbell in 1971, *The Belt and Braces Roadshow Company Ltd* set up by former members of the *Ken Campbell Roadshow* and *7:84 Company* in 1973, *The Joint Stock Theatre Group* established by Max Stafford-Clark and David Hare in 1974, *The People Show* founded by Mark Long and others in 1966, *Welfare State* formed by John Fox in 1968, and *Shared Experience* founded by Mike Alfreds in 1975. Catherine Itzin's *British Alternative Theatre Directory* (1983) gives a comprehensive list of touring theatre companies, venues, community theatre, mime companies, children's theatre, Theatre in Education (TIE) companies, and dance companies.

There has also been an important growth in women's theatre since the *Women's Theatre Group* was founded in 1973. Other women's groups include *Monstrous Regiment, Mrs Worthington's Daughters, Bloomers, The Women's Playhouse Trust* and *Spare Tyre.* The *Black Theatre Co-operative, Tara Arts* and *Temba* theatre groups represent the coloured population, and groups such as *Gay Sweatshop* the homosexual community.

Some of the most important venues (besides the Edinburgh Festival venues) which have become associated with alternative theatre are the **Royal Court** Theatre (especially the Theatre Upstairs), the King's Head (Islington), the Soho Poly, the Bush Theatre (Shepherd's Bush), the Half Moon (Tower Hamlets), and the Orange Tree Theatre (Richmond). Some of the major playwrights to emerge from 'fringe' groups in the early 1970s include David **Hare**, Howard **Barker**, Howard **Brenton**, John **McGrath**, Mike **Leigh**, Caryl **Churchill**, Snoo **Wilson** and Trevor **Griffiths**. *See also* **Happening** and **Agitprop**.

Further Reading

Peter Ansorge, *Disrupting the Spectacle,* Pitman, London, 1975.

David Bradby and John McCormick, *People's Theatre,* Croom Helm Ltd, London, 1978.

Sandy Craig (ed.), *Dreams and Deconstructions: Alternative Theatre in Britain,* Amber Lane Press, Derbyshire, 1980.

Catherine Itzin (ed.), *The British Alternative Theatre Directory,* John Offord (Publications) Ltd, Eastbourne, 1983.

Anderson, Lindsay (Gordon)

Born in Bangalore, South India, on 17 April 1923, he was educated at Cheltenham College and then at Wadham College, Oxford University. He began his career in 1949, making documentary and advertising films at a factory in Wakefield and became a film critic. With Karel Reisz he formed the Free Cinema group (1956-69) which aimed to make realist films about contemporary social issues (films by the group included *Saturday Night and Sunday Morning, A Taste of Honey* and Anderson's film, *This Sporting Life*). In 1959 he became associated with George Devine's **English Stage Company** at the **Royal Court** Theatre. There he directed a number of important plays, including Willis **Hall**'s *The Long and the Short and the Tall* (January 1959), John **Arden**'s *Sergeant Musgrave's Dance* (October 1959) and Harry Cookson's *The Lily White Boys* (January 1960). In the same period he directed Keith **Waterhouse** and Willis **Hall**'s *Billy Liar* (Cambridge Theatre, September 1960), Max Frisch's *Andorra* (**National Theatre**, **Old Vic**, 1960) and *The Fire Raisers* (Royal Court, December 1961), Gogol's *The Diary of a Madman* (Royal

Court, March 1963), which he co-adapted with Richard Harris (who took the solo part). He directed Chekhov's *The Cherry Orchard* for the **Chichester Festival** (1966) and a Polish version of John **Osborne**'s *Inadmissible Evidence* (Contemporary Theatre, Warsaw, 1966).

Lindsay Anderson returned to the Royal Court Theatre in 1969 as a joint Artistic Director of the English Stage Company with William **Gaskill** and Anthony Page, and from 1971 until 1975 was Associate Artistic Director. He particularly encouraged the work of David **Storey**, directing the following of his plays at the Royal Court: *The Contractor* (October 1969), *In Celebration* (October 1969), *Home* (September 1973), *The Changing Room* (November 1971), *The Farm* (September 1973), *Life Class* (April 1974). At the National Theatre (Cottesloe) he directed Storey's *Early Days* (April 1980), in a production starring Sir Ralph **Richardson**. Other productions have included Chekhov's *The Seagull* (Lyric, 1975), Ben Travers's *The Bed Before Yesterday* (Lyric, 1975), William Douglas **Home**'s *The Kingfisher* (Lyric, May 1977, Biltmore Theatre, New York, 1977), starring Richardson, *Hamlet* (Stratford E15, May 1981), Chekhov's *The Cherry Orchard* (Haymarket, October 1983) and Synge's *Playboy of the Western World* (**Edinburgh Festival**, Assembly Rooms, August 1984) for **United British Artists**.

Film work not already referred to includes *Thursday's Children* (1954), *O Dreamland* (1954), *Every Day Except Christmas* (1957), *The White Bus* (1966), *Raz, Dwa, Trzy* (Warsaw 1967), *If ...* (1968), *O Lucky Man!* (1973), *In Celebration* (1974), and *Britannia Hospital* (1982).

In an interview with Vincent Guy in 1969, Lindsay Anderson defined theatre as 'a game between artists and the public with the critics as umpires'. Commenting on directing in the theatre he said, 'I take responsibility for every detail of my stage productions, and work for an end-product that is detailed, finished and complete ... technicians are people who know their job and should therefore get on with it, whereas actors, one knows, have to be cossetted and pampered, in a word, *loved*.'

Further Reading

Laurence Kitchen, *Mid-Century Drama*, Faber and Faber, London, 1962, pp 175-7.

Lindsay Anderson and Vincent Guy, 'Director in Interview', *Plays and Players*, December 1969, pp. 48-9.

Andrews, Harry

Born 10 November 1911 in Tonbridge, Kent, he was educated at Wrekin College. His first appearance on the stage was as John in *The Long Christmas Dinner* (Liverpool Playhouse, September 1933) and his first appearance in London was in *Worse Things Happen at Sea* (St James's Theatre, March 1935). He appeared in *Romeo and Juliet* in October 1935, playing Abraham, the Captain, and later, Tybalt. Other pre-war appearances of note were in John **Gielgud**'s company (Queen's Theatre, September 1937 to April 1938) playing in *Richard II*, *The School for Scandal*, *Three Sisters* and *The Merchant of Venice*. Continuing classical acting he played Diomedes in *Troilus and Cressida* (Westminster Theatre, September 1938), Demetrius in *A Midsummer Night's Dream* (**Old Vic**, December 1938), Laertes in *Hamlet* (Lyceum, June 1939 and at Elsinore). He served with the Royal Artillery 15th Scottish Division during the war and returned to the stage with the Old Vic company, playing Sir Walter Blunt in *Henry IV Part 1*, Creon in *Oedipus* and Sneer in *The Critic* (New Theatre, December 1945) and a year later went with the company to perform in New York. On his return he stayed with the Old Vic company until the end of the 1948-9 season and played Cornwall in *King Lear*, Gerald Craft in *An Inspector Calls*, De Castel-Jaloux in *Cyrano* *de Bergerac*, Bolingbroke in *Richard II*, Hortensio in *The Taming of the Shrew* and the Earl of Warwick in *Saint Joan*. He also played in *The Government Inspector*, *Coriolanus*, *Twelfth Night*, *Dr Faustus*, *The Way of the World* and *The Cherry Orchard*.

In April 1949 Andrews joined the **Shakespeare Memorial Theatre** Company, Stratford-upon-Avon, and played Macduff in *Macbeth*, Don Pedro in *Much Ado About Nothing*, Theseus in *A Midsummer Night's Dream*, Pisanio in *Cymbeline* and Cardinal Wolsey in *King Henry VIII*. He toured Australia with the company in the same year and remained with it for the 1950 season playing, as well as other roles, Brutus in *Julius Caesar*. In the 1951 season he played the title-role in the *Henry IV* plays, after which he joined Sir Laurence **Olivier**'s Company for New York performances of Shaw's *Caesar and Cleopatra* and Shakespeare's *Anthony and Cleopatra*. In 1953 he returned to the Shakespeare Memorial Theatre Company for the season and played Antonio in *The Merchant of Venice*, Buckingham in *Richard III*, Enobarbus in *Antony and Cleopatra* and Kent in *King Lear*. He continued with the company on a tour of Europe and appeared with them again in the 1956 season, taking the parts of Claudius in *Hamlet*, Don Adriano in *Love's Labour's Lost* and, most notably, the title-role in *Othello*.

Andrews continued in mainly classical roles until 1960 when he played General Allenby in *Ross* (Haymarket, May 1960). He subsequently played Robert Rockhard in *The Lizard on the Rock* (Phoenix, May 1962) and Ekart in *Baal* (Phoenix, February 1963). His work since the late 1960s has included a notable performance in the title-role of Edward **Bond's** *Lear* (**Royal Court,** September 1971) and Ivan Kilner in *A Family* (Haymarket, July 1978).

He has also appeared in many films, notably *Moby Dick* (1956), *Ice Cold in Alex* (1958), *The Devil's Disciple* (1959), *55 Days at Peking* (1962), *The Informers* (1965), *Sands of Kalahari* (1965), *The Charge of the Light Brigade* (1968), *The Battle of Britain* (1969), *The Gaunt Woman* (1970) and many others since, including *Entertaining Mr Sloane*, *The Prince and the Pauper* and *Equus*. He has also worked in television in the series *Clayhanger* and played Tolstoy in *A Question of Faith*.

Physically of great stature he usually plays strong, often military-style parts. His contribution to post-war classical theatre has been enormous and he has been described by Robin May as 'quite simply the best major Shakespearian supporting actor in Britain since 1945'.

'Angries', Angry Young Man

Terms which were largely invented by critics and journalists in the 1950s in Britain for discussions of the anti-Establishment stance expressed in the works of a wave of young new writers. The terms may partly be attributed to the Irish writer, Leslie Paul, whose autobiographical work *Angry Young Man* was published in 1951. The chief artists who were described as the 'angry young men' were Lindsay **Anderson**, co-founder of British Free Cinema (which produced such films as *Saturday Night and Sunday Morning*, *A Taste of Honey* and *This Sporting Life*) the novelists John Braine, Kingsley Amis, John Wain, Alan Sillitoe and Stan Barstow, the philosopher Colin Wilson, and the playwrights who were encouraged by George **Devine** and Tony Richardson's **English Stage Company** which performed their plays at the **Royal Court** Theatre in the second half of the 1950s: John **Osborne**, John **Arden**, Ann **Jellicoe**, Willis **Hall** and Arnold **Wesker**, to name only the major ones. Nevertheless, as Lindsay Anderson has pointed out ('The Colour Supplement', Radio 4, 23 September 1984), 'the people who found themselves labelled as "angry young men" weren't really a close group', but produced a variety of works in forms as diverse as 'kitchen-sink' realism and **Brechtian**-influenced documentary and satire.

The archetype of the 'Angry Young Man' is usually cited as Jimmy Porter, the central, vigorously protesting and anti-Establishment protagonist of John Osborne's *Look Back in Anger* (Royal Court Theatre, 8 May 1956), a play which has come to be regarded as a watershed, a breakthrough to new directions in British Theatre. Kenneth **Tynan**, in a now legendary review in the *Observer* at the time, wrote that he doubted if he could love anyone who did not want to see the play and rated it 'the best young play of its decade'. The roots of the 'new wave' can, however, also be located in earlier work of the decade, such as Joan **Littlewood**'s pioneering **Theatre Workshop**.

The historical events of 1956, in particular the British invasion of Suez and the Russian invasion of Hungary, discredited both British traditional conservative imperialism and, at the other extreme, Stalinist Communism, and led to a 'new left' and, as Anderson describes it, 'a hope that there would be a kind of social democratic revival ... that we could put the past, and put conservative, traditional, imperialist Britain behind us, even escape from the old class system which had really throttled Britain after the war, and go into a period that was more egalitarian, that was freer in thought and behaviour, and more creative. We didn't really have absurd stars in our eyes, we *were* sceptical, but we did have hope and vigour.'

Tony Hancock's role in Alan Simpson and Ray Galton's film *The Rebel* (1961) parodies the 'angry young man' as artist.

Further Reading

John Russell Taylor, *Anger and After*, 2nd edn, Pelican Books, Penguin Books, Harmondsworth, 1969.

Krishan Kumar 'The Social and Cultural Setting', *The Present*, Vol. 8 (ed. Boris Ford), *The New Pelican Guide to English Literature*, Penguin Books, Harmondsworth, 1983.

Terry Browne, *Playwright's Theatre: The English Stage Company at the Royal Court*, Pitman Publishing, London, 1975.

Robert Cushman, 'In Celebration', *Plays and Players*, April 1984, pp. 14-15.

Apron Stage

In **Proscenium** theatres a projecting stage in front of the curtain, often a specially built extension into the **Auditorium**.

Arden, John

A 'theatrical poet', as he once described himself, Arden has made a unique contribution to Post-War British Theatre. Although his first plays were presented at the **Royal Court** in the mid-1950s they were very different in form and style from the social realism of plays by **Osborne** and **Wesker** or the abstraction of the **Absurd** dramatists. As he stated in 1960 (in his essay 'Telling a True Tale') the problem of 'translating the concrete life of today into terms of poetry' which could at the same time 'set it within the historical and legendary tradition of our culture' is an immense and important one for the modern dramatist because 'the English public has regrettably lost touch with its own poetic traditions'.

Arden was born on 26th October 1930 in Barnsley, Yorkshire, went to Sedbergh private school and in 1949 served in the Intelligence Corps until 1950 when he studied architecture at King's College, Cambridge and then in 1953 at Edinburgh College of Art. In 1955 he had his first play *All Fall Down* performed in Edinburgh. He moved to London and worked as an architect's assistant and wrote a radio play, *The Life Of Man*, which was broadcast in 1956. This play brought him to the attention of the Royal Court and his next play, *The Waters of Babylon*, was put on there as a Sunday night performance in October 1957. It is a play which in many ways points towards some of Arden's later interests in provincial politics and local community life: a Polish ex-patriot (Krank) who works in an architect's office by day and is also the landlord and pimp of a lodging-house tries to rig a municipal lottery in order to pay off a Polish patriot who is involved in a bomb plot. A later development of this play was *The Workhouse Donkey* (1965).

Arden's next play *Live Like Pigs* (directed by George Devine, Royal Court, September 1958) concerned the effects upon a gypsy family of living on a housing estate. Their problems of adapting to the neighbourhood and of the neighbourhood's accepting them throw into relief the prejudices of local bureaucracy and the estate community. It is a clash between disruptive freedom and ordered restriction. This disruption of a balanced, unquestioning community by an outside alien force of liberty and anarchy is a central preoccupation of many of Arden's other plays, including *Soldier, Soldier* (a television play written before *Live Like Pigs* and broadcast in 1960) which is about a soldier who abuses a small community by claiming to know the family of another soldier and draining its members of their resources. This play was a precursor to Arden's next and most celebrated play *Sergeant Musgrave's Dance* (Royal Court, October 1959) which John Russell Taylor (in *Anger and After*) has suggested involves 'the sudden explosive incursion of the extraordinary and disruptive into the normal and fairly orderly'. As in *Soldier, Soldier*, a soldier confronts a community (in this case a northern mining town already thrown into chaos by a strike). The period is some time towards the end of the nineteenth century (but implicitly parallels the Cyprus crisis in the 1950s) and the mysterious and menacing soldier (Sergeant Musgrave) leads a group of deserters who are posing as a recruiting party, on a mission to return the bones of a local youth who was encouraged by the community to go to war. The implications are that the deserters have come to punish the town. Chaos and confusion break up the community until, with the coming of a party of dragoons, order returns and is ritualised by a dance. Musgrave, too, has his 'dance' — on the gallows.

There is no doubt that *Musgrave* is a powerful and innovative play and one of the best of the period. Yet is has never been entirely successful in performance as there are some weaknesses of pace a director needs to smooth out in order to avoid some of the unevenness. Nevertheless it is perhaps the best English play in the **Brechtian** mode to have been produced. The subtle blending of prose, poetry and song achieves in great measure Arden's desire to create a 'ballad' theatre (he once stated that 'the bedrock of English poetry is the ballad' and in the ballad 'the colours are primary. Black is for death, and for coalmines. Red is for murder.') Social criticism, he maintains, needs to derive its impact from something more than 'documentary facility': it must be expressed 'within the framework of the traditional poetic truths'. As for the common dissatisfaction felt by numerous critics because Arden never seems to condemn or condone any of the various forces in the dramatic conflicts he presents (what Michael Anderson has described as his 'typically uncommitted' and 'obstinately disengaged and amoral stance') this too can be seen as part of the nature of the ballad: Arden himself has pointed out that he does not commit himself to a position because 'this does not happen in ballads'. The ambiguities of position are quite deliberate. *Musgrave* and many of Arden's other plays are only 'political' in the sense that, as Arnold Hinchliffe has commented, 'it is impossible to avoid being political since man is a political animal. Everything that man does is a political act ... any play about people is political.'

From 1959 to 1960 Arden was the Fellow in Playwriting at Bristol University and partly as a result of some of his studies of theatre traditions wrote *The Happy Haven* (Royal Court, September 1960) which employs masks similar to those of the *commedia dell 'arte* and owes something to Ben Jonson's 'comedy of humours' plays. The play is set in an old folks' home and concerns the possibilities of rejuvenation (another variation on the conflict between vitality and community security).

Arden's determination to dedicate himself to a drama preoccupied with local community life was extended in this period to a growing disillusionment with commercial **West End** theatre which carried the suggestion that drama's function was to serve the kind of audiences who attended the London theatres (and major provincial theatres). *The Business of Good Government*, a nativity play with Herod as the central figure, was staged in 1960 for the local church at the village of Brent Knoll, Somerset. He wrote it in collaboration with his wife Margaretta D'Arcy (whom he married in 1957). As different again from West End audiences are those for television and *Wet Fish*, a television play representing Krank from *The Waters of Babylon*, was broadcast by BBC Television in 1961.

In 1963 Arden adapted a play he had been familiar with as a schoolboy, Goethe's *Goetz von Berlichingen* to which he gave the title *Ironhand*. It is about a corrupt robber-knight from the medieval period who is in conflict with a developing Renaissance humanism and something of a challenge to it. Such an interest in the moral and political aspects of tradition was explored again in Arden's *Armstrong's Last Goodnight* (Chichester, July 1964), based on Arthurian legend, and in his recent versions of *Don Quixote* (1980) and *Pearl* (1978). This involvement with history, romance, legend and mythology perhaps places Arden's theatre more alongside the mytho-poetic vein of post-war British poetry represented by Dylan Thomas, David Jones, Ted Hughes, Seamus Heaney and Geoffrey Hill and less alongside the work of his contemporary dramatists.

The Workhouse Donkey (**Chichester**, June 1963) is about a local borough's attempts to appoint a police chief (Colonel Feng), a fanatic as threatening as Musgrave. The intended appointment creates social and moral anarchy — again an ordered community is disrupted and the values of collective existence questioned and again Arden's sympathies are equally divided (in particular between Feng and the alderman, Butterthwaite). It is an 'epic' and was originally intended to be 13 hours long with the audience drifting in and out as it wished. *Armstrong's Last Goodnight* (Glasgow Citizen's, 1964 and Chichester, 1965) fuses together a number of influences from a story about the Congo (Conor Cruise O'Brien's *To Katanga and Back*) and a Scottish border ballad 'The Ballad of Johnny Armstrong', set in sixteenth century Border Country. Armstrong, an aristocractic robber (like the knight in *Ironside*) creates anarchy in his conflict with Lindsay, a devious politician. In the same year Arden wrote a one-acter with Margaretta D'Arcy, called *Ars Longa, Vita Brevis* (Lamda, January 1964), for the **RSC**'s **Theatre of Cruelty** season.

Left-handed Liberty was presented at the **Mermaid Theatre** in June 1965 as part of the City of London Corporation's celebrations of the 750th anniversary of the signing of Magna Carta. The commission gave him another opportunity to explore medieval history and chivalric conflict.

Since this time Arden has worked in collaboration with Margaretta D'Arcy for most of his subsequent plays: a one-acter *Friday's Hiding* (1966), a children's play *The Royal Pardon* (1966), *Harold Muggins is a Martyr* (1969) which was developed through improvisation, *The Hero Rises Up* (1968) a musical about Nelson, *The Ballygombeen Bequest* (RSC, Aldwych, 1972) and *The Island of the Mighty* (RSC, Aldwych, December 1972). This latter play was a four-hour epic 'ballad play' about King Arthur and a Britain locked in war after the Romans had departed. It had a massive episodic and 'epic' form and was a condensation of a television series. Partly as a result of the problems of staging the play Arden and

D'Arcy had disagreements with the theatre and finally broke with the commercial West End Establishment theatre system and immersed themselves more fully in the Irish theatre and small community drama, co-founding Corrandulla Arts Centre, County Galway, Eire, in 1975. There followed *The Non-Stop Connolly Show* (Dublin, 1975), *Vandaleur's Folly* (7:84 Company, 1978), *The Little Gray House in the West* (1978) and the radio plays *To Put It Frankly* (1979) *The Menace of Ireland* (1979) and *Garland for a Hoar Head* (1982). Arden's novel *Silence Among the Weapons* appeared in Methuen in 1982.

There are many who regard Arden's shift away from the mainstream market-place he had established himself in as an unwelcome departure and one which may have, as John Russell Taylor put it in 1981, 'deprived our theatre for ever of one of its most individual voices'. Certainly, where T.S. **Eliot** failed to fulfil the hopes of a modern 'poetic drama' Arden has been more successful. Laurence Kitchin has even gone so far as to suggest that *Sergeant Musgrave's Dance* is an 'achievement to justify anyone's entire career'.

Yet even a cursory look at Arden's development shows that his move away from establishment theatre and towards a community environment and culture which has *not* 'lost touch with its own poetic traditions' was inevitable if the artist was to be true to himself. Arden's is now much more of a 'theatre of engagement' than ever before. As he himself once put it, 'the tale stands and it exists in its own right. If the poet is a true one, then the tale will be true too.'

The eventual growth of community theatre groups in the 1970s and the confidence of the Royal Shakespeare Company and **National Theatre** Company in staging 'epic' dramas (such as *Nicholas Nickleby*, *The Romans in Britain* and Marlowe's *Tamburlaine the Great*) demonstrates that Arden's views have been ahead of their time and possibly even influential.

Some of Arden and D'Arcy's recent works have been two radio plays called *The Manchester Enthusiasts* (broadcast June 1984) about Ralahine, a nineteenth-century Irish farm commune.

Further Reading

Albert Hunt, *Arden: A Study of his Plays*, Eyre Methuen, London, 1974.

Francis Gray, *John Arden*, 'Macmillan Modern Dramatists', Macmillan, London, 1982.

John Arden, *To Present the Pretence: Essays on the Theatre and its Public*, Methuen, London, 1979.

Arena Stage

A stage or acting space with the audience on three or four sides. *See* **Open Stage**.

Ashcroft, Dame Peggy (Edith Margaret Emily), DBE, CBE

Born in Croydon on 22 December 1907, she was educated at Woodford School, Croydon, and trained for the stage at the Central School of Dramatic Art. Her first professional role was Margaret in J.M. Barrie's *Dear Brutus* (Birmingham Repertory Theatre, 22 May 1926).

In the 1930s she became distinguished for her performances of the great classical heroines, in particular Desdemona in *Othello* (Savoy, May 1930) which she played to Paul Robeson's Othello, Cleopatra in Shaw's *Caesar and Cleopatra*, Imogen in *Cymbeline* and Rosalind in *As You Like It* (**Old Vic** and Sadler's Wells, September-October 1932), Perdita in *The Winter's Tale*, Juliet in *Romeo and Juliet* (Old Vic, December 1932–May 1933), Juliet again (New Theatre, October 1935) and Nina in Chekhov's *The Seagull* (New Theatre, May 1936). It is generally held that Ashcroft's performance of Juliet was the definitive performance of this century.

For John **Gielgud**'s season at the Queen's

Theatre (September 1937–June 1938) she was the Queen in *Richard II*, Lady Teazle in Sheridan's *The School for Scandal*, Irina in Chekhov's *Three Sisters* (in a cast which included Gielgud and Michael **Redgrave**) and Portia in *The Merchant of Venice*. After further roles in productions at London Theatres and on tour she played Ophelia for a tour of *Hamlet* in 1944, with Gielgud as Hamlet. For Gielgud's much-praised season at the Haymarket (October 1944–June 1945) she was once again Ophelia to his Hamlet, and in addition was Titania to his Oberon in *A Midsummer Night's Dream* and the Duchess to his Ferdinand in Webster's *The Duchess of Malfi*. Laurence Kitchin has written (in *Mid-Century Drama*, 1962) that in this period her performances had the effect of 'very sweet woodwind interludes in a robust symphony. She had ... a kind of distilled essence of sex which humanized the lyrical heroines ... Ashcroft defined an acceptable standard for this range of parts which has never been attained since.'

At the **Shakespeare Memorial Theatre**, Stratford-upon-Avon, in 1950 she played Beatrice to Gielgud's Benedick in *Much Ado About Nothing* and Cordelia to his Lear in *King Lear*. Subsequently she was Viola in *Twelfth Night* (Old Vic, March 1951), Hester in Terence **Rattigan**'s *The Deep Blue Sea* (Duchess, March 1952), Portia in *The Merchant of Venice* and Cleopatra in *Antony and Cleopatra* (Shakespeare Memorial Theatre, Stratford-upon-Avon, 1953 season, Princess Theatre, November 1953, tour of The Hague, Amsterdam, Antwerp, Brussels and Paris, 1953-4). In November 1954 she gave a superb performance in the title-role of Ibsen's *Hedda Gabler* at the Westminster Theatre and was awarded King Haakon's Gold Medal for her performance as Hedda at the New Theatre, Oslo (March 1955).

In 1956 Peggy Ashcroft extended her range considerably by playing roles in a number of modern plays, including Miss Madrigal in Enid Bagnold's *The Chalk Garden* (Haymarket, April 1956) in a production which included Edith **Evans** in the cast, and Shen Te in **Brecht**'s *The Good Woman of Setzuan* for the **English Stage Company** at the **Royal Court** (October 1956). She also played Rebecca in Ibsen's *Rosmersholm* in the Royal Court production of November 1959 (transferred to Comedy Theatre, January 1960). Her other work in the 1950s was largely at the Shakespeare Memorial Theatre, Stratford-upon-Avon (and included Rosalind, Imogen, Katherina, Paulina and the Duchess of Malfi).

In January 1961 she became a member of the re-named **Royal Shakespeare Company** and subsequently gave many performances in Stratford and London (Aldwych Theatre). These included parts in John **Barton**'s anthology *The Hollow Crown* (Stratford 1961), Emilia in *Othello* (Stratford, October 1961), Madame Ranevsky in Chekhov's *The Cherry Orchard* (Aldwych, December 1961), Margaret of Anjou in John Barton's adaptation of the *Henry VI* plays and *Richard III* into the trilogy *The Wars of the Roses* (Stratford, July 1963, Aldwych, January 1964, Stratford, July 1964), Mrs Alving in Ibsen's *Ghosts* (Aldwych, June 1967), Agnes in Edward Albee's *A Delicate Balance* (Aldwych, January 1969), Beth in Harold **Pinter**'s *Landscape* (Aldwych, July 1969) and Queen Katherine in *Henry VIII* (Stratford, October 1969, Aldwych, December 1970).

In the 1970s she divided her work between the RSC, the **National Theatre** and various London theatres. Among her roles were Claire Lannes in Marguerite Duras's *The Lovers of Viorne* (Royal Court, July 1971), Beth and Flora in Pinter's *Landscape* and *A Slight Ache* (Aldwych, October 1973), Ella in Ibsen's *John Gabriel Borkman* (National Theatre, Old Vic, January 1975), Winnie in Samuel **Beckett**'s *Happy Days* (National Theatre, Old Vic, March 1975), Lidya in Arbuzov's *Old World* (RSC, Aldwych October 1976) and she played Winnie in *Happy Days* again for the National Theatre (Lyttleton, September 1977).

For the National Theatre at the **Edinburgh Festival** in 1980 she played in a revival of Lillian Hellman's *Watch on the Rhine* (transferred Lyttleton, September 1980), in February 1981 she was Voice 2 in Pinter's *Family Voices* (Lyttleton) and for the RSC's 1981 season she played the Countess of Rousillon in *All's Well That Ends Well* (transferred Barbican, July 1982).

Film work includes *The Wandering Jew, The Thirty-Nine Steps, Rhodes of Africa, Quiet Wedding, The Nun's Story, Secret Ceremony, Hullabaloo over Georgie, Bonnie's Pictures* and *A Passage to India.* Her appearances on television include *The Cherry Orchard, The Wars of the Roses, Days in the Trees, Edward and Mrs Simpson, Caught on a Train, Cream in My Coffee, The Jewel in the Crown* and *Six Centuries of Verse.*

Recollecting his experiences of Ashcroft's past performances, Harold Hobson (in *Theatre in Britain*, 1984) wrote that 'the first thing one noticed ... (and always noticed) about Peggy Ashcroft was her quietness. She seemed stiller than the moon itself, for all its eternal silence. But, unlike the moon, she was alive.'

In 1982 a theatre named after Peggy Ashcroft was opened in her home town, Croydon.

Asher, Jane

Born in London on 5 April 1946, she was educated at North Bridge House and Miss Lambert's PNEU. Stage appearances began as a child in *Housemaster* (Frinton Summer Theatre, 1957) and *Through the Looking Glass* (Playhouse, Oxford, December 1958) in which she played Alice. Her first appearance in London was as Muriel in *Will You Walk a Little Faster?* (Duke of York's, June 1960) and in December 1961 she toured as Wendy in *Peter Pan.* Several parts followed and in 1965 she joined the **Bristol Old Vic** Company and appeared in a number of plays including *Cleo, Great Expectations* and *The Happiest Days of Your Life.* A year later she left the company to play Cassandra in *The Trojan Woman* (Pop Theatre Company, **Edinburgh Festival**, August 1966) and Perdita in *The Winter's Tale* (Pop Theatre Company, Edinburgh Festival, September 1966). She subsequently played Perdita at the Cambridge Theatre (September 1966) and then returned to Bristol to play Juliet in *Romeo and Juliet* and Julietta in *Measure for Measure* (Bristol Old Vic and North American tour, 1967).

Jane Asher's first appearance in New York was as Julietta in *Measure for Measure* (City Center, February 1967). On her return to London she played Lorette in *Summer* (Fortune, July 1968) and Alison in **Osborne**'s *Look Back in Anger* (**Royal Court** and Criterion, October 1968). Subsequent productions have included Celia in Christopher **Hampton**'s *The Philanthropist* (Royal Court, August 1970 and Barrymore, New York, 1971), Sally in *Old Flames* (New Vic Studio, Bristol, October 1975), Ann in Hampton's *Treats* (Royal Court, February 1976). In 1977 she joined the **National Theatre**, played Charlotte in Stephen Poliakoff's *Strawberry Fields* (Cottesloe, April 1977), and took part in *To Those Born Later* (Cottesloe, June 1977), a compilation of Brechtian songs and poems.

In October 1977 Jane Asher played the title-role in *Ophelia* (Oxford Playhouse and tour) and then Dr Scott in Brian Clark's *Whose Life Is It Anyway*? (**Mermaid**, March 1978). Film appearances include *Mandy, The Greengage Summer, The Girl in Headlines, Alfie, Henry VIII and His Six Wives* and *Deep End.* Appearances on television include *The Mill on the Floss* and *Brideshead Revisited* (1981).

ASM

Assistant Stage Manager.

Auditorium

Place where the audience sits.

'Aunt Edna'

See **Rattigan, Terence**.

Ayckbourn, Alan

Born in London on 12 April 1939, he was educated at Haileybury and the Imperial Service College, Hertfordshire. On leaving college in 1957 he worked as a stage-manager and took acting parts with Donald **Wolfit**'s company in Edinburgh, Worthing, Leatherhead and Oxford. He married Christine Roland in 1959.

From 1962 to 1964 he worked with Stephen **Joseph** (pioneer of **'Theatre in the Round'** in Britain), at Scarborough and Stoke-on-Trent. His acting roles included Starbuck in N. Richard Nash's *The Rainmaker*, Ben in Harold **Pinter**'s *The Dumb Waiter*, Aston in Pinter's *The Caretaker*, Vladimir in Samuel **Beckett**'s *Waiting for Godot*, Thomas More in Robert **Bolt**'s *A Man For All Seasons* and Del Bosco in Marlowe's *The Jew of Malta*. He also directed a number of plays in this period. Stephen Joseph encouraged him to write for the stage and (originally under the name of 'Roland Allen') Ayckbourn had a number of plays produced at Scarborough and Stoke-on-Trent, including *Mr Whatnot* (Victoria Theatre, Stoke-on-Trent, 1963) which subsequently was performed in London (Arts Theatre, 1964). The play is a comedy, largely in the form of mime, about a piano-tuner taking opportunities to enjoy himself during a call at a stately home. Ayckbourn was a radio drama producer for BBC Leeds from 1964 to 1970.

He achieved recognition with *Relatively Speaking* (Duke of York's, March 1967) which was first presented as *Meet My Father* in Scarborough (1965) where, at what later became the Library Theatre, most of his plays have been presented and directed by Ayckbourn before transferring to London. The play concerns the farcical misunderstandings and bewilderment caused by a young man mistaking his fiancée's lover for her father. Whilst not a traditional sex-farce the play is less dark in tone than later plays by Ayckbourn. In *How the Other Half Loves* (Scarborough, 1969, Lyric, August 1970) he sharpened his comic focus by having two family groups of different social classes presented simultaneously, an upper-class family and lower-middle-class family, whose dialogues intriguingly mix together. For one ingenious sequence of the play the audience has to follow events taking place at two dinner parties on the same set at the same time. In an interview with Bernard Levin (BBC 2, 1 July 1984) Ayckbourn commented on the willingness of audiences to accept such devices, stating that it is 'a game the audience plays ... people will play any game you want in the theatre providing you set the rules out clearly. They like to be exercised and they like to go with you.' Similarly in *Bedroom Farce*, the audience sees simultaneous action taking place in three different rooms. 'Stage time interests me,' says Ayckbourn, 'there's a stage time and there's real time to play with and if you write a play in actual time that has the effect of a sort of close-up lens.'

Time and Time Again (Scarborough, 1971, Comedy Theatre, August 1972) focuses on Leonard, an ex-teacher and something of a failure who decides to become a corporation gardener. He is caught in the lunatic life-style of the Bakers' suburban household, full of compromising situations with lovers, obsessions with garden gnomes and sport. Ayckbourn said in his interview with Levin, 'I don't tend very much to work with winners ... all my characters seem to have this terrible disappointment, this terrible gap between what they meant to achieve and what they did achieve.' Perhaps his best play to date has been *Absurd Person Singular* (Scarborough, 1972, Criterion, July 1973) which presents three separate couples in their three kitchens on three successive Christmas Eves. The least 'successful' couple, the Hopcrofts, develop towards prosperity in the play whilst the other couples, the Jacksons (an architect and his wife) and Brewster-Wrights (a bank manager and his wife), decline. Much of the comedy arises from characters' fears of social exposure and embarrassment but also from the hilarious problems people face trying to cope with household gadgets and technology. The play, as with many of Ayckbourn's other plays, has elements of pure farce mixed with sharp social observation, dark tragedies (there are three suicides) and witty insights into the way modern, technological, domestic environments have real effects upon personal lifestyles. Ayckbourn has said that he is one of those people who 'has difficulty with the system and has difficulty with machinery ... everything I buy breaks down, every time I travel I get lost. I seem to have the common touch in that sense and I just write from that viewpoint.'

Following this was *The Norman Conquests,* a trilogy comprising *Table Manners, Living Together* and *Round and Round the Garden* (Scarborough, 1973, Globe, August 1974). Each play presents the simultaneous events of the same weekend at a house, the first play set in the dining room, the second in the living room and the third in the garden. For the full effects the plays are best seen consecutively but each play stands quite successfully as a separate entity. The protagonist, Norman, creates havoc in his vain attempts to maintain relations with three women at the same time, eventually being rejected by them all. *Absent Friends* (Scarborough, 1974, Garrick, July 1975) concerns the ways in which a well-intentioned sentimentality over past friendships can be destructive of life in the present. Colin, whose fiancée has died, meets up with old friends at a tea-party but his insistent harping upon their camaraderie drives each to a deeper sense of unhappiness, and in one case to a nervous breakdown. 'What really appals me,' Ayckbourn says 'is when people do ill to each other in the guise of well-meaningness, and without actually realizing what they are doing.' After *Confusions* (Scarborough, 1974, Apollo, May 1976), *Bedroom Farce* (Scarborough, 1975, **National Theatre**, March 1977), *Just Between Ourselves* (Scarborough, 1976, Queen's, April 1977) and *Joking Apart* (Scarborough 1976, Globe, March 1979) came *Ten Times Table* (Scarborough, 1977, Globe, April 1978), described by Ayckbourn as 'a study of the committee person ... a predominantly sedentary farce with faintly allegorical overtones'. Eric, a young left-wing schoolteacher, wishes to turn a local village pageant into a rally for a worker's revolution and the play wittily explores the ideological battles between him and the rest of the village committee.

Sisterly Feelings (Scarborough, 1979, National Theatre, June 1980) introduced the innovation of four alternatives for the action in the middle scenes of the play, chosen according to the decision of an actress during performance. In September 1980 *Taking Steps* was presented at the Lyric Theatre, in February 1981 *Suburban Strains* at the Round House, in March 1982 *Season's Greetings* at the Apollo and in October 1982 *Way Upstream* at the National Theatre. In March 1983 *Making Tracks,* a musical written with Paul Todd, was performed at Greenwich Theatre and later in 1983 *It Could Be Any One of Us* at Scarborough. Previously seen in Scarborough in 1982, *Intimate Exchanges* was presented by the **Theatre of Comedy** company at the Ambassadors in August 1984. The play has 16 possible versions and over 30 scenes.

Plays of Ayckbourn's which have been televised include *Time and Time Again, The Norman Conquests* (starring Richard **Briers**), *Bedroom Farce* and *Just Between Ourselves.* A children's play called *Ernie's Incredible*

Illucinations was produced in 1971.

His ingenious experiments with the construction of his plays, his keen, perhaps often cruel, observation of middle-class frustration, and his capacity to generate farce mixed with a sombre vision of human inadequacy, anxiety and fallibility, have greatly extended the possible modes of comedy in the theatre. Ayckbourn has said 'I suppose when I started I was just obsessed with the mechanics of playwriting. After that I began to write more and more about people. I think inevitably as you write about people you scrape away the outer layers and you get to darknesses.'

1985 saw *A Chorus of Disapproval* (Lyttleton, July) and *Woman in Mind* (Stephen Joseph, Theatre-in-the-Round, Scarborough, Summer).

Further Reading

Stephen Joseph, *Theatre in the Round*, Barrie and Rockliff, London, 1967.

John Russell Taylor, *The Second Wave*, Methuen, London, 1971, pp. 154-62.

John Russell Taylor, 'Art and Commerce: The New Drama in the West End Marketplace', *Contemporary English Drama*, ed. C.W. E. Bigsby, Stratford-upon-Avon Studies, No. 19, Edward Arnold, London, 1981, pp. 182-6.

Ian Watson, *Conversations with Ayckbourn*, Macdonald, London, 1981.

B

Backcloth

A suspended canvas or surface upstage which can be lit and painted. *See also* **Cyclorama (Cyc)**.

Barbican Theatre

See **Royal Shakespeare Company**.

Barker, Howard

Born in Dulwich on 28 June 1946, he was educated at Battersea Grammar School (1958-64) and read history at the University of Sussex, Brighton (1964-8). His first play, *Cheek*, was performed at the **Royal Court** Theatre (Theatre Upstairs, July 1970) and is about a young boy's healthy sexual appetites frustrated by conventional morality. His next play, *No One Was Saved*, was performed soon afterwards (Royal Court, Theatre Upstairs, 1970) and is about an unmarried mother. Barker was invited (by director John Mackenzie) to write a screenplay based on it and it was subsequently made into a film.

At Charles **Marowitz**'s Open Space Theatre Barker's *Alpha Alpha* was presented in 1971. It is based on the story of the twin criminals, the Kray brothers. In the same year *Edward: The Final Days* was presented and *Faceache*. These were followed by *Private Parts* (**Edinburgh Festival**, 1972) and *Claw* (Open Space, 1975), a didactic play about a pimp (Noel Biledew, who takes the name 'Claw') who is weak and inadequate and victimised by the Establishment. From 1974 to 1975 Barker was Resident Dramatist at the **Open Space Theatre**. *Stripwell* (Royal Court, October 1975), which starred Michael **Hordern** as the judge, is about a criminal's taking reprisals against a judge by entering his house. *Wax* was presented at the Edinburgh Festival in 1976 and *That Good Between Us*, about a future Britain as a totalitarian state, in July 1977 (**RSC** Warehouse). Also in 1977 *Fair Slaughter* was produced and in December 1978 *The Hang of the Gaol* (RSC, Warehouse), a play about a prison governor who commits arson. This was followed by *The Love of A Good Man* (1978) about some incidents in the First World War. *The Loud Boy's Life* was seen in 1980 and *No End of Blame* in 1981 (Oxford Playhouse, then Royal Court). For the **Joint Stock Company** Barker wrote *Victory* which was performed at the Royal Court Theatre in March 1983.

Most of Barker's plays are marked by an anti-Establishment, anti-capitalist stance and present a witty and highly critical view of contemporary society's dominant ideologies. He has commented that 'the stage is the last remaining arena for the free assault of our society ... the last playground of the emotions, last public place for a critical but humane judgement of a monstrous speculative society'.

Recently Barker's plays have looked at conflict in history, politics and art: 'My plays celebrate life, energy — and belief, however mistaken. But I'm saying that the essence of things is conflict', he told Jim Hiley in interview (*Radio Times*, 29 June–5 July 1985). *The Power of the Dog* (Joint Stock Company tour, December 1984, Hampstead Theatre, January 1985) was set at the time of Yalta (1945) and the period of Stalin and Churchill's attempts to share out the division of Europe after the Second World War. Barker's excellent television play *Pity in History* (1985), set in the time of the English Civil War and about a stonemason (Gaukroger) who carves the statue of a Royalist aristocrat only to have it smashed by Roundheads, was a play of great dramatic power and intensity which went some way towards fulfilling Barker's wish that his plays should have 'a texture which is uniquely mine, and against the headlong rush of naturalism ... I think every convention is a form of decay. I'd like to rediscover the rhetoric and powerful images of an earlier theatre, say the Jacobean.'

In autumn 1985 the Royal Shakespeare Company presented his three history plays at the Barbican (Pit), *Downchild*, *Crimes in Hot Countries* and *The Castle*.

Barkworth, Peter

Born in Margate, Kent, on 14 January 1929, he was educated at Stockport and whilst still at school made his first stage appearance in *For What We Are* (Hippodrome, Stockport, 1942). Between 1946 and 1948 he studied at RADA and in 1948 joined the repertory company at Folkestone and soon after, the Sheffield Repertory Theatre Company.

His first London appearances were as Gaston Probert in Dodie Smith's *Letter From Paris* (Aldwych, October 1952), a play based on Henry James's *The Reverberator*, Gerald Arbuthnot in Oscar Wilde's *A Woman of No Importance* (Savoy, February 1953), Stefan in *The Dark is Light Enough* (Aldwych, April 1954) and Paul Cassagnon in Sam and Bella Spewack's *My Three Angels* (Lyric, May 1955).

In February 1956 Barkworth played Bentley Summerhays in George Bernard Shaw's *Misalliance* (Lyric, Hammersmith) and in April of the same year, Captain Mortlock in Noël **Coward**'s *South Sea Bubble* (Lyric). He subsequently played Bernard Taggart-Stuart in Lesley Storm's celebrated comedy *Roar Like A Dove* (Phoenix, September 1957) which ran for more than a thousand performances. Again at the Phoenix Theatre (December, 1960) he took the part of Victor in Arthur Watkyn's comedy *The Geese Are Getting Fat* and at the Haymarket Theatre (April 1962) played Sir Benjamin Backbite in Sheridan's *The School for Scandal*, appearing with the same production in January 1963 at the Majestic Theatre in New York. Subsequently he toured England in a production of *Everything Happens on Friday*, playing the part of Armitage (March 1964), and played Oliver in Enid Bagnold's comedy *The Chinese Prime Minister* (Globe, May 1965). He toured again in April 1967, taking the part of the Reverend Arthur Humphrey in *I'll Get My Man*. At the Haymarket Theatre (October 1972) he was Edward VIII in *Crown Matrimonial* (which he has subsequently appeared in on television).

Barkworth created the role of Headingley in Michael **Frayn**'s *Donkeys' Years* (Globe, July 1976) and Philip Turner in Brian Clark's *Can You Hear Me at the Back?* (Piccadilly, May 1979). He also played in Brian Clark's television series *Telford's Change* (1979). In 1982 Barkworth appeared in Ronald Millar's *A Coat of Varnish* (Haymarket, April 1982) based on a story by C.P. Snow.

He has appeared in a number of films including *Where Eagles Dare*, *Escape From the Dark*, *International Velvet* and *Mr Smith*. In television some of his best work has been in *The Power Game*, *Crown Matrimonial* and **Stoppard**'s *Professional Foul*. He gained particular acclaim for his role in *Winston Churchill: the Wilderness Years* (1981). In 1983 he appeared in the television play *The Price*.

Further Reading

Peter Barkworth, *About Acting*, Secker and Warburg, London, 1980.

Barn Doors

The four movable hinged shutters on the front of a spotlight used to alter the shape of the light cast on to the stage and sometimes to compensate for **Spill**.

Barnes, Peter

Born on 10 January 1931, in London, he was educated at Stroud Grammar School. In 1954 he became a film critic for the journal *Films and Filming* and in 1956 was a story editor for Warwick Films Ltd. In 1958 he married Charlotte Beck. His first play to be performed in Britain was *Sclerosis* (**Edinburgh Festival**, 1965), though he had an earlier play, *The Time of the Barracudas*, produced in San Francisco in 1963. The one-act play *Sclerosis* is about Cyprus's struggle for freedom against British colonial dominance in the 1950s.

His next original play, *The Ruling Class*, brought him to prominence (Nottingham Playhouse, 1968, Piccadilly, February 1969). It is a powerful and witty, somewhat Gothic comedy, criticising British aristocratic Toryism. After the Thirteenth Earl of Gurney has accidentally hanged himself, his son Jack, who believes himself to be God, persists in his riotous and unstable romps at the family seat, disconcerting the late Earl's half-brother Charles who is intent upon the family inheritance. The satirical vein of the play turns to bitter criticism in the closing stages, as the House of Lords is depicted as a collection of cobwebbed corpses, an image summarising Barnes's comment on the ruling classes, whose freedom, 'insanity' and power leads to decadence. The ultimate beneficiary of the estate is Tucker, the butler, a card-carrying Communist. A highly successful film version, with Peter **O'Toole** as Jack, was made in 1972. In a programme note to the stage version Barnes wrote that he was aiming to create 'a comic theatre of contrasting moods and opposites, where everything is simultaneously tragic and ridiculous'.

After *The Ruling Class* came *Leonardo's Last Supper* and *Noonday Demons* (double bill, **Open Space**, 1969), directed by Charles **Marowitz**. The first play studies Leonardo da Vinci, apparently dead in a charnel-house, undergoing a moment of intense creativity in a state of trance. It is an intense Gothic comedy about the decay and squalor which yet produced great Renaissance artists. This intriguing exploration of a declining society through satirical comedy is highly reminiscent of Ben Jonson's comedies of humours. The second play explores the intense quarrels of two Divines in an Egyptian cave.

There followed adaptations of Wedekind's *Lulu* plays (Nottingham Playhouse, 1970), which he also co-directed, and Ben Jonson's *The Devil is an Ass* (Nottingham Playhouse, 1973). His next original play was *Bewitched* (**RSC**, Aldwych, February 1974), which was a study, including elements of farce and song, of the declining Spanish Hapsburgs. The play extended Barnes's interests in Jonsonian and Jacobean visions of waning societies. He subsequently adapted and directed Feydeau's *The Purging* and Wedekind's *The Singer* under the title *Frontiers of Farce* (**Old Vic**, 1976). In 1976 he co-directed his adaptation of Jonson's *The Devil is an Ass* (**Edinburgh Festival**) and it was also produced the following year (**National Theatre**, May 1977). At the **Royal Court** (Theatre Upstairs), in April 1977, he put on a cabaret entertainment, based on his own translations of **Brecht** and Wedekind, under the title *For All Those Who Get Despondent*. Also at the same theatre he put on *Laughter!* (Royal Court, January 1978).

At the Round House in 1978 he directed Jonson's *Bartholomew's Fair* and at the Nottingham Playhouse in 1979 co-directed *Antonio*, an adaptation of two plays by Marston. In 1981 he published his *Collected Plays* (which also contains *Somersaults*) and in the same year directed Brien **Friel**'s *Translations* (Hampstead, May 1981, Lyttleton, August 1981). In July 1985 the RSC staged Barnes's *Red Noses* (Barbican, Pit) about a troupe of entertainers in the period of the Black Death.

Some of his many screenplays are *Violent*

Moment, The Professionals, Ring of Treason and *The Ruling Class*. In 1983 and 1984 his 'duologues' *Barnes People 2* were broadcast on Radio 3.

Jonathan Hammond (in 1976) described Peter Barnes as 'a worthy follower of Jonson, and one of the most significant, as well as one of the most entertaining, British playwrights of the day'. However, Peter Barnes has yet to produce another play equal to the originality, wit and power of *The Ruling Class*.

Barrel

A tubular metal bar, usually suspended horizontally, from which can be hung stage lights or scenery. *See also* **Boom.**

Barton, John (Bernard Adie)

Born in London on 26 November 1928, he was educated at Eton College and King's College, Cambridge. While at Cambridge he directed and acted in productions for the Marlowe Society and Amateur Drama Club (ADC). In July 1953 (Westminster Theatre) he directed *Henry V*, his first London production. In 1954 he became a fellow of King's College (and Lay Dean 1956-9) until 1960 when he was invited by Peter **Brook** to join the newly-founded **Royal Shakespeare Company**. In July of that year he directed *The Taming of the Shrew* at Stratford-upon-Avon.

He devised and took part in performance recitals of a number of anthologies (of extracts from Shakespeare's plays) for the stage: *The Hollow Crown* (Aldwych, March 1961), *The Art of Seduction* (Aldwych, March 1982) and *The Vagaries of Love* (Coventry Festival, Belgrade, June 1962). *The Hollow Crown* was also performed in New York (Henry Miller Theatre, January 1963). John Barton became an Associate Director of the RSC in 1964, a year after he had adapted and edited *Henry VI Parts 1, 2 and 3* and *Richard III* into a controversial production he co-directed, called *The Wars of the Roses* (RSC, Stratford-upon-Avon, July 1963). In Judith Cook's *Directors' Theatre*, Barton's assistant of the time, Penny Gold, is quoted as saying, 'he believes in the theory of continuous copy, the idea that Elizabethan texts were constantly modified to fit varying conditions of individual performances'. Such a view has been taken further in some of his subsequent work and it is one of Barton's achievements to have managed to erode something of the sanctity and inviolability of Shakespeare's literary texts, guarded and upheld as an orthodoxy so persistently (and sometimes dogmatically), by Shakespeare scholars, and to place the texts firmly in the creative and practical life of the constantly changing theatre — to recognise, as Jonathan **Miller** argues, that all plays have an 'afterlife' in successive productions by each new generation. Barton states in Judith Cook's article, 'in a sense, any production of a play is an adaptation of the original . . . a production cannot help creating as well as criticizing, so turning the original text into something it is not by itself'.

Some of the many productions he has directed for the RSC at Stratford and the Aldwych include *Richard II, Henry IV Parts 1 and 2* and *Henry V* (1964), *Love's Labour's Lost* (1965), his own adaptation of Tourneur's *The Revenger's Tragedy* (1966), *Coriolanus* and *All's Well That Ends Well* (1967-8), *Julius Caesar* and *Troilus and Cressida* (1968-9), *Twelfth Night* (1969-70), *When Thou Art King* (1969-70, adapted from *Henry IV Parts 1 and 2* and *Henry V*), *Measure for Measure* (1970), *The Tempest* (1970), *Othello* (1971-2), *Richard II* (1973-4, with Richard **Pasco** and Ian **Richardson** alternating the roles of King Richard and Bolingbroke), an adaptation of *King John* (1974), his own version of Marlowe's *Doctor Faustus* (1974), *Much Ado About Nothing* and *King Lear* (1976), *A Midsummer Night's Dream*, Ibsen's *Pillars of the*

Community and Congreve's *The Way of the World* (1977-8), *The Merchant of Venice* and *Love's Labour's Lost* (1979).

In January 1980 he directed *The Greeks* (Aldwych), his ten-play adaptation from Homer, Aeschylus, Sophocles and Euripides, in September 1980 *Hamlet* (Aldwych), in September 1981 an adaptation of *Two Gentlemen of Verona* and *Titus Andronicus* into a four-hour double-bill (Stratford-upon-Avon), in January 1982 a new version of Arthur Schnitzler's *La Ronde* (Aldwych) and in January 1983 he directed *The School For Scandal* (Haymarket). Later in 1983 he directed *The Vikings* (Bergen). In August 1984 he directed a revival of John **Whiting's** *The Devils* (RSC, Barbican, Pit).

Television work has included *The Wars of the Roses* (1966), the series *Playing Shakespeare* which he wrote and presented (1982), and an adaptation of Malory's *Le Morte d'Arthur* (1984), in which he gave a solo performance as Sir Thomas Malory. John Barton married Ann Righter (author of *Shakespeare and the Idea of the Play*) in 1968.

Further Reading

John Barton, *Playing Shakespeare*, Methuen, London, 1984.

Judith Cook, 'John Barton', *Directors' Theatre*, Harrap, London, 1974, pp. 9-14.

Stanley Wells, *Royal Shakespeare*, Manchester University Press, Manchester, 1977, pp. 43-81.

'King John Barton', *Plays and Players*, June 1974.

Bates, Alan (Arthur)

Born on 17 February 1934 in Derbyshire, he attended the Herbert Strutt Grammar School, Belper (Derbyshire), and trained at RADA. He first appeared with the Midland Theatre Company (Coventry) in *You and Your Wife* (1955) and at the **Royal Court** Theatre with the **English Stage Company**, in Angus Wilson's *The Mulberry Bush* (April 1956) in the role of Simon Fellowes.

He came to public attention in 1956 with his work for the English Stage Company, playing in particular the part of Cliff Lewis in John **Osborne**'s provocative play *Look Back in Anger* (May). Prior to this he played Hopkins in Arthur Miller's *The Crucible* (April) and subsequently Stapleton in Nigel Dennis's *Cards of Identity* (June) and Harcourt in Wycherley's *The Country Wife* (December). Remaining with the English Stage Company in 1957 he played le Crachton in Ronald Duncan's adaptation of Giraudoux's *The Appollo de Bellac* (May), Dr Brock in Michael **Hastings**' *Yes — And After* (June). In July of 1957 Bates again played Cliff in *Look Back In Anger*, on this occasion for the World Youth Festival in Moscow, and afterwards (in October 1958) at the Lyceum Theatre, New York. On returning to Britain in the same year he played Edmund Tyrone in the first British production of O'Neill's *Long Day's Journey Into Night* at the **Edinburgh Festival** (November 1958) and the Globe Theatre, London (September 1958).

Alan Bates achieved major acclaim as Mick in Harold **Pinter**'s *The Caretaker* (Arts Theatre, April 1960 and Lyceum, New York, 1961). In December 1964 at the Helen Hayes Theatre, New York, he took the part of Richard Ford in *Poor Richard* and in London the following year played Adam in **Wesker**'s *The Four Seasons* (Saville, August 1965). At the 1967 Shakespeare Festival in Stratford, Ontario, Bates took the title-role in *Richard III* and played Ford in *The Merry Wives of Windsor.* During this period he continued his highly successful career in films but also began his association with the new playwrights David **Storey** and Simon **Gray**, as well as taking classical roles in the theatre. He appeared as Andrew in Storey's *In Celebration* (Royal Court, April 1969), took the title-role in *Hamlet* (Nottingham Playhouse, November 1970, Cambridge Theatre, January 1971), and played the title-role in Simon Gray's *Butley* (Criterion, July 1971 and New York, 1972).

At Stratford-upon-Avon in September 1973 he played Petruchio in *The Taming of the Shrew* and in the following year was Allott in Storey's *Life Class* (Royal Court, April 1974). In July 1975 he played Simon in Simon Gray's *Otherwise Engaged* (Queen's Theatre) and in July 1976, Trigorin in Chekhov's *The Seagull* (Derby Playhouse, then Duke of York's, August 1976). He played Robert in Simon Gray's *Stage Struck* at the Vaudeville Theatre in November 1979 and he appeared in the revival of John Osborne's *A Patriot for Me* at the **Chichester Festival** and Haymarket Theatre in 1983. In March 1984 he appeared in Pinter's *Victoria Station* and *One For the Road* (Lyric Studio) and in December 1985 took the title-role in **Shaffer's** *Yonadab* at the **National Theatre.**

His highly successful career in films has included roles in *The Entertainer* (1960), *The Caretaker* (1960), *A Kind of Loving* (1961), *Far From the Madding Crowd* (1967), *The Fixer* (1968), *Women in Love* (1969), *The Go-Between*, *Nijinsky* and many others. He has made notable television appearances in *Look Back in Anger*, *The Wind and The Rain*, *The Mayor of Casterbridge*, John **Mortimer**'s *A Voyage Round My Father* (1982), Terence **Rattigan**'s *Separate Tables* (1982) and Alan **Bennett**'s *An Englishman Abroad* (1982).

In May 1985 he was Edgar in Strindberg's *The Dance of Death* (Riverside Studios).

Further Reading

Alan Bates, Interview with Peter Roberts, 'Of Bates and Redl', *Plays and Players*, June 1983.

Beckett, Samuel

One of the most distinguished writers of the century, he has written in nearly all the genres of literature and drama, including film (*Film*, starring Buster Keaton, 1965) and television (*Eh Joe*, 1966, Germany). In 1969 he won the Nobel Prize for Literature.

Born into a family of middle-class Protestants at Foxrock (nr. Dublin) on 13 April 1906, Beckett attended Portora Royal School, County Fermanagh (once attended by Oscar Wilde). At Trinity College, Dublin, he read French and Italian. He took a job lecturing in English at the École Normale Supérieure, Paris, in 1928 and in 1930 took a lectureship in French at Trinity College. He was a close friend of James Joyce in the late 1920s and during the 1930s (working for a time as his secretary). Beckett settled in Paris in 1937 and during the war was active in the French Resistance and did service with a Red Cross unit at St Lô in 1945.

Although one of his first writings was a play (*Le Kid*), produced in Dublin (1931), this was a collaboration (with Georges Pelorson) and it is not until the post-war period that Beckett emerges as a writer for the stage. Previous to the Second World War he wrote poetry (*Whoroscope*, 1930, a satirical poem about the philosopher Descartes which includes 'notes' which are something of a parody of T.S. **Eliot**'s 'notes' to *The Waste Land.* More Poems were published in 1935 as *Echo's Bones and Other Precipitates*). He wrote short stories (*More Pricks Than Kicks*, 1934, stories with Dublin as their setting, as was Joyce's similar collection *The Dubliners*).

He wrote criticism on Proust in 1931 and in 1938 wrote his first full-length novel *Murphy.* This novel begins a fascinating exploration, in comic terms, of the relationship between mind and body (a philosophical conundrum particularly expounded by Descartes in the seventeenth century). The use of the mind-body problem as stimulus for an aesthetic device comes through to much of the stage imagery of the post-war plays too (the three characters in *Play*, 1963, are in jars up to their necks, suggesting the immobilising of the body in order to free consciousness; similarly Winnie is up to her neck in a mound in *Happy Days*, 1961, Hamm is paralysed in a wheelchair in *Endgame*, 1957, and in *Not I*, 1973, the near-exclusion of the body is achieved by only lighting the speaking mouth of an actress with a tiny spotlight beam and having elsewhere on the stage the black silhouette of a human figure slowly, almost indiscernibly, moving). Beckett continued writing novels during and after the war (*Watt*, 1942 published 1953, and the trilogy *Molloy*, *Malone Dies* and *The Unnameable*, 1947-9, published 1951-5). As with nearly all the post-war writing, Beckett writes and publishes first in French and later translates into English himself. His subsequent short stories, novellas, tiny 'verbal constructs' and attempts to write 'minimal' prose pieces are too numerous to record here but *Imagination Dead Imagine* (1965) and *The Lost Ones* (1971-2) might be singled out: through ostensibly simple images (the inside of a brilliant white-hot cylinder inside a skull in the former and people endlessly walking round inside a brilliant white cylinder in the latter) Beckett reduces the human condition to its most essential and honed. He challenges us to experience the existential core of man stripped of his external world of social and political organisation, culture and 'civilisation', commerce and conventional behaviour and confronts us with what he sees as the fundamentals of human existence — and for Beckett it is most frequently a purgatorial and sisyphean existence. Habit, endless repetition, waiting, religious doubt, endurance and survival, tears and laughter, these are the keynotes of his tragi-comic vision. And it is Beckett's play *Waiting for Godot* (regarded as perhaps his finest work) which manifests this vision most fully. *En Attendant Godot* was written in the period 1947-9, first performed on 5 January 1953, at the Théâtre de Babylone, Boulevard Raspail, Paris and in the English translation *Waiting for Godot* in August 1955 at the Arts Theatre, London.

Godot has all the richness and ambiguity of Shakespeare's tragedy *King Lear* (with which there are a number of parallels), yet at the same time the knockabout farce of the music-hall, of a Laurel and Hardy film, and both the comedy and pathos of the classic circus clown. The play has a huge range of possible meanings which depend upon an ostensibly simple and concrete situation presented in the theatre: the setting is a lonely roadside somewhere in the country; there is a tree and a small mound; two characters, Vladimir and Estragon, who appear to be tramps (they eat raw carrots and turnips and sleep in ditches, for example), wait for a mysterious Mr 'Godot' to meet them; 'Didi' and 'Gogo' (their nicknames) struggle to fill this time of waiting by playing games, trying to have conversations, eating, urinating, putting boots on and taking them off, disagreeing, hugging each other; they talk about the Bible and Christ, about suicide and death but always there are silences which come upon them between their often lyrical verbal games. In these silences they (and we in the audience) feel the pressure of awesome metaphysical horrors; the tramps come back time and again to the hope that 'Godot' will come, yet it is this very hope which ties them to their immovable situation ('Let's go./We can't./Why not?/We're waiting for Godot./Ah!' is repeated like a musical refrain in the play as is the stage direction in the text *They do not move*); they are visited by the authoritarian and self-indulgent (chicken-eating, pipe-smoking and throat-spraying) Pozzo and his wretched servant Lucky who is tied to him by a rope and carries his burdensome bags; they are also visited by a small boy who tells them that 'Godot' will be coming tomorrow. This sequence of events forms the structure of the first half of the play and the second half follows exactly the same structure. There are small changes in the second half, such as leaves having appeared on the tree overnight, and Pozzo blind, but from the point of view of dramatic form the play has a repeated structure, the purpose of which seems to be to suggest habit, repetition, endlessness and the purgatorial existence of the tramps. Such a bare plot would hardly seem capable of producing theatrical or critical interest and yet directors and critics have commented, and will go on commenting, on the possible interpretations of the play — each new approach revealing felicities never before discerned in the text. There is not space here to catalogue all the possible interpretations but a few of those which might be fruitfully taken further can be included. *Waiting For Godot* can be viewed as an 'extended metaphor' for human existence, the four main characters of the play representing four aspects of one 'everyman' (as if the play is a modern morality play), Vladimir and Estragon representing warmth, humour, personal relationship, dependency, loyalty, endurance, the capacity to survive, curiosity and fear of what may lie outside of human life. Yet, for all their tragic situation, Didi and Gogo doggedly persist in their hope; Pozzo and Lucky, tied to each other as they are, could represent master and servant, landowner and peasant, capitalist and worker, monarch and subject, a wrathful, authoritarian, unmerciful God and a meek and burdened mankind, even Body (Pozzo indulges his bodily appetites) and Mind (Lucky's main function is to 'think'). In such an extended metaphor we see 'unaccommodated man' (as Lear sees Edgar) stripped down to his essence, represented by the simplest concrete details of action in the play (swapping bowler hats, changing boots, eating carrots and so on). The critical search for some explanation of who 'Godot' is is as endless as the tramps' waiting for him in the play: in spite of the word 'Godot' appearing in the French version it may be (like 'Didi' and 'Gogo') a nickname — for 'God' — in which case the tramps are 'waiting' for salvation. Godot is, after all, described (in Blakean Old Testament terms) as having a 'white beard' and the statement 'If he comes?/We'll be saved!' along with the discussions about the two thieves in Luke's account of the crucifixion, may suggest that the play can be taken, on one level, as a Christian allegory or parable. But Godot may be Death, Godot may be Revolution, Godot may be Nothingness. Perhaps Beckett's own comment is the most helpful: 'If I knew who Godot was I would have said so in the play.'

The apparently irrational situation presented on the stage — 'modernist abstraction' of a kind — makes *Godot* and many of Beckett's subsequent plays central to the group of post-war plays Martin Esslin has termed **'Theatre of the Absurd'** (in the book of that title) and the separate entry under that concept may be read alongside this entry.

Endgame was first performed in Britain in its French version (*Fin de Partie*) on 3 April 1957 at the **Royal Court** Theatre (followed by the mime *Act Without Words* on the same bill). Hamm is paralysed and blind, again an early variant of the typical Beckett stage-image of disembodied consciousness and language as a means of expression of the self. Like Pozzo in *Godot*, Hamm is master over a servant (Clov) who fetches and carries for him, pushes his chair to different positions and looks out of the window for him. Two other characters, Nagg and Nell, with their legs cut off at their thighs, live in two dustbins on the stage. When the dustbin lids are lifted they eat biscuits and tell anecdotes about the past — they perhaps represent 'Memory' (or even Hamm or Clov's parents). This is feasible if we accept Hugh Kenner's idea that the action of the play takes place inside a human skull, the two windows high up on the upstage wall of the box-set suggesting 'eyes' looking out to the external world of desolation and nothingness, Hamm representing will and Clov action and emotion. We experience a consciousness at the end of its time, almost freed from the carnate world, its last moments like an 'endgame' of chess the final moves of which lead to a stalemate (Clov and Hamm remain together at the end of the play). Other key plays which carry immobility and the retreat of the physical body further and further have already been mentioned. Each one in its own way seems to penetrate the nature of the human condition by isolating language as the expression of thought, as if to suggest that Being is language and language is thought therefore thought is Being (again a Cartesian notion: 'I think, therefore I am.') *Krapp's Last Tape* (Royal Court, 28 October 1958) concerns an isolated old man who lives alone in a small flat: he listens to tape recordings of his past life. The ultimate expression of the 'nothingness' of being is *Breath* (Oxford Playhouse, 8 March 1970). The idea of the theatre itself as a metaphor of existence pared down to its most minimal essential qualities of setting (rubbish is strewn all over the stage) and action (the sound of breathing in, a cry, and breathing out) is taken perhaps to the furthest extreme Beckett could achieve (and nothing he has written since has verged so closely on the totally abstract).

Some of his latest plays are *That Time* (part of the Royal Court season celebrating Beckett's 70th birthday, 1976) which presented a face and voice (the voice separated on three tape recordings) exploring the past, a situation reminiscent of the similar 'monodrama' *Krapp's Last Tape*; the English version of *Rockaby* and a reading of *Enough* (written and published in French in 1966) were staged at the Cottesloe in December 1982.

The recently published *Collected Shorter Plays* (Faber and Faber, London, 1984) includes *Ghost Trio* and *... but the clouds* (BBC 2, April 1977), *A Piece of Monologue* written in English for David Wirrilow (New York, 1980), *Ohio Impromptu* (Ohio State University, 1981), *Quad* (BBC 2, December 1982), *Catastrophe* (Avignon Festival, 1982), *Nacht und Träume* (German Radio, May 1983), and *What Where* (New York, June 1983).

Four celebrated performers of Beckett's work have been Jack MacGowran, Patrick Magee, Billie **Whitelaw** (for whom *Footfalls*, Royal Court, 1976, was specially written) and Max **Wall**.

Further Reading

B. Fletcher *et al.*, *A Students' Guide to the Plays of Samuel Beckett*, Faber, London, 1978.

Hugh Kenner, *A Reader's Guide to Samuel Beckett*, Thames and Hudson, London, 1973.

Deirdre Blair, *Samuel Beckett: A Biography*, Picador, London, 1978

Behan, Brendan (Francis)

Born in Dublin on 9 February 1923 and educated at the French Sisters of Charity School, Dublin, he joined the IRA at the age of 14 and was sent to Borstal for three years (which he recalled later in his novel *Borstal Boy*, 1958). In 1942 he was sentenced to 14 years' imprisonment for political offences and the attempted murder of a Special Branch detective but was released after six. Like his father before him, he worked as a housepainter but he also wrote journalism.

In 1952 he wrote two short radio plays which were broadcast by Radio Eireann in the same year, *Moving Out* and *The Garden Party*, both autobiographical and about a family's experiences moving from a Dublin slum to a suburban housing estate. The plays were later adapted for the stage and produced by Alan Simpson under the title of *The New House* together with another adapted radio play (1957) by Behan called *The Big House* (Pike Theatre Club, Dublin, May 1958).

In November 1954 Alan Simpson directed Behan's first major successful play *The Quare Fellow* (Pike Theatre Club, Dublin), set in an Irish prison on the eve of a prisoner's execution. Much of the dramatic tension of the play is motivated by the impending hanging of the condemned prisoner (who is never seen or even heard) and the waiting moments of his fellow inmates. It is a rich and startling evocation of prison life. Although ostensibly sombre and sometimes macabre in its implied criticisms of capital punishment the play is coloured by much humour (Behan called it a 'comedy-drama'). Behan sent the play to Joan **Little-**

wood and the **Theatre Workshop** in London which, as usual with most texts, explored it through improvisation sessions at rehearsals and derived a new version of the play. It was presented at the Theatre Royal, Stratford East, in May 1956, just a fortnight after John Osborne's *Look Back in Anger* had been presented at the **Royal Court** Theatre. Later in 1956 *The Quare Fellow* transferred to the Abbey Theatre Company who were at the Queen's Theatre in the **West End**. Irving Wardle, who witnessed the Theatre Workshop production, has written of 'the wonderful night of May 24th 1956 when the then unknown figure of Brendan Behan swayed towards the public he had conquered ... and announced "I did not write this play — the lags wrote it." "Screw" and "lag" went overnight into the national vocabulary. And a whole set of attitudes to imprisonment went down the drain.' (*Drama*, 2nd Quarter, 1981), and Lawrence Kitchin has described it as 'a durable masterpiece if ever there was one' and a 'polemic worthy of Swift' (*Contemporary Dramatists*, ed. J. Vinson, 1977).

Behan's next stage play, *The Hostage*, was almost as great a success. It was commissioned by the Irish language society, Gael Linn, in 1957 and first performed in Gaelic as *An Giall* (An Damer Theatre, Dublin, June 1958). The English translation by Behan was sent to Theatre Workshop who, as with *The Quare Fellow*, revised it in rehearsal and produced a new version. It was directed by Joan Littlewood and first performed at the Theatre Royal, Stratford East in October 1958, in a further revised version by Theatre Workshop at the Paris Théâtre des Nations Festival in April 1959 and at Wyndham's Theatre in June 1959. The setting of the play is a seedy brothel used as a centre for IRA activities. The location is a 'safe house' for a British soldier taken hostage by the IRA in retaliation for the impending execution of one of their members. The hostage is accidentally shot during a police raid towards the end of the play. Although less coherently shaped than *The Quare Fellow* it has all the hallmarks of Theatre Workshop's **Brechtian**-style presentation and of Behan's comic treatment of and a broad sympathy for his characters. The form of the play employs tableaux, stylisation, song and dance routine blended with realistic dialogue and it was an ideal vehicle for a Theatre Workshop approach (an approach which later developed and refined into such original productions as *Oh! What a Lovely War*).

Behan's legendary drinking bouts and semi-coherent interviews on radio and television gained him as much, if not more, personal fame than his plays (he gave a notorious performance in a *Monitor* television interview with Colin MacInnes in which, in spite of much alchoholic rambling, he was at least able to comment on his work 'I'm not a postman ... I don't deliver messages' and quoted Camus as saying when he received the Nobel Prize, 'the duty of a writer is not to those that are in power but to those that are subject to them'). He died of alchoholism and diabetes on 20 March 1964, leaving behind him an unfinished political comedy about fascism, *Richard's Cork Leg*, which was completed from extant typescripts and by his own additions by Alan Simpson ('Brendan's last play as I believe he would have wished it to be presented'). It was first performed by the Abbey Theatre Company (Peacock Theatre, Dublin, March 1972) and also presented by the **English Stage Company** (Royal Court Theatre, London, September 1972), both productions directed by Alan Simpson.

John Russell Taylor, assessing Behan's place in post-war British theatre (*Anger and After*, 1969) wrote that he was 'an Irishman among the English ... a Catholic among Protestants, a cat among the pigeons (or perhaps, all things considered, a bull in a china shop is nearer the mark), a historical accident ... he must be considered, if only because, like Everest, he is there.'

Further Reading

Peter Gerdes, *The Major Works of Brendan Behan*, Herbert Lang, Bern, 1973.
Rae Jeffs, *Brendan Behan: Man and Showman*, Hutchinson, London, 1966.
Ulick O'Connor, *Brendan Behan: A Biography*, Hamish Hamilton, London, 1970.

Bennett, Alan

Born in Armley, Leeds, on 9 May 1934, he was the son of a butcher. (In an interview with Frank Delaney in 1984 he said he once thought 'my only niche in literary history would be that I'd once upon a time delivered meat to T.S. Eliot's mother-in-law'). Bennett was educated at Leeds Modern School and Exeter College, Oxford. During National Service on the Russian Language course at the Joint Services School in 1956 he wrote and performed some revue sketches with Michael **Frayn**. At Exeter College he wrote 'smoking' concert sketches and put on a show with Russell Harty which included some material which was eventually to become part of the famous revue, *Beyond the Fringe* (1960).

Bennett first appeared in a stage revue called *Better Late* (Oxford Theatre Group, **Edinburgh Festival**, August 1959) and a year later co-wrote and appeared in *Beyond the Fringe* (Edinburgh Festival, August 1960) with Peter Cook, Dudley Moore and Jonathan **Miller**. One of his most memorable contributions was a parody of a church sermon ('life, you know, is rather like opening a tin of sardines. We are all of us looking for the key ... there's always a little bit in the corner you can't get out. I wonder — I wonder, is there a little bit in the corner of your life? I know there is in mine.') Jonathan Miller has said of Bennett's performances in the *Fringe* that 'he had a sort of pin-sharp accuracy — an absolutely unflinching accuracy of portraiture ... a miniaturist — perfect when he came on'. The revue subsequently ran in London (Fortune, May 1961) and New York (John Golden, October 1962).

Bennett appeared as the Archbishop of Canterbury in **Osborne**'s *Blood of the Bambergs* (**Royal Court**, July 1962) and the Rev. Sloley-Jones in Ben Travers's *A Cuckoo in the Nest* (Royal Court, October 1964). In December 1965 he appeared in John Bird's television play *My Father Knew Lloyd George* with John Fortune and Eleanor **Bron** and afterwards wrote sketches for Ned Sherrin's late night show *BBC3*. In 1966 he wrote and appeared in six half-hour weekly programmes of sketches, poems and observations of life, called *On the Margin*.

His first play for the stage was *Forty Years On* (Apollo, October 1968) which starred John **Gielgud** as the Headmaster (later played by Emlyn Williams) and himself as Tempest, a well-meaning junior master. The play, originally called *The Last of England*, concerns a public school's attempts to put on a play about the first half of the twentieth century. In an interview with Russell Harty (October 1977) Bennett said 'within the framework of *Forty Years On* I was able to be both sad and funny. Critics prefer you to be one or the other, but audiences have no objection if you manage to be both.' His next play, *Getting On* (Queen's, October 1971), was a witty comedy about a disillusioned middle-aged and middle-class Labour MP (George Oliver), originally played by Kenneth More. This was followed by *Habeus Corpus* (Lyric, May 1973), a play satirising the sexual lusts of the flesh (corpus) and the 'permissive society'. The leading role (Arthur Wicksteed) was taken by Alec **Guinness** and Bennett took over the part of Mrs Swabb (the cleaner) from February 1974 (Lyric Theatre). The play was also performed in New York in 1975 with Donald **Sinden** in the leading part.

The Old Country (Queen's, September 1977) was a witty exploration of the identity of the 'English', and a study of a British traitor (first played by Alec Guinness) exiled in the USSR. In some ways the play was a precursor to Bennett's television play about the spy Guy Burgess, *An Englishman Abroad.* For BBC television he wrote *A Little Outing* and *A Visit from Mrs Prothero* (1977) and for London Weekend Television: *Doris and Doreen, The Old Crowd* (directed by Lindsay Anderson), *Me! I'm Afraid of Viginia Woolf, All Day on the Sands, Afternoon Off* and *One Fine Day.* His next stage play was *Enjoy* (Vaudeville, 1980) about an elderly working-class couple, originally played by Colin **Blakely** and Joan **Plowright**.

In 1981 Bennett wrote a double-bill called *Office Suite* and contributed to *The Secret Policeman's Other Ball* (Theatre Royal, Drury Lane, September 1981). 1982 saw two much-acclaimed television plays: *A Woman of No Importance,* a monologue by an incessant talker and gossiper, Miss Schofield (played by Patricia **Routledge**), whose view of life is (to her unwittingly) both comic and pathetic – Bennett stated in his 1984 interview 'by the end of *A Woman of No Importance* you understand why she is like that and you sympathise with her'. (He also related that Miss Schofield was partly based on his Auntie Cathleen who used to say things to him such as, when they were passing the Wellington Road Gasworks in Leeds, 'Alan. This is the biggest gasworks in England ... and I know the manager.') He felt he 'wanted to write a play in which one came to understand that sort of person and that she was redeemed'. A second television play, *Intensive Care,* was about a father dying in a hospital Intensive Care Unit. Bennett played the son. Perhaps his best play for television to date is *An Englishman Abroad* (1983), a remarkable study of the spy Guy Burgess exiled in Soviet Russia and in a state of considerable decline. Alan **Bates** gave a much-acclaimed performance as Burgess. At the **Chichester Festival** in 1984 Bennett's first play, *Forty Years On,* was revived.

The majority of his plays, whether for the stage or television, tread a thin line between farcical comedy and a serious and sympathetic understanding of human life. Bennett has said about this that 'edges seem to be the most interesting thing ... it seems to me much more interesting to write about the edge between comedy and tragedy and to be able to stray from one to the other ... somehow tread the line between the two'.

Berkoff, Steven

Born in London on 3 August 1937, he was educated at Raines Foundation, Stepney, and Hackney Downs Grammar School. He trained for the stage at the École Jacques Le Coq, Paris (where he studied mime), and the Webber-Douglas Academy, London.

He first appeared as Louis in Arthur Miller's *A View From the Bridge* (Empire, Finsbury Park, August 1959), subsequently worked in repertory, and then formed the London Theatre Group for which he has written, adapted, directed and acted in a number of plays including *The Penal Colony* (Arts Lab., Drury Lane, 1968), which was an adaptation of a short story by Kafka, *The Trial* (Oval House, 1970, Round House, December 1973, Dusseldorf Playhouse, West Germany, September 1976), adapted from Kafka's novel, and *Metamorphosis* (Round House, July 1969, Hampstead Theatre Club, 1972, Collegiate Theatre, 1976, **National Theatre**, Cottesloe, 1977, Nimrod Theatre Company, Sydney, 1978, Haifa Theatre Company, Haifa, 1978), which was also adapted from a story by Kafka. Berkoff played Titorelli in the 1970 production of *The Trial* and Gregor in the 1969 production of *Metamorphosis.* In 1973 he presented *Agamemnon,* adapted from Aeschylus, in which he played the title-role, and in 1974 *The Fall of the House of Usher,* adapted from Edgar Allan Poe, in which he played Usher.

His first original play, *East,* was presented at the 1975 **Edinburgh Festival** and later at the National Theatre (Cottesloe). As with many productions by the London Theatre

Group, mime and non-verbal effects are central to the performance but in this play Berkoff also developed a mixture of parodies of Shakespearian blank-verse, punk poetry and cockney slang.

At the Edinburgh Festival in 1979 he directed and took the title-role in *Hamlet* and in the same year wrote and directed a parody of the Oedipus myth, called *Greek* (Croydon Warehouse). In 1980 he presented *The Murder of Jesus Christ*, and in 1981 *Decadence* (New End, July 1981, Arts Theatre, October 1981, revived January 1983). At the Almeida in December 1982 he gave a solo performance of *One Man* and in May 1983, at the Warehouse, *West* (a cockney version of *Beowolf*) was presented.

Berkoff has also written a collection of short stories called *Gross Intrusion*.

Most of Berkoff's work has been concerned with the lonely and private trials of individuals, often allegorically presented through myth and legend. Commenting in his preface to the published edition of *The Trial* (Amber Lane Press, Derbyshire, 1981), he stated, '*The Trial* is my life. It is anyone's trial ... To create a metaphysical concept is to condense reality into its surreal intense image: reality heightened by fear, excitement or the pathological hyper-awareness of the artist.'

Black-Out

When all the stage lights are extinguished.

Blacks

Long black curtains sometimes used when a production requires little or no scenery or when rehearsals are held on the stage.

Blakely, Colin (George Edward)

Born in Bangor, County Down, Northern Ireland, on 23 September 1930, he was educated at Sedbergh School, Yorkshire. He began his career in his family's sports retail business (Athletic Stores Ltd, Belfast) and was manager of it from 1948 until 1957. He had amateur theatrical experience with Bangor Operatic Society and in 1957 joined a children's theatre touring group. In April 1958 he made his first fully professional appearance as Dick McArdle in *Master of the House* with the Group Theatre, Belfast, and in September of the same year appeared at the **Edinburgh Festival** (Lyceum) as Kevin McAlinden in *The Bonfire*.

His first London appearance was as the Second Rough Fellow in Sean O'Casey's *Cock-a-Doodle-Dandy*, with the **English Stage Company** at the **Royal Court** Theatre (September 1959). Further parts with the company followed until 1960 when he played Baxter in *Over the Bridge* (Princes, May 1960) and Josh in *Dreaming Bandsmen* (Belgrade, Coventry, July 1960). In April 1961 he joined the **Royal Shakespeare Company** at Stratford-upon-Avon to play Hastings in *Richard III*, Touchstone in *As You Like It* and the Duke of Venice in *Othello*. Returning to the Royal Court Theatre in December 1961, parts included Schmitz in Max Frisch's *The Fire-Raisers* and, the following year, Bottom in *A Midsummer Night's Dream*. He married Margaret Whiting in 1961.

In October 1963 Colin Blakely joined the **National Theatre** Company at the **Old Vic** where he came to prominence in a number of roles, notably a highly-acclaimed Pizarro in the original production of Peter **Shaffer**'s *The Royal Hunt of the Sun* (1964), which was also played at the **Chichester Festival** Theatre. Other parts with the National included Proctor in Arthur Miller's *The Crucible*, Hobson in Harold Brighouse's *Hobson's Choice*, and the Sergeant in **Brecht**'s *Mother Courage* (1965), Boyle in O'Casey's *Juno and the Paycock* (1966), the title-role in Ben Jonson's *Volpone* (1968) and Creon in *Oedipus* (1968).

After a performance as Astrov in Christopher **Hampton**'s new version of Chekhov's *Uncle Vanya* (Royal Court Theatre, February 1970) Blakely rejoined the RSC to play Deeley in Harold **Pinter**'s *Old Times* (Aldwych, June 1971) and take part in *Titus Andronicus* (Stratford, October 1972). He then took the role of Torvald Helmer in Ibsen's *A Doll's House* (Criterion, February 1973) and directed and played Blakey in *The Illumination of Mr Shannon* (Soho Poly, March 1973). Other major parts have been Captain Shotover in Shaw's *Heartbreak House* (National Theatre at the Old Vic, February 1975), Martin Dysart in Shaffer's *Equus* (Albery, April 1976), Dennis in Alan **Ayckbourn**'s *Just Between Ourselves* (Queen's, April 1977), Soriano in de Filippo's *Filumena* (Lyric, November 1977) and the title-role in *Semmelweiss* (Kennedy Centre, Washington DC, 1978). He recently appeared in Alan **Bennett**'s *Enjoy* (Vaudeville, 1980), a revival of Arthur Miller's *All My Sons* (Wyndham's, November 1981) and in Charles Dyer's *Lover's Dancing* (Albery, October 1983). In March 1985 he was in Pinter's *Other Places* at the Duchess Theatre.

Film work includes *This Sporting Life, Decline and Fall, The Private Life of Sherlock Holmes, Murder on the Orient Express, The National Health, It Shouldn't Happen to a Vet, The Pink Panther Strikes Again, Equus, Dogs of War, Evil Under the Sun, Nijinsky* and *The Little World of Don Camillo.* Television appearances include *Son of Man* (in which he played Christ), *Peer Gynt* (in which he played Peer Gynt), *Antony and Cleopatra* (in which he was Antony), *The Red Monarch* (in which he was Stalin), *Man Friday* and *Donkey's Years.*

Blakemore, Michael (Howell)

Born in Sydney, Australia, on 18 June 1928, he was educated at the King's School, New South Wales, and the University of Sydney. He worked as a press agent for Robert Morley when he toured Australia in *Edward, My Son* in 1949 and in 1950 came to England to study at the Royal Academy of Dramatic Art. He began his career in acting and first appeared professionally as the Doctor in Rudolf Besier's *The Barretts of Wimpole Street* (Theatre Royal, Huddersfield, 1952). He played numerous parts in repertory at Birmingham, Bristol and Coventry, appeared at the **Shakespeare Memorial Theatre** in 1959 and for two seasons at the Open Air Theatre, Regent's Park (1962-3), his parts including Sir Toby Belch in *Twelfth Night* and Theseus in *A Midsummer Night's Dream.* He toured Australia as Palmer Anderson in Iris Murdoch and J.B. Priestley's *A Severed Head* (1965) and joined the company at the Glasgow Citizen's Theatre in 1966, where he also began directing (in particular he directed productions of David Halliwell's *Little Malcolm and his Struggle Against the Eunuchs,* Hugh Leonard's *Stephen D* and Ibsen's *Rosmersholm*). He married Shirley Bush in 1960.

Michael Blakemore greatly encouraged Peter **Nichols**'s writing for the stage and directed many of his plays for the first time: *A Day in the Death of Joe Egg* (Glasgow Citizen's, May 1967), *The National Health* (**National Theatre**, **Old Vic**, October 1969), *Forget-me-not Lane* (Greenwich Theatre, April 1971) and *Privates on Parade* (**Royal Shakespeare Company**, Aldwych, February 1977). Other major productions by Blakemore have been *Brecht*'s *The Resistible Rise of Arturo Ui* (1969), *Design For Living* (1973) and David **Hare**'s *Knuckle* (1974). As an Associate Director for the National Theatre at the Old Vic (1971-6) some of his productions were Adrian Mitchell's *Tyger* (1971), O'Neill's *Long Day's Journey Into Night* (1971), *Macbeth* (1972), Chekhov's *The Cherry Orchard* (1973) and Ben Travers's *Plunder* (1976). In London he also directed **Rattigan**'s *Separate Tables* (1976), Shaw's *Candida* (1977) and abroad directed Webster's *The White Devil* (Tyrone Guthrie Theatre, Minneapolis, 1977), Noël **Coward**'s

Hay Fever (Denmark, 1977) and *Deathtrap* (New York, 1978).

Recent productions include *Make and Break* (Lyric, Hammersmith, 1980), *Travelling North* (Lyric, Hammersmith, 1980), Ibsen's *The Wild Duck* (Lyric, Hammersmith, 1980), Arthur Miller's *All My Sons* (Wyndham's, 1981), Michael **Frayn**'s *Noises Off* (Lyric, Hammersmith, and Savoy Theatre, 1982) and Frayn's *Benefactors* (Vaudeville, 1984). He has written a partly autobiographical novel about actors called *Next Season* (1969).

Peter Nichols (in Ronald Hayman's *Playback 2*, 1973) commented that Michael Blakemore's directing is 'like Sandhurst — which is one of Michael's strong points ... whatever else happens, you can be sure the mechanics are going to work. Nothing is left to chance in his productions.'

Bleasdale, Alan

Born in Liverpool in 1946, he began his career in teaching but turned to writing for the stage and television. His first play, *Fat Harold and the Last Twenty Six* (Everyman Theatre, Liverpool, New End, Hampstead, 1975), was about comic and sometimes violent tensions in a bus depot. This was followed by *The Party's Over* (Everyman Theatre, Liverpool, 1975) about intrigue in a girls' probation hostel, *Down the Dock Road* (Everyman Theatre, Liverpool, 1976), an entertaining exploration of corruption among Liverpool dockers and security police, and the need to fantasise in order to escape from urban reality, and *It's a Madhouse* (Contact Theatre, Manchester, June 1976). In 1976 Bleasedale stated: 'I write about the person who is the outsider — the inspector, Fat Harold, Bernadette, the girl trapped in a Probation Hostel, the Union Man in *Dock Road*.' He was Resident Playwright at the Everyman Theatre, Liverpool, until 1977 and has since been joint Artistic Director at the same theatre. After a number of other plays (including *Feet First*, *Should Old Acquaintance* and *No More Sitting On the Old School Bench*, the latter a comedy about tensions among the staff of a multi-racial comprehensive school) he shot to fame with the highly-acclaimed television play *The Black Stuff* and subsequent series *The Boys From The Blackstuff*, about a group of men coping with unemployment.

Other stage plays include *Having a Ball* (1981 tour, Lyric, Hammersmith, June 1981) and *Are You Lonesome Tonight?* (Liverpool Playhouse, May 1985, Phoenix, July 1985) a musical about Elvis Presley. For television Bleasdale has also written *Early to Bed*, *Scully's New Year's Eve*, *A Dangerous Ambition*, *Benjamin and Mary*, *The Muscle Market* and the series *Scully*. He wrote the film script for *No Surrender* and has had two novels published.

Blocking

Strictly the initial working out of stage moves in rehearsal. *Note*: many directors prefer not to 'block' moves at the outset of rehearsals but rather allow them to evolve in the course of working with the actors.

Bloom, Claire

Born on 15 February 1931 in London, she was educated at Badminton School, Bristol and Fern Hill Manor, New Milton (near Bournemouth). She trained for the stage at the Guildhall School of Music and Drama and the Central School of Speech and Drama. In 1959 she married Rod Steiger and her second marriage was to Hillard Elkins in 1969.

Claire Bloom's first stage appearance was as Private Jessie Killigrew in *It Depends What You Mean* (Oxford Repertory Theatre, October 1946) and her first London appearance was in minor parts in Webster's *The White Devil* (Duchess, March 1947) and

Andreyev's *He Who Gets Slapped* (Duchess, June 1947). For the 1948 season she joined the **Shakespeare Memorial Theatre** company at Stratford-upon-Avon and played Ophelia in *Hamlet*, Lady Blanche in *King John* and Perdita in *The Winter's Tale.* Subsequently she played Daphne in *The Damask Cheek* (Lyric, Hammersmith, February 1949), Alizon Eliot in Christopher **Fry**'s *The Lady's Not For Burning* (Globe, May 1949) and Isabelle in Jean Anouilh's *Ring Round the Moon* (Globe, January 1950).

She joined the **Old Vic** Company for its 1952-3 season and appeared as Juliet in *Romeo and Juliet* and Jessica in *The Merchant of Venice.* After playing Ophelia in *Hamlet* at the **Edinburgh Festival** (1953) she continued with the Old Vic Company for the next season (1953-4), playing Ophelia again, Helena in *All's Well That Ends Well,* Viola in *Twelfth Night,* Virgilia in *Coriolanus* and Miranda in *The Tempest.*

She played Cordelia, with John **Gielgud** as the King, in *King Lear* (Palace, July 1955) and in June 1956 returned to the Old Vic to play Juliet. From September 1956 to March 1957 she toured with the Old Vic Company and again took the part of Juliet (Winter Garden, New York, October 1956). She was also the Queen in *Richard II* at the same theatre and for the tour.

On her return to London she took the part of Lucille in Giraudoux's *Duel of Angels* (Apollo, London, April 1958), playing opposite Vivien Leigh. Her appearances in the 1960s included Johanna in Sartre's *Altona* (**Royal Court**, April 1961), Andromache in *The Trojan Women* (Spoleto Festival of Two Worlds, Italy, July 1963) and Sasha in Chekhov's *Ivanov* (Phoenix, September 1965), again with John Gielgud. In the 1970s her roles included Nora in Ibsen's *A Doll's House* and Hedda in *Hedda Gabler* (Playhouse, New York, January 1971), Mary Queen of Scots in Robert **Bolt**'s *Vivat! Vivat! Regina* (Broadhurst Theatre, New York, January 1972), Blanche du Bois in Tennessee Williams's *A Streetcar Named Desire* (Piccadilly, March 1974) and Rebecca in Ibsen's *Rosmersholm* (Haymarket, October 1977).

Claire Bloom has subsequently taken part in Chekhov's *The Cherry Orchard* (**Chichester Festival**, 1981) and toured in *These are Women: a portrait of Shakespeare's heroines* (USA, 1981-2). She has appeared in many films (since her first, *The Blind Goddess,* in 1947), including *Limelight* (1952), *Richard III* (1956), *The Brothers Karamazov* (1958), *Look Back in Anger* (1959), *The Spy Who Came in from the Cold* (1966), *Charly* (1968), *A Severed Head* (1969) and *The Clash of the Titans* (1979). Television appearances have included *A Legacy* (1975), and, for the BBC Shakespeare productions, she played Katherine in *Henry VIII* (1979), Gertrude in *Hamlet* (1980) and the Queen in *Cymbeline* (1983). In 1980 she appeared in ITV's *Brideshead Revisited.*

Further Reading

Claire Bloom, *Limelight and After: Education of an Actress,* Weidenfeld and Nicolson, London, 1982.

Bogdanov, Michael

Born in London on 15 December 1938, and originally surnamed Bogdin, he was educated at the Lower School of John Lyon, Harrow, Trinity College (Dublin), Munich, and then at the Sorbonne, Paris. He married Patsy Warrick in 1966 and in December 1968 he directed his own musical version of Molière's *Le Bourgeois Gentilhomme* which he retitled *The Bootleg Gentleman* (Oxford Playhouse). His first London production was *A Comedy of the Changing Years* (**Royal Court**, Theatre Upstairs, February 1969). This was followed by *Rabelais* (with Jean-Louis Barrault) and *A Midsummer Night's Dream* (with Peter **Brook**) in 1970. He took up a number of directorships: Assistant Director with the **Royal Shakespeare Company** (1970), Associate Director,

Tyneside Theatre Company (1971-3), Associate Director, Leicester Theatre Trust (1973-7), Director of the Phoenix Theatre, Leicester (1974-7). Productions at Leicester included *Richard III*, *Hamlet*, and *The Tempest.* He also produced Farquhar's *The Recruiting Officer* for the opening of the Haymarket Theatre, Leicester. Some other productions at Leicester were *Lucy in the Sky*, *Twelfth Night*, *The Caucasian Chalk Circle*, *The Threepenny Opera* and *Tommy.*

For the **National Theatre** in 1977 he directed *The Magic Drum*, was Head of 'Christmas at the National', and directed his own adaptations of *Sir Gawain and the Green Knight* and *The Hunchback of Notre Dame.* For the Royal Shakespeare Company at Stratford-upon-Avon, he directed *The Taming of the Shrew* in 1978 and in the same year was Director of the Young Vic (until 1980). At the latter theatre some of his productions were Ben Jonson's *Bartholomew Fair*, his own adaptation of Chaucer's *Canterbury Tales* (1978), *Richard III*, *Hamlet*, *The Tempest* (1978-9) and *Faust!* (1979).

In 1980 Bogdanov directed Chekhov's *The Seagull* and Sean O'Casey's *The Shadow of a Gunman* for the RSC's Tokyo performances and in the same year became an Associate Director of the National Theatre. At the National in October 1980 he directed a controversial production of Howard **Brenton**'s *The Romans in Britain*, for which he was unsuccessfully prosecuted. He later directed his own adaptation of *Hiawatha* and, in April 1981, Beaumont and Fletcher's *The Knight of the Burning Pestle* (RSC, Aldwych). He then directed Dario Fo's *One Woman Plays* (National, Cottesloe, June 1981), *The Shadow of a Gunman* (RSC, Warehouse, July 1981), Calderon's *The Mayor of Zalema* (National, Cottesloe, August, Olivier, December, 1981), his own adaptation of Molière's *The Hypochondriac* (National, Olivier, October 1981), Pam **Gems'** translation of Chekhov's *Uncle Vanya* (National, Lyttleton, May 1982), his own adaptation of ad Habib Tanvir's *Charan the Thief* for the Naya Theatre of India (Riverside Studio, August 1982), Kyd's *The Spanish Tragedy* (National, Cottesloe, September 1982), John Fowles's translation of de Musset's *Lorenzaccio* (National, Olivier, March 1983), his own workshop production of *Macbeth* (National, Cottesloe, May 1983), a revival of Hart and Kaufmann's *You Can't Take It With You* (National, Lyttleton, August 1983), and Peter Tegel's translation of Rozovsky's *Strider — the Story of a Horse*, based on a short story by Tolstoy (National, Cottesloe, February 1984).

Bogdanov has also written and directed children's shows, and written reviews and song lyrics (for *The Hypochondriac*). With Terence Brady he wrote the television series *Broad and Narrow* and was a director with Telefis Eirean (1967-9).

His theatre productions are visually powerful and often politically committed: in an interview of 1982 he spoke of 'a need to express certain things I believe in deeply, and theatre provides that means of articulating social change ... Theatre is derived from the social circumstances in which it finds itself: when society needs to say something powerful about change, it produces art ... I can't approach any work unless it's in a way that is relevant to now.'

Further Reading

David Roper, 'A Young Man's Game', interview with Michael Bogdanov, *Plays and Players*, June 1982.

Bolt, Robert (Oxton), CBE

Born on 15 August 1924, at Sale, Manchester, he was educated at Manchester Grammar School and in 1940 began his career at the Sun Insurance Office, Manchester. In 1943 he began studies at the School of Economics, Manchester University. He served in the RAF and West African

Frontier Force from 1943 until 1946, stationed in South Africa and the Gold Coast and he attained the rank of Lieutenant. After the war he returned to Manchester University and gained a degree in history in 1949. He then took a teaching qualification at University College, Exeter, and was a teacher for nine years, first at Bishopsteignton village school, Devon, and then at Millfield School, Somerset. During his teaching career he began writing plays for children and also a number of radio plays, which were broadcast by the BBC (including *The Master*, *Fifty Pigs*, *Ladies and Gentlemen*, *Mr Sampson's Sundays*, *The Window* and *The Drunken Sailor*). Robert Bolt has been married three times.

His first plays for the stage were *The Critic and the Heart* (Oxford Playhouse, 1957) a play which, Bolt acknowledged, follows the plot and structure of Somerset Maugham's *The Circle*, and *The Flowering Cherry* (Haymarket, London, November 1957). The latter ran for 435 performances and was also staged at the Lyceum, New York, in October 1959. It is about a businessman disillusioned with urban life, who desperately wishes to escape to the orchard-country of his boyhood. For its time the play was not adventurous in its form and was conventionally naturalistic, yet achieved a balance of tensions comparable with some of Chekhov's plays. *The Tiger and the Horse* (Queen's, August 1960) is about a university lecturer whose family life is in tension and pressurised by university politics and the feelings of threat imposed by nuclear armaments.

A Man For All Seasons (Globe, July 1960), which starred Paul **Scofield** in the leading role, was a hugely successful and psychologically powerful historical drama about Sir Thomas More. Bolt commented in 1961 (*Encore* magazine): 'It is rare, I think, to find anybody who loves life as much as More did, who is nevertheless able quite consciously to part with it ... I wanted to show a man of extreme sophistication, wit and charm, who never lost control ... he is more or less my ideal human being.' The play focused in particular on the conflict between More's public duty (towards the demands of Henry VIII) and his private moral conscience. In form and structure Bolt moved away from the naturalism of his earlier work and gave the play a more **Brechtian** shape, in particular through the choric use of 'The Common Man' (originally played by Leo **McKern**). In the article already quoted above, Bolt stated, 'Brecht is the writer I would most wish to resemble.'

His next play, *Gentle Jack* (Queen's, 1963) was not greatly successful in performance and remains more a play of ideas and speculations about the analogy between the pagan folklore of the Maytime Jack-in-the-Green and the immorality (or otherwise) of capitalism. Bolt's interests in folk-tale and legend, history and political authority were also reflected in his play for children, *The Thwarting of Baron Bolligrew* (1965). *Vivat! Vivat! Regina!* (**Chichester Festival** August 1970 and Piccadilly, October 1970) was another historical drama. It explored the conflict between Elizabeth I and Mary Stuart ('above all, the unnaturalness of Power, the impermissible sacrifice of self which Power demands, and gets, and squanders', Bolt suggested in his Introduction to the published play). *State of Revolution* (**National Theatre**, May 1977) explored the frictions between Lenin (played by Michael **Bryant**) and Stalin.

Bolt has written screenplays for *A Man For All Seasons*, *Lawrence of Arabia*, *Doctor Zhivago*, *Ryan's Daughter*, *Lady Caroline Lamb* (which he also directed), *The Bounty* and *The Mission*.

In his 1961 interview he said: 'In the mere act of putting (a play) on the stage, you are attempting to control it — a ritual is a way of making tolerable the intolerable by the application of consciousness to it.'

Further Reading

Robert Bolt, interview with Tom Milne and Clive Goodwin (from *Encore*, 1961), in *Theatre at Work*, Charles Marowitz and Simon Trussler (eds), Methuen, London, 1967, pp. 58-77.

Bond, Edward

A controversial figure in the 1960s Bond has since become established as not only a 'committed' dramatist but a poet of the theatre and a tragedian. He was born on 18 July 1934 in London, educated at local schools and at the age of 14 left school to work in factories and offices, writing plays in his spare time. In December 1962 his first play *The Pope's Wedding* (about a young man, Scopey, who abandons everything in order to befriend a hermit and learn his wisdom) was performed at the **Royal Court** and Bond became a member of the Royal Court Writers' Group. He gained notoriety (and some acclaim) with *Saved* (Royal Court, November 1965), a play about the claustrophobic existence of a family living in a flat in working-class London; a young member of the family, Len, is 'saved' by what he comes to learn about himself through confronting death — the murder of a baby wiped with its own dirty nappies and stoned to death by a gang of youths. Len, present at the act, cannot condone it and is eventually reconciled with his family. The play was put on by the **English Stage Company** in spite of a ban by the Lord Chamberlain. The violence is, however, hardly gratuitous and has serious dramatic purpose related to the play's examination of one of the social diseases which is a consequence of contemporary technological society — as Bond has put it, 'we are now face to face with the fact that Man is a very violent creature' but 'people are not born violent by nature. The natural condition by which people are born is love, the aptitude for loving and being loved.'

Bond's third play *Narrow Road to the Deep North* (Belgrade, Coventry, June 1968) is a political and moral allegory about imperialism and presents its case through nineteenth-century Japanese history and to an extent the Noh Play tradition. In February 1969 the Royal Court Theatre presented an Edward Bond season which included *Saved*, *Narrow Road to the Deep North*, and *Early Morning* (earlier presented April 1968). This latter play was originally banned and is a surrealistic fantasy about monarchy: Queen Victoria, threatened with usurpation by Albert and Disraeli, is depicted as having Siamese twins and has a Lesbian relationship with Florence Nightingale. Bond's playful statement at the front of the published text of the play is 'The events of this play are true.' His next play was *Black Mass* (Lyceum, December 1970) which was put on as part of an evening held by the Anti-Apartheid Movement to commemorate the tenth anniversary of the Sharpeville massacre. *Passion* (Royal Court, April 1971) was put on for the CND Festival of Life. In September 1971 (Royal Court) came Bond's adaptation of Shakespeare's *King Lear* as *Lear*. It places a greater emphasis on the authoritarian aspects of Lear's character and is a remarkably exhilarating and intense play exhibiting Bond's poetic talents and his sympathy — and the credit is as much Bond's as Shakespeare's. The play is a modern tragedy in which Bond's Lear, as Ruby Cohn has put it, 'like Shakespeare's Lear ... has learned compassion, but he has also learned the necessity for socially responsible action'. *The Sea* (Royal Court, May 1973) follows the attempts of grief-stricken Willie to come to terms with the fact of death (his friend Colin is drowned at the opening of the play). Again the language of the play is vibrant, poetic and handled with great sureness. *Bingo* (first presented Exeter, 1973, Royal Court, 1974) presents a dying Shakespeare (originally played by **Gielgud**) in retirement at Stratford and *The Fool* (Royal Court, November 1975) is based on the life of the poet John Clare. *A-A-America* (*Grandma Faust* and *The Swing*) was a programme presented at the Almost-Free Theatre for Ed Berman's American Bicentennial Season and in June 1976 (Institute of Contemporary Arts) Gay Sweatshop presented Bond's *Stone*. The first contemporary play to be presented on the newly-opened **National Theatre**'s Olivier stage was Bond's *The Woman* (August 1978) which drew heavily on Greek tragedy. In December of the previous year the **RSC** staged *The Bundle* at the Warehouse, another play drawing on Japanese history.

Implying some rejection of the **Theatre of the Absurd**'s lack of historical realism Bond has described his own work as 'Rational Theatre', a theatre of ideas and action: Michael Anderson has suggested that Bond's 'excellence and originality lie in his uncompromising, pitiless view of man that strips him of his last shreds of nobility without recourse to the dubious symbolism of earlier writers'. Nevertheless Bond is as capable of highly rhetorical language and symbolic presentation as he is of raw realism. He is, like Peter **Shaffer**, capable of distilling the major post-war influences of **Brecht**, Artaud and **Beckett** and producing unique new forms of the contemporary theatre. The Royal Court Theatre in 1981 (July) presented *Restoration*, a musical play Bond has written with Nick Bicat and in 1982 (January) *Summer* was presented at the National Theatre (Cottesloe). Bond has adapted a number of plays (Chekhov's *Three Sisters* 1967, Wedekind's *Spring Awakening* 1974, Webster's *The White Devil* 1976), written libretti for operas (*We Come to the River* 1976 and *The English Cat* 1979) and written a ballet-version of *Orpheus* (1978). His screenplays include *Blow-up* (1967) and *Laughter in the Dark* (1969). Bond's *Theatre Poems and Songs* were published in 1978.

Bond has tackled such a range of genres that any simple categorisation of his work is now quite impossible and he must be regarded as one of our major writers for the theatre. His work might be summarised as disturbing, at times shocking, often richly allusive, poetic and compassionate. Bond is capable of striking a deeply destructive and tragic chord in his plays whilst always upholding humanistic values and maintaining an awareness of the dramatist's social and moral responsibilities in a world of increasing cruelty.

In May 1985 the RSC staged his trilogy *War Plays* (Barbican, Pit).

Further Reading

Tony Coult, *The Plays of Edward Bond*, Drama Books, London, 1978.

Malcolm Hay and Philip Roberts, *Edward Bond: A Companion to the Plays*, Methuen, London, 1978.

Jenny S. Spencer, 'Edward Bond's Dramatic Strategies' in *Contemporary English Drama*, C.W.E. Bigsby (ed.), Stratford-upon-Avon Studies, No. 19, Edward Arnold, London, 1981, pp. 123-37.

Simon Trussler, *Edward Bond*, 'Writers and their Work', No. 249, Longman for the British Council, London 1976.

Boom

A vertical tubular metal pole used for mounting stage lighting, usually employed in side lighting. The horizontal version is a suspended **Barrel**.

Borders

Narrow pieces of cloth used in **Proscenium** theatres to mask the ceiling of the stage and its lighting equipment. In earlier periods it formed part of the scenery and could be painted.

Box Set

A three-sided room on the stage, the open side ('fourth wall') facing the audience. It is usually constructed of **Flats**.

Braces and Weights

Extendable wooden supports which hook on to the rear of scenery **flats** and stand in 'stage weights'. *See also* **French Brace**.

Brahms, Caryl

Born in 1901, she was a novelist, playwright and ballet critic, and the co-author with S.J. Simon of several novels and wrote a number of shows and plays with Ned Sherrin. These included *No Bed For Bacon* (1959), *'Cindy-Ella' or 'I Gotta Shoe'* (Garrick, December 1962), *The Spoils* (1968), *Nicholas Nickleby* (1969), *Sing a Rude Song* (Greenwich, February 1970), an adaptation of *Fish Out of Water* (1971), *Liberty Ranch* (1972), *Nickleby and Me* (1975), *Beecham* (1980) and *The Mitford Girls* (Globe, October 1981). With Ned Sherrin her writing for television included TV revue sketches and *Little Beggars, Benbow was his Name, Take a Sapphire* and *The Great Inimitable Mr Dickens.* She died in December 1982.

Branagh, Kenneth

Born in 1961 in Ireland. From school (where he appeared in *Oh! What a Lovely War*) he went straight to the Royal Academy of Dramatic Art where he won the Bancroft Gold Medal. He immediately starred on television as Billy in *The Billy Trilogy* and took the lead in *The Boy in the Bush* television series. He shot to enormous success with his award-winning performance as Judd in Julian Mitchell's *Another Country* (Greenwich, November 1981, Queen's, March 1982). His extraordinarily quick rise to prominence at such a young age was furthered by leading roles in Caryl Phillips's *The Shelter* (Lyric Studio, September 1983) and Julian Mitchell's *Francis* (Greenwich, October 1983).

For the 1984 season at Stratford-upon-Avon Kenneth Branagh joined the **Royal Shakespeare Company** and gave a highly acclaimed performance as the King in *Henry V*. In addition he played Laertes in *Hamlet* and the King of Navarre in *Love's Labour's Lost.* One critic (Martin Hoyle in *Plays and Players*, May 1984) has commented, 'at 23, Kenneth Branagh is an actor of intelligence, toughness and sensitivity'.

Further Reading

Barney Bardsley, 'Waiting for the Renaissance of the Actor', interviews with Kenneth Branagh and Alan Rickman, *Drama*, No. 154, 4th Quarter, 1984, pp. 12-14.

Brecht, Bertolt (and Brechtian Theatre)

A major figure in European drama this century ('the most important and original in European drama since Ibsen and Strindberg', wrote Raymond Williams), the German dramatist Bertolt Brecht (1898-1956) has exerted a particularly strong influence upon dramatists and theatre practice in Britain in the post-war period. For better or worse, misinterpreted and at times only partially understood, his ideas, plays, and ways of working with his company, the Berliner Ensemble, pervade much of what we experience as theatre today. The influence ranges from the simplest of accepted conventions of 'open' production where audiences are constantly reminded (through austere sets, revealed lighting equipment, audience participation and the like) of their presence in a *theatre*, to sophisticated aesthetic forms of narrative structure in plays.

Brecht's theories are too often seen in isolation from his practices in the theatre and tend to be reduced to what appear to be simple formulae. As Michael Morley points out (in *Brecht: A Study*, 1977) 'in Brecht's case the popular game of "hunt the symbol" has re-appeared under a modified but no less dangerous guise as "hunt the *V-Effect*, or *Gestus*, or 'epic' elements",' whereas 'in both his work and his theory, Brecht was concerned with the problem of analysing the effect and function of the theatrical experience'. This is a useful corrective and points the way towards understanding Brecht as primarily a man of the theatre fascinated by actors and audiences and the complex relationship between the two. Ultimately Brecht's theories merge into a total approach to theatrical practice and performance, only testable in the live theatre. His theories are drawn from his experiences of writing plays and directing. They can also be seen as the sum of a dissatisfaction with contemporary German classical theatre and late-nineteenth and early-twentieth-century Naturalistic modes of presentation, a theatre which, Brecht argued, created an 'illusion of reality' on the stage, capable of suspending the disbelief of the audience and purging it of emotion deeply aroused through identification (empathy) with characters. This cathartic theatre he referred to as 'Aristotelian'. Two common confusions arise from this. In the first place the term 'Aristotelian', as used by Brecht, refers to Aristotle's theories of 'Imitation' in *The Art of Poetry* ('The Poetics') written some time in the fourth century BC. Greek drama of the sixth and fifth centuries BC was, in fact, much closer to Brechtian theatre than Naturalistic theatre. Brecht, in *The Messingkauf Dialogues* (first published 1963) contrasts what he calls 'Aristotelian' theatre with that of Shakespeare and the Elizabethans. Secondly, if Brecht was advocating an anti-cathartic theatre, then it might appear he wished to deny emotion in performances. This is a common misunderstanding of Brecht's position, a position inseparably linked with his techniques of distanciation (*Verfremdungseffect* or *'V' Effect*). As David Bradby puts it (in 'Brecht and his Influence', *People's Theatre*, 1978) 'far from wanting to suppress the emotions of his audience, Brecht wanted, like all great artists, to channel them'. Brecht himself wrote in *The Messingkauf Dialogues* that the Alienation effect 'consists in the reproduction of real-life incidents on the stage in such a way as to underline their causality ... This type of art also generates emotions; such performances facilitate the mastering of reality; and this it is that moves the spectator.' He refers to 'classical comedy, certain branches of popular art and the practices of the Asiatic theatre' as precedents, and, elsewhere, Elizabeth drama. His more immediate influences were Büchner, Wedekind, Piscator and Meyerhold.

The 'mastering of reality' is an emotional end, the means of attainment involving a placing of the audience in a critical and judgemental position through a variety of distancing techniques all of which have a *combined* effect upon the spectators. One form of alienation comes from the placing of the action of the play in the historical past or invented past, even the world of 'fable' or folk-tale (the *Caucasian Chalk Circle*, *Mother Courage and her Children*, *Galileo*, all, in various degrees, are examples of historical detachment). The narrative structure of a play, Brecht suggested in *A Short Organum for the Theatre* (1948), should be dialectical in form (Brecht was a committed Marxist and drew such ideas from Marxist and Hegelian views of history), in order to demonstrate (as Raymond Williams puts it) 'men producing themselves and their situations'. Brecht wrote in the *Short Organum* 'the individual events must be tied together in such a way that the knots are strikingly noticeable ... one must be able to pass judgement in the midst of them ... The parts of the fable, therefore, are to be carefully set off against one another by giving them their own structure, that of a play within the play.'

Alienation is also the responsibility of the actor, who must 'give up his *complete conversion* into the stage character' (as Stanislavski had required) but 'he *shows* the character, he *quotes* his lines, he *repeats* a real-life incident. The audience is not entirely "carried away",' (*The Messingkauf Dialogues*). The actor should also be aware of the particular 'attitude' or '*gestus*' of an event, episode, and the play as a whole, so that his emotions can be controlled in the service of communicating the various social and political issues arising from the action. More obvious performance devices integrated with other forms of detachment explored by Brecht (and most evident in actual performances by the Berliner Ensemble) were the use of chorus narration, songs, projected captions, and a minimal use of scenery and properties.

Brecht's 'epic' theatre, as he termed it, attempted to avoid the subjective, it broadened the scope of Expressionism in its aesthetic, freed the theatre from the naturalistic traditions of 'bourgeois' theatre, and opened up new possibilities for theatre as a social, political, and moral force in contemporary life. Brecht insisted, however, that 'there is no question of the theatre thereby losing its old functions of entertainment and instruction: these actually get a new lease of life ... Concern with reality sets the imagination off on the right pleasurable road. Gaiety and seriousness revive in criticism, which is of a creative kind.'

The influence of Brechtian theatre on post-war British theatre is immense, ranging from the 'ensemble' approaches towards production generated by the Berliner Ensemble (who appeared in London at the Palace Theatre in 1956 and presented *Mother Courage, The Caucasian Chalk Circle* and *Trumpets and Drums*), to direct influences upon Joan **Littlewood** and **Theatre Workshop**, John **Arden**, Peter **Barnes**, John **Osborne**, Alan **Plater** and Robert **Bolt**, to less self-evident but nevertheless important influences on Peter **Shaffer** and John **Whiting**, the directors William **Gaskill**, John **Dexter** and John **Barton**, and a whole new generation of writers in the 1970s associated with 'fringe' companies and politically-orientated theatre, such as David **Hare**, John **McGrath**, Howard **Brenton** and Trevor **Griffiths**.

Although post-war British theatre has been mostly influenced by Brecht's theories, John Willet has rightly argued for a greater concentration, in Brecht studies, on the plays themselves and on the practices and achievements of the Berliner Ensemble. All too often the plays are viewed as manifestations of the 'sacred principles of the Brechtian Theatre' (John Willett, *The Theatre of Bertolt Brecht*, revised edition 1977) and 'as a result, the Ensemble's productions get treated as examples of a new theoretical approach, when they ought to be judged primarily as realizations of the playwright's work'. For Raymond Williams (*Drama from Ibsen to Brecht*, 1983) Brechtian Theatre offers 'a way of seeing that permanently alters dramatic possibilities'.

Further Reading

John Willett (editor and translator), *Brecht on Theatre*, Eyre Methuen, London, 1978.

John Willett, *The Theatre of Bertolt Brecht*, Eyre Methuen, London, revised paperback edn, 1977.

Michael Morley, *Brecht: A Study*, Heinemann, London, 1977.

Frederic Ewen, *Bertolt Brecht: His Life, His Art and His Times*, Calder and Boyars, London, 1970.

Brenton, Howard

Born in Portsmouth on 13 December 1942, he was educated at Chichester High School and St Catherine's College, Cambridge. As an undergraduate he wrote his first play *Ladder of Fools*, a one-acter produced in 1965 at Cambridge. Following this he had another one-acter *It's My Criminal* performed at the **Royal Court** Theatre in 1966. *Winter, Daddykins* followed in the same year and was produced in Dublin. In 1969 Brenton Joined David **Hare**'s Portable Theatre touring company and wrote for it his first full-length plays *Revenge* (also seen at Royal Court, Theatre Upstairs), a play about a criminal who has a passionate urge to take revenge on a Scotland Yard police officer, and *Christie in Love* (Portable Theatre, and Theatre Upstairs, 1969) about a mass-murderer's interrogation by police (which also involves some intriguing use of flashbacks to Christie's confession and uses the symbolism of a burial compound to represent a number of aspects of contemporary life). In 1969 *Gum and Goo* (Brighton Combination), *Heads* and *The Education of Skinny Spew* (Bradford University), were also performed, all of which are plays about children and employ a form and style which have many affinities with the strip-cartoon. *Wesley* (Bradford Festival, 1970) was an exploration of Wesley's foundation of Methodism and *Scott of the Antarctic* (Bradford Festival at Bradford Ice Rink, 1971) pungently criticised public school attitudes to heroes. *A Sky Blue Life* (1971) is in episodic form and explores the artistic and political nature of Gorky. In 1972 Brenton's *Hitler Dances* jointly created with Traverse Workshop Company, was performed and focused on the sadistic aspects of extreme patriotism but lacked the form of some of his better plays.

At his best Brenton writes forceful plays which are quick-moving, energetic, full of verbal and non-verbal jokes and which criticise people's tendencies to live on illusions in a society which restricts freedom of expression. John Russell Taylor has commented (*Plays and Players*, January 1982) that 'when Brenton hits right, he hits straight to the guts'.

Also in 1972 Brenton's *How Beautiful With Badges* was performed and an adaptation of Shakespeare's *Measure for Measure* (Northcotte Theatre, Exeter). In collaboration with David Hare he wrote *Brassneck* (Nottingham Playhouse, 1973), a play about a Nottingham builder who joins the Freemasons to further his business; it is a study of how most shades of political persuasion all partake in the general decline of capitalism. *Magnificence* (Royal Court, 1973) again plays with different political opinions but this time in the context of four squatters who make a stand against a Tory Establishment and *The Churchill Play* (Nottingham Playhouse, 1974 and **RSC** 1978/9) takes a future perspective on what one critic (Johnathan Hammand) has described as 'the ideological struggle between the socialism we are painfully stumbling into and the positive political qualities of conservatism ossified into fascism'. The play is a political fantasy in many ways (Churchill runs a coalition government in 1984 and there are British Fascist prison-camps) though the handling of problems in Northern Ireland and the Falkland Crisis by Mrs Thatcher's government have given this play some ironic and predictive dimensions.

Weapons of Happiness (July 1976) was the first contemporary original play to be performed at the new **National Theatre**. It was on Communist themes and was directed by David Hare.

In 1977 Brenton wrote *Epsom Downs* for the **Joint Stock Theatre Group** (at the Round House) and in 1978 collaborated with David Hare (co-founder of Joint Stock since 1974), Trevor **Griffiths** and Ken Campbell in the writing of *Deeds* (Nottingham Playhouse). For the RSC he wrote *Sore Throats* (Warehouse, August 1979) and, with Tony Howard, a play called *A Short Sharp Shock!* (Theatre Royal, Stratford East, 1980) which takes a highly satirical view of Margaret Thatcher and the Tory Government of the late 1970s. In 1980 Brenton also translated **Brecht**'s *Galileo* (National Theatre) and wrote the controversial *The Romans in Britain* (National Theatre, October) which paralleled the British presence in Northern Ireland with the Roman invasion. Its violent scenes of bloodshed and homosexual rape caused a number of critical outbursts (notably from Mary Whitehouse who, although she did not actually attend the play, wrote in the *Guardian* about 'men being so stimulated by the play that they will commit attacks on young boys ...' and the Conservative leader of the GLC, Sir Horace Cutler, wrote in the *Daily Telegraph* that people should expect 'more responsibility from the National Theatre. It is not some Soho hovel.' His most recent plays have been *Thirteenth Night* (RSC, Warehouse, July 1981), a translation and adaptation, with Jane Fry, of Büchner's *Danton's Death* (National Theatre, Olivier, July 1982), adaptations of Alfred Fagon's *Four Hundred Pounds* and Brecht's *Conversations in Exile* (Royal Court, Theatre Upstairs, November 1982) and *The Genius* (Royal Court, September 1983) which is set in a Midlands university and is a comedy about a Nobel Prize-winning mathematician who discovers the solution to the final problems of nuclear physics but encounters a brilliant student who has done the same. Later in 1983 (November) Brenton wrote, in collaboration with Tundi Ikoli, *Sleeping Policemen* for the Theatre Upstairs.

Howard Brenton is also co-author of *Lay-By* (1971) and *England's Ireland* (1972), wrote the film *Skinflicker* (1973) and the television plays *Lushly* (1972), *The Saliva Milkshake* (1975) which was also performed as a stage play at Soho Polytechnic, *The Paradise Run* (1976) and the long-awaited *Desert of Lies* (BBC1, March 1984). This latter play is a *tour de force* of television drama and concerns the harrowing experiences of a female journalist who joins a safari to the Kalahari desert. The safari aims to follow the journey made by a Victorian missionary family (the Broom family) but becomes brutalised and corrupted in its attempts to survive disease and exposure. The play's use of flashbacks and animal imagery provides a richness of suggestion rare in the television medium.

Comparing Howard Brenton with the playwright David Hare, John Russell Taylor, in 1982, commented that 'at least wherever their work finds a home, from the fringe of Portable Theatre and Joint Stock to the National Theatre's nest of gentlefolk, they are both ruthlessly consistent in what they want to say and how they go about saying it'. Certainly Brenton is one of the best playwrights of the generation after **Osborne**, **Wesker**, and **Arden**, the generation often referred to as the 'new wave' or 'second wave'. His plays have tremendous force, theatrical energy and often an entertaining, if not relieving, comic tone: he stated once that 'the only thing that binds us together today is a profound unease, and laughter is the language of that unease'.

1984 saw his *Bloody Poetry* (Leicester Haymarket, transferred Hampstead Theatre, November).

Further Reading

John Russell Taylor, 'In and Out of Court', *Plays and Players*, January 1982.

John Russell Taylor, *The Second Wave*, Methuen, London, 1971.

Brett, Jeremy (*né* Huggins)

Born in Berkswell, near Coventry, on 3 November 1935, he was educated at Eton and studied at the Central School of Speech and Drama. He first appeared in repertory at the Library Theatre, Manchester, and made his first London appearance with the **Old Vic** Company, as Patroclus in *Troilus and Cressida*, Malcolm in *Macbeth*, Paris in *Romeo and Juliet* and the Duke of Aumerle in *Richard II* (Old Vic, 1956). He subsequently appeared in the same productions in New York (Winter Garden, October 1956) and played Troilus in a modern-dress production of *Troilus and Cressida*. He toured the United States with the company and afterwards Canada (until March 1957). On return to Britain he played numerous parts in the **West End** including Sebastian in *The Edwardians* (Saville, October 1959), the title-role in *Hamlet* (Strand, June 1961), Peter in Arnold **Wesker**'s *The Kitchen* (**Royal Court**, June-July 1961), Dunois in Shaw's *Saint Joan* (**Chichester Festival**, June 1963) and Sweetman in John **Arden**'s *The Workhouse Donkey* (Chichester Festival, July 1963).

In February 1964 Brett returned to New York and played Father Fontana in *The*

Deputy (Brooks Atkinson Theatre). On his return he took the part of Gilbert in *A Measure of Cruelty* (Birmingham Repertory Company, February 1965). He then played Beliaev in Turgenev's *A Month in the Country* (Cambridge Theatre, September 1965) and for its 1967 season, joined the **National Theatre** Company at the Old Vic, playing Orlando in *As You Like It* and Valère in Molière's *Tartuffe.* With the same company he subsequently played Kent in *Edward the Second* and Berowne in *Love's Labour's Lost* (1968), Che Guevara in John Spurling's *Macrune's Guevara* (1969) and Bassanio in *The Merchant of Venice* (1970). At the Cambridge Theatre he played Tesman in Ibsen's *Hedda Gabler* (1970) and in August 1971 at the Haymarket Theatre he took the part of the son in John **Mortimer**'s *A Voyage Round My Father.*

Some notable performances in the 1970s were Rosmer in Ibsen's *Rosmersholm* (Greenwich, May 1973), Mirabell in Congreve's *The Way of the World* and doubling Theseus and Oberon in *A Midsummer Night's Dream* (Stratford, Ontario, June 1976) and Robert Browning in *Robert and Elizabeth* (Ahmanson, Los Angeles, 1978).

He has appeared in the films *War and Peace* (1956) and *My Fair Lady* (1964) and many television plays and series, including Dorian Gray in *The Picture of Dorian Gray,* Joseph Surface in Sheridan's *The School For Scandal* and Jacques in *Dinner With the Family.*

In April 1984 he appeared as Sherlock Holmes in Alexander Baron's television dramatisation of *The Adventures of Sherlock Holmes,* and in May 1984 appeared as King Arthur in John **Barton**'s television adaptation of Malory's *Le Morte d'Arthur.*

Briers, Richard

Born on 14 January 1934 in Croydon, he was educated at Wimbledon and then privately. For a time he worked as a clerk and then trained at the Royal Academy of Dramatic Art. Whilst a student he played the title-role in *Hamlet* (and later once commented, 'I may not have been a great Hamlet but I was about the fastest.' W.A. Darlington in the *Daily Telegraph* said that Briers 'played Hamlet like a demented typewriter'). He won a scholarship to Liverpool Playhouse Repertory Company where he appeared from 1956 to 1957. In October 1957 he toured as Blisworth in *Something About a Sailor* and in 1958 continued in repertory at Leatherhead and Coventry (Belgrade Theatre). He toured as Joseph Field in *Gilt and Gingerbread* (November 1958) and made his first London appearance in the same production (Duke of York's, April 1959).

He played Bill in *Special Providence* (in the double-bill *Double Yoke*) at St Martin's Theatre (February 1960) and Christian Martin in *It's in the Bag* (Duke of York's, May 1960). In 1961 he appeared in a number of plays at the Arts Theatre, including the tramp in Harold **Pinter**'s *A Slight Ache* (January 1961, and subsequently at the Criterion, February 1961). At the Criterion in September 1962 he played David Madison in Leonard Gershe's *Miss Pell is Missing* and subsequently appeared at the **Edinburgh Festival** as Lieutenant Hargreaves in *Hamp* (Lyceum, Edinburgh, August 1964).

After a tour as Gerald Popkiss in Ben Travers's *Rookery Nook* (November 1964) he played Roland Maule in Noël **Coward**'s *Present Laughter* (Queen's, April 1965), Mortimer Brewster in *Arsenic and Old Lace* (Vaudeville, February 1966), Greg in Alan **Ayckbourn**'s *Relatively Speaking* (Duke of York's, March 1967) and William Falder in *Justice* (St Martin's, January 1968).

Richard Briers is best known for his comedy parts and is gifted with a quick and lively speech delivery and superb sense of comic timing. His acting has rarely been mannered or lacking in fluency and from the late 1960s onwards he created roles in some important new plays and revivals including the part of Moon in Tom **Stoppard**'s *The Real Inspector Hound* (Criterion, June 1968), Bois d'Enghien in *Cat Among the Pigeons*, which was John **Mortimer**'s translation of Feydeau's farce *Un Fil à la Patte* (Prince of Wales, April 1969) and played five parts, opposite Lynne Redgrave, in the first production of Michael **Frayn**'s dialogues, *The Two of Us* (Garrick, July 1970).

In February 1972 he took over the title-role in Simon **Gray**'s *Butley* at the Criterion Theatre and in Autumn 1972 toured with the **Prospect Theatre Company** as Richard in its production of *Richard III.* Briers's attempt to portray an almost 'vaudeville' Richard, treating his devious route to the throne as a sort of wicked and prankish game, made the character unexpectedly endearing and almost admirable in his good-humoured audacity. Rarely has the character been made to laugh at himself and his crimes to the extent that, in the final stages of the play when all is lost, many of our sympathies are with Richard. It was a skilful performance and an original interpretation which showed Briers to be quite at home in a major classical role.

In July 1973 he played Sidney Hopcroft in Alan Ayckbourn's *Absurd Person Singular* at the Criterion and in July 1975 took the part of Colin in Ayckbourn's *Absent Friends* (Garrick Theatre). He played Colin in *Middle-Age-Spread* in October 1979 (Lyric), and more recently appeared as Hjalmar in Ibsen's *The Wild Duck* in 1980 and Bluntschli in Shaw's *Arms and the Man* (Lyric, October 1981). As a member of Ray **Cooney's Theatre of Comedy** Company he played John Smith, a bigamous taxi-driver, in Cooney's *Run for Your Wife* (Shaftesbury, March 1983).

Briers has made many television appearances (first appearing on television in 1956) including parts in *Brothers in Law, Marriage Lines, OneUpManShip, The Other One, Ever Decreasing Circles* and Alan Ayckbourn's *Norman Conquests.* Perhaps his most popular and well-known television appearance was as Tom in *The Good Life* comedy series with Felicity **Kendal**, Penelope **Keith** and Paul **Eddington**.

Further Reading

Richard Briers, *Natter Natter*, Dent, London, 1981.

Bristol Old Vic

The oldest working theatre in England, built in 1766 in King Street, Bristol, and originally called the Theatre Royal. After being saved from complete closure in 1943 by CEMA (Council for the Encouragement of Music and the Arts, later the Arts Council) it was re-opened under its present name and with the formation of a repertory company. In 1946 a drama school based at the theatre was created and in 1972 a new studio theatre with flexible staging, the New Vic, was added. From 1963 until 1980 the Bristol Old Vic Company also staged plays, many of which were experimental and international in scope, at Bristol Corporation's Little Theatre in Colston Street. The Bristol Old Vic is closely associated with Bristol University Drama Department.

Many of the Old Vic's productions in the post-war period have transferred to London and elsewhere for further runs, notably the musical *Salad Days* (July 1954, transferred to Vaudeville, August 1954), *Love's Labour's Lost* (August 1964, transferred Old Vic, London, September 1964, **Edinburgh Festival** and world tour) directed by Valentine May, Frank Marcus's *The Killing of Sister George* (May 1965, Duke of York's, June 1965, Belasco Theatre, New York, October 1966) which starred Beryl **Reid**, Peter **Nichols**'s *Born in the Gardens* (September 1979, Globe, January 1980) and *Troilus and Cressida* and Farquhar's *The Recruiting Officer* (both Edinburgh Festival, August 1979).

Bron, Eleanor

Born at the beginning of the Second World War in Stanmore, Middlesex, she was educated at North London Collegiate School. She did not enter her family's music-publishing business but went to Newnham College, Cambridge (1958-60) where she studied for a degree in Modern Languages. During this period she appeared in the Cambridge Footlights Club revue called *The Last Laugh* (Cambridge Theatre Royal, June 1959). Alistair Cooke wrote of her performance in the *Manchester Guardian* (10 June 1959), 'she has a wolf-whistle figure, a confident pout, and needs only to practise singing in pitch ... to be something of a threat to the hoydens of the London Pavilion'. On leaving Cambridge (and after a stay in hospital for a spinal operation and working in the personnel department of the De La Rue Company) she made her first professional appearance in revues at the Establishment Club in Greek Street, London W1 (January 1962). In 1963 she appeared in New York with the same company. Roger Wilmut (in *From Fringe to Flying Circus*, 1980) wrote of her work at this time: 'Bron in particular showed herself to be an excellent actress, the mistress of the subtle inflexion and the expressive pause.'

She continued in revue work, mainly on BBC Television's satirical shows (directed by Ned Sherrin) *That Was The Week That Was* (1963), *Not So Much a Programme More a Way of Life* (1964) in which she worked with John Fortune, and other revue shows including *BBC-3* and *The Late Show* (1966). Later, with John Fortune, she co-wrote and appeared in the television series *What Did You Say This Thing Was Called Love?* (June 1968) and *Where Was Spring?* (1968, second series 1969).

Bron's work in stage plays began in June 1966 with the role of Jennifer Dubedat in Shaw's *The Doctor's Dilemma* (Comedy). Subsequent roles included Jean Brodie in Jay Presson Allen's *The Prime of Miss Jean Brodie* (**Bristol Old Vic**, 1967), the title-role in Shaw's *Major Barbara*, Hilda Wangel in Ibsen's *The Master Builder* and Sheila in Peter **Nichols**'s *A Day in the Death of Joe Egg* (all at the Bristol Old Vic, 1969). She was Hedda in Ibsen's *Hedda Gabler* and Pegeen Mike in Synge's *The Playboy of the Western World* (both at the Connaught Theatre, Worthing, 1969-70), the Countess of Chell in Willis **Hall** and Keith **Waterhouse**'s *The Card* (Bristol Old Vic, June 1973, Queen's, July 1973), Portia in *The Merchant of Venice* (Yvonne Arnaud, Guildford, October 1975), Mrs Faber in John **Mortimer**'s *The Prince of Darkness* (Greenwich, May 1976) and Amanda in Noël **Coward**'s *Private Lives* (Nottingham Playhouse, July 1976).

In April 1976 Eleanor Bron took part in the first Amnesty International review concert *A Poke in the Eye with a Sharp Stick* (Her Majesty's) with a cast which included Alan **Bennett**, Jonathan **Miller**, John Cleese, Michael Palin, Bill Oddie, John Bird and Peter Cook. She later joined the company at the Manchester Royal Exchange Theatre (1977-8) and played Elena in Chekhov's *Uncle Vanya*, Monica in Coward's *Private Lives* and Margaret Barrett in *A Family* (which she also later played at the Theatre Royal, Haymarket, July 1978). In January 1978 she played Charlotta in Chekhov's *The Cherry Orchard* (Riverside Studios) and in November 1979 she was in her one-woman show *On Her Own* (Playhouse Upstairs, Liverpool). In 1979 she also appeared in the Amnesty International review concert *The Secret Policeman's Ball* (Her Majesty's, June 1979). In 1980 she was in *The Amusing Spectacle of Cinderella and her Naughty, Naughty Sisters* (Lyric, Hammersmith) and later took the roles of Emma in Harold **Pinter**'s *Betrayal* and Hesione in Shaw's *Heartbreak House* (Manchester Royal Exchange, 1981), Stephanie Abrahams in Tom Kempinski's *Duet for One* (tour of provinces, 1982) and the title-role in Webster's *The Duchess of Malfi*, the latter for Ian **McKellen** and Edward **Pether-**

bridge's actors' company at the **National Theatre** (Lyttleton, July 1985).

Television work (other than already mentioned) has included N.F. **Simpson**'s *World in Ferment*, *Beyond a Joke* which she co-wrote with Michael **Frayn**, *Making Faces* which was a series written by Frayn, *Pinkerton's Progress*, *Nina*, *My Dear Palestrina*, *Dr Who*, *Moving on the Edge* and *A Month in the Country*. Films include *Help!*, *Alfie*, *Two for the Road*, *The National Health*, *Women in Love*, *Bedazzled* and *The Day that Christ Died*.

Further Reading

Eleanor Bron, *Life and Other Punctures*, Andre Deutsch, London, 1978.

Eleanor Bron, *The Pillow Book of Eleanor Bron*, Jonathan Cape, London, 1985.

Brook, Peter

Director and theorist, born 21 March 1925 in Chiswick, London, of Russian parents who were both scientists. Brook is probably the greatest and most innovative post-war British director and has notably proved that 'Director's Theatre' is a valid and exciting possibility for furthering the theatre arts. He went to Westminster School, spent two years in Switzerland and then attended Gresham's School. In 1942 he went up to Oxford at Magdalen College but previous to this, in the summer of 1942, produced *Dr Faustus* at the Torch Theatre, London, for the Aid to Russia Fund. Whilst a student he made a film of Sterne's *A Sentimental Journey* and in 1944 he joined a London film company. His first major directing was at Birmingham Repertory Theatre where he directed Shaw's *Man and Superman* (1945) and Shakespeare's *King John* (1945). Also in 1945 he directed Cocteau's *The Infernal Machine* at the Chanticleer Theatre Club, London, and Shaw's *Pygmalion* for an ENSA tour. Joining the company at the **Shakespeare Memorial Theatre**, Stratford-upon-Avon in 1946, Brook began his long association with Stratford and Shakespearian productions (later, in 1961, when the company became the **RSC**, Brook was made co-director). In that year Brook presented *Love's Labour's Lost* with settings evoking the paintings of Watteau, and in 1947 he presented *Romeo and Juliet* with stylised sets. 1950 saw his production of *Measure for Measure* with costuming reminiscent of characters in the paintings of Breughel and Bosch. Brook directed a ritualistic version of *Titus Andronicus* in 1955 and in the same year (at the Phoenix Theatre, London), a *Hamlet* with Paul **Scofield** in the title-role. Brook's association with Scofield began in 1945 (Scofield played Tanner in *Man and Superman*) and in 1956 Scofield was in Brook's production of **Eliot**'s *The Family Reunion* (Phoenix Theatre, London) and in the much-acclaimed *King Lear* of 1962 which was eventually adapted as a film.

Brook's talents extend to design and musical composition. In 1957 he directed *The Tempest* at Stratford-upon-Avon, making innovative use of gauzes and traps and his own 'concrete' music. In the 1960s Brook's productions became more sombre and existential, his 1962 *King Lear* being influenced by **Beckett** and the **Theatre of the Absurd**, an affinity which had been proposed by the Polish Scholar Jan Kott in a chapter comparing *King Lear* with Beckett's *Endgame* in his book *Shakespeare Our Contemporary* (Brook wrote the introduction to the English translation). Brook, whilst maintaining a fervently independent, creative approach to the theatre, has thus shown himself to be open to influences, as also instanced by his **Theatre of Cruelty** season with the RSC and Charles **Marowitz** at the LAMDA Theatre in 1964 which absorbed the influences of Artaud and Grotowski. In the same year came a powerful production of Peter Weiss's *Marat/Sade* at the Aldwych Theatre, London, with the RSC. This was heavily Artaudian in influence and struck a new note of unconventionality in the English theatre. In 1965 Brook toured *Marat/Sade* to New York and in 1966 devised, through rehearsals with the RSC company, a play about American involvement in Vietnam called *US*, presented at the Aldwych theatre.

Recently Brook seems constantly to have been attempting to probe into the fundamentals of theatre and its social functions. It is as if he wishes to use every production as an experimental laboratory for finding out some new detail of what constitutes the nature of theatrical enactment. His theoretical writings, the chief of which is *The Empty Space* (1968), are thus more a distillation of practical experience than the product of private academic study carried out apart from active engagement with the theatre itself. He said in an interview with Ronald Hayman in *The Times* (29 August 1970) that 'where someone in a library uses intellectual and analytical methods to discover what a play is about, actors try to discover through the voice, through the body, through experiment in action' and it may not be too exaggerated an idea to suggest that since the 1960s Brook's own career has been a kind of 'experiment in action'. J.C. Trewin, Brook's biographer, stated that 'Peter Brook's life is a prolonged and peripatetic experiment.' His remarkable production of *A Midsummer Night's Dream* with the RSC at Stratford-upon-Avon in 1970 was an encounter with what he has called 'dark and powerful currents' of magic and sensuality, but also with the question 'What is theatre?' The white box set, though not deliberately meant to be so, appeared fully to represent Brook's well-known view in *The Empty Space* that 'I can take any empty space and call it a bare stage. A man walks across this empty space whilst someone else is watching him, and this is all that is needed for an act of theatre to be engaged.' Brook has commented on the white box-set that 'the white walls are not there to state something, but to *eliminate* something. On a nothingness, moment by moment, something can be conjured up — and then made to disappear. The bare stage is a form of nothingness.' The production was memorable for its ability to throw the language of the play into relief and this was made possible by the extraordinary appropriateness of the visual spectacle. The fairies flew on circus trapezes and spun a plate on a stick to conjure their magic. The simplicity of circus costume and movement created space for the words and for the potency of the play to emerge in a way no other presentation has managed this century.

If Brook's presentation of *A Midsummer Night's Dream* was a theatrical 'safari' later developments in his work have literally turned out to be safaris into a deeper and deeper understanding of theatrical art. With the formation of his International Centre of Theatre Research in Paris, Brook has appeared to be probing into what seems to be a universal language of theatre — the essence of theatrical action which can work within any culture. As part of this experiment he took his Paris theatre group (which is made up of actors from many different nationalities) to Persepolis in 1972 to perform *Orghast* which used an 'international' language invented by the poet Ted Hughes. In the same year Brook took the group on an African safari through the Sahara desert performing spontaneous improvisations to native tribes and a play based on a Persian tale called *Conference of the Birds* (a book of this title by John Heilpern gives a superb first-hand account of the events of the safari). Brook's position has taken him to the recognition of the *necessity* of theatre and away from Western conventions: as he puts it, 'how to make theatre absolutely and fundamentally *necessary* to people, as necessary as eating and sex? Make-believe is *necessity*, It's this quality, lost to Western industrialized societies, I'm searching for.' On return from Africa Brook's group staged a new play called *The Ik* which was based on Colin Turnbull's research into an African tribe who chose to starve to death rather than accept a modern way of life. Brook has also revealed an interest in the systems of consciousness and mystical experience propounded by Gurdjieff and Ouspenski. He returned briefly to Stratford in 1978 where he directed *Antony and Cleopatra* and in 1984 he directed a film of the opera *The Tragedy of Carmen.*

Controversial though his productions and theories are Brook remains a remarkably influential director and a major innovative force in post-war European drama. His ceaseless questioning of and insatiable curiosity about the nature of theatre art will doubtless continue to push the limits of Western theatre further and prove beyond doubt the validity of the concept of the 'director-as-artist'. In summer 1985 at the Avignon Festival, Brook presented a day-long production of a Sanskrit epic the *Mahabharata.*

Further Reading

Peter Brook, *The Empty Space*, Penguin Books, Harmondsworth, 1983.
J.C. Trewin, *Peter Brook: A Biography*, Macmillan, London, 1971.

Bryant, Michael

Born on 5 April 1928, in London, he was educated at Battersea Grammar School, served in the Merchant Navy in 1945 and was in the Army from 1946 to 1949. He trained for the stage at the Webber-Douglas School (1949-51) and first appeared as the Young Collector in Tennessee Williams's *A Streetcar Named Desire* at the Palace Pier, Brighton (Summer 1951).

Among his chief roles before he joined the **Royal Shakespeare Company** in 1964 were Walter Langer in Peter **Shaffer**'s *Five Finger Exercise* (Comedy, July 1958, New York, December 1959 and USA tour, 1960), the title-role in Terence **Rattigan**'s *Ross* (Haymarket, London, January 1961) and Rudge in James **Saunders**'s *Next Time I'll Sing to You* (New Arts, January 1963). With the RSC he gave particularly memorable performances of Selim Calymath in Marlowe's *The Jew of Malta* (Aldwych, August 1964), the Dauphin in *Henry V* (Aldwych, May 1965), Teddy in Harold **Pinter**'s *The Homecoming* and Captain von Blixen in Graham **Greene**'s *The Return of A.J. Raffles* (Aldwych, December 1975).

In 1977 Michael Bryant became a **National Theatre** player, his work having since included Lenin in Robert **Bolt**'s *State of Revolution* (May 1977), the title-role in Ibsen's *Brand* (April 1978), Sir Paul Plyant in Congreve's *The Double Dealer* (September 1978), David in Galsworthy's *Strife* (November 1978), Von Aigner in Tom **Stoppard**'s version of Schnitzler's *Undiscovered Country* (June 1979), Jacques in *As You Like It* (August 1979), Gregers Werle in Ibsen's *The Wild Duck* (December 1979), Iago in *Othello* (March 1980), Julius Caesar in Howard **Brenton**'s *The Romans in Britain* (Olivier, 1980), Pedro Crespo in Adrian Mitchell's adaptation of Calderon's *The Mayor of Zalemea* (Cottesloe, August 1981, Olivier, December 1981), Béralde in Molière's *The Hypochondriac* (Olivier, October 1981), the title-role in Pam **Gems**'s version of Chekhov's *Uncle Vanya* (Lyttleton, May 1982), Hieronymo in Kyd's *The Spanish Tragedy* (Cottesloe, September 1982, Lyttleton, June 1984), Carlo in N.F. **Simpson**'s English version of de Filippo's *Inner Voices* (Lyttleton, June 1983), Peter Cauchon in Shaw's *Saint Joan* (Olivier, February 1984) and the Mariner in *The Ancient Mariner* (November, 1984), a stage adaptation by Michael **Bogdanov**, of Coleridge's 'The Rhyme of the Ancient Mariner'.

Films include *Nicholas and Alexandra, The Ruling Class* and *Caravan to Vaccares.* On television he appeared in the highly-acclaimed play *Talking to a Stranger* by John Hopkins and has also appeared in *The Roads to Freedom* and *The Duchess of Malfi.*

'Bums on Seats'

Colloquial term for the selling of tickets. Directors, managers, and companies hope their production will put 'bums on seats' (that is, will sell plenty of tickets).

Burlesque

Parody of a play or person.

Business ('Stage Business')

A term used to describe a short sequence of stage actions often using objects or articles of dress but it can also be a sequence of gesture. Sometimes stage business is performed with dialogue and sometimes without.

C

Caird, John

Born 22 September 1948, he was educated at Magdalen College School and the **Bristol Old Vic** Theatre School. He has directed mainly for the **RSC** and productions of note have been *The Dance of Death* (1977), *Savage Amusement* (1978), *Nicholas Nickleby* (co-directed with Trevor **Nunn**, 1980), *Twin Rivals* (1981), *Our Friends in the North* and *Peter Pan* (1982) and *Twelfth Night* (1983). He also directed the musical *Song and Dance* at the Palace Theatre (1982). For the 1984 season at Stratford-upon-Avon he directed *The Merchant of Venice* and at the Barbican in September 1985 he adapted and co-directed (with Trevor Nunn) *Les Misérables.*

Callow, Simon

Born in London on 15 June 1949, educated at Oratory Grammar School, London, and Queen's University, Belfast, he trained for the stage at the Drama Centre. His first professional appearance was in *The Thrie Estates* (Assembly Hall, Edinburgh, July 1973) after which he was in repertory at Lincoln and Edinburgh. Parts included Crown Prince Maximilian in *Schippel* (Traverse Theatre, Edinburgh, August 1974, subsequently at the **Open Space**, London, October 1974). In February 1975 he appeared in *Mrs Grabowski's Academy* at the **Royal Court** (Theatre Upstairs) and in the same year played Redpenny in Shaw's *The Doctor's Dilemma* (**Mermaid**, April 1975) and Crown Prince Maximilian in *Schippel,* renamed *Plumber's Progress* (Prince of Wales, October 1975). The following year saw him as Pieter de Groot in *Soul of the White Ant* (Bush, March 1976), and he also appeared at the Bush Theatre in *Blood Sports* by David **Edgar** (June 1976) and *Juvenalia* (July 1976).

He joined the **Joint Stock Theatre Company** and in 1977 played Kutchevski in *Devil's Island* (Royal Court, February), in 1978 Sayers in *A Mad World, My Masters* (Young Vic, May) and Sandy in Howard **Brenton**'s *Epsom Downs* (Round House, August). In April 1978 he took the title-role in *Titus Andronicus* (**Bristol Old Vic**) and in June played Boyd in *Flying Blind* (Royal Court). Also in 1978 he played Ui in Brecht's *The Resistable Rise of Arturo Ui* (Half Moon, October), a number of parts in *The Machine Wreckers* (Half Moon, November) and Eddie in David Edgar's *Mary Barnes* (Birmingham Repertory, Studio, September 1978, later transferring to the Royal Court, January 1979).

In 1979 Callow joined the **National Theatre** Company and played Orlando in *As You Like It* (August) and Mozart in Peter **Shaffer**'s *Amadeus* (November). At the Lyric, Hammersmith, he took the role of Verlaine in Christopher **Hampton's** *Total Eclipse* (May 1981) and subsequently appeared in Edward **Bond**'s musical play *Restoration* at the Royal Court Theatre (July 1981). In September 1981 he played Beefy in J.P. Donleavy's *The Beastly Beatitudes of Balthazar B* (Duke of York's) and in 1983 he directed Snoo **Wilson**'s *Loving Reno* (Bush, July) and appeared as Fashion in Vanbrugh's *The Relapse* (Lyric, Hammersmith, October 1983). He played a Chicago gangster in Edgar Wallace's *On the Spot* at the Albery Theatre in May 1984. At the National Theatre he has also given a one-man recital of John Padel's compilation of Shakespeare's sonnets.

Simon Callow is a versatile and powerful young actor (Victoria Radin in the *Observer,* 25 March 1984, stated that he is 'probably the most flamboyant character actor since Laughton') and he has expressed strong views on acting and directing in his book *Being an Actor.* He sees, for example, the dominance of 'director's theatre' as a 'directocracy' which has diminished the actor's vital contributions to the interpretations of a writer's text: 'the director has interposed himself between actor and writer, claiming they cannot speak each other's language ... the crucial element of the theatre, the actor's delight in the theatre, has been abolished'. Callow suggests that the director 'should be at the service of the company, realising the group's understanding of the play and its needs'.

Further Reading

Simon Callow, *Being an Actor*, Methuen, London, 1984, Penguin Books, Harmondsworth, 1985.

Campbell, Cheryl

Born in St Albans, the daughter of an airline pilot, she trained for the stage at LAMDA and subsequently worked with the companies at the Glasgow Citizens Theatre, the Palace Theatre, Watford, and the Birmingham Repertory Theatre. She was Freda in Ibsen's *John Gabriel Borkman* with the **National Theatre (Old Vic**, January 1975) which starred Sir Ralph **Richardson**, and played Maggie in W.S. Gilbert's *Engaged* in the same season at the **Old Vic**. She came to prominence in Dennis **Potter**'s television play *Pennies from Heaven* and gave an award-winning performance in the television version of Vera Brittain's *Testament of Youth.*

Subsequently she joined the **Royal Shakespeare Company** to play Nora in Ibsen's *A Doll's House* (Stratford-upon-Avon, the Other Place, 1981 season, Barbican, Pit, June 1982) and Diana in *All's Well That Ends Well* (Stratford-upon-Avon, 1981 season, Barbican, July 1982). She took the title-role in Strindberg's *Miss Julie* (Lyric Studio, January 1983, Duke of York's, March 1983), Asta in Ibsen's *Little Eyolf* (Lyric, Hammersmith, March 1985) and Minnie in D.H. Lawrence's *The Daughter-in-Law* (Hampstead Theatre, August 1985).

Other television appearances besides those mentioned include *A Winter Harvest* and *Absurd Person Singular.* She was also in the films *Chariots of Fire* and *The Shooting Party.*

Cargill, Patrick

Born in London on 3 June 1918, he was educated at Haileybury College and the Royal Military College, Sandhurst. He was in the Indian Army but did not pursue a military career after the Second World War. Instead (having worked in repertory in Bexhill and with Anthony Hawtrey's company in Buxton, Croydon and London, Embassy Theatre), he joined the company at the Theatre Royal, Windsor in 1946, remaining with them until 1953. He then began to appear in **West End** productions, including the revue *High Spirits* (London Hippodrome, May 1953) and Kenneth Horne's *Wolf's Clothing* (Strand, March 1959) in which he played Andrew Spicer.

In the later 1950s and early 1960s he was well known as one of the comic foils for Tony Hancock in the television series *Hancock's Half Hour* (written by Ray Galton and Alan Simpson). Continuing his work in theatre comedy he played Bernard in Beverley Cross's translation of Marc Cannoletti's *Boeing-Boeing* (Apollo, February 1962). Further roles included Stuart Wheeler in Keith **Waterhouse** and Willis **Hall**'s *Say Who You Are* (Yvonne Arnaud, Guildford, August 1965, Her Majesty's, October 1965), Charles in Noël **Coward**'s *Blithe Spirit* (Globe, July 1970), George in Richard Harris and Leslie Darbon's *Two and Two Make Sex* (Cambridge Theatre, September 1973, Australian and Canadian Tour, 1974-

5), Andrew Wyke in Anthony Shaffer's *Sleuth* (Savoy, March 1978), Gordon in John Chapman and David Freeman's *Key for Two* (Vaudeville, September 1982), King-Rat in *The Wind in the Willows* (Sadlers Wells, December 1984) and Simpson the butler in William Douglas **Home**'s *After the Ball is Over* (**Old Vic**, March 1985).

In a recent interview with Al Senter Patrick Cargill remarked 'comedy is instinctive. You know it's there but the moment you consciously search for it you're lost. Timing is a skill which you develop over the years — it gives you the necessary courage to wait — to pause while the audience gathers in anticipation.'

Cargill's filmwork includes *Carry on Jack*, *Help!* and *Inspector Clouseau.* Television appearances include *Top Secret*, *Father, dear Father*, *Hancock's Half Hour*, *Ooh La La!*, *The Many Lives of Patrick* and *Barnet.*

Carteret, Anna (*née* Wilkinson)

Born in Bangalore, India, on 11 December 1942, she was educated at the Arts Educational Schools, Tring, Herts, where she also trained for the stage. Her first professional appearance was as a Cloud and a Jumping Bean in *Jack and the Beanstalk* (Palace, Watford, December 1957) and her first London appearance was as Wendy in *Peter Pan* (Scala, December 1960). She worked in repertory at a number of theatres, including Windsor and Lincoln (1962-3) and the **Bristol Old Vic** (1964-6). Some of her roles at the latter were Honey in Albee's *Who's Afraid of Virginia Woolf?*, Titania in *A Midsummer Night's Dream*, Mariana in *Measure for Measure* and the Green Woman in Ibsen's *Peer Gynt.*

In 1967 she joined the **National Theatre** at the **Old Vic**. Parts included a member of the Chorus in *Oedipus* (1968), Nurse Sweet in Peter **Nichols**'s *The National Health* (1969), Jacquenetta in *Love's Labour's Lost* (1969), Nerissa in *The Merchant of Venice* (1970), Lucille in Büchner's *Danton's Death* (New Theatre, 1971), the Secretary in Tom **Stoppard**'s *Jumpers* (1972), Anabella in Ford's *'Tis Pity She's A Whore* (tour 1972), Anya in Chekhov's *The Cherry Orchard* (1973), Olivia in *Twelfth Night* (tour, 1973) and Susie in Trevor **Griffiths**'s *The Party* (1973).

Returning briefly to Bristol, she was Eliza in the Bristol Old Vic's production of Shaw's *Pygmalion* (Theatre Royal, Bristol, September 1974) and then, again with the National, she played Fanny in Ibsen's *John Gabriel Borkman* (Old Vic, January 1975, Lyttleton, March 1976). For the 1977 season she was a member of the company at St George's Theatre Islington, and played Portia in *The Merchant of Venice*, Isabella in *Measure for Measure* and Mistress Page in *The Merry Wives of Windsor.* Work at the Greenwich Theatre has included Olivia in *Twelfth Night* (March 1977), Mrs Cheveney in Oscar Wilde's *An Ideal Husband* (February 1978) and Dona Elvira in *Don Juan* (March 1978). In 1979 she returned to the National Theatre to play a number of roles in *Lark Rise* (Keith Dewhurst's adaptation of Flora Thompson's *Lark Rise to Candleford*), Adele in Tom Stoppard's version of Arthur Schnitzler's *Undiscovered Country* (June), Phoebe in *As You Like It* (August) and Queen Elizabeth in *Richard III* (November). In January 1981 she was in Shaw's *Man and Superman* (Olivier), after which she performed in *In The Pink* (Riverside, August 1981), with Raving Beauties, a woman's cabaret, dance and recital group of which she is Director. Later the same year she appeared in Molière's *The Hypochondriac* (Olivier, October).

Some of her numerous television appearances have included *The Pallisers*, *The Glittering Prizes* and *Send in the Girls.* She is especially well known as Inspector Kate Longton in the police series *Juliet Bravo.* Anna Carteret is married to Christopher Morahan.

Catwalk

A narrow bridge between two raised locations on the stage.

Chichester Festival and Theatre

The hexagonal theatre in Oaklands Park, Chichester was opened on 3 July 1962. The idea for the theatre was Leslie Evershed-Martin's and was much influenced by the theatre at Stratford, Ontario, which was partly designed by Tyrone **Guthrie** on the principle of the open-stage 'arena' theatre. The first Director of the Chichester Festival was Laurence **Olivier** and the theatre opened for an annual summer festival which put on two or three productions. Olivier's company became the **National Theatre** company in September 1963 and opened at the **Old Vic**, subsequently many of its productions being transferred there from the initial Chichester Festival productions. In 1966 the festival was taken over by John Clements who extended the season to four months and created a 'Festival of Acting'. Keith Michell took over as Director in 1974, Peter Dews in 1978 and Patrick Garland in 1980.

Some of the most celebrated Chichester Festival productions have included John **Arden**'s *The Workhouse Donkey* and Olivier's production of *Uncle Vanya* (1963 season), Peter **Shaffer**'s *The Royal Hunt of the Sun* and Olivier's highly-acclaimed *Othello* (1964 season), Wycherley's *The Country Wife* (1969 season) which starred Maggie **Smith**, Robert **Bolt**'s *Vivat, Vivat Regina!* (1970 season), Turgenev's *A Month in the Country* (1974 season) which starred Dorothy **Tutin** and N.C. Hunter's *Waters of the Moon* (1977 season) which starred Ingrid Bergman. In 1985 a revival of Noël **Coward**'s *Cavalcade* saw the up-and-coming Robert Demeger (who later in the year played King Lear to great acclaim with the Kick Theatre Company at the **Edinburgh Festival**) play Tom Jolly.

The Festival annually presents four plays from May to September and during the rest of the year the theatre has Sunday readings and one-night-stands and is also used by amateur companies.

Churchill, Caryl

A successful socialist and feminist playwright, she has become the leading woman stage-writer of the 1970s and 1980s, perhaps only rivalled by Pam **Gems**. She was born in London on 3 September 1938, educated at Trafalgar School, Montreal (1948-55), and read English at Lady Margaret Hall, Oxford (1957-60). She married David Harter in 1961.

As a student she wrote her first play, a one-acter called *Downstairs* (Oxford, 1958 and NUS festival, London, 1959), and subsequently, *Having a Wonderful Time* (London, 1960), *Easy Death* (Oxford, 1962), and a number of radio plays for Radio 3: *The Ants* (1962), *Lovesick* (1966), *Identical Twins* (1968), *Not ... not ... not ...not enough oxygen* (1971), *Schreber's Nervous Illness* (1972, also at the King's Head) and *Henry's Past* (1972).

Caryl Churchill came to prominence with her stage play *Owners* (**Royal Court**, Theatre Upstairs, 1972), a play which explores the capitalist effects of ownership and 'possession' upon a personal relationship (between Clegg, a butcher, and his wife Marion, an estate agent and property developer). Churchill followed this with another radio play, *Perfect Happiness* (1973) which was later also staged (Soho Poly, 1974). In 1974 she became Resident Dramatist for a year at the Royal Court Theatre where most of her subsequent work has been presented.

Objections to Sex and Violence (Royal Court, January 1975) concerns a divorced woman who is being blackmailed by a wealthy man and whose other lover is attracted to her younger sister. This sister is involved with a left-wing terrorist gang. Ronald Hayman has suggested that the play was a 'conversation piece' and that terrorism was a theme for little else than 'wordy variations'. For the **Joint Stock Company**, Churchill wrote *Light Shining in Buckinghamshire* (Royal Court, September 1976) about a revolution in 1647 which was eventually suppressed by Cromwell. In this play she achieved a mature historical perspective for contemporary issues about freedom, democracy, sex and religion. As Christian W. Thomsen puts it, she is concerned with 'the suppression of women, of the poor and powerless, with the displacement of social and political evil onto sexual morality'. *Vinegar Tom* was written for the feminist theatre group Monstrous Regiment (Royal Court, 1976) and concerned the suppression and humiliation of women in a male-dominated world. This was followed by *Traps* (Joint Stock Company at the Royal Court, Theatre Upstairs, January 1977) about alternative life-styles, and *Cloud Nine* (Joint Stock Company, Royal Court and tour, 1979), a sex-farce in the tradition of Joe **Orton**'s *What the Butler Saw*. The play's first half is set in Victorian Africa and its second half in contemporary Britain and satirises sexual freedoms and taboos. It was also performed in 1981 at the De Lis Theatre, New York.

In 1980 *Three More Sleepless Nights* was presented at Soho Poly, and this was followed by *Top Girls* (Royal Court, September 1982 and Joseph Papp's Public Theatre, New York, November 1982). In an interview with Lynne Truss (*Plays and Players*, January 1984) Caryl Churchill said that *Top Girls* was 'about a lot of dead women having coffee with someone from the present and an idea about women doing all kinds of jobs'. *Fen* (Joint Stock Company on tour and at the Almeida, February 1983; also the Public Theatre, New York, 1983), set in East Anglia, demonstrates material impoverishment in the form of changes in patterns of land ownership and the connections between this land and the emotional and cultural lives of people in a small farming community. The 'land' itself is depicted visually on stage and serves as interior settings as well as exterior, thus underlining the main issues of the play by a single all-embracing stage image.

Softcops (RSC, Barbican Pit, January 1984) made the distinction (influenced by Churchill's acknowledged reading of Michel Foucault's *Discipline and Punish*) between 'hardcops' who use force to attain their goal and 'softcops' who base their approach on friendly but detached relationships. Again Churchill sets the play in the past, in this case in Paris in the nineteenth century (*c.* the 1830s) in order to draw parallels with the present. Discussing the play in her interview with Lynne Truss she said 'I think it shows how hospitals, schools, crime, prisons ... are connected up' and what the effects of 'control' are upon these and individuals. It is about authority itself as a kind of 'softcop'. Caryl Churchill's television plays have been *The Judge's Wife* and *The Legion Hall Bombing.*

Further Reading

Christian W. Thomsen, 'Three Socialist Playwrights', *Contemporary English Drama,* C.W.E. Bigsby (ed.), Stratford-Upon-Avon Studies No. 19, Edward Arnold, London, 1981, pp. 165-9.

Lynn Truss, 'A Fair Cop', interview with Caryl Churchill, *Plays and Players,* January 1984, pp. 8-10.

Claque

Hired applauders.

Community Theatre

See **Alternative Theatre.**

'Comps' ('complimentaries')

Free tickets.

Console

Stage lighting control unit, often with lighting-plot computer storage facility.

Cooney, Ray (Raymond George Alfred)

Born in London on 30 May 1932, and educated at Alleyn's School, Dulwich, he first appeared on the stage as a boy actor in Homer Curran's *Song of Norway* (Palace, March 1946). At the end of his National Service in 1952 he worked in repertory and then in 1956 appeared with Brian **Rix**'s company at the Whitehall Theatre in John Chapman's *Dry Rot* and in March 1958 *Simple Spymen* (in which he was Corporal Flight) by the same author.

His first play was the comedy *One for the Pot* (Whitehall, August 1961) co-written with Tony Hilton. It ran for over 1,000 performances, as nearly did his second play *Chase Me, Comrade* (Whitehall, July 1964), a farce about a Russian ballet dancer seeking political asylum in Britain. Both these productions starred Brian Rix. Cooney's collaboration with John Chapman led to some highly successful farces including *Not Now, Darling* (Strand, June 1967, Brooks Atkinson, New York, October 1970), *Move Over, Mrs Markham* (Vaudeville, March 1969) and *There Goes the Bride* (Criterion, October 1974). With Gene Stone he wrote *Why Not Stay for Breakfast?* (Apollo, December 1973). His own *Run For Your Wife* (Yvonne Arnaud, Guildford, Autumn 1982, Shaftesbury, March 1983) and *Two Into One* (Shaftesbury, October 1984) were presented by Cooney's 'Theatre of Comedy' Company which he founded in 1983 at the Shaftesbury Theatre, a second company, the 'Little Theatre of Comedy' Company, being based at the Ambassadors' Theatre. Ray Cooney said in an interview in 1984 (*Plays and Players*, January): 'For a long time I've had the feeling that we've got the best comedy writers in the world. The RSC and the National get the awards and the publicity, and of course they deserve them, but the general public don't go to those plays. I wanted to present truly popular plays of high quality.'

Besides acting in and directing many of his own plays and directing plays by other writers, Cooney has presented numerous others for the theatre, including William Douglas **Home**'s *Lloyd George Knew My Father* (Savoy, July 1972), Richard Harris and Lesley Darbon's *Two and Two Make Sex* (Cambridge, August 1973), William Douglas Home's *The Dame of Sark* (Wyndham's, October 1974), Ron Pember and Denis Demarne's *Jack the Ripper* (Ambassadors', September 1974), Agatha Christie's *Murder at the Vicarage* (Savoy, July 1975), Ben Travers's *Banana Ridge* (Savoy, July 1976), Jack Good, P.J. Proby, Shakin' Stevens and Timothy Whitnall's *Elvis* (Astoria, November 1977), Brian Clark's *Whose Life Is It Anyway?* (**Mermaid**, March, Savoy, June 1978), James **Saunders**'s *Bodies* (Ambassadors', April 1979), Michael Stewart and Jerry Herman's *Hello, Dolly!* (Theatre Royal, Drury Lane, September 1979), Margaret Monnot and Alexandre Breffort's *Irma La Douce* (Shaftesbury, November 1979), Mark Medoff's *Children of a Lesser God* (Mermaid, August 1981), Shaw's *Pygmalion* (Shaftesbury, May 1984), Philip King's *See How They Run* (Shaftesbury, February 1984, and September 1984), Joe **Orton**'s *Loot* (Ambassadors', March 1984) and Arne Sultan and Earl Barret's *Wife Begins at Forty* (Yvonne Arnaud, Guildford, September 1985).

Actors associated with Cooney's Theatre of Comedy Company include Maureen **Lipman**, Richard **Briers**, John **Alderton**, Donald **Sinden**, Anton **Rodgers**, Paul

Eddington, Geoffrey Palmer, Derek Nimmo, Eric Sykes, Terry Scott, Maria Aitken, Richard O'Sullivan, Liza Goddard, Lionel Jeffries, Barbara Murray and Michael **Williams**. The late Leonard **Rossiter** was also associated with the company.

'Corpse'

A verb used by actors meaning 'to unavoidably get the giggles' during a performance.

Courtenay, Tom (Thomas Daniel)

Born in Hull, Yorkshire, on 25 February 1937, he was educated at Kingston High School, Hull, University College, London, and trained for the theatre at RADA. His first appearance on the professional stage was as Konstantin Treplyef in Chekhov's *The Seagull* (**Old Vic** Company, Lyceum Theatre, Edinburgh, August 1960, Old Vic, September 1960).

He remained with the Old Vic Company for a further year, taking two Shakespearean roles (Poins and Feste) and in June 1961 left to take over from Albert **Finney** as Billy Fisher in Keith **Waterhouse** and Willis **Hall**'s *Billy Liar* (Cambridge Theatre). With the **National Theatre** Company he played Andri in George Tabori's *Andorra* (Old Vic, January 1964) and at the **Chichester Festival** in 1966 was Trofimov in Chekhov's *The Cherry Orchard* (July 1966) and Malcolm in *Macbeth* (August 1966).

Since the mid-1960s Courtenay's work has been mainly in Manchester (with London transfers). He joined the 69 Theatre Company in Manchester in 1966 with whom his roles include Lord Babberley in Brandon Thomas's *Charley's Aunt*, a role he later played in August 1971 and at the Apollo in December 1971 (a performance which Frank Marcus said 'reminded me of Whistler's Mother'). With the 69 Theatre Company he also took the title-role in *Hamlet* at the 1968 **Edinburgh Festival** ('his Hamlet was a man who believed in his religion, and yet was ruined by it', wrote Harold Hobson in *Theatre in Britain*, 1984). At the University Theatre, Manchester, he took the title-role in Ibsen's *Peer Gynt* (December 1970) and in May 1973 was Captain Bluntschli in Shaw's *Arms and the Man*.

One of Courtenay's major successes was as the original Norman in Alan **Ayckbourn**'s trilogy *The Norman Conquests* (Greenwich, May 1974, Globe, August 1974). At the Manchester Royal Exchange Theatre further work has included Faulkland in Sheridan's *The Rivals* (September 1976), Raskolnikov in *Crime and Punishment* and Norman in Ronald Harwood's *The Dresser* (March 1980, transferred Queen's April 1980) with Freddie **Jones** in the main-role.

He was recently Andy in Alan Price's *Andy Capp* (Manchester Royal Exchange, July 1982, Aldwych, September 1982) and George in a revival of Tom **Stoppard**'s *Jumpers* (Manchester Royal Exchange, March 1984).

Filmwork includes *The Loneliness of the Long Distance Runner, Private Potter, Billy Liar, Doctor Zhivago, The Night of the Generals, A Dandy in Aspic, One Day in the Life of Ivan Denisovitch, Otley, Catch me a Spy* and *The Dresser*.

Coward, Sir Noël

Born on 16 December 1899, at Teddington, Middlesex, the son of a piano salesman, and educated at Chapel Road School, he made his first professional stage appearance at the age of ten as Prince Mussel in the Christmas Show *The Goldfish* at the Little Theatre.

Whilst most of his best work as a playwright was done in the years between the two wars Coward continued writing in the 1950s and 1960s. He also exerted some influence on the writers of this latter period, indeed Ronald Hayman has gone so far as to suggest (in *Playback*, 1973) that 'if a family tree were drawn up to represent the heritage of post-war drama, Wilde and Shaw would have to be shown as ancestors of Coward and Osborne; Pinter and Orton would be among his [Coward's] descendants', and Harold Hobson (in *Theatre in Britain*, 1984) recently wrote 'throughout the middle years of the century Coward was a potent theatrical influence ... it finally dawned on the newest generation of the young [in the 1970s] that Noël Coward, despite his predilection for titled people, and the boiled shirts and ropes and pearls of his characters, was a revolutionary writer'. His best plays have been consistently revived in the post-war theatre.

Coward came to recognition as a playwright with *The Vortex* (Everyman Theatre, Hampstead, November 1924), a witty comedy which caused considerable controversy over its daring treatment of the social and sexual mores of the leisured English upper middle-class 'social set' of the 1920s. As with his best plays the dialogue was economical, impudent and satirical and the structure of the action superbly balanced and 'well-made'. It was after the success of *The Vortex* that Coward began to develop a public image reflecting a life-style of wit and leisure (with a hint of decadence) which seemed to summarise a whole élitist generation of the period — he wrote 'with this success came many pleasurable trappings. A car. New suits. Silk shirts. An extravagant amount of pyjamas and dressing gowns, and a still more extravagant amount of publicity. I was photographed, and interviewed, and photographed again.'

He wrote revue sketches, musicals and a host of songs which he performed with fashionable ostentation. His best stage plays of the period were *Hay Fever* (Ambassadors', June 1925, Criterion, September 1925), *Private Lives* (Phoenix, September 1930) in which he starred with Laurence **Olivier** and Gertrude Lawrence, *Cavalcade* (Theatre Royal, Drury Lane, October 1931), *Blithe Spirit* (Piccadilly, July 1941, St James's, March 1942, Duchess, October 1942) which was directed by Coward and had a record run of 1,997 performances, and *Present Laughter* (H.M. Tennant tour, 1942, Theatre Royal, Haymarket, April 1943).

During the war Coward wrote the script, co-directed, and played Captain 'D' for David Lean's film *In Which We Serve* (1942) and entertained troops in the Middle East, South Africa, Ceylon, India and Australia (1943-4). After the war he lived mainly in Bermuda. His most successful post-war works for the stage were *Relative Values* (Theatre Royal, Newcastle, October 1951, Savoy, London, November 1951) which ran for 477 performances, *Waiting in the Wings* (Olympia, Dublin, August 1960, Duke of York's, September 1960) with Dame Sybil **Thorndike** as Lotta Bainbridge, and *Suite in Three Keys* (Queen's Theatre, April 1966) which comprised *A Song at Twilight*, *Shadows of the Evening* and *Come into the Garden Maud*. These three were Coward's last plays and in them he gave his last performances as an actor. He died in Jamaica on 26 March 1973.

Coward wrote over 60 plays and more than 200 songs, acted, directed and worked as a cabaret performer (in particular at the *Café de Paris* in London from 1951). Perhaps his best acting role outside parts in his own plays was as King Magnus in G.B. Shaw's *The Apple Cart* (Haymarket, May 1953). On acting Coward once commented 'you have got to listen for those coughs which might start — which means that you've either got to play more softly or hurry the scene a little bit or something ... regulate your audience as well as be the character — as well as consider the other people on stage with you'. Less seriously he is credited with giving the advice 'learn your lines — speak up — and don't fall over the furniture'. Ned Sherrin, reviewing a recent revival of *Cavalcade* (**Chichester Festival**, June 1985) stated (*Plays and Players*, July 1985) that 'Coward is a lesson in knowing when to stop, when not to say too much and to let silence or understatement find its own eloquence.'

One of the great post-war revivals of *Hay Fever* was for the **National Theatre (Old Vic**, October 1964) which Coward directed and which had a cast including Dame Edith **Evans**. In 1969, for Coward's 70th birthday celebrations, some of his major plays were presented on BBC Television.

Noël Coward's plays will be remembered for their brilliance and wit, their capacity to expose eloquently and stylishly the opulent and pretentious life-style of a particular kind of fashionable, moneyed social class and for their superbly crafted dramatic structuring. Coward was undoubtedly a master of high comedy, the modern heir to a tradition of comedy begun by Oscar Wilde. He wrote in the New York *Herald Tribune* (8 December 1963) 'I'm sick of the assumption that plays are "important" only if they deal with some extremely urgent current problem ... I was brought up in the belief that the theatre is primarily a place of entertainment. The audience wants to laugh or cry or be amused.' He possessed, as he himself put it, 'a talent to amuse'.

Further Reading

John Lahr, *Coward the Playwright*, Methuen, London, 1982.

Raymond Mander and Joe Mitchenson, *Theatrical Companion to Coward*, Rockliff, London, 1957.

Noël Coward, *Present Indicative*, Heinemann, London, 1937, and *Future Indefinite*, Heinemann, London, 1954.

Sheridan Morley, *A Talent to Amuse*, Heinemann, London, 1969.

Crew

Scene-Shifters and general 'dogsbody' stage hands.

Croft, Michael

See **National Youth Theatre**.

Cruelty, Theatre of

A visionary approach to theatre involving disturbance of the imagination and deeper levels of the psyche in an audience. Such theatre possesses metaphysical and mystical dimensions which are overtly anti-rationalistic and largely created by the use of ceremonial and ritual, incantatory language, music and all the devices of theatre which can be brought to bear on the eliciting of a transcendent experience. The use of such a wide range of theatrical devices has led to it being described as 'total' theatre, a theatre appealing to all mental and emotional levels at once.

The term 'Theatre of Cruelty' was coined by the French actor, dramatist and theorist Antonin Artaud (1896-1948) in his book *The Theatre And Its Double* (1938). In using the term 'cruelty' Artaud did not mean that bloodshed and violence should be presented in the theatre but that actors and writers needed to inflict an intense rigour into explorations of their own inner lives. He also meant that the spectators in the audience would be assaulted by a 'total' experience and find their civilised Western mentality and rational intelligence bypassed by the psychological disruption of their sensibility. Such traditions as Balinese dance and folk-drama appealed to Artaud as the kind of theatre the West was alienated from: 'In Oriental theatre with its metaphysical tendencies, as compared with Western theatre with its psychological tendencies, forms assume their meaning and significance on all possible levels ... We ought to consider staging from the angle of magic and enchantment, not as reflecting a script, the mere projection of actual doubles arising from writing, but as the fiery projection of all the objective results of gestures, words, sounds, music or their combinations.' He suggested that such non-verbal devices could rediscover 'the idea of figures and archetypal symbols which act like sudden silences, fermata, heart stops, adrenalin calls, incendiary images surging into our abruptly woken minds'. The task of theatre was to express the inexpressible, the ineffable. Both cast and audience together should be 'victims burnt at the stake, signalling through the flames'.

Artaud was inspired by Surrealism as well as Oriental theatre and, although he presented only one play *Les Cenci* (1935), wrote a few others and the script of the Surrealist film *La Coquille et le Clergyman* (1927), nevertheless the influence of his theories has been profound and far-reaching on modern theatre. His own life was haunted by mental illness and suffering which grew worse throughout his life (he was confined in mental institutions at various times between 1937 and 1946 and eventually died of cancer in 1948).

On the Continent his influence has been greatest on the directors Jean-Louis Barrault (France), Jerzy Grotowsky (Poland) and in the USA on Julian Beck's 'Living Theatre'. In Post-War British Theatre his strongest influence has been on Peter **Brook** who, together with Charles **Marowitz**, formed a company of actors in Autumn 1963 for a 'Theatre of Cruelty' season (LAMDA Theatre, 1964) which included a performance of Artaud's *Le Jet de Sang*. The influences of Artaud can also be felt strongly in Brook's production of *King Lear* (**RSC**, 1962) and particularly in his production of Weiss's *Marat/Sade* (RSC, 1964). It could also be argued that Peter **Shaffer**'s *The Royal Hunt of The Sun* (1964) and *Equus* (1973), though owing much to **Brecht**, are also strongly indebted to Artaud's ideas about 'Theatre of Cruelty'. Artaud's influences can be felt in many other plays performed since the war and must be regarded as of major importance alongside Brecht's influence.

Artaud's view of the theatre has implications beyond the theatre itself, as a challenge to Western civilisation's dualism which has (Artaud maintained) placed too much emphasis upon the head and too little upon the divine soul: 'Theatre is like heightened waking ... Using breathing's hieroglyphics, I can rediscover a concept of divine theatre.'

Further Reading

Antonin Artaud, *The Theatre and Its Double* (1938), translated Victor Corti, John Calder Ltd, London, 1977.

Ronald Hayman, *Artaud and After*, Oxford University Press, London, 1977.

Cusack, Sinead

Born in Ireland on 18 February 1948, the daughter of Cyril and Maureen Cusack, she was educated at Holy Child Convent, Killiney, and the University of Dublin. She first appeared on the stage when she was twelve, playing the deaf mute Phoebe in *The Importance of Mr O* (Olympia, Dublin, 1960).

After leaving university she played a number of roles at the Abbey Theatre, Dublin, and at the Gardner Centre, Brighton (in 1971). Her chief parts since have included Juliet in *Romeo and Juliet* (Shaw, February 1972), Grace Harkaway in Boucicault's *London Assurance* (New, July 1972), Laura Wingfield in Tennessee Williams's *The Glass Menagerie* (Gardner Centre, Brighton, September 1973), Desdemona in *Othello* (Ludlow Festival, 1974), Raina Petkoff in Shaw's *Arms and the Man* (Oxford Festival, 1976, and tour) and Lady Amaranth in John O'Keeffe's *Wild Oats* (Piccadilly, April 1977).

With the **Royal Shakespeare Company** her roles include Lisa in Gorky's *Children of the Sun* (Aldwych, October 1979), Isabella in *Measure for Measure* (Aldwych, November 1979), Celia in *As You Like It* Stratford-upon-Avon, 1980 season, Aldwych, July 1981), Evadne in Beaumont and Fletcher's *The Maid's Tragedy* (Stratford, 1980 season, Warehouse, October 1981), Katharina in *The Taming of the Shrew* (Stratford, 1982 season, Barbican, April 1983), Beatrice in *Much Ado About Nothing*

(Stratford, 1982 season, Barbican, April 1983) playing opposite Derek **Jacobi**'s Benedick, She-in-the-Green in David **Rudkin**'s translation of Ibsen's *Peer Gynt* (Barbican, Pit, June 1983) with Jacobi in the title-role, and Henrietta Van Es in Nicholas Wright's *The Custom of the Country* (Barbican, Pit, October 1983). In March 1984 she toured Europe as Beatrice in the RSC's production of *Much Ado About Nothing*.

Her film work includes *Alfred the Great, Hoffman* and *The Last Remake of Beau Geste.* She has appeared on television in *The Shadow of a Gunman, Trilby* and *Twelfth Night.*

'Cyc'

Short for 'cyclorama', a plain or scenically painted **Backcloth** or wall.

D

Dark

Term derived from the absence of illuminated signs, used to describe a theatre which has closed.

Delaney, Shelagh

Born in Salford, Lancashire, on 25 November 1939, and educated at Broughton Secondary School, she worked as a salesgirl, an usherette and a photographer's laboratory assistant. She was only 18 years old when her first play, *A Taste of Honey*, was staged by Joan **Littlewood**'s **Theatre Workshop** at the Theatre Royal, Stratford East (May 1958, revived January 1959) and transferred to Wyndham's Theatre (February 1959) with a run of 350 performances. It was subsequently performed at the Lyceum Theatre in New York (October 1960) and has been revived in Britain and abroad many times since. The play centres on a teenage girl, Jo, whose promiscuous mother goes to live with a car-salesman, Jo being also abandoned by a young coloured sailor who has made her pregnant. An art student comforts Jo and forms a sensitive relationship with her but leaves when the mother returns. Written in a lively northern idiom and incorporating music-hall jokes, games, nursery-rhymes, songs, jazz music, rhythmical repetitions and silence (elements largely introduced by Joan Littlewood's company) the play remains a *tour de force* of theatricality, moral questioning and the search for individuality and wholeness in the face of an alienating reality. Jo says in the play that she is a 'contemporary', ironically asking 'I really live at the same time as myself, don't I?'

Her next play, *The Lion in Love*, first performed at the **Royal Court** Theatre (December 1960), which was about the tensions in a family of market-stall traders, was less successful than *A Taste of Honey* but nevertheless once again offered a powerful statement about human relationships. The title of the play derives from one of *Aesop's Fables* which carries the moral 'nothing can be more fatal to peace than the ill-assorted marriages into which rash love may lead'.

The promise of further stage plays of the calibre of *A Taste of Honey* remains unrealised, although Shelagh Delaney's *The House that Jack Built* (New York, 1979), adapted from her six television plays of that title, was quite successful, as was her screenplay for the film *Charley Bubbles* (1968). Other films include *The White Bus*, the film version of *A Taste of Honey* and *Dance With A Stranger.* Other television plays have been *Did Your Nanny Come from Bergen?*, *St Martin's Summer* and *Find Me First.* Delaney has also written radio plays and the novel *Sweetly Sings the Donkey* (Methuen, London, 1964).

Dench, Judi (Judith Olivia), OBE

Born in York on 9 December 1934, she was educated at the Mount School, York, where she first became interested in acting. She trained for a year at York School of Art and was briefly involved in stage design for the York Repertory Company at the Theatre Royal, York. She then studied for the stage at the Central School of Speech Training and Dramatic Art, London. On leaving in 1957, she made her first professional appearance as Ophelia in *Hamlet* with the **Old Vic** Company, (Royal Court, Liverpool, Old Vic, London, September 1957). She stayed with this company until 1961, her roles including

Juliet in *Measure for Measure*, Katherine in *Henry V*, Juliet in *Romeo and Juliet* and Kate Hardcastle in Goldsmith's *She Stoops to Conquer*.

In 1961 she joined the **Royal Shakespeare Company** to play Anya in Chekhov's *The Cherry Orchard* (Aldwych, December 1961), and later took the roles of Isabella in *Measure for Measure* (Stratford-upon-Avon, April 1962) and Dorcas Bellboys in John **Whiting**'s *Penny for a Song* (Aldwych, August 1962). She played Lady Macbeth in *Macbeth* (Nottingham Playhouse, January 1963, and West Africa) and in 1964 joined the Oxford Playhouse Company with whom her roles included Irina in Chekhov's *Three Sisters* and Dol Common in Ben Jonson's *The Alchemist* (1965). Returning to Nottingham Playhouse she was Isabella in *Measure for Measure* (September 1965) and, among other parts, was Joan in Shaw's *Saint Joan* (March 1966). She made her musical début as Sally Bowles in *Cabaret* (Palace Theatre, February 1968).

She returned to the RSC for the 1969 season at Stratford-upon-Avon to play Bianca in Middleton's *Women Beware Women*, Hermione and Perdita in *The Winter's Tale* and Viola in *Twelfth Night*. She toured Australia in the latter production (January 1970) and on her return appeared again as Viola and Hermione, and also as Grace Harkaway in Boucicault's *London Assurance* and Barbara in Shaw's *Major Barbara* (Aldwych 1970-1 season). Subsequent work with the RSC included the title-role in Webster's *The Duchess of Malfi* (Stratford-upon-Avon, 1971), Viola in *Twelfth Night* (Tour of Japan, January 1972), the Nurse in *Too True to be Good* (Aldwych, October 1975, Globe, December 1975), Beatrice in *Much Ado About Nothing*, Lady Macbeth in *Macbeth*, Adriana in *The Comedy of Errors* and Regan in *King Lear* (Stratford-upon-Avon, 1976), Adriana and Beatrice again, Lona Hessell in Ibsen's *Pillars of the Community*, Millamant in Congreve's *The Way of the World* (Aldwych 1977-8) and Lady Macbeth in *Macbeth* (Warehouse 1978). In 1979 she played Imogen in *Cymbeline* (Stratford-upon-Avon) and in 1980 she gave a much-praised performance as Juno in O'Casey's *Juno and the Paycock* (Aldwych). Recently she appeared in Frank Hauser's version of Shaw's *Village Wooing* (New End, October 1981) and at the **National Theatre** was Lady Bracknell in Wilde's *The Importance of Being Ernest* (Lyttleton, September 1982) and Deborah in Harold **Pinter**'s *A Kind of Alaska* (Cottesloe, October 1982) which was part of the trilogy, *Other Places*. She appeared in Hugh Whitemore's *Pack of Lies* (Lyric, October 1983) and took the title-role in **Brecht**'s *Mother Courage* with the RSC (Barbican, November 1984). In January 1985 she was Amy O'Connell in the RSC's revival of Harley Granville Barker's *Waste* (Barbican, Pit).

Judi Dench is married to the actor Michael **Williams** with whom she starred in the television series *A Fine Romance*. Some of her major television roles have been in *Talking to a Stranger*, *Major Barbara*, *Go Down*, *Macbeth*, *The Comedy of Errors*, *Saigon*, *The Cherry Orchard* and *Going Gently*. She has also appeared in a number of films.

In an interview with Richard Findlater she said, 'I do try to keep on doing something different. I don't want people to think I'm content doing the same kind of work.'

Further Reading

Judi Dench and Richard Findlater, 'A Fine Romance', *The Observer* Colour Supplement, 21 October, 1984

Gerald Jacobs, *A Great Deal of Laughter*, Weidenfeld & Nicholson, London, 1985.

Denham, Maurice

Born in Beckenham, Kent, on 23 December 1909, he was educated at Tonbridge School and began his career in engineering. His first stage appearance was as Hubert in *The*

Marquise (Little Theatre, Hull, August 1934). He was in repertory and a number of London productions until 1939 when he was associated with the radio series *ITMA* and served in the Army during the Second World War. After the war he was Davenport in radio's *Much Binding in the Marsh* and worked in films.

Since 1949 he has appeared in many plays and most notably was the original Fowle in John **Mortimer**'s *The Dock Brief* (Lyric, Hammersmith, April 1958, Garrick, May 1958) and with the **Old Vic** Company played the title-role in *King John* (**Edinburgh Festival**, August, Old Vic, September 1961) and the title-role in *Macbeth* (Old Vic, December 1961). Other roles have included Nathan in *Nathan the Wise* (**Mermaid**, September 1967), Proteus in Shaw's *The Apple Cart* (Mermaid, March 1970), Pierre in *The Lovers of Viorne* (**Royal Court**, July 1971), Serebriakov in Chekhov's *Uncle Vanya* (Hampstead, November 1979) and Henry Hopkins in Harold **Pinter**'s production of Robert East's *Incident at Tulse Hill* (Hampstead, December 1981).

Of his many television performances the most notable have been the Father in John Hopkins's highly-acclaimed *Talking to a Stranger* (1966) and Joe in Caryl Phillips's *The Hope and the Glory* (1984). He also appeared in *Madame Curie.* Filmwork includes *London Belongs to me, The Spider and the Fly, Our Man in Havana, Sink the Bismarck, The Seventh Dawn, Hysteria, After the Fox, The Virgin and the Gypsy* and numerous others.

Denison, (John) Michael (Terence Wellesley), CBE

Born in Doncaster, Yorkshire, on 1 November 1915, he was educated at Harrow and Magdalen College, Oxford. He studied for the theatre at the Webber-Douglas School and his first professional appearance was as Lord Fancourt Babberly in Brandon Thomas's *Charley's Aunt* (Frinton-on-Sea, August 1938). He went into repertory at the Westminster Theatre, London, where his parts included Paris in *Troilus and Cressida* (September 1938) and Reverend Alexander Mill in Shaw's *Candida* (March 1939) and Stephen Undershaft in Shaw's *Major Barbara* (October 1939). During the war he was in the Royal Signals and Intelligence Corps, after which he appeared in a number of **West End** plays, mainly in comedies and thrillers. With Dulcie Gray, to whom he was married in 1939, he toured South Africa in Noël **Coward**'s *Private Lives* and Jan de Hartog's *The Fourposter* (December 1954, February 1955).

Denison joined the **Shakespeare Memorial Theatre** Company at Stratford-upon-Avon in April 1955 to play Aguecheek in *Twelfth Night*, Bertram in *All's Well That Ends Well*, Dr Caius in *The Merry Wives of Windsor* and Lucius in *Titus Andronicus.* He directed his wife Dulcie Gray's first play, *Love Affair* (Alexandra Theatre, Birmingham, November 1955) and at the 1956 **Edinburgh Festival** played A in Shaw's *Village Wooing* (Lyceum, September 1956, Berlin Festival, October 1956), a role he played many times later in his career. Subsequent roles included the Reverend James Morell in Shaw's *Candida* (Piccadilly, June 1960) and Hector Hushabye in Shaw's *Heartbreak House* (Wyndham's, November 1961) in both of which he partnered Dulcie Gray. Later he gave performances in Melbourne, Brisbane (April-July 1962), Hong Kong (August 1962), Berlin (Berlin Festival, September 1962) and, for the opening of the Ashcroft Theatre in Croydon, he played Henry VIII in *The Royal Gambit.* He was Philip Herriton in Elizabeth Hart's adaptation of E.M. Forster's novel *Where Angels Fear to Tread* (New Arts, June 1963, St Martin's, July 1983), Sir Robert Chiltern in Wilde's *An Ideal Husband* (Strand, December 1965), and, after other roles in the West End, was Hjalmar Ekdal in Ibsen's *The Wild Duck* (Criterion, November 1970),

Lord Ogleby in Garrick and Colman's *The Clandestine Marriage* (tour, April 1971), Prospero in *The Tempest* and Malvolio in *Twelfth Night* (tour and Open Air, Regent's Park, Summer 1972) and Pooh-Bah in *The Black Mikado* (Cambridge Theatre, April 1975). In 1977 he toured as Edward Moulton Barrett in Ronald Millar and Ron Grainer's musical *Robert and Elizabeth* and as Sir Julian Twombley in his own version of Pinero's *The Cabinet Minister.*

Michael Denison joined the **Prospect Theatre Company** in 1978 to play Malvolio in *Twelfth Night,* Hebble Tyson in Christopher **Fry**'s *The Lady's Not For Burning* and Lebedev in Chekhov's *Ivanov* (tour and **Old Vic**). For the **National Theatre** at the Prince of Wales Theatre (May 1979) he took over the role of Ernest in Alan **Ayckbourn**'s *Bedroom Farce.* Recent parts at the Haymarket Theatre have included Humphrey Leigh in Ronald Millar's *A Coat of Varnish* (April 1982), Sir Howard Hallam in Shaw's *Captain Brassbound's Conversion* (June 1982) and Sir Oliver Surface in Sheridan's *The School for Scandal* (January 1983, Duke of York's, December 1983). For the Open Air Theatre, Regent's Park, he played Sir Toby Belch in *Twelfth Night* (June 1985) and Messerschmann in Jean Anouilh's *Ring Round the Moon* (June 1985).

Appearances in films include *The Glass Mountain, The Importance of Being Earnest* and *The Truth About Women.* Television work includes the series *Boyd QC* in which he made over 80 appearances in the title-role (1957-63).

Further Reading

Michael Denison and Dulcie Gray, *The Actor and His World,* Victor Gollancz, London, 1964

Michael Denison, *Overture and Beginners,* Victor Gollancz, London, 1973

Devine, George

See **Royal Court Theatre.**

Dexion

Lengths of angled metal resembling 'Meccano' which can be used in stage-construction.

Dexter, John

Began his career as a television and radio actor and in the late 1950s turned to directing. He directed 15 plays at the **Royal Court** Theatre, including Arnold **Wesker**'s trilogy *Chicken Soup With Barley* (1958, 1960), *Roots* (1959) and *I'm Talking About Jerusalem* (1960), Wesker's *The Kitchen* (1959) and *Chips With Everything* (1962) and John **Osborne**'s *Plays for England* (1962). For the periods 1963-6 and 1971-5 he was an Associate Director of the **National Theatre** at the **Old Vic** where his productions included the highly-acclaimed Othello with Laurence **Olivier** in the title-role (1964), Peter **Shaffer**'s *The Royal Hunt of the Sun* (also **Chichester Festival**, 1964), John **Arden**'s *Armstrong's Last Goodnight* (1965, also Chichester), Shaffer's *Black Comedy* (Chichester 1965, Old Vic, 1966), John Osborne's *A Bond Honoured* (1966), Heywood's *A Woman Killed With Kindness* (1971), Shaffer's *Equus* (1973) and Trevor **Griffiths**'s *The Party* (1973). In 1972 he directed Wesker's *The Old Ones* at the Royal Court Theatre.

In an interview with Ronald Hayman in 1973 (*Playback 2*) he revealed that his approach to directing a play is largely intuitive: 'You have an idea in the gut or somewhere about what the play's about for you, and you draw certain physical conclusions about the clearest way to make it. From then on, everything else is almost a series of intuitive jumps ... Directing is offering possibilities to actors.' In another interview (*Plays and Players,* October 1972) he said, 'You sit and watch and react — the director's the only litmus paper there is, not even an author can do that.'

From 1974 until 1981 Dexter was Director

of production at the Metropolitan Opera House, New York, where his opera productions included *Aida* (1976), *Dialogues of the Carmelites* (1977), *Rigoletto* (1977), *Billy Budd* (1978), *The Bartered Bride* (1978), *Don Carlo* (1979), *Le Rossignol* (1981) and *Oedipus Rex* (1981). During this period he also directed *Phaedra Britannica* (1975) and **Brecht**'s *The Life of Galileo* (1980) for the National Theatre, London. Since 1981 he has been Production Advisor to the Metropolitan Opera, New York, and joint Artistic Director of the Mermaid Theatre, London. At the Mermaid he has directed Christopher **Hampton**'s adaptation of George Steiner's *The Portage to San Christobal of AH* (1982) and at the Haymarket Theatre Shaw's *Heartbreak House* (1983). In 1984 he directed Sartre's *The Devil in the Good Lord* (Lyric, Hammersmith).

He told Ronald Hayman (in the interview previously mentioned), 'you've got to be able to make a fool of yourself at rehearsal without disturbing the cast too much'.

Further Reading

Ronald Hayman, 'Arnold Wesker and John Dexter', *Playback 2*, Davis-Poynter, London, 1973.

Judith Cook, 'John Dexter', *Directors' Theatre*, Harrap, London, 1974.

Dock

A location close to or adjoining the stage and used for storing scenery.

Dotrice, Roy

Born in Guernsey, Channel Islands, on 26 May 1925, he was educated at Dayton Academy and began his acting career while a prisoner-of-war in Stalagluft 3, Silesia, Germany, during the Second World War. His first appearance in the theatre was in 1945 in a revue called *Back Home*, performed by ex-prisoners-of-war to raise funds for the Red Cross. For the next ten years he appeared in repertory (including Liverpool, Manchester and Oldham) and in 1955 he founded the Guernsey Repertory Theatre Company with which he both appeared and directed until 1957.

He joined the **Shakespeare Memorial Theatre** Company at Stratford-upon-Avon in July 1958 (re-named the **Royal Shakespeare Company** in 1961) and remained with it until 1965. His major roles at Stratford and in London (Aldwych Theatre) for the RSC included Burgundy in *King Lear* (1959), Antenor in *Troilus and Cressida* (1960), Father Ambrose in John **Whiting**'s *The Devils* (1961), Firs in Chekhov's *The Cherry Orchard* (1961), Simon Chachara in **Brecht**'s *The Caucasian Chalk Circle* (1961), Caliban in *The Tempest* (1963), the title-role in *Julius Caesar* (1963), Edward IV in John **Barton**'s adaptation *The Wars of the Roses* (1963, 1964), John of Gaunt in *Richard II* (1964), Hotspur in *Henry IV Part 1* (1964) and the title-role in Brecht's *Puntila* (1965).

Roy Dotrice is a distinguished performer of one-man shows and in this genre holds the world record for the greatest number of performances (by 1985 the figure had reached 1,700). Without doubt the finest of these performances has been that of John Aubrey in *Brief Lives*, first performed at the Hampstead Theatre Club (January 1967) and subsequently Broadway, New York (John Golden Theatre, December 1967), the Criterion (February 1969, for a run of 213 performances), tours of England, Canada, USA (1973), Mayfair Theatre (1974, over 150 performances), Broadway season (1974) and an Australian tour (1975). He has also given the show on television.

Some of his other appearances have been as Peer in Christopher **Fry**'s version of Ibsen's *Peer Gynt* (**Chichester Festival**, May 1970), James Blanch in Denis Cannan's *One at Night* (**Royal Court**, April 1971), Dr Arnold in *Tom Brown's Schooldays* (Cambridge Theatre, May 1972), the title-role in *Gnomes* (Queen's, November 1973), Sir Anthony Eden in *Suez* (tour, April 1977), Iago in *Othello* (Chichester Festival Company, tour of Australia, 1978), Abraham Lincoln in the one-man play *Mister Lincoln* (Capital Theatre, Edmonton, Alberta, 1979, the Morosco Theatre, New York, February 1980, Fortune Theatre, London, 1981), Drumm in Hugh Leonard's *A Life* (New York 1980-1), the title-role in *Henry V* and Falstaff in *Henry IV Parts 1 and 2* (American Shakespeare Theatre, Stratford, Connecticut, 1981) and the title-role in *Winston Churchill*, a one-man play (USA, 1982). In December 1984 he appeared at the **Old Vic** as Magwitch in *Great Expectations*.

Work in films includes *Heroes of Telemark, Twist of Sand, Lock Up Your Daughters, Buttercup Chain, Tomorrow, One of Those Things, Nicholas and Alexandra, Corsican Brothers* and *Amadeus*. Television work includes *Dear Liar, Brief Lives, The Caretaker, Imperial Palace, Clochemerle, Dickens of London, The Family Reunion* (USA), *Mister Lincoln* (USA), *Winston Churchill* (USA) and *Tales of the Gold Monkey* (USA).

Doubling

When an actor plays two or more roles in the same play. *See also* **Walter Plinge**.

Dramaturg

Literary Advisor to a company.

'Dressing the Set'

Putting details onto a set, for example small properties, curtains, ornaments, etc.

Drugget

See **Stage Cloth**.

'Dry'

To forget one's lines.

E

Eddington, Paul

Born in London on 18 June 1927, he was educated at the Friends School, Sibford Ferris in Oxfordshire. He began his acting career with ENSA in 1944 and then worked in repertory at Birmingham and Sheffield. He trained at RADA (1951-3) and then played in repertory and television. His first London appearance was as the Rabbi in Paddy Chayefsky's *The Tenth Man* (Comedy Theatre, April 1961). Soon after this he joined the **Bristol Old Vic** Company and played numerous major roles including the title-role in Ibsen's *Brand*, Henry II in Anouilh's *Becket*, Brutus in *Julius Caesar*, Biedermann in Max Frisch's *The Fire Raisers* and Palmer Anderson in Iris Murdoch's *The Severed Head* (all at Bristol Old Vic, September 1962-3 season). He also appeared as Anderson at the Criterion (June 1963) and at the Royale Theatre, New York (October 1964). Returning to the Bristol Old Vic in February 1965 he was Disraeli in William Francis's *Portrait of a Queen* (transferred Vaudeville, May 1965). He remained in the **West End** for a number of productions including Alan **Bennett**'s *Forty Years On* (Apollo, October 1968) in which he was Franklin. He did another season with the Bristol Old Vic in 1973, playing James Tyrone in Eugene O'Neill's *Long Day's Journey into Night* and Osborne in R. C. Sherriff's *Journey's End*.

Eddington took over the part of Ronald in Alan **Ayckbourn**'s *Absurd Person Singular* (Criterion, April 1974) and took over Headingley in Michael **Frayn**'s *Donkey's Years* (Globe, April 1977). He has also played Ray in Ayckbourn's *Ten Times Table* (Globe, April 1978), Sir Oliver Cockwood in Etherege's *She Would If She Could* (Greenwich, April 1979), Reg in Roger Hall's *Middle-Age Spread* (Lyric, October 1979), George in Edward Albee's *Who's Afraid of Virginia Woolf?* (**National Theatre**, Lyttleton, August 1981) and Lloyd Dallas in Michael Frayn's *Noises Off* (Lyric, Hammersmith, February 1982, Savoy, March 1982).

He recently appeared in Charles Dyer's *Lovers Dancing* (Albery, October 1983), returned to the Bristol Old Vic in 1984 to play in Rattigan's *The Browning Version* and **Shaffer**'s *Black Comedy*, played the Headmaster in a revival of Alan Bennett's *Forty Years On* (Chichester, July 1984, Queens, August 1984) and George Moore in a revival of Tom **Stoppard**'s *Jumpers* (Aldwych, March 1985).

He has appeared in numerous television plays and became a household name as Jerry in *The Good Life* and Jim Hacker, MP, in *Yes, Minister.* Other television appearances have included *Robin Hood, Plain Jane, Brother and Sister, Man at the Top, Fall of Eagles, Leo, Outside Edge, Ten Commandments, Special Branch, Let There Be Love,* and *Hay Fever.* In an interview with Claire Colvin, given while he was playing the theatre producer in *Noises Off*, Paul Eddington said of acting: 'If you say "I love you" to a girl on the stage and you don't mean it, then it doesn't work. You must mean it when you say it and at the same time you don't mean it, and the audience knows that as well. There is a double perspective at work all the time.'

Further Reading

Claire Colvin, 'Hobson's Choice?', *Plays and Players*, March 1982.

Edgar, David

Born 26 February 1948 in Birmingham, he went to Manchester University where he took a degree in drama. From 1969 to 1972 he was a journalist on the *Telegraph and Argus* in Bradford and in this period began writing plays, his first being *Two Kinds of Angel* (Bradford, 1970, transferred to London 1971) and *A Truer Shade of Blue* (Bradford, 1970). Most of his plays deal with topical social and political issues and hence have an ephemeral quality (like many television plays) which disadvantages them compared with some other stage plays of the 1970s and 1980s. On this problem of 'topicality' Edgar has commented that often his plays are 'plays about current events that die with the events they portray'. Nevertheless Edgar's plays are very committed and often have a great deal of theatrical energy and a careful mixture of serious socialist polemic and sheer comedy. On occasions we witness 'political' drama which has become richly entertaining as well as at the same time demonstrating a firm didacticism and a keen sense of 'documentary' theatre (very much derived from his 'journalistic' approach to creating a play).

Edgar is a prolific writer and many of his plays have been written for touring companies in the first instance. Some of his best known plays are the one-acter *The National Interest* (General Will, 1972) about industrial problems, *State of Emergency* (General Will, 1972), the documentary on housing called *Rent, or Caught in the Act* (General Will, 1972) and *A Fart for Europe* (with Howard **Brenton**, Theatre Upstairs, **Royal Court** Theatre, 1973) a play expressing an anti-EEC position. Written for Paradise Foundry touring company in 1973, *Operation Iskra* explores terrorism in the 'future' of 1977. *Dick Deterred* (Bush Theatre, London, 1974) extends its punning title by having Richard Nixon meet with Richard III in a Washington hotel (a comic device for exploring the Watergate scandal). In June 1976 we had *Blood Sports* (Bush Theatre) and, perhaps one of Edgar's best plays, *Destiny* (**RSC**, The Other Place, Stratford-upon-Avon, March 1976) which uses a time-shift to create historical parallels, ideological contradictions and paradoxes: we see soldiers in London in 1947 celebrating Indian independence then shift to a by-election in the Midlands of 1976 where there are problems with Asian workers; the racial issues become election issues (as they did with the National Front at this time) and towards the end of the play Adolf Hitler appears. *Wreckers* (for 7:84 Company, 1977) also employs a time-shift, the first half of the play set in 1972 with five dock-workers imprisoned under the Industrial Relations Act and the second half set in 1976 when the dockers are trying to 'wreck' a constituency Labour party whose MP has supported the law over their case.

Recent plays have been *Our Own People* (1977), *The Jail Diary of Albie Sachs* (RSC, Warehouse, January 1978), *Teendreams* (with Susan Todd, Monstrous Regiment touring company, January 1979), the much acclaimed adaptation *The Life and Adventures of Nicholas Nickleby* (RSC, Aldwych, June 1980) and *Maydays* (RSC, Barbican, October 1983). *Maydays* is a documentary about post-war protest and covers the vast sweep of the period since 1945 dealing with what Steve Grant has described as 'post-war optimism, CND, Hungary, Vietnam, 1968 student unrest, The Angry Brigade, feminism, the rise of the British ultra-left, the rapid growth of the rightist reaction in the seventies until a bleak, open-ended but strangely powerful climax in which bicycling Russian dissidents and camped-out anti-nukers celebrate the innate resistance of the human spirit'. It does seem as if Edgar is shifting away from a total commitment to the left (or any other extreme) and has produced a play here which shows a wider and deeper capacity to respond very fully to his own historical, political and cultural period in which sectarianism itself has become a 'holly human (humanist and humanitarian) roblem. As one critic (Misha Glenny) has ut it 'David Edgar is no longer writing bout socialists and for socialists.'

urther Reading

avid Edgar, 'Ten Years of Political Theatre', *Theatre Quarterly*, VIII, xxxii, Winter 1979.

:dinburgh Festival (Of Music and Drama)

'he international festival founded in 1947 by :udolph Bing, an Austrian-born opera npresario who was general manager of the ilyndebourne Opera festival and later the 1etropolitan Opera House, New York. .lthough the Edinburgh Festival has placed reater emphasis upon music than drama iere have been many distinguished theatre roductions for both the main festival and ie **fringe**, and numerous foreign theatre ompanies have brought their work (includ-ıg the Piccolo Teatro Della Citta Di Milano, ie Comédie-Française and the Théâtre lational Populaire).

Noteworthy British productions at the :stival include Tyrone **Guthrie**'s production f Sir John Lindsay's play of 1540 *The Three :states* (1947), world premières of T.S. **:liot**'s *The Cocktail Party* (1949), *The :onfidential Clerk* (1953) and *The Elder 'tatesman* (1958), Michael **Blakemore**'s roduction of Bertholt **Brecht**'s *The Resist-ble Rise of Arturo Ui* (1968) and John **1cGrath**'s *Random Happenings in the lebrides* (1970). Many repertory companies nd touring companies have visited the :stival including the **English Stage :ompany**, **7:84 Theatre Company**, the **Royal Shakespeare Company**, **The Joint tock Theatre Group**, Belt and Braces, **The ctors' Company**, **Prospect Theatre :ompany**, the **National Theatre** Company nd numerous companies from regional heatres. The fringe has brought many new talents into prominence, notably Jonathan **Miller**, Alan **Bennett**, Dudley Moore and Peter Cook in the Cambridge Footlights revue *Beyond the Fringe* (1960), Tom **Stoppard** with his play *Rosencrantz and Guildenstern Are Dead* (1966), and numerous revue artists and small alternative theatre groups.

The festival usually opens in mid-August and runs until mid-September.

Eliot, Thomas Stearns

See **Verse Drama**.

Elliott, Denholm.

Born in London on 31 May 1922, he was educated at Malvern College and trained for the theatre at RADA. During the war he served in Royal Air Force Bomber Command and was a prisoner of war in Germany from 1942 until 1945. His first stage appearance was as Arden Rencelaw in a version of W.H. Smith's nineteenth-century melodrama *The Drunkard* (Playhouse, Amersham, July 1945).

After a number of productions in London he came to prominence with an award-winning performance as Edgar in Christopher **Fry**'s *Venus Observed* (St James's, January 1950). Subsequent appearances include Hugo in Jean Anouilh's *Ring Round the Moon* (Martin Beck, New York, November 1950), Private Able in Fry's *A Sleep of Prisoners* (St Thomas's Church, Regent Street, London, May 1951), Colby Simpkins in T.S. **Eliot**'s *The Confidential Clerk* (**Edinburgh Festival**, August 1953, Lyric, London, September 1953), Jan Wicziewsky in Julian Green's *South* (Arts, March 1955), Alex Shanklin in Lesley Storm's *The Long Echo* (St James's, August 1956), Gaston in Anouilh's *Traveller Without Luggage* (Arts, London, January 1959) and Shem in the original production of James

Saunders's *The Ark* (Westminster, September 1959).

Elliott joined the **Shakespeare Memorial Theatre** Company at Stratford-upon-Avon for the 1960 season, during which he played Bassanio in *The Merchant of Venice*, Troilus in *Troilus and Cressida* and Valentine in *The Two Gentlemen of Verona.* He later toured the United States with the National Repertory Theatre Company (October 1963), playing Trigorin in Chekhov's *The Seagull* and the Rev. John Hale in Arthur Miller's *The Crucible* (both also at Belasco, New York, April 1964). Also in the United States he appeared as Dr Diaforus in Molière's *The Imaginary Invalid* and Cornelius Melody in Eugene O'Neill's *A Touch of the Poet* (American National Theatre and Academy, New York, May 1967).

Returning to London his work included four roles in John **Mortimer**'s *Come As You Are* (New Theatre, January 1970, Strand, June 1970), Judge Brack in Ibsen's *Hedda Gabler* (**Royal Court**, June 1972), Dick in Peter **Nichols**'s *Chez Nous* (Globe, February 1974), the title-role in the **Royal Shakespeare Company**'s production of Graham **Greene**'s *The Return of A.J. Raffles* (Aldwych, December 1975), Lewis Luby and the Rev. A.K. Bulstrode in Mortimer's double-bill *Heaven and Hell* (Greenwich, June 1976), Vershinin in Chekhov's *Three Sisters* (Brooklyn Academy, New York, April 1977), the title-role in Strindberg's *The Father* (**Open Space**, London, November 1979) and the lead in Jonathan Gems's *The Paranormalist* (Greenwich, September 1982).

Denholm Elliott has worked prolifically in film and television, his film work including *Sound Barrier, The Cruel Sea, They Who Dare, Pacific Destiny, King Rat, The High Bright Sun, You Must Be Joking, Alfie, Here we go round the Mulberry Bush, The Seagull, A Doll's House, Russian Roulette, The Hound of the Baskervilles, A Game for Vultures, A Bridge Too Far, Brimstone and Treacle, The Missionary* and *The Wicked Lady.* Television appearances include *Sextet, Clayhanger, Donkey's Years* and *Bleak House.*

English Stage Company

See **Royal Court Theatre.**

Ensemble

A way of approaching company productions whereby all the actors are considered part of the performance as much as each other – 'teamwork'. Often seen as opposed to the 'star-system' whereby a few 'stars' dominate the production. The 'ensemble' approach has been promoted by such directors as John **Gielgud**, Trevor **Nunn** and companies such as the **Prospect Theatre Company**, the **Actors' Company**, and many independent touring companies such as the **Joint Stock Theatre Group** and **7:84 Theatre Company**.

Evans, Dame Edith (Mary Booth)

Born in Pimlico, London, on 8 February 1888, she was educated at St Michael's School, Chester Square, and made her first stage appearances with Miss E.C. Massey's Streatham Shakespeare Players, as Viola in *Twelfth Night* (October, 1910) and Beatrice in *Much Ado About Nothing* (April, 1912). In December 1912 she was Cressida in *Troilus and Cressida* (Elizabethan Stage Society, King's Hall, Covent Garden) in a production directed by William Poel. J.C. Trewin has commented on her performance as Cressida that 'she was able to suggest beauty without being, in the conventional way, beautiful: her tones had a mocking glint and curl, her acting an intuitive assurance. That night a great actress was born.'

Most of Edith Evans's roles in the years

before the Second World War were in the great classics but she was also in the first performances of many of George Bernard Shaw's plays and in some popular plays of the period. Her chief roles included Mistress Ford in *The Merry Wives of Windsor* (London Coliseum, November 1917) in which Ellen Terry also appeared, Nerissa in *The Merchant of Venice* (**Royal Court** Theatre, October 1919), Aquilina in Thomas Otway's *Venice Preserv'd* (Lyric, Hammersmith, November 1920), Lady Utterword in Shaw's *Heartbreak House* (Royal Court, October 1921), Cleopatra in John Dryden's *All for Love* (Phoenix Society, March 1922), Serpent, Oracle, She-Ancient and Ghost of the Serpent in Shaw's *Back to Methuselah* (October 1923), Mrs Millament in Congreve's *The Way of the World* (Lyric, Hammersmith, February 1924, Wyndham's, November 1927), Mrs George Collins in Shaw's *Getting Married* (Everyman, Hampstead, July 1924) and Helena in *A Midsummer Night's Dream* (Drury Lane, December 1924). In May 1926 she was in Andrew Leigh's season at the **Old Vic**, playing roles in 13 plays, notably Cleopatra in *Antony and Cleopatra*, Rosalind in *As You Like It* and the Nurse in *Romeo and Juliet* (a part she also played to great acclaim on a number of occasions later in her career). She played Florence Nightingale in Reginald Berkeley's *The Lady With a Lamp* (Arts Theatre, Garrick Theatre, January 1929), Orinthia in Shaw's *The Apple Cart*, Lady Utterword in a revival of Shaw's *Heartbreak House* (Malvern Festival, August 1929) and Mrs Sullen in Farquhar's *The Beaux' Stratagem* (Royalty, June 1930). In February 1932 she again played the Nurse in *Romeo and Juliet*, this time for John **Gielgud**'s OUDS production (New Theatre, Oxford) and in December 1934 she played the same part in a production at the Martin Beck Theatre, New York. She also played the Nurse in Gielgud's production at the New Theatre (April 1935) which had Gielgud and Laurence **Olivier** alternating Romeo and Mercutio. In February 1937 she was Rosalind in *As You Like It* (New Theatre) with Michael **Redgrave** and Alec **Guinness**. Edith Evans's other famous great performance came in January 1939 at the Globe Theatre when she was Lady Bracknell in John Gielgud's production of Wilde's *The Importance of Being Earnest*, with Gielgud as Jack Worthing. Her intonation on the line 'In a handbag?' is still remembered with affection in the profession and set a precedent difficult to erase in performances by other actresses since.

With the onset of the Second World War she toured the provinces as Epifania Fitzfassenden in Shaw's *The Millionairess* (August 1940), in revue entertained troops in Gibraltar (December 1942) and toured as Hesione Hushabye in *Heartbreak House* for ENSA. After further tours and a period at the Garrison Theatre, Salisbury (1944) she was in India with a production of *The Late Christopher Bean* (1945).

On her return from India Edith Evans appeared as Mrs Malaprop in Sheridan's *The Rivals* (Criterion, September 1945). The post-war period of her career was marked by performances of strong, often comic, older women's parts and by many roles in film and television (particularly after 1959). Her best-known performances for the stage were as Katerina in Rodney Ackland's adaptation of Dostoevsky's *Crime and Punishment* (New Theatre, June 1946), Lady Wishfort in Congreve's *The Way of the World* (Old Vic Company at the New Theatre, October 1948), Madame Ranevsky in Chekhov's *The Cherry Orchard* (New Theatre, November 1948), Lady Pitts in James Bridie's *Daphne Laureola* (Wyndham's, March 1949), Helen Lancaster in N. C. Hunter's *Waters of the Moon* (Haymarket, April 1951) which ran for nearly two years, Countess Ostenburg in Christopher **Fry**'s *The Dark is Light Enough* (Aldwych, April 1954) directed by Peter **Brook**, and Mrs St Maugham in Enid Bagnold's *The Chalk Garden* (Alexandra Theatre, Birmingham, March 1956, Haymarket, May 1956) directed by John Gielgud.

For the 1959 season Edith Evans joined the **Shakespeare Memorial Theatre** Company at Stratford-upon-Avon to play Countess Rousillon in Tyrone **Guthrie**'s production of *All's Well That Ends Well* and Volumnia in Peter **Hall**'s production of *Coriolanus.* Ken **Tynan**, in a review of *All's Well That End's Well*, wrote that the Countess was 'played by Dame Edith in her characteristic later manner — tranquillized benevolence cascading for a great height, like royalty opening a bazaar'. With the newly-formed **Royal Shakespeare Company** in 1961 at Stratford-upon-Avon she played Queen Margaret in William **Gaskill**'s production of *Richard III* and made what was her last appearance as the Nurse in *Romeo and Juliet*, directed by Peter Hall.

In December 1962 she gave a recital with Christopher Hassall at the Marlowe Theatre, Canterbury, and in November 1963 was Violet in the first performances of Robert **Bolt**'s *Gentle Jack* (Queen's Theatre). She then played Judith Bliss in Noël **Coward**'s *Hay Fever* (**National Theatre**, Old Vic, October 1964) in a production directed by Coward.

Most of her subsequent work was in television and films, with the exception of recital parts from time to time and the role of Carlotta in Jean Anouilh's *Dear Antoine* (**Chichester Festival**, May 1971). Her final performances on stage were in *Edith Evans ... and Friends*, devised by Roger Clifford (Theatre Royal, Brighton, October 1973, Richmond Theatre, November 1973, Haymarket, April 1974, Oxford Playhouse, July 1974, Phoenix Theatre, September 19–October 5 1974). Dame Edith Evans died at her home in Kilndown, Kent, on 14 October 1976.

Film work included *The Importance of Being Earnest, Look Back In Anger, The Nun's Story, Tom Jones, Young Cassidy, The Whisperers, The Chalk Garden, Prudence and the Pill, The Madwoman of Chaillot, A Doll's House, David Copperfield* and *The Slipper and the Rose.* On television she appeared in *The Importance of Being Earnest, A Question of Fact, The Old Ladies, The Country Wife, Hay Fever, Time Remembered* and *I Caught Acting Like the Measles* (a documentary of her life).

In an interview with Laurence Kitchin (31 July 1959) John Gielgud commented on the way Edith Evans created a role: 'Dame Edith Evans refines by cutting away the dead wood until she has chosen the relevant emotion, cadence or nuance. Then it is played so that no one can miss it, like the right place for a vase of flowers in a room.'

Further Reading

Bryan Forbes, *Dame Edith Evans: Ned's Girl*, Little, Brown and Co., Boston and Toronto, 1977.

Extra

An actor who has a non-speaking part to swell the number of people on the stage, such as in crowd scenes. Also known as a 'supernumerary'.

F

-alse Proscenium

ₜemovable wing-**flats** or **wing**-curtains and **order** forming a **proscenium** up-stage of the eal proscenium.

-inlay, Frank

3orn in Farnworth, Lancashire, on 6 August 926 and educated at St Gregory the Great chool, Farnworth, he left school to work as n apprentice butcher, as a grocer's assistant nd for Exide Batteries. During this period e spent most of his spare time acting for mateur drama groups and eventually ecame an assistant stage manager in the rofessional theatre, taking small acting parts n various productions. After 18 months vork of this kind he won a scholarship to ₜADA where he trained as an actor. He narried Doreen Shepherd in 1954, the same ear as his first fully professional engagement urely as an actor. He was in repertory from 954 until 1957 in which year he was Mr 'innock in R.C. Sherriff's *The Telescope* Guildford, April-May 1957), the Gaoler in ₜosemary Anne Sisson's *The Queen and the Velshman* (Lyric, Hammersmith, August 957) and Peter Cauchon in Shaw's *Saint oan* (Belgrade, Coventry, May 1958).

Finlay came to prominence in the late 950s and early 1960s with the **English tage Company** when he played in many of he radical new plays, mostly at the **Royal ourt** Theatre, by writers of John **Osborne**'s eneration. In Arnold **Wesker**'s plays he was Iarry Kahn in *Chicken Soup With Barley* Belgrade, Coventry, June 1958, Royal ourt Theatre, London, July 1958 and June 960), Stan Man in **Roots** (Royal Court, une 1960), Libby Dobson in *I'm Talking About Jerusalem* (Royal Court, July 1960) and Corporal Hill in *Chips with Everything* (Royal Court, April 1962, Vaudeville, June 1962). He was Percy Elliott in John Osborne's *Epitaph for George Dillon* (John Golden Theatre, New York, November 1958), Eric Watts in Donald Howarth's *Sugar in the Morning* (Royal Court, April 1959), Private Attercliffe in John **Arden**'s *Sergeant Musgrave's Dance* (Royal Court, June 1960), Mr Crape Robinson in Arden's *The Happy Haven* (Royal Court, September 1960) and Alderman Butterthwaite in Arden's *The Workhouse Donkey* (**Chichester Festival**, July 1963).

In October 1963 Finlay joined Laurence **Olivier**'s **National Theatre** Company at the **Old Vic** to play the First Gravedigger in *Hamlet*, the company's inaugural production (with Peter **O'Toole** in the title-role). He remained with the company for seven years, during which time his chief roles were Chaplain de Stogumber in *Saint Joan* (1963 season), Willie Mossop in John **Dexter**'s production of Harold Brighouse's *Hobson's Choice* and a highly-acclaimed Iago in John Dexter's production of *Othello* (1964 season and Chichester Festival, 1964, Moscow and Berlin, 1965) in which Olivier took the title-role. In an interview with Gordon Gow (*Plays and Players*, November 1973) Finlay commented: 'I just played Iago as near as I could to the truth of the matter ... It got progressively better. I never stopped studying it all the time we were playing it — never ever.' In 1965 the production was made into a film.

Other roles with the National Theatre at the Old Vic included Giles Corey in Arthur Miller's *The Crucible*, Dogberry in *Much Ado About Nothing* and the Cook in William **Gaskill**'s production of **Brecht**'s *Mother Courage* (1965 season). Temporarily leaving the National, in 1969 Finlay became the first actor to play Jesus Christ in the English theatre (other than the part acted in medieval Mystery Plays) when he was in Dennis **Potter**'s *Son of Man* (Phoenix, Leicester, October 1969, Round House, November 1969). Further roles included Bernard in David **Mercer**'s *After Haggerty* (**RSC**, Aldwych, February 1970, Criterion, February 1971) and, back with the National Theatre at the Old Vic, Peppino (with Joan **Plowright** in the same cast) in Franco Zeffirelli's production of Eduardo de Filippo's, *Saturday, Sunday, Monday* (October 1973, Queen's, October 1974), Sloman in John Dexter's production of Trevor **Griffiths**'s *The Party* (December 1973), Freddie Malone in Ben Travers's *Plunder* (January 1976, also Lyttleton, March 1976), Ben Prosse in John Osborne's *Watch it Come Down* (February 1976, Lyttleton, March 1976), Josef Frank in Howard **Brenton**'s *Weapons of Happiness* (Lyttleton, July 1976), Henry in the musical *Kings and Clowns* (Phoenix, March 1978), Domenico (taken over from Colin **Blakely**) in de Filippo's *Filumena* (Lyric, 1978, St James's, New York, February 1980) in a cast which again included Joan Plowright.

Frank Finlay took over the role of Salieri from Paul **Scofield** when Peter **Shaffer**'s *Amadeus* transferred from the National Theatre to Her Majesty's Theatre (September 1981). In a review at the time Peter Roberts wrote, 'Finlay simply had the audience eating out of his lap ... the final image of him toothily grinning like a deathshead will linger.' In October 1983 he was Lopakhin in Chekhov's *The Cherry Orchard* (Haymarket) and in July 1985 was Captain Bligh in David Essex's musical *Mutiny* (Piccadilly Theatre).

Filmwork includes *The Longest Day, The Loneliness of the Long Distance Runner, Othello, The Jokers, Robbery, Inspector Clouseau, Twisted Nerve, Cromwell, Gumshoe,* the *Van Der Valk* films, *The Three Musketeers, The Wild Geese, Enigma, Return of the Soldier, Ploughman's Lunch,* and *The Key.* Appearances on television include *Julius Caesar, Les Misérables, The Lie, Casanova, The Death of Adolf Hitler, Don Quixote, Voltaire, A Bouquet of Barbed Wire* and *The Merchant of Venice.*

In a radio interview with Sally Magnusson (19 July 1985) Frank Finlay said: 'Life's a risk, the theatre's a risk ... they talk about acting on the stage as doing a high wire act without a safety net, which it is. You can't do retakes or go back. You're there in the full glare of the audience and you've got to be absolutely on the ball — every night.'

Finney, Albert

Born in Salford on 9 May 1936, and educated at Salford Grammar School, he trained for the stage at the Royal Academy of Dramatic Art. He has been married twice, first to actress Jane Wenham and then to Anouk Aimée. His first professional appearance was as Decius Brutus in *Julius Caesar*, with the Birmingham Repertory Company (Birmingham Repertory Theatre, April 1956). He stayed with this company for two years playing parts which included the title-roles in *Macbeth* and *Henry V* and Face in Jonson's *The Alchemist.*

His first London appearance was as Belzanor in Shaw's *Caesar and Cleopatra* with the Birmingham Repertory Company (**Old Vic**, July 1956). In April 1959 he joined the **Shakespeare Memorial Theatre** Company, Stratford-upon-Avon, for the celebration of its 100th season, taking the parts of Edgar in *King Lear* (with Charles Laughton as Lear), Cassio in *Othello* and Lysander in *A Midsummer Night's Dream.* He also took over from Laurence **Olivier** in the title-role of *Coriolanus.*

Finney came into prominence when he played the title-role in Willis **Hall** and Keith **Waterhouse**'s *Billy Liar* (Cambridge Theatre, September 1960) and Martin Luther in John **Osborne**'s *Luther* (Theatre des Nations' Festival, Paris, Holland Festival and **Royal Court Theatre**, July 1961; **Edinburgh Festival**, August 1961, Phoenix Theatre, September 1961). In March 1963 he played the title-role in Pirandello's *Henry IV* at the Glasgow Citizens' Theatre and directed Harold **Pinter**'s *The Birthday Party* and Sheridan's *The School for Scandal.* In September of the same year he made his New York début repeating his performance of Martin Luther in *Luther* (St James's Theatre, New York).

In February 1965 Albert Finney joined the **National Theatre** company and played Don Pedro in *Much Ado About Nothing* (Old Vic). He played the role of John Armstrong in John **Arden**'s *Armstrong's Last Goodnight* (**Chichester Festival**, July 1965, Old Vic, October 1965) and also played Victor and Poche in John **Mortimer**'s version of Feydeau's farce *A Flea in her Ear*, (Old Vic, February 1966). In the same season he also played Jean in Strindberg's *Miss Julie* and Harold Gorringe in Peter **Shaffer**'s *Black Comedy.*

Memorial Enterprises Ltd, a film, television and theatre production company, was formed by Albert Finney in June 1965 and in July 1967 Finney co-presented Peter **Nichols**'s *A Day in the Death of Joe Egg* (Comedy Theatre) which had been first presented by Michael **Blakemore** at the Glasgow Citizens' Theatre with Alan **Bates** in the leading part of Bri. Finney played Bri in the New York production (Brooks Atkinson, February 1968). Subsequently he played Mr Elliot in E.A. Whitehead's *Alpha Beta* (Royal Court, January 1972, Apollo, March 1972) and became an associate Artistic Director of the Royal Court Theatre for the period 1972-5, himself appearing there as Krapp in Samuel **Beckett**'s *Krapp's Last Tape* (January 1973) and directing Joe **Orton**'s *Loot* (June 1975). In addition to his work at the Royal Court he played Phil in the first production of Peter Nichols's *Chez Nous* (Globe, February 1974).

Rejoining the National Theatre in December 1975 he played the title-role in *Hamlet* at the Old Vic and for the opening production at the Lyttleton Theatre (March 1976). For the Olivier Theatre he played the title-role in Marlowe's *Tamburlaine the Great* (October 1976). Some of his roles since have been the lead in *Macbeth* (Olivier, June 1978) and John Bean in Charles **Wood**'s *Has 'Washington' Legs?* (Cottesloe, November 1978). In May 1984 Finney returned to the Old Vic to direct and play the lead in a revival of John Arden's *Sergeant Musgrave's Dance.* He has also founded, with others, the **United British Artists** Company.

Film work has included *Saturday Night and Sunday Morning, Tom Jones, Night Must Fall, Two for the Road, Charley Bubbles, Scrooge, Gumshoe, Alpha Beta, Murder on the Orient Express, Annie, John Paul II, The Dresser* and *Under the Volcano.*

Albert Finney has great stature and presence on stage and a strikingly rich voice. He has often been regarded as having brought a Northern solidity to **West End** acting styles. Nevertheless, he has shown himself capable of playing an immense range of parts, from farce to epic and tragedy. He is one of the most versatile British actors to emerge in the first two decades of the post-war period.

Fit-Up

Putting the set and lighting together for a production. As a noun it refers to a portable stage for use when touring.

Flat

Canvas-covered wooden frame which can be painted and used as scenery. It stands vertically, usually supported by **Braces** and **Weights**.

Flies

The space above the stage from where scenery can be 'flown' (raised and lowered) by the use of ropes and pulleys.

Floats

Footlights.

Flood

A stage light which gives a broad spread of light to part of the **Acting Area** or **Cyclorama**.

Fly Gallery

A walkway from where the ropes can be operated to 'fly' the scenery. Also used for access to lighting over the stage.

FOH

'Front of house', that is, **Auditorium**, box office, foyer, etc. and all those staff designated to work in these areas.

Follow Spot

A spotlight manned by one of the lighting crew and which follows the performers as they move about the **Acting Area**.

Fox, Edward

Born on 13 April 1937 and educated at Ashfold School and Harrow School, he trained for the stage at RADA. After National Service (1956-8) he appeared in many provincial repertory productions, films, television plays and series. Appearances in stage plays include **Eliot**'s *The Family Reunion* (Vaudeville, 1979), John Wells's *Anyone For Denis?* (Whitehall, May 1981), Simon **Gray**'s *Quartermaine's Terms* (Queen's, July 1981) and the title-role in *Hamlet* (Young Vic, August 1982). Some of his best known film appearances have been in *The Go-Between* (1971), *The Day of the Jackal* (1973), A Doll's House (1973), *Galileo* (1976), *The Squeeze* (1977), *A Bridge Too Far* (1977), *The Duellists* (1977), *Force Ten From Navarone* (1978), *The Mirror Crack'd* (1980), *Gandhi* (1982) and *Anna Pavlova* (1983). He has made numerous appearances on television including *Hard Times* (1977) and *Edward and Mrs Simpson* (1978). He is the elder brother of the film actor, James Fox.

Frayn, Michael

Born in London on 8 September 1933 he was educated at Kingston Grammar School, Surrey, and Emmanuel College, Cambridge, where he read Philosophy. Whilst an undergraduate he wrote for a student newspaper and was active in the Cambridge Footlights. Prior to going up to university he did National Service in the Royal Artillery and Intelligence Corps and took a Russian language course. On graduation from Cambridge in 1957 he became a journalist with the *Guardian* until 1962 and then with the *Observer* until 1968. He wrote four novels in this period: *The Tin Men* (1965), *The Russian Interpreter* (1966), *Towards the End of the Morning* (1967) and *A Very Private Life* (1968). He published another novel, *Sweet Dreams*, in 1974. He married Gillian Palmer in 1960.

His first professional production was a group of four short plays (*Black and Silver, The New Quixote, Mr Foot,* and *Chinamen*) under the collective title of *The Two Of Us*, presented at the Garrick Theatre, July 1970, which starred Richard **Briers** and Lynne Redgrave. Subsequently he wrote *The Sand-*

boy (Greenwich Theatre, September 1971) which starred Eleanor **Bron** and Joe Melia as a couple whose private lives are invaded by a elevision crew and all its equipment. Like *The Two Of Us* the play depends more on lialogue and repartee than on the author's haping of events.

Far more acclaimed and successful was *Alphabetical Order* (Hampstead Theatre Club, May 1975) which established Frayn as a writer of comedy and farce blended with erious explorations of human social ehaviour. The play, which starred Dinsdale **anden** and Billie **Whitelaw**, is set in the ibrary of a provincial newspaper where its haotic, rather muddled, but reasonably ompetent librarian acquires a female assisant (Lesley) who proceeds to reorganise the ibrary on highly efficient lines, ultimately to ittle purpose since the paper closes down. In n outburst of orgiastic chaos the library is mashed and order breaks down. Frayn has ommented that, besides being about order nd disorder, the play is 'about how we rganise the world around us in knowledge nd language and how that organisation can ecome destroyed'. In the next year *Donkey's Years* was performed (Globe, July 976). Set at an Oxford University college eunion 20 years after its participants had een undergraduates, the play explores the hanges which have occurred in its charcters' life-styles and how easily and ridicuously they revert to their student elationships and views. In the process of this eversion the play moves from social comedy almost a 'comedy of manners') to pure arce. *Clouds* (Hampstead Theatre Club, 976, Duke of York's, November 1978), vhich starred Tom **Courtenay**, is about Owen, a journalist who goes on an assignnent to Cuba, only to find that a woman eporter from a rival magazine has been here too. The idea of placing a Westerner in n alien, strange and mythologised culture llowed Frayn to explore the difficulties eople have in not allowing their view of the vorld to be coloured by their preconceptions and received illusions about the world — just as people will read familiar shapes into clouds.

Frayn's next play *Balmoral* (Yvonne Arnaud, Guildford, 1978) was largely unsuccessful and reappeared a second time as *Liberty Hall* (Greenwich, 1979) but did not transfer to the **West End**. A year after this his next play, *Make and Break* (Theatre Royal, Haymarket, April 1980), starring Leonard **Rossiter** and Prunella **Scales**, was a great success. It is about a businessman who is attending an international trade fair in Germany, develops a relationship with a secretary, has a lesson in Buddhism and mystical thought, and is forced into a confrontation with death by an apparent heart attack. His all-consuming and compulsive obsession with his business is stripped away by these events and he has to face up to his real existential state as a human being. Again the play is a blend of comedy and seriousness.

In a television interview with Melvyn Bragg ('The South Bank Show', ITV, 29 April 1984), Michael Frayn discussed the blending of comedy and seriousness in his plays in terms of what he had discovered when engaged in the close details of translating some of Chekhov's plays from Russian into English. He suggested that what he had learned was that 'organisation and tightness and density, and never ever letting go of the central material of the play, is the essence of what makes a play work on the stage'. Frayn's translation of Chekhov's *The Cherry Orchard* was presented in February 1978 at the **National Theatre** and was directed by Sir Peter **Hall** and was followed by his translation of Tolstoy's *Fruits of Enlightenment* in March 1979. Frayn has also translated Chekhov's *Three Sisters* (1983) and *Wild Honey* (1984), the latter a version of *Platanov*.

One of Michael Frayn's most acclaimed plays, *Noises Off*, was first performed in March 1982 at the Savoy Theatre. It is, in effect, a 'farce within a farce': in the first of three acts we see a director rehearsing the actors of a small touring company in a sex-farce called (in witty contrast to Frayn's main title), *Nothing On*; in the second act the whole set is turned round so that we can see the real problems the cast face backstage in trying to keep up with their exits and entrances through eight different doors, and props required for the complicated stage-business of a farce. We also learn of the director's relationships with two female members of the company, adding further complication to the production; finally the set is turned round again and we experience the chaos of the farce on stage caused by the cast's problems and difficulties backstage. As Frayn has explained: 'Doors are marvellous things: they are what separate the visible world of the stage from a world we don't see and we are not supposed to think about ... all those props are objects that go back and forth between two worlds.'

In *Benefactors* (Vaudeville Theatre, March 1984) four characters give different points of view on life and exist in different times from one another. In remembering their past there are flashbacks, re-enactments of experiences, and the characters sometimes address the audience and sometimes each other, techniques Frayn learned from the Russian playwright Trifinov. In April 1984 *Number One*, a translation and adaptation from a play by Jean Anouilh, appeared at the Queen's Theatre and starred Leo **McKern**.

Fravn has commented on farce that it is 'about panic, it's about the threat of some kind of social exposure; and I think everyone, however well-balanced, must feel the possibility that the whole performance they are keeping up in public is going to go astray at some point and they are not going to be able to go on with it — and the feeling of panic that that engenders is very powerful'.

In July 1984 Frayn's translation of Chekhov's first play, *Wild Honey*, appeared at the National Theatre and starred Ian **McKellen**. Commenting on Chekhov's lack of commitment to any particular party, or political beliefs, or philosophy, and his desire to be a 'free artist', Frayn has stated 'I would like humbly to subscribe to the same philosophy.'

French Brace

Hinged triangular piece of wood used for supporting a stage **Flat**.

Fresnel

Spotlight which produces a soft-edged beam. It contains a simple dish reflector the position of which can be altered for focusing. The ribbed formation of the fixed lens is characteristic. Fresnels are mainly used for lighting the **Acting Area** from **FOH** positions and spot bars. Any **Spill** can be controlled by attaching a **Barn Door** to the front of the lamp. *See also* **Follow Spot** and **Profile Spot**.

Friel, Brian

Born in Omagh, County Tyrone, Ireland, on 9 January 1929, he was educated at St Columb's College, Derry (1941-6), St Patrick's College, Maynooth (1946-9) and St Joseph's Training College, Belfast (1949-50). He was a teacher for ten years in primary and intermediate schools (1950-60), since when he has been a full-time writer. In 1954 he married Anne Morrison and in 1963 lived for five months in Minneapolis during the opening season of the Tyrone **Guthrie** Theatre.

His first stage play was *The Francophile* (Belfast, 1960) and his major plays since have included *The Enemy Within* (Dublin, 1962) and *Philadelphia, Here I Come* (Dublin Theatre Festival, 1964, New York, 1966, Lyric, London, September 1967). This latter play, which brought Friel to success, concerns Gareth O'Donnell, whose public and private selves are acted out by two different actors as he explores his frustrations with life and his restless urge to emigrate to America. Other plays have included *The Loves of Cass McGuire* (New York, 1966, Dublin, 1967), about an old woman who retreats into her dreams through disillusionment with her life, *Crystal and Fox* (Dublin, Globe Theatre, November 1968, New York, 1973) about a man trying to recapture his youth, *The Freedom of the City* (Dublin, London, **Royal Court** and Chicago, 1973), about the contemporary political strife in Ulster, *Volunteers* (Dublin, 1975), *Living Quarters* (Dublin, 1977) and *Faith Healer* (New York, 1979, Dublin, 1980, Royal Court, London, March 1981), *Aristocrats* (Dublin 1979) and *Translations* (Hampstead Theatre, May 1981, **National Theatre**, Lyttleton, August 1981), this latter a highly successful play which parallels the visit of a British Army map-making unit to Donegal in 1833, with the British military presence in Northern Ireland in the 1970s and 1980s.

In 1981 he also translated Chekhov's *Three Sisters* (Londonderry) and in May 1983 his play *The Communication Cord* was presented in London (Hampstead Theatre).

Brian Friel has also written a number of short stories (collected in *The Saucer of Larks*, Gollancz, 1962, and *The Gold in the Sea*, Gollancz, 1966) and radio plays.

Further Reading

D.E.S. Maxwell, *Brian Friel*, Bucknell University Press, Lewisburg, Pennsylvania, 1973.

'Fringe' Theatre

See **Alternative Theatre.**

Frisby, Terence

Born in New Cross, London, on 28 November 1932, he was educated at Dobwalls Village School, Dartford Grammar School and trained for the stage at the Central School of Speech Training and Dramatic Act. He has had substantial repertory experience as an actor and has also directed and written plays. His first professional appearance was at High Wycombe in August 1957. Under the pseudonym of Terence Holland he directed and acted in many plays (1957-66) and later appeared as the First Man in John **Osborne**'s *A Sense of Detachment* (Theatre Upstairs, **Royal Court**, December 1972), the father in Barry Reckord's *X* (Theatre Upstairs, August 1974), General Wax in Howard **Barker**'s *Wax* (Edinburgh Festival, 1976), Scrooge Birdboot in Tom **Stoppard**'s *The Real Inspector Hound* (Young Vic, 1977-8 season) and Leslie in his own play *Seaside Postcard* (Young Vic, 1977-8 season).

He directed his own play, *The Subtopians* (Arts Theatre, April 1964), which is a comedy about an imaginary London suburb called 'Subtopia', the dreariness of which is rejected by Tom Mann, who escapes into the world of art and into a love affair with a talented girl called Helen. The comedy is enriched when she is brought to Subtopia to meet Tom's family, the members of which have anything but harmonious relationships. Perhaps Frisby's best-known play is the comedy *There's a Girl in My Soup* (London Globe, June 1966, New York 1967), about a food and wine connoisseur's relationship with a girl much younger than himself. It ran in London for six years.

Other plays include *The Bandwagon* (London 1969), *It's All Right if I Do It* (Mermaid, March 1977) and *Seaside Postcard* (1978). In June 1983 Frisby presented Mtwa, Ngeni and Simon's *Woza Albert!* at the Criterion Theatre.

Terence Frisby's television plays include *Take Care of Madam, Don't Forget the Basics* and the series *Lucky Feller.*

Fry, Christopher

See **Verse Drama.**

FX

Special effects.

G

Gambon, Michael

Born in Dublin on 19 October 1940, he was educated at St Aloysius School, London. Before becoming an actor he had a career in engineering. His first professional stage appearance was as the Second Gentleman in *Othello* (Gaiety, Dublin, 1962, and European tour).

In 1963 he joined the **National Theatre Company** at the **Old Vic**, where he played roles which included Coster Pearmain in Farquhar's *The Recruiting Officer*, Diego in Peter **Shaffer**'s *The Royal Hunt of the Sun* (which he also played at the 1964 **Chichester Festival**), Herrick in Arthur Miller's *The Crucible* (1965), Eilif in **Brecht**'s *Mother Courage* (1965) and Snap in Congreve's *Love for Love* (1965). Some of his roles with the Birmingham Repertory Company (1967-8) were Patrick in Shaw's *The Doctor's Dilemma*, Cauchon in Shaw's *Saint Joan*, the Button Moulder in Ibsen's *Peer Gynt* and the title-role in *Othello.* In 1968 at the Forum Theatre, Billingham, he took the title-role in *Macbeth.* The following year he was at Liverpool Playhouse, playing Andrew in David **Storey**'s *In Celebration* and the title-role in *Coriolanus.*

For the **Royal Shakespeare Company** 1970-1 season at the Aldwych Theatre his chief roles were Charles Lomax in Shaw's *Major Barbara* and Surrey in *Henry VIII*, and at the Round House he was Hotspur in John **Barton**'s *When Thou Art King.* He later played Robin in Leonard Webb's *Not Drowning But Waving* (Greenwich, September 1973), Tom in Alan **Ayckbourn**'s *The Norman Conquests* (Greenwich, May 1974, Globe, August 1975), Simon in Simon **Gray**'s *Otherwise Engaged* (Queen's, 1976), Neil in Ayckbourn's *Just Between Ourselves* (Queen's, April 1977) and Bertie in *Alice's Boys* (Savoy, May 1978).

He again became a member of the National Theatre Company in 1978 and has played Jerry in Harold **Pinter**'s *Betrayal* (November 1978), Henry in Simon Gray's *Close of Play* (May 1979), Buckingham in *Richard III* (February 1980), Roderigo in *Othello* (March 1980) and Benedick in *Much Ado About Nothing* (August 1981). For the 1982 season at Stratford-upon-Avon and the 1983 season at the Barbican, he was with the Royal Shakespeare Company, playing the title-role in *King Lear* and Antony in *Antony and Cleopatra.* Returning to the National Theatre he was Von Horvath in Christopher **Hampton**'s *Tales from Hollywood* (Olivier, September 1983).

Gantry

An overhead supporting structure from which lights can be suspended. Frequently used by touring companies and rock groups as a substitute for permanent lighting systems.

Gaskill, William

Born in Shipley, Yorkshire, on 24 June 1930, he was educated at Salt High School, Shipley, and Hertford College, Oxford. He was a male nurse, a factory worker and a baker before he went into the theatre as a director. His first production was St John Ervine's *The First Mrs Fraser* (Redcar, Yorkshire, February 1954) and after working with Joan **Littlewood**'s **Theatre Workshop** and at the Q Theatre in 1955 he directed a number of plays at the **Royal Court** Theatre including N.F. **Simpson**'s double-bill *A*

Resounding Tinkle and *The Hole* (the former December 1957, both April 1958), John **Osborne** and Anthony Creighton's *Epitaph for George Dillon* (February 1958), Donald Howarth's *Sugar in the Morning* (April 1959), N.F. Simpson's *One Way Pendulum* (December 1959) and John **Arden**'s *The Happy Haven* (September 1960).

After two years with the **Royal Shakespeare Company** at Stratford-upon-Avon, where he directed a number of plays including *Richard III* (1961 season) and *Cymbeline* (1962 season) and in London where he directed Bertholt **Brecht**'s *The Caucasian Chalk Circle* (Aldwych, January 1962) and *Baal* (Phoenix, 1963), he became an Associate Director of the **National Theatre** at the **Old Vic** (1963-5). Productions he directed for the company included Farquhar's *The Recruiting Officer* (December 1963), **Brecht**'s *Mother Courage and her Children* (May 1965) and Arden's *Armstrong's Last Goodnight* (October 1965, earlier at **Chichester Festival**, July).

Gaskill subsequently returned to the Royal Court and became Artistic Director of the **English Stage Company** (1965-73). His directing for the company included Edward **Bond**'s *Saved* (November 1965), Arnold **Wesker**'s *Their Very Own and Golden City* (May 1966), *Macbeth* (October 1966), Charles **Wood**'s *Fill the Stage with Happy Hours* (English Stage Company at the Vaudeville Theatre, September 1967) and *Dingo* (November 1967), Bond's *Early Morning* (March 1968) and *Narrow Road to the Deep North* (February 1969), Brecht's *Man is Man* (March 1971) and Bond's *Lear* (September 1971) and *The Sea* (May 1973).

In 1974 he became Director of the **Joint Stock Theatre Group** which he co-founded that year with David **Hare** and Max **Stafford-Clarke**. Productions he has co-directed for Joint Stock include David Hare's *Fanshen* (tour 1975), Barry **Keeffe**'s *A Mad World, My Masters* (Traverse, Edinburgh, January 1977 and tour) and Howard **Brenton**'s *Epsom Downs* (Round House, June 1977 and tour). For Joint Stock he has also directed Stephen **Lowe**'s adaptation of Robert Tressell's novel *The Ragged Trousered Philanthropists* (tour 1978), and *An Optimistic Thrust* (tour 1980).

For the National Theatre he directed Middleton and Rowley's *A Fair Quarrel* (Olivier, February 1979) and, at the Royal Court Theatre, productions of Nicholas Wright's *The Gorki Brigade* (Joint Stock, 1979), Stephen Lowe's *Touched* (January 1981) and *Tibetan Inroads* (September 1981). Recently he directed Goldsmith's *She Stoops to Conquer* (Lyric, Hammersmith, August 1982), Nicholas Wright's *The Crime of Vautrin* (Joint Stock, Almeida, June 1983), Vanbrugh's *The Relapse* (Lyric, Hammersmith, October 1983), Michael Wilcox's *Rents* (Lyric, Hammersmith, February 1984) and Congreve's *The Way of the World* (Chichester Festival, August, 1984, Haymarket, November 1984).

In an interview with David Roper in 1982 Gaskill said, 'directing is a terrible profession. It's lonely and it's frustrating; it has no real satisfaction in it. You only live in what you live in, and notices in history books ... once a thing is on, it's on, and however much you try to involve yourself in it, that's something which it's very difficult to continue working on. The first night is like *death* — it's like something that's just finished, which it never is for the actor.'

Further Reading

David Roper, 'Royal Court and After', *Plays and Players*, August 1982.

Gauze

Thin open weave cloth which when painted and lit from the front appears to be solid but when lit from behind 'dissolves'. Useful for creating mysterious and magical effects.

Gems, Pam

Born on 1 August 1925, in Bransgrove, Hampshire, she was educated at Brockenhurst County Grammer School and Manchester University. She is married to Keith Gems. In May 1973 she formed the Women's Theatre Group.

She is particularly well-known for plays which explore the problems of female sexual identity and the role of women in a male-dominated society. Plays include *Betty's Wonderful Christmas* (Cockpit, 1971), *My Warren* and *After Birthday* (Almost Free, 1973), *The Amiable Courtship of Miz Venus and Wild Bill* (Traverse, Edinburgh, 1973, Almost Free, 1973), *Go West, Young Woman* (Round House, 1974) and *Dead Fish* (1976) which later became *Dusa, Fish, Stas and Vi* (**Edinburgh Festival**, 1976, Hampstead Theatre Club, December 1976). This latter play explores the many roles available to women and, as C.W.E. Bigsby puts it in *Contemporary English Drama* (1981), all the female characters 'are deeply vulnerable. It is a female world: men are the objects of pursuit or scorn. No one is happily married. They all pay some kind of price for their sexual identity.'

There followed a number of plays which concentrated on celebrated women of the past: *Guinevere* (double-bill with *The Project*, 1976, separate fringe performance by **RSC** at Gulbenkian Theatre, Newcastle, March 1979), *Queen Christina* (RSC, the Other Place, Stratford-upon-Avon, 1977, and Tricycle Theatre, May 1982) and, perhaps her most acclaimed play to date, *Piaf* (RSC, the Other Place, October 1978, the Warehouse, June 1979, Aldwych, December 1979, Wyndham's, January 1980 and Piccadilly, February 1980), with Jane **Lapotaire** in the title-role. *Piaf* blends fragmented dialogue with song and thereby achieves a highly successful balance between Piaf's neurotic sensibility in a world of pressurising fame, and her more private and deeply-felt emotions.

Further plays have included *Sandra* and *Ladybird, Ladybird* (King's Head and tour, April 1979), a translation of Chekhov's *Uncle Vanya* (Hampstead Theatre Club, November 1979, and **National Theatre**, Lyttleton, May 1982), a translation and adaptation of Chekhov's *The Cherry Orchard* (Leicester Haymarket, May 1984), *Aunt Mary* (Omega Projects, Warehouse, June 1984) and a new version of Dumas' *La Dame aux Camelias* titled *Camille* (RSC, the Other Place, Stratford-upon-Avon, 1984 season).

Further Reading

'Women in the Workshop', *Plays and Players*, November 1973.

'Get In'

Noun used by touring companies for arrival at a venue and setting up of equipment. A 'get out' is the opposite.

'Ghost Walks on Friday, The'

Colloquialism for wages and payday in the theatre. The term allegedly derives from an actor who refused to enter as Hamlet's father's ghost until he was given his wages.

Gielgud, Sir (Arthur) John

Born in London on 14 April 1904, the great-grandson of the Polish actress Madame Aszperger and grand-nephew of the actress Ellen Terry, John Gielgud was educated at Westminster School (where he took a great interest in drawing and painting and at one time wanted to become a designer in the theatre). He trained as an actor at Lady Benson's school and at RADA.

His first stage appearance was as the Herald in *Henry V* at the **Old Vic**, 7 November

1921. Prior to the Second World War he played a variety of parts ranging widely from the classics to comedy: King Lear three times (Old Vic, 1921, Sadler's Wells Theatre, 1931, Old Vic, 1940), Hamlet on six occasions (Old Vic, 1929, Queen's 1930, New 1934, St James, 1936, Lyceum and Elsinore 1939, Haymarket, 1944-5), Macbeth twice (Old Vic 1929, Piccadilly 1942), Romeo on three occasions (Regent, 1924, Old Vic, 1929, New, 1935, alternating the part of Mercutio with Ralph **Richardson**), Richard II twice (Old Vic, 1929, Queen's, 1938). Some of his other major classical roles prior to the war were in *The Cherry Orchard* (Lyric, Hammersmith 1925), *The Seagull* (Little Theatre, 1925), *Three Sisters, Ghosts* and *Julius Caesar* (Old Vic, 1929), *A Midsummer Night's Dream* (Old Vic, 1929), *Henry IV Part 1* (Old Vic, 1930), *The Tempest* (Old Vic, 1930 and 1940), the much acclaimed part of the title-role in *Richard of Bordeaux* (New, 1932) and numerous Shakespearean and other substantial roles.

His excursions into comedy included **Coward**'s *The Vortex* (Little Theatre, 1925), Margaret Kennedy's *The Constant Nymph* (New Theatre, 1926), Brandon Thomas's *Charley's Aunt* (Comedy, 1923), Sheridan's *The School For Scandal* (Queen's, 1937-8) and the most famous of all his comic roles, John Worthing in Oscar Wilde's *The Importance of Being Earnest* (Lyric, Hammersmith, 1930, Globe, 1939 to Dame Edith **Evans**'s legendary playing of Lady Bracknell). Gielgud also directed many plays before the war and recently commented on the sense of continuity with the great traditions of Victorian and Edwardian theatre this gave him: 'I was so fortunate to begin to direct in the early 1930s when there was a wonderful pool of elderly actors who had worked with Tree, Playfair, Granville-Barker, Forbes-Robertson, Alexander ... They taught me a good deal.' He took on the management of the Queen's Theatre 1937-8 for a season, during which, among other parts, he played Shylock in *The Merchant of Venice* (which **Olivier** has said is one of the best performances Gielgud has ever given) and Vershinin in *Three Sisters*, directed by Michel St Denis. It has often been suggested that this season laid the foundations of English '**ensemble**' acting (that is, the shifting away from the actors, or a few members of a cast, as 'stars' who are given a dominant presence on stage, and more towards the importance of the director-as-artist — in other words it places emphasis upon 'Director's Theatre').

During the war-period Gielgud toured with ENSA and played in repertory for a season at the Haymarket Theatre. After the war he gave superb performances as Raskolnikoff in *Crime and Punishment* (New, June 1946) and Mendip in Christopher **Fry**'s *The Lady's Not for Burning* (Globe, May 1949) which he also directed. He toured the USA 1947-8 and on return to England entered a period of successful directing which included *The Glass Menagerie* (Haymarket, July 1948), *Medea* (Globe, September 1948) and *The Heiress* (Haymarket, February 1949). At Stratford-upon-Avon he directed *Much Ado About Nothing* (June 1949) and on return to London directed three more plays.

Gielgud made his first appearance at the **Shakespeare Memorial Theatre**, Stratford-upon-Avon in the 1950 season, playing Angelo in *Measure for Measure*, Benedick in *Much Ado About Nothing*, Cassius in *Julius Caesar* (which he also played in the 1952 film) and the title-role in *King Lear*. His Leontes in *The Winter's Tale* (Phoenix, June 1951) was highly acclaimed and there followed a number of directing activities including *Macbeth* (Shakespeare Memorial Theatre, 1952), *Richard II* (Lyric, December 1952) and *The Way of the World* (Lyric, February 1953). He took his own company on tour to Rhodesia in 1953 during which he appeared as Richard II.

Gielgud's craft as an actor, it has often been remarked, emphasises the voice and minimises the importance of the body on the stage. Reviewing Gielgud's Romeo of 1924

Ivor Brown wittily remarked 'Mr Gielgud has the most meaningless legs imaginable' and Kenneth **Tynan**, reviewing *The Ages of Man* (a Shakespeare anthology) in 1959 stated 'I have always felt that Sir John Gielgud is the finest actor on earth from the neck up.' More seriously, however, Gielgud has suggested that the control of bodily movement and expression in order to permit the language of a play to dominate is particularly important in Shakespearean productions: in 1959 he stated that young actors 'need first to learn how to stand still and speak beautifully, without fidgeting and byplay ... There are many passages in Shakespeare that really are arias.' It is a view of acting which emphasises 'naturalness' as the way to convince the audience. This means the reduction of artifice to a minimum — the 'effect' of acting, Gielgud once said, should be 'something you produce in yourself to make the audience convinced. But if it becomes too consciously a trick, it's apt to become a debit rather than an asset.' He told Margaret Tierney in 1971 that 'the point is to find the style of the play you're playing, and try to steep yourself in that so that you can act it naturally and do justice to the playwright'. In an interview with Ronald Hayman he once located the beginnings of a consistency in his acting discipline as the 1950 Stratford season when he played Angelo in *Measure for Measure*: 'Ever since then I've really prided myself that I don't add very much or put in very much or take out very much. I simplify as much as possible.'

Since 1953 Gielgud has played a tremendous variety of parts as well as the great classical roles (though rarely has he played 'character-parts'), directed a large number of plays and appeared, as also before the war, in many films. Perhaps his major contributions to post-war theatre have been his own adaption of *The Cherry Orchard* which he also directed (Lyric, May 1954), the Shakespeare Memorial Theatre Company tour of 1955 in which he played a memorable Benedick in *Much Ado About Nothing* (and also directed it) and the title-role in *King Lear*. He played Prospero at Stratford (August 1957) and Drury Lane (December 1957), Cardinal Wolsey in *Henry VIII* (Old Vic, May 1958) and directed Peter **Shaffer**'s first successful play *Five Finger Exercise* (Comedy, July 1958).

Peter Roberts has pointed out that (unlike Olivier who played in **Osborne**'s *The Entertainer*) Gielgud had to wait for the next generation of writers after the 1950s before his style of acting (often the 'grand manner') could be adapted to the new drama. His work after the war as a **West End** director for the H.M. Tennant management and his appearances in the great classical roles tended to keep him apart from the moves in the theatre to present plays which were critical of contemporary Britain and also kept him apart from the controversies surrounding Lee Strasbourg's 'Method' acting (which was loosely based on Stanislavski's ideas). Roberts suggests (in *Theatre In Britain*, 1975) that 'Gielgud took refuge in the world of the one-man show, with his Shakespearean recital *The Ages of Man*.' This was a selection from George Rylands' anthology of extracts from Shakespeare and was one of Gielgud's major and most extensively toured performances from 1956 to 1964 (as well as London he performed it in the USA and Canada, Haifa, Jerusalem, Tel Aviv, Australia, New Zealand, Scandinavia, Finland, Poland and the USSR).

In the 1960s Gielgud continued in major classical roles such as Othello (Aldwych, October 1961) and Julius Caesar (Haymarket, August 1963) and toured South America and the USA with another Shakespeare recital *Men and Women of Shakespeare* (November–December 1966). He played Oedipus at the Old Vic in 1968 and then began something of a breakthrough into the 'second wave' of plays by dramatists of the next generation after Osborne. In October 1968 he played the Headmaster in Alan **Bennett**'s *Forty years On* (Apollo Theatre) and then, as well as acting in and directing classics, there followed the parts of

Gideon in Peter Shaffer's *The Battle of Shrivings* (Lyric, February 1970), and Harry in David **Storey**'s *Home* (**Royal Court**, June 1970) which was one of his most acclaimed contemporary performances (in partnership with Sir Ralph Richardson). At the Royal Court (March 1972) Gielgud played Sir Geoffrey Kendle in Charles **Wood**'s play *Veterans* (with Sir John **Mills**) which appeared to be something of a biographical celebration of Gielgud himself, his recent appearance in the film *The Charge of the Light Brigade* (1968) and his great aunt Ellen Terry's famous role in Shaw's *Captain Brassbound's Conversion* — as Ronald Bryden put it, the play explains 'to the future why, since Ellen Terry, no actor has been more beloved by his peers'.

In March 1974 Gielgud played Prospero (Old Vic) and in August of the same year the dying Shakespeare in Edward **Bond**'s *Bingo*. Perhaps one of his most memorable performances was as Spooner (whom Gielgud modelled on the poet W.H. Auden) in Harold **Pinter**'s *No Man's Land* (Old Vic, April 1975), again in a superb partnership with Richardson. At the **National Theatre** (Olivier, March 1977) he played the title-role in *Julius Caesar*, Sir Politic Wouldbe in *Volpone* (April, 1977) and Sir Noel Cunliffe in Julian Mitchell's *Half-Life* (Cottesloe, November 1977).

More recently Gielgud has continued his work in films and television, notably *The Elephant Man* (1979), *Chariots of Fire* (1980), *Arthur* (1980), *Inside the Third Reich* (1981) and *Brideshead Revisited* (1981). He has remarked that playing the butler in *Arthur* 'was a kind of summing-up of all the work I'd ever done in the theatre, how I'd learnt to act over sixty years'.

Although many think of Gielgud as one of the finest actors of the post-war period he is also one of its major directors. He has achieved a certain notoriety for never making up his mind at rehearsals, a product of his fertile and utterly creative approach. Richard Findlater (*Observer*, 18 March 1984) has written that he possesses a 'mercurial, questing conscience as a director', and Ralph Richardson once said that 'Johnny's rather like a catherine wheel. He springs out with a thousand ideas.' His acting is always refined and controlled, sometimes in the grand manner if the play demands and sometimes subtly muted as in *Home* and *No Man's Land*. Gielgud seemed to express something of the enigma, detachment and isolation of the actor and his art in *Early Stages* (1938) when he wrote that 'No-one cares, or is even aware that he works for many months to correct some physical trick, or fights against his vocal mannerisms ... No-one knows if he is suffering in his heart while he plays an emotional scene, or if he is merely adding up his household bills.'

Further Reading

John Gielgud, *An Actor In His Time*, Penguin Books, Harmondsworth, 1979.

Ronald Harwood, *The Ages of Gielgud: An Actor at Eighty*, Hodder and Stoughton, London, 1984.

Gyles Brandreth, *John Gielgud: A Celebration*, Pavilion Books, London, 1984.

Richard Findlater, *These Our Actors*, Elm Tree Books, London, 1984.

Gill, Peter, OBE

Born in Cardiff on 7 September 1939, he was educated at St Illtyd's College, Cardiff, and began his career as an actor in 1957. He turned to directing in 1965 and worked mainly at the **Royal Court** Theatre (Theatre Upstairs), directing such plays as D.H. Lawrence's *A Collier's Friday Night* (August 1965), Joe **Orton**'s *The Ruffian on the Stair* (August 1966), *A Provincial Life* (October 1966) which was his own adaptation of Chekhov's *My Life*, Thomas Otway's *The Soldier's Fortune* (January 1967), D.H. Lawrence's *The Daughter-in-Law* (March 1967), Joe Orton's *Crimes of Passion* (June 1967), and a season of the D.H. Lawrence plays *A Collier's Friday Night* (February 1968), *The Daughter-in-Law* and *The*

Widowing of Mrs Holroyd (March 1968).

In 1969 he directed *Much Ado About Nothing* (Stratford, Connecticut, USA) and in 1970 Harold **Pinter**'s *Landscape and Silence* (Lincoln Centre, New York) and Ibsen's *Hedda Gabler* (Stratford, Ontario). Back in London he became Associate Artistic Director of the Royal Court Theatre for two years and directed Webster's *The Duchess of Malfi* (Royal Court, January 1971) and John Antrobus's *Crete and Sergeant Pepper* (Royal Court, May 1972). For the **Royal Shakespeare Company** he directed *Twelfth Night* (Stratford-upon-Avon, 1974 season, Aldwych, January 1975) and for the **Edinburgh Festival** and the opening of the Riverside Studios (formerly a television studio) in 1975 he directed *As You Like It.* In November 1975 he directed Edward **Bond**'s *The Fool* at the Royal Court and the following year became Director of the Riverside Studios, Hammersmith. Productions at the latter directed by Gill include his own version of Chekhov's *The Cherry Orchard* (January 1978), Middleton and Rowley's *The Changeling* (1978) and *Measure for Measure* (1979).

In 1980 he became Joint Director with Peter **Hall** of the **National Theatre** where he has directed Turgenev's *A Month in the Country* (Olivier, February 1981), Molière's *Don Juan* (Cottesloe, April 1981), *Much Ado About Nothing* (Olivier, August 1981), Howard **Brenton**'s adaptation of Büchner's *Danton's Death* (Olivier, July 1982), Shaw's *Major Barbara* (Lyttleton, October 1982), Christopher **Hampton**'s *Tales From Hollywood* (Olivier, September 1983), Sophocles' *Antigone* (Cottesloe, October 1983), Otway's *Venice Preserv'd* (Lyttleton, April 1984) and Sam Shephard's *Fool For Love* (Cottesloe, October 1984). Since the re-organisation of the National Theatre in 1984 Peter Gill has had responsibility for the encouragement of new writing and experimental drama for company members (housed in the 'National Theatre Studio' in the **Old Vic** Annexe).

Peter Gill has also written a number of quite successful plays including *The Sleepers' Den* (Royal Court, February, 1965) about Mrs Shannon, a poverty-stricken housewife pressurised into mental collapse by her indifferent and demanding family, *Over Gardens Out* (Royal Court, Theatre Upstairs, August 1969) an allegory about two misunderstood boys driven to violence, and *Kick for Touch* (Cottesloe, February 1983).

Further Reading

David Roper, 'Royal Court and After', *Plays and Players*, August 1982.

Gobo

See **Profile Spot.**

'Going Up'

Starting the performance.

Gray, Simon (James Holliday)

Born on Hayling Island, Hampshire, on 21 October 1926, he was educated in England at Westminster School and then studied literature at Dalhousie University, Halifax, Nova Scotia, Canada, and Trinity College, Cambridge (1954-61). He was then a Harper-Wood Student at St John's College, Cambridge (1961-2) and Research Student at Trinity College, Cambridge (1962-3). *Colmain,* his first novel, was published by Faber in 1963 and in that same year he became a Lecturer in English at the University of British Columbia, Vancouver. A year afterwards he became Supervisor in English at Trinity College, Cambridge (1964-6). In 1965 his second novel, *Simple People,* was published by Faber and in the same year he married Beryl Kevern. Since 1966 he has been a Lecturer in English at Queen Mary

College, University of London.

Little Portia, a third novel, was published by Faber in 1967 and in the same year a television play called *Sleeping Dog* was broadcast. Gray's first stage play was *Wise Child* (Wyndham's, October 1967), about a criminal on the run (Jack Masters) who disguises himself as a tarty middle-aged woman ('Mrs Artmaster'), the role originally being played in a fine performance by Alec **Guinness**. In its explorations of sexual ambiguity against the background of crime the play is a comedy of morality rather in the vein of Joe **Orton**'s plays (such as *Entertaining Mr Sloane*).

In March 1969 the **Royal Shakespeare Company** presented Gray's *Dutch Uncle* directed by Peter **Hall** at the Aldwych Theatre. The strong original cast included Warren Mitchell who played Godboy, a shy chiropodist who hero-worships a police inspector, and Patrick Magee who played Inspector Hawkins. One of the ways in which Godboy tries to gain Hawkins's attention is by attempting to be a wife-murderer. Again Gray is more than a farceur here and extends his work to an exploration of characters' frustrations in a restricted, oppressive and conventional society. His fourth novel, *A Comeback for Stark* was published in 1979, and his next play was an adaptation of Dostóevsky's novel *The Idiot* (**National Theatre** at the **Old Vic**, July 1970) with Derek **Jacobi** in the title-role. In a programme-note to this production Gray referred to the 'futility of a world gone mad with convention'.

In *Spoiled* (Theatre Royal, Haymarket, February 1971) we saw a sexually frustrated schoolmaster whose wife is pregnant and who tutors a young boy in their home for a week, the teacher's relationship with the boy growing gradually towards homosexuality.

Gray received particular acclaim for his next play, *Butley* (Criterion, July 1971), which was directed by Harold **Pinter** and starred Alan **Bates** in the title-role. The play is a 'campus' comedy about Ben Butley, a university lecturer whose marriage is breaking up and who has an intense relationship with Joey, a former student who now shares his flat and study. Butley has some superbly written and very witty monologues about university politics, student dissidents and campus life in general, topics which Gray, as a university lecturer himself, knows intimately.

Otherwise Engaged (Queen's, July 1975) concerns a publisher (Simon) who constantly attempts to escape from the demands of other people (to be 'otherwise engaged'), by absorbing himself in such distractions as his collection of the latest technological domestic equipment and comforts. In 1977 *Dog Days* appeared and the following year *The Rear Column* was presented (Globe, February 1978) under Pinter's direction. The latter play is about a group of explorers in the Congo Jungle who are waiting frustratedly, under orders from Henry Morton Stanley and his intransigent representative Barttelot, to transport relief supplies. Gillian Reynolds (in *Plays and Players*, April 1978), described it as a 'drama of character which debates reason, honour and moral standards'.

In October 1978 Billie **Whitelaw** took the title-role in Gray's murder story *Molly* (Comedy Theatre). *Close of Play* (National Theatre, Lyttleton, May 1979) concerns Jasper, an academic, who keeps his own counsel while the relationships of those around him collapse. The lead part was originally played by Michael **Redgrave**. *Stage Struck* (Vaudeville, November 1979) is a comedy thriller about a failed actor (originally played by Alan Bates) on the brink of rejection by his wife, a successful actress.

One of his most acclaimed plays other than *Butley* was *Quartermaine's Terms* (Queen's, July 1981) which explored the tensions and lack of communication experienced by teachers in a Cambridge language school. Michael Billington (in the *Guardian*) wrote of the play, 'Mr Gray pins down that particular English quality of embarrassment in the face of real emotion: the sense of relief at a ringing telephone when someone is about to break down.' In 1982 Simon Gray adapted Molière's *Tartuffe* (for Washington DC) and in June 1984 *The Common Pursuit* was directed by Harold Pinter at the Lyric, Hammersmith. Stuart, an undergraduate at Trinity College, Cambridge, in 1964, attempts to start a literary magazine (the *New Literary Review*) with five of his student friends. The majority of the play, set in the London offices of the magazine, examines the interrelated lives of the six graduates over the subsequent 15 years — up to middle-age, disillusionment and the early death of the most talented of the group. The title of the play is taken from the liberal humanist and moralist critic F.R. Leavis's influential critical work *The Common Pursuit.* Michael Ratcliffe (in the *Observer,* 8 July 1984) suggested the play is about these Cambridge English graduates who 'fail to match up to their Leavisite ideals of scholarly truthfulness in the service of great art'. Television plays other than those already mentioned include *Death of a Teddy Bear, Plaintiffs and Defendants* and *Two Sundays.*

Further Reading

John Russell Taylor, *The Second Wave,* Methuen, London, 1979, pp. 169-71.

Green

A green cue light used for 'go', located at the **SM**'s prompt-desk and, in addition, sometimes at the lighting console. **FOH** manager can cue the SM for the start of a performance by this means.

Greene (Henry) Graham, CH

Born in Berkhamsted, Hertfordshire, on 2 October 1904, educated at Berkhamsted School and Balliol College, Oxford University, he worked on *The Times* (1926-30) and the *Spectator* (1937-41) before becoming Director of the publishing firms of Eyre and Spottiswoode (1944-8) and the Bodley Head (1958-68). During the war he worked in the Foreign Office (1941-4). Although his work as a novelist is internationally acclaimed and is the greatest part of his writing achievement, Greene has made a small but strong contribution to the theatre.

Other than an adaptation of *Heart of the Matter* (1950, with Basil Dean as co-writer) his first play for the theatre was *The Living Room* (Wyndham's, April 1953) about the relationship between a young girl (played by Dorothy **Tutin** in the original production) and a married man which ends in her tragic suicide. A central figure in the play is the girl's uncle, a crippled priest. This was followed by his now much-revived *The Potting Shed* (Bijou, New York, January 1957, Globe, London, February 1958) which starred John **Gielgud** and was about a priest's search to refind his faith after sacrificing it in order to bring a dead boy back to life. *The Complaisant Lover* (Globe, June 1959) was a comedy about a dentist's wife who has an affair with a bookseller. It starred Ralph **Richardson** and Paul **Scofield**. *Carving a Statue* (Haymarket, September 1964) starred Richardson as a sculptor obsessed, to the point of destructive disregard for his family and friends, with the creation of a religious sculpture. Denholm **Elliott** played the lead in Greene's *The Return of A.J. Raffles* for the **Royal Shakespeare Company** (Aldwych, December 1975), a play about an upper-class burglar's involvement in the quarrel of Lord Alfred Douglas with the Marquess of Queensbury. *The Living Room, The Potting Shed* and *Carving a Statue* are plays more interesting in their content — the struggles of man with religious faith and the mysteries of God — than in their form (which is in the tradition of the 'well-made-play'), but have nevertheless retained their capacity to create dramatic energy.

Other plays include *Yes and No* (1980),

For Whom the Bell Chimes (1980) and *The Great Jowett* (1981). Greene has written film scripts for *21 days*, *The Green Cockatoo*, *The New Britain*, *Went the Day Well?*, *Brighton Rock* (co-written with Terence **Rattigan**), *The Fallen Idol*, *The Third Man*, *Saint Joan*, *Our Man in Havana* and *The Comedians*.

His major novels and stories include *Stamboul Train* (1932), *Brighton Rock* (1938), *The Power and The Glory* (1940), *The Heart of the Matter* (1948), *The Quiet American* (1955), *Our Man in Havana* (1958), *A Burnt-Out Case* (1961), *The Honorary Consul* (1973), *The Human Factor* (1978) and *Monsignor Quixote* (1982).

Further Reading

John Spurling, *Graham Greene*, 'Contemporary Writers' series, Methuen, London, 1983.

Graham Greene, *A Sort of Life* (1970) and *Ways of Escape* (1980), republished by Penguin Books, Harmondsworth, 1982.

Green Room

A waiting room backstage, or sometimes beneath the stage.

Grid

The framework constructed of bars and **Barrels** from which lights can be suspended over the stage. Some theatres and halls have additional grids in **FOH** positions.

Griffiths, Richard

Born on 31 July 1947 in Thornaby-on-Tees, North Yorkshire, he studied art (between 1966 and 1970) at Manchester School of Art, English and Drama at Manchester Polytechnic, and did postgraduate Theatre Studies at Manchester University.

His first stage appearance was as Darnforth in Arthur Miller's *The Crucible* at Stockton-Billingham Technical College (July 1964) and his first professional appearance was as Salinas in Peter **Shaffer**'s *The Royal Hunt of the Sun* (Harrogate, July 1970). He came to prominence in the 1970s and parts have included Edward in *Henry VI* (BBC Radio, 1971), Doolittle in Shaw's *Pygmalion* (Orchard Theatre, Dartford, 1973), the chaplain in **Brecht**'s *Mother Courage* (Orchard, 1973), Macduff in *Macbeth* (Belfast, 1973), York in *Richard II* (Manchester Library, 1974) and the Jew in Georg Büchner's *Woyzek* (Newcastle, 1975). In 1974 he appeared as the Park Keeper in the television play *Norma*.

In 1974 Griffiths joined the **Royal Shakespeare Company** at Stratford-upon-Avon and for that season played the Officer in *Twelfth Night* and Abhorson in *Measure for Measure* at the Royal Shakespeare Theatre. At the Other Place he played Gonzalo in *The Tempest* and Tiny in David **Rudkin**'s *Afore Night Come* (1974). Subsequently he has played the Officer and Sailor in *Twelfth Night* (Stratford and Aldwych, 1975), Tanky in *Dingo* (the Other Place, 1976), Paris's Servant in *Troilus and Cressida* and Peter in *Romeo and Juliet* (Stratford 1976, and Aldwych 1977).

One of his outstanding performances was as Bottom in John **Barton**'s production of *A Midsummer Night's Dream* (Stratford, 1977 and Aldwych, 1978). In this production Griffiths revealed a considerable mastery of comic timing and balletic movement (particularly effective was his ability to gesture with his feet). In the same season he played Trinculo in Clifford **Williams**'s production of *The Tempest*, the Clown in *Antony and Cleopatra*, Navarre in *Love's Labour's Lost* and Pompey in *Measure for Measure*. In the 1979 Aldwych season he continued in these parts but also played Larion in Bulgakov's *The White Guard* and George in Kauffman and Hart's *Once in a Lifetime* (transferred to the Piccadilly, March 1980).

Some of his latest work has included appearances in a number of films: Delmas' Assistant in *Ragtime* (1980), Collins in *Ghandi* (1981), the Bishop's Son in *The French Lieutenant's Woman* (1981), Billings in *Greystoke Tarzan*, Anton in *Gorky Park* (1983) and Allardyce in *A Private Function* (1984).

Richard Griffiths became a popular television actor as Sam in the comedy series *Nobody's Perfect* (1980) which ran for a second series (1981) on London Weekend Television. He appeared as Falstaff in the BBC Shakespeare production of *The Merry Wives of Windsor* (1982). He also appeared as Ptolemy in *The Cleopatras* (1982). Other television appearances have included *Norma, Parole, Red Letter Day, When the Boat Comes In, It's Only Rock and Roll, Bird of Prey,* and *Bergerac.*

With the RSC at Stratford he played the title-roles in *Henry VIII* (May 1983) and *Volpone* (September 1983) and played them again in 1984 at the Barbican Theatre, in addition playing Nikolai in Charles **Wood**'s *Red Star* (Barbican, July 1984).

Griffiths, Trevor

One of the leading socialist playwrights and television dramatists to emerge in the 1970s, he was born in Manchester on 4 April 1935, educated at St Bede's College, Manchester (1945-52) and Manchester University (1952-5), where he read English. He served in the Manchester Regiment (1955-7) and then became a teacher and Further Education lecturer. He married Janice Stansfield in 1960. From 1965 until 1972 he was a Further Education Officer for BBC Television in Leeds.

His first play performed for the stage was a one-acter called *The Wages of Thin* (Stables, Manchester, November 1969). This was followed by his first full-length play, *Occupations* (Stables, Manchester, 1970, **RSC** at the Place, October 1971), set during the 1920 Fiat strike in Italy. Through the central conflict between the Italian Marxist theorist, Gramsci, and a Soviet agent, Kabak, Griffiths explores different aspects of revolutionary action and the problems of creating solidarity in the working class. Two one-act plays, *Apricots* and *Thermidor*, were performed by John **McGrath**'s **7:84 Company** at the **Edinburgh Festival** in 1971 and Griffiths also collaborated with David **Hare** in writing *Lay By* (Edinburgh Festival, Traverse Theatre, 1971). The one-act play *Sam, Sam* (Open Space, 1972), to a certain extent autobiographical, is about two brothers (both called Sam), of working-class background, one of whom remains in his social position and the other of whom enters the middle-class bourgeoisie through his education and his marriage to the daughter of a bank manager. The latter brother is shown to be the unhappier and more isolated, making the play a penetrating comment on capitalism's permeation of the social structure.

The Party (**National Theatre**, **Old Vic**, December 1973), originally performed with Sir Laurence **Olivier** in the part of the veteran Trotskyite, John Tagg, is set in a Kensington flat in May 1968, the time of the Paris revolutionary *événements.* The play's central conflict is between Tagg, the leader of the 'Revolutionary Socialist Party', and Professor Ford of the LSE, and it concerns the problem of how the British Left should respond to the political upheaval in France. The apparent analytical seriousness and commitment of the play is, however, tempered by Griffith's command of linguistic wit and comic ambiguity, in such a way that the play is able to focus attention upon its characters' reassessment of their personal life-styles as well as their political beliefs. Much of the ambiguity of the play is expressed through the private and public uncertainties of the owner of the flat, Joe Shawcross, a trendy TV producer. *The Party* was revived by the **Royal Shakespeare Company** (the Other Place, Stratford-upon-

Avon, August 1984) and, in a review of this production, Ros Asquith (*Observer*, 2 September) stated, 'class-consciousness is precisely what imbues his writing with such muscle and anger, but his ear is finely tuned to psychological nuance and he oils the wheels with a liberal wit'.

Griffiths's next stage play (and his best known) was *Comedians* (Nottingham Playhouse, February 1975, National Theatre, Old Vic, September 1975, New York, 1976), which included Jimmy Jewel and Jonathan **Pryce** in the cast. Ostensibly a comedy about an evening class for stand-up comics (the play is full of gags), it is also an extremely successful exploration of the analogy between revolutionary political action and the effects of comedy upon audiences. As Eddie Waters says in the play, 'most comics feed prejudice and fear and blinkered vision, but the best ones ... illuminate them. We've got to make people laugh till they cry. Cry. Till they find their pain and beauty. Comedy is a medicine. Not coloured sweeties to rot their teeth with.' Discussing the play in an interview in 1976 (*Theatre Quarterly*, Vol. 6, No. 22) Griffiths suggested he wanted to write a work which was 'more immediately accessible to people who haven't had a background in revolutionary theory or revolutionary history.'

With Howard **Brenton**, Ken Campbell and David **Hare** he co-wrote *Deeds* (Nottingham Playhouse, March 1978). A stage adaptation of his television play, *Oi for England* was performed at the **Royal Court**, Theatre Upstairs in June 1982.

In March 1984 the British Film Institute celebrated the work of Trevor Griffiths by a season devoted to screenings of his television plays. He is one of the leading television dramatists to emerge in the last two decades and even once stated (*Plays and Players*, June 1974), 'theatre is ... not a thing to which I can express total commitment as a writer. I have a prior commitment to television. Writing for television provides me with the widest spectrum for communication that is available in this society. It cuts right across the classes.' His work for television includes a television version of *Occupations*, the series *Adam Smith*, *Dr Finlay's Casebook*, *The Silver Mask* (in the series *Between the Wars*), *Absolute Beginners* (in the series *Fall of Eagles*), *All Good Men*, the series *Bill Brand*, *Destiny*, *Through the Night*, a television version of *Comedians*, an adaptation of *Sons and Lovers*, *Reds* (co-written for USA), an adaptation of *The Cherry Orchard*, *Country* and *Oi For England*.

Interviewed on Radio 4 (*Kaleidoscope*, 13 March 1984) during the BFI season, he said, 'my sort of writing isn't about ego-massage. It's really about impact and penetration. It's about opening up possibilities for a different social reality from the one we have.'

Further Reading

Trevor Griffiths, interview with Catherine Itzin and Simon Trussler, 'Transforming the Husk of Capitalism', *Theatre Quarterly*, Vol. 6, No. 22, Summer 1976, pp. 25-46. Also in Simon Trussler (ed.), *New Theatre Voices of the Seventies*, Methuen, London, 1981, pp. 121-33.

Peter Ansorge, interview with Trevor Griffiths and David Hare, 'Current Concerns', *Plays and Players*, July 1974, pp. 18-22.

Christian W. Thomsen, 'Three Socialist Playwrights', *Contemporary English Drama*, C.W.E. Bigsby (ed.), 'Stratford-upon-Avon Studies', No. 19, Edward Arnold, London, 1981, pp. 169-75.

Mike Poole and John Wyver, *Powerplays: Trevor Griffiths in Television*, BFI Publications, London, 1984.

Ground Cloth

Same as **Drugget** or **Stage Cloth**.

Ground Row

An arrangement of **Floods** at ground level usually for lighting the **Cyclorama** or **Backcloth**. Such lights are normally masked by a 'groundrow' of scenery.

Group Theatre, The

See **Verse Drama**.

Guinness, Sir Alec

Born in Marylebone, London, 2 April 1914, he was educated in Sussex at Pembroke Lodge, Southbourne, and Roborough, Eastbourne. (In an interview for *TV Times* in May 1984, he said, 'I wasn't miserable — children accept what happens — but I had a lonely childhood and I suppose acting came from inventing things for myself'). On leaving school he began his career as a copywriter with Arks Publicity, Advertising Agents, in Lincoln's Inn. After 18 months in this job he trained for the stage at the Fay Compton Studio of Dramatic Art.

His first stage appearance was a walk-on part in Edward Wooll's *Libel!* (Playhouse, April 1934). Some of his most important appearances before the war were as Sampson and the Apothecary in *Romeo and Juliet* (New Theatre, October 1935) and Yakov in Chekhov's *The Seagull* (New Theatre, May 1936) and, joining the **Old Vic** company in September 1936, he played in many productions including *Love's Labour's Lost*, *Hamlet* (in which he took the parts of Reynaldo and Osric), *Twelfth Night* (playing Aguecheek) and *Henry V* (playing Exeter). In September 1937 he joined John **Gielgud**'s company at the Queen's Theatre where his roles included Snake in Sheridan's *The School for Scandal*, Feodotik in Chekhov's *Three Sisters* and Lorenzo in *The Merchant of Venice*. Rejoining the Old Vic company in September 1938, his most memorable performance was as Hamlet (in a modern dress production). From January to April 1939 he toured with the Old Vic company's *Hamlet* and, in addition to other roles, played the Chorus in *Henry V*. On return to the Old Vic he took the part of Michael Ransom in Auden and Isherwood's *The Ascent of F6*. In December of 1939 he appeared as Herbert Pockett in his own adaptation of Dickens's *Great Expectations* (Rudolf Steiner Hall) and in 1940 toured as Charleston in Robert Ardrey's *Thunder Rock*.

He joined the Royal Navy in 1941 as an ordinary seaman, received a commission in 1942, and at the end of the same year was temporarily released in order to play Flight Lieutenant Graham in Terence **Rattigan**'s *Flare Path* (Henry Miller Theatre, New York, December 1942).

After the war he appeared as Mitya in his own adaptation of Dostoevsky's *The Brothers Karamazov* (Lyric, Hammersmith, June 1946) and Garcin in Sartre's *Vicious Circle* (*Huis Clos*) at the Arts Theatre, July 1946. He rejoined the Old Vic company at the New Theatre in September 1946 and in seasons up to May 1948 his parts included the Fool in *King Lear*, Eric Birling in J.B. Priestley's *An Inspector Calls*, Comte de Guich in Rostand's *Cyrano de Bergerac*, Abel Drugger in Ben Jonson's *The Alchemist*, the title-role in *Richard II* and Klestakov in Gogol's *The Government Inspector*. In September 1948 Guinness directed *Twelfth Night* for the Old Vic company at the New Theatre, and in the following year he played the Unidentified Guest in T.S. **Eliot**'s *The Cocktail Party* (Lyceum, **Edinburgh Festival**, August 1949, and Henry Miller Theatre, New York, January 1950). Subsequently he directed *Hamlet* and played the title-role himself (New, May 1951). According to a review of the time (*Evening Standard*) Guinness portrayed Hamlet as a 'middle-aged Hamlet instead of the youthful, pitiful, self-infatuated Prince ... we felt last night that Mr. Disraeli had come to Elsinore. If there was something rotten in the State of Denmark this was the very man to put it right.'

Alec Guinness had, by this time, established his ability as a virtuoso character-actor who had the uncanny knack of erasing his own appearance and personality behind a disguise and a skilfully crafted persona (in the film *Kind Hearts and Coronets*, 1949, he played all eight victims of a murderer, including Lady Agatha). Margaret Tierney (*Plays and Players*, September 1971) has commented on 'Sir Alec's ability to disappear behind a change of expression' and Ronald Hayman (*Playback 2*, 1973) maintains that there is 'no living actor who has succeeded better than Alec Guinness at creating characters without recognisable resemblance, facial or vocal, to himself or to each other'. Kenneth **Tynan** (in *Alec Guinness*, 1961) stated: 'The whole presence of the man is guarded and evasive. Slippery sums him up ... he will communicate intimacy, but always from a considerable distance, as if through a reversed telescope ... You might easily take him for a slightly tipsy curate on the verge of being unfrocked.'

Guinness played the title-role in *Richard III* and the King in *All's Well That Ends Well* at the Stratford Shakespearean Festival (Ontario, July 1953). Other work in this period included Boniface in Feydeau's farce *Hotel Paradiso* (Winter Garden, May 1956) and the title-role in Terence Rattigan's *Ross* (Haymarket, May 1960). At the Edinburgh Festival in 1963 he played Berenger the First in Eugène Ionesco's *Exit the King* (transferring to the **Royal Court** Theatre, September 1963) and in January 1964 went to the USA and played Dylan Thomas in Sydney Michaels's *Dylan* (Plymouth Theatre, New York). In 1966 he returned to London and took the part of Von Berg in Arthur Miller's *Incident at Vichy* (Phoenix, January 1966). He played the title-role in *Macbeth* in October 1966 at the Royal Court Theatre in a production by William **Gaskill**. The presentation was experimental, non-illusionistic, used a bare, heavily-lit set, and was much influenced by **Brechtian** ideas. In October 1967 Guinness played in the first production of Simon **Gray**'s *Wise Child* (Wyndham's, October 1967), taking the comedy role of Mrs Artminster.

He directed T.S. Eliot's *The Cocktail Party* at the **Chichester Festival** in May 1968 and played the part of Harcourt-Reilly himself. This production later transferred to Wyndham's (November 1968) and the Haymarket (February 1969).

From this point on Guinness took part in a number of new plays, appearing as the Father in John **Mortimer's** *A Voyage Round My Father* (Haymarket, August 1971), Dr Wickersteed in Alan **Bennett**'s *Habeus Corpus* (Lyric, May 1973) and Dudley in Julian Mitchell's adaptation of Ivy Compton-Burnett's *A Family and a Fortune* (Apollo, April 1975). Following this he co-devised, with Alan Strachan, a play about Jonathan Swift called *Yahoo* (Queen's, October 1976), in which he played the part of Swift. In September 1977 he took the part of Hilary (a British defector in Russia), in Alan Bennett's *The Old Country* (Queen's), and in July 1984 played Shylock in *The Merchant of Venice* (Chichester Festival).

Sir Alec Guinness has been one of Britain's most versatile and successful film actors. Among his many film appearances the best known are: *Great Expectations* (1946) in which he played Herbert Pockett, *Oliver Twist* in which he played Fagin, *Kind Hearts and Coronets* (1949) in which he played eight parts, *The Lavender Hill Mob* (1951), *The Man in the White Suit* (1951), *Father Brown* (1954), *The Bridge on the River Kwai* (1957), *The Horse's Mouth* (1959), *Our Man in Havana* (1959), *Tunes of Glory* (1960), *Lawrence of Arabia* (1962), *Doctor Zhivago* (1966), *The Comedians* (1967), *Cromwell* (1969), *Scrooge* (1972), *Hitler: the Last Ten Days* (1973), *Star Wars* (1980), *Return of the Jedi* (1982), *A Passage to India* (1984).

Guinness's television work has included *The Wicked Scheme of Jebel Jacks* (USA), *Conversation at Night* and *Caesar and Cleopatra.* Recently he gave a highly-acclaimed performance as George Smiley, a government agent, in adaptations of John le Carré's *Tinker, Tailor, Soldier, Spy* (1979) and *Smiley's People* (1982).In 1985 he was in *Monsignor Quixote* (1985). Guinness once said that 'an actor's faculties consist of his voice, his eyes and his physical presence' and in the part of Smiley he was able to finely tune these to create a complex and enigmatic figure who was also authoritative and likeable. Some time ago, in 1961, Kenneth Tynan (in *Alec Guinness*) wrote of Guinness's eyes: 'superficially guileless, they are in truth sly and wary'. In 1984 he played the retired judge in John Mortimer's *Edwin*.

In his interview with Ronald Hayman, Guinness said 'I think a lot of acting, after all, is fooling oneself ... you have a great capacity, if you're a performer, for playing children's games, and how real do children think games are when they're playing them? It's the same thing, I think.'

Further Reading

John Russell Taylor, *Alec Guinness: A Celebration*, Pavilion Books, London, 1983.

Kenneth Tynan, *Alec Guinness*, Barrie and Rockliff, London, 1961.

Ronald Hayman, 'Alec Guinness', *Playback 2*, Davis-Poynter, London, 1973, pp. 37-47.

Alec Guinness, *Blessings in Disguise*, Hamish Hamilton, London, 1985.

Guthrie, Sir (William) Tyrone

Great-grandson of the Irish actor Tyrone Power, he was born on 2 July 1900, in Ireland, and educated at Wellington College and subsequently St John's College, Oxford. He began his career as an actor, first appearing at the Oxford Playhouse in 1924. His directing career began with productions for the Scottish National Players (1926-7) and then at the Festival Theatre, Cambridge (1929-30). His first London production was James Bridie's *The Anatomist* (Westminster Theatre, 1931).

His productions of Shakespearean plays at the **Old Vic** a little later were often controversial and provocatively experimental. Some of the most notable were *Measure for Measure* (1933) in which Charles Laughton was Angelo and Flora **Robson** was Isabella, *A Midsummer Night's Dream* (1937, 1938) which incorporated Mendelssohn's incidental music and a modern dress production of *Hamlet* (1938) which starred Alec **Guinness** in the title-role and which was also performed at Elsinore. From 1939 until 1945 he was the Director and administrator of the Old Vic and Sadler's Wells theatres.

In 1944 Guthrie directed Ralph **Richardson** in the title-role of Ibsen's *Peer Gynt* (Old Vic company at the New Theatre) and in 1951 directed Donald **Wolfit** in the title-role of a visually spectacular production of Marlowe's *Tamburlaine the Great* (Old Vic). 1953 saw his notoriously unconventional production of *Henry VIII* at the Old Vic. For the 1948 **Edinburgh Festival** Guthrie directed one of his greatest successes, *The Three Estates*, a Scottish morality play by the medieval poet Sir David Lyndsay. The production used a thrust stage and was indicative of Guthrie's advocacy of '**open**' **stage** production, particularly for plays written before 1660 and especially for Shakespeare's plays. Commenting on his production of *The Three Estates* (in *A Life in the Theatre*, 1960), Guthrie wrote: 'Here was an opportunity to put into practice some of the theories which, through the years, I had been longing to test. Scene after scene seemed absolutely unplayable on the proscenium stage, almost meaningless in terms of "dramatic illusion"'. This view of the physical space of a theatre as an open arena was more fully realised in 1953 when Guthrie became one of the founders of the Festival Theatre, Stratford, Ontario, which was built partly to his designs for a thrust-stage with audience seating on three sides. As Guthrie put it in a 1959 interview with Laurence Kitchin (*Mid-Century Drama*, 1962), 'They scooped a big cement arena from the side of a hill, put a stage in the middle and a tent on top. In this way a great many things which are problems in the proscenium theatre solve themselves at once.' For its opening in 1953 Guthrie directed *Richard III* with Alec Guinness in the title-role and later in the same year *All's Well that Ends Well* starring Guinness and Irene **Worth**, both of the productions presented in partly ritualistic mode, the former pageant-like and the latter highly balletic.

At the Old Vic Guthrie directed *Troilus and Cressida* (1956) in a modern dress production. In 1958 he started planning another arena theatre, this to be in Minneapolis, Minnesota, which opened as the Minneapolis Theatre in May 1963 (later, in 1971, re-named the Guthrie Theatre). Some of his productions there included Chekhov's *Three Sisters* (1963), *Hamlet* (1963), *Henry V* (1964), Jonson's *Volpone* (1964), Chekhov's *The Cherry Orchard* (1965), *Richard III* (1965) and *Twelfth Night* (1965). After directing a number of productions in the Middle East, Australia, New Zealand and elsewhere he directed Molière's *Tartuffe* for the **National Theatre**, London, (Old Vic, 1967).

Often viewed as an eccentric (he even had a jam-making factory in Ireland) and an *enfant terrible*, Guthrie was nevertheless an extremely influential figure in the theatre. His vision of greater freedom of interpretation and of physical action in the theatre has had a great impact on post-war theatre in Britain and elsewhere. His revival of interest in 'arena' staging (common to the Greeks and Elizabethans) and its possibilities for a more intimate relationship between stage and audience laid the foundations for such open stages as the National Theatre's Olivier stage, the stage at the **RSC**'s Barbican Theatre, and many of the newer provincial theatres in Britain including some employing forms of 'theatre-in-the-round'. So far as directing is concerned Guthrie sometimes took unexpected risks in many of his productions yet generated a great sense of '**ensemble**' acting from the casts with whom he worked. As he put it in his 1962 talk for Folkways Records *Directing a Play*, 'the scales have got to be held — the powerful and rich and important actors must not oppress the small-part people ... A play is players playing. And if that sounds too obvious to be a distinction, then try it this way: a play is people pretending, for it is as simple as that.' In his book *Tyrone Guthrie on Acting* (1971) he wrote that acting 'implies pretending to be someone or something other than yourself; or even, while retaining your own identity, expressing thoughts or feelings which do not in fact correspond with your own thoughts and feelings at a particular moment. Indeed in this sense of the word we all spend a great deal of our lives in acting, a greater part, I suspect, than most of us realise.'

Tyrone Guthrie died on 15 May 1971.

Further Reading

Tyrone Guthrie, *A Life in the Theatre*, Hamish Hamilton, London, 1960.

Tyrone Guthrie, *Tyrone Guthrie on Acting*, Cassell and Collier Macmillan, London, 1971.

James Forsyth, *Tyrone Guthrie: A Biography*, Hamish Hamilton, London, 1976.

H

Haigh, Kenneth

Born on 25 March 1931 in Yorkshire and educated at Gunnersbury Grammar School, London, he trained at the Central School of Speech and Drama. His first professional stage appearance was as Cassio in *Othello* (Drogheda, Eire, 1952) and first London appearances were as Geoffrey Baines in *Dear Little Liz* (New Lindsey Theatre, September 1954) and in a Shakespeare season at the Open Air Theatre, Regent's Park.

Kenneth Haigh joined the **English Stage Company** for its first season at the **Royal Court** Theatre (1956-7) and besides appearing in other plays created the legendary role of Jimmy Porter in John **Osborne**'s *Look Back in Anger* (May 1956). Subsequently he played the part in New York (Lyceum Theatre, 1957) and toured the USA with the production. In February 1960 he played the title-role in Albert Camus's *Caligula* (54th Street Theatre, New York) and in London played Jerry in Edward Albee's *The Zoo Story* (Arts Theatre, August 1960) and Gerlach in Sartre's *Altona* (Royal Court, April 1961, and Saville, June 1961).

In 1962 he joined the **Royal Shakespeare Company** and played the Friend in Strindberg's *Playing With Fire* and James in **Pinter**'s *The Collection* (Aldwych, June 1962), the latter jointly directed by Harold Pinter and Peter **Hall**. Later with the RSC he took the part of Mark Antony in *Julius Caesar* (Royal Shakespeare Theatre, Stratford-upon-Avon, April 1963).

In the following year he again played the title-role in Camus's *Caligula* (Phoenix, April 1964) and in 1965 played the Burglar in *Too True to be Good* at the **Edinburgh Festival** (and later the Strand, September 1965). From 1967 until 1969 Haigh worked in the USA and on his return to England took over the part of Laurie in Osborne's *The Hotel in Amsterdam* (Duke of York's, January 1969).

In the 1970s his most important roles have been the title-role in *Prometheus Bound* (Mermaid, June 1971), Rupert Foster in John **Whiting**'s *Marching Song* (Greenwich, October 1974), the title-role in Strindberg's *The Father* (Haymarket, Leicester, 1975), Benedict in *Much Ado About Nothing* (69 Theatre Company, Manchester Cathedral, January 1976), Dysart in Peter **Shaffer**'s *Equus* (Citadel, Edmonton, Alberta, 1977) and Henry Jarvis in *The Aspern Papers* (**Chichester Festival**, 1978).

At the American Shakespeare Festival (Stratford, Connecticut, 1979) he played Malvolio in *Twelfth Night*, Brutus in *Julius Caesar* and Prospero in *The Tempest.* He played F. Scott Fitzgerald in *Clothes for a Summer Hotel* (Cort, March 1980) and in September 1982 played the title-role in *Othello* at the Young Vic.

Appearances in films include *Saint Joan* (1957), *Cleopatra* (1962), *A Hard Day's Night* (1964), *A Lovely Way to Die* (1968), *Eagle In a Cage* and *The Bitch.* Work in television has included *Man at The Top, Search for the Nile, Moll Flanders* and *Hazlitt in Love* and in April 1984 he played Robert in Don Taylor's television verse-play *The Testament of John* to Anthony **Quayle**'s John.

Hall, Sir Peter (Reginald Frederick)

With Peter **Brook**, he is the most acclaimed British director of his generation, and perhaps the post-war period of theatre in Britain up to the present time. Both directors worked together with the **Royal Shakespeare**

Company in the 1960s but since that time have taken their work in very different directions which, in many ways, can be seen to mark their different artistic temperaments — Brook forming the International Centre of Theatre Research in Paris, a small ensemble group of international actors, Hall becoming Director of the **National Theatre** in London, first at the **Old Vic** (succeeding **Olivier** in 1973) and then at the new triple-theatre complex on the South Bank of the Thames (from 1976).

Peter Hall was born on 22 November 1930, at Bury St Edmunds, Suffolk, the son of a stationmaster. When his father was transferred to Cambridge, Hall attended the Perse School where he played the title-role in the school production of *Hamlet* and in the Mummery Theatre (Hall wrote in *The Times*, 22 December 1958) the pupils 'improvised scenes from *The Odyssey* and Shakespearian productions'. During the war Sadler's Wells Opera Company had been evacuated to Cambridge and the young Hall saw some of their productions; he also experienced **Gielgud**'s playing of the title-role in *Hamlet* and many of the Marlowe Society's Shakespearean productions. He proceeded to St Catherine's College, Cambridge, where he directed one-night stands for the Arts Council and many Shakespeare productions for the Marlowe Society.

After graduation his first professional production was at the Theatre Royal, Windsor, in 1953. He subsequently directed several plays for repertory companies and then in January 1954 was appointed Assistant Director of the Arts Theatre, London. There he directed *Blood Wedding* and *The Immoralist* in 1954 and in 1955 he was made Director of the theatre. At the Arts between 1955 and 1956 he directed several plays, most notably Ionesco's *The Lesson* (1955), Anouilh's *The Waltz of the Toreadors* (1956) and the first performance of Samuel **Beckett**'s English version of *Waiting for Godot* (August 1955). He also directed *Love's Labour's Lost* at the Shakespeare Memorial Theatre in 1956, and in the same year married Leslie Caron.

In 1957 Hall formed his own producing company, the International Playwright's Theatre, and directed the first production for this company, *Camino Real* (Phoenix, April 1957). In May of the same year he directed his first opera, *The Moon and Sixpence* (Sadler's Wells), and in July directed *Cymbeline* at the Shakespeare Memorial Theatre, Stratford-upon-Avon. Later, in November 1957, he staged *The Rope Dancers* at the Cort Theatre, New York, his first production on Broadway. Hall has written that this period was a formative one in his development as a young director and in particular about how much he was influenced by the Old Vic Company's productions at the New Theatre which, he wrote, 'made me want to be a director. They were of a blazing and total theatrical quality which is unforgettable.'

In 1958 he directed a number of plays in London and continued his growing association with Stratford-upon-Avon with his production of *Twelfth Night* and then in 1959 he staged his much-acclaimed productions of *A Midsummer Night's Dream* and *Coriolanus*. The *Dream* used a permanent set (realised for Hall by Lila di Nobili) consisting of a balustraded gallery-platform with two great staircases leading to it: the whole set changed its functions with each scene of the play (and different dimensions of the play, from the fantasy-world of the fairies to the realities of Theseus' court nuptials). As J.L. Styan has put it (in *The Shakespeare Revolution*) it was as if 'the play were being presented in non-illusory fashion by the members of an Elizabethan wedding party'. *Coriolanus*, which starred Laurence Olivier in the title-role, and Edith **Evans** as Volumnia, again used a variety of levels in a set which represented any location but which also had a projection representing the Tarpeian rock, upon which, according to Laurence Kitchin (in *Mid-Century Drama*), Olivier stood 'like the apparition of an eagle'.

The set, which was designed for Hall by Boris Aronson, was not received entirely favourably: Kenneth **Tynan** said it was 'mountainous, which is fine, and full of mountainous steps, which is not', a comment which, Tynan suggested, recalled a remark once made by Alec **Guinness** about Shakespearian productions in general 'that he himself had very few conversations on the stairs of his own house'. Most of Peter Hall's reasons for these kinds of set were related to his attempts to break down the restrictions of the Memorial Theatre's proscenium arch, an obstacle inherited from the 1930s when the theatre was built. The *Coriolanus* production also used *musique concrète* composed by Roberto Gerhard and prerecorded sound effects.

In 1960, at the age of 29, Peter Hall became Director of what was renamed the **Royal Shakespeare Company** (RSC) at Stratford-upon-Avon, and from this time until 1969 introduced artistic policies which created the company as we know it today. In 1960 he directed *The Two Gentlemen of Verona*, *Twelfth Night* and, with an associate director, John **Barton**, *Troilus and Cressida.* In his period as Director of the RSC he introduced the policy of having a permanent company at Stratford which enabled the development of an **ensemble** approach to performance and he also emphasised the need for Shakespeare's plays to be understood in terms of their meanings and significance for modern society. As Peter Brook put it (in 1970), the 'first great change in Shakespeare at Stratford was introduced by Peter Hall, when he announced this vital principle that it was actors in touch with contemporary life — through contemporary works — who had to be the people to interpret Shakespeare ... eventually *all* that has grown from the Royal Shakespeare Company, has come from that policy'. Hall broadened the RSC's repertoire to include contemporary plays and classics other than Shakespeare's plays. The company acquired a London base at the Aldwych Theatre and presented a number of important contemporary plays, as well as classics.

Some of Hall's most notable productions during this influential period with the RSC were *Troilus and Cressida* (1960), *Romeo and Juliet* (1961), Harold **Pinter**'s *The Collection* (1961, co-directed), *The Wars of the Roses* (1963) which was an adaptation, with John Barton, of four of Shakespeare's Histories (*Henry VI Parts 1, 2 and 3*, and *Richard III*, renamed *Henry VI*, *Edward IV* and *Richard III*), *A Midsummer Night's Dream* (1963), *Richard II* (1964), and for the 400th anniversary of Shakespeare's birth, *Henry IV Parts 1 and 2* and *Henry V* (1964). Hall strongly emphasised the political aspects of the Histories in this period. In an interview with Charles Marowitz in 1967, Hall said that he 'was on a political kick. I was fascinated by power politics in Shakespeare.'

The 1965 Stratford season saw Hall's legendary production of *Hamlet*, which starred David **Warner**, very much the Hamlet of the younger generation of the 1960s. Hall commented (in 1967) on the selection of Warner that 'I'd been looking for a young actor who, in the broadest sense, represented the young intellectual of today' and that 'what triggered it off was a particular feeling about the powerlessness of the intellectual in a political state'. In his lecture to the Shakespeare Institute in May 1965 Hall argued that *Hamlet* is 'one of mankind's great images' which 'turns a new face to each century, even to each decade. It is a mirror which gives back the reflection of the age that is contemplating it.' Yet, at the same time, he suggested that in thinking about *Hamlet* this way a director was 'in peril of over-stressing certain elements at the expense of others'. His interpretation of the play was, in spite of such qualifications, related to the apparent disillusionment of the younger generation of the mid-1960s — 'for our decade', he said, 'I think the play will be about the disillusionment which produces an apathy of the will so deep that commitment to politics, to religion or to life is impossible.'

In one of the best essays on this production, Stanley Wells (in *Royal Shakespeare*, 1977), remarks that Warner's performance in particular 'did much to emphasise Hamlet's noncomformity, his inner rebellion against the Establishment by which he was surrounded. This was a young man who made his own rules and did not mind appearing ridiculous or eccentric ... a disaffected young man, an existentialist drop-out, a beatnik.'

In the same year as *Hamlet* Peter Hall also directed the first performance of Harold Pinter's *The Homecoming* (RSC at the Aldwych, June 1965), in 1966 directed a production of Gogol's *The Government Inspector* and a year later *Macbeth* (1967) starring Paul **Scofield**. Hall resigned as Managing Director of the RSC in 1968, being succeeded by Trevor **Nunn**, but he remained on the Directorial Board and continued to direct plays for the company. Some impressive productions were the first performances of Pinter's *Landscape* and *Silence* (RSC, Aldwych, July 1969), Peter **Shaffer**'s *The Battle of the Shrivings* (RSC, Lyric Theatre, February 1970) and Pinter's *Old Times* (RSC, Aldwych, June 1971). He married Jacqueline Taylor in 1965.

Peter Hall commented in the early 1970s that in his work with the RSC, 'We caused a revolution in the speaking of Shakespeare's verse ... theatre begins with the word. In the beginning is the word ... without the word there is little possibility for all the other things of the theatre ... a silence on the stage means nothing — unless it's surrounded with the most marvellous words. The more marvellous the words are the better the silence.' This kind of awareness is also reflected in his directorial attitude towards Pinter's plays — in the 1967 interview with Marowitz, for example, he stated that 'when Pinter writes three dots, he means something different than when he writes "Silence"', and in 1975 (in an interview with Chris Barlas, published in *Gambit*, Vol. 7, No. 28, 1976) he suggested that acting is 'a delicate matter of communicating the instinctive and unspoken'.

Hall went to New York in 1972 and directed *All Over*, *Via Galactica* and *Macbeth*. In November 1973 he took over from Sir Laurence Olivier as Director of the National Theatre, then at the Old Vic, and subsequently directed *The Tempest* (1973), Ibsen's *John Gabriel Borkman* (1974), Samuel Beckett's *Happy Days* (1974) and Pinter's *No Man's Land* (1975), starring Sir John **Gielgud** and Sir Ralph **Richardson**. During this first half of the 1970s Hall was involved in the complicated administrative and financial problems of establishing the National Theatre in its new premises (designed by Denys Lasdun) on the South Bank of the River Thames. Some of the anguish and pleasure this gave him is recorded in his diaries which were begun in 1972 (*Peter Hall's Diaries: The Story of a Dramatic Battle*, 1983). So far as his artistic policy is concerned his intentions have been to have a theatre capable of presenting a variety of drama from classics to experimental drama, British and foreign drama and to attract the work of regional theatre companies as well. As Peter Roberts put it (in *Theatre In Britain*, 1975) Hall wanted an atmosphere 'where patrons in dinner jackets may feel as much at home as those in jeans'. Hall himself (*Gambit*, 1976) stated that the establishment of a permanent National Theatre offered an unrivalled opportunity 'to put the theatre right in the centre of creation, of society's debate with itself'.

Two of the new theatres opened with productions by Hall: *Hamlet* (Lyttleton, March 1976) and Marlowe's *Tamburlaine the Great* (Olivier, October 1976), both starring Albert **Finney**.

Subsequently Hall co-directed Alan **Ayckbourn**'s *Bedroom Farce* (1977), directed Jonson's *Volpone* (1977), Wycherley's *The Country Wife* (1977), Chekhov's *The Cherry Orchard* (1978), *Macbeth* (1978) and Pinter's *Betrayal* (1978).

Peter Hall's production of Shaffer's

madeus was staged at the Olivier in Jovember 1979 and in 1980 he directed a pro-luction of *Othello.* In February 1981 he irected Pinter's *Family Voices* (Lyttleton) nd in November of the same year Aeschy-is' *The Oresteia* (Olivier). His production of Oscar Wilde's *The Importance of Being Earnest* was presented in September 1982 Lyttleton) and in October 1982 Pinter's *Other Places* (Cottesloe). At the Olivier 'heatre in December 1983, Hall put on *Jean eberg* (a musical by Martin Hamlish) and, at ne Cottesloe in April 1984, his own adapta-ion of George Orwell's *Animal Farm.* He narried Maria Ewing in 1982.

In addition to his work with plays Peter Iall has a distinguished career as a director f opera, some of his major work having een (at Covent Garden) *Moses and Aaron* 1965), *The Magic Flute* (1966), *Eugene Onegin* and *Tristan and Isolde* (1971). He as also directed at Glyndebourne, including roductions of *The Marriage of Figaro* 1973), *Don Giovanni* (1977), *Cosi fan Tutte* (1978), *Fidelio* (1979), *A Midsummer Night's Dream* (1981) and *Orfeus and Euri-ice* (1982). He directed Verdi's *Macbeth* for he Metropolitan Opera, New York, in 1982, nd at the Bayreuth Festival in 1983 directed Vagner's *The Ring.*

For the Fiftieth Anniversary season at Glyndebourne in 1984, Hall directed four peras: Monteverdi's *The Coronation of Poppea,* Mozart's *Cosi fan Tutte* and *The Marriage of Figaro* and Benjamin Britten's *A Midsummer Night's Dream.*

His film work includes *A Midsummer Night's Dream* (1969), *The Homecoming* 1973) and his autobiographical film set in he Suffolk of his childhood, *Akenfield* 1974) from the novel by Ronald Blythe.

It is difficult to summarise a director and heatre manager of such range, talent and chievement but perhaps Peter Hall came lose to describing his own career when he aid (in his 1967 interview with Marowitz) hat 'I find the theatre an obsession because is always changing, like life itself … creation is produced by the pressure of now.'

Further Reading

David Addenbrooke, *The Royal Shakespeare Company: The Peter Hall Years,* Kimber Press, London, 1974.

Peter Hall, interview with Chris Barlas, *Gambit,* Vol. 7, No. 28, 1976.

Peter Hall, *Peter Hall's Diaries: The Story of a Dramatic Battle,* John Goodwin (ed.), Hamish Hamilton, London, 1983

Hall, Willis

Born in Leeds, Yorkshire, on 6 April 1929, he was educated at Cockburn High School, Leeds. He did his National Service as a radio playwright for Radio Malaya.

He came to prominence as a playwright with *The Long and the Short and the Tall* (**Edinburgh Festival**, 1958, **Royal Court** Theatre, January 1959), a play about a group of British soldiers and a Japanese prisoner trapped in a hut in the Malayan jungle, eventually all but one of them killed in an ambush. J.W. Lambert commented in a 1959 introduction to the play that its strength 'lies in the cross currents of fear, hatred, nostalgia, despair, courage and rare kindliness which may be expected of any group of men in a hopeless situation, and which it is a privilege to share'. Other than a few one-act plays and some writing for film and television, Willis Hall has written his stage plays with Keith Waterhouse.

Waterhouse was also born in Leeds and, to a day, is two months older than Hall. Born on 6 February 1929, he was educated at Osmondthorpe Council School, Leeds, and has been a journalist since 1950 and a novelist and playwright since the publication of his novels *There is a Happy Land* (1957) and *Billy Liar* (1959). Hall and Waterhouse's first joint venture was a much-acclaimed stage adaptation of *Billy Liar* (Cambridge Theatre, September 1960) which was directed by Lindsay **Anderson** with Albert

Finney in the title-role. The comedy is focused on Billy, a northern working-class lad who fantasises and lies to himself and others about his life and relationships. Billy's life treads the thin tightrope between fantasy and reality as he struggles to find a true identity.

Celebration (Nottingham, 1961) juxtaposed a wedding celebration with a funeral, *England, Our England* (1962) was a satirical revue with music written by Dudley Moore and *All Things Bright and Beautiful* (Bristol Old Vic, 1962) was about a family trapped by bureaucracy as it moves from a condemned house to a block of flats. Hall and Waterhouse have also written review sketches, in particular for BBC's *That Was The Week That Was.*

The one-acters *The Sponge Room* and *Squat Betty* were produced as a double-bill at the Royal Court Theatre (December 1962) and in 1964 *Come Laughing Home* was presented at Bristol and a year later at Wimbledon. This latter play explored the conflicts between an unmarried pregnant girl and her family. The highly successful farce *Say Who You Are* (Her Majesty's, October 1965), which partly takes place in a phone booth (hence the title of the play), follows the hilarious confusions surrounding a group of South Kensington people involved in the use of a flat for their assignations. Another big success was *Saturday, Sunday, Monday* for the **National Theatre** (**Old Vic**, October 1973, Queen's, October 1974, Martin Beck, New York, November 1974) which was based on a comedy by Eduardo de Filippo about an Italian family in a Naples flat whose disagreements (on a Saturday evening) over the preparation of a Sunday meal lead to a momumental row (on the Sunday) which is peacefully resolved (on the Monday). The original cast was led by Laurence **Olivier** and Joan **Plowright**. In 1977 another joint adaptation of a de Filippo play, *Filumena,* was produced (Lyric, November) starring Joan Plowright as the long-standing mistress of a man (played by Colin **Blakely**) she wishes to marry for the sake of respectability. Hall and Waterhouse's recent play *Lost Empires* (Birmingham Repertory, May 1985) was based on J.B. Priestley's book about variety theatres at the turn of the century.

Hall and Waterhouse's filmscripts include *Whistle Down the Wind, A Kind of Loving, Billy Liar, Man in the Middle, Lock Up Your Daughters* and *Torn Curtain.* They co-wrote the television series *Budgie* and *Worzel Gummidge* but have also written separately for television. Keith Waterhouse is a regular writer for the *Daily Mirror* and *Punch.* He recently wrote the television series *Charters and Caldicott.*

Hampton, Christopher

Born in Fayal, the Azores, on 26 January 1946, he was educated at Lancing College, Sussex, and from 1964 to 1968 studied French and German at New College, Oxford. His first play, *When Did You Last See My Mother?* (OUDS, 1964, **Royal Court**, June 1966, Sheridan Square Playhouse, New York, January 1967), was written before he went to Oxford University and is about two school-leavers. In 1968 he became Resident Dramatist at the Royal Court Theatre where *Total Eclipse* (September 1968), about the relationship between Rimbaud and Verlaine, was staged. This was followed by *The Philanthropist* (August 1970) which is a witty comedy set in a university where a sheltered and rather ineffectual linguist (Don) inhabits a world detached from such realities as his own students' suicidal tendencies. Hampton married Laura de Holesch in 1971. With his next successful play *Savages* (Royal Court and Comedy Theatre, April and May 1973, Mark Taper Forum Theatre, Los Angeles, 1974), he moved away from the realistic modes of his earlier work and explored a more poetic and allegorical form of play. He juxtaposes two sets of events, each of which throws light on the other: the mass murder of American Indians in Brazil and the story of a British diplomat (Alan West) held hostage by a guerrilla (Carlos) who is also something of a poet. Inventive in form and part-ritualistic in presentation, the play is, as Ronald Hayman put it in *British Theatre Since 1955*, 'not merely a polemical condemnation of genocide but a balanced theatrical investigation of attitudes that have been adopted towards an insoluble political problem: how to integrate Indian culture into an industrial society'.

This was followed by *Treats* (Royal Court and Mayfair, February and May 1976), *Signed and Sealed* (1976, an adaptation of a play by Feydeau and Desvalliers), *After Mercer* (**National Theatre**, 1980), a revised version of *Total Eclipse* (Lyric, Hammersmith, May 1981), *The Portage to San Cristobal of A.H.* (Mermaid, February 1982, an adaptation of a novel by George Steiner) and *Tales From Hollywood* (Mark Taper Forum Theatre, Los Angeles, 1982, National Theatre, Olivier, September 1983). This latter play concerns a group of European emigrés living in Hollywood in the late 1930s and centrally involves a confrontation between the Austro-Hungarian playwright Odon von Horvath and Bertholt **Brecht** (who was working in Hollywood as a hack-writer at the time).

Christopher Hampton has translated and adapted many plays for the stage, including Isaac Babel's *Marya* (1967), Chekhov's *Uncle Vanya* (1970), Ibsen's *Hedda Gabler* (1970), *A Doll's House* (1970), *Ghosts* (1978), *The Wild Duck* (1979), Von Horvath's *Tales From the Vienna Woods* (1977) and Molière's *Tartuffe* (1983). He has adapted Graham **Greene**'s novel *The Honorary Consul* for a film (1983) and films have been made of his own versions of *A Doll's House* (1973) and *Tales From the Vienna Woods* (1979). Television plays have included *Able's Will*, an adaptation of Malcolm Bradbury's novel *The History Man*, and television versions of *Total Eclipse*, *The Philanthropist*, *Savages*, *Treats* and *Marya*.

In a television interview with Frank Delaney (17 October 1983) Hampton said, 'I think my career has proceeded in a somewhat haphazard way: that is to say that I'm not conscious of having any grand plan ... I think I've written the theatre plays I've wanted to write as and when I've wanted to write them.' John Russell Taylor (in *Plays and Players*, January 1982), described Hampton's work as a striving for 'a highly literate (without being dryly intellectual) theatre. Hampton is a civilized voice in the modern British theatre we cannot well do without.'

Further Reading

Julian Hilton, 'The Court and its Favours', *Contemporary English Drama*, C.W.E. Bigsby (ed.), Stratford-upon-Avon Studies, No. 19, Edward Arnold, London, pp. 138-43.

Ronald Hayman, *British Theatre Since 1955*, Oxford University Press, Oxford, 1979, pp. 69-72.

Theatre Quarterly, Vol. III, No. xii.

Hands, Terry (Terence David)

Born in Aldershot, Hampshire, on 9 January 1941, he attended Woking Grammar School and Birmingham University, later training for the theatre at RADA (1962-4). He founded the Everyman Theatre, Liverpool, in 1964, and directed there until 1966 (his productions including **Wesker**'s *The Four Seasons*, **Osborne**'s *Look Back in Anger* and Shakespeare's *Richard III*). In that year (1966) he joined the **Royal Shakespeare Company** as Artistic Director of the touring company Theatregoround (for whom his directing included *The Second Shepherd's Play*, **Pinter**'s *The Dumb Waiter*, Dylan Thomas's *Under Milk Wood* and his own compilation of readings and play extracts *Pleasure and Repentence*).

From 1967 to 1977 he was an associate director for the RSC and from 1978 he has been Joint Artistic Director with Trevor **Nunn**. Some of his major productions for the

RSC include *The Merry Wives of Windsor* (Stratford, 1968 season, Aldwych 1968-9 season), Middleton's *Women Beware Women* (Stratford, 1969 season) Jonson's *Bartholomew Fair* (Aldwych, 1969), *The Merchant of Venice* (Stratford, 1971 season), Jean Genet's *The Balcony* (Aldwych, 1971), T.S. **Eliot**'s *Murder in the Cathedral* (Aldwych, 1972) and *The Actor* (Australian tour, 1974) which he devised.

For the Stratford Shakespeare Centenary Season in 1975 he directed *Henry IV Parts 1 and 2, Henry V* and *The Merry Wives of Windsor* with Alan **Howard** as Hal and King Henry and Brewster Mason as Falstaff (also Aldwych, 1976). For the 1977 season at Stratford-upon-Avon he directed the three parts of *Henry VI* and *Coriolanus* (also Aldwych, 1978). Later he directed *Twelfth Night* (Stratford, 1979 season, Aldwych 1980), Gorky's *Children of the Sun* (Aldwych, 1979), *Richard II* and *Richard III* (Stratford, 1980 season) both of which starred Alan Howard in the title-roles, *Troilus and Cressida* (Stratford, 1981 season), *Much Ado About Nothing* (Stratford, 1982 season, Barbican, May 1983), Peter **Nichols**'s *Poppy* (Barbican, October 1982), Rostand's *Cyrano de Bergerac* (Barbican, July 1983) which starred Derek **Jacobi**, Howard **Brenton**'s *The Genius* (**Royal Court**, September 1983), Peter **Barnes**'s *Red Roses* (Barbican, July 1985) and *Othello* (Stratford-upon-Avon, September 1985).

Terry Hands has also directed Shakespearian plays for the Comédie Française, the Burgtheater, Vienna, and operas for the Royal Opera at Covent Garden. From 1975, in addition to continuing as Joint Artistic Director of the RSC, he has been a consultant director of the Comédie Française. In an interview with Ronald Hayman (*Playback*, 1973) he said: 'For a director to express himself or his ego, or his talent, he has to operate through other people. The director, therefore, is forced, over a number of years, to develop the arts of persuasion, and patience, and *care* of the actors because it is the only means of getting his way.' He described the actor as needing to be a mixture of 'a monk and a madman'.

Further Reading

Ronald Hayman, 'Terry Hands', *Playback 1*, Davis-Poynter, London, 1973, pp. 79-109.

Happening

A short theatrical 'event' intended to appeal to its audience's subconscious. Happenings were particularly popular in the late 1950s and early 1960s when such American artists as Allan Kaprow (who first used the term 'happening' in 1959) and Claes Oldenburg developed their work into what became known as Pop Art, some of which involved the construction of 'environments' and 'actions' designed to break down the barriers between audience and artists' presentations. Elements of chance, spontaneous creation and audience participation were sometimes involved. John Cage, in the 1950s, developed mixed-media events at Black Mountain College (USA) and performed a silent piano piece which lasted four minutes and thirty-three seconds (called *4′ 33″*). Happenings can be traced back to the Italian Futurists, the Dada movement, and the **Absurd** tradition of Jarry, Artaud and Ionesco. Some of Kaprow's best known events were *Overtime, The Night, Chicken, A Happening in Paris, Sea* and *Fight.* In *Art News* (May 1961) Kaprow described part of a happening in the following way: 'Suddenly, mushy shapes pop up from the floor and painters slash at curtains dripping with action. A wall of trees tied with coloured rags advances on the crowd, scattering everybody ... coughing you breathe in noxious fumes, of the smell of hospitals and lemon juice.' Some forms of Street Theatre and Theatre-in-Education in Britain owe much to the

Iappening genre. *See also* **Alternative Theatre**.

Further Reading

Darko Suvin, 'Reflections on Happenings', *The Drama Review*, Vol. 14, No. 3 (T47), 1970, pp. 125-44.

New Writers IV, 'Plays and Happenings', Calder and Boyars, London, 1967.

Hardy, Robert

Born on 29 October 1925 and educated at Rugby School and Magdelen College, Oxford, he started his acting career with the **Shakespeare Memorial Theatre** Company in 1949 with whom his major role was Banquo in *Macbeth.* His first appearance in London was as Claudio in *Much Ado About Nothing* (Phoenix, January 1952).

In 1953 he joined the **Old Vic** Company with whom his roles included the Lord Chamberlain in *Henry V* (May 1953), Laertes in *Hamlet,* Ariel in *The Tempest,* Dumaine in *Love's Labour's Lost,* Hortensio in *The Taming of the Shrew* (1953-4) and Prince Hal in *Henry IV Parts 1 and 2* (January 1955). After appearances at the 1955 **Edinburgh Festival** and New York in 1956 he was Lieutenant Keith in Herman Wouk's *The Caine Mutiny Court-Martial* (Hippodrome, June 1956). After playing Byron in Tennessee Williams's *Camino Real* (Phoenix, April 1957) he rejoined the Shakespeare Memorial Theatre Company (Stratford-upon-Avon, 1959 season) and played, among other roles, Oberon in *A Midsummer Night's Dream* and Edmund in *King Lear.*

At the **Bristol Old Vic** he was the Count in Jean Anouilh's *The Rehearsal* (March 1961, transferred Globe, April 1961) and Martin in Iris Murdoch's *A Severed Head* (May 1963, transferred Criterion, July 1963). In August 1964 he played the title-roles in *Henry V* and *Hamlet* (Ravinia Festival, Illinois) and for the **Prospect Theatre Company** in June 1967 he was Sir Harry Wildair in Farquhar's *The Constant Couple* (New Theatre). Further parts have included Dr Wicksteed in Alan **Bennett**'s *Habeus Corpus* (Lyric, February 1974) which he took over from Alec **Guinness**, after which Hardy worked in television and film until his return to the stage in May 1982 to play George Bernard Shaw in *Dear Liar* (Mermaid Theatre), an adaptation by Jerome Kilty of correspondence between Shaw and Mrs Patrick Campbell (played by Sian Phillips).

Some of his extensive work in television includes *An Age of Kings, Henry V, Twelfth Night, Elizabeth R, Edward VII, Sir Gawain and the Green Knight, Mogul, Manhunt, Jenny's War, Churchill: The Wilderness Years* and, perhaps his best known appearance, as Siegfried in *All Creatures Great and Small.* Film appearances include *Ten Rillington Place, Young Winston* and *Yellow Dog,* and he has written the filmscripts for the documentary films *The Picardy Affair, The Longbow* and *Horses in Our Blood.*

Hare, David

Born on 5 June 1947, in Bexhill, Sussex, he was educated at Lancing College and Jesus College, Cambridge. On leaving university he worked for A.B. Pathe, making 'Pathe Pictorials' films. In 1968, with Tony Bicat, he co-founded the experimental touring group Portable Theatre. He came to notice with his second play, *Slag* (Hampstead Theatre Club, 1970, **Royal Court**, May 1971), ostensibly about three schoolmistresses but, more subtly, a play (as Hare has described it) 'about every institution I had known — school, Cambridge, Pathe and so on'.

From 1969 until 1970 he was Literary Manager of the Royal Court Theatre and then became Resident Dramatist at the same theatre (1970-1). His next play was *The Great Exhibition* (Royal Court, 1972), about a disillusioned Labour MP. As in many of the plays which followed, Hare concentrated upon a Britain in decline or in a period of decaying principles and moral values. Though he is not as wholly committed to the Left as some of his contemporaries (Trevor **Griffiths**, for example) a number of his plays examine the inadequacy of capitalism in creating a morally, politically and domestically satisfying society. *Lay-by* (Traverse Theatre, **Edinburgh Festival**, 1971), was a collaborative experiment with Trevor Griffiths and five other writers, and was based on a newspaper article about a roadside rape and the subsequent trial. With Howard **Brenton** he wrote (and also directed) *Brassneck* (Nottingham Playhouse, 1973) about a builder in Nottingham who joins the Freemasons to improve business; the play is a reflection upon the decline of Midlands England (and on another level, Europe) under commercialisation, and follows the gradual corruption of a family over three generations. In a radio interview in 1984 (*Kaleidoscope*, Radio 4, 28th September) Hare stated, 'Europe's been arguing about the same things for at least a hundred and fifty years. We've argued among ourselves about how our society should be organised for so long, without healing the divisions in our society, that we're like cripples.' For 1973 he was Resident Dramatist at Nottingham Playhouse. *Knuckle* (Comedy Theatre, March 1974, New York, 1975), another attack on capitalism, was less overtly 'political' in that it took the form of a comedy detective thriller combining elements of the Joe **Orton** and Micky Spillane traditions.

In 1974 David Hare co-founded the **Joint Stock Theatre Group** with Bill **Gaskill** and Max **Stafford-Clark**. His next play, *Fanshen* (Joint Stock Company, Sheffield, and Hampstead Theatre Club, 1975), moves away from England as a focus of attention and is set in the Chinese Revolution (the play being an adaptation of a book by William Hinton). It optimistically demonstrates the processes of a successful revolution and the construction of a realistic socialist state ('fanshen' being Chinese for 'to transform'). *Teeth 'n' Smiles* (Royal Court, September 1975, Wyndham's, May 1976, New York, 1979) had, as its female protagonist, a rock-singer (originally played by Helen **Mirren**), who, together with her rock-group, performs at a Cambridge May Ball. The friction between the group and the class-privileged audience provides a conflict which allows Hare to explore the absorption of the popular values of the 1960s into those of the Establishment. In 1978 Hare collaborated with Ken Campbell, Trevor Griffiths and Howard Brenton in writing *Deeds* (Nottingham Playhouse) and in April of the same year his next play, *Plenty*, was produced at the **National Theatre**. As in *Teeth 'n' Smiles* the central figure is a woman, but in this play Hare is more compassionate towards his character. Through a series of time-shifts the play compares the protagonist's war-time ideals in the French Resistance with her disillusionment and lack of fulfilment after the war.

In May 1981 Hare directed a revival of Christopher **Hampton**'s *Total Eclipse* (Lyric, Hammersmith) and in 1983 he directed his own play, *A Map of the World* (National Theatre, Lyttleton, January 1983) which was first performed at the Adelaide Festival (Opera Theatre, Adelaide) and Sydney Opera House, 1982. It is a play which uses time-shifts and changes in location as formal devices for exploring the emotional and sexual frustrations of a group of people attending a UN Conference on world poverty being held at a hotel in Bombay. In 1984 he became an Associate Director (with special responsibility for new plays), of the National Theatre.

David Hare founded Greenpoint Films in 1982 and his own films include *Wetherby* and *Plenty*. Television plays include *Man Above Men*, *Dreams of Leaving*, *Licking Hitler*, *Fanshen*, and *Saigon: Year of the Cat*. Something of Hare's view of *Knuckle*, *Licking Hitler* and *Plenty*, is revealed by the fact that he had them published under the title of

History Plays in 1984.

In an interview for *Theatre Quarterly* in 1975 Hare said of the theatre, 'Journalism, however intelligent, will always fail you. It is glib by nature. Words can *only* be tested by being spoken. Ideas can *only* be worked in real situations. That is why the theatre is the best court society has.'

Further Reading

David Hare, 'From Portable Theatre to Joint Stock ... via Shaftesbury Avenue', Theatre Quarterly, Vol. V, No. 20, Winter 1975; republished as 'Commanding the Style of Presentation', *New Theatre Voices of the Seventies*, Simon Trussler (ed.), Eyre Methuen, London, 1981, pp. 110-20.

David Hare, Trevor Griffiths and Peter Ansorge, 'Current Concerns', *Plays and Players*, July 1974, pp. 18-22.

Hastings, Michael (Gerald)

Born in Brixton, London, on 2 September 1938, and educated at the Imperial Services College, Windsor (1944-6), Dulwich College Preparatory School (1946-9) and Alleyn's College (1949-53), he began his career as an apprentice to a bespoke tailor and then became a trainee actor and writer at the **Royal Court** Theatre. His first play was *Don't Destroy Me* (New Lindsey, July 1956) performed when Hastings was 18 years old. It is about the fraught relationships between a young couple and their parents. The award-winning *Yes — And After* ('Sunday Night' production, Royal Court, 9 June 1957) again explored conflicts between generations, this time between a rape victim and her parents.

Another noteworthy play was *The Silence of Lee Harvey Oswald* (Hampstead Theatre Club, 1966) which explored the psychological tensions and personality of President Kennedy's assassin. It was an example of the kind of documentary stage play which was fashionably labelled the 'Theatre of Fact' at the time. *The Cutting of the Cloth* (unperformed, 1973) was an autobiographical play in a similar mode. Other plays include the political comedy about Meadowlark Rachel Warner, *Gloo Joo* (Hampstead Theatre Club, transferred to Criterion, November 1978), *Full Frontal* (Royal Court Upstairs, February 1979), *Carnival War a Go Hot* (Royal Court, August 1979), a farce about the Notting Hill Carnival, *Midnite at the Starlite* (1980), a comedy about a ballroom dancing competition, and the highly successful *Tom and Viv* (Royal Court, February 1984, New York, 1985, Royal Court, March 1985) which was a biographical documentary of the relationship between T.S. **Eliot** and his first wife Vivienne Haigh-Wood. In his introduction to the published edition of *Tom and Viv* (1985) Hastings wrote 'in all theatre all biography is fiction, and some fiction is autobiography. The idea of omniscient narrative in straightforward biography doesn't apply to the stage ... What a play can achieve is to take time past and present and thread it through the needle of the years and provide the audience with a pictorial statement.' Hastings's use of comedy and farce as a weapon for moral, social and political comment is powerfully integrated with his plays' subjects. As he said in his article 'Glum Theatre' (*Plays and Players*, September 1979) he shares with a number of playwrights such as Dario Fo, Bill Morrison and Caryl **Churchill** the intention of treating 'antic comedy as a weapon. Antic and blissful, capable of being elevated into realms of pantomime, or fantasia, at last as a political weapon, farce might be allowed to emerge ... Laughter is a leveller.'

Michael Hastings's plays for television include *For the West (Congo), Gloo Joo, Murder Rap, Midnight at the Starlight* and *Stars of the Roller State Disco.* He has also written five novels and two biographies (of Rupert Brooke and Richard Burton).

Helpmann, Sir Robert (Murray)

Born at Mount Gambier, Australia, on 9

April 1909, he was educated at Prince Alfred's College, Adelaide, began his career as a dancer in *The Ugly Duckling* (Theatre Royal, Adelaide, 1922) and subsequently appeared in many ballets in Australia. His acting career before the Second World War included playing Septimus Barrett in Rudolf Besier's *The Barretts of Wimpole Street* (Criterion, Sydney, April 1932) and, for his London début, a role in *I Hate Man* (Gate, February 1933).

In ballet Helpmann worked in London for the Vic–Wells Ballet (1933) and Sadler's Wells Ballet (1933-50). His roles in plays included Oberon in *A Midsummer Night's Dream* (**Old Vic**, December 1937), Felix, Mr Cricket and Chief of Yellow Ants in Karel Čapek's *The Insect Play* (Playhouse, April 1938) and Gremio, Nicholas and the Tailor in *The Taming of the Shrew* (Old Vic, March 1939). In November 1938 at the Mercury Theatre he was guest dancer with the Ballet Rambert.

At the New Theatre in February 1944 he played the title-role in *Hamlet* and in December 1946 he was Oberon in the masque entertainment *The Fairy Queen* (Covent Garden). He took over as Artistic Director of the Duchess Theatre in 1947, himself appearing there as Flamineo in Webster's *The White Devil* (March 1947) and the Prince in Andreyev's *He Who Gets Slapped* (June 1947).

For its 1948 season Robert Helpmann joined the **Shakespeare Memorial Theatre** Company at Stratford-upon-Avon to play the title-roles in *King John* and *Hamlet* and was also Shylock in *The Merchant of Venice.* The following year he worked abroad in ballet and in January 1950 directed *Madame Butterfly* at Covent Garden, later in the same year appearing as a guest artist at La Scala, Milan (April), directing *Golden City* (Adelphi, June) and touring in ballet with Margot Fonteyn (June-July 1950).

His major acting roles from this time onwards were Apollodorus in Shaw's *Caesar and Cleopatra* and Octavius Caesar in Shakespeare's *Antony and Cleopatra* (St James's, May 1951) in casts which included Laurence **Olivier** and Vivien Leigh, and the Doctor in Shaw's *The Millionairess* (New, June 1952, also Shubert Theatre, New York, October 1952). After directing T.S. **Eliot**'s *Murder in the Cathedral* (Old Vic, March 1953), *The Tempest* (Old Vic, April 1954) and Noël **Coward**'s *After the Ball* (Globe, June 1954), he played Oberon in *A Midsummer Night's Dream* at the 1954 **Edinburgh Festival**, also touring in the same role with the Old Vic Company (United States and Canada, September 1954). In March 1955 he directed *As You Like It* at the Old Vic.

He subsequently toured Australia as Shylock in *The Merchant of Venice*, Petruchio in *The Taming of the Shrew* and Angelo in *Measure for Measure* (Old Vic Company tour, May 1955), directed *Romeo and Juliet* (Old Vic, June 1956, Winter Garden, New York, October 1956), played the title-role in *Richard III* (Old Vic, 1956-7 season) and directed *Antony and Cleopatra* (Old Vic, 1956-7 season). At the Edinburgh Festival (1957) he played George de Valera in Sartre's *Nekrassov* (transferred **Royal Court**, September 1957).

In November 1957 Helpmann took over the role of Sebastian from John **Gielgud** in Noël Coward's **Nude with a Violin** (Globe) and played the same part on tour in Australia (1958-9). He then directed a number of plays including *Twelfth Night*, Dumas's *The Lady of the Camelias* and Giraudoux's *Duel of Angels* for an Old Vic World Tour (1961) and in 1963 directed *Swan Lake* (Covent Garden) and Dame Margot Fonteyn's world tour. He was the narrator for the ballet *A Wedding Bouquet* (Metropolitan Opera House, New York, May 1965, Royal Ballet Company, Covent Garden, November 1969) and in 1970 was the director of the Adelaide Festival of Arts. From 1965 until 1976 he was Director of the Australian Ballet Company, choreographing numerous ballets including *Comus*, *The Birds*, *Hamlet*,

Elektra, Yugen, Sun Music, The Sleeping Beauty and *The Merry Widow.* For the Australian Ballet Company's 1969-70 season he was Don Quixote in *Dr Coppelius.*

In 1977 he was guest artist with the Royal Ballet (Sadler's Wells, London) and a year later co-directed the Australian tour of 'Stars of World Ballet' in *Gala Performances* (1978-9). For the **Chichester Festival** in May 1982 he played Cardinal Pirelli in Sandy Wilson's musical version of Ronald Firbank's novel *Valmouth.*

An artist of remarkable range and talent (ballet dancer, choreographer, actor, producer, director of opera, ballet and stage plays) Helpmann has made a distinguished contribution to the theatre arts of the post-war period in Britain, Australia and elsewhere. He has appeared in numerous films including *One of our Aircraft is Missing, Caravan, Henry V, Tales of Hoffman, The Iron Petticoat, Big Money, Red Shoes, Fifty-five Days in Peking, The Soldier's Tale, Chitty Chitty Bang Bang, Alice in Wonderland, Don Quixote, The Mango Tree* and *Patrick.* He has also given solo performances on Australian television.

Hiller, Dame Wendy

Born on 15 August 1912 in Bramhall, Cheshire, she was educated at Winceby House School, Bexhill. She became a student-actress with the Manchester Repertory Company in 1930 and made her first stage appearance as the Maid in *The Ware Case* (Manchester Repertory Theatre, September 1930) after which, in 1931, she understudied a number of parts and became assistant stage-manager to the theatre. Her first London appearance was as Sally in a highly successful production of Ronald Gow's adaptation of Walter Greenwood's novel *Love on the Dole* (Garrick, June 1935) and she appeared in the same production in New York (Shubert Theatre, February 1936). At the Malvern Festival (July 1936) she was Joan in Shaw's *Saint Joan* and Eliza Doolittle in his *Pygmalion.* In 1937 she married Ronald Gow. During the Second World War she played Viola in *Twelfth Night* for a factory tour (August 1943), appeared in a few **West End** productions and made a number of films.

In 1946 she joined the **Bristol Old Vic** Company to play Tess in Ronald Gow's adaptation of Thomas Hardy's novel *Tess of the D'Urbervilles* (transferred New Theatre, November 1946, Piccadilly, May 1947) and other roles including Pegeen Mike in J.M. Synge's *The Playboy of the Western World.* In January 1950 she replaced Peggy **Ashcroft** as Catherine in Ruth and Augustus Goetz's *The Heiress* based on Henry James's novel *Washington Square* (Haymarket Theatre). She was Evelyn Daly in the two-year run of N.C. Hunter's *Waters of the Moon* (Haymarket, April 1951).

For the 1955-6 season Wendy Hiller joined the **Old Vic** Company with whom her roles included Mistress Page in *The Merry Wives of Windsor*, Hermione in *The Winter's Tale* and Helen in Tyrone **Guthrie**'s modern dress production of *Troilus and Cressida.* Her chief roles in London and elsewhere have since included Isobel in Robert **Bolt**'s *Flowering Cherry* (Lyseum, New York, October 1959), Miss Tina in Michael **Redgrave**'s adaptation of Henry James's novel *The Aspern Papers* (Playhouse, New York, February 1962), Susan Shepherd in Christopher Taylor's adaptation of Henry James's *The Wings of the Dove* (Lyric, London, December 1963), Irene in Ibsen's *When We Dead Awaken* (**Edinburgh Festival**, August 1968), Enid in Peter **Shaffer**'s *The Battle of the Shrivings* (Lyric, February 1970) and Mrs Alving in Ibsen's *Ghosts* (Arts, Cambridge, February 1972). She gave a highly-acclaimed performance as Queen Mary in Royce Ryton's *Crown Matrimonial* (Haymarket, October 1972) and followed this with a fine performance as Gunhild Borkman for the **National Theatre**'s production of Ibsen's *John Gabriel*

Borkman (Old Vic, January 1975, Lyttleton, March 1976) in which Ralph **Richardson** played the title-role. At the **Chichester Festival** in May 1977 she played Mrs Whyte in a revival of N.C. Hunter's *Waters of the Moon* (also Haymarket, January 1978) and in March 1984 she was seen as Miss Bordereau in a revival of *The Aspern Papers* (Haymarket) the cast of which also included Vanessa **Redgrave** and Christopher Reeve.

Wendy Hiller's work in films includes *Pygmalion, Major Barbara, An Outcast of the Islands, Separate Tables, Sons and Lovers, A Man for All Seasons, David Copperfield, Murder on the Orient Express* and *The Elephant Man.* Television appearances include *When We Dead Awaken, Peer Gynt, Clochemerle, Richard II, The Kingfisher* and *Witness for the Prosecution.*

Holm, Ian (Ian Holm Cuthbert)

Born at Goodmayes, Ilford, Essex, on 12 September 1931, he was educated at Chigwell Grammar School and trained for the stage at the Royal Academy of Dramatic Art.

He made his début as a Spear Carrier in *Othello* at the **Shakespeare Memorial Theatre**, Stratford-upon-Avon, in March 1954. Further work at the same theatre included Donalbain in *Macbeth* and Mutius in *Titus Andronicus* (1955). His first London role was Rupert Bliss in *Love Affair* (Lyric, Hammersmith, June 1956). After a European tour as Mutius in *Titus Andronicus* with Sir Laurence **Olivier** (June 1957, then Stoll Theatre, July 1957) he returned to the Shakespeare Memorial Theatre Company at Stratford-upon-Avon with whom his roles included Sebastian in *Twelfth Night* (1958 season), Puck in *A Midsummer Night's Dream* (1959 season), Lorenzo in *The Merchant of Venice* and Gremio in *The Taming of the Shrew* (both 1960 season). On the renaming of the company as the **Royal Shakespeare Company** in 1961 Ian Holm became an actor on a long-term contract with them.

His main work with the RSC has since incuded Mannoury in John **Whiting**'s *The Devils* (Aldwych, February 1961), Claudio in *Measure for Measure* (Stratford, April 1962), Troilus in *Troilus and Cressida* (Aldwych, October 1962), Ariel in *The Tempest* (Stratford, 1963 season), Richard of Gloucester in John **Barton**'s trilogy *The Wars of the Roses* (Stratford, 1963 season) an adaptation of *Richard III* and the three parts of *Henry VI*, Prince Hal in *Henry IV Parts 1 and 2* and the title-role in *Henry V* (Stratford, April 1964), Lenny in Harold **Pinter**'s *The Homecoming* (Aldwych, June 1965), Malvolio in *Twelfth Night* and repeat performances as Prince Hal and King Henry V (Stratford, April 1966) and Romeo in *Romeo and Juliet* (Stratford, September 1967).

Holm left the RSC after the 1967 season and has subsequently worked mainly in London, his chief roles being Manfred in Arnold **Wesker**'s *The Friends* (Round House, May 1970), Nelson in Terence **Rattigan**'s *A Bequest to the Nation* (Haymarket, September 1970), Hatch in Edward **Bond**'s *The Sea* (**Royal Court**, May 1973), Dave in Mike **Stott**'s *Other People* (Hampstead, July 1974) and Voinitsky in Pam **Gems**'s version of Chekhov's *Uncle Vanya* (Hampstead, November 1979). Recently he has worked more in film and television than in the theatre.

Film appearances include *A Midsummer Night's Dream, The Fixer, Oh! What a Lovely War, The Bofors Gun, Alien, All Quiet on the Western Front, The Homecoming, Juggernaut, Shout at the Devil, Chariots of Fire, Return of the Soldier, Greystoke* and *Laughter House.* Television work includes *The Lost Boys, We the Accused, The Bell, The Sweeney* and *Helen.*

Home, Hon. William Douglas

Born in Edinburgh on 3 June 1912, the son of the 13th Earl of Home and younger brother of Sir Alec Douglas Home (Prime Minister of Great Britain 1963-4), he was educated at Eton and read History at New College, Oxford. He trained as an actor at RADA and began his career at the Brighton Repertory Theatre (1937). His first London appearance was as Brian in Dodie Smith's *Bonnet Over the Windmill* (New Theatre, September 1937) and he subsequently appeared in a number of other productions. During the Second World War he was a Captain in the Royal Armoured Corps.

Success as a playwright came in August 1947 with *The Chiltern Hundreds* (Theatre Royal, Brighton, Vaudeville, London), a political comedy about the effects of a Socialist victory in 1945 upon the aristocratic household of the Earl of Lister, including the promoting of the butler (Beecham) as a Conservative candidate in the local by-election. In contrast, *Now Barabbas* (Vaudeville, March 1947) was a study of prison life during the time when a condemned murderer awaits execution. Extending his range even further Home's *The Thistle and the Rose* (1949) was a romantic historical drama about the events leading to the Battle of Flodden in which the Scots were defeated. Home's plays are commercially popular, naturalistic 'well-made' plays and came in for a good deal of criticism from the supporters of the new wave of dramatists of John **Osborne**'s generation which emerged in the mid-1950s. Yet, although most of his plays from this period onwards have been rooted in the traditions of his aristocratic background, Home treats the privileged classes as material for comedy and entertaining criticism. *The Reluctant Debutante* (Cambridge Theatre, May 1955), about the refusal of a young girl (Jane) to conform to her mother's expectations of the London 'season' and arranged escorts, was followed by little of note until *The Reluctant Peer* (Duchess Theatre, January 1964), based on Home's brother's renunciation of his peerage in order to become Prime Minister.

Other stage plays have been *The Secretary Bird* (Savoy, October 1968), *The Jockey Club Stakes* (Vaudeville, September 1970), *Lloyd George Knew My Father* (Savoy, July 1972) which starred Peggy **Ashcroft** and Ralph **Richardson**, *The Kingfisher* (Lyric, May 1977) which starred Richardson, and *After the Ball is Over* (Compass Company, **Old Vic**, March 1985).

Further Reading

William Douglas Home, *Half-Term Report: An Autobiography*, Longman, London, 1954.
William Douglas Home, *Mr. Home Pronounced Hume: An Autobiography*, Collins, London, 1979.

Hopkins, Anthony

Born in Port Talbot, Wales, on 31 December 1937, he was educated at Cowbridge Grammar School, Glamorgan, and (1961-3) trained for the stage at the Royal Academy of Dramatic Arts and subsequently Cardiff College of Drama. He married his second wife, Jennifer Lynton, in 1973. Anthony Hopkins's first professional stage appearance was as Mickser in Brendan **Behan**'s *The Quare Fellow* (Library Theatre, Manchester, 1960), after which he was in repertory at Leicester, Liverpool and Hornchurch. He made his London début as Metellus Cimber in *Julius Caesar* (**Royal Court**, November 1964).

From 1966 to 1973, as a member of the **National Theatre** at the **Old Vic**, his roles included an Irregular Mobiliser in O'Casey's *Juno and the Paycock* (1966), Etienne in Feydeau's *A Flea in Her Ear* (1966), Edgar in Strindberg's *The Dance of Death* (1967), Andrei Prosorov in Chekhov's *Three Sisters* (1967), Audrey in an all-male production of *As You Like It* (1967), the Emperor in Jack Hibberd's *The Architect* *and the Emperor of Assyria* (1971), Frankford in Heywood's *A Woman Killed with Kindness* (1971) and the title-roles in *Coriolanus* (1971) and *Macbeth* (1972).

In July 1972 he was at the **Chichester Festival** to play Petruchio in *The Taming of the Shrew*, after which the greater part of his work has been done in American theatres and in films and television. In October 1974 he took over from Richard Burton in the part of Dysart in Peter **Shaffer**'s *Equus* (Plymouth Theatre, New York) and also played the part in August 1977 (Huntington Hartford Theatre, Los Angeles). In April 1979 he was Prospero in *The Tempest* (Mark Taper Theatre, Los Angeles), and in 1984, for the 18th anniversary of the Roundabout Theatre, New York, he played Deeley in Harold **Pinter**'s *Old Times*. In April 1985 he was Lambert le Roux in **Brenton** and **Hare**'s *Pravda* at the National Theatre.

Anthony Hopkins's work in films is extensive and he is one of Britain's most successful film actors, generally playing very powerful roles with great authority and screen presence. He came to prominence in *The Lion in Winter* (1967) and subsequent films include *The Looking Glass War* (1968), *Hamlet* (1969), *When Eight Bells Toll* (1971), *Young Winston* (1972), *A Doll's House* (1973), *All Creatures Great and Small* (1974), *Dark Victory* (1975), *A Bridge Too Far* (1976), *International Velvet* (1977), *Magic* (1978), *The Elephant Man* (1980), *A Change of Seasons* (1980), *The Bounty* (1984) and *Hollywood Wives* (1985). Appearances on American television include *QB VII* (1973), *The Voyage of the Mayflower* (1979), *The Acts of Peter and Paul* (1980) and *The Hunchback of Notre-Dame* (1981).

For British television his most acclaimed and popular performance was as Pierre in the serial, *War and Peace* (1972). Other appearances include *Kean* (1978), *Othello* (1981) and *Little Eyolf* (1982).

Hordern, Sir Michael

Born in Berkhamstead on 3 October 1911, the son of a Naval officer, he was educated at Brighton College where he played in school productions (for example, the Duchess in *The Gondoliers*, 1926). He went into business with the Educational Supply Association and at the same time played in amateur productions, in particular at Edith Neville's St Pancras People's Theatre. His first professional appearance was as Ludovico in *Othello* (People's Palace, March 1937). He toured abroad with Westminster Productions and then from 1937 to 1939 appeared in repertory at the Little Theatre, Bristol. He married Grace Mortimer in 1943. During the war he served with the Navy (two and a half years of the war were spent on an aircraft carrier) and was demobilised as a Lieutenant Commander.

In the immediate post-war years his most important roles were Torvald Helmer in Ibsen's *A Doll's House* (Intimate Theatre, Palmer's Green, January 1946) and Bottom in *The Fairy Queen* (Covent Garden, December 1946). With the **Shakespeare Memorial Theatre** Company at Stratford-upon-Avon he played Mr Toad in *Toad of Toad Hall* (December 1948 and again in December 1949). He played Nikolai Ivanov in Chekhov's *Ivanov* (Arts Theatre, April 1950) and Macduff in Shakespeare's *Macbeth* (Arts Theatre, June 1950). In September 1951 he created the part of Paul Southam in John **Whiting**'s *Saints Day* (Arts Theatre), presented to mark the occasion of the Festival of Britain.

Hordern joined the Shakespeare Memorial Theatre Company, Stratford-upon-Avon (then run by Anthony **Quayle** and Glen Byam-Shaw) for the 1952 season, playing Caliban in *The Tempest*, Jaques in *As You Like It*, Menenius Agrippa in *Coriolanus* and Sir Politick Wouldbe in Jonson's *Volpone*.

In an interview with Ronald Hayman (published in *Playback 2*, 1973) Hordern's view of acting was that the actor should always be partly 'conscious of *acting*' and that, at least for him, every new part should be a fresh start: 'I would hope not to let one part influence another in any way, either negatively or positively.' Perhaps Hordern's lack of formal drama school training has helped him retain this freshness of approach, together with the fact that, as he put it, he is 'almost literally on the ground. I'm a countryman and not a townsman, and I like the earth. I like fishing, I like animals and trees and birds ... I believe that to be able to shake off the artificiality of the theatre, and enjoy the reality that is the country is of marvellous therapeutic value.' He is very much of an '**ensemble**' player ('I think one takes a great deal from other people. To some extent their performance would indeed show you your character'), and a 'director's actor' ('I rely on a director tremendously. To give and take from me.')

He played Polonius in *Hamlet* (**Edinburgh Festival**, 1953) and again for the **Old Vic** 1953-4 season, as well as Parolles in *All's Well That Ends Well*, Malvolio in *Twelfth Night* and Prospero in *The Tempest.* In October 1955 he played Sir Ralph Bloomfield Bonnington in *The Doctor's Dilemma* (Saville Theatre) and in April 1958 Morgenhall and Tony Peters in John **Mortimer**'s double-bill of *The Dock Brief* and *What Shall We Tell Caroline?* (Lyric, Hammersmith) which he said was 'one of the top evenings of enjoyment I've ever had as an actor'.

Rejoining the Old Vic Company for the 1958-9 season he played Cassius in *Julius Caesar*, Pastor Manders in Ibsen's *Ghosts,* Mr Posket in *The Magistrate* and the title-role in *Macbeth.* At the Edinburgh Festival (October 1962) he played Ulysses in *Troilus and Cressida* after earlier in the same year (June 1962) playing Harry in **Pinter**'s *The Collection* for the **RSC** at the Aldwych Theatre. In January 1963 he took the role of Herbert Georg Butler in Dürrenmatt's *The Physicists* (RSC, Aldwych).

One of his finest creations was Paul Southam in John Whiting's *Saint's Day* (Royal, May 1965) and he also played Philip in **Ayckbourn**'s first major success *Relatively Speaking* (Duke of York's, March 1967). In 1968 Hordern began his highly successful association with Tom **Stoppard**, playing George Riley in *Enter a Free Man* (St Martins, March 1968) and a year later joined the RSC and played Tobias in Albee's *A Delicate Balance* (Aldwych, January 1969). He played the title-role in *King Lear* under the direction of Jonathan **Miller** at Nottingham Playhouse (October 1969) and the Old Vic (February 1970) and the title-role in David **Mercer**'s *Flint* (Criterion, May 1970).

Hordern gave a memorable performance as George Moore, a confused moral philosopher, in Stoppard's *Jumpers* (**National Theatre** at the Old Vic, January 1972). He said in *Plays and Players* (May 1983) that the first night of *Jumpers* 'was about the high point of my career ... that night was just unbelievable — it brings tears to one's eyes to remember the reception'. At the National Theatre at the Old Vic he also played John of Gaunt in *Richard II* (March 1972), Gayev in Chekhov's *The Cherry Orchard* (May 1973) and at the Royal Court played the title-role in Howard **Barker**'s *Stripwell* (October 1975). In April 1976 he appeared at the **Bristol Old Vic** as Feyda in *Once Upon a Time* and a year later was Pinfold in an adaptation of Waugh's *The Ordeal of Gilbert Pinfold* (Royal Exchange, Manchester, September 1977).

Hordern joined the RSC for its 1978 season at Stratford-upon-Avon and there played Prospero in *The Tempest* and Don Adriano in *Love's Labour's Lost.* In February 1979 he again took the role of Gilbert Pinfold in *The Ordeal of Gilbert Pinfold* (the Round House).

At the National Theatre in May 1983 he played Sir Anthony Absolute in Sheridan's *The Rivals.*

Television appearances have been

numerous and include Mortimer's *The Dock Brief*, the title-role in *King Lear* which he has played twice for television, *Tartuffe*, *The Magistrate*, *Romeo and Juliet* and the narrator for *Paddington Bear*. He has appeared in over 60 films including *England Made Me*, *Cleopatra*, *The Spy Who Came in From the Cold*, *The Possession of Joel Delaney* and *Joseph Andrews*.

It is well recognised that Hordern is a master of comic timing and certainly some of his finest performances have been in 'the portrayal of quixotic eccentrics' (the phrase used in the *Oxford Companion*) and elderly character-parts. Yet his range has also extended to major classical roles (notably his Prospero). He has said in interview that 'I'm afraid I'm that terrible thing, an instinctive actor.' It is this which has perhaps enabled him to make such a unique and fresh contribution to the interpretation of his roles, especially in the many important original plays he has appeared in since the war.

'I think an actor should be fifty per cent confidence and fifty per cent humility,' he once remarked.

Further Reading

Ronald Hayman, 'Michael Hordern', *Playback 2*, Davis-Poynter Ltd, London, 1973, pp. 80-96.

Michael Hordern and Christopher Edwards, 'Parts Ancient and Modern', *Plays and Players*, May 1983, pp. 10-12.

House Lights

Auditorium lights, dimmed or switched off during the performance.

House Tabs

Front curtains of a **Proscenium** stage. *See* **Tabs**.

Howard, Alan (Mackenzie)

Born in London on 5 August 1937, and educated at Ardingly College, he made his first stage appearance as a footman in the musical *Half in Earnest* (Belgrade, Coventry, April 1958). He went, with the company from Coventry's Belgrade Theatre, to the **Royal Court** Theatre, London, to play in Arnold **Wesker**'s Trilogy which he originally appeared in at the Belgrade. He was Frankie Bryant in *Roots* (Royal Court, June 1959, Duke of York's, July 1959, Royal Court, June 1960), Monty Blatt in *Chicken Soup with Barley* (Royal Court, June 1960) and 1st Removal Man in *I'm Talking About Jerusalem* (Royal Court, June 1960). Also at the Royal Court he was de Piraquo in Middleton's *The Changeling* (February 1961).

At the **Chichester Festival** in July 1962 he played the Duke of Ferrara in Fletcher's *The Chances*, Nearchus in Ford's *The Broken Heart* and Loveless in Vanbrugh's *Virtue in Danger* (transferred Strand, June 1963). He played Bassanio in *The Merchant of Venice* and Lysander in *A Midsummer Night's Dream* for a European and South American tour in 1964 and in May 1965 gave a highly-acclaimed performance as Simon in Julian Mitchell's adaptation of Ivy Compton-Burnett's novel *A Heritage and Its History* (Phoenix), which brought him to prominence.

After playing Angelo in *Measure for Measure* and Bolingbroke in *Richard II* (Nottingham Playhouse, 1965) Alan Howard joined the **Royal Shakespeare Company** in 1966. Parts for seasons at Stratford-upon-Avon included Orsino in *Twelfth Night*, Burgundy in *Henry V*, Lussurio in Tourneur's *The Revenger's Tragedy* (1966 season), Jacques in *As You Like It* (also Los Angeles, 1968), Edgar in *King Lear*, Achilles in *Troilus and Cressida* and Benedick in *Much Ado About Nothing* (1968 season, 1968-9 Aldwych season).

For the Stratford 1970 season Howard

took the title-role in *Hamlet*, played Mephistophilis in Marlowe's *Doctor Faustus* and Ceres in *The Tempest* and doubled the roles of Oberon and Theseus in Peter **Brook**'s highly-acclaimed production of *A Midsummer Night's Dream* (the latter also at Billy Rose Theatre, New York, January 1971, Aldwych 1971-2 season, World Tour: Western and Eastern Europe, USA, Japan, Australia, August 1972–August 1973).

Other work for the RSC has included Carlos II in Peter **Barnes**'s *The Bewitched* (Aldwych, May 1974), the title-role in *Henry V* and Prince Hal in *Henry IV Parts 1 and 2* (Royal Shakespeare Theatre Centenary, Stratford-upon-Avon, 1975 season, Aldwych, January 1976), Rover in O'Keefe's *Wild Oats* (Aldwych, December 1976), the title-role in *Henry V*, King Henry in the three parts of *Henry VI* and the title-role in *Coriolanus* (Stratford, 1977 season, Aldwych, summer 1978), and Mark Antony in *Antony and Cleopatra* (Stratford, October 1978, Aldwych, July 1979) with Glenda **Jackson** taking the role of Cleopatra. In the same year (1979) he was Chepurnoy in Gorky's *Children of the Sun* (Aldwych, October 1979).

In the last few years Howard has played in John **Barton**'s *The Hollow Crown* and Terry **Hands**'s *Pleasure and Repentance* (Fortune, July 1981), and has taken the roles of Gennady in Ostrovsky's *The Forest* (The Other Place, Stratford-upon-Avon, April 1981, Warehouse July 1981), Halder in C.P. Taylor's *Good* (the Other Place, June 1981, Warehouse, September 1981) and the title-roles in *Richard II* and *Richard III* (Stratford 1980 season, Aldwych, November 1981). In 1982 at the Aldwych he again played Gennady (February) and Halder (April). He recently appeared in Christopher Logue's *War Music* (Almeida, April 1984) and played Nikolai Pesiakoff in Stephen **Poliakoff**'s *Breaking the Silence* (RSC, Pit, October 1984, Mermaid, April 1985).

Alan Howard, in an interview with W. Stephen Gilbert, said of his creation of a role 'I really find the best way to approach any role is to do with collaboration ... If everyone is encouraged to contribute and not feel shy about it, so many ideas come up that it's better than reading a hundred books ... the two essential things for me are the text and what a group of people can do by questioning it.'

His film-work includes *The Heroes of Telemark*, *Victims* and *Work is a Four-Letter Word*. Television appearances include *Philoctetes*, *The Way of the World*, *Comet Among the Stars*, *Cover*, *Banting and Best* and *Poppyland*.

Further Reading

Alan Howard and W. Stephen Gilbert, 'Howard's Ends and Means', *Plays and Players*, July 1975.

Humberside Theatre

See **Plater, Alan**.

I

Irons, Jeremy

Born on 19 September 1948, on the Isle of Wight, the son of a hovercraft engineer, he was educated at Sherborne, Dorset (where, at his school there, he appeared as Mr Puff in Sheridan's *The Critic*) and trained for the stage at the **Bristol Old Vic** Theatre School (1966-9). At the Bristol Old Vic he played Florizel in *The Winter's Tale,* Simon in **Coward**'s *Hay Fever,* Nick in **Orton**'s *What the Butler Saw,* and took part in Shaw's *Major Barbara,* Goldini's *The Servant of Two Masters, Macbeth* and *The Boy Friend* (1969), *As You Like It* (1970), *Oh! What a Lovely War* and *The School for Scandal* (both these latter at the Little Theatre, Bristol, 1970).

He had been working as a gardener and part-time builder of kitchen extensions when in November 1971 he played John the Baptist and Judas in *Godspell* (Round House and later at Wyndham's) which he remained with until 1973 when he left to play the Madman in *Diary of a Madman* (Act Inn, 1973), Don Pedro in *Much Ado About Nothing* and Mick in **Pinter**'s *The Caretaker* (Young Vic, 1974), Petruchio in *The Taming of the Shrew* (Round House, 1975) and Harry Thunder in John O'Keefe's *Wild Oats* (Aldwych and Piccadilly, March and April 1977). He has appeared on television in *The Pallisers, Notorious Woman, Churchill's People, Playaway, Love for Lydia* and (his most acclaimed television performance) in *Brideshead Revisited.* Films include *The French Lieutenant's Woman* and *Swann in Love.*

In 1983 he appeared in New York in Tom **Stoppard**'s *The Real Thing,* and at the Globe Theatre, Utah, took the title-role in *Hamlet.* When interviewed by Maureen Cleave in 1984 (the *Observer*) he said the actor's aim is 'to engulf people in an oceanic feeling, to make them exercise dangerous and exciting emotions that they perhaps deny themselves in everyday life'.

J

Jackson, Sir Barry (Vincent)

Born in Birmingham on 6 September 1879, he trained as an architect but founded the Pilgrim Players, an amateur theatre company, in 1907. This company became the original Birmingham Repertory Theatre Company in 1913 when Jackson built the Repertory Theatre in Birmingham. In the First World War he served in the Royal Navy. A wealthy entrepreneur, he maintained the Birmingham building and directed a wide variety of plays for 22 years, notably promoting the plays of George Bernard Shaw (*Back to Methuselah*, 1923), presenting experimental drama (Andreyev's *He Who Gets Slapped*, 1926) and classics (*Cymbeline*, 1923, *Hamlet*, 1925 and a modern dress *Macbeth*, 1929). In 1929 he founded the Malvern Festival, which lasted for over twelve years, and presented, among others, seven plays by Shaw and a number by James Bridie and J.B. Priestley.

Although he handed over the Birmingham Repertory Theatre to a Board of Trustees in 1935, Jackson still produced plays there, among which were his own versions of Wyss's *The Swiss Family Robinson* (1938), Dickens's *The Cricket on the Hearth* (1941) and Fielding's *Jonathan Wild* (1942). Immediately after the Second World War he became Director of the **Shakespeare Memorial Theatre**, Stratford-upon-Avon, and remained in the post until 1948. During this period he introduced such reforms as having a different director for each play, and he built extensions to the building. He attracted such figures as director Peter **Brook** (*Love's Labour's Lost*, 1946), Paul **Scofield** (who played the title-role in a Victorian-style production of *Hamlet*, 1948) and Anthony **Quayle** (who directed *The Winter's Tale*, and acted in *Othello*, *Hamlet* and *The Taming of the Shrew*, 1948). Quayle became Director of the Shakespeare Memorial Theatre when, in 1948, Jackson became Director of the Royal Opera House, Covent Garden, where he remained until his retirement in 1955. He died on 3 April 1961.

Jackson was one of the great influences upon the strengthening of theatre in the provinces and, especially with his development of Birmingham Repertory Theatre, showed it was possible to have thriving, creative and important drama outside London. Some of the actors and actresses who emerged from his patronage were Laurence **Olivier**, Ralph **Richardson**, Paul **Scofield**, Margaret Leighton, Edith **Evans**, Peggy **Ashcroft**, Cedric Hardwicke and Albert **Finney**.

Jackson, Glenda, CBE

Born in Birkenhead, Cheshire, on 9 May 1936, she was educated at West Kirby Grammar School for Girls and trained for the stage at RADA. Her first appearance was in Terence **Rattigan**'s *Separate Tables* (Worthing, February 1957) and she first appeared in London as Ruby in *All Kinds of Men* (Arts, September 1957). She worked with a number of repertory companies and was a stage manager for Crewe Repertory Company.

In 1963 she joined the **Royal Shakespeare Company** and played in their **Theatre of Cruelty** Season (LAMDA, January 1964). At Stratford-upon-Avon for the 1965 season her roles included Ophelia in *Hamlet*, and at the Aldwych she was Eva in *Puntila* (July 1965) and a reader in *The Investigation* (October 1965). In the same year she gave a superb performance as Charlotte Corday in

Peter **Brook**'s production of Weiss's *Marat/ Sade* (Aldwych, November 1965, Martin Beck Theatre, New York, December 1965). Subsequent roles have included a part in *US* (RSC, Aldwych, October 1966), Masha in Chekhov's *Three Sisters* (**Royal Court**, April 1967), Tamara in David Pinner's *Fanghorn* (Fortune, November 1967), Katherine Winter in John **Mortimer**'s *The Collaborators* (Duchess, April 1973) and Solange in Genet's *The Maids* (Greenwich, February 1974).

One of her most acclaimed performances was as Hedda in Ibsen's *Hedda Gabler* (RSC tour of Great Britain, USA and Australia, 1975, Aldwych, July 1975). This was followed by the major roles of Vittoria Corombona in Webster's *The White Devil* (**Old Vic**, July 1976), Stevie Smith in Hugh Whitemore's *Stevie* (Vaudeville, March 1977) and Cleopatra in Peter Brook's production of *Antony and Cleopatra* (RSC, Stratford-upon-Avon, October 1978, Aldwych, July 1979). In March 1980 she took the title-role in Andrew Davies's *Rose* (Duke of York's) and also played it on Broadway. She followed this with the roles of Eva Braun in David MacDonald's *Summit Conference* (Lyric, April 1982), Lotte in Botho Strauss's *Great and Small* (Vaudeville, October 1983, Nina in O'Neill's *Strange Interlude* (Duke of York's, March 1984) and the title-role in Racine's *Phèdre* (Aldwych, October 1985).

Glenda Jackson has appeared in a great many films, including *This Sporting Life* (1963), *Marat/Sade* (1967), *Negatives* (1968), *Women in Love* (1970), *The Music Lovers* (1971), *Sunday, Bloody Sunday* (1971), *The Boyfriend* (1972), *Mary, Queen of Scots* (1972), *Triple Echo* (1972), *The Tempter* (1973), *A Touch of Class* (1973), *The Maids* (1974), *The Romantic Englishwoman* (1974), *Hedda Gabler* (1975), *Stevie* (1978), *Lost and Found* (1979), *Return of the Soldier* (1982), *Health* (1982), *Giro City* (1982) and *Sakharov* (1984). On television her best-known role was Queen Elizabeth I in *Elizabeth R* (1971), and on radio in 1984 she played Galactia in Howard **Barker**'s *Scenes From An Execution* (with Freddie **Jones** as the Doge).

In 1983 she became Director of the production company, **United British Artists** which has among its members Dianna **Rigg**, Albert **Finney**, Richard **Johnson** and Ben **Kingsley**. She said in a 1982 interview, 'I'd love to do Cleopatra again. She's so rich. Even on your very best night you come off knowing that there are aspects you haven't touched upon. And then there's Beatrice and Lady Anne. I'd like to do a season. I'd like the discipline of doing a variety of parts. But only for a short while. I'm not a good company person. I don't like to depend upon the company of actors all the time.'

Further Reading

Linda Christmas and Glenda Jackson, 'Jackson's Choices', *Plays and Players*, May 1982.

Jacobi, Derek (George)

Born in London on 22 October 1938, he was educated at Leyton County High School and St John's College, Cambridge. At Cambridge he took leading roles in productions by the ADC (Amateur Dramatic Club) and Marlowe Society. He also appeared with the **National Youth Theatre**.

His first professional roles were with Birmingham Repertory Company, which he joined in 1960, and included the part of Honeybone in N,F. **Simpson**'s *One Way Pendulum* (Birmingham Repertory Theatre, September 1960). He appeared as Brother Martin in George Bernard Shaw's *Saint Joan* and PC Liversedge in John **Arden**'s *The Workhouse Donkey* at **Chichester Festival** Theatre in 1963. Immediately after this season he joined the **National Theatre Company** at the **Old Vic**. Appearances included Laertes in *Hamlet* (October 1963), Felipillo in Peter **Shaffer**'s *The Royal Hunt* *of the Sun* (1964), Cassio in *Othello* (1964), Simon in Noël **Coward**'s *Hay Fever* (1964), Brindsley Miller (the leading role) in Shaffer's *Black Comedy* (Chichester and Old Vic, 1965-6), Tusenbach in Chekhov's *Three Sisters* (1967), the King of Navarre in *Love's Labour's Lost* (1968), Adam in Shaw's *Back to Methuselah* (1969), Lodovico in John Webster's *The White Devil* (1970) and Sir Charles Mountford in John Heywood's *A Woman Killed With Kindness* (1971).

From 1972 to 1978 Jacobi was with the **Prospect Theatre Company** for a number of productions. Parts included the title-role in Chekhov's *Ivanov* (November 1972), Buckingham in *Richard III* (1972), Aguecheek in *Twelfth Night* (1973) and the title-role in *Pericles* (1973, and tour abroad). In 1974 he again played Pericles (Her Majesty's, June 1974) and, afterwards, Raketin in Turgenev's *A Month in the Country* (Chichester Festival, July 1974). In January 1975 he toured in *The Hollow Crown.*

One of Jacobi's finest performances in the 1970s was as Hamlet (Old Vic, 1977 and 1979) which he also played with Prospect Theatre on tours in Scandinavia (including Elsinore), Australia, Japan and China. At the Old Vic he also played Thomas Mendip in a revival of Christopher **Fry**'s *The Lady's Not for Burning* (1978), and took part in *The Lunatic, The Lover and The Poet* and *The Grand Tour* (two parts of the triple-bill *Great English Eccentrics*) in 1978. In 1980 he appeared for the first time in New York, in Erdman's *The Suicide.*

For the 1982-3 season Jacobi joined the **Royal Shakespeare Company** at Stratford-upon-Avon and the Barbican, playing Benedick in *Much Ado About Nothing,* the title-role in *Peer Gynt* and Prospero in *The Tempest.* Of this latter Richard Findlater wrote in *Plays and Players* (October 1982) 'he shows a commanding authority, technical range, stamina, insight and voice ... seeing the play afresh, this seems the way to do the part, even to *be* it'. In 1983 he also played the title-role in Anthony Burgess's version of Rostand's *Cyrano de Bergerac* (Barbican, Pit). In March 1984 he toured Europe as Benedick.

Television appearances include *She Stoops to Conquer, Man of Straw, The Pallisers, Burgess and Maclean, Philby, Inside the Third Reich, I, Claudius, Hamlet* and *Richard II.* Film work has included *The Odessa File, Othello, The Day of the Jackal, The Medusa Touch, Three Sisters, The Human Factor, Charlotte* and *Enigma.*

Jacobi has taken only a few parts in new plays of the 1960s and 1970s but must be ranked as one of the leading and most versatile classical actors to emerge in the last 20 years. He said in a radio interview (*'So You Want to be an Actor?*' broadcast on Radio 4, June 1984) that when playing a part on the stage 'I'm in control and I am functioning much better in the unreality of the acting world than I am in the real world. I can cope, I know the plot, I know how the piece ends, I know what to say, I know how to react. In the real world I don't know any of those things.'

James, Emrys

Born in Wales just before the Second World War, he trained for the stage at the Royal Academy of Dramatic Art and in 1958 joined the **Bristol Old Vic** Company for a year, during which time parts included Touchstone in *As You Like It* and a Narrator in Dylan Thomas's *Under Milk Wood.* In 1959 he made his first London appearance as Private Evans in Lindsay **Anderson**'s production of Willis **Hall**'s *The Long and the Short and the Tall* (New Theatre) and later for the 1962 season played at the **Old Vic**, his parts including the title-role and Octavius Caesar in *Julius Caesar,* Malcolm in *Macbeth* and Richmond in *Richard III.* In 1964 he played Juryman No. 9 in *Twelve Angry Men* and subsequently appeared in a number of television plays.

In 1968 he joined the **Royal Shakespeare Company** at Stratford-upon-Avon and took the part of Evans in *The Merry Wives of Windsor.* Except for television work he has remained with the RSC taking numerous supporting roles and some leading parts, ranging from comic and character parts to more serious and heavyweight roles. Some of his many appearances with the RSC have been Gower in *Pericles* (Stratford, 1969), Feste in John **Barton**'s production of *Twelfth Night* (Stratford, 1970), the Cardinal in Webster's *The Duchess of Malfi,* Iago in *Othello* and Shylock in *The Merchant of Venice* (all at Stratford, 1971), The Boss in Gunter Grass's *The Plebeians* (Aldwych, December 1971), Merlin in John **Arden**'s *The Island of the Mighty* (Aldwych, December 1972), the title-role in *King John* (Stratford, 1974), Mephistophilis in Marlowe's *Doctor Faustus* (Aldwych and Tour, 1974), King Henry in Terry **Hands**'s production of *Henry IV Parts 1 and 2,* Chorus in *Henry V* and Evans in *The Merry Wives of Windsor* (Stratford 1975) for the centenary of the Royal Shakespeare Theatre.

Emrys James's many television appearances include roles in *Pygmalion, Twelfth Night, Softly, Softly, Fall of Eagles* and *Wessex Tales.* In 1983 he played Malvolio in *Twelfth Night* (RSC, Stratford-upon-Avon) and Cassius in *Julius Caesar* (RSC, Stratford-upon-Avon, 1983, and Barbican, London, May 1984).

Jarvis, Martin

Born in Cheltenham on 4 August 1941, he was educated at Whitgift School and studied for the theatre at the Royal Academy of Dramatic Art where he played the title-role in *Henry V* for the **National Youth Theatre** and received the Vanbrugh Award in 1962. His first professional performance was as Sebastian in *Twelfth Night* (Library Theatre, Manchester, October 1962) and he subsequently made his first London appearance as Frank Delanoue in Jean Anouilh's *Poor Bitos* (Duke of York's, January 1964, transferred from Manchester). Other parts followed, including Octavius Robinson in Shaw's *Man and Superman* (New Arts, November 1965, Vaudeville, January 1966), Jack Absolute in Sheridan's *The Rivals* (Thorndike, Leatherhead, April 1972, and University Theatre, New York), the title-role in *Hamlet* (Theatre Royal, Windsor, September 1973), Father Michael in David Turner's *The Prodigal Daughter* (1974 tour), Arnold in W. Somerset Maugham's *The Circle* (**Chichester Festival**, July 1976, Haymarket, October 1976) and Young Marlow in Goldsmith's *She Stoops to Conquer* (Canada and Hong Kong, 1978).

In September 1981 he was in Trevor Cowper's comedy *Caught in the Act* (Garrick) and subsequently appeared in the **National Theatre** Company's productions of Oscar Wilde's *The Importance of Being Earnest* (Lyttleton, September 1982), Harold **Pinter**'s *Other Places* (Cottesloe, October 1982) and a revival of Christopher **Fry**'s version of Giraudoux's *The Trojan War Will Not Take Place* (Lyttleton, May 1983).

He has made frequent television appearances, including parts in *The Forsyte Saga, Nicholas Nickleby,* the comedy series *Rings on Their Fingers* and *Breakaway.* His radio work is extensive and he also writes for the medium (his play, *Bright Boy,* has been broadcast by the BBC). Martin Jarvis is frequently seen and heard as a story-narrator (on *Jackanory* and recently, in 1984, as a reader of stories by Oscar Wilde). He is married to the actress Rosalind Ayres.

Jayston, Michael (*né* James)

Born on 29 October 1936 in Nottingham, he was educated at Becket Grammar School, Nottingham, Nottingham University and the Guildhall School of Music and Drama. Prior to training for the stage he was a trainee accountant. His first professional stage appearance was as Corporal Green in Anthony Kimmins's *The Amorous Prawn* (Salisbury Playhouse, July 1962) with Salisbury Repertory Company. In 1963 he joined the **Bristol Old Vic** Company with whom his parts included roles in *Beyond the Fringe* (Bristol Old Vic, April 1964), following which he joined the **Royal Shakespeare Company** and played numerous roles, the chief of which were Exeter in *Henry V* (Aldwych, May 1965), Laertes in *Hamlet* (Stratford-upon-Avon, April 1966), Lenny in Harold **Pinter**'s *The Homecoming* (Music Box, New York, July 1967), Oswald in Ibsen's *Ghosts*, reader in John **Barton**'s *The Hollow Crown* and Young Fashion in Vanbrugh's *The Relapse* (Aldwych, 1968). At the Yvonne Arnaud Theatre in Guildford in March 1972 he played King Henry II in Anouilh's *Becket*.

Joining the **National Theatre** at the **Old Vic** in 1974 he took over the part of Martin Dysart in Peter **Shaffer**'s *Equus* and played Charles Appleby in J.B. Priestley's *Eden End*. In 1976 he toured as Dysart in *Equus* and also played the role at the Albery Theatre (September 1976). In 1980 he played Elyot Chase in Noël **Coward**'s *Private Lives* (Greenwich Theatre, March, Duchess, April 1980).

From August 1981 to September 1982 he was in Rogers and Hammerstein's *The Sound of Music* (Apollo Victoria) and in October 1983 he was in Olwen Wymark's *Buried Treasure* (Tricycle Theatre).

Michael Jayston's work for films includes *Nicholas and Alexandra*, *A Bequest to the Nation*, *The Homecoming*, and *Zulu Dawn*. He has appeared frequently in television plays and series, including *The Power Game*, *Beethoven*, *Jane Eyre*, *The Last Romantic*, *Gossip from the Forest* and *Tinker, Tailor, Soldier, Spy*. He is married to Elizabeth Smithson.

Jefford, Barbara (Mary), OBE

Born in Plymstock, near Plymouth, Devon, on 26 July 1930, she was educated at Weirfield School, Taunton and studied for the stage at the Hartley Hodder Studio, Bristol, and the Royal Academy of Dramatic Art (where she won the Bancroft Gold Medal). Her first professional appearance was a walk-on part in Thornton Wilder's *Our Town* (Dolphin, Brighton, April 1949) and she made her first London appearance as Bertha in *Frenzy* (Q Theatre, June 1949).

In 1950 she joined the **Shakespeare Memorial Theatre** Company and played Isabella (to John **Gielgud**'s Angelo) in *Measure for Measure* (Stratford-upon-Avon, April 1950). Remaining with the Stratford company for four years her roles included Hero in *Much Ado About Nothing* (also a tour of Germany, 1950), Lady Percy in *Henry IV Parts 1 and 2* (1951 season), Desdemona in *Othello* and Rosalind in *As You Like It* (tour of Australia and New Zealand, 1953), Helena in *A Midsummer Night's Dream*, Katherina in *The Taming of the Shrew* and Helen in *Troilus and Cressida* (all 1954 season).

With the New Zealand Players Company, she played Jennett Jourdemayne in Christopher **Fry**'s *The Lady's Not For Burning* (New Zealand tour, 1954-5) and on her return to London appeared as Andromache in Giraudoux's *Tiger at the Gates* (Apollo, June 1955), remaining with the production when it transferred to New York (Plymouth Theatre, October 1955).

From 1956 until 1962 she was a member of the **Old Vic** Company, her major and highly successful roles being Portia in *The Merchant of Venice* (1956), Beatrice in *Much Ado About Nothing* (1956), Tamora in *Titus Andronicus* (1957), Queen Margaret in *Henry IV Parts 1, 2 and 3*, Regan in *King Lear* (1958) and Viola in *Twelfth Night* (1958). She toured America with the company (1958-9) and in 1960 gave one of the finest performances of her career as Joan in Shaw's *Saint Joan* and, for the same tour, also played Lady Macbeth in *Macbeth* and Gwendolen in Wilde's *The Importance of Being Earnest* (tour of Great Britain, September–December 1960, tour of USSR and Poland, January 1961).

At the Paris Festival in June 1961 she performed her own recital, *Heroines of Shakespeare* (also touring in Finland and West Germany, August–September 1961). She subsequently played Lavinia in O'Neill's *Mourning Becomes Electra* (Old Vic, November 1961) and toured the USA and Europe as Lady Macbeth and again in the title-role of *Saint Joan* (Old Vic Company, February–August 1962). She later played Lina in Shaw's *Misalliance* (Oxford Playhouse, October 1962, **Royal Court** and Criterion, January 1963) and the Step-Daughter in Pirandello's *Six Characters in Search of an Author* (Mayfair, June 1963).

After a South American tour (playing Portia and Helena) Barbara Jefford played Nan in David **Mercer**'s *Ride a Cock Horse* (Piccadilly, June 1965). Subsequent roles included Cleopatra in *Antony and Cleopatra* (Oxford Playhouse, September 1965–January 1966, Nottingham Playhouse, October 1966) and Patsy in Jules Feiffer's *Little Murders* (**RSC**, Aldwych, July 1967). In 1969 she performed in *The Labours of Love* (tour of Canada, West Africa and the Middle East), which she devised with John Turner (her husband, whom she married in 1967), and in Spring 1971 she toured South America as Katherina in *The Taming of the Shrew* and Hedda in Ibsen's *Hedda Gabler* in productions with the **Bristol Old Vic** Company. In 1972 she toured Australia in *The Labours of Love* and in the following year she was Portia in *The Merchant of Venice* (Oxford Playhouse). At the 1975 **Chichester Festival** she played Roxane in Rostand's *Cyrano de Bergerac* and Katherine in Ibsen's *An Enemy of the People.*

She played other parts after this until joining the **National Theatre** Company with whom she played Gertrude in *Hamlet* (Lyttleton, May 1976) and Zabina in Marlowe's *Tamburlaine the Great* (Olivier, October 1976) for the opening of the company's new theatre complex on the South Bank of the Thames. In March 1977 she joined the **Prospect Theatre Company** and played a number of parts, including Gertrude in *Hamlet* and Cleopatra in *Antony and Cleopatra*, in seasons at the Old Vic and the **Edinburgh Festival**. In 1979 she took over from Joan **Plowright** in the title-role of de Filippo's *Filumena* (Lyric, January) and in the same year played the Nurse in *Romeo and Juliet* (Old Vic, June). In July 1983 she was Grace Winslow in a revival of Terence **Rattigan**'s *The Winslow Boy* (Lyric, Hammersmith).

Barbara Jefford's film work includes *Ulysses, A Midsummer Night's Dream, Hitler: the Last Ten Days,* and *And the Ship Sailed On.* Appearances on television include *Edna, the Inebriate Woman, The Visitors, Skin Game* and *Canterbury Tales.* She has also performed in numerous radio productions.

Jellicoe, (Patricia) Ann

Born in Middlesborough, Yorkshire, on 15 July 1927, educated at Polam Hall, Darlington, and Queen Margaret's School, Castle Howard, Yorkshire, she studied for the theatre at the Central School of Speech and Drama. When she left the latter in 1947 she worked as a stage manager, actress and director in London and elsewhere until, in 1951, she founded the Cockpit Theatre Club in London. Experimenting with **open stage** production at the Cockpit she directed a number of plays including Sir John Vanburgh's *The Confederacy* (1952), Aristophanes' *The Frogs* (1952), Strindberg's *Miss Julie* (1952), John **Whiting**'s *Saint's Day* (1953), *The Comedy of Errors* (1953) and Ferenc Molnar's *Olympia* (1953). From 1953 until 1955 she lectured and directed at the Central School of Speech and Drama.

Ann Jellicoe came to recognition as a playwright with *The Sport of My Mad Mother* presented at the **Royal Court** Theatre (February 1958) which she co-directed with George **Devine**. It was a play about Teddy boys and demanded a great deal of fleshing out in terms of spectacle and stage presentation. John Russell Taylor has described it as 'director's theatre to the nth degree' and suggested that it can be seen as 'a sort of visceral theatre, rather like that advocated by Antonin Artaud under the label of '**Theatre of Cruelty**': it seeks to bypass our intellects and play instead upon our instincts, using more than the normal theatrical channel of verbal communication to make its effect'. Her most resounding success was *The Knack* (Arts, Cambridge, 1961, Royal Court, March 1962, New Theatre, New York, May 1964) about three men and their various capacities to seduce girls. Once again, the dialogue of the play is not where the emphasis in production lies but more in the non-verbal or, on occasions, onomatopoeic spheres (such as when a bed is imagined to be a piano). More verbal and conventional in narrative form was *Shelley: or, The Idealist* (Royal Court, October 1965), a study of the poet Shelley. *The Giveaway* (Garrick, 1969) was a farce about the absurdities which arise for a family who have received eight crates of breakfast cereal, enough for ten years, as a competition prize.

From 1973 until 1975 Ann Jellicoe was Literary Manager of the Royal Court Theatre. Towards the end of the 1970s she became interested in community theatre, particularly in the West Country where she lives (Lyme Regis). In 1978 at Lyme Regis she presented *The Reckoning* (also Medium Far Touring Company, November 1979) and has subsequently developed other community plays such as *The Bargain* (South West Music Theatre, 1979), *The Tide* (Axe Valley, 1980) and *The Western Women* (Lyme Regis, 1984) which was based on a story by Fay Weldon and historical research by John Fowles about the seventeenth-century ancestors of the population of Lyme Regis. *The Knack* was revived at the Oxford Playhouse in June 1984.

In 1980 Jellicoe founded the Colway Theatre Trust for the promotion and production of community drama. She has also written a number of plays for children (known as 'Jelliplays') and adapted Ibsen's *Rosmersholm*, *The Lady from the Sea* and Chekhov's *The Seagull* (with Ariadne Nicolaeff). She stated in her preface to *Shelley* that she writes plays 'for the pleasure of creating something, for the exhilaration of defining and trying to answer certain questions, because writing is a process of self-discovery and self-enrichment, for the sake of communication'.

Further Reading

Ann Jellicoe, *Some Unconscious Influences in the Theatre*, Cambridge University Press, London, 1967.

Johnson, Richard

Born on 30 July 1927, in Upminster, Essex, he was educated at Parkfield School and Felstead. He studied for the stage at the Royal Academy of Dramatic Art and made his first professional appearance in a small part in *Hamlet* (Opera House, Manchester, July 1944 and Sir John **Gielgud**'s repertory season at the Haymarket, September 1944). He did his National Service in the Royal Navy (1945-8) and afterwards was in repertory at Perth (1948-9) and a number of productions in London including Giraudoux's *The Madwoman of Chaillot* (St James's, February 1951) and *A Midsummer Night's Dream* (Open Air Theatre, May 1951). He joined the **Bristol Old Vic** Company for its 1953 season and then went into broadcasting for a short time. In May 1955 he was Beauchamp in Anouilh's *The Lark* (Lyric, Hammersmith) and later played Laertes in Peter **Brook**'s production of *Hamlet* (Moscow, November 1955, Phoenix,

London, December 1955). After further **West End** appearances he joined the **Shakespeare Memorial Theatre** Company at Stratford-upon-Avon with whom his roles included Orlando in *As You Like It*, Mark Antony in *Julius Caesar* (1957), Romeo in *Romeo and Juliet*, Aguecheek in *Twelfth Night* and the title-role in *Pericles* (1958).

With the newly-named **Royal Shakespeare Company** he again played Aguecheek in *Twelfth Night* (Aldwych, December 1960). Subsequent roles with the RSC included Grandier in John **Whiting**'s *The Devils* (Aldwych, February 1961) and one of the actors in John **Barton**'s anthology *The Hollow Crown* (Aldwych, June 1961). After an appearance as Clive Root in Graham **Greene**'s *The Complaisant Lover* (Ethel Barrymore, New York, November 1961) he again played Grandier (Aldwych, October 1962). He devised his own show, *The Golden Age* (Lyceum, New York, November 1963) and toured Europe in *The Hollow Crown.*

In 1969 Richard Johnson founded a production company called Pageant Entertainments Ltd, and, for the RSC's 1972 season at Stratford, played Mark Antony in *Julius Caesar* and *Antony and Cleopatra.* For the **National Theatre** he has played Charles in Noël **Coward**'s *Blithe Spirit* (Lyttleton, June 1976), Pontius Pilate in *The Passion* (1977), Pinchwife in Wycherley's *The Country Wife* (1977), and Nandor in *The Guardsman* (1978). In 1982 a production company, United British Artists, was formed by Diana **Rigg** (Director) and a number of other actors and actresses including Albert **Finney** and Glenda **Jackson**. Richard Johnson has been chairman of the group and promoted a number of projects, notably the films *Champions* (1984), in which he also acted, and *Turtle Summer* (1984) which he produced.

Other film appearances include *Captain Hornblower, The Haunting, The Pumpkin Eater, Operation Crossbow, Moll Flanders, Khartoum, Danger Route, Oedipus the King, Lady Hamilton, Julius Caesar* and *The Beloved.*

Joint Stock Theatre Group

See **Alternative Theatre**; **Gaskill, William,** and **Hare, David**.

Jones, Freddie

Born in 1927 at Stoke-on-Trent, Staffordshire, he was educated at his local high school where he appeared in school plays. He left school and became a laboratory technician for a scientific company and in his spare time was a great amateur dramatics enthusiast. After ten years he decided to take up acting professionally and won a scholarship to the Rose Bruford College where he trained for two years. After repertory work he joined the **Royal Shakespeare Company** and played Cucurucu in Peter **Brook**'s celebrated production of Peter Weiss's *The Marat/Sade* (Aldwych, August 1964).

Subsequent roles for the stage have included Alec, the ageing novelist, in Stanley Eveling's *Dear Janet Rosenberg* (Hampstead Theatre, September 1969), the title-role in the original production of David **Mercer**'s *Flint* (Oxford Playhouse, March 1970), Mathias in a revival of Leopold Lewis's *The Bells* (Greenwich, January 1976) and Robert in David Mamet's *A Life in the Theatre* (**Open Space**, July 1979).

Freddie Jones gave a highly-acclaimed performance as Sir, the actor-manager, in Ronald Harwood's *The Dresser* (Royal Exchange, Manchester, March 1980, Queen's, London, April 1980) with Tom **Courtenay** as Norman. He also played Arthur Langley in Ronald Harwood's *Tramway Road* (Lyric, Hammersmith, October 1984) and was recently Willie Loman in Arthur Miller's *Death of a Salesman* at the Yvonne Arnaud Theatre, Guildford.

His acting career has been spread with

equal success over film and television and he is a distinguished actor in these media. Television appearances include *Uncle Vanya, Nana, Germinal, The Caesars* (in which he gave an award-winning performance as Claudius), *Joe's Ark, Pennies from Heaven, Fall of Angels, The Ghosts of Motley Hall, Through the Looking Glass, Secret Orchards, Tiny Revolutions, Silas Marner, The Secret Diary of Adrian Mole Aged 13¾* and *Time After Time.* Films include *Antony and Cleopatra, The Marat/Sade, The Bliss of Mrs Blossom, Accident, Far From the Madding Crowd, Juggernaut, Zulu Dawn, The Elephant Man* and *Firefox.* He took the leading role in Peter Yates's film *Krull* and Federico Fellini's *And the Ship Sailed On.* Other films are *Dune, Firestarter, Lost in London* and *Comrades.* In 1985 he was the Doge of Venice, with Glenda **Jackson** as Galactia, in Howard **Barker**'s award-winning radio play *Scenes from an Execution.*

Freddie Jones recently commented ('An Actor's Life For Me', BBC 2, 18 August 1985) that acting is rather 'like climbing when you're first on the rope: there may be an anchor somewhere belay down below but you're alone and it is you related to your fears and the rock that is *all*'. The 'very mainspring of our being as actors' is a dependence on 'intuition, flashes, rather than logical perambulations'. In his interview with Richard Barber (see below) he said 'any actor is an actor because he *needs* to act'.

Further Reading

Richard Barber, 'Who is Freddie?', *Plays and Players,* June 1980.

Joseph, Stephen

See **Theatre-in-The-Round**.

K

Keeffe, Barrie (Colin)

Born in East Ham, London, on 31 October 1945, he was educated at East Ham Grammar School and afterwards had various jobs, including working in a tin box factory, as a soft drinks salesman and as a gravedigger's mate. He worked as a freelance journalist and then for five years as a journalist on the *Stratford Express*, an East London newspaper.

Keeffe's long association with the **National Youth Theatre** began when he was an actor-member (for five years) and he has subsequently written some of his plays for the company. His plays are marked by their preoccupation with the hardships and deprivation of working-class youth in London's East End, by their comedy and by a savage realism deriving from Keeffe's interest in Jacobean drama (in his late teens he adapted Ben Jonson's *Volpone*, and the title of his own play *A Mad World, My Masters* (1977) is taken directly from a play of 1606, by Thomas Middleton).

His first stage play was *Only a Game* (Shaw, March 1973), about the waning career of a football star. *A Sight of Glory* (National Youth Theatre, Cockpit, August 1975) is set in an East End boxing club, *Scribes* (Tyneside Theatre, 1975, Greenwich, October 1976) is set in the office of an East End newspaper hit by a strike, *My Girl* (Soho Poly, 1975) portrays a social worker who, on the eve of his thirtieth birthday, questions his vocation, and *Here Comes the Sun* (National Youth Theatre, Jeanetta Cochrane, August 1976) follows the experiences of a group of young office workers on holiday on the Costa Brava.

His future as a playwright was assured with the success of his trilogy *Gimme Shelter* (*Gem*, *Gotcha* and *Getaway*, Soho Poly and **Royal Court** Theatre, February 1977), which portrayed class warfare resulting from the frustrations of poorly-employed working-class youth. In 1969 he commented (in an interview with Catherine Itzin), 'I think the plays are asking questions of the people who are running the world, who have forgotten what it's like, or who never knew.' This trilogy was followed by another, entitled *Barbarians* (*Killing Time*, *Abide With Me* and *In the City*, Greenwich, September 1977). *A Mad World, My Masters* (**Joint Stock Company**, Young Vic, May 1977), loosely based on Thomas Middleton's play of the same title, is a romping and bawdy comedy which explores the greed of both the Establishment (represented chiefly by an industrialist and Royalty) and the anti-Establishment (represented by an avaricious grandmother, alcoholic doctor, and trade-unionist with a double who plays the trombone). *Frozen Assets*, first performed by the **Royal Shakespeare Company** (Warehouse, December 1977), is an exposé of the inadequacy of the social system, which is thrown into relief by following the experiences of a Borstal boy on the run.

A particularly successful play was *Sus* (Soho Poly, **Royal Court** and Theatre Royal, Stratford, October–November 1979, Round House 1982) about the injustices of the 'Sus' laws (detention on suspicion only) which are seen savagely used against a Jamaican by two racist policemen. Barry Keeffe has gone on to write plays with music, such as *Bastard Angel* (RSC, Warehouse, 1980), *She's So Modern* (Queen's, Hornchurch, 1980) and *Chorus Girls* (Theatre Royal, Stratford East, April 1981), which features Prince Charles who, as a result of falling down a trap-door, spends some hilarious hours with some chorus girls beneath a theatre stage. Other plays include *Black Lear*

(Temba tour, 1980), an adaptation of *King Lear* with a tube-train driver as the protagonist, and *Better Times* (Half Moon, September 1984), about the London Borough of Poplar, which, in 1921, refused to comply with Government legislation over rates.

Keeffe wrote the screenplay for the film *The Long Good Friday* (1981) and his television plays include *Substitute, Gotcha, Not Quite Cricket, Nipper, Champions, Hanging Around, Waterloo Sunset* and the series *No Excuses.* He was married to Julia Lindsay in 1983.

In his interview with Malcolm Hay (1984) he commented on his blend of comedy and tough social criticism: 'Listen to people in the East End talking about something painful — they'll tell you five funny stories before they get through the pain of it. It's an instinctive way of making serious points through humour.'

Further Reading

Malcolm Hay, 'Portraits of Angry Young Underdogs', *Drama*, 4th Quarter, No. 154, 1984, pp. 9-11.

Keith, Penelope (Anne Constance)

Born in Sutton, Surrey, she was educated at Annecy Convent, Seaford, Sussex, and at Bayeaux. She trained for the stage at the Webber-Douglas School, London. In 1978 she was married to Rodney Timson.

Her first professional role was as Alice Pepper in Jerome Chodorov's *The Tunnel of Love* (Civic Theatre, Chesterfield, September 1959) and, after playing in repertory at Lincoln, Salisbury and Manchester, she joined the **Royal Shakespeare Company** in 1963, appearing in John **Barton**'s Shakespearian trilogy *The Wars of the Roses* (Stratford-upon-Avon, July 1963, Aldwych, January 1964). Her chief parts since have been in comedy and include Sarah in Alan **Ayckbourn**'s *The Norman Conquests* (Greenwich, May 1974, Globe, August 1974), Lady Driver in Michael **Frayn**'s *Donkey's Years* (Globe, July 1976), Orinthia in Shaw's *The Apple Cart* (**Chichester Festival**, 1977, Phoenix, November 1977), Epifania in Wolf Mankowitz's *The Millionairess* (Haymarket, December 1978), Sarah in Stanley Price's *Moving* (Queen's, January 1981), Maggie in Harold Brighouse's *Hobson's Choice* (Haymarket, February 1982), Lady Waynflete in Shaw's *Captain Brassbound's Conversion* (Haymarket, June 1982) and Judith Bliss in Noël **Coward**'s *Hayfever* (Queen's, October 1983–April 1984), which she also co-produced. She said, in an interview with Edward Lucie-Smith (*Plays and Players,* December 1983), that comedy 'is rooted in character. You've got to make them believe in the character. If they laugh out loud, that's a bonus. They may just be satisfied even if they don't. And you must never sacrifice the meaning for the laugh.'

Her television roles as Margot in *The Good Life* and Audrey Fforbes-Hamilton in *To the Manor Born* gained her national popularity. She has also appeared on television in *Kate, Private Lives, The Norman Conquests, Donkey's Years* and *Sweet Sixteen.* Films include *Every Home Should Have One, Penny Gold, Take a Girl Like You* and *The Priest of Love.* When asked about her capacity to draw theatre audiences because of her television fame she said, 'I'm grateful for anything which brings people into the theatre . . . When they're here you've got to convince them that live theatre's a different experience — you do your very best for them.'

Kendal, Felicity

Born in Olton, Warwickshire, on 25 September 1946, she was brought up and educated in India where she toured with her parents' theatre company (at nine months she was the Changeling Boy in *A Midsummer Night's*

Dream, at nine years she was Puck, and later played such parts as Viola, Jessica and Ophelia). In 1965 she returned to England when *Shakespeare Wallah*, a film about her family's life in India, was shown. She has remained in England ever since, where her roles have included Katherine in *Henry V* (Phoenix, Leicester, 1968), Amaryllis in Shaw's *Back to Methuselah* (**National Theatre, Old Vic**, August 1969), Hermia in *A Midsummer Night's Dream* (Open Air Theatre, Regent's Park, 1970), Anne Danby in Peter Stone's *Kean* (Playhouse, Oxford, September 1970, Globe, January 1971) and Juliet in *Romeo and Juliet* (Oxford Playhouse, February 1972).

In 1972 she joined the **Actors' Company** and played Annabella in Ford's *'Tis Pity She's a Whore* (**Edinburgh Festival**, September, and tour). She gave award-winning performances as Annie in Alan **Ayckbourn**'s trilogy *The Norman Conquests* (Greenwich Theatre, May 1974, Globe, August 1974) and as Mara in Michael **Frayn**'s *Clouds* (Duke of York's, November 1978). Since joining the National Theatre in 1979 she has played Constanze in Peter **Shaffer**'s *Amadeus* (Olivier, November 1979), Desdemona in *Othello* (Olivier, March 1980), Christopher in Tom **Stoppard**'s *On the Razzle* (Lyttleton, September 1981) and Paula in Pinero's *The Second Mrs Tanquary* (Lyttleton, December 1981). In 1982 she was Annie in Tom Stoppard's *The Real Thing* (Strand, November 1982).

On television she is best-known for her performances in *The Good Life* and *Solo*. Other television work includes *Edward VIII*, *Clouds of Glory* and *Twelfth Night*. Films include *Shakespeare Wallah*, and *Valentino*.

Kestelman, Sara

Born in London on 12 May 1944, she was educated at Camden School for Girls and trained as a ballet dancer with Laura Wilson. She made her first professional appearance as a dancing nymph in Robert Atkins's production of *The Tempest* (Open Air Theatre, Regent's Park, 1960). Between 1962 and 1965 she trained at the Central School of Speech and Drama, after which she was in repertory at Liverpool Playhouse and the Library Theatre, Manchester.

In 1968 she joined the **Royal Shakespeare Company** at Stratford-upon-Avon and played Lechery in Marlowe's *Doctor Faustus*. She made her London début as Cassandra in *Troilus and Cressida* (RSC, Aldwych, June 1969) and also played Margaret in *Much Ado About Nothing* (Aldwych, July 1969). A major success followed when she was chosen to double the roles of Hippolyta and Titania in Peter **Brook**'s production of *A Midsummer Night's Dream* (RSC, Stratford-upon-Avon, August 1970, Billy Rose Theatre, New York, January 1971, Aldwych, June 1971). In an interview with Christopher Edwards (*Plays and Players*, April 1982) she said, 'For me, the success of *The Dream* was a rather painful mystery. On stage this tigress materialised — that's how it was described to me — but inside there was this mouse doing effective things but not knowing *how* to embrace them; it was very weird.' This part was followed by a fine performance as Natasha in Robert Montgomery's play with music, *Subject to Fits* (The Place, October 1971).

At Birmingham Repertory Theatre she was Lady Macbeth in *Macbeth* and Ruth in Harold **Pinter**'s *The Homecoming* (September 1972), and at the **Bristol Old Vic** appeared as Yelena in Chekhov's *Uncle Vanya* (October 1973). She returned to the RSC to play Countess Werdenfels in Wedekind's *The Marquis of Keith* (Aldwych, November 1974) and tour in *The Hollow Crown* and *Pleasure and Repentence* (USA, 1974, Japan, 1975).

In 1976 she played Sally Bowles in John van Druten's *I am a Camera* with the Cambridge Theatre Company and then joined the **National Theatre** for its 1977-8 season, her roles including Alexandra in

Robert **Bolt**'s *State of Revolution*, Susannah in Alan **Ayckbourn**'s *Bedroom Farce*, Lady Touchwood in William Congreve's *The Double Dealer* and Enid Underwood in John Galsworthy's *Strife*. At the National in 1979 she was Rosalind in *As You Like It*, the Lady with a Monocle in *The Fruits of Enlightenment* and Mrs Wahl in Tom **Stoppard**'s adaptation of *Undiscovered Country*. After appearing in Romulus Linney's *Childe Byron* at the Young Vic (July 1981) she returned to the RSC and played Lady Macbeth in *Macbeth* (Stratford-upon-Avon, March 1982, Barbican, May 1983), Goneril in *King Lear* (Stratford, June 1982, Barbican, May 1983) and Bodice in Edward **Bond**'s *Lear* (the Other Place, Stratford, June 1982, Barbican, May 1983). At the **Chichester Festival** in July 1984 she played Mrs Marwood in Congreve's *The Way of the World*.

Her film work includes *Zardoz*, *Lisztomania*, *Break of Day* and *The Life of Nobel*. She has appeared on television in the series *Walls of Justice*, *Crown Court*, *The New Avengers* and in a number of plays, including *The Caucasian Chalk Circle*, *Peer Gynt*, *Under Western Eyes* and *Kean*.

Kingsley, Ben

Born in Snainton, North Yorkshire, on 31 December 1943, he attended Manchester Grammar School and became a laboratory assistant. Although he initially wanted to become a doctor he took up a career in the theatre when he joined a schools tour for Theatre Centre in 1964. He was subsequently in repertory with Peter Cheeseman's company at Stoke-on-Trent and later played the First Murderer in *Macbeth* and a Party Guest in Chekhov's *The Cherry Orchard* for the 1966 **Chichester Festival**.

In 1967 he joined the **Royal Shakespeare Company** at Stratford-upon-Avon to play small parts. He has remained with the company for the majority of his stage career, his chief parts being Aeneas in *Troilus and Cressida* (Stratford, 1968 season), Winwife in Jonson's *Bartholomew Fair* (Aldwych, 1969 season), Claudio in *Measure for Measure*, Ariel in *The Tempest* and Demetrius in Peter **Brook**'s hugely successful production of *A Midsummer Night's Dream* (all at Stratford, 1970 season), Demetrius for a tour of the United States of America (later also at the Aldwych, June 1971), Gramsci in Trevor Griffiths's *Occupations* (the Place, October 1971) and Johnnie in Athol Fugard's *Hello and Goodbye* (King's Head and The Place, October 1973).

For a short period Kingsley left the RSC to appear as Errol Philander in Fugard's *Statements After an Arrest* at the **Royal Court** Theatre (January 1974) and European tour (returning to the Royal Court, January 1975). He rejoined the RSC in 1975 and subsequent roles included Slender in *The Merry Wives of Windsor*, the title-role in Buzz Goodbody's production of *Hamlet* (the Other Place, Stratford-upon-Avon, 1975 season, Round House, February 1976).

In 1977 he was with the **National Theatre** for the roles of Mosca in Jonson's *Volpone* (Olivier), Vukhov in Barry Collins's *Judgment* (Cottesloe) and Trofimov in Chekhov's *The Cherry Orchard* (Olivier). Returning to the RSC for the 1979 season at Stratford, he was Frank Ford in *The Merry Wives of Windsor*, Iachimo in *Cymbeline* and Brutus in *Julius Caesar*. He was also at the Other Place for the same season, playing the title-role in Brecht's *Baal* (also the Warehouse, 1980 season) and later played Squeers in David **Edgar**'s stage version of Dickens's *Nicholas Nickleby* (Aldwych, 1980 season). In 1981 he took the title-role in Marlowe's *Doctor Faustus* (Manchester Royal Exchange), the title-role in Ray Fitzsimmons's *Edmund Kean* (Harrogate, 1981, later at the Lyric Hammersmith, April 1983, Theatre Royal, Haymarket, June 1983) and the title-role in *Othello* (RSC, Stratford-upon-Avon, September 1985).

In an interview with Colin Chambers in 1978 Kingsley said of working with the RSC, 'you can develop lazy habits in a stable working environment but not necessarily so ... We've had our dreams and aspirations hammered out in real sweat and real spade with people who are constantly provoking us.'

His work in films includes *Fear is the Key, Ghandi* and *Betrayal.* Television appearances include *Hard Labour, Misfortune, Barbara of Grebe House, Need for the Nightmare, The Love School, Every Good Boy Deserves Favour, Edmund Kean* and *Silas Marner.*

Plate 1 The first production of John Osborne's *Look Back in Anger*, Royal Court Theatre, May 1956: (left to right) Mary Ure, Alan Bates, Helena Hughes, Kenneth Haigh *Photo*: Houston Rogers Collection, Theatre Museum, Victoria and Albert Museum

Plate 2 The first London production of Samuel Beckett's *Waiting for Godot,* Arts Theatre, August 1955, directed by Peter Hall: (left to right) Timothy Bateson (Lucky), Paul Daneman (Vladimir), Peter Bull (Pozzo), Peter Woodthorpe (Estragon) *Photo* Times Newspapers Ltd

Plate 3 Peter Brook's production of *A Midsummer Night's Dream* for the Royal Shakespeare Company, Stratford-upon-Avon, 1970: (centre) Sara Kestelman as Titania, (background, left to right) Ralph Cotterill (Moth), Celia Quicke (Peaseblossom), Hugh Keays Byrne (Cobweb), John York (Mustardseed) *Photo*: The Shakespeare Birthplace Trust

Plate 4 A recent revival of John Arden's *Sergeant Musgrave's Dance*, Old Vic, May 1984, with Albert Finney as Musgrave (also directed) *Photo*: The Old Vic

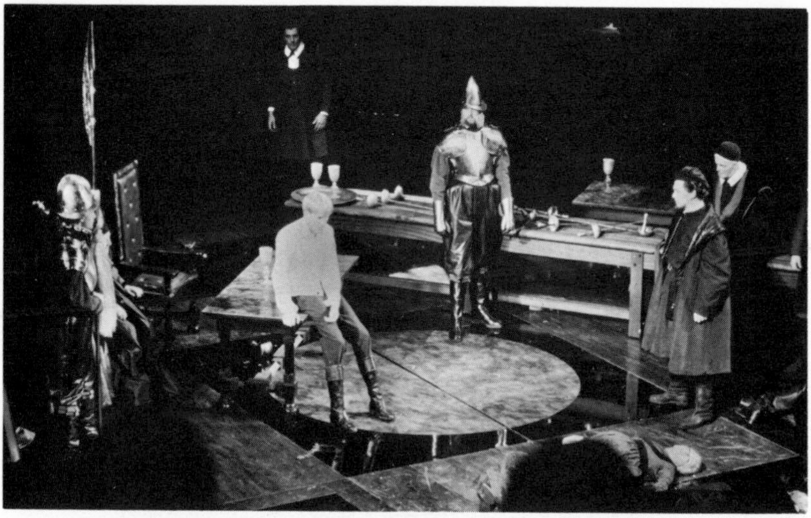

Plate 5 Peter Hall's production of *Hamlet* for the Royal Shakespeare Company, Stratford-upon-Avon, 1965: (table centre) David Warner as Hamlet. *Photo*: The British Tourist Authority

Plate 6 Ian McKellen as King Richard and Andrew Crawford as the Bishop of Carlisle in the Prospect Theatre Company's production of *Richard II*, November 1968 *Photo*: Michael Peto, University Library, Dundee

Plate 7 The National Theatre on London's South Bank *Photo*: Philip Barnes and John Marshall

Plate 8 The Old Vic Theatre, Waterloo Road *Photo*: Philip Barnes and John Marshall

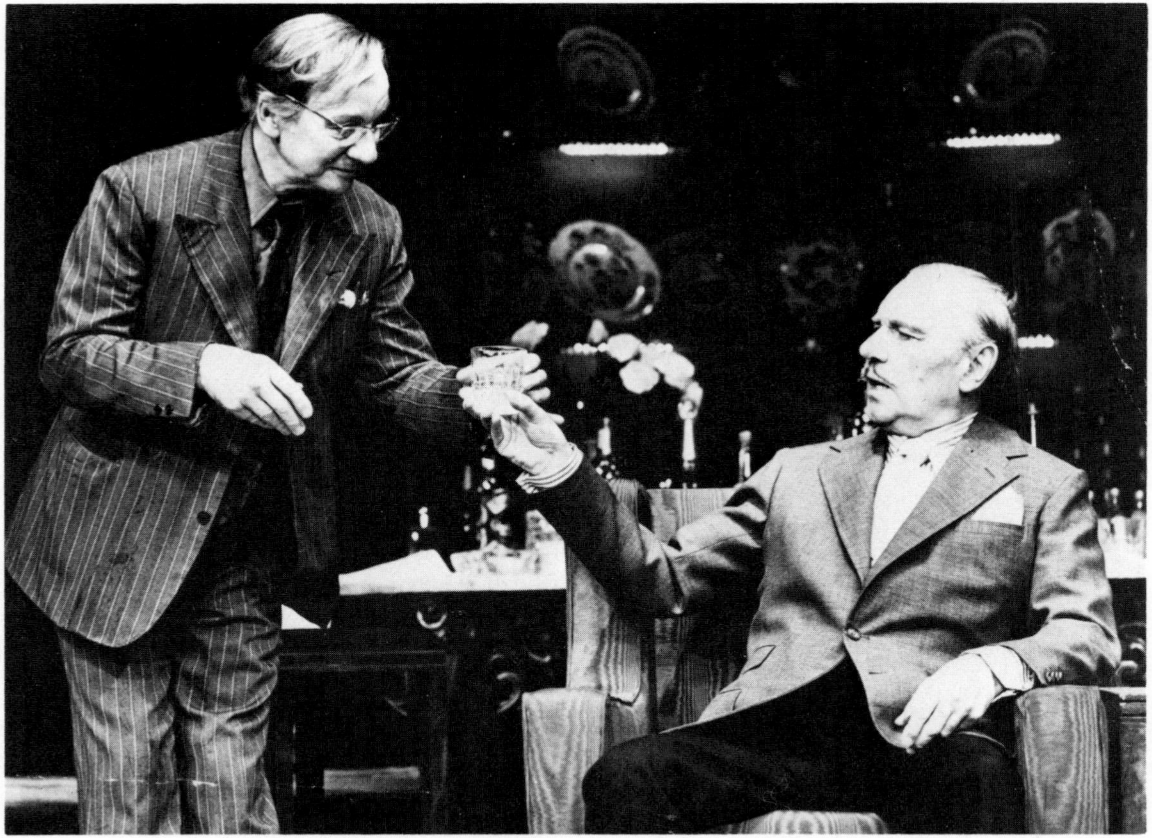

Plate 9 The first production of Harold Pinter's *No Man's Land*, National Theatre at the Old Vic, April 1975: (left) Sir John Gielgud as Spooner, (right) Sir Ralph Richardson as Hirst *Photo*: Anthony Crickmay

Plate 10 The Royal Court Theatre, Sloane Square
Photo: Philip Barnes and John Marshall

Plate 11 The Barbican Theatre, Barbican Centre, London base of the Royal Shakespeare Company
Photo: Philip Barnes and John Marshall

Plate 12 The first production of Peter Shaffer's *The Royal Hunt of the Sun*, National Theatre, Chichester Festival, July 1964 (transferred Old Vic, December 1964): Robert Stephens as Atahuallpa *Photo*: Angus McBean, Harvard Theatre Collection, Cambridge, Massachusetts

L

Landen, Dinsdale

Born in Margate, Kent, on 4 September 1932, he was educated at King's School, Rochester, and studied for the stage at the Florence Moore Theatre Studios, Hove, Sussex. His first professional appearance was as Bimbo in Ian Hay's comedy *Housemaster* (Dolphin, Brighton, November 1948) and, after an Australian tour with the **Old Vic** Company in 1955, he made his London début as Archie Gooch in Rodney Ackland's *A Dead Secret* (Piccadilly, May 1957).

After other **West End** appearances he joined the **Shakespeare Memorial Theatre** Company for the 1960 Stratford-upon-Avon season to play a number of roles including Launcelot Gobbo in *The Merchant of Venice.* At the Open Air Theatre, Regent's Park, he played the title-role in *Henry V* and Petruchio in *The Taming of the Shrew* (July 1964). In 1968 he toured with Toby Robertson's **Prospect Theatre Company** as Aguecheek in *Twelfth Night* and Bluntschli in George Bernard Shaw's *Arms and the Man.* In August 1970 he was at the **Royal Court** Theatre playing Donald in Christopher **Hampton**'s *The Philanthropist* (later transferred to May Fair Theatre, September 1970) and in April 1972 he was Dazzle in Dion Boucicault's *London Assurance* (New Theatre).

Other roles have included Robert in Snoo **Wilson**'s *The Pleasure Principle* (Royal Court, Theatre Upstairs, December 1973), John in Michael **Frayn**'s *Alphabetical Order* (Hampstead, March 1975, May Fair, April 1975) and, for the **National Theatre** at the Old Vic, D'Arcy in a revival of Ben Travers's *Plunder* (transferred to Lyttleton, March 1976). In February 1978 he was Mervyn in James **Saunders**'s *Bodies* (Hampstead, February 1978) and in May of the same year he returned to the National to play D'Arcy again, and also played Leonard Charteris in Shaw's *The Philanderer.* In the following year he again played Mervyn in *Bodies* (Ambassadors' Theatre, April 1979). He subsequently appeared in Tom **Stoppard**'s *On the Razzle* (Lyttleton, September 1981), and played Astrov in Pam **Gems**'s version of Chekhov's *Uncle Vanya* (Lyttleton, May 1982), and Jack Barker in Dennis **Potter**'s *Sufficient Carbohydrate* (Albery, December 1983). In October 1984 he took over from the late Leonard **Rossiter** as Inspector Truscot in the revival of Joe **Orton**'s *Loot* at the Lyric Theatre, and in September 1985 he appeared with the **Theatre of Comedy** Company in Ray **Cooney**'s production of Arne Sultan and Earl Barret's *Wife Begins at Forty* (Yvonne Arnaud, Guildford).

Television appearances include *The Glittering Prizes, Fathers and Families, Devenish, Pig in the Middle, This Office Life, Radio Pictures* and *The Irish RM.* Films include *The Valiant, Every Home Should Have One* and *Morons from Outer Space.*

Lapotaire, Jane

Born in Ipswich on 26 December 1944, she was educated at Northgate Grammar School, Ipswich, and trained for the stage at the **Bristol Old Vic** Theatre School. Her first professional appearance was as Ruby Birtle in J.B. Priestley's *When We Are Married* (Bristol Old Vic, September 1965). Further parts with the Bristol Old Vic Company, with whom she remained until 1967, included Vivie in Shaw's *Mrs Warren's Profession* and Ruth in **Pinter**'s *The Homecoming.* From 1967 to 1971 she was with the **National Theatre** at the **Old Vic** appearing in numerous roles, the chief of which were Judith in

The Dance of Death (February 1967), Mrs Fainall in Congreve's *The Way of the World*, Zanche in Webster's *The White Devil* (May and November 1969), Jessica in *The Merchant of Venice* (April 1970) and Lieschen in John **Mortimer**'s adaptation of Zuckmayer's *The Captain of Kopenick* (March 1971). She also worked with the Young Vic (1970-1), her parts including Katherina in *The Taming of the Shrew* and Jocasta in *Oedipus*.

She subsequently joined the **Royal Shakespeare Company** and played Viola in *Twelfth Night* (Stratford, August 1974, Aldwych, February 1975), Lady Macduff in *Macbeth* (Stratford, October 1975) and Sonya in Chekhov's *Uncle Vanya* (The Other Place, December 1975).

In October 1975 she toured with the **Prospect Theatre Company** and appeared with the same company as Vera in Turgenev's *A Month in the Country* (Albery, November 1975) and Lucy in *A Room with a View* (Albery, November 1975). In May 1976 she played Rosalind in *As You Like It* (Riverside Studios) and at the Bristol Old Vic took the title-role in Webster's *The Duchess of Malfi.* For the RSC 1978 season at Stratford-upon-Avon she played Rosaline in *Love's Labour's Lost* (also at the Aldwych, April 1979).

She gave a highly acclaimed performance in the title-role of Pam **Gems**'s *Piaf* at the Other Place (October 1978), the Warehouse (June 1979), the Aldwych (December 1979), Wyndham's (January 1980) and the Piccadilly (February 1980).

In February 1983 she was in Peter **Gill**'s *Kick for Touch* with the National Theatre Company (Cottesloe) and later appeared in the musical *Dear Anyone* (Cambridge Theatre, November 1983). In April 1984 she played Belvidera in Otway's *Venice Preserv'd* (National Theatre, Olivier).

Television work includes *Stocker's Copper, The Other Woman, Marie Curie, The Devil's Crown* and *Playing Shakespeare.* Jane Lapotaire is married to Roland Joffé.

Legs

Vertical lengths of cloth used to mask the **Wings**.

Leigh, Mike

Born in Salford, Lancashire, on 20 February 1943, the son of a medical doctor, he was educated at Salford Grammar School and attended RADA where he trained as an actor from 1960 until 1962. He then went to the Camberwell and Central Schools of Art and the London School of Film Technique. In 1965 he directed the original production of David Halliwell's *Little Malcolm and His Struggle Against the Eunuchs* at the Unity Theatre and in the same year became Associate Director at the Midlands Arts Centre, Birmingham, where, in 1966, his first original play for the stage, *The Box Play,* was performed. He also acted at the Victoria Theatre, Stoke-on-Trent in 1966.

From 1967 until 1968 he was an Assistant Director with the **Royal Shakespeare Company** and directed Ann **Jellicoe**'s *The Knack* (RSC, Theatregoround touring company, 1967).

Mike Leigh's plays, as is usually stated in their published form, are 'evolved from scratch entirely by rehearsal through improvisation'. As he put it in an interview in 1975: 'It's necessary that the improvisations serve a particular theme or idea. I discover the substance of the plays during rehearsals … I assume that people who write plays, to the extent that the plays are truly organic, make similar discoveries during the process of writing.' Plays written by these methods of collective authorship have included *Bleak Moments* (**Open Space**, March 1970) about a woman whose freedom is constrained by the demands of caring for her retarded sister, *Babies Grow Old* (Royal Shakespeare Company, The Other Place, Stratford-upon-Avon, April 1974, ICA, February 1975) which explored the political and social responsibilities of doctors, *Abigail's Party*

Hampstead Theatre Club, April 1977) bout rising tensions at a neighbours' wel-:oming party as the teenage daughter of one f the guests is having her own party nearby, ınd *Goose-Pimples* (Hampstead, March 981, Garrick, April 1981) which, like the revious play, parodies lower-middle-class alues, on this occasion through the presence f an Arab (called Muhammed, played by \nthony **Sher** in the original production) vho mistakes a domestic situation for a visit o a brothel, becomes the butt of the other haracters' jokes, and is ultimately reduced o an alcoholic stupor by their 'hospitality'.)ther stage plays have included *Wholesome ;lory* (**Royal Court**, 1973), *The Jaws of)eath* (Traverse, Edinburgh, 1973), *Oh Vhat!* (Hull Truck Company tour, 1975, 3ush, November 1975), and *Ecstasy* (Hamp-tead, 1979). He married the actress Alison teadman in 1973.

Leigh has written over 20 plays for tele-ision using the same method of group reation as for his stage plays. Television lays include *A Mug's Game, Hard Labour, Vho's Who, Old Chums, Grown-Ups, The 'ermissive Society, Knock for Knock, Five-1inute Films, The Kiss of Death, Nuts in 1ay, Home Sweet Home, Four Days in July* nd a television production of *Abigail's 'arty.* Clive Hodgson (*Radio Times,* 4-10 eptember 1982) has commented: 'His omedies make as many serious points about ontemporary Britain as the hard-hitting ocumentary, while his dramas contain more ıughs than most comedies ... comic dramas, ramatic comedies, character studies — the ıbels provide only an approximate descrip-on of something which is not quite like any-ıing else.'

urther Reading

ıul Clements, *The Improvised Play: The Work of Mike Leigh,* Methuen Theatrefile, Methuen, London, 1983.

:ter Ansorge, 'Making up the Well Made Plays for Today', *Plays and Players,* October 1975.

Lesser, Anton

Born in 1952 this youthful actor came to prominence with the **Royal Shakespeare Company** when he played Richard in the second and third parts of *Henry VI* (Stratford-upon-Avon, 1977 season, Aldwych, April 1978), Michael in David **Rudkin**'s *The Sons of Light* (RSC, Warehouse, May 1978) and Romeo in *Romeo and Juliet* (RSC, Stratford, 1980 season, Aldwych, October 1981).

He has subsequently played Constantine Desmond in Thomas Kilroy's new version of Chekhov's *The Seagull* at the **Royal Court** Theatre (April 1981) and Darkie in Edward **Bond**'s *The Fool* (RSC, The Other Place, Stratford-upon-Avon, Summer 1981, Warehouse, September 1981). In 1982 he played the title-role in *Hamlet* (Omega Projects, Warehouse, August, Piccadilly, September) directed by Jonathan **Miller**, and recently appeared as Harry in Phil Young's *The Kissing God* (Hampstead, December 1984) and Troilus in *Troilus and Cressida* (RSC, Stratford-upon-Avon, 1985 season).

Television appearances include *Freud, Anna of the Five Towns* and *Sakharov.*

'Lime'

A **Follow Spot**.

Lipman, Maureen

Born in Hull on 10 May 1946, she was educated at Newland High School, Hull, and trained for the stage at LAMDA. She is married to Jack Rosenthal. Her first professional appearance was as Nancy in Ann **Jellicoe**'s *The Knack* (Watford, 1967). She was in repertory with the Stables Theatre Company, Manchester (1968-70) and, in 1971, joined the **National Theatre** Company, with whom parts included the Second Randy Woman in Adrian Mitchell's

Tyger (New, July 1971), Hospital Visitor in Peter **Nichols**'s *The National Health* (**Old Vic**, January 1972) and Molly in Billy Wilder's *The Front Page* (Old Vic, July 1972).

With the **Royal Shakespeare Company** at Stratford-upon-Avon for the 1973 season she was Celia in *As You Like It.* Subsequent roles have included Proserpine in Shaw's *Candida* (Albery, June 1977), Janis in *The Ball Game* (**Open Space**, May 1978) and Maggie in Richard Harris's *Outside Edge* (Hampstead, July 1979, Queen's, September 1979). In 1981 she was in Neil Simon's *Chapter Two* (Lyric, Hammersmith, August) and in 1982 Alan **Plater** and Alex Glasgow's musical, *On Your Way, Riley!* (Stratford E15, April) and Martin Sherman's *Messiah* (Hampstead, December, transferred to the Aldwych, February 1983). As a member of Ray **Cooney**'s **Theatre of Comedy** Company at the Shaftesbury Theatre she appeared in a revival of Philip King's *See How They Run* (February 1984 and September 1984).

Film work includes *Up the Junction, The Knowledge, Dangerous Davies, St Trinian's,* and *Gumshoe.* Television appearances include a number of plays and her own series *Agony* and *Dissident.* In a radio interview with Sarah Kennedy ('The Colour Supplement', *Radio 4*, 22 September 1984) Maureen Lipman said, 'I am regarded as a comedienne and very often this is a great compliment. On the other hand, occasionally you think to yourself that it's rather like saying your son is going to be a doctor and he turns out to be an aroma therapist. Because it's funny, therefore it's somehow suspect. People think that life as a comedian is terribly funny. In fact it's very, very serious ... Most comics are deeply melancholy people. Most comics, I should think, are hell to live with because they are observing the human situation from a distance and not taking part in it.'

Littlewood, (Maudie) Joan

Born in London in 1914, the illegitimat daughter of a poor sixteen-year-old girl, sh attended schools in London and then went t RADA. She left before completing he studies and in 1933 founded a street theatr company called the Manchester Theatre o Action. Later she founded the Theatr Union and during the war made programme for the BBC. Considerably disillusioned an dissatisfied by the established theatre, sh founded a company in Manchester calle Theatre Workshop (1945) which sh devoted to the presentation of plays whic had some relevance to contemporary socia and political issues. Between 1945 and 195 the company toured the British Isles, Scandinavia, Germany and Czechoslovakia. I this period Littlewood developed th company as an **ensemble** which could creat original plays as well as fresh interpretation of stage classics. As a committed socialist an extremely talented director (partly influence by the ideas of Constantin Stanislavsky an Rudolf Laban) she evolved unique method of working with actors and staged productions which were radical departures fro existing post-war theatre. In an intervie with Tom Milne ('Working with Joan' *Encore*, 1960) Clive Goodwin said, 'I thin her greatest asset is her ability to draw peopl out, to give them confidence and build the up' and pointed out that her attempts to fin a style of presentation for a play was ' voyage of exploration for both director an actors, and sometimes even for the play wright ... she doesn't come to the firs rehearsal knowing all the answers.'

In October 1947 she directed *Operatio Olive Branch* (Rudolf Steiner Hall) and i May 1952, *Uranium 235* (Embassy Theatre in addition to her Theatre Workshop wor up to 1953. In this year she, her husban Ewan McColl and her artistic director Gerr Raffles moved Theatre Workshop to th Theatre Royal, Stratford East, in Londor and from its establishment and through 195 it presented original plays, new plays and adaptations including *The Fire Eaters*, *The Flying Doctor*, *The Cruel Daughters*, *The Good Soldier Schweik* and *The Prince and the Pauper*.

The 1955-6 season included some very fine productions of classics directed by Littlewood, including *Richard II* (in which she also played the Duchess of Gloucester), Jonson's *Volpone*, the anonymous *Arden of Faversham* and Marlowe's *Edward II*. She directed and played the title-role in the first English production of **Brecht**'s *Mother Courage and Her Children* (Devon Festival, Barnstaple, June 1955) and encouraged the work of the controversial and radical Irish playwright Brendan **Behan** by staging his *The Quare Fellow* (May 1956) and *The Hostage* (October 1958). Other important productions by Theatre Workshop were Shelagh **Delaney**'s *A Taste of Honey* (May 1958), Frank Norman and Lionel Bart's *Fings Ain't Wot They Used T'Be* (February 1959) and Stephen Lewis's *Sparrers Can't Sing* (March 1960).

Based on Littlewood's methods of directing through improvisation and miming to music, Theatre Workshop developed a remarkably successful play about the First World War called *Oh! What a Lovely War* (1963) for the re-opening of the company after its closure for two years. It was a documentary 'collage' in the manner of such work as had been done in the USA by the Federal Theatre Project and the Living Newspaper companies in the 1930s. It was also indebted to Italian Commedia dell'Arte and French Pierrot traditions and to **Brechtian** theatre techniques. Songs of the period were included and projected photographs and captions of the war. The total effect was an ironic and satirical undermining of the political and military authorities of the time. The play was made into a film in 1969.

Other productions of note were Littlewood's left-wing interpretation of *Henry IV* at the **Edinburgh Festival** in August 1964 and (at Stratford East), *A Kayf Up West* (March 1964), *Macbird* (April 1967), *The Marie Lloyd Story* (November 1967), *Up Your End* (October 1970), *The Projector* (December 1970), *The Londoners* (March 1972) and *So You Want to Be in Pictures?* (June 1973). From 1968 to 1975 Joan Littlewood also experimented with the creation of children's environments outside the Theatre Royal. In 1975 she left England for France where she has since lived and worked. Stanley Reynolds ('Oh What a Lovely', *Guardian*, 25 June 1984) has written of Littlewood's achievement: 'She it was who got rid of middle-class conventions. Not only in the plays, in the style of acting ... but also in the structure of the theatre itself. She, for example, got rid of the proscenium arch ... ditto the curtain, likewise fussy sets.'

Her flair for unconventional theatre, her radicalism and her anti-Establishment position-taking made Joan Littlewood a very necessary *enfant terrible* of post-war British theatre (Kenneth **Tynan** once said 'she would have been burnt as a witch a few years ago') and the contribution she and Theatre Workshop made is of unique and lasting importance.

Further Reading

Howard Goorney, *The Theatre Workshop Story*, Eyre Methuen, London, 1981.

Mike Coren, *Theatre Royal: 100 Years of Stratford East*, Quartet Books, London, 1985.

Livings, Henry

Born in Prestwich, Lancashire, on 20 September 1929, he was educated at Park View Primary School, Stand Grammar School, Prestwich, and Liverpool University (where he read Hispanic Studies). He left the latter at the end of his second year (1947) and served in the RAF (1948-50). He was married in 1957.

Livings began his career in the theatre as an actor, his roles including Curio and Sebastian in *Twelfth Night* (Century Mobile

Theatre, Hinkley, Leicestershire, February 1954) and Prisoner C in Joan **Littlewood**'s **Theatre Workshop** production of Brendan **Behan**'s *The Quare Fellow* (Theatre Royal, Stratford East, May 1956, Comedy, July 1956).

His chief plays are comedies and farces with a critical seriousness behind them, usually set against a Northern working-class background. They explore the humble, ordinary and ignored 'underdog' in conflict with authority but possessing qualities of resilience and indestructibility which allow him to win through. *Stop It, Whoever You Are* (Arts Theatre, February 1961) is about a factory lavatory attendant, aptly named William Perkin Warbeck (Perkin Warbeck, *c.* 1474-99, claiming to be Richard, son of Edward IV, challenged the Kingship of Henry VII, invaded Cornwall, proclaimed himself King and then was captured and hanged). William, having been accosted by two pugnacious apprentices and seduced by a girl, is falsely charged by the police. He takes revenge by sabotaging the public opening of a library by his landlord but ultimately suffers a mental breakdown (in which he thinks he is a clock) and dies. Towards the end of the play he communicates his thoughts and feelings to his wife during a seance. As with N.F. **Simpson**'s plays, farce becomes surreal fantasy (a feature of some other Livings plays too).

Subsequent comedies have included *Big Soft Nellie* (Century, October 1961, Theatre Workshop, Theatre Royal, Stratford East, November 1961) about a 'mother's boy' (Stanley) who is victimised by his workmates, *Nil Carborundum* (**Royal Shakespeare Company**, New Arts, April 1962) which presented life in an RAF kitchen (the title deriving from 'carborundum' industrial abrasive, thus suggesting something like 'don't let them grind you down') and *Eh?* (Royal Shakespeare Company, Aldwych, October 1964, Circle-in-the-Square, New York, October 1966) about a rather dim-witted boiler-man (Valentine Brose) who rebels against the factory in which he works, the play being largely set in a boiler-room where he grows enormous mushrooms. The lead was originally played by David **Warner**.

Other plays have included *Kelly's Eye* (**Royal Court**, June 1963) about violent tensions beneath the surface of a developing love relationship, *Honour and Offer* (Fortune, 1969), *Pongo Plays* (various venues, 1970) which were short sketches based on folk-tales and Japanese Kyogen plays, about one Sam Pongo, a sharp-witted Lancashire weaver, *The Ffinest Ffamily in the Land* (Lincoln Theatre Royal, 1970) about a family leading a life of isolation in a high-rise flat, and *Jug* (Nottingham Playhouse, 1975) an adaptation of Heinrich von Kleist's play *The Shattered Jug* (first produced in 1808).

Henry Livings has been associated with the radio show *The Northern Drift* and appeared in the television series *Get the Drift* and *Cribbins, Livings and Co.* He has written numerous television plays including *Arson Squad, Jack's Horrible Luck, A Right Crusader, Glorious Miles, There's No Room For You Here For a Start, Brainscrew, Don't Touch Him He Might Resent It, The Mayor's Charity, Three Days That Shook The Branch, We Had Some Happy Hours* and *Pennine Tales.*

In James Vinson's *Contemporary Dramatists* Henry Livings wrote 'I go mostly for laughter, because for me laughter is the shock reaction to a new way of looking at something: even a pun questions our security in the solidity of words.'

Further Reading

John Russell Taylor, 'Henry Livings', *Anger and After*, Methuen, London, 1983, pp. 286-300.

London Theatre Group

See **Berkoff, Steven**.

.owe, Stephen

Born in Nottingham in 1948 and educated at ocal schools, he acted in many amateur pro- uctions before attending Birmingham Jniversity where he read Drama and English. His first plays to be performed were *Cards* and *Stars* which formed the double- ill *Comic Pictures* (Theatre-in-the-Round, carborough, 1976) directed by Alan **Ayck- ourn**. He stayed on for two years in Scar- orough as a resident playwright at the 'heatre-in-the-Round where his controver- ial one-acter about rape, called *Shooting, Fishing and Riding* was shown in 1977. Also n 1977 came his play about working-class vomen at the close of the Second World Var, *Touched* (Nottingham Playhouse, 977), later shown in revival at the **Royal Court** Theatre (January 1981).

Lowe gained considerable recognition for is adaptation of Robert Tressell's *Ragged Trousered Philanthropists* which was created n collaboration with the **Joint Stock Theatre Group** and director William **Gaskill** for a 978 tour. *Glasshouses* (Royal Court, 'heatre Upstairs, April 1981) examined the ves of two Nottingham families who have recently moved to a council estate, *Tibetan Inroads* (Royal Court, September 1981) explored the Chinese 'take-over' of Tibet and *Strive* (Crucible, Sheffield, 1983) was about the return of a Falklands War soldier to his peace-campaigning girlfriend.

In 1984 Stephen Lowe was writer-in-residence at the Riverside Studios at Hammersmith where *Sea Change* was shown in July. It was an allegorical play about a group of people cruising through the Aegean Sea during the period of the Falklands conflict. The war between the sexes was paralleled with the war between nations in *Keeping Body and Soul Together* (Royal Court, Theatre Upstairs, November 1984). The connections between human relationships and politics seems recently to have emerged as a major preoccupation in Lowe's work. Stephen Lowe's plays for television include *Cries from a Watchtower* and *Shades.*

LX

'Electrics', that is, lighting and any electrical special effects.

M

McCowen, Alec (Alexander Duncan), OBE

Born in Tunbridge Wells on 26 May 1925, he attended Skinner's School, Tunbridge Wells, and studied for the theatre at the Royal Academy of Dramatic Art. His first professional work was at Macclesfield Repertory Theatre where he played Paddy in *The Next Best Thing* (August 1942). During the rest of the Second World War he was in repertory and ENSA, then afterwards continued in repertory, first appearing on the London stage as Maxim in Chekhov's *Ivanov* (Arts Theatre, April 1950). In the 1950s he played in many **West End** productions (and also appeared in John Osborne's *Look Back in Anger* at the **Royal Court** Theatre in 1956) and came to prominence when he joined the **Old Vic** Company in 1959, after an appearance at the 1958 **Edinburgh Festival** as Michael Claverton-Ferry in T.S. **Eliot**'s *The Elder Statesman* (transferred to Cambridge Theatre, September 1958).

Parts in the Old Vic 1959-60 season included Touchstone in *As You Like It*, Algernon in Wilde's *The Importance of Being Earnest*, Ford in *The Merry Wives of Windsor*, the Dauphin in Shaw's *St Joan* and the title-role in *Richard II*. In the following season he played Mercutio in *Romeo and Juliet*, Malvolio in *Twelfth Night* and Oberon in *A Midsummer Night's Dream*.

Joining the **Royal Shakespeare Company**, Alec McCowen's chief roles were Antipholus of Syracuse in *The Comedy of Errors* (Stratford-upon-Avon, September 1962, Aldwych, December 1962), the Fool in *King Lear* (Stratford, October 1962, Aldwych, December 1962) and Father Fontana in Rolf Hochhuth's *The Representative* (Aldwych, September 1963). He repeated his performances of Antipholus (Aldwych, December 1963) and the Fool (Aldwych February 1964) and toured in these role (British Council tour, USSR, Europe and th USA, February–June 1964).

After a period of free-lance work he gav a highly-praised performance as Rolfe an Hadrian in Peter Luke's *Hadrian the Sevent* (Repertory Theatre, Birmingham, May 1967 Mermaid, April 1968, Helen Hayes Theatre New York, January 1969). Subsequent part have included the title-role in *Hamle* (Repertory Theatre, Birmingham, Januar 1970), Philip in Christopher **Hampton**'s *Th Philanthropist* (Royal Court, August 1970 May Fair, September 1970, Ethel Barry-more, New York, March 1971), the title-rol (taking over from Alan **Bates**) in Simo **Gray**'s *Butley* (Criterion, August 1972) Martin Dysart in Peter **Shaffer**'s *Equus* (Ol Vic, July 1973), Professor Higgins in Shaw' *Pygmalion* (Albery, May 1974), Ben i Felicity Browne's *The Family Dance* (Criterion, June 1976) and a repeat performance o Dysart in *Equus* (Helen Hayes, New York February 1977).

In 1977 Alec McCowen was with th **Prospect Theatre Company** at the Edinburgh Festival, playing Antony in *Anton and Cleopatra* (transferring Old Vic, November 1977) and in 1978 he devised and gav solo performances of *St Mark's Gospe* (Riverside Studios, Mermaid, Comedy, an Marymount Manhatten and Playhous Theatres, New York).

At the **National Theatre** he appeared in double-bill of Terence **Rattigan**'s *Th Browning Version* and *Harlequinade* (Ma 1980) and later, at the Mermaid, he playe Hitler in Christopher Hampton's adaptatio of George Steiner's *The Portage to San Crist obal of A.H.* (February 1982). In Octobe 1982 he took *Saint Mark's Gospel* to th USA and in May 1984 played the title-rol in Brian Clark's *Kipling* (Mermaid).

Film work has included *The Cruel Sea*, *Frenzy*, *Travels with My Aunt* and *Stevie*. McCowen has appeared in many television plays, including Tom **Stoppard**'s television film *Squaring the Circle* (1984) and the series *Mr Palfrey of Westminster* (1984), in which he played the title-role. He is also in demand as a radio performer, has written two volumes of autobiography and published his stage version of St Mark's Gospel under the title of *Personal Mark* (1984).

Further Reading

Alec McCowen, *Young Gemini*, Elm Tree Books, London, 1979.

Alec McCowen, *Double Bill*, Elm Tree Books, London, 1980.

McEwan, Geraldine (*née* McKeown)

Born on 9 May 1932 in Old Windsor, she was educated at Windsor County School. She appeared in a number of small parts at the Theatre Royal, Windsor, whilst still at school (her first appearance being an attendant of Hippolyta in *A Midsummer Night's Dream*, October 1946), took an office job for six months and then (at the age of 16), became an Assistant Stage Manager with the Windsor Repertory Company with whom she also appeared in plays. In 1951 she appeared as Christine Deed in John Dighton's *Who Goes There!* which transferred to the Vaudeville Theatre (April 1951) and made her an overnight star.

She married Hugh Cruttwell in 1953 and after a number of **West End** performances joined the **Shakespeare Memorial Theatre** Company at Stratford-upon-Avon in July 1956, playing the Princess of France in *Love's Labour's Lost*. The following year she played Frankie Adams in Carson McCullers's *The Member of the Wedding* (**Royal Court**, February 1957) and Jean Rice in John **Osborne**'s *The Entertainer* (Palace, December 1957). Returning to Stratford-upon-Avon she played Olivia in *Twelfth Night*, Marina in *Pericles* and Hero in *Much Ado About Nothing* (Shakespeare Memorial Theatre, 1958 season, Moscow and Leningrad, December 1958). For the 1961 Stratford season she played Beatrice in *Much Ado About Nothing* and Ophelia in *Hamlet*. A number of parts in London and abroad followed, the chief of which were Jenny Acton in Giles Cooper's *Everything in the Garden* (Arts, March 1962), Lady Teazle in Sheridan's *The School for Scandal* (Haymarket, October 1962, Majestic, New York, January 1963), Doreen and Belinda in Peter **Shaffer**'s double-bill *The Private Ear* and *The Public Eye* (Wimbledon, September 1963, Morosco Theatre, New York, October 1963, and USA tour) and Fay in Joe **Orton**'s *Loot* (tour, February 1965).

At the **Chichester Festival** Theatre Geraldine McEwan played A Lady in John **Arden**'s *Armstrong's Last Goodnight* (**National Theatre** Company, July 1965) and later played Angelica in Congreve's *Love For Love* (National Theatre Company tour, Moscow and Berlin, September 1965). Subsequently with the National Theatre at the **Old Vic** her parts included Raymonde in John **Mortimer**'s version of Feydeau's farce *A Flea in Her Ear* (1966, also at the Queen's), Alice in Strindberg's *The Dance of Death* (1967), Queen Anne in **Brecht**'s *Edward the Second* (1968), Victoria in W. Somerset Maugham's *Home and Beauty* (1968), Millamant in Congreve's *The Way of the World* (1969) and Vittoria Corombona in Webster's *The White Devil* (1969).

Roles in the 1970s included Alkmena in Giraudoux's *Amphitryon 38* (National Theatre Company at the New, July 1971), Diana in Peter **Nichols**'s *Chez Nous* (Globe, February 1974) and Lulu in Feydeau's *Look After Lulu* (Chichester Festival, 1978, Haymarket, October 1978).

In 1980 she played in a Terence **Rattigan** double-bill, *The Browning Version* and

Harlequinade (National Theatre, Lyttleton, May) and Vanbrugh's *The Provoked Wife* (National Theatre, Lyttleton, October), and in 1983 she was Mrs Malaprop in Sheridan's *The Rivals* (National, Olivier, April) and took part in Hart and Kaufman's *You Can't Take It With You* (National, Lyttleton, August). In 1983 at the National and elsewhere she also played in her own solo entertainment, *Two Inches of Ivory,* which she devised from the writings of Jane Austen.

She has appeared in many television plays, including *Hopcraft into Europe, Dear Love, The Statue and the Rose, The Prime of Miss Jean Brodie,* and *The Barchester Chronicles.*

In an interview with Gordon Gow (*Plays and Players,* March 1974), Geraldine McEwan commented on acting, 'The most exciting acting one sees — and does — is bound to have a sort of abandon to it. Not without a certain control ... The seed of a character, the centre of it must be your own. Nobody else can give it to you. And without it you're kidding yourself and everybody else ... but you never get away with it to yourself.'

Further Reading

Peter Roberts, 'From ASM to National Star', interview with Geraldine McEwan, *Plays and Players,* August 1983, pp. 9-14.

McGrath, John (Peter)

Born in Birkenhead, Cheshire, on 1 June 1935, he was educated at Alun Grammar School and St John's College, University of Oxford, where he read English. Between 1953 and 1955 he did his National Service with the British Army. His first play *A Man Has Two Fathers* (OUDS, Oxford Playhouse, 1958), about the imperialistic struggle between Russia and the United States of America, was written in his third year as a student at Oxford. It approached some of the characteristics of the **Theatre of the Absurd** in its form and allegorical handling of the dramatic situation. McGrath wrote for the television series *Z Cars* (other writers were Alan **Plater** and John Hopkins) and worked as a writer at the **Royal Court** Theatre where he was a joint author with John **Arden** and others, of *Actors' Rehearsal Group* (October 1958) one of the directors of which was Ann **Jellicoe**. *Events While Guarding the Bofors Gun* (Hampstead Theatre Club, 1966), about a self-protecting NCO on his last night in Germany, confronted by a suicidal Irish soldier, was well received and brought McGrath to greater recognition. The play was eventually filmed as *The Bofors Gun,* starring Nicol **Williamson**, David **Warner** and Ian **Holm**.

Random Happenings in the Hebrides (Edinburgh, 1970) was a 'chronicle' play about a young man who gradually grows towards political awareness. McGrath worked for a short period with the Liverpool Everyman Theatre where productions of his plays included *Soft or a Girl* (1971). In 1971 he founded the 7.84 Theatre Company, thus named because of a statistic published in *The Economist* in 1966 which stated that 7 per cent of the population of Great Britain owned 84 per cent of the capital wealth. McGrath comments in a textual note of 1974, 'Although this proportion may have fluctuated marginally over the years, we continue to use it because it points to the basic economic structure of the society we live in, from which all the political, social and cultural structures grow.' In 1973 a Scottish 7.84 Theatre Company was also set up. 7.84 (England) began its work at the **Edinburgh Festival** in August 1971 with McGrath's *Trees in the Wind* (about three girls living in a flat) and Trevor **Griffiths**'s *Apricots* and *Thermidor.* Afterwards the company went on tour and had a second tour in early 1972, later followed by tours of Trevor Griffiths's *Occupations,* McGrath's *Underneath,* John **Arden** and Margaretta D'Arcy's *The Ballygombeen Bequest* and McGrath's trilogy of one-act plays *Plugged In* (May-December 1972), all directed by McGrath. In a 1983 interview McGrath, commenting on this period of 7:84, stated: 'We were trying to produce the kind of *theatre of the left* that would be able not just to go into a community centre and have fun with the audience, but would also contest the values of the theatre itself.'

As well as developing and directing the work of 7:84 McGrath continued writing for the Liverpool Everyman Theatre which presented his play *Fish in the Sea* (1973) partly based on **Brecht**'s *The Caucasian Chalk Circle* and Arden's *The Island of the Mighty*. It was about romantic love and focused on the life of a family. The form of the play was that of popular entertainment and included rock music, song lyrics, jokes and variety show elements.

Perhaps the most successful play developed by John McGrath and 7:84 (Scotland) was *The Cheviot, the Stag and the Black, Black Oil* (April 1973) which in form drew upon the folk tradition of the Scottish 'ceilidh' community entertainment. It toured throughout the seven crofting counties including the Orkneys and many locations in southern Scotland, travelling 17,000 miles and playing to over 30,000 people. The play is essentially a chronicle of Highland history, in particular focusing on the nineteenth-century 'clearances' of land and tenants (documented in such books as John Prebble's *The Highland Clearances*) by such wealthy aristocrats as the Duke of Sutherland, in order to develop the Cheviot sheep-farming industry. The experiences of whole communities being violently driven out of their homes to the coastal areas was paralleled in the play with the contemporary exploitation of northern Scottish communities through the development of the off-shore oil industry, both the landlords of the clearances and the coming of the oil moguls being seen as symptomatic of a cruelly oppressive capitalist imperialism at its most corrupt. 'Socialism, and the planned exploitation of natural resources for the benefit of all humanity, is the alternative the play calls for ... socialism that measures progress by human happiness rather than by shareholders' dividends, that liberates minds rather than enslaving them', wrote McGrath in a note to the published text (1974).

Other 7:84 plays written and developed by McGrath have included *Yobbo Nowt* (1975 tour) and *Blood Red Roses* (Edinburgh Festival and Scottish tour, 1980, London 1981). In October 1984 7:84 (England) presented Miles Malleson and Harry Brook's *Six Men of Dorset* at the Shaw Theatre and in January 1985 presented McGrath's play about the 1984-5 miners' strike *The Garden of England* (Shaw Theatre and tour).

McGrath and his work with the two 7:84 companies have achieved the creation of a popular socialist theatre in which, as he put it in an interview in *Theatre Quarterly* (Summer 1975), the theatre is about self-evident truths 'being stated publicly, socially, in an entertaining way ... uncovering and giving expression to what is there, and to the realities of people's lives'.

Further Reading

John McGrath, *A Good Night Out. Popular Theatre: Audience, Class and Form*, Eyre Methuen, London, 1981.

Catherine Itzin, 'John McGrath', in Simon Trussler (ed.), *New Theatre Voices of the Seventies*, Eyre Methuen, London, 1981, pp. 98-109.

McKellen, Ian (Murray)

Born on 25 May 1939 he attended Wigan Grammar School, Bolton School and graduated from St Catherine's College, Cambridge in 1961. He had given some very successful performances when a student (for example as Sir Toby Belch) and after graduation went straight into the company at the Belgrade Theatre, Coventry, to play Roper in Robert **Bolt**'s *A Man For All Seasons* (1961). He gained repertory experience at Ipswich (1962-3), in particular playing the title-roles in John **Osborne**'s *Luther* and Shakespeare's *Henry V*. In repertory at Nottingham Playhouse (1963-4) his parts included Arthur in an adaptation of Sillitoe's novel *Saturday Night and Sunday Morning* and the title-role in *Sir Thomas More* (June 1964). His first appearance in London was as Godfrey in James **Saunders**'s *A Scent of Flowers* (Duke of York's, September 1964) and a year later he joined the **National Theatre** Company at the **Old Vic** and played Claudio in *Much Ado About Nothing* (February 1965), the Evangelist in John **Arden**'s *Armstrong's Last Goodnight* (**Chichester Festival**, July 1965) and Captain de Feonix in Arthur Pinero's *Trelawny of the 'Wells'* (Chichester Festival, July 1965). He gave a memorable and much acclaimed performance as Alvin in Donald Howarth's play *A Lily in Little India* (Hampstead, November 1965 and St Martin's, January 1966). Another success in a contemporary play was the part of Andrew Cobham in **Wesker**'s *Their Very Own and Golden City* (**Royal Court**, May 1966) and in September 1966 he played in *O'Flaherty* and *The Man of Destiny* at the Mermaid Theatre.

McKellen made his debut in New York, on Broadway, as Leonidik in Arbuzov's *The Promise* (November 1967) and returned to London to play in Peter **Shaffer**'s double-bill *The White Liars* and *Black Comedy* (Lyric, February 1968).

His work with the **Prospect Theatre Company** from this period established McKellen's reputation as one of the best actors of his generation, in particular his performances in the title-roles of *Richard II* (November 1968 tour and again in 1969) and Marlowe's *Edward II* (August 1969–January 1970). He directed his first production, *The Prime of Miss Jean Brodie*, at the Liverpool Playhouse in May 1969.

In October 1970 McKellen toured as Captain Plume in Farquhar's *The Recruiting Officer* and Corporal Hill in Wesker's *Chips With Everything* (Cambridge Theatre Company tour) and then toured with the Prospect Theatre Company in the title-role of *Hamlet* (March–July, 1971).

McKellen developed a great enthusiasm for regional tours and touring company principles in the early 1970s and for the **Edinburgh Festival** in 1972 helped to found the Actors' Company which was run on democratic lines whereby the actors each received the same pay, could choose their own plays, shared equal billing, and all had the same opportunities to play leading roles. With the Actors' Company on tour McKellen played the page-boy in *Ruling the Roost*, Giovanni in *'Tis Pity She's a Whore* and the Prince in Iris Murdoch's *The Three Arrows* (all 1972). Again with this company he played Michael in Chekhov's *The Wood Demon* and a footman in Congreve's *The Way of the World* (both at Edinburgh Festival and on tour 1973). He joined the **Royal Shakespeare Company** at the Edinburgh Festival in 1974, playing the title-role in Marlowe's *Dr Faustus* (which transferred to the Aldwych in September 1974), subsequently played Aubrey Bagot in Shaw's *Too Good to be True* (Aldwych, October 1975), and in the Stratford-upon-Avon 1976 season took the roles of Romeo in *Romeo and Juliet*, Leontes in *The Winter's Tale* and Macbeth. In the next season he again played the title-role in *Macbeth* and also Face in Jonson's *The Alchemist*.

He created the role of Alex in Tom **Stoppard**'s play for actors and symphony orchestra *Every Good Boy Deserves Favour* (Royal Festival Hall, July 1977) and at the 1977 Edinburgh Festival presented his second solo show *Acting Shakespeare* (his first having been *Words, Words, Words*, Edinburgh 1966).

In *Acting Shakespeare* McKellen demonstrates what the active and shifting consciousness of a performer of some of Shakespeare's roles might consist of. As Lionel Gracey-Whitman puts it (*Plays and Players*, April 1984) McKellen is 'like the

Shakespearean character speaking directly to the audience, sharing with them his innermost thoughts', as he shares with the audience 'the inner workings of the actor in performance'. In 1976 McKellen observed that at its most rewarding acting involves 'an intense combination of intellect, imagination and hard work, belying the popular distorted image of dressing-up, booming voices and shrieking exhibitionism'.

With the RSC at the Aldwych (1977-8 season) he again played Romeo and Face. He also took the parts of Bernick in Ibsen's *Pillars of the Community* and Langevin in **Brecht**'s *Days of the Commune.* At the Warehouse he again played Macbeth (September 1977) and in 1978 directed an RSC tour which included him playing Sir Toby Belch in *Twelfth Night* and Andrei in Chekhov's *Three Sisters.* McKellen wrote at the time that the tour had been planned as an 'experiment in touring' that would continue 'where the RSC's Theatregoround left off'. At the Royal Court Theatre he played Max in Martin Sherman's *Bent* (May 1979), and in 1981 played D.H. Lawrence in the film *The Priest of Love.* After touring his *Acting Shakespeare* and filming in the United States he returned in 1984 to play in Otway's *Venice Preserved,* Chekhov's *Wild Honey* and Shakespeare's *Coriolanus* at the National Theatre in the same year forming an actors' company with Edward **Petherbridge** for this theatre.

Further Reading

Ian McKellen, 'The Spirit of the National Theatre', *Plays and Players,* April 1976.
Lionel Grace-Whitman and Ian McKellen, 'Return by Popular Demand', *Plays and Players,* April 1984.

McKern, Leo (Reginald McKern)

Born in Sydney, Australia, on 16 March 1920, he attended Sydney Technical High School and became an apprentice in electrical engineering. He went into commerical art for a period and served in the Army Engineering Corps in Victoria, Australia, during the Second World War. He also began acting with May Holingworth's amateur company in Sydney and acted in radio drama. In 1946 he came to England for the love of an Australian actress, Jane Holland, to whom he was married in that same year. In England he took various jobs (including that of a porter at Sainsbury's) but in 1947 acted with the Combined Services Entertainment Unit (CSEU) on a tour of Germany and with an Arts Council tour of Welsh and Yorkshire mining areas (for which tour he played Simon in Tony **Guthrie**'s production of Molière's *The Miser*).

In October 1949 he joined the **Old Vic** Company to play the Forester in *Love's Labour's Lost* (New Theatre). Later parts included Guildenstern in *Hamlet* (February 1950) to Michael **Redgrave**'s Hamlet, Simon in *The Miser* (January 1950), the Confectioner in Chekhov's *The Wedding* (March 1951) and the Fool in *King Lear* (March 1952) to Stephen Murray's Lear.

With the **Shakespeare Memorial Theatre** Company in 1953 he toured Australia, his parts including Iago in *Othello* and Touchstone in *As You Like It.* After further parts with the company at Stratford-upon-Avon in 1954 he returned to London and appeared as Toad in *Toad of Toad Hall* (Princes, December 1954). Subsequent successes have included Tyepkin in *Brouhaha* (Aldwych, August 1958), the title-role in Marcel Achard's *Rollo* (Strand, October 1959) and the Common Man in Robert **Bolt**'s *A Man for All Seasons* (Globe, July 1960). He directed *The Shifting Heart* (Duke of York's, September 1959) by the Australian playwright Richard Beynon.

He joined the Old Vic Company for its closing season (1962-3), playing Peer in Ibsen's *Peer Gynt,* Subtle in Jonson's *The Alchemist* and Iago in *Othello.* For the opening of the new Nottingham Playhouse he was Menenius in *Coriolanus* (December 1963) and in 1965 was Baron Bolligrew in Bolt's play for children *The Thwarting of Baron Bolligrew* (Aldwych, December). The following year he played the title-role in Jonson's *Volpone* (Oxford Playhouse, September 1966, subsequently the Garrick, January 1967).

In 1970 Leo McKern and his family went on a holiday expedition in a touring van through the outback of Australia. In 1971 he appeared as Captain Bligh in *The Man Who Shot the Albatross* (Melbourne Theatre Company) by the Australian playwright Ray Lawler. On returning to England he played Shylock in *The Merchant of Venice* (Oxford Playhouse, summer 1973), Keleman in Molnar's *The Wolf* (Oxford Playhouse, summer 1973, Apollo, October 1973, Queen's, November 1973), Vanya in Chekhov's *Uncle Vanya* (Royal Exchange, Manchester, 1978), the title-role in *Rollo* (Royal Exchange, Manchester, March 1980), Matt Quinlan in Frank Gilroy's *The Housekeeper* (Apollo, February 1982) and Leon Saint-Pé in Michael **Frayn**'s adaptation of Anouilh's comedy *Number One* (Queen's Theatre, April 1984).

Leo McKern has become nationally popular as Rumpole in John **Mortimer**'s television series *Rumpole of the Bailey.* Other television work includes roles in *The Tea Party* by Harold **Pinter**, *Reilly — Ace of Spies, King Lear* (in which he played Gloucester to **Olivier**'s Lear) and *Monsignor Quixote.* Filmwork includes *A Man For All Seasons, Ryan's Daughter, Help, The French Lieutenant's Woman* and a full-length film of *Rumpole of the Bailey.*

Leo McKern is a rugged, heavily-built actor with a voice of rich tonal qualities. His view of acting was summarised when he stated (in *Just Resting*, 1983) that 'acting is a personal mystery about which the less said the better both for ourselves and the public ... it is a private indulgence that one hopes will be noticed'.

Further Reading

Leo McKern, *Just Resting*, Methuen, London, 1983.

Marie Tempest

A door hinge which can be altered by a screw lever adjustment in order to prevent the door swinging open of its own accord due to the **raked** incline of a stage. Named after Dame Marie Tempest (1864-1962) who insisted on their use in one of her performances.

Marowitz, Charles

Born in New York City on 26 January 1934, he came to England in the 1950s and studied at the London Academy of Music and Dramatic Art (LAMDA). Before coming to England he had already directed plays in New York. His first London production was Gogol's *Marriage* (Unity, 1958). In 1962 Marowitz was an assistant director for Peter **Brook**'s production of *King Lear* with the **Royal Shakespeare Company** (Stratford-upon-Avon, 1962 season) and in the following year he worked with Brook to form an **ensemble** group of actors (associated with the RSC) to experiment with some ideas about acting and theatre influenced by the theories of Antonin Artaud in *The Theatre and Its Double* (1938). The result was a five-week '**Theatre of Cruelty**' season at the LAMDA Theatre Club in 1964 and a production of Peter Weiss's *Marat/Sade* which was eventually presented by the main company of the RSC (Aldwych, August 1964) under Brook's direction. In his 'Notes on the Theatre of Cruelty' (1966) Marowitz stated: 'The quest for Artaud, if it's lucky, will not simply discover sounds, cries, groans and gestures, but new areas that never even occurred to Artaud ... the existential horror behind all social and psychological façades.' Marowitz's experiments with Artaud's ideas were a help in finding 'a new way of generating he actor into action, the playwright into neaning, and the public into consciousness'.

In 1966 Marowitz began presenting a eries of radical adaptations of Shakespear-an tragedies in the form of fragmented collage' productions. The first was *Hamlet* LAMDA Theatre Club), based on 'the ssumption … that there was a smear of *Hamlet* in everyone's collective unconscious, nd that it was possible to predicate a per-ormance on that mythic memory'. In 1968 e opened his own theatre, the Open Space, n Tottenham Court Road (in 1977 moving o Euston Road). It had experimental flexible taging and audience seating which were ften used creatively to alter the relationships etween audiences and actors. At the Open pace Marowitz presented *Macbeth* (1969) nd *An Othello* (June 1972), the latter intro-ucing strong elements of the 'Black Power' novement. Further Shakespeare adaptations vere *The Taming of the Shrew* (1973), *Measure for Measure* (1975) and *Variations n 'The Merchant of Venice'* (April 1977). Other plays directed by Marowitz at the Open Space included Sam Shepard's *The Tooth of Crime* (July 1972) co-directed with Walter Donohue, Büchner's *Woyzeck* February 1973) which Marowitz also dapted, *Artaud at Rodez* (December 1975) which he wrote, Frank Marcus's adaptation f Schnitzler's *Anatol* (February 1976), Andrew Carr's *Hanratty in Hell* (July 1976), Philip Magdalany's *Boo Hoo* (July 1978) nd Strindberg's *The Father* (November 979) which Marowitz also adapted. This atter production was the final one at the Open Space which had to close down hrough lack of funds. The company con-inued and presented work such as Jarry's *Ubu* plays (1980) and *Hedda* (Round House, 1981) based on Ibsen's *Hedda Gabler*, but went bankrupt in 1981. Besides irecting and adapting plays Marowitz was he editor of *Encore* theatre magazine.

Of the building up of an ensemble ompany of actors Marowitz has written: The building of any company sense demands the construction of those delicate vertebrae and interconnecting tissues that transform an aggregation of actors into an ensemble … it means, in rare cases, being linked by a group rhythm … the sort of thing that exists between certain kith and kin, certain husbands and wives, certain kinds of lovers or bitter enemies.'

Further Reading

Charles Marowitz, *The Act of Being*, Secker and Warburg, London, 1978.

Charles Marowitz, *Confessions of a Counterfeit Critic*, Methuen, London, 1973.

Masking

When (i) one or more actors stand in front of another actor and block the audience's view of him, or (ii) **Flats** and **Legs** are attached backstage of doors to suggest adjoining rooms or entrance lobbies.

Massey, Anna

Born in Thakeham, Sussex, on 11 August 1937, the daughter of actor Raymond (Hart) Massey, she was educated in London, New York, Switzerland, Paris and Rome. Her first stage appearance was as Jane in William Douglas **Home**'s *The Reluctant Debutante* (Theatre Royal, Brighton, and Cambridge Theatre, London, May 1955, Henry Miller, New York, October 1956). She was Monica in the original performance of T.S. **Eliot**'s *The Elder Statesman* at the **Edinburgh Festival** (Lyceum, Edinburgh, August 1958, transferred Cambridge Theatre, September 1958), Annie in William Gibson's *The Miracle Worker* (Royalty, March 1961) and Lady Teazle in Sheridan's *The School for Scandal* (Haymarket, April 1962).

Other important roles have included Jennifer in Shaw's *The Doctor's Dilemma* (Haymarket, May 1963), Virginia Crawford in M.

Bradley-Dyne's *The Right Honourable Gentleman* (Her Majesty's, May 1964), Laura Wingfield in Tennessee Williams's *The Glass Menagerie* (Yvonne Arnaud, Guildford, October 1965, Haymarket, December 1965), Jean Brodie in Jay Presson Allen's *The Prime of Miss Jean Brodie* (Wyndham's, November 1966) taking over the part from Vanessa **Redgrave**, Candida in Hugh and Margaret Williams's comedy *The Flip Side* (Apollo, August 1967) and Ophelia in *Hamlet* (Birmingham Repertory Theatre, January 1970).

In May 1971 she appeared at the **Royal Court** Theatre as Ann in David **Hare**'s *Slag* and in February 1975 for the **National Theatre** at the **Old Vic** as Ariadne in Shaw's *Heartbreak House.* With the **Royal Shakespeare Company** she was Gwendoline in Charles **Wood**'s *Jingo* (Aldwych, August 1975) and at the Royal Court Theatre was the First Woman in Samuel **Beckett**'s *Play* (May 1976).

As an actress with the National Theatre her roles have included Marianne in Simon **Gray**'s *Close of Play* (Lyttleton, May 1979), Xenia in Edward **Bond**'s *Summer* (Cottesloe, January 1982), Miss Prism in Wilde's *The Importance of Being Earnest* (Lyttleton, September 1982), Voice Two in *Family Voices* and Pauline in *A Kind of Alaska* which were two plays from Harold **Pinter**'s trilogy *Other Places* (Cottesloe, October 1982).

Anna Massey's work in films includes *Gideon's Day, Peeping Tom, Bunny Lake is Missing, The Looking Glass War, David Copperfield, De Sade, Frenzy, A Doll's House, Sweet William, The Corn is Green* and *Five Days One Summer.* She has appeared in numerous plays on television including *The Mayor of Casterbridge, Rebecca, You're Not Watching Me, Mummy, Journey into the Shadows, Pity in History* and *Hotel du Lac.*

Massey, Daniel (Raymond)

Son of the Canadian actor Raymond Massey (who worked mostly in the British theatre before the Second World War), he was born in London on 10 October 1933 and educated at Eton and King's College, Cambridge. He was in the Cambridge Footlights Club for the revue *Anything May* (June 1956) and made his professional début as Terry in *Peril at End House* (Connaught, Worthing, July 1956).

His chief roles have included Charlie in Wolf Mankowitz's musical *Make Me An Offer* (Theatre Royal, Stratford East, October 1959, New, December 1959), Charles Surface in Sheridan's *The School for Scandal* (Haymarket, April 1962), George Holyoake in John **Osborne**'s *A Subject of Scandal and Concern* (Nottingham Playhouse, November 1962), Mark Antony in *Julius Caesar* (**Royal Court**, April 1964), Beliaev in Turgenev's *A Month in the Country* (Yvonne Arnaud, Guildford, May 1965), Captain Absolute in Sheridan's *The Rivals* (Haymarket, October 1966), John Worthing in Wilde's *The Importance of Being Earnest* (Haymarket, February 1968), Abelard in Ronald Millar's *Abelard and Heloise* (Wyndham's, December 1970), Tusenbach in Chekhov's *Three Sisters* and Tom Wrench in Pinero's *Trelawney of the 'Wells'* (both for Cambridge Theatre Company tour, October 1971).

In October 1976 Massey played the title role in *Othello* (Nottingham Playhouse) and subsequently played Rosmer in Ibsen's *Rosmersholm* (Haymarket, October 1977). He joined the **National Theatre** company in 1978 and for it has played the name-part in Von Horvath's *Don Juan Comes Back from the War* (April 1978), Macduff in *Macbeth* (Olivier, June 1978), Robert in Harold **Pinter**'s *Betrayal* (November 1978), John Tanner in Shaw's *Man and Superman* (Olivier, January 1981), Captain Don Alvaro de Ataide in Calderon's *The Mayor of Zalamea* (Cottesloe, August 1981, Olivier, Decembe

1981) and Argan in Molière's *The Hypochondriac* (Olivier, October 1981).

Soon after this period with the National Theatre Daniel Massey joined the **Royal Shakespeare Company** with whom his parts have included Duke Vincentio in *Measure for Measure* (Stratford-upon-Avon, 1983 season, Barbican, April 1984), Sir Andrew Aguecheek in *Twelfth Night* (Stratford, 1983 season, Barbican, August 1984), Nikolai in Stephen **Poliakoff**'s *Breaking the Silence* (Barbican, Pit, November 1984) and Henry Trebell in Granville-Barker's *Waste* (Barbican, Pit, January 1985).

Film work includes *Girls at Sea, Upstairs and Downstairs, The Entertainer, The Queen's Guard, Go to Blazes, Moll Flanders, Star, The Incredible Sarah, The Cat and the Canary, Escape to Victory* and *The Devil's Advocate.* Television appearances include *The Roads to Freedom, The Golden Bowl, Wings of Song, Able's Will* and *Heartbreak House.*

Mercer, David

Born in Wakefield on 27 June 1928, the son of an engine driver, he left school at the age of 14 and trained and worked for three years as a laboratory technician in a hospital and between 1945 and 1948 served as a Royal Navy laboratory technician. On leaving the Navy he went to King's College, Newcastle-upon-Tyne to study chemistry but after six months changed to study fine art, which he did for four years (under Lawrence Gowing) and graduated in 1953. In the same year he married Dafna Hamdi.

While living briefly in Paris after his graduation he began writing and on returning to England in 1955 he took a job as a supply teacher in London schools and from 1959 to 1961 he taught at Barrett Street Technical College. In about 1960 he had something of a nervous breakdown at the same time as his marriage was in difficulty and he was treated at Tavistock Clinic. In 1962 he became a full-time writer.

Mercer's Northern working-class background, experiences in hospitals and schools, his treatment for psychiatric disorder and the death of his mother in 1968, have all in their ways shaped the dramatic preoccupations of his stage plays, television dramas (of which he has written many) and film work. Though disillusioned in the late 1960s Mercer earlier leant towards Communism and political and social questions in his plays, mixed with an exploration of the psychological problems of the individual — 'what I call that synthesis between individual fulfilment and social change', he told Ronald Hayman in an interview (*Playback 2*, 1973). His award-winning film *Morgan — A Suitable Case for Treatment* (1965), which starred David **Warner**, followed the unconventional behaviour of an eccentric, restless, freedom-loving young man at odds with a rigid and constraining society — a society which treats him as 'insane' rather than a person attempting to achieve full individuality. The powerful image of Morgan in a strait-jacket and dangling from a crane in the final scene, stands as a penetrating comment on the feelings of a whole generation about society in the 1960s.

Mercer's first stage play was *The Buried Man* (Library Theatre, Manchester, 1962), about a young couple who attempt to free themselves from the constraints of their seemingly immutable family backgrounds of fishing and mining folk. *The Governor's Lady* (Radio broadcast, 1960, **RSC** at the Aldwych, 1965) is a one-act fantasy about a colonial governor who turns into a gorilla and is murdered by his wife — the governor, as Mercer once stated, 'being only a projection of his Lady's less avowable suppressed desires and instincts'. His next stage play was *Ride a Cock Horse* (Nottingham, then Piccadilly, June 1965) which explores the destructive relationships between a successful writer of working-class origins and his wife, his mistress and a prostitute. After his next play, *Belcher's Luck* (RSC, Aldwych, November 1966), came his best-known stage plays, *After Haggerty* (RSC, Aldwych, February 1970, Criterion, April 1971) and *Flint* (Criterion, May 1970). *Flint* is a farcical melodrama about an agnostic and lecherous vicar, another anarchic figure trapped in a conventional institution (as was Morgan), who eventually commits suicide. *After Haggerty* is episodic in form, and employs flashbacks and sharp cuts (as often seen in television drama) to represent the memories of two characters, Bernard, a retired drama critic, and an American girl who has come to Bernard's flat in search of Haggerty (who never appears on the stage but whose presence is felt much of the time and whose death, fighting in Africa, is announced towards the end of the play). The play depicts these characters', and Bernard's father's, retreat from reality into the irrevocable past. *White Poem* (produced in London for the Sharpeville commemoration in 1970) was a short monologue for a white Rhodesian racialist.

In the late 1960s and early 1970s Mercer suggested, on a number of occasions, that he suffered great personal upheavals and was disillusioned with most political solutions to the problems faced by individuals. He felt he needed to concentrate more on the inner lives of his characters: 'What I feel, having entered my forties, is on the one hand a steady, consistent grief for all of us, for the monumental disasters we've made of creating societies on this planet. And coupled with this grief, I think, is a feeling of compassion which can, at times, amount almost to a sense of joy.' He began to deepen his explorations with *Let's Murder Vivaldi* (television 1968, King's Head 1972) about the moral consequences of infidelity and violence in the behaviour of two couples, and *Duck Song* (RSC, Aldwych, February 1974) which is centrally concerned with the effects upon middle-aged people of an intensified awareness of the fact of death. The first half of the play is set in the house of a wealthy dilettante artist where a number of people meet, but in the second half all of the furniture is removed — all the known and secure physical reality — and the characters' monologues deepen into self-assessment as the sense of an inescapable mortality grows. As Mercer said in an interview at the time of writing *Duck Song* (*Theatre Quarterly*, Vol. III, No. 9, 1973), 'When you get into your forties, you begin to have a relationship to death which is qualitatively different from when you're a younger person ... I would hope to develop one or two comedies of death, and comedies of relationship to death. I think death is something I've got to deal with now.' *Cousin Vladimir* (RSC, Aldwych, September 1978) concerns a Soviet Russian refugee who comes to a Britain of declining moral values in the 1970s. *Then and Now* (Hampstead) appeared in 1979 and his last stage play, *No Limits to Love* (RSC, Aldwych), about an eternal triangle of relationships between an Oxford history don, Edward, a professional cellist, and his wife Marna, was performed in 1980. David Mercer died in August 1980.

Mercer was a distinguished and prolific writer of plays for television. His large output includes the trilogy *The Generations* (1961, 1962, 1963), *A Suitable Case for Treatment* (1962), *And Did Those Feet?* (1965), *In Two Minds* (1967), *The Parachute* (1968), *On the Eve of Publication* (1968), *The Cellar and the Almond Tree* (1970), *The Bankrupt* (1972), *An Afternoon at the Festival* (1973), *Find Me* (1974), *Huggy Bear* (1976), *Shooting the Chandelier* (1977) and *The Ragazza* (1978). Films include *Morgan — A Suitable Case for Treatment* (1965) and *Providence* (1977).

Inevitably, since the medium is so naturalistic, his television plays have been less inclined to create and explore comic fantasy than his stage plays. Fantastic and formally risky though many of the stage plays are, Mercer is quoted (in Gordon Snell's *Book of Theatre Quotes*, 1982) as stating that for him the theatre is a place for the 'discovery and the demonstration of the truth about what's happening in a society at a given time ... I think that the theatre is concerned with reality'.

It should be added, of course, that 'reality' does not always mean only social and political reality.

Further Reading

Ronald Hayman, 'David Mercer', *Playback 2*, Davis-Poynter, London, 1973, pp. 122-44.

John Russell Taylor, 'David Mercer', *The Second Wave*, Methuen, London, 1971, pp. 36-58.

David Mercer, interview with Francis Jarman *et al.*, *Theatre Quarterly*, Vol. III, No. 9, Jan.–March 1973, pp. 43-55.

Khalid Mustafa, 'David Mercer', *British Television Drama*, edited by George W. Brandt, Cambridge University Press, London, 1981, pp. 82-109.

Mermaid Theatre, The

See **Miles, Sir Bernard.**

Miles, Sir Bernard (James)

Baron of Blackfriars in the City of London. Born in Hillingdon, Middlesex, on 27 September 1907, the son of a partner in a large firm of nurserymen, he was educated at Uxbridge County School (where he appeared in a number of stage roles, including Feste in *Twelfth Night*). He attended Pembroke College, Oxford, taught for a year at a boys' prep school in Filey, East Yorkshire, and left in 1930 to make his first stage appearance as the Second Messenger in *Richard III* at the New Theatre (1 September 1930). He subsequently worked as a scenery-painter and property-manager (as well as making stage appearances) with a number of repertory companies (including those at Sheffield, Windsor, York, Brighton, Birmingham and Bournemouth). He married the actress Josephine Wilson in 1931.

From 1938 he appeared in a number of roles in the **West End**, notably Iago in *Othello* with the **Old Vic** Company (New Theatre, July 1942), Christopher Sly in *The Taming of the Shrew*, the Bishop of Carlisle in *Richard II*, Robert de Baudricourt and the Inquisitor in Shaw's *Saint Joan*, Antovitch in Gogol's *The Government Inspector* and Face in Jonson's *The Alchemist* (Old Vic Company, New Theatre, 1947-8 season).

He developed a solo music-hall act, in particular the characterisation of a West Country rustic who tells country stories (some of which were derived from stories passed on to Miles by his grandfather). He appeared at a number of theatres including the London Palladium. In 1951 Bernard Miles and his wife founded the first Mermaid Theatre, an Elizabethan-style playhouse, in a disused schoolhouse behind their home in St John's Wood. In September 1951 Miles put on a production of Purcell's *Dido and Aeneas* and Shakespeare's *The Tempest* (himself appearing as Caliban). The following year he played the title-role in his production of *Macbeth*.

For the Coronation celebrations in 1953 the Mermaid stage was reconstructed at the Royal Exchange (May 1953) and for a three-month season housed performances of *As You Like It, Macbeth, Dido and Aeneas* and Jonson's *Eastward Ho!*. The success of this season determined Miles and his wife to raise the money for a permanent Mermaid Theatre and, on the site of a blitzed warehouse at Puddle Dock, building began in the mid-1950s and the theatre officially opened on 29 May 1959. The first production was the musical play *Lock Up Your Daughters*, which Bernard Miles adapted from Henry Fielding's *Rape Upon Rape*. In December 1959 Miles appeared as Long John Silver in his own adaptation of *Treasure Island*, much-performed ever since at the Mermaid, with Miles in the same role.

Since this period Bernard and Josephine Miles have devoted their time and energies to the running of the Mermaid Theatre. Bernard Miles has also directed and appeared in many productions there, including **Brecht**'s *The Life of Galileo* in which he was Galileo (June 1960), Ibsen's *John Gabriel Borkman* in which he took the title-role (June 1961), Brecht's *Schweyk in the*

Second World War in which he was Schweyk (August 1963), Sophocles' *Oedipus the King* and *Oedipus at Colonus* in which he played Oedipus (May 1965) and John **Arden**'s *Left-Handed Liberty* in which he was the Archbishop (June 1965). In January 1966 he apeared in the one-man show *On the Wagon,* in 1970 (April–May) he was Falstaff in *Henry IV Parts 1 and 2,* and in April 1971 he presented his one-man show *Back to Square One.*

He was Iago in *Othello* (September 1971), adapted and played the King in *The Point* (December 1976), adapted and directed *The Fire That Consumes* (October 1977) and, at the Riverside Studios in January 1980 he appeared in his own one-man show, *The Hindsight Saga.* In October 1981 he co-adapted and directed *Shakespeare's Rome* and at the Haymarket Theatre in October 1983 was in Chekhov's *The Cherry Orchard.*

Bernard Miles has appeared in and written for many films, including *Channel Crossing, In Which We Serve, Moby Dick, Thunder Rock, Great Expectations, Nicholas Nickleby, Tawny Pipit* and *Four Thousand Brass Halfpennies.*

Besides his talents as a classical actor and character-actor on the stage and in films, music-hall entertainer, writer and director, Lord Miles will always be recognised and acclaimed for establishing the Mermaid Theatre, the City of London's first theatre to be built for over 300 years. He and Lady Miles also founded the Mermaid Molecule Theatre, a touring company developing and performing plays which teach science to children.

Further Reading

Bernard Miles, *The British Theatre,* Collins, London, 1947.

J.C. Trewin and Bernard Miles (eds), *Curtain Calls,* Lutterworth, London, 1981.

Miller, Jonathan (Wolfe), Dr

Born 21 July 1934 the son of a physician, Jonathan Miller attended St Paul's School and later qualified as a medical doctor at St John's College, Cambridge and University College, London (1959). He married Helen Collett in 1956. Whilst at Cambridge he appeared in the now legendary revue *Beyond the Fringe* (Lyceum Theatre, Edinburgh, August 1960 and later the Fortune Theatre, London, May 1961) and was its co-author with Alan **Bennett**. The other members of the cast were Peter Cook and Dudley Moore. *The Fringe* was the product of a long tradition of Cambridge Footlights revues and 'smoking concerts' (which later also led to television's *That Was the Week That Was, The Goodies, Monty Python's Flying Circus* and *Not the Nine O'Clock News*). Miller's interest in the theatre was very much engendered by the opportunities at Cambridge (some of his undergraduate humour in *The Fringe* took the form of lampooning Shakespearean productions 'not because I had a burning indignation against them but because I just wanted to get them right'). Miller once said that 'If you look at the world at all, you're bound to become satirical about it' and it was the case that *Beyond the Fringe* was constantly described as 'satire', a term with which Miller and Bennett have never really felt happy. After the long run of *The Fringe* (including New York) Miller's first production was John **Osborne**'s *Under Plain Cover* which he directed at the **Royal Court** Theatre (July 1962). He returned to the States and directed *The Old Glory* (1964) by Robert Lowell and *Come Live With Me* (1967) by Minoff and Price. Later in 1967 he directed a play based on a story by Herman Melville called *Benito Cereno* (Mermaid Theatre, March 1967) and was the editor of BBC Television's arts programme *Monitor* from 1965.

Productions at Nottingham Playhouse were *The School for Scandal* (1968), *The Seagull* (1969) and *King Lear* with Michael

Hordern in the title-role (1969). **Olivier** played Shylock in a production of *The Merchant of Venice* for the **National Theatre** Company at the **Old Vic** (April 1970) and there Miller also directed Buchner's *Danton's Death* (August 1971) and *The School for Scandal* (March 1972). He put on *The Tempest* at the Mermaid in June 1970 and at the **Chichester Festival Theatre** he staged *The Taming of the Shrew* (1972 season) and *The Seagull* (1973 season). As an associate director of the National Theatre Company (1973-5) he directed *Measure for Measure*, Peter **Nichols**'s *The Freeway* and Beaumarchais's *The Marriage of Figaro* (1974).

Miller has said that on the whole 'I'm not very interested in modern plays. I work best with classical plays ... the ones that really set my juices moving are classical texts with very rich allusions.' His approach to directing is very free and open, respecting the actors' creativities as much as his own (although he tends to research and absorb the iconography of a period and its historical background in order to provide him with stage images, setting and costume ideas — but these researches are never prescriptive). He has a marked talent for '**ensemble** rehearsal' which involves all the contributors to the production. He sees the connection between being a director and medical doctor as quite close: 'There is a diagnostic task involved, in recognising human behaviour and reconstituting it.' In an interview with John Miles-Brown (*Directing Drama*, 1980) he remarked that a director needs to be 'sensitive and humorous and alive to human encounters, which really means keeping his eyes open on buses and trains and watching how people behave'.

At Greenwich Theatre he has staged a number of plays: *Hamlet* (March 1974), *Ghosts* (January 1974), *The Importance of Being Earnest* (February 1975) and *All's Well That Ends Well* (November 1975). One of his great successes was Chekhov's *Three Sisters* (Cambridge Arts Theatre, June 1976), and in April 1979 he returned to the Greenwich Theatre to direct Etherege's *She Would if She Could*.

Miller has never channelled all his energies and interests into directing plays but also leads a distinguished intellectual and academic life. He has been a Fellow in the History of Medicine (University College, London 1970-3), a Visiting Professor of Drama (London University, Westfields College 1977), has edited a book on Freud, written a book on McLuhan (which reveals much about Miller himself as well as his subject), wrote and presented a medical series called *The Body in Question* for BBC Television (1978) and delivered a series of stimulating lectures for the Faber and Faber-sponsored T.S. Eliot Memorial Lectures (University of Kent, 1977) to which he gave the title *The Afterlife of Plays*. His central argument for these lectures was that any play has a 'natural life' (the short initial period of its productions in the theatre when it is realised the closest to the writer's intentions) and an 'afterlife' (when the play has a 'free-floating life in the public domain' which is part of the play's 'biography'). As Miller stated at the International Writers' Festival Conference in 1980 (broadcast BBC Radio 4, 31 January 1981): 'One of the ways in which we relate to previous periods is by allowing this complicated and rather ambiguous survival of the works in reproduction as the years go by and in which one knows perfectly well that what are the "intentions" may or may not be actually expressed in the peformance.'

In April 1976 (Her Majesty's Theatre) Miller directed a show called *A Poke In The Eye With A Sharp Stick* for Amnesty International. It brought together nearly all the actors from *Beyond the Fringe*, *The Goodies*, *Monty Python's Flying Circus* and various shows derived from Footlights revues. From 1979 to 1981 he was an executive producer for the BBC Television Shakespeare series and in August 1982 directed *Hamlet* at the Donmar Warehouse.

Since the mid-1970s he has concentrated

mainly on directing Opera, notably productions for the English National Opera (*The Marriage of Figaro* 1978, *The Turn of the Screw* 1979, *Arabella* 1980, *Otello* 1981, and *Rigoletto* 1982) and for Kent Opera (*Orfeo* 1976, *Eugene Onegin* 1977, *La Traviata* 1979, *Falstaff* 1980-1). He has also recently made something of a return to medicine. In *Who's Who 1985* Miller states his recreation is 'deep sleep'.

His achievements as a director amount to a major contribution to Post-War British Theatre and Opera bringing a vitality, energy and freshness to his productions all of which, as Roger Wilmut has aptly put it, 'demonstrate a fiercely burning intelligence which illuminates whatever he is working on in quite a new light. It is not always a comfortable light.'

Further Reading

Jonathan Miller, *The Afterlife of Plays*, 'T.S. Eliot Memorial Lectures' (1977), Faber and Faber, London (awaiting publication).

Jonathan Miller, *McLuhan*, 'Fontana Modern Masters', Fontana/Collins, London, 1971.

Roger Wilmut, *From Fringe to Flying Circus*, Eyre Methuen, London, 1980.

Mills, Sir John (Lewis Ernest Watts), CBE

Born in Suffolk on 22 February 1908, he was educated at Norwich and began his career as a clerk. Although most of his acting career has been in films (he has appeared in over a hundred) he began it in the theatre and has periodically returned there over the years. His first stage appearance was as a member of the chorus of *The Five O'Clock Girl* (London Hippodrome, 21 March 1929) and he played his first role on a Far East tour, as Lieutenant Raleigh in R.C. Sherriff's *Journey's End* (India, 1929). He appeared in *Mr Cinders* and *Hamlet* on the same tour. During the 1930s and 1940s his parts included Babberley in *Charley's Aunt* (New Theatre, December 1930), Joe in *Cavalcade* (Drury Lane, October 1931), Private Summers in *Red Night* (Queen's, March 1936), Puck in *A Midsummer Night's Dream*, Young Marlow in Goldsmith's *She Stoops to Conquer* (both at **Old Vic**, December 1938–February 1939), George in *Of Mice and Men* (Gate, April 1939, Apollo, May 1939), Stephen Cass in (his second wife) Mary Hayley Bell's *Duet For Two Hands* (Lyric, June 1945).

His main stage appearances since the war have been Candy in *The Uninvited Guest* (St James's, May 1953), the title-role in *Ross* (Eugene O'Neill Theatre, New York, December 1961), Otto Moll in *Power of Persuasion* (Garrick, London, September 1963) which he also co-directed, Laurence D'Orsay in Charles **Wood**'s *Veterans* (**Royal Court**, March 1972) in which he starred with Sir John **Gielgud**, Henry Jackson in William Douglas **Home**'s *At the End of the Day* (Savoy, October 1973), Jess Oakroyd in J.B. Priestley's *The Good Companions* (Her Majesty's, July 1974), Joe Gargery in *Great Expectations* (Arnaud, Guildford, December 1975, and tour), Mr Malcolm and Major Pollock in Terence **Rattigan**'s *Separate Tables* (tour 1976, Apollo, January 1977), Chips in *Goodbye, Mr Chips* (**Chichester Festival**, 1982) and Mr Posket in *Little Lies* (Wyndham's, July 1983) which was an adaptation by Joseph Caruso of Pinero's *The Magistrate*.

His distinguished and extensive film career includes appearances in *OHMS*, *The Young Mr Pitt*, *Goodbye, Mr Chips*, *In Which We Serve*, *We Dive at Dawn*, *This Happy Breed*, *The Ways to the Stars*, *Scott of the Antarctic*, *Hobson's Choice*, *The History of Mr Polly* (also produced), *The Rocking Horse Winner* (also produced), *War and Peace*, *Ice Cold in Alex*, *I Was Monty's Double*, *Dunkirk*, *Tiger Bay*, *Summer of the Seventeenth Doll*, *Tunes of Glory*, *The Singer Not the Song*, *The Chalk Garden*, *The Valiant*, *Operation Crossbow*, *Red Waggon*, *Oh! What a Lovely War*, *Ryan's Daughter*, *Lady Hamilton*, *Young Winston*, *The Devil's*

Advocate, *Great Expectations*, *The Big Sleep*, *The Thirty-nine Steps*, *The Human Factor* and *Ghandi*.

Television work includes *The Zoo Gang*, *Dr Strange*, *Quatermass*, *Young at Heart*, *Tales of the Unexpected* and *A Woman of Substance*.

Further Reading

John Mills, *Up in the Clouds, Gentlemen Please*, Weidenfeld and Nicolson, London, 1980, and Penguin Books, Harmondsworth, 1981.

Mirren, Helen

Born in 1946, she began acting with the **National Youth Theatre**, playing numerous roles including Cleopatra in *Antony and Cleopatra* which was seen at the **Old Vic** (September 1965). After appearing as Nerissa in *The Merchant of Venice* (Manchester, 1967) she joined the **Royal Shakespeare Company** with whom her roles have included Castiza in Tourneur's *The Revenger's Tragedy* (Stratford-upon-Avon, 1967 seasons), Cressida in *Troilus and Cressida* (Stratford, August 1968, Aldwych, June 1969 season), Win-the-Fight Littlewit in Ben Jonson's *Bartholomew Fair* (Aldwych, October 1969), Ophelia in *Hamlet* (Stratford, June 1970), Julia in *The Two Gentlemen of Verona* (Stratford, July 1970, Aldwych, December 1970), Tatyana in Maxim Gorky's *Enemies* (Aldwych, July 1971), the title-role in Auguste Strindberg's *Miss Julie* (the Place, September 1971) and Elyane in Jean Genet's *The Balcony* (Aldwych, November 1971).

From 1972 until 1973 Helen Mirren was with Peter **Brook**'s Centre Internationale de Recherches Théâtrales for its Sahara Desert tour of *The Conference of the Birds* and other plays, and a tour of the United States of America. Returning to the RSC at Stratford-upon-Avon she was Lady Macbeth in *Macbeth* (October 1974) which she also played at the Aldwych (March 1975).

She subsequently played Maggie in the original production of David **Hare**'s *Teeth 'n' Smiles* at the **Royal Court** Theatre (September 1975), Nina in Chekhov's *The Seagull* (Lyric, November 1975), Queen Margaret in *Henry VI, Parts 1, 2 and 3* (RSC, Stratford, June 1977, Aldwych, April 1978), Isabella in *Measure for Measure* (Riverside Studios, May 1979), the title-role in Webster's *The Duchess of Malfi* (Manchester, Royal Exchange, 1980, Round House, April 1981), Cleopatra in *Antony and Cleopatra* (RSC Stratford, Other Place, October 1982, Barbican, Pit, April 1983), Moll Cutpurse in Middleton and Dekker's *The Roaring Girl* (RSC, Barbican, April 1983) and Marjorie in William Mastrosimone's *Extremities* (Duchess, November 1984).

Her work in films includes *Savage Messiah*, *Age of Consent*, *O Lucky Man* and *Cal*. Television appearances include *Miss Julie*, *The Collection*, *The Apple Cart*, *Blue Remembered Hills* and *The Little Minister*.

Moore, Stephen

Born in Brixton, he was educated at a prep school and Archbishop Tenison's Grammar School, at both of which he showed himself to be a keen actor (he played Shylock, Macbeth and Mrs Malaprop among his roles). He trained for the stage at the Central School of Speech and Drama (1956-9) and then spent a year at the **Old Vic** playing small parts. He subsequently spent some time in repertory (parts including George in *Who's Afraid of Virginia Woolf?*, Lövborg in *Hedda Gabler*, Petruchio in *The Taming of the Shrew* and Azdak in *The Caucasian Chalk Circle*) and at a number of London theatres, in particular the **Royal Court** Theatre where, among his roles in the first half of the 1970s, he gave a fine performance as Patrick in Christopher **Hampton**'s *Treats*. He was Arthur in Tom **Stoppard**'s *Dirty Linen* and *New-Found-Land* at the Almost-

Free Theatre in 1976.

In 1977 he joined the **National Theatre** where he had a long run as Trevor in Alan **Ayckbourn**'s *Bedroom Farce* and there then followed a number of parts including Lunacharsky in Robert **Bolt**'s *State of Revolution*, Brock in David **Hare**'s *Plenty*, Hjalmar in Ibsen's *The Wild Duck* (in a cast which included Sir Ralph **Richardson**), Simon in Ayckbourn's *Sisterly Feelings*, Cassio in *Othello* (with Paul **Scofield** as Othello) and the Cardinal Inquisitor in **Brecht**'s *A Life of Galileo*.

He joined the **Royal Shakespeare Company** in 1982 and gave a highly-acclaimed performance as Torvald in Ibsen's *A Doll's House*. Other parts with the RSC have included Parolles in *All's Well That Ends Well*, Jack Idle in Peter **Nichols**'s *Poppy*, Sir Toby Belch in *Twelfth Night*, Cardinal Wolsey in *Henry VIII* and the Chaplain in Brecht's *Mother Courage* (in which Judi **Dench** was the Mother).

Stephen Moore is a familiar television actor and his appearances include *Dinner with the Family, All Good Children, Three Men in a Boat, Rock Follies, Keep Smiling, Bedroom Farce, Just Between Ourselves, Solo, The Book Tower* and *The Last Place on Earth*. Film work includes *The White Bus, A Bridge Too Far, Diversion, To Catch a King* and *Laughterhouse*.

Mortimer, John (Clifford), QC

Born 21 April 1923 in Hampstead, London, the son of a barrister, he attended Harrow School from 1937 to 1940. (When asked on *TV AM* in April 1985 whether he was ever lonely at the age of 14 he said he was not because he was able to 'read all of Shakespeare's plays taking all the parts myself'). He attended Brasenose College, Oxford, where he read Law. During the war he was a scriptwriter with the Crown Film Unit and afterwards completed his degree and was called to the Bar in 1948. He married his first wife Penelope Dimont in 1949.

John Mortimer's first play to be performed was a radio play *The Dock Brief* (BBC Radio, May 1957) about an unsuccessful barrister. The play was first staged as part of a double-bill of one-acters with his next play *What Shall We Tell Caroline?* (Lyric, Hammersmith, April 1958, Garrick, May 1958). This latter play was set in a prep schoolmaster's living room and Michael **Hordern** played the eccentric schoolmaster Tony Peters. Hordern also played Morgenhall (the barrister) in *The Dock Brief* and both performances were in a highly successful partnership with Maurice **Denham**. *The Dock Brief* explores the thin divide between freedom and legal restriction, fantasy and reality, and in the confrontation between the inadequate barrister and prisoner in a cell it is at times implied that the barrister is more constrained and 'imprisoned' than the prisoner (*Morgenhall*: 'Mr Fowle, I'm a barrister.'/ *Fowle*: 'Tragic.'/ *Morgenhall*: 'I know the law.'/ *Fowle*: 'It's trapped you.'). His next play was *I Spy* (BBC Radio, November 1957, BBC Television January 1958, Salisbury Playhouse, March 1959) and takes place in a Norfolk seaside town and London lawyer's office. In 1970 Mortimer commented on the 1950s that 'pre-war attitudes still lingered. The middle-aged formed hopeless and isolated pockets of resistance, in law-courts and seaside hotels and private schools' and that in his one-act comedies he had attempted to 'chart the tottering course of British middle-class attitudes in decline'. Michael Anderson has suggested that Mortimer was 'little influenced by the new stance of the period' and it is the case that his plays of the period depart little from pre-war Naturalism and do not have the angry energy and protest of **Osborne** and **Wesker**. Nevertheless Mortimer does see himself as having benefited from the achievements of Osborne: as he puts it in *Clinging to the Wreckage*, 'none of us who lived through that time can fail to be grateful to John Osborne' and he states that his early desires to work and write for the theatre 'might have remained a well-guarded secret but for the change his (Osborne's) success brought about'. He suggests there was a good deal of truth in Emlyn Williams's remark (made to Mortimer at a rehearsal in 1960) 'Well, you just got into the New Wave as the Tube doors were closing!'

Mortimer's next play was another one-acter *Lunch Hour* (BBC Radio, June 1960, Salisbury Playhouse, June 1960, Arts Theatre and Criterion, 1961). It is an exploration of the tensions between sexual freedom and received expectations about conventional moral behaviour — a respectable businessman tries to arrange lunchtime assignations with a secretary. In February 1960 Mortimer had his first full-length play *The Wrong Side of the Park* performed (Cambridge, directed by Peter **Hall**), in which a woman (Elaine) blames her failures in her first marriage upon the husband of her second. It is an illusion she creates in order to protect herself but gradually she is forced into accepting the truth. Another full-length play, *Two Stars for Comfort*, appeared in April 1962 (Garrick) and starred Trevor Howard. It is set in Mortimer's home town of Henley and is something of a celebration of the life and fashionable pleasures associated with the River Thames. The main character (Sam Turner) owns a riverside hotel and lives on the fantasy of the regatta which will make him forget the harsh realities of his debts and personal decline. As John Russell Taylor has pointed out 'he is worn out with feeding other people fantasies and incapable of speaking the truth'. Sam's relationship with the Regatta Queen (in the absence of his wife who is arranging a legal separation) develops to a point where he comes to terms with the truth about himself. Again one of the chief conflicts of this play, like those before, is the tension between illusion and reality. Mortimer has suggested it is about the 'harsh inequalities caused by beauty', how no 'power on earth can abolish the merciless distinction between those who are physically desirable and the lonely, pallid, spotted, full-length silent, unfancied majority.'

Mortimer's highly successful translation of Feydeau's farce *Puce a l'Oreille* appeared as *A Flea In Her Ear* in February 1966 (**National Theatre** at the **Old Vic**), starring Albert **Finney** and Geraldine **McEwan** and he also translated Feydeau's *Un Fil a la Patte* as *Cat Among the Pigeons* (Prince of Wales, April 1969).

The Judge (1967), Mortimer's third original full-length play, moves slightly away from the Naturalism of previous plays and takes on something of an allegorical form. It concerns a judge (originally played by Patrick Wymark) who suffers psychological and moral pressure through his functions as a dispenser of punishment to others for misdemeanours. In January 1970 four short plays about middle-aged sexual relationships (*Mill Hill, Bermondsey, Gloucester Road, Marble Arch*) were performed under the title *Come As You Are* (New Theatre) and in October the same year his greatest success and best known full-length play *A Voyage Round My Father* was performed in its first version at the Greenwich Theatre. The final version was presented in August 1971 (directed by Ronald Eyre) at the Haymarket Theatre. The father was played by Alec **Guinness**, later by Michael **Redgrave** and when the play was made into a television film in 1982 he was played by Laurence **Olivier**.

A Voyage Round My Father is a strongly autobiographical play which portrays a blind lawyer, the authoritarian father of a family in which a young man grows to adulthood. The play contains many nostalgic memories and evocations of the Second World War and what one critic called 'the nuances of English eccentricity'.

In 1971 Mortimer married Penny Gollop, his second wife. In the same year he translated and adapted Zuckmayer's play *The Captain of Köpenick* and a year later in 1972 adapted two novels by Robert Graves as *I, Claudius.* In 1973 we had the comedy *Collaborators*, about a collaborative venture by a husband and wife to write a film about their own relationship.

Apart from the acknowledged achievements of *A Voyage Round My Father* Mortimer's full-length plays have been perhaps less successful in the theatre than his one-act plays (many of which began life as radio or television plays). He has made his major contribution to Post-War British Theatre in pioneering the one-act form. Mortimer has himself suggested 'there are no rules, and a play can be as long as a piece of string ... a play is a demonstration, in which an audience can recognise something about themselves. As with a picture, this can be achieved by a few lines of dialogue in the right position ... In a one-act play the enthusiasm has no time to die.' He has seen an important future for the one-act play where a number might be experienced (through continuous performance) by audiences in much the same way as pictures in an art gallery (where one would 'stare at one or two pictures that take your eye, and depart as soon as your feet start to ache'). Most of his plays have been comedies and he has commented that comedy is 'the only thing worth writing in this despairing age'. Much of his success has been achieved through an ability to characterise like Dickens the eccentricities of people and through his capacity to write sharply-turned dialogue (which Ronald Hayman once described as 'Mortimer's after-dinner speech style').

In May 1976 a double-bill called *Heaven and Hell* was presented (Greenwich Theatre), made up of two one-act plays *The Fear of Heaven* set in an Italian hospital ward, and *The Prince of Darkness* (revised as *The Bells of Hell* in 1977) which is about an ex-padre from the Royal Air Force who is really the Devil in disguise. The National Theatre (October 1977) performed another of Mortimer's translations of Feydeau, *The Lady from Maxim's* and in 1981 he adapted Evelyn Waugh's *Brideshead Revisited* for ITV and it was enormously successful. So too was his television film version of *A Voyage Round My Father* (1982). *John Mortimer's Casebook* (*The Dock Brief, The Prince of Darkness* and *Interlude*) was performed at the Young Vic in January 1982.

John Mortimer has written many successful radio plays (recently *Edwin*, BBC radio October 1982, starring Emlyn Williams) and television plays (including the television version of *Edwin* in May 1984, starring Alec Guinness, and notably the award-winning series *Rumpole of the Bailey*, starring Leo **McKern**), six novels, an autobiography, a collection of interviews (called *In Character*) and he has remained a working barrister (being made Master of the Bench, Inner Temple, 1975).

He once wrote 'I have to confess to a low threshold of boredom ... The only rule I have found to have any meaning in writing is to try and not bore yourself.'

Further Reading

John Russell Taylor, 'John Mortimer', *Anger and After* (2nd edn), Penguin Books, Harmondsworth, 1969.

John Mortimer, 'Introduction' to *Five Plays*, Methuen, London, 1970.

John Mortimer, *Clinging to the Wreckage*, Penguin Books, Harmondsworth, 1982.

N

National Theatre, The

The permanent state-subsidised theatre designed by Denys Lasdun on the South Bank of the River Thames immediately below Waterloo Bridge. It comprises three theatres, each offering different theatrical possibilities: the Olivier, a large open stage with a revolve, the Lyttleton, a traditional proscenium stage, and the Cottesloe, a small flexible theatre in which the size and shape of the stage and audience can be changed. The term 'National Theatre' is also used to refer to the company which stages the productions. This company pre-dates the South Bank complex which opened in 1976 and was originally founded in 1962 under the directorship of Lord Laurence **Olivier** and housed at the **Old Vic**. Since 1973 Sir Peter **Hall** has been the Director.

Although the principle of a state-supported theatre for Britain was suggested by David Garrick in the eighteenth century and Henry Irving in the nineteenth century, it was a London publisher called Effingham Wilson who first put forward a practical scheme in 1848. In 1903 Harley Granville Barker and William Archer published a book which formulated plans for such a theatre and in 1908 a different trend of development emerged when a committee was set up to look into the possibility of opening a theatre in 1916 to celebrate the tercentenary of Shakespeare's death. In 1910 the schemes proposed by this committee and those of Barker and Archer were combined and the new body was called the Shakespeare Memorial National Theatre Committee. A foundation stone was laid in Gower Street but the outbreak of the First World War in 1914 halted the continuation of work. In 1930 Barker revised his book (prophetically suggesting the South Bank as one of the possible sites) but it wasn't until 1937 that a new site was purchased opposite the Victoria and Albert Museum in South Kensington and a second foundation stone laid (by George Bernard Shaw). Further delays were caused by the Second World War until 1946 when the Joint Council of the National Theatre and the Old Vic was set up to negotiate with the LCC for a site on the South Bank. In 1949 the National Theatre Bill was passed by both houses, empowering the government to contribute up to one million pounds towards the fabric and equipment of the theatre. Implementation of the bill was left to the discretion of the Chancellor of the Exchequer and on 13 June 1951, the Queen, on behalf of her husband George VI, laid the third foundation stone, this time on a South Bank site adjacent to the Royal Festival Hall.

Progress was again halted when yet another site, adjoining County Hall, was suggested and agreed upon in 1952. In 1958 Laurence Olivier was appointed a trustee of the National Theatre and in 1960 and 1961 there were schemes proposed for the **Royal Shakespeare Company** and Sadler's Wells to be amalgamated into a National Theatre housed in the same complex. However, in July 1962 the Chancellor appointed a National Theatre Board and this body secured an agreement for the Old Vic to become the temporary home of the National Theatre. In August of the same year Olivier was appointed Director and on 22 October 1963 an inaugural production of *Hamlet* was staged. By 1967 there was a refusal on the part of the Government and GLC to finance the Opera House part of the scheme but plans for the theatre complex continued, the proposed South Bank site being abandoned in favour of the present position on Princess Meadow immediately downstream of Waterloo Bridge. On 3 November 1969 work on the site was inaugurated by Lord Cottesloe, Miss Jennie Lee, Lord Chandos and Mr Desmond Plummer.

Meanwhile the stage company at the Old Vic had established itself with many excellent productions such as Peter **Shaffer**'s *The Royal Hunt of the Sun,* Tom **Stoppard**'s *Rosencrantz and Guildenstern are Dead* and *Jumpers,* Peter **Nichols**'s *The National Health,* William **Gaskill**'s production of Farquhar's *The Recruiting officer,* Olivier's of Chekhov's *Uncle Vanya,* Clifford **Williams**'s all-male *As You Like It,* Jonathan **Miller**'s production of *The School For Scandal* and Michael **Blakemore**'s of O'Neill's *Long Day's Journey into Night,* to name only a few. The list of distinguished performers appearing there included Dame Peggy **Ashcroft**, Sir Laurence **Olivier**, Sir John **Gielgud**, Sir Ralph **Richardson**, Sir Michael **Redgrave**, Robert **Stephens**, Frank **Finlay**, Derek **Jacobi**, Sir Michael **Hordern**, Diana **Rigg**, Joan **Plowright**, Colin **Blakely**, Albert **Finney** and Ronald Pickup.

On 2 May 1973, the topping-out ceremony of the National Theatre on the South Bank was performed by Lord Cottesloe and Lord Olivier. In November of the same year Olivier resigned as Director because of ill health and was succeeded by Peter **Hall**. On 16 March 1976, the Lyttleton Theatre opened with *Hamlet,* starring Albert Finney and on October 25th the Olivier Theatre opened with a production of Marlowe's *Tamburlaine the Great,* also starring Albert Finney. On 4 November 1977 the Cottesloe Theatre opened with Ken Campbell and Chris Langham's *Illuminations.* Sir Peter Hall, who is still the overall Director, stated in an interview (*Gambit,* Vol. 7, No. 28, 1976) at the time of its opening that the National Theatre puts 'the theatre right in the centre of creation, of society's debate with itself'.

In 1984 the theatre was reorganised into six companies, one of them an actors' company led by Ian **McKellen** and Edward **Petherbridge**.

Further Reading

Plays and Players (special issue on the National Theatre), May 1976.

Gambit, 'Special Issue: The National Theatre', Vol. 7, No. 28, 1976.

Peter Hall, *Peter Hall's Diaries: The Story of a Dramatic Battle,* John Goodwin (ed.), Hamish Hamilton, London, 1983.

National Youth Theatre, The

Annually-formed commercially subsidised theatre company for young people (equivalent to the National Youth Orchestra and National Youth Jazz Orchestra in music). It was founded in 1956 by Michael Croft (OBE), a former actor and English teacher who, at Alleyn's School, Dulwich, had directed some remarkable productions of plays by Shakespeare. It was from these school productions that the NYT grew when Croft left to devote his time to writing (born 8 March 1922 in Manchester, educated there and at Keble College, Oxford, he had enormous success with his first novel *Spare the Rod* in 1955). The NYT's first production was *Henry V* (Toynbee Hall, Aldgate East, September 1956).

The company's major productions have included *Hamlet* (Queen's Theatre, August 1959, Paris Festival 1960, Scala, September 1963), *Henry V* and *Julius Caesar* (Sadler's Wells, August 1962), *Coriolanus* (Queen's, August 1964) and *Antony and Cleopatra* (**Old Vic**, September 1965) in which Helen **Mirren** played Cleopatra. In August 1966 the company staged Jonson's *Bartholomew Fair* at the **Royal Court** Theatre and in October David Halliwell's *Little Malcolm and his Struggle Against the Eunuchs* at the same theatre.

From the latter part of the 1960s the NYT has had a highly successful association with the playwright Peter **Terson** whose plays specially written for the company have included *Zigger Zagger* (Jeannetta Cochran, August 1967), *The Apprentices* (Jeannetta

Cochran, August 1968), *Fuzz* (Jeannetta, Cochran, August 1969), *Good Lads at Heart* (Jeannetta Cochran, August 1971), *The Geordie's March* (Shaw, August 1973), *The Bread and Butter Trade* (Shaw, August 1976), *England My Own* (Shaw, August 1978) and *Soldier Boy* (Jeannetta Cochran, August 1978).

Since the NYT took over the Shaw Theatre in 1971, its major productions, other than Terson's work, have included Dekker's *The Shoemaker's Holiday* (Shaw, August 1971), Skelton's *Magnificence* (Shaw, August 1974), Barry **Keefe**'s *Here Comes the Sun* (Jeannetta Cochran, August 1976), *Romeo and Juliet* (Young Vic, February 1977), *A Midsummer Night's Dream* (Round House, September 1979), *Macbeth* (Shaw, November 1981), Henry Miller's *The Crucible* (Jeannetta Cochran, September 1982), Christopher Smart's *For Those in Peril* (Shaw, August 1983), Peter **Shaffer**'s *The Royal Hunt of the Sun* (Jeannetta Cochran, September 1983), *Hamlet* (Shaw, September 1983), Robert **Bolt**'s *A Man For All Seasons* (Jeannetta Cochran, September 1984), *As You Like It* (Open Air, Regent's Park, September 1985) and *Othello* (Shaw, September 1985).

Some of the artists who have gone into the professional theatre from the NYT include Simon Ward, Martin **Jarvis**, Helen **Mirren**, Derek **Jacobi**, John Shrapnel, Diana Quick, Hywel Bennett, Barrie Rutter, David Weston, Clive Emsley, Robert East and Simon Cadell. Simon Masters, a past member of the NYT, writes in his book about the company: 'It is a communal existence, and that well-worn saying "All for one and one for all", could not find a happier, more truthful expression anywhere else than with the NYT ... Maybe it's unorthodox, but it is only what each member makes of it, for each member has to make his or her own decisions. It is an exercise in accepting responsibility, in learning how to live, while enjoying at the same time a quite unforgettable experience.' Since the Arts Council withdrew its grant in 1981 the NYT has had to be commercially supported.

Further Reading

Simon Masters, *The National Youth Theatre*, Longmans, London, 1969.

Nichols, Peter (Richard)

Born in Bristol on 31 July 1927, he was educated at Bristol Grammar School, did National Service in the RAF in India and Malaya and in 1948 trained for the stage for two years at **Bristol Old Vic** Theatre School. He acted in repertory, television and films for five years until 1955 when he trained to be a teacher at Trent Park Teacher Training College, Hertfordshire. Between 1957 and 1960 he worked as a teacher of general subjects in primary and secondary schools. He has also been a park keeper, a teacher of English language in Italy, a cinema commissionaire and a clerk.

During his career as a schoolteacher he began writing plays for television (*Walk on the Grass, After All, Promenade*, 1959, *Ben Spray*, 1961) and has continued to do so very successfully every since. Peter Nichols's first stage play was a remarkable tragi-comic exploration of the pressures on a couple whose child is a paraplegic, *A Day in the Death of Joe Egg* (Glasgow Citizens, May 1967). At the time it was first performed (Gary O'Connor has commented in *Contemporary Dramatists*) there was 'a sudden rush of approval as a new barrier of inhibition was swept away'. The subject of the play is serious and harrowing yet balanced by sharp comedy and irony, a tragi-comic mix revealing Nichols to be a writer of great compassion and saving wit. Indeed the tragic force of the play is intensified and deepened because the comedy is the parents' (and in particular the father, Bri's) attempt to compensate for what they are going through. Nichols and his wife (Thelma Reed, whom he married in 1960), themselves had a spastic child and the play is, like Nichols's subsequent plays, openly autobiographical. (In an interview with Ronald Hayman in *Playback 2*, 1973, Nichols said, 'Everybody writes autobiography, but a lot of writers manage to clothe it in disguises of various kinds. With me there's no disguise ... all my plays are written from a diary.')

His next stage play was *The National Health* (**National Theatre** at the **Old Vic**, October, 1969), set in a hospital ward of suffering and dying patients, one of whom (Mackie) suffers from terminal cancer and who is a parallel figure to the spastic child, Joe, in *Joe Egg*. In *The Second Wave* John Russell Taylor comments that Joe and Mackie are both victims of 'the twisted pseudo-humanity of a system which moves heaven and earth to resuscitate someone whose life cannot be more than a vegetable existence or a constant battle with pain'. The play's form is interesting for its inclusion of an ironic subplot, a television soap-opera called *Nurse Norton's Affair* which is 'broadcast' at various times on a mock-up television screen. Another formal interest of the play is the choric role of Barnet, a hospital porter, who addresses the audience directly (as did Bri in *Joe Egg*) and is both narrator and a sort of stand-up comic. In Nichols's next play, *Forget-Me-Not Lane* (Greenwich Theatre, April 1971), Frank, similarly, is a narrator and chorus figure who addresses the audience directly. The play is a recalling of 20 years' experiences, in particular Frank's childhood during the war, the purpose of which seems to be to explain how the past has conditioned his unsuccessful marriages. In the juxtaposing of past and present and the interweaving of events the play is technically a fine achievement, possessing (as Taylor puts it) 'the richness and unpredictable intricacy of veined marble'.

Chez Nous (Globe, February 1974) which starred Albert **Finney**, Geraldine **McEwan** and Denholm **Elliott**, explored the complex relationships between two married couples on holiday in France. *The Freeway* (National Theatre at the Old Vic, October 1974) was an amusing comedy about a group of people marooned in a motorway traffic-jam and how they pass the time entertaining each other. *Harding's Luck* (Greenwich, December 1974) was an adaptation of a children's novel by E. Nesbit, about a crippled pauper child (Dickie) who is taken in by a sympathetic family and who discovers he has good connections. The play involves time-shifts from the Edwardian and Jacobean periods, to Dickie's childhood and youth. This fascination with theatrical forms continued with *Privates on Parade* (**Royal Shakespeare Company**, Aldwych, February 1977) which is a play with songs, in the form of a variety show. Drawing on Nichols's National Service experiences, it is about a Concert Party in the Malayan jungle of 1948, the constant menace of Communist guerilla activity and the sexual foibles of some of the soldiers. The play is something of a moral allegory about authority, freedom, honesty and sexuality. *Born in the Gardens* (Bristol Old Vic, September 1979, Globe, January 1980) is about Maud (originally played by Beryl **Reid**), a freshly widowed eccentric whose middle-aged son lives with her in contentment, in contrast to her other more frustrated and less happy progeny who return for the funeral of their father. Nichols directed the play himself.

Peter Nichols's most acclaimed play since *Joe Egg* has been *Passion Play* (Royal Shakespeare Company, Aldwych, January 1981, revived Leicester Haymarket, March 1984, and Wyndham's, April 1984) which is a witty examination of the pressures and strains of contemporary middle-class marriage relationships in the context of the art world. One critic (Michael Ratcliffe in the *Observer*, 22 April 1984) has suggested the play 'dramatises the paradox by which Christian art continues to console and absorb people brought up to believe they have inherited the post-Christian age'. In October 1982 (RSC, Barbican) what may be Nichols's last play for the stage, *Poppy*, was presented. It is a mixture of music-hall, pantomime and political satire set in the mid-nineteenth-century opium war with China. Music and songs were written by Monty Norman. The play was not received particularly well by theatre critics but did run successfully at the Adelphi Theatre later.

Interviewed by James Allister (*Plays and Players*, June 1984) Nichols stated: 'I've had enough of sacrificing my work to directors' whims, trusting it to inexpert actors and being trampled on by philistine managements', a statement underlining his intention to leave the theatre and concentrate on other writing. In 1983 he wrote the television series *Funny Ideals* and in 1984 an autobiography, *Feeling You're Behind*.

Peter Nichols is highly regarded as a television playwright and he has been a prolific writer for the television medium. His plays for television include *The Reception* (1961), *Continuity Man* (1963), *The Heart of the Country* (1963), *When the Wind Blows* (1964), *Daddy Kiss It Better* (1968), *Hearts and Flowers* (1971), *The Common* (1973) and the six-part serial *The Atkinsons* (1978). He has written filmscripts, in particular for *Catch Us If You Can* (1965), *Georgy Girl* (1967), *A Day in the Death of Joe Egg* (1971), *The National Health* (1973), *Privates on Parade* (1983).

In *Feeling You're Behind* (1984) Peter Nichols seemed to sum up his dramatic achievements quite precisely when he wrote, 'To make an audience cry or laugh is easy — they want to. In reviews of *Joe Egg* it became a critical truism to speak of its capacity to do both at the same time, yet this is only worth doing if one thereby catches a whiff of life, a true tang of the bitter mixture we all have to drink.'

Further Reading

John Russell Taylor, *The Second Wave: British Drama for the Seventies*, Methuen, London, 1971, pp. 16-35.

Oleg Kerensky, *The New British Drama*, Hamish Hamilton, London, 1977, pp. 59-77.

Ronald Hayman, 'Peter Nichols', *Playback 2*, Davis-Poynter, London, 1973, pp. 47-62.

Peter Nichols, *Feeling You're Behind*, Weidenfeld and Nicolson, London, 1984.

Noises Off

'Live' sound effects performed offstage during a performance. Also called 'spot effects'.

Notices

Magazine and newspaper reviews of a production.

Nunn, Trevor (Robert), CBE

Born on 14 January 1940 in Ipswich, Suffolk, the son of a cabinet maker, he was educated at Northgate Grammar School, Ipswich, and Downing College, Cambridge (where he studied under Dr F.R. Leavis). During his student days he acted in and directed many plays for the Marlowe Society and ADC. He also directed the Cambridge Footlights review *Double Take* (1962) which had in its cast John Cleese, Graham Chapman, Tim Brooke-Taylor and Robert Atkins.

Later in 1962 Nunn went on an ABC scholarship to the Belgrade Theatre, Coventry, as a trainee director, later taking a job as resident producer until 1965. His productions at the Belgrade in this period included Gwyn Thomas's *The Keep*, **Brecht**'s *The Caucasian Chalk Circle*, Arthur Miller's *A View From the Bridge*, Ibsen's *Peer Gynt* and some of Shakespeare's plays. In 1965 he became an Associate Director of the **Royal Shakespeare Company** with whom in May of the same year he co-directed (with John **Barton**) *Henry V* and in December directed Robert **Bolt**'s *The Thwarting of Baron Bolligrew* at the Aldwych Theatre.

For the 1966 season at Stratford-upon-Avon he directed Tourneur's *The Revenger's*

Tragedy which was a highly-acclaimed production, and co-directed the two parts of *Henry IV*. The following year saw his productions of *The Taming of the Shrew* (Stratford-upon-Avon, 1967, Los Angeles, 1968) and Vanbrugh's *The Relapse* (Aldwych, August 1967). In 1968 Trevor Nunn suceeded Peter **Hall** as Artistic Director of the RSC, becoming the youngest director ever to hold the position. In that year he directed *King Lear* (with Eric **Porter** in the title-role) and *Much Ado About Nothing* (Stratford-upon-Avon, 1968 season, Aldwych, July 1969) and for the following season at Stratford directed *The Winter's Tale* (also tour of Japan and Australia, 1969, Aldwych, July 1970), and *Henry VIII* (also Aldwych, December 1970). He married the actress Janet **Suzman** in the same year (1969).

Other major productions for the RSC have included *The Romans* which was a season of Shakespeare's Roman plays *Coriolanus, Julius Caesar, Antony and Cleopatra* and *Titus Andronicus* (Stratford, 1972, Aldwych, July 1973), *Macbeth* (Stratford, 1974, Aldwych, January 1975) which starred Ian **McKellen** in the title-role, his own adaptation of Ibsen's *Hedda Gabler* (Australia and Aldwych, 1975), a musical version of *The Comedy of Errors* (Aldwych, May 1977), Tom **Stoppard**'s *Every Good Boy Deserves Favour* (Royal Festival Hall, July 1977, **Mermaid**, June 1978), Jonson's *The Alchemist* (Stratford, The Other Place, 1977 season), *As You Like It* (Stratford, 1977 season), *The Merry Wives of Windsor* (Stratford, 1979, Aldwych, January 1980), Chekhov's *Three Sisters* (Stratford, The Other Place, 1979, Warehouse, 1980) and David **Edgar**'s adaptation of Charles Dickens's novel *Nicholas Nickleby* (Aldwych, June 1980) which he co-directed with John **Caird**.

In 1978 Nunn became Chief Executive of the RSC and shared the post of Artistic Director with Terry **Hands**. Productions in the 1980s include Andrew Lloyd Webber's musical *Cats* (New London Theatre, May 1981), *Henry IV Parts 1 and 2* (Stratford, 1981 season, Barbican, June 1982) for the opening of the RSC's new London theatre (the Barbican), *All's Well That Ends Well* (Stratford, 1981 season, Barbican, July 1982), Andrew Lloyd Webber and Richard Stilgoe's *Starlight Express* (Apollo Victoria, March 1984) and J.M. Barrie's *Peter Pan* (Barbican, December 1984).

For television he directed *Antony and Cleopatra* and wrote and presented *Shakespeare Workshop*. For film he has directed *Hedda Gabler*. In an interview with Judith Cook (*Directors' Theatre*, 1974) he said that 'the true relationship that must exist during the performance of a play is between the dramatist and the audience, through the actors. For too long it has been between the director/designer and the critics. Interpretation — "I see this play as" — that's the unimportant top layer of a production.' Such views are borne out by Nunn's emphasis upon '**ensemble**' playing in the development of the RSC.

Further Reading

Judith Cook, 'Trevor Nunn', *Directors' Theatre*, Harrap, London, 1974, pp. 111-24.

O

Old Vic

Theatre off Waterloo Road, London, first opened on 11 May 1818 as the Royal Coburg Theatre. Productions were mainly popular sensational melodramas in some of which Kean and Macready performed. In 1833 the theatre was closed for redecoration and opened again as the Royal Victoria Theatre. It soon became generally known by the nickname the 'Old Vic' and continued to present melodramas for local, often riotous and unruly audiences. The theatre's work declined to the level of the Victorian 'gaff' and 'blood-tub' (Charles Kingsley called it 'a licensed pit of darkness') and it closed in 1871 even after J.A. Cave had attempted to turn it into a music-hall. It was auctioned, renamed the New Victoria Palace, and closed yet again in 1880.

In December 1880 the theatre re-opened as the Royal Victoria Hall and Coffee Tavern, having been bought by Emma Cons, the first woman to serve on the LCC. William Poel was the manager from 1880 until 1883 and the theatre became something of a social centre. Emma Cons's niece, the indefatigable Lilian Baylis who had been assisting her aunt since 1898, succeeded to the management in 1912 and increased the theatre's output of classics, especially Shakespeare's plays. From 1914 to 1922 all of Shakespeare's 37 plays from the First Folio were presented. Prominent in the casts was the young Sybil **Thorndike**. On one occasion her brother Russell, who had been invalided from the army, played King Lear, giving rise to the incident recounted by J.C. Trewin (*Shakespeare on the English Stage 1900-1964,* London, 1964): 'There is no more famous story from Waterloo Road than that of the *Lear* night during an air-raid. Striding downstage, his white-faced fool at his heels, the King cried "Crack nature's mould, all *Germans* spill at once!" as a Zeppelin rode high over London and bombs crashed down upon Waterloo Station.' Most of the Shakespeare productions were directed by Ben Greet and George Foss. The theatre also staged operas in this period.

In 1927 the theatre closed for repairs and alterations. The company was temporarily housed in the Lyric Theatre but returned in February 1928. From 1931, when Lilian Baylis also reopened and managed the Sadler's Wells Theatre, the Old Vic and Sadler's Wells alternated its programmes of drama, opera and ballet. Baylis died in 1937 and the Old Vic closed in 1939 with the outbreak of the Second World War. It re-opened, after bomb-damage repairs, in November 1950. Under Michael Benthall the theatre for the second time presented all the plays of Shakespeare contained in the First Folio.

In October 1963, Laurence **Olivier**'s company (largely drawn from the **Chichester Festival**) moved into the Old Vic as the **National Theatre** company prior to the building of the triple theatre complex on the South Bank. The company gave notable productions of *Othello* (1964) which starred Olivier in the title-role, Peter **Shaffer**'s *The Royal Hunt of the Sun* (1964) and *Equus* (1973), Tom **Stoppard**'s *Rosencrantz and Guildenstern are Dead* (1967) and *Jumpers* (1971), an all-male *As You Like It* (1967), Molière's *Tartuffe* (1967) with John **Gielgud** in the title-role, and a modern dress production of Seneca's *Oedipus* starring Gielgud and directed by Peter **Brook**. In 1970 the company also performed at the Cambridge Theatre and the New Theatre whilst some of the Old Vic's programme included visiting companies. This, together with a scandal over the censorship problems of presenting

Hochhuth's *Soldiers* (which was unsuccessfully promoted by the company's Literary Manager Kenneth **Tynan**) caused a good deal of criticism but the company returned to the Old Vic a year later. Peter **Hall** took over the management in 1973 and the last production before the National Theatre left the Old Vic for its new premises was *Tribute to the Lady* (1976), a compilation of readings and anecdotes remembering the life and work of Lilian Baylis.

In 1977 the Old Vic became the London base for Toby Robertson's **Prospect Theatre Company** which disbanded in 1981 with the loss of its financial support from the Arts Council. After threats of closure and the efforts of pressure groups to save the theatre, the Old Vic has continued, under new management, to present both classics and new plays. Some of the artists (other than those already mentioned) who have appeared there over the years include Edith **Evans**, Richard Burton, Harry **Andrews**, Robert **Stephens**, Colin **Blakely**, Vanessa **Redgrave**, Ralph **Richardson**, Albert **Finney** and Paul **Scofield**.

Further Reading

Raymond Mander and Joe Mitchenson, *The Theatres of London*, New English Library, London, 1975.

Olivier, Laurence (Kerr)

Baron Olivier of Brighton, Knight. He was born the son of a clergyman on the 22 May 1907 in Dorking and went to All Saints School, London and St Edward's School, Oxford. His first appearances were in school plays: the parts of Katherine in a boys' performance of *The Taming of the Shrew* (1922 Stratford-upon-Avon Shakespeare Festival) and Puck in *A Midsummer Night's Dream* (1923, St Edward's School, Oxford). After training at the Central School of Speech Training and Dramatic Art he joined Birmingham Repertory Company in 1927 and acted in a variety of plays there and also in the **West End**, including Malcolm in Barry **Jackson**'s modern-dress version of *Macbeth* (**Royal Court**, 1928). He was the original Captain Stanhope in Sherriff's *Journey's End* (Apollo, 1928), the original Victor Prynne in Noël **Coward**'s *Private Lives* (Phoenix, September 1930) and his first major Shakespearean roles were Mercutio and Romeo (alternating the parts with John **Gielgud**) in *Romeo and Juliet* (New Theatre, September 1935). He married Jill Esmond in 1930.

After joining the **Old Vic** Company in 1937 he played a range of parts which established him as a classical actor: Sir Toby Belch in *Twelfth Night* and the title-roles in *Henry V*, *Macbeth* and *Hamlet* (all 1937), Iago to Ralph **Richardson**'s *Othello* (February 1938) and Caius Marcius in *Coriolanus* (April 1938). He dissolved his marriage to Jill Esmond in 1940 and married Vivien Leigh.

During the war he was in the Fleet Air Arm and in 1943 directed the film of *Henry V* in which he also took the part of Henry. It was a film which in many ways seemed to reflect the patriotic feelings of the British people during the war years. (Much later, in an interview with Ronald Hayman, he remembered how important flying aeroplanes had been to his acting: 'I learnt a lot about a very essential factor in acting — poise, the feeling of poise — from flying an aeroplane. . .a very exact poise, between your feet being too heavy on the rudder, or your hand too heavy on the stick or too savage on the throttle. You learn a very special poise.')

Olivier co-directed the Old Vic Company 1944-9 and acted his celebrated role as Richard III in September 1944. Robin May has suggested that this performance 'ushered in a rebirth of great acting in the Kean and Irving tradition'. It was certainly in the decade immediately after the war that Olivier established himself as the major Shakespearean and classical actor of his generation.

In January 1945 he also played Astrov in Chekhov's *Uncle Vanya* (New Theatre) and n September 1945 (New) Hotspur in *Henry 'V Part 1* (a role he made controversial and amous by giving Hotspur a stammer). He layed the title-role in Sophocles' *Oedipus he King* (New, October 1945) and Kenneth **Tynan** recalls how during this remarkable erformance Olivier 'let out those two amous cries that all but shattered the alcony of the New Theatre in London' and hat 'after a quarter of a century, there is still sort of kinship between those who were here and heard him, as if they'd been on the omme together'. September 1946 saw him n *King Lear* (New) and in 1947 (the year of is knighthood) he directed and took the itle-role in his film of *Hamlet.* He played the itle-role in *Richard III* again (New, January 949) and starred in Christopher **Fry**'s *Venus Observed* (St James's, January 1950) vhich was specially written for him. He was he Grand Duke in Terence **Rattigan**'s *The leeping Prince* (Phoenix, November 1953) nd directed and starred in his own film of *Richard III* in 1954.

One of the high points of Olivier's career s undoubtedly the 1954-5 Stratford season vhen he played Macbeth ('Yes, at last, the lefinitive Macbeth,' remarked Terence Rattigan at the time) with Vivien Leigh playng Lady Macbeth. He played Malvolio in *Twelfth Night* with Vivien as Viola and the itle-role in *Titus Andronicus* with Vivien as avinia. *Titus* had not been performed at tratford before and in this production, irected by Peter **Brook**, Olivier gave a brilant and historic performance. In his autoiography (*Confessions of an Actor*, 1982) Olivier recalls himself at the time being 'now escribed as a Shakespearean actor' and 'in he plenitude of my powers'. He remembers hat he had 'lungs like organ-bellows, vocal ower and range that no infection could eemingly affect, and bodily expression alanced by a technique that could control ll physical expressiveness from dead stillness an almost acrobatic agility; my performnces were apt to have, if anything, too much itality'.

In his acting-style Olivier places much emphasis upon the posturings and gesturings of the physical body — he once said that 'a mannerism is something you develop in order to make you feel more comfortable...there are a lot of things that one does with one's body that one does unknowingly in search of a refuge'.

He played the down-and-out Music Hall artist Archie Rice in John **Osborne**'s *The Entertainer* (Royal Court, April 1957), perhaps his greatest success in a modern play. In 1958 he became a trustee of the **National Theatre** and at Stratford-upon-Avon gave a brilliant performance as Coriolanus in April 1959 (and according to Laurence Kitchin 'the audience quivered at the sound of Olivier's voice like Avon swans at a sudden crack of thunder'). From 1961-5 Olivier was Director at the **Chichester Festival** Theatre which he planned and developed with Tyrone **Guthrie**. He was also Director of the National Theatre at the Old Vic 1962-73 (becoming an Associate Director 1973-4) and a member of the South Bank Theatre Board from 1967. He is perhaps one of the last great actor-managers (he has had his own company, Laurence Olivier Productions Ltd, and in 1950 he leased the St. James's Theatre for six years).

In the 1960s his most acclaimed acting roles at the Old Vic were Astrov in *Uncle Vanya* (National Theatre at the Old Vic, 1963), Brazen in Farquhar's *The Recruiting Officer* (December 1963), the title-role in *Othello* (April 1964, filmed in 1965), Tattle in Congreve's *Love for Love* (October 1965), Edgar in Strindberg's *The Dance of Death* (February 1967) and in 1970, the year he was made a life peer (the first actor to be made one), he played Shylock in Jonathan **Miller**'s production of *The Merchant of Venice* (April). The 1970s saw him as a superb Tyrone in *Long Day's Journey Into Night* (New, December 1971). In 1973 he resigned as Director of the National Theatre (being succeeded by Sir Peter **Hall**) after which his last appearance on the London

Stage was as John Tagg in Trevor **Griffiths**'s *The Party* (Old Vic, December 1973): there is an interesting account of this last appearance in the journal *Plays and Players* (January–April, 1984). He married Joan **Plowright** in 1961.

Most of Olivier's work in the 1970s has been in film and television and it is perhaps always important to remember that Olivier has been a great film actor and director as well as stage actor, director and theatre manager. Some of his best-known films are *Wuthering Heights* (1939), *Rebecca* (1939), *Henry V* (1943-4), *Hamlet* (1947), *Richard III* (1954), *Khartoum* (1966), *Oh! What a Lovely War* (1968), *Three Sisters* (1969), *Long Day's Journey Into Night* (1972). His notable television appearances in Britain have been in *The Collection* (1976), *Brideshead Revisited* (1981) and *A Voyage Round My Father* (1982).

One critic has described Olivier as possessing 'striking eyes, commanding, thrilling voice. . .sheer magnetism, and a sense of danger that makes for theatrical electricity. By any standards, he ranks as head of his profession in Britain, possibly in the world.'

Further Reading

Richard Findlater, *These Our Actors*, Elm Tree Books, London, 1984.

Laurence Olivier, *Confessions of an Actor*, Coronet Books, Hodder and Stoughton, London, 1984.

OP

'Opposite prompt', that is, stage right (which is opposite the promptside). *See* **PS**.

Open Space Theatre

See **Marowitz, Charles.**

Open Stage

A general term referring to a stage without a **Proscenium** arch and which often has its audience on three sides of a 'thrust' stage as in the Elizabethan Globe Theatre, or in a semi-circle as at the **National Theatre**'s Olivier Theatre. Tyrone **Guthrie** promoted the revival of interest in open stages and helped in the design of the Festival Theatre Stratford, Ontario, a fine example of this type of theatre. Open stages vary in their shape from 'thrust' to **Arena** and **Theatre-in-the-Round.**

Orton, Joe (John Kingsley Orton)

Born in Leicester on 1 January 1933, he was educated at Clark's College (a private commercial college where he learned shorthand and typing) and left at the age of 16 to work in clerical jobs. From 1951 to 1953 he trained for the stage at the Royal Academy of Dramatic Art where he befriended Kenneth Halliwell, a fellow-student with whom he maintained a homosexual relationship for the rest of his life. On leaving RADA they collaborated on a number of novels (which were not successful). Their eventful lives together included a six-month prison sentence for defacing and stealing public library books (1962). In 1963 Orton was commissioned to write a radio play and this was performed as *The Ruffian on the Stair* for BBC Radio (1964). It was a play about a young man seeking revenge on the murderer of his dead brother and at the same time trying to effect his own suicide by being caught making love to the murderer's mistress. The play shows Orton's emerging gifts for writing black comedy which blends sexual tensions with macabre criminal action. In the same year his first stage play *Entertaining Mr Sloane* was performed (New Arts, May 1964, Wyndham's, June 1964, revived **Royal Court**, April 1975). In this play an intruder (Sloane) disrupts a household (a situation owing something to the influence of Harold **Pinter**'s plays) and it is discovered he is the murderer of a photographer of pornographic material. The play involves further killing, heterosexual and homosexual attractions and blackmail. Martin Esslin has commented (in *Contemporary English Drama*, 1981) that the play 'while still, outwardly, structured like a comedy' can be clearly assigned to the realm of farce because of 'the mechanical nature of its characters and the explicitness of its language' and Simon Trussler (in *Contemporary Dramatists*, 1977) writing of the play stated, 'if the farceur wishes to add mortality and murder to his usual themes of adultery and fraud, the loss of control is more likely to be tragic than comic in its implications. Orton triumphantly transcends that likelihood.'

Loot (London, Traverse Theatre Company, Jeanette Cochrane Theatre, September 1966, revived Royal Court, June 1975, Ambassadors', March 1984, this latter production with the late Leonard **Rossiter** as Inspector Truscott) satirises police corruption through a series of macabre incidents surrounding the hiding of two bank-robbers' loot in a coffin containing a corpse. It is a play, as C.W.E. Bigsby suggests (in *Joe Orton*, 1982), which deliberately sets out 'to flout all normal standards of good taste' and to present 'a society of the self-seeking'. It is 'anarchic farce'. *Loot* is also something of a parody of the conventions of the detective thriller. *The Erpingham Camp*, originally written for television, was adapted for the stage and formed part of the double-bill with the stage version of *The Ruffian on the Stair*, both performed as *Crimes of Passion* (Royal Court, June 1967). *The Erpingham Camp* was described by Orton himself as a modern version of Euripides' *The Bacchae.* The link is only tenuous, however, and the play is more of an anarchic romp in protest against all forms of authority, a subversive farce set in a holiday camp run by a tyrant, Erpingham, and chief 'Redcoat', Riley, who are challenged by the holiday-makers. The camp is an image of Britain itself (Erpingham 'the state', an inadequate Padre 'the Church' and the holiday-makers 'the Public') but the hubris of both the 'Establishment' and 'Revolutionaries' is equally satirised and undermined by Orton's deft use of techniques of comic deflation (superbly carried out, for example, by portraying Erpingham's 'fall' and death as a result of his office floorboards giving way so that he lands on the dancing holiday-makers in the ballroom below). *The Good and Faithful Servant* and *Funeral Games* were television plays (Rediffusion, 6 April 1967 and Yorkshire Television, 25 August 1968, respectively), the latter a satirical mockery of religious pretentiousness.

The circumstances of Orton's death were like some of the bizarre juxtapositions presented in his later plays: on 9 August 1967, Halliwell battered the sleeping and naked Orton to death with a hammer. Immediately after the murder Halliwell committed suicide by taking an overdose of sleeping pills.

Orton's last play, *What the Butler Saw*, was first performed at the Queen's Theatre in March 1969 (and later revived at the Royal Court, July 1975) with Sir Ralph **Richardson** as Dr Rance in the original cast. Taken from Tourneur's *The Revenger's Tragedy*, the published epigraph to *What the Butler Saw* indicates the play's setting and preoccupation: 'Surely we're all mad people, and they whom we think are, are not.' The action takes place in a mental hospital which can be seen as an image of British society in the late 1960s: as C.W.E. Bigsby puts it, 'a paradigm of a world in which authority seeks to define reality, impose rules, coerce the individual, and in which the individual can respond only with corrosive anarchy, for, as one of the play's central characters remarks, "You can't be a rationalist in an irrational world. It isn't rational."' The central character, Dr Prentice, a psychiatrist, has an adulterous relationship with his new secretary (as part of his interview procedure) but meanwhile Mrs Prentice has seduced a page-boy in a hotel linen-closet. She brings the page-boy to the clinic just as a government inspector (Dr Rance) is paying a visit. The rest of the play is a complex of Feydeau-like confusions of identity, concealments and embarrassments which lead to the revelation that the page-boy and the new secretary are twins, conceived by Mrs Prentice in the same linen-cupboard of the same hotel, the lover, so it falls out, being Dr Prentice. Thus the twins are the Prentices' children who therefore have committed incest with their parents, all of which is excellent sales fodder for Dr Rance's new book about mental illness. Orton sets all regard for established authority upside down and asks his audience to re-examine the insanity of the apparently ordered world. In his method of standing received ideas and conventions on their heads he has much in common with Shaw, whilst in wit and style his major plays are reminiscent of Wilde.

Orton wrote the television plays already mentioned and also the screenplay for a film *Up Against It* for the Beatles, which was never filmed. His novel, *Head to Toe*, was published posthumously in 1971. John Lahr, in his superb biography, quotes Orton as stating (*Radio Times*, 29 August 1964) that 'laughter is a serious business and comedy a weapon more dangerous than tragedy'. On another occasion Orton claimed that he developed a 'mocking, cynical way of treating events because it prevented them being too painful'.

Further Reading

C.W.E. Bigsby, *Joe Orton*, 'Contemporary Writers', Methuen, London, 1982.

John Russell Taylor, 'The Late Lamented Joe Orton', *Plays and Players*, October 1970.

Martin Esslin, 'Joe Orton: The Comedy of (Ill) Manners' in *Contemporary English Drama*, C.W.E. Bigsby (ed.), Stratford-Upon-Avon Studies, No. 19, Edward Arnold, London, 1981.

John Lahr, *Prick Up Your Ears: The Biography of Joe Orton*, Penguin Books, Harmondsworth, 1980.

Osborne, John (James)

He was born on 12 December 1929 in Fulham, London, the son of a barmaid and a commercial artist (he once said that his parents were from the 'impoverished middle class'). He attended various suburban schools and then a minor public school, Belmont College, Devon, until 1946 when he worked as a journalist on trade magazines such as *Gas World*. In 1948 he took a job as an assistant stage-manager and also acted, mainly in seaside repertory. The actress Pamela Lane became his first wife in 1951.

His career as a playwright began with two collaborative ventures *The Devil Inside Him* with Stella Linden (Huddersfield, 1950) and *Personal Enemy* with Anthony Creighton (Harrogate, 1955). The latter play had its homosexual elements suppressed by the Censor.

Without doubt the play considered most important (though not necessarily his best) was *Look Back in Anger* the first performance of which took place on 8 May 1956 with George **Devine**'s newly-formed **English Stage Company** at the **Royal Court** Theatre. The play has been variously described as a 'landmark', a 'watershed in modern theatre' and as heralding the beginning of a 'renaissance' of British drama. John Russell Taylor called it 'a breakthrough', Michael Anderson has suggested that it 'enlarged the scope of contemporary drama as much as it extended its emotional range' and the now celebrated comment of Kenneth **Tynan** in the *Observer* at the time read, 'I doubt if I could love anyone who did not wish to see *Look Back in Anger*. It is the best young play of its decade.'

The play was controversial, bitterly critical of the post-war Establishment, middle-class complacency and an inert Toryism. It was not, as many plays before, a polite 'conversation-piece' reinforcing the values of middle-class audiences. As Michael Anderson has commented, the play rid the theatre of 'the smug suggestion that the English drawing room, preserved almost unchanged from Edwardian days by playwrights and directors, represents a high point in civilisation and wit'.

The main character, Jimmy Porter, has come to be regarded as the archetype of the 'angry young man' of the 1950s (a phrase attributable to the Irish writer Leslie Paul's autobiographical work *Angry Young Man* published in 1951) and Osborne himself the central writer of the so-called **'Angries'** (some others being Willis **Hall**, John **Arden**, Arnold **Wesker**, the novelists Kingsley Amis and John Wain and the philosopher Colin Wilson. The whole atmosphere of the 'angry young man' was parodied by Tony Hancock in the film *The Rebel* of 1961). Yet, if there was anything like a common response of a post-war generation, in the theatre the 'Angries' thrust was shortlived and in any case produced very different kinds of play. There was, as John Russell Taylor has pointed out, 'no question of a clear, consistent Royal Court "line"'. Osborne has described *Look Back in Anger* as 'a formal, rather old fashioned play' (its realism, for example, gave rise to the popular term 'kitchen-sink drama') and a 'lesson in feeling'. Perhaps today the play has lost some of its capacity to disquiet its audiences and it has become something of a period piece (for example Cliff, played by Alan **Bates** in the original production, is a traditional jazz fanatic — the mid-1950s was a period of revival for traditional jazz in Britain, the period of the Suez Crisis, problems in Hungary, CND protests and so on. The topicality of the play apart, we can nevertheless see in the frustrated anti-hero of the play a modern *angst* which is still perhaps relevant — he is a man raging for a life of feeling and enthusiasm in a society which appears inert and bereft of feeling and who learns to care, to love, and to value a personal relationship. Jimmy's rebellious rage against the dying of the light is at the same time a rage for life: 'there aren't any good brave causes left' he complains and he longs for 'a little ordinary human enthusiasm. Just enthusiasm — that's all. I want to hear a warm, thrilling voice cry out Hallelujah! Hallelujah! I'm alive.'

Osborne's play *Epitaph for George Dillon* (Royal Court, February 1958, written prior to *Look Back in Anger* with Anthony Creighton) is partly autobiographical, with its protagonist an aspiring playwright and struggling actor. Some of George's monologues anticipate those of Jimmy Porter. In April 1957 (the year he married Mary Ure, his second wife), Osborne's *The Entertainer* was staged at the Royal Court with Laurence **Olivier** as Archie Rice, a seedy second-rate music-hall artist. Although the play is set very much in the period of the Suez Crisis and has much to say about the decay of post-war Britain, it is a remarkably different form of play from *Look Back in Anger*, integrating as it does a non-realistic 'music-hall performance' structure with realistic domestic episodes, songs and comic turns, the whole reminiscent of **Brechtian** theatre. There are burlesques and parodies (such as in the sequence when Archie sings 'Thank God we're normal, normal, normal' against a background of 'Land of Hope and Glory' and a nude wearing Britannia's helmet and holding a bulldog and trident — the last line of his song runs 'this is our finest shower'). There are music-hall jokes (for example, Archie says his wife is 'very cold. Cold and stupid. She's what they call a moron glacée. Don't clap too hard — it's a very old building'), and there are the notes of protest ('all that Trafalgar Square stuff') such as we encountered in *Look Back in Anger*. Archie in a more serious moment says 'we're characters out of something nobody believes in...We don't get on with anything. We don't ever succeed in anything', and on another occasion 'I'm dead behind these eyes. I'm dead, just like the whole inert, shoddy lot out there...I don't feel a thing, and neither do they.' Osborne's attempt at a musical play *The World of Paul Slickey* (1959) was not successful but *A Subject of Scandal and Concern* (1960) and *Luther* (English Stage

Company at Theatre Royal, Nottingham, 1961, Royal Court, July 1961 with Albert **Finney** as Luther) were more successful. Osborne has perhaps too easily been regarded as a playwright of 'protest' and 'anger' whereas he has actually taken his writing in many different fruitful (and sometimes less fruitful) directions. Simon Trussler has described him as an 'ad hoc playwright with no predetermined sense of direction' and Arnold Hinchliffe explains (in his essay 'Whatever Happened to John Osborne?') that this virtuosity and variety 'often seems to derive from restlessness'.

At the Royal Court in July 1962 two one-acters were performed under the title *Plays for England* (*The Blood of the Bambergs* and *Under Plain Cover*). In 1963 he married the writer Penelope Gilliat, his third wife, and in September 1964, perhaps his best play since *Look Back in Anger* and *The Entertainer* was performed, a powerful drama called *Inadmissible Evidence*. It is a harrowing exploration of the personal and psychological breakdown of a solicitor (originally played by Nicol **Williamson**). *A Patriot for Me* (June 1965/6) is a historical drama about a homosexual spy in the pre-1914 Austrian Army — the play had to be performed privately by the English Stage Society because the performance licence was refused by the Lord Chamberlain. Such opposition from the Establishment and reactionary press reviewers has led to Osborne's legendary hatred of theatre critics: he once said, for example, that 'theatre critics should be regularly exposed, like corrupt constabularies or faulty sewage systems ... I regard them as something like kinky policemen on the cultural protectionist make, rent collectors, screws, insurance men, customs officers and Fairy Snowmen. One should simply not open one's door to them.'

His next plays at the Royal Court, *The Hotel in Amsterdam* (July 1968), *Time Present* (May 1968) and *West of Suez* (August 1971) mark something of a turning point in Osborne's writing and Hinchliffe has suggested they should be regarded as a trilogy, each focusing on a central figure who dies. Each of these figures is 'like their creator, older, wealthier and more "successful" than before' and not concerned with anti-social rebellion but 'the values of civilized life'. These plays are rather static 'conversation-pieces' about show-business people who are comfortably well-off. In the first Laurie says 'I work my drawers off and get written off twice a year as not fulfilling my earlier promise by some philistine squirt drumming up copy' — as if Osborne's autobiographical strain could view the work in the 1950s as merely one direction his writing had taken. The actress Jill Bennett (married to Osborne in 1968) starred in *The Hotel in Amsterdam* and *Time Present*. The central figure of *West of Suez*, the writer Wyatt Gillman, was played by Sir Ralph **Richardson**, and the play bears some resemblance to Shaw's *Heartbreak House* (Gillman is rather like the ageing and eccentric inventor Captain Shotover, surrounded by family and friends in a house which appears to symbolise English civilisation voyaging to disaster).

In *A Sense of Detachment* (Royal Court, November 1972) Osborne experimented with the relationships between audience and stage by having two actors in the auditorium (a football fan and a reactionary Tory) who heckled the actors (who play actors) on the stage. The play deliberately exploits controversy in having excerpts read from a pornographic catalogue contrasted with Elizabethan love lyrics and classical music, in parodying much contemporary drama and in giving theatre critics plenty of flak. *The End of Me Old Cigar* (about female militancy) and *Jill and Jack* were performed at a John Osborne Season at Greenwich Theatre in January 1975 as was an adaptation of Wilde's *The Picture of Dorian Gray*. *Watch It Come Down* (**National Theatre** at the **Old Vic**, March 1976) is about a retired film director who lives in a country railway station (which collapses during the play) with his family — very much an exposé of the illusions of 'pastoral' England in the Home Counties. Here Osborne has moved his focus of attention to rural England and the nostalgic values which are the last vestiges of a vanished culture. This is also his focus in the television play *Try a Little Tenderness* (1978) which is about a village community which protests about the staging of a pop festival in its locality.

Osborne has written a number of adaptations: *A Bond Honoured* (1966) based on a play by Lope de Vega, Ibsen's *Hedda Gabla* (1972), *A Place Calling Itself Rome* (1973) an adaptation of Shakespeare's *Coriolanus* and *The Picture of Dorian Gray* (1975) from Oscar Wilde's novel. He has also written screenplays for *Tom Jones* (1964), *Look Back in Anger* (1959), *The Entertainer* (1960) and *Inadmissible Evidence* (1968). His other works have been the television plays *The Right Prospectus* (1970), *Very Like a Whale* (1971), *A Gift of Friendship* (1972), *Jill and Jack* (1974), *Try a Little Tenderness* (1978) and *You're Not Watching Me, Mummy* (1979).

A Patriot for Me was revived at the 1983 **Chichester Festival** and subsequently the Haymarket Theatre in August 1983.

Osborne has not stood still in his writing for the stage and cannot easily be categorised, and although some would see him as perhaps the *enfant terrible* of Post-War British Theatre he broadened the social basis of English drama in a more dynamic way than Shaw was able. He has certainly remained controversial but never at the cost of a sympathy for the human condition at the private as well as public level. As Hinchliffe put it 'he does not hate mankind; only those who give it a bad name (usually with four letters)'. It will be interesting to see what fresh departures he makes in the future: his natural and creative restlessness will certainly not allow him to stagnate.

Further Reading

Simon Trussler, *The Plays of John Osborne*, Gollancz, London, 1969.

Arnold P. Hinchliffe, 'Whatever Happened to John Osborne?' in *Contemporary English Drama*, Stratford-upon-Avon Studies, No. 19, C.W.E. Bigsby (ed.), Edward Arnold, London, 1981.

John Osborne, *A Better Class of Person*, Penguin Books, Harmondsworth, 1982.

O'Toole, Peter

Born in Ireland on 2 August 1932, he was educated in Leeds, Ireland and Gainsborough. He began his career as a journalist and then trained for the stage at the Royal Academy of Dramatic Art, making his first professional appearance at the Civic Theatre, Leeds in 1949. From 1955 until 1958 he was a member of the **Bristol Old Vic** Company and played numerous roles, including Cabman in Thornton Wilder's *The Matchmaker* (1955), Cornwall in *King Lear* (1956, with Eric **Porter** as Lear and Alan Dobie as the Fool), Bullock in Farquhar's *The Recruiting Officer* (1956), Peter Shirley in George Bernard Shaw's *Major Barbara* (1956), Lodovico in *Othello* (1956), Alfred Doolittle in Shaw's *Pygmalion* (1957), Lysander in *A Midsummer Night's Dream* (1957), Jimmy Porter in John **Osborne**'s *Look Back in Anger* (1957), the General in Peter Ustinov's *Romanoff and Juliet* (1957), John Tanner in Shaw's *Man and Superman* (1958), the title-role in *Hamlet* (1958) and Jupiter in Jean Giraudoux's *Amphitryon '38* (1958).

O'Toole made his first appearance on the London stage as Shirley in Shaw's *Major Barbara* (Bristol Old Vic Company at the **Old Vic**, July 1956). After leaving the Bristol Old Vic Company in 1958 he played Private Bamforth in Willis **Hall**'s *The Long and the Short and the Tall* (**Royal Court**, January 1959, New, April 1959), and then joined the **Shakespeare Memorial Theatre** Company for its 1960 season at Stratford-upon-Avon, playing a highly acclaimed Shylock in *The Merchant of Venice*, Petruchio in *The Taming of the Shrew* and

Thersites in *Troilus and Cressida.* After this he began to divide his time between film and stage work and became a highly successful film actor. Nevertheless, he returned to the stage on a number of occasions, playing some major roles such as the title-role in **Brecht**'s *Baal* (Phoenix, February 1963), the title-role in *Hamlet* (**National Theatre**, inaugural production at the Old Vic, October 1963), Peter in David **Mercer**'s *Ride-a-Cock Horse* (Piccadilly, June 1965), Captain Boyle in Sean O'Casey's *Juno and the Paycock* (Gaiety Theatre, Dublin, August 1966), Vladimir in Samuel **Beckett**'s *Waiting For Godot* (Abbey Theatre, Dublin, December 1969, where he also directed Beckett's *Happy Days*), the title-role in Chekhov's *Uncle Vanya* (Bristol Old Vic, October 1972), King Magnus in Shaw's *The Apple Cart* (Bristol Old Vic, November 1973), three parts in *Dead-Eyed Dicks* (Dublin Festival, October 1976), the title-role in Chekhov's *Uncle Vanya* and a part in Noël Coward's *Present Laughter* (both in Chicago, 1978).

In 1980 he appeared in the title-role of *Macbeth,* in a remarkably controversial production (**Prospect Theatre Company** at the Old Vic), which was heavily criticised and sensationalised by the press-critics but which nevertheless (perhaps because of the publicity) was a huge box-office success. Irving Wardle (in *The Times*) wrote that O'Toole, 'walks around the stage as if he were inspecting a property he has just acquired', and Michael Billington wrote (in the *Guardian*), 'he delivers every line with a monotonous tenor bark as if addressing an audience of deaf Eskimos'. He played Tanner in Shaw's *Man and Superman* in November 1982 (Theatre Royal, Haymarket) and in May 1984 was Professor Higgins in Ray **Cooney**'s production of Shaw's *Pygmalion* for the **Theatre of Comedy** Company (Shaftesbury), a performance described by Michael Ratcliffe (in the *Observer*) as full of 'zest, rhythm and tonal variety...monstrous, eccentric, secretive, arrogant, asexual, childlike, cross and vain...he is rather a good listener ... his tenderness is gallant and touching ... a star performer who knows precisely what he is at'.

O'Toole's very successful film career has included *Lawrence of Arabia* (1962), *Becket* (1963), *Lord Jim* (1964), *What's New, Pussycat?* (1965), *The Night of the Generals* (1967), *The Lion in Winter* (1968), *Under Milk Wood* (1971), *The Ruling Class* (1972), *Rosebud* (1975), *Power Play* (1978), *The Antagonists* (1981) and *My Favourite Year* (1981). Television work includes *Rogue Male, Strumpet City, Masada, Svengali* and *Pygmalion.*

O'Toole is an energetic and animated actor in performance, given to outbursts of eccentricity in voice and bodily movement, yet he is capable of great sensitivity. He said in an interview with Michael Anderson (in 1974), 'I'm a very physical actor, and I use everything — toes, teeth, ears, everything...I don't simply mean physical in the sense of movement and vigour; I find myself remembering the shape of a scene by how I'm standing, what I'm doing.'

Further Reading

Michael Anderson, 'Way out West with Peter O'Toole', *Plays and Players*, February 1974, pp. 15-17.

Nicholas Wapshott, *Peter O'Toole*, New English Library, London, 1983.

P

'Paper The House'

Fill the empty seats with complimentary ticket holders.

Pasco, Richard (Edward)

Born in Barnes, London, on 18 July 1926, he was educated at Colet Court, King's College School, Wimbledon, and trained at the Central School of Speech and Drama. His first appearance on the stage was as Diggory in Oliver Goldsmith's *She Stoops to Conquer* (Q Theatre, February 1943). He served in HM Forces (1944-8) and joined the **Old Vic** Company in September 1950. Parts with the company included Curio in *Twelfth Night* (December 1950), Gloucester in *Henry V* (January 1951), Simple in *The Merry Wives of Windsor* (May 1951), Old Man in *King Lear* (March 1952) and Lucilius in *Timon of Athens* (May 1952).

In 1952 he joined Birmingham Repertory Theatre Company, playing many different parts including Fortinbras in *Hamlet* for the 1955 tour, followed by performances in Moscow and the Phoenix Theatre, London (December 1955).

At the Lyric, Hammersmith, Pasco played Jimmy Porter in a revival of John **Osborne**'s *Look Back in Anger* (November 1956) and then in February 1957 joined the **English Stage Company** at the **Royal Court** Theatre. Some of his roles at the Royal Court were Frank Rice in Osborne's *The Entertainer* (April 1957) and the Orator in Ionesco's *The Chairs* (May 1957). Following this he made his first New York appearance as Frank Rice in *The Entertainer* (Royale, New York, February 1958) and appeared at the Moscow Youth Festival (1959) as Jimmy Porter in *Look Back in Anger.* At the Queen's Theatre, London (March 1961), he took the part of Lyngstrand in Ibsen's *The Lady from the Sea* and in 1963 took over the role of Julian in Peter **Shaffer**'s *The Public Eye* (part of the double-bill with *The Private Ear*, Globe, June 1963).

Pasco took the title-role in *Henry V* at the **Bristol Old Vic** (May 1964) and played Berowne in *Love's Labour's Lost.* He toured with both these productions to Austria, Scandinavia, Germany, Belgium, Holland, Israel, Yugoslavia and the Paris Festival. In September 1964 these productions were repeated at the Old Vic and later at the Venice Festival.

In March 1965 he played the title-role in *Hamlet* (Bristol Old Vic) and in September 1965 Yevgeny Konstantinovitch in Chekhov's *Ivanov.* At the Bristol Old Vic in 1966, he again played the title-role in *Hamlet* and took a number of other parts including Angelo in *Measure for Measure,* the title-role in Ibsen's *Peer Gynt* and Tanner in Shaw's *Man and Superman.* After a tour the next year, he played Edmund in Iris Murdoch and James **Saunders**'s *The Italian Girl* (Bristol Old Vic, November 1967).

With the **Royal Shakespeare Company** at Stratford-upon-Avon (1969 season) Richard Pasco played Polixenes in *The Winter's Tale,* Leantio in Middleton's *Women Beware Women,* Proteus in *The Two Gentlemen of Verona* and Buckingham in *Henry VIII.* He toured with the company in 1970 to Japan and Australia and subsequently played numerous parts including Adolphus Cusins in Shaw's *Major Barbara* (Aldwych, July 1970), Richard in *Richard II* (RSC 'Theatregoround' company, Stratford, 1971), Don John in *Much Ado About Nothing* (Stratford, 1971), Orsino in *Twelfth Night* (Stratford, 1971) and contributions to Terry **Hands**'s entertainment *Pleasure and Repent-*

ance (Stratford, 1971). In the following year he toured Japan as Orsino in *Twelfth Night* (February–March, 1972) and, on his return, his roles included Becket in **Eliot**'s *Murder in the Cathedral* (Aldwych, June 1972) and Medraut in John **Arden**'s *The Island of the Mighty* (Aldwych, December 1972).

In April 1973 at Stratford-upon-Avon, Pasco played both Richard and Bolingbroke in John **Barton**'s production of *Richard II*, alternating the parts with Ian **Richardson**. Stanley Wells (in *Royal Shakespeare*) said of these performances, 'Pasco, taller and of bigger build, has the more obviously "committed" acting style. He is an emotional actor; his large eyes easily command pathos, his rich, vibrant voice, with a wide tonal range, can be both thrilling and moving. Ian Richardson, slighter in build, is more obviously intellectual.' It was an interesting experiment and certainly one of Pasco's most acclaimed performances. The production was later put on at Brooklyn Academy of Music (January 1974), was repeated for the 1974 Stratford season, and played at the Aldwych (September 1974). Also in the 1974 Stratford season Pasco played Philip the Bastard in *King John* and in the same year and in 1975 took part in the Aldeburgh Festival. At the Malvern Festival in May 1977 he played Tanner in Shaw's *Man and Superman* (afterwards on tour and then Savoy Theatre, August 1977). In 1978 he toured the USA in performances for Poetry International and on return to England played Trigorin in Chekhov's *The Seagull* (Theatre Royal, Bristol, August 1978). Later rejoining the Royal Shakespeare Company he played the title-role in *Timon of Athens* (Other Place, October 1980), took part in John Barton's *The Hollow Crown* and Terry Hands's *Pleasure and Repentance* (Fortune, July 1981), played in Ostrovsky's *The Forest* (Warehouse, July 1981), repeated the role of Timon (Warehouse, November 1981) and played the title-role in *Richard III* (Aldwych, November 1981). In January 1982 he appeared in John Barton's new version of Schnitzler's *La Ronde* (Aldwych and Stratford) and the next month was again in *The Forest* (Aldwych).

Film work has included *Room at the Top*, *Yesterday's Enemy*, *A Watcher in the Woods* and *Wagner*; television appearances have been numerous and include *The Three Musketeers*, *Disraeli*, *The Houseboy* and *Sorrell and Son*. Pasco is also well known as a radio–drama performer and poetry reader.

Peck, Bob

Born and educated in Yorkshire, he appeared, at the age of 13, as Maria in *Twelfth Night*. He trained for four years in Fine Art at Leeds Art College and took numerous parts in amateur productions. He worked in repertory for seven years at Birmingham, Scarborough (under Alan **Ayckbourn**), Exeter (under Jane Howell) and the **Royal Court** Theatre (under Lindsay **Anderson**). Parts included Sir Epicure Mammon in Jonson's *The Alchemist*, Inspector Truscott in Jo **Orton**'s *Loot*, Pat in Brendan **Behan**'s *The Hostage*, Old Alan in Edward **Bond**'s *The Pope's Wedding*, Shakespeare in Bond's *Bingo* and Abercrombie in David **Storey**'s *Life Class*. In 1975 he joined the **Royal Shakespeare Company** for its Centenary of the Royal Shakespeare Theatre at Stratford-upon-Avon and subsequently played Lord Mowbray in *Henry IV Part 2*, Macduff in *Macbeth*, Soliony in Chekhov's *Three Sisters*, Malvolio in *Twelfth Night*, Iago in *Othello*, the title-role in *Macbeth*, Caliban in *The Tempest*, John Browdie and Sir Mulberry Hawk in *Nicholas Nickleby* and perhaps his finest performance to date, the title-role in Edward **Bond**'s *Lear* which was highly acclaimed abroad when the RSC took it on a European tour in 1984.

Pennington, Michael

Born on 7 June 1943, he was educated at Marlborough College and then studied English at Trinity College, Cambridge. He joined the **Royal Shakespeare Company** for the 1964-5 seasons and from 1966 to 1974 appeared in a number of **West End** productions and at the **Royal Court** Theatre. On rejoining the RSC in 1974 his parts included Edgar (to Donald **Sinden**'s Lear) in *King Lear* (Stratford-upon-Avon, 1966), Mercutio in *Romeo and Juliet* (Stratford, 1966) and Hector in *Troilus and Cressida* (Stratford, 1966), these productions being transferred to the Aldwych in 1977 where he also appeared as Major Rolfe in David **Edgar**'s *Destiny.* Subsequently he played Mirabell in Congreve's *The Way of the World* (Aldwych, January, 1978), Berowne in *Love's Labour's Lost* and the Duke in *Measure for Measure* (Stratford 1978, Aldwych, November 1979) and Leonid in Michael Glenny's translation of Mikhail Bulgakov's *The White Guard* (Aldwych, May 1979). In 1981 he played in John **Barton**'s *The Hollow Crown* and Terry **Hands**'s *Pleasure and Repentance* (RSC, Fortune Theatre, July), took part in O'Casey's *The Shadow of a Gunman* (the Warehouse, July) and played the title-role in John Barton's production of *Hamlet* (Aldwych, September). In September 1983 he appeared in Lyubimov and Kariakin's adaptation of Dostoevsky's *Crime and Punishment* (Lyric, Hammersmith). With the **National Theatre** in 1984 he played Jaffier in Otway's *Venice Preserv'd* (Lyttleton, April), took part in Peter Tegel's adaptation of Rozovsky's *Strider — The Story of a Horse* (Cottesloe, January) and gave a highly acclaimed solo performance in the title-role of *Anton Chekhov* (Cottesloe, July), a biographical performance–anthology of Chekhov which Michael Pennington himself devised.

Petherbridge, Edward

Born in Bradford on 3 August 1936 he was educated at the Grange Grammar School, Bradford, and trained for the stage at the Northern Theatre School, Bradford. He first appeared in 1956 as Gaveston in Marlowe's *Edward II* (Ludlow Festival) and then toured extensively and played in provincial repertory. His first London appearance was as Demetrius in *A Midsummer Night's Dream* (Open Air, Regent's Park, June 1962) and from 1964 to 1970 he was a member of the **National Theatre** Company at the **Old Vic**. He took numerous parts, the most important of which were Ferdinand Gadd in Pinero's *Trelawny of the 'Wells'*, Guildenstern in the original production of Tom **Stoppard**'s *Rosencrantz and Guildenstern are Dead* (1967), and Ludovico in Webster's *The White Devil.* Among other roles he has subsequently played Alceste in *The Misanthrope* (Nottingham Playhouse, September 1970), Laurence Doyle in Shaw's *John Bull's Other Island* (Mermaid, May 1971), been the solo performer in *Who Thought It?* (Arts Theatre, May 1972), Soranzo in Ford's *'Tis Pity She's a Whore* (**Actors' Company** at the **Edinburgh Festival**, September 1972) and Prospero in *The Tempest* (Northcott, Exeter, April 1973). With the Actors' Company he devised, directed and performed in *Knots* (Edinburgh Festival, September 1973, and tour), a compilation based on R.D. Laing's volume of poems of the same title. He directed and played in *The Bacchae* (Edinburgh Festival, August 1974, and with the Actors' Company, Wimbledon, June–August 1975).

Petherbridge joined the **Royal Shakespeare Company** in 1976 and played in *The Hollow Crown* and *Pleasure and Repentance* (Australia and New Zealand tour) and in 1977 toured with the Cambridge Theatre Company in *Dog's Dinner* and directed Chekhov's *Uncle Vanya.* In the period December 1977–January 1978 he adapted and played in R.D. Laing's *Do You Love Me?* (Actors' Company tour and Round House).

In November 1978 Petherbridge rejoined the RSC and played Orsino in *Twelfth Night* and Vershinin in Chekhov's *Three Sisters* (tour). He again played the latter in September 1979 (RSC, The Other Place, Stratford-upon-Avon) and later Newman Noggs in *Nicholas Nickleby* (RSC, Aldwych, June 1980). In April 1982 he devised and acted in *Bumps* (Lyric, Hammersmith) and later played in *Twelfth Night* (London Shakespeare Company, Warehouse, December 1982), *The Rivals* (National Theatre, Olivier, April 1983), J.M. Barrie's *Peter Pan* (RSC, Barbican, December 1983) and O'Neill's *Strange Interlude* (Duke of York's, March 1984). He has appeared in a film version of *Knots* (1975) and on television his appearances include *The Soldier's Tale*, *After Magritte*, *A True Patriot*, *Schubert* and *Pyramid of Fire*. In 1984 Petherbridge became joint director with Ian **McKellen** of the Actors' Company section of the National Theatre.

Pinter, Harold

Perhaps the leading English dramatist of post-war British theatre, he is also an actor and director. His plays have gained international acclaim and together with **Beckett** he is the central British playwright of what Martin Esslin has called the **Theatre of the Absurd**.

Born on 10 October 1930 in Hackney, East London, Pinter (da Pinta) was the son of a Jewish tailor. He was educated at Hackney Downs Grammar School and trained as an actor both at RADA and the Central School of Speech and Drama. Under the stage name of 'David Baron' he worked for nine years as an actor, starting with a Shakespearean Company touring Ireland, followed by provincial repertory work. He wrote poetry for small magazines and in 1954-5 two short stories *The Black and White* and *The Examination.* He also started to write a novel *The Dwarfs* (which eventually became a radio play broadcast on BBC Third Programme, 1960). He began to write plays in 1957 and his first, a one-act play *The Room* was performed on May 15th of that year by students in the Drama Department of Bristol University. In the same year he wrote a one-act play *The Dumb Waiter* (performed **Royal Court**, March 1960) and his first full-length play *The Birthday Party* (performed April 1958 at the Arts Theatre, Cambridge, and subsequently the Lyric Opera House, Hammersmith. Pinter directed it himself in 1959 at Birmingham). *The Dumb Waiter* is a small classic of Absurd Theatre: like Didi and Gogo waiting for some indefinable visitor 'Godot' in Beckett's *Waiting for Godot*, two gangsters Gus and Ben, wait in a hotel flat for their orders from an unknown and menacing source. The 'dumb waiter', a food lift, sends menus and food down to the two men and they can communicate with the mysterious presence 'upstairs' via a speaking tube. They fill in their time by rehearsing what they will do if someone comes in and quibbling over details of language (such as whether or not one 'lights the kettle' or 'lights the gas'). The sense of threat and menace is ever-present in the play and we never find out who is 'upstairs'. Enigmatic threats to the security of characters in a play and of audiences in the theatre are a feature of most of Pinter's plays and reveal his intimate knowledge (as a trained and experienced actor) of how the expectations, satisfactions and curiosity of audiences can be manipulated and disturbed. In *The Birthday Party*, set in a seaside boarding-house, the sense of menace and puzzlement is aroused by two potential lodgers (Goldberg and McCann) met by chance on the beach by Petey the landlord. In *A Slight Ache* (BBC Third Programme, July 1959, performed in 1961 at the Arts Theatre Club), the mysterious intruder is a match-seller who lurks outside the country house of a married couple. He is invited inside but remains silent throughout the whole play. His presence exacerbates the tensions of the relationship between the married man and woman by pressing them to reveal to each other the deeper thoughts they have never communicated. In Pinter's subsequent plays uncertainties, doubts and contradictions are deliberately aroused by many such apparently motiveless figures whose origins and backgrounds are obscure. Pinter has stated that a 'character on stage who can present no convincing argument or information as to his past experience, his present behaviour or his aspirations, nor give a comprehensive analysis of his motives, is as legitimate and as worthy of attention as one who, alarmingly, can do all these things'.

It was with *The Caretaker* (Arts Theatre, April, starring Donald **Pleasance** and Alan **Bates**, and the Duchess Theatre, May, 1960) that Pinter became established as a major successful playwright. Mick and Aston invite a strange down-and-out figure, Davies, into their seedy flat. All three rely on fantasies about their futures and these give them some foothold, some secure anchorage, against having to face their true existential state: Aston believes he will convert the house, refurbish it and build a shed in the garden, Mick dreams of being a successful salesman, and Davies has his 'papers' at Sidcup and a bag containing his 'things'. Nevertheless, as the play develops Davies is increasingly threatened (even violently) and cornered by the two men whose nervous tensions are aroused by his presence. As with nearly all Pinter's plays the ambiguities of human existence are partly manifested through the apparently realistic setting (a room with recognisably real and ordinary furniture is common) and fine rendering of ordinary language conversation, beneath both of which lie irrational fears, doubts and uncertainties about what is real. The 'silences' between *and* beneath utterances (as in many of Beckett's plays too) press the pathos and agonising tragedy of human existence upon the characters (and the audience in the theatre) and suggest an unknown, metaphysical and horrendous nothingness and mystery beyond the here and now. Pinter said (in 1962) that there are 'two silences: one when no word is spoken, the other when perhaps a torrent of language is being employed. This speech is speaking of a language locked beneath it. That's its continual reference. The speech we hear is an indication of what we don't hear. It is a necessary avoidance, a violent, sly, anguished or mocking smokescreen which keeps the other in its place. When true silence falls we are still left with the echo but are nearer nakedness.' Whereas with a Beckett play we know clearly we are in an abstracted 'poetic' realm (in physical stage setting especially) in Pinter's plays the ordinary and realistic are inextricably intertwined with the irrational and absurd. Martin Esslin put his finger on precisely this subtlety in the way the plays work when he wrote that we are confronted by 'images of the real world which are raised to metaphors of the human condition by the mysteriousness inherent in reality and the difficulties of drawing a line between the real, the imagined and the dream'.

The short plays *A Night Out* (1960), *The Collection* (1961) and *The Lover* (1963) explore the hidden powers of sexual energy which lurk beneath the surface of relationships, producing anxieties, jealousies and absurdities of behaviour and dialogue. Pinter's television plays *The Tea Party* (broadcast on 25 March 1965) and *The Basement* (20 February 1967, with Pinter himself as Stott) also focus upon disturbing sexual encounters.

The Homecoming (presented by the **RSC**, Aldwych Theatre, June 1965) involves the 'homecoming' of a professor (Ted) and his wife (Ruth) to their home in London only to find his family still living there (his uncle, father and two brothers). Reactions to each other are often inexplicably and strangely casual as if Ted has never been away and Ruth becomes the centre of threats and sexual attractions, surrounded as she is by five men (one of whom turns out to be a professional pimp). It is a play with unexpected turns and sudden surprises such as might be found in dreams which are manifestations of desires and fears (there are occasions when Ruth is regarded as a surrogate mother for the two brothers; when Sam collapses towards the end of the play we never know, even when the play has finished, whether he is really dead or alive).

The double-bill of *Landscape* and *Silence* (RSC, Aldwych, July 1969), attempted some new formal experiments with dialogue and 'silences'. In the first there are two characters who (as the stage direction instructs) do '*not appear to hear*' each other when they speak. The dialogue is more like two monologues which loosely refer to the same memories and anecdotes of the past. *Silence* has three characters and each on occasion is even more isolated in a monologue than we find in *Landscape*, yet on other occasions one of the two men (Bates and Rumsey) moves into dialogue with the woman Ellen. Both plays are essays in human isolation and the problems of communication through attempts to recall the past. There seem to be many affinities here with Beckett's *Play* and *Lessness* (a radio play for six voices, one of which was originally read by Pinter). *Old Times* (RSC Aldwych, June 1971) possesses a similar rather static quality and dwells upon memory and the attempt of three people to share the past. These shifting perspectives on the past, the inadequate grip characters have on reality and truth, give rise to what C.W.E. Bigsby has described as 'a threatening world in which the desire for verification, the need for full knowledge and genuine communication, is necessarily frustrated'.

The remarkable partnership between those two knights of the theatre Sir Ralph **Richardson** and Sir John **Gielgud** (so successful in David **Storey**'s *Home*) formed the centrepiece of the first staging of Pinter's *No Man's Land* (**National Theatre** at the **Old Vic**, April 1975) and the play seemed almost to have been written for them. The location of the play is neither an actual historical location in an easily recognisable place and time (what appears to be a realistic setting becomes ambiguous) nor the 'nowhere' of a symbolic landscape (such as we have in *Silence* or Beckett's *Endgame*). It is rather something between these two extremes, a credible metaphor for the 'no man's land' of human existence perceived through a semi-alcoholic haze, almost a mysterious dream. Supposedly a house near Hampstead Heath, the location is at times doubted and at other times symbolic of different places according to who is describing it; Hirst says at one point 'Let me perhaps be your boatman', suggesting he may be something like the ferryman of the Styx in the classical underworld; Foster, on the other hand, says 'But I still like a nice lighthouse like this one' and in the original production the upstage part of the room was in the form of very tall windows set in a semicircle and when the window-curtains were thrown back for the second half of the play a richly ambiguous image was created: was actual daylight streaming in, was 'light' from the room-as-lighthouse beaming out of the windows, or was *darkness* 'shining' out and in? Such finely wrought moments in the play abound and possess an uncanny economy of statement. Referring to his work with director Sir Peter **Hall** in particular, Pinter has remarked that 'the key word is economy, economy of movement and gesture, of emotion and its expression, both the internal and the external in specific and exact relation to each other, so that there is no wastage and no mess'. Anyone who saw the first production will know how appropriate that statement is to *No Man's Land*. Perhaps the play expresses an 'eternal present' ('No Man's Land ... does not move ... or change ... or grow old ... remains ... forever ... icy ... silent,' says Hirst) where people use language in each other's presence but remain strangers.

In an interview on London Weekend

Television (September 1975) Sir Ralph Richardson (Hirst) said of the characters in the play: 'They don't quite know who they are. But that's rather natural in a way. We don't know exactly who we are, do we? We hardly know anybody else, really completely... We're a mystery to ourselves, and to other people.' Even the truth of the past is in doubt and the only truly accurate expression is the 'essentially poetic' (Spooner holds) because that kind of truth is outside time and space, transcendent. When the lights go out in a theatre it usually only denotes the end of a scene or act or the whole performance: in *No Man's Land* it creates fear and insecurity, like that of a child terrified of the dark, a place where it is difficult to find one's bearings. One is reminded of the lines from T.S. **Eliot**'s *Four Quartets*, 'let the dark come upon you/Which shall be the darkness of God. As, in a theatre,/The lights are extinguished, for the scene to be changed/With a hollow rumble of wings, with a movement of darkness upon darkness,' (indeed allusions to Eliot's poetry abound in *No Man's Land* – 'now and in England and in Hampstead and for all eternity', 'All we have left is the English language. Can it be salvaged?', 'Can you imagine two of us gabbling away like me? It would be intolerable', 'I have known this before. The voice unheard', 'I am your Chevalier'). Gielgud's appearance was modelled on W.H. Auden's.

In 1978 came the short play *Betrayal* (National Theatre, November) and in 1981 the radio play for three voices *Family Voices* (BBC Radio 3, January) later staged (National Theatre, February). It seems that since *Landscape* Pinter has become more and more experimental in exploring the complex relationships between language, reality and human consciousness. This has brought him very close to the preoccupations of Beckett's later plays and monologues (Pinter's *Monologue* was televised in April 1973). Yet Pinter's plays and Pinter himself defy categories and explanations: he has said 'What am I writing about? Not the weasel under the cocktail cabinet. I am not concerned with making general statements ... I can sum up none of my plays. I can describe none of them, except to say: That is what happened. That is what they said. That is what they did.'

In October 1982 the National Theatre staged Pinter's trilogy *Other Places* at the Cottesloe and in March 1984 his double bill *One for the Road* and *Victoria Station* was performed at the Lyric Studio.

Further Reading

Steven Gale, *Butter's Going Up: A Critical Analysis of Harold Pinter's Work*, Durham, N. Carolina, 1977.
Martin Esslin, *Pinter: A Study of his Plays*, Eyre Methuen, London, 1973.
Ronald Hayman, *Harold Pinter*, Heinemann Educational Books, London, 1976 (and subsequently).

Pit

The ground floor or below ground-floor area of the theatre between the front of a stage and the first row of the audience, usually for orchestras or musicians.

'Plant'

An actor deliberately placed in the audience in order to address or heckle the actors on the stage.

Plater, Alan (Frederick)

Born in Jarrow-on-Tyne, County Durham, on 15 April 1935, he was educated at Pickering Road Junior and Infant School, Hull, Kingston High School, Hull (1946-53), and King's College (Durham University), Newcastle-upon-Tyne (1953-7) where he studied architecture (fully qualified in 1961). From 1957 until 1960 he worked in an architect's office in Hull and in 1961 became a full-time writer.

Many of Plater's television plays have been rewritten for the stage and vice versa, his first successful play *The Referees*, originally a television play transmitted in 1961, being performed as a stage play at the Victoria Theatre, Stoke-on-Trent in 1963. This was later followed by other plays at the same theatre including *A Smashing Day* (1965), originally a television play (transmitted in 1962) about a restless youth (Lennie) and his relationship with the opposite sex.

Plater's greatest success for the stage has been *Close the Coalhouse Door* (Jesmond Playhouse, Newcastle, 1968) which was a musical documentary, based on a story by Sid Chaplin, celebrating the coalmining industry and the Durham miners in particular. Songs for the play were written by Alex Glasgow. Another musical with Alex Glasgow was *Simon Says!* (Leeds Playhouse, 1970) a satirical attack on the ruling classes epitomised by the Marylebone Cricket Club (MCC).

Alan Plater has for many years been associated with the Hull Arts Centre which he eventually helped to establish as the Humberside Theatre (Spring Street Theatre, Hull). *The Tigers are Coming, OK* (Hull Arts Centre, 1973) explored the experiences of a Hull City ('The Tigers') football supporter. Subsequent plays performed in Hull and elsewhere have included *Swallows on the Water* (Hull Arts Centre, 1973), *Trinity Tales* (Birmingham Repertory, 1975) which were adaptations (with Alex Glasgow's music) of some of Chaucer's *Canterbury Tales* shifting them to the context of a Rugby League trip to Wembley, *Tales of Humberside* (Humberside Theatre, 1975) based on local stories, *The Fosdyke Saga* (Bush, London, 1976) adapted from Bill Tidy's *Daily Mirror* strip-cartoon, *Well...Good Night Then* (Humberside Theatre, Hull, February 1978) about people who are reluctant to go home, *On Your Way, Riley!* (Theatre Royal, Stratford East, April 1982) about Arthur Lucan and Kitty McShane, and *Prez* (Humberside Theatre, Hull, April 1984), a musical documentary about the jazz saxophonist Lester Young (the title of the play deriving from his nick-name 'president') with jazz music arranged by Bernie Cash.

Alan Plater is one of Britain's most distinguished and prolific television playwrights. His numerous plays and contributions to series include *Z Cars, Ted's Cathedral, Softly Softly*, the trilogy *To See How Far It Is, Close the Coalhouse Door, The Whips Are Out, Softly Softly Task Force, Rest In Peace, Uncle Fred, Tonight We Meet Arthur Pendlebury, The Reluctant Juggler* (for *The Edwardians*), *The Land of Green Ginger, Trinity Tales, Middleman, On Your Way, Riley*, an episode of *The Adventures of Sherlock Holmes, The Barchester Chronicles, The Beiderbecke Affair* and *Edward Lear on the Edge of the Sand.* Filmscripts include *The Virgin and the Gypsy, Juggernaut* (additions), *All Things Bright and Beautiful* and *It Shouldn't Happen to a Vet.*

His stage plays are mostly comedies with a working-class appeal set in the North-East of England and characterised by a socialist viewpoint. He wrote in 1977: 'The evidence of the more-or-less knockabout shows we've done around the regions is that people laugh the louder if the fun is spiced with a couple of centuries of inherited prejudice.'

Pleasence, Donald

Born on 5 October 1919, in Worksop, Nottinghamshire, he was educated at Ecclesfield Grammar School, Yorkshire, and made his first stage appearance at the Playhouse, Jersey in May 1939, playing Hareton in *Wuthering Heights.* He married Miriam Raymond in 1940 and first appeared in London at the Arts Theatre in June 1942, as Valentine in *Twelfth Night*, and then served with the Royal Air Force during the war. He was a prisoner-of-war from 1944 until 1946, and returned to the theatre in June 1946, playing Mavriky in Alec **Guinness**'s adaptation of *The Brothers Karamazov* (Lyric, Hammersmith). From 1948 to 1950 he worked with the Birmingham Repertory Company and in 1951 appeared briefly with the **Bristol Old Vic** Company. In September 1951 he appeared as the Reverend Giles Aldus in the first production of John **Whiting**'s *Saint's Day* (Arts Theatre), directed by Stephen Murray for the Festival of Britain. He first appeared in New York with Sir Laurence **Olivier**'s company in *Antony and Cleopatra* and Shaw's *Caesar and Cleopatra* (Ziegfeld Theatre, December 1951).

In 1952 Donald Pleasence appeared at the **Edinburgh Festival** as Huish in his own play, *Ebb Tide*, which subsequently transferred to the **Royal Court** Theatre in London. The following year he appeared for a season at the **Shakespeare Memorial Theatre**, Stratford-upon-Avon, as Lepidus in *Antony and Cleopatra* (with Michael **Redgrave** and Peggy **Ashcroft** in the title-roles). In November 1953 the production transferred to the Prince's Theatre, London.

Following this he took many roles in London productions including the Dauphin in Anouilh's *The Lark* (Lyric, Hammersmith, May 1955) and Gunner in Shaw's *Misalliance* (Lyric, Hammersmith, February 1956). His second marriage was to Josephine Crombie in 1959 and the next year he played one of his most memorable roles as Davies in the first production of Harold **Pinter**'s *The Caretaker* (Arts Theatre, April 1960, Duchess, May 1960, Lyceum, New York, October 1961). In July 1967 he played Arthur Goldman in Robert Shaw's *The Man in the Glass Booth* (St Martin's, July 1967, Royale, New York, September 1968). In 1970 his third marriage was to Meira Shore and in the same year he played Law in Pinter's *The Basement* and Disson in Pinter's *Tea Party* (Duchess, September 1970). In February 1972 he played Mrs Artminster in Simon **Gray**'s *Wise Child* (Helen Hayes Theatre, New York) and subsequently concentrated largely on film, television and radio acting. In 1980 he appeared on the stage as George Greive in John Peacock's *Reflections* (Theatre Royal, Haymarket, March 1980) which also starred Dorothy **Tutin**.

Donald Pleasence has been a prolific film actor, usually in character parts. Some of the many films he has appeared in are, *The Beachcomber, The Great Escape, The Caretaker, The Greatest Story Ever Told, Cul-de-Sac, The Night of the Generals, The Mad Woman of Chaillot, Outback, Soldier Blue, Kidnapped, Henry VIII and His Six Wives, Tales From Beyond the Grave, Escape to Witch Mountain, Journey Into Fear, The Eagle Has Landed, Golden Rod, Halloween, Power Play, Dracula, Escape from New York, A Rare Breed,* and *Warrior of the Lost World.* Television work has included *Occupations, Call Me Daddy, Shades of Greene, The Captain of Kopenick, Mrs Colombo* and *The Ghost Sonata.* In 1982 he appeared in *Barchester Towers* and in 1983, *The Falkland Factor.*

Although he has played a range of character-parts Donald Pleasence is best known for his playing of sinister, rather menacing and mysterious figures: witness his solo performance of Caesar as the first modern dictator in *The Private Thoughts of Julius Caesar*, a television adaptation (by Christopher Burstall) of Rex Warner's novel *Imperial Caesar*; witness also his superb playing of Pinter roles.

Plowright, Joan (Ann), CBE, Lady Olivier

Born in Brigg, Lincolnshire, on 28 October 1929, she was educated at Scunthorpe Grammar School. Her father edited a Scunthorpe newspaper. She became a supply-teacher before studying for the stage at the **Old Vic** Theatre School (with such distinguished directors as Michel St Denis, Glen Byam Shaw and George **Devine**). Her first professional appearance was as Hope in *If*

Four Walls Told at the Grand Theatre, Croydon, in July 1951. After a period in repertory at the **Bristol Old Vic** and a tour of South Africa in 1952 with the Old Vic Company she appeared in the **West End** and at Nottingham Playhouse (1955-6).

She joined the **English Stage Company** at the **Royal Court** Theatre in April 1956, where her roles included Mary Warren in Arthur Miller's *The Crucible*, Mrs Shin in **Brecht**'s *The Good Woman of Setzuan* and the part which brought her to prominence, Margery Pinchwife in Wycherley's *The Country Wife* (Royal Court, December 1956). She then played in a number of important contemporary plays including the Old Woman in Ionesco's *The Chairs* (Royal Court, May 1957) and Jean Rice in John **Osborne**'s *The Entertainer* (Palace, September 1957), with Laurence **Olivier** whom she married in 1961. She repeated her role as the Old Woman in Ionesco's *The Chairs* and also played the Pupil in the same playwright's *The Lesson* at the Phoenix Theatre, New York (January 1958) and played Jean Rice in *The Entertainer* at the Royale, New York (February 1958). On returning to the Royal Court Theatre in June 1958 she again played in *The Lesson* and *The Chairs* and subsequently played the title-role in Shaw's *Major Barbara* (Royal Court, August 1958).

Joan Plowright was the original Beattie Bryant in Arnold **Wesker**'s *Roots* (Belgrade, Coventry, May 1959, Royal Court, June 1959), a part which she has said 'leapt off the page at me and I'd have gone anywhere to have done it' (*Plays and Players*, July 1982). This was followed by other parts in avant-garde and contemporary plays including Daisy in Ionesco's *Rhinoceros* (Royal Court, April 1960) and Josephine in Shelagh **Delaney**'s *A Taste of Honey* (Lyceum Theatre, New York, October 1960).

She gave highly praised performances of Sonya in Chekhov's *Uncle Vanya* (**Chichester Festival**, July 1962 and June 1963, **National Theatre** Company, Old Vic, October 1963) and the title-role in Shaw's *Saint Joan* (Chichester, June 1963, **Edinburgh Festival**, September 1963, National Theatre, Old Vic, October 1963). Other roles with the National Theatre at the Old Vic included Hilda in Ibsen's *The Master Builder* (1964), Masha Sergueevna in Chekhov's *Three Sisters* (1967), Dorine in Tyrone **Guthrie**'s production of Molière's *Tartuffe* (1967), Rosaline in *Love's Labour's Lost* (1968), Portia in *The Merchant of Venice* (1970) and Mistress Ann in Heywood's *A Woman Killed With Kindness* (1971).

In an interview with Mavis Nicolson ('A Plus Four', Channel 4, 7 January 1985) she suggested that acting is an extension of what children engage in when playing but exactly why actors should continue to play the game of 'let's pretend' in adult life is something which, she said, actors and actresses can never really explain. She offered her own point of view as feeling 'there were a lot of creatures inside me which I could find no means of expressing in ordinary life, because in ordinary life you've got to become one person in order to function properly...I've been able to lead a lot of lives...I think I am only really totally free on stage and in another character.' She summarised her views of theatre and acting in an earlier interview with Linda Christmas (*Plays and Players*, July 1982): 'The theatre is a tightrope, you don't *know* what is going to happen: one night you might soar to the heights for no explicable reason...I want to be part of something that is essential. Acting is essential if it offers God-given illumination of the human dilemma.'

At the Chichester Festival Theatre in 1972 she was Jennifer in Shaw's *The Doctor's Dilemma* (May) and Katharina in *The Taming of the Shrew* (July). Following these appearances she played Rebecca West in Ibsen's *Rosmersholm* at Greenwich Theatre (May 1973). Subsequent roles have included Rosa in de Filippo's *Saturday, Sunday, Monday* (Old Vic, October 1973), Stella in J.B. Priestley's *Eden End* (Old Vic, April 1974), Irena in Lindsay **Anderson**'s production of Chekhov's *The Seagull* (Lyric, October 1975) and Alma in Ben Travers's *The Bed Before Yesterday* (Lyric, December 1975). She was highly acclaimed in the title-role of de Filippo's *Filumena* (Lyric, November 1977, St James Theatre, New York, February 1980). With Colin **Blakely** as the elderly husband she played the wife in Alan **Bennett**'s *Enjoy* (Vaudeville, 1980) and in July 1982 she took the title-role in Keith Baxter's *Cavell* (Chichester Festival). She appeared in Chekhov's *The Cherry Orchard* in October 1983 at the Haymarket Theatre and in July 1984 she was Lady Wishfort in Congreve's *The Way of the World* at Chichester Festival and in November 1984 at the Haymarket.

Pre-performance preparations are, Joan Plowright told Mavis Nicolson, essential rituals for shedding the preoccupations of the day and for 'becoming whoever you are going to be playing that night'. It is vital that 'you feel prepared for an audience, prepared for your character, that you have tuned up your instrument — which in an actor's case is his voice and his body — that the blood is racing through and that the mind is alert and the emotions are ready to be turned on ... because that's your job'.

Film appearances include *Moby Dick, The Entertainer, Three Sisters, The Merchant of Venice, Equus, Britannia Hospital, Brimstone and Treacle, A Dedicated Man* and *Wagner*. Television work includes *Odd Man In, The Secret Agent* and *The School For Scandal*. She has also directed a number of plays.

Further Reading

Joan Plowright and Linda Christmas, 'Acting is not Enough', *Plays and Players*, July 1982.

'Poetic' Drama

See **Verse Drama**.

Poliakoff, Stephen

Born in London in 1952, his education included studying for a degree at Cambridge University. His major plays have been *Clever Soldiers* (Hampstead Theatre Club, November 1974) set in the period of the First World War and which explores and criticises the class-privileges which follow a public school education, and *City Sugar* (Bush Theatre, October 1975) about an ex-teacher who, as a Radio Leicester disc jockey (Leonard Brazil), is disillusioned by the falsities and fantasies of the pop record shows he presents to his teenage audiences, audiences who appear to be almost totally distracted from the realities of the world (such as those presented in the news bulletins). They prefer such false dreams as Leonard's phone-in 'Competition of the Year'.

The one-act play *Hitting Town* (Bush, March 1975) also explored the disillusionment of a central character, this time an ex-student of Birmingham University who seeks solace in an incestuous relationship with his sister in Leicester. *Strawberry Fields* (**National Theatre**, April 1977) was about a boy and girl who are extreme fascists, and *American Days* (ICA, May 1979), set in the offices of a record company, examines the short-lived potential of three hopeful pop-stars and reveals how subservient they become to the whims of fashion and consumerism. Other plays have included *Shout Across the River* which was performed by the **Royal Shakespeare Company** (Warehouse, September 1978), *The Summer Party* (1979) about an unsuccessful pop-concert which leaves its audience to focus its attentions on a senior police officer, *Favourite Nights* (Lyric, Hammersmith, November 1981), and *Breaking the Silence* (Royal Shakespeare Company, Barbican, Pit, November 1984, Mermaid, May 1985) which is set in Russia in the period immediately after the Russian Revolution and is about an inventor (Pesiakoff) on the brink of developing movie 'talkies' as he travels in a railway carriage.

His persecuted journey leads to a deeper recognition of his own tragic existence.

Although his plays are not as overtly 'political' as David **Hare**'s, nevertheless, as Christopher Bigsby put it (in *Contemporary English Drama*, 1981) Poliakoff's plays, like some of those of Barrie **Keefe**, have an 'air of bafflement, stunted hopes, betrayed ideals and spiritual capitulation'.

Poliakoff has written a number of screen plays including *Runners*, *Soft Targets*, *Stronger than the Sun*, *Bloody Kids*, and *Caught on a Train*.

Porter, Eric (Richard)

Born in London on 8 April 1928, he was educated at schools in London and at Wimbledon Technical College. He made his first stage appearance in a walk-on part for the **Shakespeare Memorial Theatre** Company's production of *Twelfth Night* (Arts Theatre, Cambridge, February 1945). He remained with the company for the 1945 season at Stratford-upon-Avon and in autumn of the same year joined Lewis Casson's Travelling Repertory Theatre Company, making his first London appearance as Dunois' Page in Shaw's *Saint Joan* (King's Theatre, Hammersmith, March 1946). After National Service with the RAF (1946-7) he joined Donald **Wolfit**'s Company on tour in Britain and Canada. Subsequently he was with Birmingham Repertory Company under the direction of Barry **Jackson** (1948-50) and then took a contract with H.M. Tennant Ltd (1951-3), playing a number of roles including Jones in Galsworthy's *The Silver Box* (Lyric, Hammersmith, March 1951), Solyoni in Chekhov's *Three Sisters* (Aldwych, May 1951), the Boy in *Under the Sycamore Tree* (Aldwych, April 1952) and, (for the John **Gielgud** season at the Lyric, Hammersmith) Bolingbroke in *Richard II* (December 1952), Fainall in Congreve's *The Way of the World* (February 1953) and Reynault in Otway's *Venice Preserv'd* (May 1953).

With the **Bristol Old Vic** Company his parts included Becket in T.S. **Eliot**'s *Murder in the Cathedral* and Father Browne in Graham **Greene**'s *The Living Room* (Bristol, 1954). Joining the **Old Vic** Company in London his chief roles were Banquo in *Macbeth*, Bolingbroke in *Richard II*, and King Henry in *Henry IV Parts 1 and 2* (1954-5). He returned to the Bristol Old Vic where his main parts were the title-roles in Chekhov's *Uncle Vanya*, Ben Jonson's *Volpone* and Shakespeare's *King Lear* (1955-6). Subsequently he appeared in many plays at a variety of theatres, some of his most important parts being the Burgomaster in Durrenmatt's *Time and Again* (Theatre Royal, Brighton, December 1957, renamed *The Visit* when later performed at the Lunt–Fontanne Theatre, New York, May 1958), and Rosmer in Ibsen's *Rosmersholm* (**Royal Court**, November 1959).

In 1960 he joined the Shakespeare Memorial Theatre Company at Stratford-upon-Avon and the Aldwych, where parts included Malvolio in *Twelfth Night* (1960), Ulysses in *Troilus and Cressida* (1960), Leontes in *The Winter's Tale* (1960), the title-roles in Anouilh's *Becket* (1961) and Shakespeare's *Macbeth* (1962), Iachimo in *Cymbeline* (1962), Bolingbroke in *Richard II* (1964), King Henry in *Henry IV Parts 1 and 2* (1964), Barabas in Marlowe's *The Jew of Malta* (1965), Shylock in *The Merchant of Venice* (1965), Ossip in Gogol's *The Government Inspector* (1966) and the title-roles in *King Lear* and Marlowe's *Doctor Faustus* (1968). He toured in this latter role in the USA (1969) and then played Paul Thomsen in *My Little Boy, My Big Girl* which he also directed (Fortune, October 1969). At the Brighton Festival in May 1971 he took the title-role in *The Protagonist* (Gardner Theatre, Brighton). For the opening of the St George's Theatre, Islington, he played Malvolio in *Twelfth Night* (April 1976).

Eric Porter is perhaps as highly regarded

a film and television actor as he is a stage actor. Film work has included *The Fall of the Roman Empire* (1964), *The Pumpkin Eater* (1964), *The Lost Continent* (1968), *Nicholas and Alexandra* (1971), *Antony and Cleopatra* (1971), *Hitler: the Last Ten Days* (1973), *The Day of the Jackal* (1973), *The Belstone Fox* (1973), *Hennessy* (1975), *The Thirty-Nine Steps* (1978), *Little Lord Fauntleroy* (1980). His most acclaimed performance on television has undoubtedly been Soames in *The Forsyte Saga* (1967) but he has given equally fine performances in many other television plays and series (since 1945), some of which are: *Cyrano de Bergerac, Man and Superman, Separate Tables, The Statue and the Rose, Why Didn't They Ask Evans?* Some recent television roles include Karenin in *Anna Karenina* (1977), Alanbrooke in *Churchill and the Generals* (1979), Polonius in *Hamlet* (1980), Darnforth in *The Crucible* (1981) and Neville Chamberlain in *Winston Churchill: The Wilderness Years* (1981). In 1983 he appeared in *The Jewel in the Crown* and in 1985 was Fagin in *Oliver Twist.*

Potter, Dennis (Christopher George)

Born the son of a miner in Joyford Hill, Coleford, Gloucester on 17 May 1935, he was educated at Christchurch Village School, Bell's Grammar School, Coleford and St Clement Danes Grammar School, London. After National Service as a War Office clerk he read philosophy, politics and economics at New College, Oxford and gained his degree in 1959, the year he married Margaret Morgan. He began his career on the Current Affairs Staff of BBC Television and then in 1961 became a journalist and television critic for the *Daily Herald*, in 1964 a Leader Writer for the *Sun* and has subsequently been a television critic for the *New Statesman* and a book reviewer for *The Times* and the *Guardian.* In 1964 he stood as a Labour candidate for East Hertfordshire.

He has written plays primarily for television (well over 20) and this is undoubtedly his first medium. Indeed, it is often claimed that Potter is our most distinguished television playwright. Most of his plays which have appeared in the theatre are stage versions of plays originally written for television and include *Vote, Vote, Vote, for Nigel Barton* (televised 1965, stage version **Bristol Old Vic**, 1968), a semi-autobiographical play about a miner's son who goes up to Oxford, stands as a Labour candidate and then becomes disillusioned with party politics, and *Son of Man* (televised 1969, stage version Leicester, Phoenix, 1969), about the mission, trial and crucifixion of Christ, but with the emphasis upon Christ as a 'man' agonising over his own divinity. In an interview with Marcel Berlins (Channel 4, 17 June 1984) Potter said that Christian morality 'seems to carry within it certain truths, or even half-truths — and half-truths will sometimes do — in grappling with physical materiality, the deadness of "things", callousness of "things"'. In the late 1960s and through until about 1977 (when it was controlled by drug treatment) Potter suffered from a crippling disease (psoriatic arthropathy) but managed to keep writing for television and newspapers. His television play *Only Make Believe* was broadcast in 1973 and presented as a stage play at the Playhouse, Harlow, in 1974, and concerns a crippled writer trying to write a television play. *Brimstone and Treacle* was written in 1976 for television but the then BBC Director of Programmes (Alastair Milne) would not allow its transmission because of its rape scenes. A video of the play was shown at the 1977 Edinburgh Television Festival and a stage version performed in October 1977 at the Studio Theatre, Sheffield, and in February 1979 at the **Open Space**, London. The play explores the moral redemption of a girl (Pattie) from seemingly irredeemable corruption. In the same interview quoted earlier Potter said, 'nobody is without morality. That's an assumption I start from.

The question is: is one form of morality better than another? The answer to that must be yes.'

Potter's first play written originally for the stage was *Sufficient Carbohydrate* (Hampstead, December 1983, later transferred to the Albery Theatre), about two senior executives who sharply disagree over company policy, and who are on a conflict-ridden holiday in a Greek villa with their families.

Dennis Potter's best television plays, besides *Nigel Barton* and *Son of Man* already mentioned, have undoubtedly been *Pennies from Heaven* (1978), which broke new ground in its form of musical television drama presenting the story of a sheet-music salesman in the 1930s, and *Blue Remembered Hills* (1979), a remarkable piece in which seven adult performers play seven small children engaged in their gang's games on a summer's day in the country during the Second World War. Other television plays include *Where the Buffalo Roam* (1966), *The Bonegrinder* (1968), *A Beast with Two Backs* (1968), *Paper Roses* (1971), *Follow the Yellow Brick Road* (1972), *Joe's Ark* (1974), *Schmoedipus* (1974), *Late Call* (1975, an adaptation of Angus Wilson's novel), *The Mayor of Casterbridge* (1978, an adaptation of Thomas Hardy's novel), and *Cream in My Coffee* (1980). Filmscripts have been written for *Pennies From Heaven* (1981), *Brimstone and Treacle* (1982) and *Gorky Park* (1983). In addition, Potter's novels *Hide and Seek* (1973) and *Pennies From Heaven* (1982) have been published.

Potter has said that a writer has to have the 'impulse towards understanding that mortal human beings have a difficult journey to make...it's not pessimistic to say everything is not alright. Everything is capable of change, including oneself.'

Further Reading

Philip Purser, 'Dennis Potter', *British Television Drama* George W. Brandt (ed.), Cambridge University Press, London, 1981, pp. 168-93.

John Ashton, S.J., *The Month*, March 1970.

Powell, Robert

Born in Salford, Lancashire, on 1 June 1944, he was educated at Manchester Grammar School and Manchester University (where he acted in student productions). He began his professional career under Peter Cheeseman at the Victoria Theatre, Stoke-on-Trent, in 1964. In July 1966 he appeared as messengers and guests in Alfred Jarry's *Ubu Roi* (**Royal Court** Theatre) and in 1971 played the title-role in *Hamlet* (Leeds Playhouse). Subsequent parts have included Lingstrand in Ibsen's *The Lady from the Sea* (Greenwich Theatre, April 1971), Jean in *Pirates* (Royal Court, Theatre Upstairs, December 1971), Scythrop Glowery in Anthony Sharp's dramatisation of Thomas Love Peacock's *Nightmare Abbey* (Arnaud, Guildford, November 1972), Oberon in *The Fairy Queen* (Newcastle University, 1973) and Branwell Brontë in Noel Robinson's *Glasstown* (Westminster Theatre, July 1973).

Robert Powell came to prominence with his much-praised performance as the Dada artist Tristan Tzara in Tom **Stoppard**'s *Travesties* (**Royal Shakespeare Company**, Aldwych, May 1975). In 1981 he appeared in Richard Maher and Roger Michell's *Private Dick* (Lyric, April 1981, Whitehall, June 1982).

His appearances in films include *Running Speed, Mahler, Tommy, Jesus of Nazareth, The Thirty-Nine Steps* and *Harlequin.* Television work includes *Doomwatch, Jude the Obscure, Sentimental Journey, Shelley, Rolls and Royce, Mrs Warren's Profession, The Caucasian Chalk Circle* and *Looking for Clancy.* He is also much in demand as a film narrator and recent work included the television documentary series *The World of Wildlife* (BBC TV, 1983).

Profile Spot

FOH spotlight with a hard clear-cut edge to

the beam. Unlike the **Fresnel Spot** the lens is movable in order to slightly soften or harden its edge. This is also facilitated by shutters at the front of the lantern (in the 'gate'). Profiles can take silhouette cut-outs (called 'gobos') and project them for special effects, and they also take electrically driven colour wheels.

Promenade

A play performed 'in promenade' is usually one where different scenes are moved around the audience which itself is permitted to move where it wishes in relation to the location of acting areas, an example being *The Mysteries* (Cottesloe, January 1985).

Prompt Copy

Text of a play with all cues marked in. Usually used by the **Stage Manager** in conjunction with a cue board.

Prompt Corner

The area stage left where the **Stage Manager** sits (and sometimes a prompter).

Proscenium

A term used to describe both an architectural feature of the theatre and a tradition of theatrical presentation. The former refers to the 'picture-frame' arch between the stage and orchestra **Pit** and **Auditorium**, usually possessing curtains. The latter refers to the presentation of plays with a 'fourth wall' (as if the audience were looking into a room through one of its four walls) and is a practice over 300 years old. Today the term is often associated with traditions of Naturalism. *See also* **Box Set**.

Prospect Theatre Company

Originally set up in 1961 in Oxford as Prospect Productions it ran plays for three summer seasons and then, taking advantage of Arts Council support through DALTA (the Dramatic and Lyric Theatre Association), in 1964 became a touring company with a base at the Arts Theatre, Cambridge. Its artistic director from 1964 to 1979 was Toby Robertson (born in Chelsea, 29 November 1928 and educated at Stowe and Trinity College, Cambridge; he was an actor, then became a director in the late 1950s). The company quickly gained a reputation for its **ensemble** playing and the high standard of its productions and acting (attracting a number of major actors and actresses to its ranks, notably Ian **McKellen**, Dorothy **Tutin**, Alec **McCowen** and Derek **Jacobi**). As a touring company it required low-budget minimal sets which were easily transferred from theatre to theatre and it was a pioneer in this field of stage design. Any emphasis on spectacle was provided more by the superb costumes than by the sets, especially in productions of the classics.

Among its many notable productions (of which Robertson directed over 50) were *The Soldier's Fortune* (1964), *The Importance of Being Earnest* (1964), *The Man of the Mode* (1965), *Macbeth* and *The Tempest* (1966). In 1967 Prospect began its fruitful association with the **Edinburgh Festival**. Many of its productions were presented at the festival during tours and before appearing in London, some of which were: *A Room with a View* (1967), *Twelfth Night*, *No Man's Land*, *The Beggar's Opera* (all 1968) and the much-acclaimed *Richard II* (1968) and *Edward II* (1969) with superb performances by Ian McKellen in the title-roles. McKellen's Richard was also seen on BBC Television in 1969. In the same year Prospect was no longer able to use the Cambridge Arts Theatre as its base but continued as a subsidised touring company, presenting in 1970 *Much Ado About Nothing*, a play based on Boswell's *Life of Johnson*, and in 1971 *Hamlet* (with McKellen as Hamlet), *King Lear* (with Timothy **West** as Lear) and *Love's Labour's Lost* (which also toured Australia). Richard **Briers** played the title-role in *Richard III* in 1972 and in the same year Prospect presented Chekhov's *Ivanov* (starring Derek Jacobi).

One of the Prospect Theatre Company's most ambitious and successful touring seasons was in July and August 1973 when it took *Pericles* (with Jacobi in the title-role), *Twelfth Night* and **Shaffer**'s *The Royal Hunt of the Sun* round Britain and also (sponsored by the British Council) to many places abroad including Cyprus, Egypt, Jordan, Lebanon (Baalbeck Festival), Greece (Athens Festival), Yugoslavia (Dubrovnik Festival), USSR (Moscow and Leningrad) and Hong Kong. *Pericles* was also part of the opening week of the 1973 Edinburgh Festival.

In 1975 Dorothy Tutin starred with Derek Jacobi in Prospect's production of Turgenev's *A Month in the Country* and at the **Old Vic** with Alec McCowen in the production of *Antony and Cleopatra* in 1977. The 1978 programme included *Ivanov* and *King Lear* and in 1979 Derek Jacobi toured extensively in the title-role of *Hamlet* which was performed at Elsinore, in Australia, and as part of the first-ever Western theatre tour of China.

The actor Timothy West, who had been a member of the Prospect Theatre Company since 1966 and a co-director since the 1975 season, took over from Toby Robertson as artistic director in 1980 and in that year the company presented a highly successful but very controversial production of *Macbeth* starring Peter **O'Toole**, and a production of *The Merchant of Venice* (with West as Shylock). At the end of 1980 it was announced that the Arts Council grant would have to be withdrawn, the company went bankrupt and was dissolved, at great artistic loss to the theatre in Britain and abroad. Ian McKellen, who has for much of his career been an enthusiastic supporter of touring companies such as the Prospect Theatre Company, the **Actors' Company** and the **Royal Shakespeare Company**'s 'Theatregoround', once commented (*Plays and Players*, April 1976) on an important principle of theatre in the 1960s and 1970s (which had certainly been manifested by the Prospect Company): 'The best theatre is no longer synonymous with London and the West End. . .the national theatre of Great Britain is spread throughout the country.'

Further Reading

W. Stephen Gilbert, 'Prospect for the Future', *Plays and Players*, October 1973, pp. 24-7.

Pryce, Jonathan

An Associate Actor of the **Royal Shakespeare Company**, he emerged in the mid-1970s as one of Britain's most promising leading actors. He has also played many parts in repertory (particularly at the Everyman Theatre, Liverpool) and directed plays.

His acting appearances include Edgar in *King Lear*, Richard in *Richard III*, the lead in Adrian Mitchell's *Mind Your Head*, Andy in John **McGrath**'s *Fish in the Sea*, Sidney in Howard **Brenton** and David **Hare**'s *Brassneck*, the title-role in Gogol's *The Government Inspector*, John Proctor in Arthur Miller's *The Crucible*, Andrei in Chekhov's *Three Sisters*, Harry Poulson in *Bendigo*, Gethin Price in Trevor **Griffiths**'s *The Comedians* (which was played in Nottingham, London and New York and won him *Plays and Players* and Tony awards), the title-role in Mike **Stott**'s *Lenz*, Ludovico in Webster's *The White Devil*, Petruchio in *The Taming of the Shrew* and the title-role in *Hamlet*. In 1982 he appeared as Malt in Lanford Wilson's *Talley's Folly*.

He appeared in the film *The Voyage of the Damned* and television work includes *Death of a Young Man*, *Playthings*, *Glad*

Day and *For Tea on Sunday.*

He has directed a number of plays includ-ng *A Taste of Honey, The Sea Anchor* and *The Taming of the Shrew.*

PS

'Prompt side', that is, stage left (where the **Prompt Corner** is usually located).

Q

Quayle, Sir (John) Anthony

Born in Ainsdale, Lancashire, on 7 September 1913, he was educated at Rugby School and trained for the stage at RADA. He made his first professional appearance as Richard Coeur de Lion and Will Scarlett in *Robin Hood* (Q Theatre, December 1931). In the pre-war years he played in Shakespearean plays and other classics including seasons at the **Old Vic** (1932-3) and Chiswick Empire (1933). He appeared as Laertes in *Hamlet* with the Old Vic Company at Elsinore (June 1937) and worked with the Old Vic in 1938 and again in 1939 (European and Egyptian tour) when he was King Henry in *Henry V*. In the Second World War he served in the Royal Artillery, attaining the rank of Major. In September 1945 he returned to the stage when he was Jack Absolute in Sheridan's *The Rivals* at the Criterion Theatre. He subsequently directed *Crime and Punishment* (New Theatre, June 1946) and Vanbrugh's *The Relapse* (Lyric, Hammersmith, December 1947, Phoenix, January 1948) and was Iago in *Othello* (Piccadilly, March 1947). In 1947 he married Dorothy Hyson, his second wife.

In an interview with Jim Grace (*Radio Times*, 28 April–4 May 1984) he said: 'I almost abandoned acting after the war. I felt I had a handicap with my face; it could never win me leading parts. It was wrong, pudgy and round. It's not a face, it's a currant bun.' However, in 1948 he was asked by Tyrone **Guthrie** to be an actor–manager and director of the **Shakespeare Memorial Theatre** at Stratford-upon-Avon, a position he held until 1956 (he was joined in 1953 by Glen Byam Shaw). In the same year as his appointment he played Iago, Claudius and Petruchio and in the next two seasons (1949 and 1950) he directed *Macbeth*, *Julius Caesar*, and *King Lear* and played Benedick, Henry VIII and Mark Antony. The company at this time had in its ranks John **Gielgud**, Godfrey Tearle, Diana Wynyard, Harry **Andrews**, Peggy **Ashcroft**, Barbara **Jefford**, Andrew Cruikshank, John Slater and Gwen Ffrangcon-Davies.

Anthony Quayle told Diana Hutchinson (*Daily Mail*, 12 January 1985), 'If I died now and went to heaven's gate, I would still have to ask St. Peter to look at 1951 as my time of major achievement.' It was in 1951 that he made some major structural changes to the Memorial Theatre, extending the circle and building an apron stage over the orchestra pit, thus laying the foundations for the more '**open stage**' productions of Shakespeare which were developed further by Quayle's successors, in particular Peter **Hall** and Trevor **Nunn**. In the same season he directed *Richard II* (with Michael **Redgrave** in the title-role), *Henry V* (with Richard Burton as King Henry), co-directed *Henry IV Part I* (with Richard Burton as Prince Hal and Michael Redgrave as Hotspur) and played the role of Falstaff. The casts that season also included Hugh Griffith and Alan Badel.

In 1952 he took the title-role in Glen Byam Shaw's production of *Coriolanus* and then took productions of *Othello*, *As You Like It*, and *Henry IV Part 1* on a tour of Australia and New Zealand (January–October 1953). Quayle played the title-role, with Barbara Jefford as Desdemona, in *Othello*, which, on returning to Stratford ran for the 1954 season. Also in the season Quayle was Bottom in George **Devine**'s production of *A Midsummer Night's Dream* and Pandarus in Glen Byam Shaw's production of *Troilus and Cressida*. The 1955 season (which included Laurence **Olivier** and Vivien Leigh in *Twelfth Night* and *Macbeth*) saw him as Falstaff in *The Merry Wives of*

Windsor and Aaron, the Moor, in Peter **Brook**'s production of *Titus Andronicus* (which had Olivier in the title-role). In his final season at the Shakespeare Memorial Theatre he directed *Measure for Measure.*

In his introduction to *Shakespeare Memorial Theatre 1954-56* (1956) Ivor Brown wrote: 'During recent years theatrical planning at Stratford has had a broadly-based intention. In Anthony Quayle's words Stratford has been seeking to provide both "a testing-ground for the experienced actor to pit himself against the most exciting parts in our tongue" and a nursery "where the young player can take his first uncertain steps towards becoming a classical actor".' Anthony Quayle's 'nursery' produced, among others, Laurence Harvey, Richard Burton, Prunella **Scales**, Robert Shaw, Alan Badel, Leo **McKern**, Harry **Andrews**, Keith Michell, Ian **Holm**, Barbara **Jefford**, Nigel Davenport, Emrys **James** and Geraldine **McEwan**.

On leaving Stratford Anthony Quayle's work included playing the title-role in Marlowe's *Tamburlaine the Great* (Winter Garden, New York, January 1956) and a tour, as Aaron in *Titus Andronicus,* which visited Paris, Venice, Belgrade, Zagreb, Vienna and Warsaw, returning to London for a run at the Stoll Theatre (July 1957). His chief acting and directing work has since included Moses in Christopher **Fry**'s *The Firstborn* (Coronet Theatre, New York, April 1958, Habimah Theatre, Tel-Aviv, July 1958) which he himself directed, James Tyrone in O'Neill's *Long Day's Journey Into Night* (**Edinburgh Festival**, September 1958), Nachtigall in *Power of Persuasion* (Garrick, September 1963) which he co-directed, Sir Charles Dilke in Bradley-Dyne's *The Right Honourable Gentleman* (Her Majesty's, May 1964), the title-role of **Brecht**'s *Galileo* (Vivian Beaumont Theatre, New York, April 1967), General Fitzbuttress in Peter Ustinov's *Halfway Up the Tree* (Atkinson Theatre, November 1967) and Andrew Wyke in Anthony Shaffer's *Sleuth* (St Martin's February 1970, Music Box, New York, November 1970). He directed an adaptation of Dostoevsky's *The Idiot* for the **National Theatre** (Old Vic, July 1970) and played Rodion Nikolayevich in Arbuzov's two-character play *Old World* (RSC, Aldwych, October 1976) playing opposite Peggy Ashcroft's Lydia.

In June 1978 Quayle took over the part of Hilary in Alan **Bennett**'s *The Old Country* (Queen's Theatre) and later played Sir Anthony Absolute in Sheridan's *The Rivals* (Old Vic, September 1978) which he also directed. He subsequently played the title-role in *King Lear* for the **Prospect Theatre Company** (Old Vic, October 1978), Hobson in Harold Brighouse's *Hobson's Choice* (Theatre Royal, Haymarket, February 1982), Dr Berryman in Ronald Millar's *A Coat of Varnish* (Haymarket, April 1982) which he also directed, and directed Piradello's *The Rules of the Game* (Haymarket, September 1982, Phoenix, December 1982).

In 1984 Quayle, at the age of 70, began to formulate plans for a new touring company, the Compass Company, which he said 'will produce high-quality plays and keep ourselves small and close-knit, unlike the National and the Royal Shakespeare' (*Observer,* 7 April 1984). The company's first production was Garrick's *The Clandestine Marriage* which Quayle directed and in which he played Lord Ogleby (Leeds, Plymouth, Norwich, Bath, Croydon, Nottingham, Brighton, 1984 tour, Albery, June 1984). Next the company had Quayle as the Duke of Drayton in William Douglas **Home**'s *After the Ball is Over* (Compass, Old Vic, March 1985).

Anthony Quayle has appeared in numerous films including *Hamlet, The Battle of the River Plate, Ice Cold in Alex, Tarzan's Greatest Adventure, The Guns of Navarone, HMS Defiant, Lawrence of Arabia, Anne of a Thousand Days, Moses the Lawgiver, The Eagle has Landed, The Antagonists* and *Dial M for Murder.* Television work includes *Treasure Island, Strange Report, Ice Age,*

Henry IV Parts 1 and 2, Masada, Lace and *The Testament of John.*

As a stage actor, director and theatre company manager, Anthony Quayle has made an astonishing and important contribution to post-war British theatre. He said in a 1984 interview with Al Senter, 'living is an extraordinary adventure and you must live on the frontier'.

Further Reading

Anthony Quayle, *Eight Hours from England* (novel), Heinemann, London, 1945.

Anthony Quayle, *On Such a Night*, Heinemann, London, 1947.

R

Rake

A slope, particularly of the stage from the back down to the front, and of the **Auditorium** from the rear seats down to the front row. **Rostra** can also be raked.

Rattigan, Sir Terence (Mervyn)

Born on 10 June 1911, educated at Harrow School (Scholar), Middlesex, and Trinity College, Oxford University where he read history (1930-3), he came to prominence as a dramatist in the 1930s with *French Without Tears* (Criterion, November 1936), a comedy about a party of English people in France taking a crash course in French. The play ran for 1,039 performances. His other great success in the pre-war period was *After the Dance* (St James's, June 1939).

During the Second World War Rattigan was a Flight Lieutenant air gunner in Royal Air Force Coastal Command (1940-5). In May 1946 his highly successful play based on a true story about a father who tried to defend his naval-cadet son against charges of theft, *The Winslow Boy*, was performed at the Lyric Theatre. *Playbill* (Phoenix, September 1948) comprised two plays, *The Browning Version* about a frustrated teacher taking enforced retirement, and *Harlequinade* about an ageing theatre couple. *The Deep Blue Sea* (Duchess, March 1952, Morosco, New York, November 1952) which starred Peggy **Ashcroft**, was a profoundly moving study of a woman who leaves her husband for a man who does not return her love, and *The Sleeping Prince* (Phoenix, November 1953) with Laurence **Olivier** and Vivien Leigh in the leading roles, was a romantic fairy tale about a prince who falls in love with a musical comedy artist.

Separate Tables (St James's, September 1954, Music Box, New York, October 1956) presented a double-bill about frustrated love relationships in a Bournemouth hotel. *Ross: a Dramatic Portrait* (Haymarket, May 1960) was a study of T.E. Lawrence, originally played by Alec **Guinness** and a year later played in New York by John **Mills** (O'Neill, December 1961). The play took advantage of the loosening of censorship and was able to explore Lawrence's homosexuality — all the more keen-edged a study because Rattigan too was a self-confessed homosexual who hated the tendency in himself.

Although, as is nearly always mentioned when discussing his work, Rattigan wrote commercially successful 'well-made plays' for what he called 'Aunt Edna' (his term for conservative audiences of theatre-goers with little or no interest in experimental or avant-garde plays, what he called in a preface of 1963, 'a nice, respectable, middle-class, middle-aged, maiden lady, with time on her hands and the money to help her pass it ... a hopeless lowbrow') this view belies a deeper and more tragic dimension beneath the surface craftsmanship so carefully handled: the pain of emotional and sexual repression, the frustrations of loneliness and unrequited love, the destructive effects of the breakdown of relationships on the inner lives of his characters. David **Rudkin**, in a letter to Anthony Curtis (quoted in 'Professional Man and Boy', *Plays and Players*, February 1978) stated: 'I detect in his plays a deep personal, surely sexual pain, which he manages at the same time to express and disguise. The craftsmanship of which we hear so much loose talk seems to me to arise from deep psychological necessity, a drive to organise the energy that arises out of his own pain.' The generation of playwrights and theatre-goers before Rudkin's, that of John **Osborne**, John **Arden** and Arnold **Wesker**, had rejected Rattigan's work as belonging to an outmoded tradition. With the newer generation of the 1970s Rattigan's work has been better understood and it has again found a strong place in the modern repertoire.

In Praise of Love (Duchess, September 1973, Morosco, New York, December 1974) which starred Donald **Sinden** and Joan Greenwood in John **Dexter**'s original production, comprised *Before Dawn* and *After Lydia* and explored the suffering of a married couple who both suppress their knowledge of the wife's incurable disease. A further tension in the play is the fraught relationship between the husband and his son which only gradually leads towards reconciliation (imaged in a game of chess at the end of the play). Rattigan's last play, *Cause Célèbre* (Her Majesty's, July 1977, earlier premièred at Haymarket, Leicester, 1977) was based on the real-life case of a woman who murders her husband with the help of her lover.

Rattigan adapted many of his own plays for film and television and wrote the screenplays for *Quiet Wedding, The Day Will Dawn, Way to the Stars, The Sound Barrier, The Prince and the Showgirl, The VIPs, The Yellow Rolls Royce, Goodbye, Mr Chips* and *Conduct Unbecoming.* Television plays include *The Final Test, Heart to Heart, Ninety Years On, Nelson, All on Her Own,* and *High Summer.*

Terence Rattigan died in Bermuda on 30 November 1977.

Further Reading

John Russell Taylor, *The Rise and Fall of the Well-Made Play*, Methuen, London, 1967.

Michael Darlow and Gillian Hodson, *Terence Rattigan: The Man and his Work*, Quartet Books, London, 1980.

Redgrave, Sir Michael (Scudamore)

Born on 20 March 1908 in Bristol, the son of parents who were members of the acting profession (and who gave him his début on the stage as a babe-in-arms in an Australian theatre), he was educated at Clifton College and at Magdalen College, Cambridge. His first job was as a schoolmaster, teaching modern languages at Cranleigh School. He joined Liverpool Repertory Company in 1934, when his first professional appearance was as Roy Darwin in *Counsellor-at-Law* (Playhouse, Liverpool, August 1934). He played in repertory for two years and then joined the company at the **Old Vic** where he made his London début as Ferdinand in *Love's Labour's Lost* (September 1936), and in the same season also played Orlando in *As You Like It,* Warbeck in *The Witch of Edmonton,* Laertes in *Hamlet* and Horner in Wycherley's *The Country Wife.* He married Rachel Kempson in 1935.

After playing further roles in the **West End** Redgrave joined John **Gielgud**'s company in 1937 (at the Queen's Theatre), which included such players as Alec **Guinness** and Peggy **Ashcroft**. His chief roles with this company were Bolingbroke in *Richard II,* Charles Surface in Sheridan's *The School for Scandal* and Tuzenbach in Chekhov's *Three Sisters.* After this highly successful season, which established him as a major leading actor on the London stage, he appeared as Alexei Turbin in Bulgakov's *The White Guard* (Phoenix Theatre, October 1938) and Aguecheek in *Twelfth Night* (Phoenix Theatre, December 1938). The company was directed by Michel Saint-Denis. Just before the outbreak of the Second World War Redgrave created the role of Harry in T.S. **Eliot**'s *The Family Reunion* (Westminster, March 1939) and subsequently toured in 1939 as the name-part in *Springtime for Henry.*

At the Haymarket Theatre in March 1940 he played Macheath in Gay's *The Beggar's*

Opera, followed by Charleston in Ardrey's *Thunder Rock* (Neighbourhood, June 1940 and Globe, July 1940). During the war he served with the Royal Navy as an Ordinary Seaman, was released to the Reserve in 1942 and discharged on medical grounds (November 1942). In March 1943 he played Rakitin in Turgenev's *A Month in the Country* (St James's Theatre), in June 1943 played Lafont in *Parisienne* (St James's) and also directed this latter play. Other roles in the wartime period included the title-role in Thomas Job's *Uncle Harry* (Garrick, March 1944), which he co-directed (with William Armstrong), and Colonel Stjerbingsky in S.N. Behrman's adaptation of Franz Werfel's *Jacobowsky and the Colonel* (Piccadilly, June, 1945), which he also directed.

After the war Redgrave played a number of major classical parts, the chief of which were the title-role in *Macbeth* (Aldwych, December 1947, and the National, New York, March 1948) and the Captain in Strindberg's *The Father* (Embassy, London, November 1948, and Duchess, January 1949). On joining the Old Vic Company at the New Theatre for the 1949-50 season he played Berowne in *Love's Labour's Lost*, Marlow in Goldsmith's *She Stoops to Conquer*, Rakitin in Turgenev's *A Month in the Country* and the title-role in *Hamlet*. He later played Hamlet at the Zurich Festival, Holland Festival and at Krönberg Castle, Elsinore (June, 1950). For the 1951 season he joined the **Shakespeare Memorial Theatre** Company at Stratford-upon-Avon, appearing as Richard in *Richard II*, Hotspur in *Henry IV Part I*, Chorus in *Henry V* and Prospero in *The Tempest*. In addition he directed *Henry IV Part II*. In the 1953 season he was Shylock in *The Merchant of Venice*, Lear in *King Lear* and Antony in *Antony and Cleopatra*.

It was in 1953 that Michael Redgrave published *The Actor's Ways and Means*, a series of Rockefeller Foundation Lectures he had given, in the 1952/3 academic year, to the Drama Department at Bristol University. In these lectures he articulated many of the artistic challenges which face an actor and in doing so revealed a great deal about his own approaches to acting at this time: a 'well placed, resonant and pleasing voice...can be almost as fatal as an exquisite face and a beautiful body. When the actor has gained some mastery of these things ... he must know how not to use these powers to the full. He must know, in fact, what to leave out.' He also gave some sound warnings about possible misunderstandings and misapplications of Stanislavsky's methods (he had written on Stanislavsky in an earlier paper called 'The Stanislavsky Myth', published in *New Theatre*, Vol. III, No. 1, London, June, 1946).

Following this period he played fewer classical roles and his work included Hector in Giraudoux's *Tiger at the Gates* (Apollo, June 1955 and the Plymouth Theatre, New York, October 1955), the Prince in Terence **Rattigan**'s *The Sleeping Prince* (Coronet, New York, November 1956), which he also directed, and Philip Lester in N.C. Hunter's *A Touch of the Sun* (Saville, January 1958). His daughter Vanessa also appeared with him in this latter production. In June 1958 he rejoined the company at Stratford-upon-Avon and played the title-role in *Hamlet* and Benedick in *Much Ado About Nothing*, subsequently touring as Hamlet in Leningrad and Moscow.

In August 1959 Redgrave played Jarvis in his own adaptation of Henry James's *The Aspern Papers* (Queen's Theatre) and in August 1960 he was Jack Dean in Robert **Bolt**'s *The Tiger and the Horse* (Queen's Theatre). Chief performances in the 1960s were Victor Rhodes in Graham **Greene**'s *The Complaisant Lover* (Ethel Barrymore, New York, November 1961), the title-role in Chekhov's *Uncle Vanya* (at the first **Chichester Festival**, July 1962 and **National Theatre** at the Old Vic, November 1963), Claudius in the National Theatre Company's opening production of *Hamlet* at the Old Vic (October 1963), Hobson in Harold Brighouse's *Hobson's Choice* (Old Vic, January 1964), Solness in Ibsen's *The Master Builder* (Old Vic, June 1964) and Rakitin in Turgenev's *A Month in the Country* (opening festival of the Yvonne Arnaud Theatre, Guildford, May 1965) which latter play he also directed. Most of Redgrave's other work in the 1960s was directing but in July 1971 he created the role of Mr Jaraby in William Trevor's *The Old Boys* (Mermaid) and in April 1972 took over (from Alec Guinness) the part of the Father in John **Mortimer**'s *A Voyage Round My Father* (Haymarket), subsequently touring in the part in Canada and Australia. He toured with the **Royal Shakespeare Company** in John **Barton**'s *The Hollow Crown* (USA and Australia, 1974-5), beween 1976 and 1978 toured South America, Canada and Britain in Alan Strachan's anthology *Shakespeare's People* and in May 1979 he played Jasper in Simon **Gray**'s *Close of Play* (National Theatre, Lyttleton). *The Aspern Papers* was revived at the Haymarket in March 1984 with Vanessa **Redgrave** as Miss Tina.

A highly respected director as well as one of our most distinguished actors, Michael Redgrave (in an interview with Margaret Tierney, *Plays and Players*, September 1971), observed that 'a lot of direction — and having directed myself I know this — comes from what the director can see is in the actor trying to come out. It's therefore not "put in" there by the director, but emerging from the actor through the medium of the director.' He has written a novel (*The Mountebank's Tale*, 1959) and appeared in numerous films, including *The Lady Vanishes*, *Thunder Rock*, *The Browning Version*, *The Importance of Being Earnest*, *The Dam Busters*, *The Quiet American*, *Oh! What a Lovely War*, *The Loneliness of the Long-Distance Runner*, *The Battle of Britain*, *Goodbye Mr Chips*, *The Go-Between* and *Nicholas and Alexandra*. Television work includes the series *Great War* and *Lost Peace*. In addition to *The Actor's Ways and Means* (1953) he has written *Mask or Face* (1958), a number of plays and adaptations, and an autobiography. The theatre at Farnham is named after him.

Redgrave stated in *The Actor's Ways and Means*: 'To act well and to act well repeatedly has to become an obsession...the business of drama is to move...it is our job to communicate the size of what is happening as greatly as we can, the depth as deeply.'

Sir Michael Redgrave died on 21 March 1985.

Further Reading

Michael Redgrave, *The Actor's Ways and Means*, Mercury Books, London, 1966 and Theatre Arts, New York, 1979.

Michael Redgrave, *In My Mind's I: An Actor's Autobiography*, Viking Press, New York, 1983.

Redgrave, Vanessa, CBE

Born in London on 30 January 1937, the daughter of Sir Michael **Redgrave** and his wife Rachel (Kempson), she was educated at Queensgate School, London, and trained for the theatre at the Central School of Speech and Drama. From 1962 until 1967 she was married to the director Tony Richardson.

Her first professional role was as Clarissa in William Douglas **Home**'s *The Reluctant Debutante* at the Frinton Summer Theatre in July 1957. Her first London appearance was as Caroline in N.C. Hunter's *A Touch of the Sun* (Saville, January 1958), with her father in the same cast. She was subsequently at the **Royal Court** Theatre where she played Sarah in Shaw's *Major Barbara* (August 1958) and then became a member of the **Shakespeare Memorial Theatre** Company for the 1959 season at Stratford-upon-Avon and played Valeria in *Coriolanus* and Helena in *A Midsummer Night's Dream*. Again in a cast which included her father, she was Stella Dean in Robert **Bolt**'s *The Tiger and the Horse* (Queen's, August 1960). In March of the following year she was Boletta in Ibsen's *The Lady From the Sea*, at the same theatre.

In July 1961 she joined the **Royal Shake-peare Company** and played Rosalind in *As 'ou Like It* (Stratford-upon-Avon). emaining with the RSC she was Katharina *The Taming of the Shrew* (Aldwych, eptember 1961, Stratford-upon-Avon, pril 1962), Rosalind again (Aldwych, Janu-ry 1962) and Imogen in *Cymbeline* (Strat-ord, July 1962). She then left the RSC and ubsequent parts included Nina in Chekhov's *'he Seagull* (Queen's, March 1964), Jean rodie in Jay Presson Allen's *The Prime of liss Jean Brodie* (Wyndham's, May 1966), 'olly Peachum in Bertholt **Brecht**'s *The 'hreepenny Opera* (Prince of Wales, Febru-ry 1972), Viola in *Twelfth Night* (Shaw, lay 1972) and Cleopatra in *Antony and 'leopatra* (Bankside Globe, August 1973). n March 1976 she was Ellida in Ibsen's *The ady From the Sea* (Circle in the Square, lew York) and played the same role at the lanchester Royal Exchange Theatre (1978) nd the Round House (1979). The produc-ion at Manchester was directed by Michael lliott and at the time Vanessa Redgrave tated (in an interview with Ria Julian) that n actor or actress should be a 'tool in the irector's hand', both director and actress eing creative artists. 'A director, just as an ctress,' she said, 'is concerned with material nd putting it at the highest point...We are ll instruments, very high precision instru-nents. Or we can be.' In March 1984 she layed Miss Tina in a revival of Sir Michael edgrave's adaptation of Henry James's *The spern Papers* (Haymarket).

Vanessa Redgrave is not only one of the nost original actresses of her generation but as also taken an active (and sometimes ontroversial) interest in left-wing politics. Vith her brother Corin Redgrave she ecame a Trotskyite in the 1970s and ttempted to make the actor's union, Equity, nore militant and radical. She has stood wice as a candidate of the Worker's Revolu-ionary Party in parliamentary elections but vas not elected.

Her extensive film career includes roles in *Morgan — A Suitable Case for Treatment, Blow-Up, Camelot, Charge of the Light Brigade, Isadora, A Quiet Place in the Country, The Seagull, The Trojan Women, The Devils, Mary, Queen of Scots, Murder on the Orient Express, Julia, Agatha, Playing for Time, My Body, My Child, Wagner, The Bostonians* and *Wetherby*. She has also worked in television including appearances as Helena in *A Midsummer Night's Dream* and Rosalind in *As You Like It*.

Rees, Roger

Born in Aberystwyth, Wales, on 5 May 1944, he was educated at Balham Secondary School and trained as a fine artist and litho-grapher at Camberwell School of Art and the Slade School of Fine Art. He appeared in the chorus of Ralph Reader's *Gang Show* (Golder's Green Hippodrome, October 1963) and made his first professional appear-ance as Alan in *Hindle Wakes* (Wimbledon, 1964).

He joined the **Royal Shakespeare Company** in 1967 and played small parts in *The Taming of the Shrew* and *As You Like It* (Stratford-upon-Avon, 1967 season, Los Angeles, 1968). Subsequent roles included Fenton in *The Merry Wives of Windsor* (1968 season), Curio in *Twelfth Night* (1969 season), and in 1970 he toured Japan (in *The Merry Wives of Windsor* and *The Winter's Tale*) and Australia (in *The Winter's Tale* and *Twelfth Night*). He played Stephen Undershaft in Shaw's *Major Barbara* at the Aldwych in the same year. In 1971 his parts included Claudio in *Much Ado About Noth-ing* and Roderigo in *Othello* (both at Strat-ford, 1971, then Aldwych, 1971-2). At the Aldwych he took the part of Balin in John **Arden**'s *The Island of the Mighty* (December 1972) and subsequently appeared as March-banks in Shaw's *Candida* at the Neptune Theatre, Halifax, Nova Scotia (April 1973).

Between 1973 and 1974 he toured with

the Cambridge Theatre Company in roles which included Fabian in *Twelfth Night* and Marlow in Goldsmith's *She Stoops to Conquer.* With the RSC he then toured the USA as Charles Courtly in *London Assurance,* making his first New York appearance in the part (Palace Theatre, New York, December 1974). Again with the Cambridge Theatre Company on tour, he took the parts of Algernon in Wilde's *The Importance of Being Earnest* and Stanley in Harold **Pinter**'s *The Birthday Party.*

For the RSC's 1976 season at Stratford he played Benvolio in *Romeo and Juliet,* Malcolm in *Macbeth* (this latter production at The Other Place), and Antipholus of Syracuse in *The Comedy of Errors.* Chief roles since, with the RSC, have been Ananias in Ben Jonson's *The Alchemist* (Other Place, May 1977), Nazzar in *Factory Birds* (Warehouse, September 1977), Petulant in *The Way of the World* (Aldwych, January 1978). For an RSC tour in 1978, led by Ian **McKellen**, he was Sir Andrew Aguecheek in *Twelfth Night* and Tusenbach in Chekhov's *Three Sisters.* He also devised the recital *Is There Honey Still For Tea?* Subsequently he played Postumus in *Cymbeline* (Stratford, 1979 season), Tusenbach in *Three Sisters* and Semyon in *The Suicide* (both at The Other Place, Stratford, 1979, Newcastle and the Warehouse, 1980).

In June 1980 he gave a highly-acclaimed performance as Nicholas in David **Edgar**'s adaptation of Dickens's *Nicholas Nickleby* (Aldwych) and in March 1982 took part in Rod Argent's musical, *Masquerade* (Young Vic). He played Henry in Tom **Stoppard**'s *The Real Thing* (Strand, November 1982) and for the RSC played the title-role in *Hamlet* (Stratford-upon-Avon, August 1984).

Television work includes *Place of Peace, Under Western Eyes, A Bouquet of Barbed Wire, The Comedy of Errors, Macbeth, Saigon* and *Imaginary Friends.*

Reid, Beryl

Born in Hereford on 17 June 1920, of Scottish parents, she was educated at Lady Barnes House School, Withington High School and Levenshulme High School, Manchester.

Her first appearance was in a concert party at the Floral Hall, Bridlington, in May 1936 and she later established herself as a comedienne, notably creating the character of 'Monica' in the BBC radio show *Educating Archie* which ran for four years. From 1951 until 1964 she appeared in revues, pantomimes and variety. She created another much-loved comic character, 'Marlene of the Midlands', who became extremely popular in the 1950s.

A breakthrough into 'serious' theatre came when she played Sister George for two years in Frank Marcus's *The Killing of Sister George* (**Bristol Old Vic**, April 1965, Duke of York's, June 1965, Belasco, New York, October 1966). After this enormous success (which included her receiving a Tony Award) she gave notable appearances as Madame Arcati in Noël **Coward**'s *Blithe Spirit* (Arnaud, Guildford, June 1970, Globe, July 1970, O'Keefe Theatre, Toronto, January 1971), Frau Bergmann in *Spring Awakening* (**Old Vic**, May 1974 and **National Theatre** tour), the Nurse in *Romeo and Juliet* (Old Vic and tour, July 1974), Kath in Joe **Orton**'s *Entertaining Mr Sloane* (**Royal Court**, April 1975, Duke of York's, June 1975), Donna Katherina in *Il Campiello* and She in *Counting the Ways* (National Theatre, 1976). She appeared with the **Royal Shakespeare Company** as Lady Wishfort in Congreve's *The Way of the World* (Aldwych, January 1978) and then with the Bristol Old Vic Company as Maud in Peter **Nichols**'s *Born in the Gardens* (Bristol Old Vic, September 1979, Globe, January 1980). Recently she starred as Mrs Candour in Sheridan's *The School for Scandal* (Haymarket, January 1983, Duke of York's, December 1983) and in *Gigi* at the 1985 **Edinburgh Festival**.

Film appearances include *The Belles of St Trinians, Star, The Extra Day, The Dock Brief, Two Way Stretch, Psychomania, No Sex Please, We're British, Late Flowering Love, Joseph Andrews, Entertaining Mr Sloane* and *Yellowbeard.* On television she has taken part in many quiz-shows and variety shows. She had her own six-week television series, 'Beryl Reid says Good Evening' (BBC) and gave strong performances in *Tinker, Tailor, Soldier, Spy* and *Smiley's People.*

In an interview with Al Senter (*Plays and Players,* October 1984) she described herself as a 'comedy actress', which she defined as 'being an actress but showing a sense of comedy'.

Further Reading

Beryl Reid and Al Senter, 'Reid All About It', *Plays and Players,* October 1984, p. 21.
Beryl Reid, *So Much Love,* Hutchinson, London, 1984.

'Resting'

Actor's euphemism for 'out of work'.

Reveal

A board attached at a right angle to suggest a window or doorway thickness.

Richardson, Ian

Born in Edinburgh, Scotland, on 7 April 1934 he was educated at Tynecastle School, Edinburgh, and as a youth played a number of roles in amateur repertory with the Edinburgh People's Theatre. For his National Service he was a Duty Announcer for the Forces Broadcasting Service and then trained for the stage (1955-7) at the Glasgow College of Dramatic Art which was linked with Glasgow University where Richardson was taught for a time by the Shakespearean scholar Peter Alexander.

In August 1958 he joined the Birmingham Repertory Theatre Company with whom his parts included the title-role in *Hamlet.* He joined the **Shakespeare Memorial Theatre** Company at Stratford-upon-Avon in January 1960 when his roles included Sir Andrew Aguecheek in *Twelfth Night.* He remained with the company (renamed the **Royal Shakespeare Company** in January 1961) at Stratford-upon-Avon and the Aldwych Theatre, London. Some of his most important roles with the RSC have been Count Malatesti in Webster's *The Duchess of Malfi* (Aldwych, December 1960), Don John in *Much Ado About Nothing* (1961 season), Oberon in *A Midsummer Night's Dream* (1962 season), Antipholus of Ephesus in *The Comedy of Errors* (1962 season), Edmund in Peter **Brook**'s production of *King Lear* (Stratford 1964, European and Russian tour, State Theatre, New York, 1964) in which Paul **Scofield** was Lear, the Herald in Brook's production of Peter Weiss's *Marat/Sade* (October 1964) and Marat in the same play (Aldwych, November 1965, Martin Beck, New York, December 1965). He also played the Chorus in John **Barton**'s production of *Henry V* and Vendice in Trevor **Nunn**'s production of Tourneur's *The Revenger's Tragedy* (1966 season), the title-role in *Coriolanus* (1967 season) and Prospero in *The Tempest* (1970 season).

He left the RSC in 1970 and later appeared in the musical *Trelawny* (Sadler's Wells, June 1972, Prince of Wales, August 1972) but returned to the RSC to play in John Barton's highly-acclaimed production of *Richard II* (1973 season, Brooklyn Academy, January 1974) in which he alternated the roles of Richard and Bolingbroke with Richard **Pasco**. Other parts with the RSC have included Shalimov in Gorky's *Summerfolk* (Aldwych, 1974), Berowne in *Love's Labour's Lost* (Aldwych, April 1975), Ford in *The Merry Wives of Windsor*

(Stratford, 1975 season), the title-role in *Richard III* (The Other Place, Stratford, 1975 season).

At the Shaw Festival Theatre, Niagara, Ontario, he was Jack Tanner in Shaw's *Man and Superman* and the Doctor in *The Millionairess* (1977). He played Mercutio in *Romeo and Juliet* and Khlestakov in Gogol's *The Government Inspector* at the **Old Vic** in September 1979 and in 1981 he was in *Lolita* on Broadway.

Richardson's work in films includes *The Darwin Adventure, Man of la Mancha, Ike — the War Years* and *King Lear*. Appearances on television include *Danton's Death, Churchill and the Generals, Tinker, Tailor, Soldier, Spy, The Master of Ballantrae, Number 10, Brass, Slimming Down* and *Six Centuries of Verse*.

In an interview with Gordon Gow (*Plays and Players*, August 1979) he suggested that the best stage performances come from 'a knowledge of, and a sympathy with, what your opposite numbers are up to and doing ... Theatre is so much a business of sharing. Sharing with each other on the stage — and that shared experience on the stage communicates to an audience.'

Richardson, Sir Ralph (David)

Affectionately known as 'Raffles' he died on 10 October 1983 at the age of 80 having recently appeared in Eduardo de Filippo's *Inner Voices* (**National Theatre**, Lyttleton).

Kenneth **Tynan** once wrote that, along with **Gielgud** and **Olivier**, Richardson forms 'a map that covers most of the high points of English theatre in the past five decades'. Yet he remained unique in the trio of knights in not being a tragedian. (His attempt at Othello with Olivier as Iago in 1938 was unsuccessful as was his 1952 performance as Macbeth, directed by Gielgud. He never played Lear or Hamlet.) It has often been argued, with some justification, that his greatest achievements have been in character-parts, playing the ordinary 'common man': but it could also be argued that his unique talent was such that he could make the ordinary extraordinary. His Falstaff (**Old Vic** at New Theatre, September 1945) was, according to Gielgud, 'his greatest performance' and Robin May has described the performance as 'the greatest Falstaff of modern times'. Sir Peter **Hall** has written that 'He was a dangerous actor, able to express the complex spiritual side of apparently very ordinary men.'

He was one of London's great eccentrics (riding a motorbike at speed through the London streets — and at higher speeds in some of its parks — keeping a parrot called José and at one time a pet ferret). He had a natural comic style which was adored by the profession and general public and it was a humour often prankish and childlike, undermining conventions of behaviour and people's expectations (especially those of interviewers, as with Russell Harty and Michael Parkinson on two memorable occasions) but that humour always revealed a penetrating and serious intelligence behind it — and a pathos born of the knowledge of human isolation. He could be seen as the genial *enfant terrible* of his acting generation. ('I would much rather be able to terrify than to charm. I like malevolence,' he once said.) Always self-effacing ('As for my face, I've seen better-looking hot cross buns', 'I've never given a good performance that has satisfied me in any play', 'Clearly I don't belong to the first division. It could be that my place is in the doomed second', 'I am a printer, that is all'), Richardson's acting had a mysterious and deceptive simplicity about it (some would say even a 'mannered' quality), but this was always the result of an intense care for his art and a totally perfectionist crafting of a performance. Gielgud said in 1976 (the year after appearing with him in **Pinter**'s *No Man's Land* at the National Theatre, Lyttleton) that Richardson 'loves the craftsmanship of his art. He prepares his work and exhibits it with the utmost finesse.' Often this would be to a point of precision almost akin to an engineer's (precision engineering was greatly admired by Richardson — his obsession with motorbikes is an example — yet the analogy with acting was profounder than that of implying a 'mechanical' performance: 'The theatre is an instrument,' he said, 'in much the same way that a microscope is...If you think of acting as an instrument, it looks into the soul of people very sharply, very penetratingly and it magnifies them'). In a lighter moment he once defined acting as 'keeping people from coughing', but in a more serious mood suggested that 'Acting is make-believe, and to make other people believe you must partly believe yourself. In a way acting is dreaming to order.'

Like Rembrandt in his famous sequence of self-portraits Richardson explored many parts in his life: he once said that every part is a new beginning and his biographer Garry O'Connor wrote that 'he is someone he himself has invented'.

He was born on 19 December 1902, the son of painter and art teacher at Cheltenham but was brought up at Shoreham-by-Sea by his mother (separated from Ralph's father who had taken a mistress). They lived in two disused railway carriages in near-poverty. Ralph attended several Roman Catholic schools including the priests' seminary Xavierian College at Brighton (from which he ran away) and was an incense-boy at St John's Church, Brighton. He moved later to Norwood near Crystal Palace and it was here that he was able to revel in the great firework displays held there. This love of firework spectacle stayed with him throughout his life — there is a famous incident when he let off a rocket in Laurence Olivier and Vivien Leigh's house in Chelsea in 1937: the incident gave him the idea later of sending up a rocket every time a new production opened at the National Theatre, the first one being launched by Sir Ralph himself in March 1976. (Ever since the rocket has been known as 'Ralph's Rocket'. He said at the time 'I love fireworks ... they are so unnecessary.') In 1917 he and his mother returned to Brighton where he took a job with an insurance firm, attended Brighton Art School briefly and then in 1920 joined the semi-professional F.R. Growcott Repertory Company. In 1921 he joined his first professional company, the Charles Doran Shakespeare Company and played his first professional role as Lorenzo in *The Merchant of Venice* (August 1921). In 1924 he married the actress Muriel Hewitt. It was a difficult marriage due to her long illness and she died in 1942. He was married again in 1944 to actress Meriel Forbes.

Richardson's pre-war career covered many classical roles at the **Old Vic** and elsewhere (including Henry V in 1931 and a notable Bottom in 1937 under the direction of Tyrone **Guthrie**) and he also played parts in a number of new plays (especially Priestley's). During the war he served in the Fleet Air Arm and in 1944 rejoined the company at the Old Vic, his memorable performances being the leads in *Peer Gynt* (August 1944), *Uncle Vanya* (January 1945) and magnificent performances as Sir John Falstaff (September 1945) and Cyrano de Bergerac (November 1946). In 1947 (January) he played Gaunt in *Richard II* and directed the play himself. Some notable performances in the 1950s were Vershinin in Chekhov's *Three Sisters* (May 1951), the Grand Duke in **Rattigan**'s *The Sleeping Prince* and Major Pollock in *Separate Tables* (tour of Australia and New Zealand, 1955), Timon in *Timon of Athens* (September 1956), Cherry in Robert **Bolt**'s *The Flowering Cherry* (November 1957) and Victor Rhodes in Graham **Greene**'s *The Complaisant Lover* (June 1957).

In the 1960s his outstanding performances were as the Father in Pirandello's *Six Characters in Search of an Author* (June 1963), Shylock in *The Merchant of Venice* and Bottom in *A Midsummer Night's Dream* for the British Council Shakespeare Anniversary Tour (February–May 1964) and the

Father in Graham Greene's *Carving a Statue* (September 1964). In 1966 (September) he played Sir Anthony Absolute in Sheridan's *The Rivals* and in 1967 (September) Shylock in *The Merchant of Venice.* Richardson will always be remembered for his performances in new plays as well as classics and in the last 14 years of his career he contributed much to the development of the new drama of the 1970s and 1980s, appearing as Dr Rance in Joe **Orton**'s *What the Butler Saw* (March 1969), Jack in David **Storey**'s *Home* (June 1970) in which he gave a superb performance in partnership with Gielgud, Wyatt Gilman in **Osborne**'s *West of Suez* (August 1971), General Sir William Boothroyd in **Home**'s *Lloyd George Knew My Father* (July 1972), and Hirst in Pinter's *No Man's Land* (April 1975), again in partnership with Gielgud. Richardson's enigmatic performance as Hirst created a marvellous sense of mystery, Pinteresque ambiguity and absurdity in the theatre (Richardson appropriately commented in 1977 that 'the ability to convey a sense of mystery is one of the most powerful assets possessed by the theatre'). He was a great success in a part written specially for him by William Douglas Home, Cecil in *The Kingfisher* (May 1977) and in 1980 (April) he played Kitchen in David Storey's *Early Days.* His last performances were as Leonard in Angela Huth's *The Understanding* (May 1982) and Alberto in Eduardo de Filippo's *Inner Voices* (June 1983). He has also taken part in over 60 films.

Richardson's is a life and career marked by tragedy and loneliness but much more by huge success (he was knighted in 1947) and great popularity in the British Theatre and with the theatre-loving public. O'Connor has pointed out how appropriate to himself was the comment Richardson made on the Michael Parkinson Show in 1980 when describing Chaplin: 'The audience didn't realize how odd he was because he was so near to reality in his madness.'

Further Reading

Garry O'Connor, *Ralph Richardson*, Coronet Books, Hodder and Stoughton, London, 1983.

Kenneth Tynan, 'Tynan on Richardson', *Observer Magazine*, 18 December 1977

Richard Findlater, *These Our Actors*, Elm Tree Books, London, 1984.

Rickman, Alan

Born and brought up in Acton, he trained and worked as a graphic designer and founded Design Group. At the age of 26 he went to RADA and trained for the theatre. He worked in repertory (chiefly Birmingham Repertory Theatre, the **Bristol Old Vic** and the Sheffield Crucible Theatre), his roles including Daniel in *The Carnation Gang*, the title-role in *Nijinsky*, Rubek in *When We Dead Awaken*, the title-role in *Sherlock Holmes*, Jacques in *As You Like It*, Laertes in *Hamlet*, Mère Ubu in *Ubu Roi* and Uriah Shelley in *A Man's a Man.* He was Wittipol in Peter **Barnes**'s adaptation of Jonson's *The Devil is an Ass* (Nottingham Playhouse, 1973, **Edinburgh Festival** and European tour).

For the 1978 season he was with the **Royal Shakespeare Company** in Stratford-upon-Avon, playing Ferdinand in *The Taming of the Shrew* and Angelo in *Measure for Measure.* He appeared in Russia in a version of Dostoevsky's *The Brothers Karamazov.* Following this Rickman has involved himself more in fringe theatre, and particularly in Women's Theatre movements and the CND. When recently asked, by D.A.N. Jones, if he is a political actor, Rickman said, 'I think if you set one foot on a stage it's a political act. To say: "Life is all about cucumber sandwiches — one lump or two?" is as political as anything else.' (*Radio Times*, 13-19 October 1984, p. 22). In an interview with Barney Bardsley (*Drama*, 1984) he said, 'theatre is an act of challenge, born out of a relentless optimism for the possibility of change'.

He has appeared in Dusty Hughes's

Commitments (Bush, 1979), Stephen Davis's *The Last Elephant* (Bush, November 1981) played Trigorin in Chekhov's *The Seagull* (**Royal Court**, April 1981), Bob in Dusty Hughes's *Bad Language* (Hampstead, August 1983), Dennis in Snoo **Wilson**'s *Grass Widow* (Royal Court, November 1983) and Gayman in Aphra Behn's *The Lucky Chance* (Women's Playhouse Trust, Royal Court, July 1984).

Alan Rickman has directed Ruby Wax's *Desperately Yours* in America and in May 1983 at the Royal Court Theatre he was an Assistant Director of Robert Holman's *Other Worlds.* Television appearances include Tybalt in *Romeo and Juliet,* Simon, the lawyer, in *Busted* and the Rev. Obadiah Slope in *The Barchester Chronicles,* a role which has earned him national popularity.

In his interview with Bardsley he commented on the art of acting that 'the "stillness" acclaimed in great actors in fact comes from a body so connected to mind and heart that in a way it vibrates. That's really centred acting.'

Further Reading

Barney Bardsley, interview with Alan Rickman, 'Waiting for the Renaissance of the Actor', *Drama,* 4th Quarter, No. 154, 1984, pp. 12-15.

Rigg, Diana

Born on 20 July 1938 in Doncaster, Yorkshire, she attended Fulneck Girls School, Pudsey and trained at the Royal Academy of Dramatic Art. Her first stage appearance was as Natella Abashwili in **Brecht**'s *The Caucasian Chalk Circle* in a RADA production for the York Festival (Theatre Royal, York, Summer 1957). She played in repertory at Chesterfield and York and then, in 1959, joined what was later named the **Royal Shakespeare Company** at Stratford-upon-Avon.

Her first London appearance was as 2nd Ondine and Violanta in Jean Giraudoux's fantasy play, *Ondine* (Aldwych, January 1961). Continuing in repertory at the Aldwych she played Phillipe in John **Whiting**'s *The Devils,* Gwendolen in Anouilh's *Becket* and Bianca in *The Taming of the Shrew* (1961) Touruel in *The Art of Seduction* (1962) and at Stratford-upon-Avon played Helena in *A Midsummer Night's Dream,* Bianca again, Lady Macduff in *Macbeth,* Adriana in *The Comedy of Errors,* and Cordelia in *King Lear* (1962 season). At the Aldwych she played Cordelia again (December 1962) and Monica in Dürrenmatt's *The Physicists* (January 1963). She subsequently toured the provinces with the RSC and appeared at Stratford and the Aldwych, toured Soviet Russia and the United States as Adriana and Cordelia in 1964, and at Stratford in the 1966 season appeared as Viola in *Twelfth Night.*

In the 1970s parts included Heloise in Ronald Millar's *Abelard and Heloise* (Wyndham's, May 1970, Brooks Atkinson Theatre, New York, March 1971), Dottie in Tom **Stoppard**'s *Jumpers* (**National Theatre** at the **Old Vic**, February 1972), Lady Macbeth in *Macbeth* (Old Vic, 1972), Eliza Doolittle in Shaw's *Pygmalion* (Albery, May 1974), Governor's Wife in *Phaedra Britannica* (Old Vic, September 1975), Ilona in Molnar's *The Guardsman* (National Theatre, Lyttleton, January 1978), and Ruth in Stoppard's *Night and Day* (Phoenix, November 1978). In 1982 she appeared in *Colette* in the United States and in March 1983 Shaw's *Heartbreak House* at the Haymarket Theatre.

Some of her many film appearances include *A Midsummer Night's Dream, Assassination Bureau, On Her Majesty's Secret Service, Julius Caesar, A Little Night Music* and *Evil Under the Sun.* Television appearances include *The Comedy of Errors, Married Alive, Diana* (US series), *Three Piece Suite, The Serpent Sun, Hedda Gabler, The Marquise, Little Eyolf* and, one of her most popular appearances, the series *The Avengers.*

In 1982 she became a founder-member and Director of the actors' collective called **United British Artists** and in the same year published an anthology of worst-ever theatrical reviews called *No Turn Unstoned*, in which she unashamedly republished a review of her nude scene in *Aberlard and Heloise* which said, 'Diana Rigg is built like a brick mausoleum with insufficient flying buttresses.' In a fascinating introduction to the book she wrote: 'There are so many wonderful qualities to be found in the theatre, and courage predominates...I think it takes guts to act...the courage I speak of is there every time an entrance is made, every time an actor or actress undertakes the daring and delicate task of making an audience believe. And another great quality is generosity of spirit.'

Rix, Brian (Norman Roger), CBE

Born in Cottingham, near Hull, Yorkshire, on 27 January 1924 he was educated at Bootham School, York, and made his first stage appearance as a Courtier in *King Lear* (Prince of Wales, Cardiff, August 1942). He subsequently joined the Donald **Wolfit** company (1942-3) and made his first London appearance as Sebastian in *Twelfth Night* (St James's, January 1943). From 1943 to 1944 he appeared with the White Rose Players (Harrogate) and then served in the Royal Air Force until 1947.

On his return to the theatre he formed his own repertory company, Rix Theatrical Productions, at Ilkley (March 1948) and Bridlington (November 1948). He formed a second company at the Hippodrome, Margate in 1949, the year of his marriage to Elspet Gray. He toured Colin Morris's farce *Reluctant Heroes* in 1950 and later (from September 1950) presented it, and played Gregory, for almost four years at the Whitehall Theatre. This run initiated what came to be known as 'Whitehall farce' and included the later long-running plays at the Whitehall, John Chapman's *Dry Rot* (1954-8, in which Rix played Fred Phipps) and *Simple Spymen* (1958-61, in which he played Percy Pringle), Ray **Cooney** and Tony Hilton's *One for the Pot* (1961-4, in which he played Hickory Wood) and Ray Cooney's *Chase Me Comrade!* (1964-6, in which he played Gerry Buss).

In March 1967 he and the company moved to the Garrick Theatre to present a repertoire of farces including Ray Cooney and Tony Hilton's *Stand By Your Bedouin* (Rix himself playing Fred Florence), Anthony Marriott and Alistair Foot's *Uproar in the House* (Rix playing Nigel Pitt) and Harold Brooke and Kay Bannerman's *Let Sleeping Wives Lie* (which ran until April 1969 and in which Rix took the part of Jack).

Some of Brian Rix's subsequent appearances and presentations included Hubert Porter in Michael Pertwee's *She's Done It Again* (Garrick, October 1969), Barry in Pertwee's *Don't Just Lie There, Say Something* (Garrick, September 1971) and Fogg in Pertwee's *A Bit Between the Teeth* (Cambridge Theatre, September 1974). Returning to the Whitehall Theatre in 1976 he co-presented Peter Yeldham and Donald Churchill's *Fringe Benefits* (playing Colin Hudson himself) and at the Astoria Theatre in October 1979 he co-presented *Beatlemania*, devised by Steven Leber, David Krebs and Jules Fisher. Also in 1979 (November) he presented *Lunatic Fringe* (Shaftesbury Theatre).

From 1956 to 1972 many Whitehall productions were televised (Rix appearing in over 70 parts) and he has also appeared on television in *Men of Affairs* and *A Roof Over My Head* and presented the pioneering television series for the mentally handicapped, *Let's Go* (1978-83). Many of his productions have also been made into films. He was also a radio disc-jocky 1978-80.

In 1977 Brian Rix was awarded the CBE for his work with the mentally handicapped and in 1980 he left the theatre to become

Secretary General of *Mencap* (the Royal Society for Mentally Handicapped Children and Adults). In 1981 he also became Chairman of the Independent Development Council for People with Mental Handicap, and in 1983 became a Trustee of Ray Cooney's **Theatre of Comedy** Company which is based at the Shaftesbury Theatre.

Further Reading

Brian Rix, *My Farce from My Elbow*, Secker and Warburg, London, 1975.

Robertson, Toby

See **Prospect Theatre Company**.

Robson, Dame Flora

Born in South Shields, County Durham, on 28 March 1902, she went to Palmer's Green High School, North London. From an early age she took lessons in singing and dancing and when only five years old appeared on stage reciting 'Little Orphan Annie' for a school performance. She trained for the stage at RADA (under the principalship of Kenneth Barnes who gave her much encouragement) and continued her voice and ballet training at the same time (1919-21). Her first professional appearance was as Queen Margaret in Clemence Dane's *Will Shakespeare* (Shaftesbury, 17 November 1921) after which she was in Shakespearean repertory with Ben Greet's company (1922) and in repertory with J.B. Fagan's company at the Oxford Playhouse (1923). In 1925 she left the theatre to work as a liaison officer at the Shredded Wheat factory in Welwyn Garden City. At the factory she directed a number of amateur productions in a small theatre which was specially built for her.

In 1929 Tyrone **Guthrie** encouraged her to return to the professional theatre and in October of that year she joined Anmer Hall's company at the Festival Theatre, Cambridge, of which Guthrie was director. After a little over a year with this company Dame Flora appeared in a number of roles in London theatres including Abbie Putnam in Eugene O'Neill's *Desire Under the Elms* (Gate Theatre, February 1931) and Herodias in Oscar Wilde's *Salome* (Gate Theatre, May 1931).

Recognition came with her critically-acclaimed performance as Mary Paterson in James Bridie's *The Anatomist* (Westminster, October 1931) and she went on to play a number of parts including the Stepdaughter in Pirandello's *Six Characters in Search of an Author* (Westminster, February 1932), Bianca in *Othello* (St James's, April 1932) which was a performance James Agate described as 'a little miracle', Olwen Peel in Priestley's *Dangerous Corner* (Lyric, May 1932) and Eva in Somerset Maugham's *For Services Rendered* (Globe, November 1932). In March 1933 at the Embassy Theatre she played Ella Downey, opposite Paul Robeson, in Eugene O'Neill's *All God's Chillun Got Wings*.

Joining the **Old Vic**–Sadler's Wells Company in October 1933 she was (for the 1933-4 season) Varya in Chekhov's *The Cherry Orchard*, Queen Katherine in *Henry VIII* (with Charles Laughton as King Henry) and Isabella in *Measure for Measure* (with Laughton as Angelo). It was in this same season that Flora Robson played Lady Macbeth to Charles Laughton's lead in *Macbeth*. Harold Hobson described her performance as 'the most memorable Lady Macbeth of her generation' and said she was potentially another Ellen Terry. J.C. Trewin (in *Shakespeare on the English Stage*, 1964) wrote: 'Flora Robson, defying the Siddons tradition, knew Lady Macbeth as a woman ambitious, unimaginative, and loving, who revealed herself in the agonised remorse of the Sleepwalking.' Dame Flora, in an interview with Joanna Lumley (published in the *Listener*, 19 July 1984) said of her now legendary performance of the sleepwalking scene: 'most people play it mad and you can see they're not asleep. I played it very sleepy.' After several years in **West End** productions she gave almost as greatly-acclaimed performances of Lady Catherine Brooke in Margaret Kennedy's *Autumn* (St Martin's, October 1937).

Dame Flora next spent seven years (including most of the Second World War) in the USA appearing in New York, Los Angeles and making films in Hollywood. On her return to Britain in 1944 she played Thérèse Raquin in *Guilty* (Lyric, Hammersmith, April 1944), an adaptation of Zola's novel *Thérèse Raquin.* In the post-war years she played roles ranging from classic heroines to comedy and character parts. She played Lady Macbeth again (National Theatre, New York, March 1948) and after highly successful runs as Lady Cicely Waynflete in Shaw's *Captain Brassbound's Conversion* (Theatre Royal, Windsor, July 1948, Lyric, Hammersmith, October 1948), appeared as Christie in Lesley Storm's *Black Chiffon* (Westminster, May 1949, 48th Street Theatre, New York, September 1950) and again as Lady Brooke in a revival of *Autumn* (Q Theatre, London, April 1951). Under Peter **Brook**'s direction she was Paulina in *The Winter's Tale* (Phoenix, June 1951) in which John **Gielgud** played Leontes.

Over the next 15 years Dame Flora's chief roles were Janet in Hugh Mills's *The House by the Lake* (Duke of York's, May 1956) which had a run of over 700 performances, Mrs Alving in Ibsen's *Ghosts* (Old Vic, November 1958, Prince's, April 1959), an award-winning Miss Tina in Michael **Redgrave**'s adaptation of Henry James's *The Aspern Papers* (Queen's, August 1959, South African tour, August–December 1960), Grace Rovarte in *Time and Yellow Roses* (St Martin's, May 1961), Miss Moffatt in Emlyn Williams's *The Corn is Green* (Connaught Theatre, Worthing, November 1961, South African tour, January 1962) which was also a role she repeated for the opening of the Flora Robson Playhouse, Newcastle-upon-Tyne (October 1962).

She was with Donald **Wolfit** (who took the title-role) when she played Gunhild Borkman in *John Gabriel Borkman* (Duchess, December 1963) and a year later played Lady Bracknell in Wilde's *The Importance of Being Earnest* (Flora Robson Playhouse, Newcastle, 1964). Subsequent roles included Hecuba in Euripides' *The Trojan Women* (**Edinburgh Festival**, 1966), Miss Prism in *The Importance of Being Earnest* (Haymarket, February 1968) and the Mother in Jean Anouilh's *Ring Round the Moon* (Haymarket, October 1968).

Dame Flora's last appearance on the London stage was as Agatha Payne in Rodney Ackland's adaptation of Hugh Walpole's 1924 novel *The Old Ladies* (Westminster, November 1969, Duchess, December 1969). At the 1970 Edinburgh Festival she was Elizabeth I in *Elizabeth Tudor, Queen of England.* She retired from the stage in 1970 but continued working in television and films. She made an appearance at the Brighton Festival in May 1974 as the narrator for a performance of Prokofiev's *Peter and the Wolf.*

Her extensive film work since 1933 includes performances in *Catherine the Great, Fire Over England, Wuthering Heights, Caesar and Cleopatra, Black Narcissus, Frieda, Romeo and Juliet, High Tide at Noon, 55 Days at Peking, Young Cassidy, Those Magnificent Men in their Flying Machines, Seven Women, Eye of the Devil, The Beloved, Alice in Wonderland* and *Clash of the Titans.* On television she has appeared in *Heidi, A Legacy, Mr Lollipop, The Shrimp and the Anemone, Eustace and Hilda, The Oresteia of Aeschylus, Les Misérables, The Turn of the Screw, A Tale of Two Cities* and *Mother Courage.*

In her interview with Joanna Lumley Dame Flora said of acting: 'The important thing is to feel a part. . .the audience really teaches you how to act. . .as Tolstoy said, an actor must feel what the author felt, feel it in himself and pass it on to the audience. If he can make an audience feel, that is art.'

Dame Flora Robson died on 7 July 1984.

Further Reading

Kenneth Barrow, *Flora*, Heinemann/David and Charles, London, 1981.
Janet Dunbar, *Flora Robson*, Harrap, London, 1960.

Rodgers, Anton

Born on 10 January 1933, and educated at Westminster City School, he appeared in the professional theatre at the age of 14 when he was in Bizet's opera *Carmen* (Royal Opera House, Covent Garden, 1947). This was followed by other boyhood roles when he toured as Pip in *Great Expectations* (1948) and in the title-role of Terence **Rattigan**'s *The Winslow Boy* (1949). After playing in repertory at Birmingham, Northampton and Hornchurch he trained at Italia Conti and LAMDA.

On leaving drama school in 1957 he was in musicals and revues until, in July 1962, he played Withers in John **Osborne**'s double-bill *Plays for England* at the **Royal Court** Theatre. Since then he has appeared in many musicals, classic plays, comedies, and he has also directed a number of productions. His chief work as an actor includes the title-role in *Henry V* (Belgrade, Coventry, March 1968), Vladimir in Samuel **Beckett**'s *Waiting for Godot* (University Theatre, Manchester, 1968), Stockmann in Ibsen's *An Enemy of the People* (Harrogate, August 1969), Frank in Peter **Nichols**'s *Forget-Me-Not-Lane* (Greenwich and Apollo, April 1971), Dr Rank in Ibsen's *A Doll's House* (Criterion, February 1973), Hildy Johnson in Hecht and MacArthur's *The Front Page* (**National Theatre**, Australian tour, 1974), Astrov in Chekhov's *Uncle Vanya* (Oxford Playhouse, December 1975), Jack Manningham in Patrick Hamilton's *Gaslight* (Criterion, March 1976), Jim in Peter Nichols's *Passion Play* (**Royal Shakespeare Company**, Aldwych, January 1981), Walter Burns in Dick Vosburgh and Tony Macaulay's musical *Windy City* (Victoria Palace Theatre, July 1982) and the Earl of Warwick in Shaw's *Saint Joan* (National Theatre, Olivier, February 1984).

Directing includes Tom Jones's musical *The Fantasticks* (Hampstead, May 1970), N. Richard Nash's comedy *The Rainmaker* (Ibiza Festival, 1970), *The Taming of the Shrew* (Northcott Theatre, Exeter, January 1971), Arthur Miller's *Death of a Salesman* (Oxford Playhouse, October 1975) and Garrard Thomas's *Flashpoint* (New End, December 1978, Mayfair, February 1979).

Anton Rodgers has made numerous appearances in television plays and series since 1958, recently in *The Flaxborough Chronicles, Lily Langtry* and *Disraeli.* He became well known as Arthur Fields in John Chapman's situation-comedy series *Fresh Fields.*

Rossiter, Leonard

Born in Liverpool on 21 October 1926, he was educated at Liverpool Collegiate Secondary School, served as a Sergeant in the Education Corps of the Army for two years in Germany and then worked for the Commercial Union Insurance Company in Liverpool for six years. During this period he was in numerous amateur stage productions and took voice lessons. He was married to Gillian Raine in 1972.

His first professional appearance was as Bert in *The Gay Dog* (Repertory Theatre, Preston, September 1954) and, after a period in repertory at Wolverhampton, he played John and a Reporter in *Free As Air* (Savoy, 1958). From 1959 until 1961 he was a member of the **Bristol Old Vic** Company. Reflecting on his early years as an actor he said in one of his last interviews ('The John Dunn Show', Radio 4, 27 February 1984) that at the time he felt he was 'not a genuine actor because genuine actors all start by how the character feels. And I always seemed to be worried about the shoes. Then I read an article by Olivier and I found he did the same. I felt a good deal relieved after that.' Leonard Rossiter played in a number of **West End** productions (and also David Turner's *Semi-Detached* at the Music Box, Broadway, New York, October 1963) until he came to prominence with his highly-acclaimed performance in the name-part of Bertholt **Brecht**'s *The Resistible Rise of Arturo Ui* (**Edinburgh Festival**, August 1968, Saville, July 1969).

Major roles followed, including the title-role in *Richard III* (Nottingham Playhouse, October 1971), Davies in Harold **Pinter**'s *The Caretaker* (**Mermaid**, March 1972), Brian in John Antrobus's *The Looneys* (Hampstead, October 1974), Followvoine and Dhuring in Peter **Barnes**'s *The Frontiers of Farce* (Old Vic, October 1976), the title-role in *Tartuffe* (Greenwich, December 1976) and Garrard in Michael **Frayn**'s *Make and Break* (Lyric, Hammersmith, April 1980). In 1982 he appeared in Pirandello's *Rules of the Game* (Haymarket, September, Phoenix, December) and in 1984 he played P.C. Truscott in a revival of Joe **Orton**'s *Loot* for the **Theatre of Comedy** Company (Ambassadors, March), the production still running when he died on 5 October 1984. In his interview with John Dunn earlier in 1984 (see above) he said of acting that it demands the technical ability to 'reproduce the thing night after night to roughly the same level, because the audience who've come that night are as entitled to as good a performance as the first night'.

Leonard Rossiter appeared in many films, including *A Kind of Loving, Billy Liar, This Sporting Life, Oliver, 2001: A Space Odyssey, Voyage of the Damned, Rising Damp, Hotel Paradiso, Luther, Otley* and *Britannia Hospital.* He achieved huge popularity in the television series *Rising Damp, The Rise and Fall of Reginald Perrin* and *Tripper's Day.* Together with Joan Collins (whom he spilt his drinks over) he made a series of greatly-loved advertisements for Cinzano. His last appearances in television plays were Arthur in Richard Harris's *Dog Ends* and the King in *King John.*

In a radio tribute (*Kaleidoscope*, Radio 4, 8 October 1984), Alan Coren said of Leonard Rossiter: 'The suit acted, the shoes acted, the whole body had a force. It was a force-field. You had the feeling, somehow, that if some forensic scientist went into a room in which Rossiter had recently been he would be able to identify the ex-presence as Rossiter. He ionized the world he moved through.'

Further Reading

Leonard Rossiter, *The Devil's Bedside Book*, Hamlyn, London, 1980.

Leonard Rossiter, *The Lowest Form of Wit*, James, London, 1981.

Rostra

(Plural of rostrum) Platforms or stage blocks used to vary the height of different parts of the **Acting Area**.

Routledge, Patricia

Born in Birkenhead, Cheshire, on 17 February 1929, she was educated at Birkenhead High School and the University of Liverpool and studied for the stage at the **Bristol Old Vic** Theatre School. Her first professional appearance was as Hippolyta in *A Midsummer Night's Dream* (Liverpool Playhouse, August 1952). She was in repertory for a number of years at Liverpool, Guildford, Worthing and Windsor and made her first London appearance as Carlotta in the musical *Duenna* (Westminster Theatre, July 1954). Patricia Routledge is a talented singer as well as actress and has appeared in many musicals and musical plays (including a musical version of *The Comedy of Errors* (1956), *Virtue in Danger* (1963), *Darling of* *the Day* (1968) and the opera *The Grand Duchess of Gerolstein* (1978) by Offenbach).

Her roles in plays have ranged from comedy parts such as Victoria in W. Somerset Maugham's farce *Home and Beauty* (Ashcroft, Croydon, January 1964), Violet, Nell and Rover in Roger Milner's *How's The World Treating You?* (Hampstead Theatre Club, August 1965), to more serious roles including the Mother-in-Law in **Brecht**'s *The Caucasian Chalk Circle* (**Chichester Festival**, 1969), Madame Ranevsky in Chekhov's *The Cherry Orchard* (Bristol Old Vic Company, Theatre Royal, Bristol, May 1975) and Emilia in *Othello* (Chichester, 1975). Other major parts have been Lady Fidget in Wycherley's *The Country Wife* (Chichester, 1969), Agatha in Pinero's *The Magistrate* (Chichester 1969, Cambridge Theatre, September 1969), Georgina in Pinero's *Dandy Dick* (Chichester, July 1973, Garrick, October 1963), Mrs Malaprop in Sheridan's *The Rivals* (Royal Exchange, Manchester, September 1976), Julia in *Semmelweiss* (Washington, Eisenhower Theatre, May 1978) and Dottie Otley in Michael **Frayn**'s *Noises Off* (Lyric, Hammersmith, February 1982, Savoy, March 1982).

Television work includes *When We Are Married, The Years Between, Doris and Doreen, Nicholas Nickleby* and *A Woman of No Importance.*

Royal Court Theatre

The theatre in Sloane Square which has been the home of the English Stage Company since 1955. It was built in 1888 to replace a previous theatre established in 1870 in Lower George Street, Chelsea. In the early years of this century it presented productions under J.E. Vedrenne and Harley Granville-Barker (including plays by Shakespeare, Shaw and Galsworthy), after which the theatre was less successful until J.B. Fagan took over after the Great War, followed by Barry **Jackson**'s seasons with his Birmingham Repertory Company in the 1920s (which included productions of plays by Shaw and Shakespeare, notably the controversial modern dress productions, in 1928, of *Macbeth* and *The Taming of the Shrew*). The theatre became a cinema in 1932 and was bombed during the Second World War. It reopened in 1952 but presented little of interest until George Devine set up the English Stage Company in 1955 with its policy of presenting new and experimental drama. The Berliner Ensemble presented **Brecht**'s *The Threepenny Opera* there in 1955 and in April 1956 Devine directed Angus Wilson's *The Mulberry Bush* and Arthur Miller's *The Crucible.* The company changed the course of British theatre almost overnight when it staged John **Osborne**'s *Look Back in Anger* (May 1956), directed by Tony Richardson and starring Kenneth **Haigh** as Jimmy Porter.

Following on from the inroads *Look Back in Anger* made into the post-war Establishment and the conventional theatre of the period, the Royal Court presented Osborne's *The Entertainer* (April 1957), starring Laurence **Olivier** as the waning music-hall comedian, Archie Rice. This was followed by a number of new and provocative plays by a group of playwrights whom the press tended to label (along with Osborne), '**Angry Young Men**': Arnold **Wesker** (the trilogy comprising *Chicken Soup With Barley*, 1958, *Roots* and *I'm Talking About Jerusalem*, 1959) and John **Arden** (*Sergeant Musgrave*'s *Dance*, 1959). In addition Devine in particular encouraged plays, both British and foreign, which Martin Esslin later grouped under the form of theatre he called '**Theatre of the Absurd**': Samuel **Beckett**'s *Fin de Partie* (April 1956), *Krapp's Last Tape* (October 1958), *Happy Days* (November 1962) and *Waiting for Godot* (December 1964), Eugene Ionesco's *The Chairs* (May 1956), *The Lesson* (June 1958), *Rhinoceros* (April 1960) and *Jacques* (March 1961), Jean-Paul Sartre's *Nekrassov* (September 1957), *Altona* (April 1961), N.F. **Simpson**'s

A Resounding Tinkle (April 1958) and *One Way Pendulum* (December 1959), and Harold **Pinter**'s *The Room* and *The Dumb Waiter* (March 1960). Other playwrights Devine encouraged included Nigel Dennis, Ronald Duncan, Michael **Hastings**, Ann **Jellicoe**, Donald Howarth, Willis **Hall**, Alun Owen and Keith Johnstone.

In 1964 the theatre closed for building work and in 1965 George Devine died. His place as Artistic Director was taken by William **Gaskill** and, from 1972, Oscar Lowenstein. In this period (1965-77) there were productions of new plays by David **Storey**, Edward **Bond**, Charles **Wood**, Christopher **Hampton**, David Cregan, E.A. Whitehead, Howard **Barker**, Howard **Brenton** and David **Hare**, to name only a few. In 1977 Stuart Burge took over as Artistic Director and he was succeeded in 1979 by Max Stafford-Clark, previously Director of the **Joint Stock Theatre Group**.

With the addition, in 1969, of the Theatre Upstairs, an adapted rehearsal space, the Royal Court has also encouraged experimental theatre by staging short runs and one-night stands of low-budget plays by new and previously unknown writers. With the growth of small **Alternative Theatre** groups and touring 'fringe' groups in the 1970s the Royal Court has also attracted visits by many such companies, including the Joint Stock company, Portable Theatre, and from abroad, the Bread and Puppet Theatre and La Mama company.

Although its unique role of encouraging new writers and plays is also now shared by the **National Theatre** and the **Royal Shakespeare Company**, the Royal Court remains a vital force in post-war British theatre.

Further Reading

Terry Browne, *Playwright's Theatre: the English Stage Company at the Royal Court*, Pitman, London, 1975.
Richard Findlater (ed.), *25 Years of the English Stage Company at the Royal Court*, Amber Lane Press, Derbyshire, 1981.

Royal Shakespeare Company (RSC)

Possibly the most distinguished theatre company in Great Britain, it was formed in 1961 when the Shakespeare Memorial Theatre Company at Stratford-upon-Avon was reorganised (largely by Peter **Hall**). In addition, the Memorial Theatre was renamed the Royal Shakespeare Theatre. The Company plays there and at the Other Place in Stratford and in London at the Barbican Theatre and Pit and at the Warehouse. It also organises national and foreign tours. Previous to the opening of the Barbican Theatre in 1982 the RSC's London base was the Aldwych Theatre.

The first Shakespeare Memorial Theatre was donated by a local Stratford-upon-Avon brewer called Charles Flower and it opened in 1879 on Shakespeare's birthday, April 23rd. Frank Benson was its director from 1886 to 1919 and from then until 1934 the director was William Bridges-Adams. The theatre was destroyed by fire on 6 March 1926 and the present one, designed by Elizabeth Scott, was opened on 23 April 1932. Bridges-Adams was succeeded in 1935 by Ben Iden Payne who was Director until 1943 when Milton Rosmer took over. In 1944 Robert Atkins succeeded him for a year and in 1945 Sir Barry **Jackson** took over. Although the company prior to Jackson's directorship was often considered provincial, there were fine performances by such actors as Randle Ayrton, Donald **Wolfit** and Baliol Holloway.

Jackson attracted Peter **Brook** to his company and such actors as Paul **Scofield** and Robert **Helpmann**. He initiated policies of spreading the first nights over the season and the use of a different director for each play, as well as making alterations to the fabric of the theatre in order to create more space backstage. In 1949 Jackson was replaced by Anthony **Quayle** as Director who stayed until 1956 when Glen Byam Shaw took over for four years. In 1960 Peter

Hall became Director.

In spite of the fact that up until Hall's time companies were formed and disbanded every season, the period from Quayle to Hall saw some extremely fine performances from such leading players as John **Gielgud**, Peggy **Ashcroft**, Edith **Evans**, Ralph **Richardson**, Laurence **Olivier**, Michael **Redgrave** and Dorothy **Tutin**. Most notable were Peter Brook's production of *Titus Andronicus* (1955), starring Olivier, Byam Shaw's *Antony and Cleopatra* (1953) with Ashcroft and Redgrave, and Tyrone **Guthrie**'s *All's Well That Ends Well* (1959).

A new phase of development began when Peter Hall became director (1960) at the age of 29. He made some radical changes such as establishing a permanent company with actors on long-term contracts which included provision for them to work elsewhere between seasons. He established a permanent base in London, at the Aldwych Theatre, where Shakespearean plays could be transferred from Stratford but also where modern and non-Shakespearean plays could be performed, thus extending the company's repertoire (which included plays by Harold **Pinter**, David **Mercer** and Edward Albee). So far as Shakespeare's plays were concerned there were changes in emphasis: as Peter Brook stated in 1970: 'The first great change in Shakespeare at Stratford was introduced by Peter Hall, when he announced this vital principle that it was actors in touch with contemporary life — through contemporary works — who had to be the people to interpret Shakespeare...The notion of a Shakespeare company as something cut off from the world could no longer be tolerated...eventually *all* that has grown from the Royal Shakespeare Company, has come from that policy.'

A number of talented directors, besides Peter Hall himself, gave expression to this policy of artistic freedom and contemporary relevance: Peter Brook, John **Barton**, Terry **Hands**, Trevor **Nunn** and Clifford **Williams**. The designer John Bury contributed much to the development of a distinctively bold style of visual presentation.

In 1968 Trevor Nunn succeeded Hall as Artistic Director and in 1970 the RSC was the first British theatre company to visit Japan. 'Theatregoround', a touring ensemble, was established in the mid-1960s and took plays to local communities, factories and schools in the provinces. In 1971, when Theatregoround had to be abandoned, a small theatre in London, The Place, was used as a continuation of the development, eventually being superseded by The Other Place at Stratford in 1974. Another London base, the Warehouse, was established in 1977 and in 1978 Nunn was joined by Terry Hands as Joint Artistic Director. In June 1982 the RSC were able to move into their new and long-awaited London base, the Barbican Theatre and its small experimental basement, the Pit.

Some of the most acclaimed productions by the RSC have been *King Lear* (1962,) *The Wars of the Roses* (1963-4), Weiss's *Marat/Sade* (1964), *The Revenger's Tragedy* (1966), *Hamlet* (1965), *The Winter's Tale* (1969), *The Jew of Malta* (1964), *The Merry Wives of Windsor* (1968), *King Lear* (1968), *A Midsummer Night's Dream* (1970), *Richard II* (1973), *Henry V* (1975), *The Tempest* (1978), *The Taming of the Shrew* (1978), *Antony and Cleopatra* (1979), *Nicholas Nickleby* (1981) and plays by Chekhov, Ibsen, Strindberg, Pinter, **Stoppard**, Mercer, **Shaffer**, **Nichols** and numerous others. Some of the company's best known performers, other than the major figures already mentioned have been Ben **Kingsley**, Brewster Mason, Janet **Suzman**, Glenda **Jackson**, David **Warner**, Eric **Porter**, Susan Fleetwood, Elizabeth **Spriggs**, Helen **Mirren**, Sarah **Kestelman**, Donald **Sinden**, Michael **Hordern**, Richard **Pasco**, Ian **Richardson**, Alan **Howard**, Patrick **Stewart**, Jonathan **Pryce** and Emrys **James**.

Recent directors have included John **Caird**, Michael **Bogdanov**, Howard Davies, David Jones, Ron Daniels and Adrian

Noble. In July 1985 the RSC opened the Whitbread Flowers Warehouse as a third theatre in Stratford-upon-Avon.

Further Reading

Sally Beauman, *The Royal Shakespeare Company: A History of Ten Decades*, Oxford University Press, London, 1982.

Paul Addenbrooke, *The Royal Shakespeare Company: the Peter Hall Years*, Kimber Press, London, 1974.

J.L. Styan, *The Shakespeare Revolution*, Cambridge University Press, London, 1977.

Rudkin, (James) David

Born on 29 June 1936, he was educated at King Edward's School, Birmingham, and St Catherine's College, Oxford, after which he became a music teacher. His first play to be performed was a radio play, *No Accounting for Taste* (broadcast 1960), about three partners in an accountancy firm who turn out to be one man.

His first stage play, *Afore Night Come*, which was performed by the **Royal Shakespeare Company** at the New Arts Theatre in June 1962, was highly acclaimed and remains his finest play. Set on a fruit farm somewhere in the Black Country, the play's superbly-evoked surface of rustic life (in a pear-orchard) has beneath it growing forces of darkness, violence and menace which finally erupt in the ritual murder of an Irish tramp, performed as a helicopter hovers above, spraying insecticide. The play has been regarded as the best example of the **Theatre of Cruelty** by a British playwright, though John Russell Taylor has argued that it owes less to the influences of Artaud and Genet and more to Thomas Hardy, D.H. Lawrence and Arthur Machen. A review by Tom Milne (*Encore*, July 1962) stated: 'Basically, the theme is that of [Golding's] *Lord of the Flies* — the incredible, primitive savagery and blood-lust latent in mankind, so easily brought to the surface by fear or isolation.'

Rudkin married Sandra Thompson in 1967 and in 1968 his play for children, called *Burglars*, was performed. *The Filth Hunt* followed in 1972 as a fringe production at the Almost Free Theatre, and in 1973 *Cries from Casement as His Bones Are Brought to Dublin* (originally a radio play broadcast earlier in 1973). In July 1974 came *Ashes* (**Open Space**), an intense play about a marriage breakdown which is brought about partly by the childless couple's submission to medical authority and partly by one of the partner's private feelings about the problems of Northern Ireland. *No Title* was produced at Birmingham Repertory Theatre in the same year, and in March 1976 *The Sons of Light* was performed at Newcastle University Theatre. This latter play was influenced by Rudkin's acquaintance with the psychotherapist Robert Ollendorff (to whom the play is dedicated) and some of the work of the psychiatrist R.D. Laing. It is an excursion into a mytho-poetic vision of isolation and oppression set on a remote island (perhaps symbolic of the unconscious).

His next stage play was *Sovereignty under Elizabeth* (1978) and this was followed by an adaptation of Euripides' *Hippolytus* (RSC, Other Place, June 1979).

David Rudkin has translated the libretto for the London production of Schoënberg's opera *Moses and Aaron* (Covent Garden, 1965), he wrote the libretti for the opera *The Grace of Todd* (Aldeburgh, 1966) and for *Sabbatai Zevi* (1966). In November 1981 his translation of *Hansel and Gretel* was performed by the Royal Shakespeare Company (Warehouse) and in June 1983 his translation of Ibsen's *Peer Gynt* was performed (RSC, Barbican, Pit), starring Derek **Jacobi**.

His plays for television include *The Stone Dance, Children Playing, House of Character, Blodwen, Home from Rachel's Marriage, Bypass, Atrocity, Penda's Fen*, two episodes of *Churchill's People, The Ash Tree* and others. He collaborated with Francois Truffaut on the screenplay for *Fahrenheit 451* and he has translated Aeschylus' *The Persians* and Euripides' *Hecuba* for the radio.

Further Reading

Interview with David Rudkin, *Encore*, Vol. XI, No. 4, 1964.

David Rudkin, 'Seeing the Light', *Plays and Players*, May, 1976.

S

Saunders, James

Born in Islington, London, on 8 January 1925, and educated at Wembley County School and the University of Southampton, he began his career as a chemistry teacher. He wrote a number of one-act plays influenced by Ionesco and the **Theatre of the Absurd** and came to prominence with his major full-length play *Next Time I'll Sing to You* (Questors, 1962, revised January 1963, New Arts) which explores the motives behind a man (Jimmy Mason) rejecting society and becoming a hermit. The play was based on Raleigh Trevelyan's book *A Hermit Disclosed* (which also had some influence on Henry **Livings**'s television play *Jim All Alone* and Edward **Bond**'s *The Pope's Wedding*).

A Scent of Flowers (Duke of York's, September 1964, New York 1969), possibly Saunders's finest play, takes place on the day of the funeral of a girl (Zoë) who has committed suicide. She is present on stage, existing somewhere between life and death, and provides for the play some fascinating formal interest through retrospectives and time-shifts as she relives the conflicts of her family, her love and her Roman Catholic faith. Along with Harold **Pinter**, George Melly, Alan **Ayckbourn** and others, Saunders contributed sketches to *Mixed Doubles* (Comedy Theatre, April 1969). *The Borage Pigeon Affair*, about a councillor whose pigeon-keeping creates conflict in a provincial town, was also presented in the **West End** in 1969.

Saunders continued writing both full-length and one-act plays, nearly all of which were presented at the Questors Theatre, Ealing, or the Orange Tree Theatre, Richmond, Surrey. These include the one-act plays *Games* and *After Liverpool* (**Edinburgh Festival**, Questors Theatre, 1971) both of which have actors as their characters, the former play exploring the rehearsal of a play, the latter exploring the emergence of relationships between the actors. These two plays focus more overtly on the nature of theatre than some of Saunders's other plays but it is a preoccupation to be found in most (including *Next Time I'll Sing to You*). Another one-act play was *Bye Bye Blues* (Orange Tree, Richmond, November 1973), a conversation-piece involving the accidental confrontation between three pairs of strangers who, in the course of the play, investigate their various responsibilities towards each other in relation to their freedom. The full-length play *Bodies* (Orange Tree, Richmond, April 1977, revised version Hampstead Theatre, London, February 1978, Ambassadors, 1979) had a highly successful run. It explores the changed life-styles and differing values of two couples who meet again after a ten year gap, prior to which the husbands have had affairs with one another's wife. Formal experiments with shifts from monologue to dialogue and group conversation are mixed with changes of location and more conventional and naturalistic elements. *The Girl in Melanie Klein*, based on a novel by Ronald Harwood and originally a radio play broadcast in 1973, was performed as a stage play in 1980 (Palace Theatre, Watford, Questors Theatre, Ealing) as was another radio play *Random Moments in a May Garden* (originally broadcast 1974). *Fall* (Hampstead Theatre, September 1984) is an exposé of the tormented inner lives of three sisters who return to their mother after the death of their father. An intriguing aspect of the play is that its 'author', in the character of Roache, comments on the action whilst on stage.

An innovator and writer of plays which

are both profoundly moving and comic, James Saunders is somewhat like some of his central characters and once described himself (according to Frederick Lumley in *New Trends in 20th Century Drama*, 1967) as a man 'beyond the confines of conventional society and looking in, observing, criticising and maybe envying a little'. Jonathan Hammond (in James Vinson's *Contemporary Dramatists*, 1982) described Saunders as 'a liberal humanist, someone who values the virtues of common humanity, tolerance and understanding above everything else, and would like society organised in such a way that these qualities would be encouraged'.

Saunders's television plays include *Just You Wait, Watch Me I'm a Bird, The White Stocking, Beast in the Bloomers* and *The Captain's Doll.* He has also written numerous radio plays.

Scales, Prunella (Margaret Rumney)

Born in Sutton Abinger, Surrey, she was educated at Moira House, Eastbourne and then trained for the stage at the **Old Vic** Theatre School, London, and the Herbert Berghov Studio, New York. She married Timothy **West** in 1963.

Prunella Scales first appeared on the stage as the Cook in Jean Anouilh's *Traveller Without Luggage* (Theatre Royal, Bristol, September 1951) and her first London appearance was as Lucrezia in *The Impresario from Smyrna* (Arts Theatre, May 1954). Her first appearance on Broadway was as Ermengarde in Thornton Wilder's *The Matchmaker* (1954). Some of her most important roles have been Nerissa in *The Merchant of Venice*, Jacquenetta in *Love's Labour's Lost* and Juliet in *Measure for Measure* (**Shakespeare Memorial Theatre**, Stratford-upon-Avon, 1956 season), the pupil in Eugène Ionesco's *The Lesson* (Oxford Playhouse, 1957) and Margie in Eugene O'Neill's *The Iceman Cometh* (Arts, January 1958).

With the Oxford Playhouse Company she toured Europe in 1959, taking the parts of Olivia in *Twelfth Night* and Hermia in *A Midsummer Night's Dream.* She subsequently played Anna Bowers in Donald Howarth's *All Good Children* (Bromley Little Theatre, November 1960), Hermione in *The Winter's Tale* (Birmingham Repertory, 1965), Cherry in Farquhar's *The Beaux's Strategem* (**Chichester Festival**, June 1967), Jackie Coryton in Noël **Coward**'s *Hay Fever* (Duke of York's, February 1968) and the Wife in *The Unknown Soldier* (Chichester Festival, May 1968).

In 1969 she took the part of Emma Partridge in Keith **Waterhouse** and Willis **Hall**'s *Children's Day* (Mermaid, September) and in April 1970 appeared in Tom **Stoppard**'s *After Magritte* (Ambiance lunchtime production). The following year she appeared as Natasha in Chekhov's *Three Sisters* and Avonia Bunn in Pinero's *Trelawny of the 'Wells'* (Arts, Cambridge, and tour, October 1971).

She joined the **Prospect Theatre Company** in Spring 1972 and toured Australia in productions of *King Lear, Love's Labour's Lost* and Samuel **Beckett**'s *Endgame.* Subsequently she appeared as Lady Brute in Vanbrugh's *The Provok'd Wife* (Watford Palace, February 1973), Katherina in *The Taming of the Shrew* (Playhouse, Nottingham, September 1973), Joyce in Joe **Orton**'s *The Ruffian on the Stair* (Soho Poly, December 1973) and Henrietta in Terence **Frisby**'s *It's All Right If I Do It* (Mermaid, March 1977). In May 1979 she returned to The **Bristol Old Vic** to play Natalya Petrovna in Turgenev's *A Month in the Country.* She then appeared with the reformed Old Vic Company, playing Tag in *Miss in Her Teens* (September 1979), Mrs Prentice in Joe Orton's *What the Butler Saw* (October 1979) and Queen Caroline in *The Trial of Queen Caroline* (November 1979).

In March 1980 she took the part of Mrs

Rogers in Michael **Frayn**'s *Make and Break* (Lyric, Hammersmith, then Haymarket) and in the same year performed a one-woman show called *An Evening with Queen Victoria* in which she appeared as Queen Victoria reading her letters. In 1981 she appeared in *The Merchant of Venice* (Old Vic, April) and Simon **Gray**'s *Quartermaine's Terms* (Queen's, July).

Prunella Scales has appeared in many films, including *Waltz of the Toreadors, The Boys from Brazil, The Hound of the Baskervilles* and (in 1982) *The Wicked Lady.* She has appeared in many television plays and is perhaps best known for her parts in the series *Marriage Lines* and *Fawlty Towers.* She has directed plays at a number of theatres and is a frequent performer in radio plays and reader at poetry recitals.

Scofield, (David) Paul

An actor of great talent and skill, he is one of the most acclaimed performers to emerge after the Second World War. He wrote in 1961: 'I feel I'm part of no group in the theatre. I come sort of half-way between two schools — one exemplified by John Gielgud, with the classic style of speaking, and the other by the **Royal Court Theatre**, which puts on the work of so many good new playwrights.'

He was born in Birmingham on 21 January 1922, but was brought up in Hurstpierpoint, Sussex. His father was the headmaster of a Church of England school in Brighton. Paul Scofield was educated at Varndean School for Boys in Brighton and, whilst there, played Juliet and Rosalind. As a member of the crowd in *The Only Way* he made an appearance at the Theatre Royal, Brighton, in 1936. He went briefly to Croydon Repertory Theatre School and then trained at the London Mask Theatre School, attached to Westminster Theatre, where he made his first professional appearance in *Desire Under the Elms* (January 1940). Subsequently he joined the Bideford Repertory Company (Spring 1941), toured for ENSA, and in 1942 joined Birmingham Repertory Theatre (which was then under the direction of Sir Barry **Jackson**). He married the actress Joy Parker in 1943. Some of his parts at Birmingham Rep. were Undershaft in Shaw's *Major Barbara,* Horatio in *Hamlet,* Reginald in *Getting Married,* the Prince in *Circle of Chalk,* the Clown in *The Winter's Tale,* Young Marlow in *She Stoops to Conquer,* Konstantin in *The Seagull,* Tanner in *Man and Superman* and Philip the Bastard in *King John.* When Jackson became administrative director of the **Shakespeare Memorial Theatre**, Stratford-upon-Avon, in 1946, Scofield was asked to join him and did so, at the same time as Peter **Brook** with whom he was to work on many notable productions. In the 1946 and 1947 seasons he took a number of parts, including the title-role in *Henry V,* Don Armado in *Love's Labour's Lost,* Malcolm in *Macbeth,* Lucio in *Measure for Measure,* Aguecheek in *Twelfth Night,* Cloten in *Cymbeline,* Mercutio in *Romeo and Juliet,* the title-tole in *Pericles* and Mephistophilis in Marlowe's *Doctor Faustus.* Between seasons at Stratford he played a number of parts in London, including Tegeus-Chromis in **Fry**'s *A Phoenix Too Frequent* (Arts Theatre, November 1946), and Young Fashion in Vanbrugh's *The Relapse* (Phoenix, January 1948). In a third season at Stratford (1948) his most important parts were Troilus in *Troilus and Cressida* and the title-role in *Hamlet* (alternating with Robert **Helpmann**), the latter production being Barry Jackson's somewhat controversial version presented in Victorian dress. Scofield has written of this period at Stratford that he was 'now exploring aspects of human nature that I wanted to make clear to the audience. Shakespeare is particularly well suited to an actor who wants to make his own comment.'

In March 1949 he played Alexander in Terence **Rattigan**'s *Adventure Story* (St James's Theatre) and in autumn of the same year, Konstantin in Chekhov's *The Seagull* (Lyric, Hammersmith, October, and St James's Theatre, November). A year later he played the twins, Hugo and Frederick, in Jean Anouilh's *Ring Around the Moon* (Globe, January 1950) and the title-role in his own production of *Pericles* (Rudolf Steiner Hall, July 1950). He played Philip Sturgess in Charles Morgan's *The River Line* at the 1952 **Edinburgh Festival**, and afterwards transferred to the Lyric, Hammersmith (September 1952) and the Strand (October 1952). He then joined Sir John **Gielgud**'s season at the Lyric, Hammersmith (December 1952–July 1953), appearing as Richard in *Richard II*, Witwould in Congreve's *The Way of the World* and Pierre in Otway's *Venice Preserv'd*. A number of other parts in London followed, including Prince Troubiscoi in Anouilh's *Time Remembered* (Lyric, Hammersmith, December 1954).

In October 1955 Scofield toured in the title-role of *Hamlet*, including appearances at the Moscow Art Theatre. This production was then seen at the Phoenix Theatre (December 1955) where Scofield next gave one of his most acclaimed performances as the 'whisky-priest' in Denis Cannan and Pierre Bost's stage adaptation of Graham **Greene**'s novel *The Power and the Glory* (Phoenix, April 1956). The play was directed by Peter Brook. Writing in 1961, Scofield noted that this part 'gave me the opportunity to work in a completely nonclassical, realistic style, in which I could still use more of my classical training than ever before'.

In June 1956 he played Harry in a revival of T.S. **Eliot**'s *The Family Reunion* (Phoenix) and in May 1957 played Fred Dyson in Rodney Ackland's *A Dead Secret* (Piccadilly). He made his first appearance in a musical playing Johnnie in *Expresso Bongo* (Saville, April 1958) and took the part of Clive Root in Graham Greene's *The Complaisant Lover* (Globe, June 1959).

His two finest performances to date have been as Thomas More in Robert **Bolt**'s *A Man for All Seasons* and Lear in Shakespeare's *King Lear*. He first appeared as More at the Globe Theatre in July 1960, and, after a season at the Stratford Shakespearean Festival, Ontario, where he played Coriolanus and Don Armado (June-September 1961), he played More again, this time on Broadway (ANTA, November 1961). He wrote of his attempts to find a way of playing More, that much depended on finding the right voice: 'I used an accent for More that was absolutely a bastard thing of my own...the way More sounded just came out of my characterization of him as a lawyer. His dryness of mind, I thought, led him to use a sort of dryness of speech. It evolved as I evolved the character.' Scofield also discovered 'More's humour and knew that that would be the thing to make him not smug' and also that the man 'was fully alive and sensual, in the true sense of the word'.

At Stratford-upon-Avon, a year later, Peter Brook directed *King Lear* with Scofield in the title-role (Royal Shakespeare Theatre, November 1962, subsequently Aldwych, December 1962). Scofield played the part again in the following year in Paris (Théâtre Sarah-Bernhardt, May 1963) for the 10th Season of the 'Théâtre des Nations' festival and between February and May 1964 played the part on tour with the **RSC** in Berlin, Prague, Budapest, Belgrade, Bucharest, Warsaw, Helsinki, Leningrad, Moscow and New York. He also played Lear in Brook's film version of *King Lear* (1969). Scofield's Lear of the early scenes was described by J.C. Trewin (*Birmingham Post*, 7 November 1962) as a 'figure of cold arrogance, set in tarnished gold, his hands clenched upon the arms of a crudely fashioned throne'. The performance has been acclaimed by many critics (in particulr Robin May, who has described it as 'an astonishing, earthy, primitive, detailed, pathetic and magnificent portrayal', and W.A. Darlington, who wrote at the time that it was 'the best all-round performance of this tremendous play in modern times'). In July 1965 Scofield played the title-role of *Timon of Athens*

(Royal Shakespeare Theatre, Stratford-upon-Avon) and subsequently a number of other roles with the RSC including Charlie, the homosexual barber, in Charles Dyer's *Staircase* (Aldwych, November 1966), the title-role in *Macbeth* (Stratford, August 1967, and tour of Finland and Russia, November-December 1967). In the following year he appeared in John **Osborne**'s *Hotel in Amsterdam* at the Royal Court Theatre (July 1968) and gave a superb performance in the title-part of Chekhov's *Uncle Vanya* later at the same theatre (February 1970).

In an interview with Ronald Hayman (*Playback*, 1973) Paul Scofield said: 'I feel drawn to attempting by means of acting what maybe a painter attempts', and remarked how he had become 'more interested in what the writer has opened up for me and how I can best illustrate this, almost without feeling that I am present'. He once described himself as possessing 'an intuitive approach' to acting, by which he meant that, for him, acting involves 'constant communication between thinking and feeling'.

His first performance with the **National Theatre** was as Voigt in Zuckmayer's *The Captain of Kopenick* (**Old Vic**, March 1971). Among his roles in the 1970s have been Alan West in Christopher **Hampton**'s *Savages* (Royal Court, April 1973), Prospero in *The Tempest* (Leeds Playhouse, November 1974), the title-role in Athol Fugard's *Dimetos* (Nottingham Playhouse, April 1976), the title-role in Jonson's *Volpone* (National Theatre, Olivier, April 1977), Salieri in Peter **Shaffer**'s *Amadeus* (National Theatre, Olivier, November 1979) and the title-role in *Othello* (National Theatre, Olivier, March 1980), these latter two plays being directed by Sir Peter **Hall**. For *Othello* he developed a hybrid accent (as he had done for Thomas More in 1960) which was highly effective (though not to everyone's taste: the magazine *Field* said he sounded like 'a man wrestling with a new set of National Health teeth' and Peter Jenkins in the *Spectator* wrote that Scofield's form of speech 'got lost somewhere between Jamaica and Berkeley Square'). In June 1982 he played the title-role in Keith Dewhurst's adaptation of Cervantes' *Don Quixote* (National Theatre, Olivier) and in November 1982 appeared as Oberon in *A Midsummer Night's Dream* (National Theatre, Cottesloe). Filmwork has included *The Train* (1964), *A Man for All Seasons* (1966), *King Lear* (1969) and *A Delicate Balance* (1974).

Paul Scofield is an actor of great range who has always remained open to new possibilities in the parts he has attempted ('when I'm working on a part I'm thinking about it all the time, going over all the possibilities in my mind'). 'The English theatre,' he said in 1973, 'should be explored by an actor in every area' and Scofield has certainly kept himself free from stagnation in a safe repertoire, and has not allowed himself to lapse into a cosy artistic security: 'The more one learns about such work as we do in the theatre, the less one can feel sure of one-self.'

Further Reading

Paul Scofield, 'The Intuitive Approach', *The Player*, Simon and Schuster Ltd, New York, 1961, pp. 180-7.

Ronald Hayman, 'Paul Scofield', *Playback*, Davis-Poynter, London, 1973.

'Scottish Play, The'

Shakespeare's *Macbeth*, so referred to in dressing rooms because of a superstition that if actors mention the real title it will bring bad luck to the performance.

7:84 Theatre Company

See **McGrath, John.**

Shaffer, Peter

Born 15 May 1926 in Liverpool he was educated at St Paul's School and took a degree at Trinity College, Cambridge. Having been a 'Bevin Boy' (a young man conscripted but choosing to work in the coal industry under a scheme devised by Ernest Bevin) during the war, he worked in a New York library and then for Boosey and Hawkes, the music publishers, in London. Between 1961 and 1962 he was a music critic for *Time and Tide.* He broke into the theatre with the highly successful *Five Finger Exercise* (July 1958) at the Comedy Theatre, London. As with many of Shaffer's plays the central conflict is a clash of opposing dramatic forces and viewpoints — in this case the clash of the Harrington's middle-class family values with those of a foreign tutor, the freedom-loving German, Walter. Two one-act plays *The Private Ear* and *The Public Eye* followed in May 1962 and the epic *The Royal Hunt of the Sun* in summer 1964 (**Chichester Festival** and **Old Vic**). This latter play concerns the conflict between Pizarro, leader of a Spanish Conquistador expedition to Peru in 1532 and Atahuallpa, the Sun King of the Incas. The confrontation is not only between the acquisitive values of the West and the highly perfected morality of the Incas but is also a clash of religious visions in which Christianity and Western faith (Pizarro's in particular) are put in doubt by the potent religious energies of Inca sun-worship. Pizarro's contact with Atahuallpa changes, or at least shifts, his vision but this leads to tragedy as Atahuallpa dies and it is recognised by Pizarro that immortality is an illusion. The play thus assumes the proportions of a religious allegory heightened by the magnificent spectacle required of the production (in the original staging, Inca masks, a giant golden sun with hinged petals which opened, mime, dance, gymnastics and richly feathered Inca costumes) and by the ritual language of the play (chants and the ritual repetition of the word 'INCA' to quote one memorable example). Shaffer wished to employ a form of '**total**' theatre and commented at the time: 'Why did I write *The Royal Hunt*? To make colour? Yes. To make spectacle? Yes. To make magic? Yes — if the word isn't too debased to convey the kind of excitement I believed could still be created out of "total" theatre.'

A year later at Chichester Festival (July 1965) we had *Black Comedy*, a one-acter which uses the brilliant device of stage-lighting representing darkness and darkness representing light: the main character, Brinsley, has to swap back the furniture borrowed from the flat next door but unfortunately the lights have fused. The comedy arises because the audience sees all this hilarious activity in a stagelit 'dark'. Another one-act play was *The White Liars* (February 1968) and 1973 saw *Equus* (**National Theatre** at the Old Vic), a remarkable play about a 17-year-old boy (Alan Strang) who has stabbed the eyes out of six horses and is undergoing treatment from a psychiatrist (Martin Dysart). It is the classical conflict between 'Dionysius' and 'Apollo', passion and freedom (Strang) and reason and control (Dysart). Though apparently a naïve conflict about the opposing sides of human nature the play has an aura of religious mystery and energy (like *Royal Hunt* it is a religious allegory with tragic dimensions) particularly in the boy's obsessive worship of a horse — the god 'Equus' — in marked contrast to the psychiatrist's attachment to the god 'Normal'. Dysart is driven to both professional and personal (religious) doubt, emphasised by the fact that the whole play is an enactment of Dysart's recalled experiences. The performance of *Equus* demands stylised horses and part of the audience is required to sit on the stage (as if in a medical dissecting theatre). At times, as with *Royal Hunt,* the language becomes incantatory and ritualistic and there are moments of extraordinary symbolism, particularly when Alan 'rides' the horse on a revolving stage at the end of the first half of the play: it is a moment of ecstasy and a magnificently conceived theatrical event (Shaffer once said 'a great production is a revelation ... a moment, a leap of excitement inside onself ... and it comes bolting out like rabbits out of the hedge' — *Arena: Theatre*, BBC 2, 1976). The anguish of both protagonists could be seen as reaching tragic proportions. Indeed John Russell Taylor has suggested that *Equus* 'is the only play of the 1970s which can put in a serious claim' to being a modern form of 'tragedy' and Shaffer himself has suggested that tragedy, instead of being a conflict between a right and a wrong, can be a conflict between 'two kinds of right' (*ibid.*, 1976) and in a note to *Shrivings* (1970) states that 'the coming to any sort of awareness of tragic ambiguity must always be new and painful'.

Shaffer's recent play *Amadeus* (National Theatre, November 1979) centres once again on a conflict of two opposing forces, Mozart and the jealous and ghostly figure of Salieri. The climax of the play is Mozart's recognition of Salieri as a messenger of God and as Death beckoning his end as he composes the *Requiem.* The 'Venticelli' (voices of gossip and rumour) give the play a near-musical form, totally appropriate to its subject. Taken with *Royal Hunt* and *Equus* one can sense behind the presentations (which Shaffer always publicly acknowledges as the achievement of his designers and directors, such as Michael Annals, John Napier, John **Dexter** and Sir Peter **Hall**) perhaps the great traditions of Japanese *Noh* theatre, **Brecht** and Artaud, not to mention the Greek and Elizabethan Chorus in Shaffer's fascinating formal uses of the 'narrator-within-narrator'. The title-part of Yonadab (National Theatre, December 1985) is also a narrator figure.

Writing in the *Observer Review* (4 November 1979), Shaffer stated: 'I have myself, in writing plays, been "haunted" three times by apocryphal images: pictures of events which may be real or imaginary, and which either way emit an immense power.' He was referring to the Incas waiting over the dead body of the Sun God Atahuallpa for the sun to rise, a young boy striking in terror at the eyes of six horses in a stable at midnight, and a spectral watching figure of Death or Envy (a 'macabre and yet pitiable icon of consuming artistic jealousy'). These he says are 'apocryphal images seeking their confirmation in public show'.

Further Reading

John Russell Taylor, *Peter Shaffer*, 'Writers and Their Work', No. 244, Longman for British Council, 1974.

Shakespeare Memorial Theatre

See **Royal Shakespeare Company**.

Shepherd, Jack

Born in Leeds, Yorkshire, on 29 October 1940, he was educated at Roundhay School, Leeds, and King's College, Newcastle. He began his career as an art teacher and a jazz musician and then trained for the theatre at the Drama Centre, London.

His first appearance in London was as an Officer of Dragoons in John **Arden's** *Sergeant Musgrave's Dance* (**Royal Court**, January 1966). Other parts at the Royal Court followed and in particular included Paul Dobson in Arnold **Wesker**'s *Their Very Own and Golden City* (May 1966), Arnold in David **Storey**'s *The Restoration of Arnold Middleton* (July 1967, transferred Criterion later the same month), Malvolio in *Twelfth Night* (April 1968) and Shogo in Edward **Bond**'s *Narrow Road to the Deep North* (February 1969).

Subsequent work includes the directing of Charles Dizenzo's *Disaster Strikes Home* (Traverse Theatre, Edinburgh, October 1970) and the roles of Bill Maitland in John **Osborne**'s *Inadmissible Evidence* (Cambridge Theatre Company tour, January

1971), Gil Martin in James Hogg's *Confessions of a Justified Sinner* (**Edinburgh Festival**, Lyceum, August 1971) and Alceste in Molière's *The Misanthrope* (Lyceum, Edinburgh, October 1971).

In November 1971 Shepherd directed his own adaptation of Aubrey Beardsley's *Under the Hill* (Cockpit, November 1971). As a founder member of the **Actors' Company** his parts included Vasques in Ford's *'Tis Pity She's a Whore* (Edinburgh Festival and tour, 1972). He later took the title-role and collaborated in the writing of *Dracula* (Bush, January 1973) and was co-author and director of *Sleep of Reason* (Edinburgh Festival, Traverse, September 1973). He played the title-role in *Hamlet* (University, Newcastle-upon-Tyne, February 1974), toured as Sloman in Trevor **Griffiths**'s *The Party* (**National Theatre** tour, September 1974), played Arthur in David **Hare**'s *Teeth 'n' Smiles* (Royal Court, September 1975) and Flamineo in Webster's *The White Devil* (**Old Vic**, July 1976).

Since 1978 he has been a player at the National Theatre where his major work has been Teach in David Mamet's *American Buffalo* (Cottesloe, June 1978), Boamer in *Lark Rise* (Cottesloe, September 1978), Smitty in O'Neill's *The Long Voyage Home* (Cottesloe, January 1979), Hickey in O'Neill's *The Iceman Cometh* (Cottesloe, March 1979), Gines de Pasamonte in Keith Dewhurst's adaptation of Cervantes' novel *Don Quixote* (Olivier, June 1982), Puck in *A Midsummer Night's Dream* (Cottesloe, November 1982, Lyttleton, April 1983), Richard Roma in David Mamet's *Glengarry Glen Ross* (Cottesloe, September 1983), Eddie Fuseli in Clifford Odets's *Golden Boy* (Lyttleton, May 1984) and Judas and Lucifer in Tony Harrison's *The Mysteries* (Cottesloe, January 1985).

Jack Shepherd also devised and directed *Real Time* with the **Joint Stock Company** (ICA, February 1982) and wrote *Revelations* (Bridge Lane, June 1983). His television appearances include *Bill Brand* (series), *Occupations, Ready When You Are Mr MacGill, Nina* and *Underdog.*

Sher, Antony

Born in 1951 in Cape Town, South Africa, he was educated in South Africa, where he showed considerable talent for the visual arts. He trained for the stage at the Webber-Douglas Academy in London and took a post-graduate course jointly run by Manchester University, Manchester Polytechnic School of Theatre and Granada TV at the Stables Theatre, Manchester. He worked in repertory at Liverpool, Manchester and Nottingham, playing parts which included Malvolio in *Twelfth Night,* Joxer in Synge's *Playboy of the Western World* and Ringo in Willie Russell's musical, *John, Paul, Ringo ... and Bert* (which transferred to the Lyric from the Everyman, Liverpool, in 1974).

He came to prominence in 1975 when he took the title-role in Bill **Gaskill**'s production of Gogol's *The Government Inspector* (**Edinburgh Festival**) and appeared in David **Hare**'s *Teeth 'n Smiles* (**Royal Court** and Wyndham's). One of his most successful roles since has been Muhammad, the Saudi Arabian businessman, in Mike **Leigh**'s *Goose Pimples* (Hampstead Theatre, March, and Garrick, April 1981), which he created in the face of the Saudi Arabian protest over the showing on television of *The Death of a Princess.* He was in Sam Shepherd's *True West* at the **National Theatre** (Cottesloe, December 1981) and in 1982 joined the **Royal Shakespeare Company** at Stratford-upon-Avon where he gave a much-praised performance as the Fool in *King Lear* (Stratford, 1982, Barbican, May 1983). For the RSC he has subsequently appeared in the title-role of Christopher **Hampton**'s translation of Molière's *Tartuffe* (Barbican, Pit, July 1983), in the title-role of Bulgakov's *Molière* (Barbican, Pit, September 1983) and as Martin Glass in David **Edgar**'s *Maydays*

(Barbican, October 1983). For the 1984 Stratford season he gave a fascinating performance as a semi-invalid Richard in *Richard III* (transferred to the Barbican, May 1985), which Michael Ratcliffe described as a 'performance inspired by the sheer joy of acting; unpredictable, dangerous but wholly under control'.

Television work has included *Cold Harbour* and (perhaps his best-known role on television) the part of Howard Kirk in *The History Man.*

Antony Sher is a physically energetic actor ('I go to the gym at least three times a week,' he said in one interview) whose visual sense contributes much to his work. In *Plays and Players* (October 1983) he said: 'I see acting as an extension of painting. In my mind acting and painting are very closely linked — acting is painting a different character within one's body. My rehearsal scripts are littered with drawings of the character I'm trying to visualise. I always know when a character is starting to take shape because I know how to draw him.'

In October 1985 he played Arnold Beckoff in Harvey Fierstein's *Torch Song Trilogy* (Albery).

Further Reading

Peter Roberts and Antony Sher, 'Virtuoso Actor', *Plays and Players*, October 1983, pp. 9-13.

Antony Sher, *Year of the King*, Chatto and Windus, London, 1985.

Simpson, N.F. (Norman Frederick)

Born in London on 29 January 1919, he was educated at Emanuel School, London (1930-7) and London University (1950-4). Prior to the war he worked in a bank for two years and during the war he served in the Royal Artillery (1941-3) and Intelligence Corps (1943-6). Before attending university he was a teacher and remained so afterwards.

Simpson came to prominence as a dramatist in the 1950s with a number of plays performed at the **Royal Court Theatre**. These were surreal comedies which had affinities with the '**Theatre of the Absurd**' (especially Ionesco's work) and the zany humour of *The Goon Show.* J.C. Trewin has described Simpson as a 'dramatist of the *non-sequitur* governed by absolute logic', and in a much-quoted speech by the fictional 'author' who appears in Simpson's first play *A Resounding Tinkle* we have the statement: 'The retreat from reason means precious little to anyone who has never caught up with reason in the first place; it takes a trained mind to relish a *non-sequitur.*'

A Resounding Tinkle (Royal Court, December 1957) follows the surreal lives of the Paradocks, a couple who keep a pet elephant but wish to change it for a snake, *The Hole* (Royal Court, April 1958) is about a group of people having a debate as they stand round a hole, and *One Way Pendulum* (Royal Court, December 1959), his best and most successful play by far, explores the eccentric Groomkirbys, especially Arthur, who, in addition to attempting to teach the 'Hallelujah Chorus' to an assembly of speak-your-weight machines, builds a replica of an Old Bailey court from a do-it-yourself kit, acquires a Judge and puts himself and family on trial. *The Cresta Run* (Royal Court, October 1965), a comic thriller about international espionage, was less successful, as were other later plays at the Royal Court such as *Playback 625* (1970), written with Leopoldo Maler, and *Was He Anyone?* (1972).

Simpson has written sketches and plays for television as well as the theatre. His television work since 1966 has included the series *Three Rousing Tinkles, Four Tall Tinkles, World in Ferment* and *Charley's Grants,* and the plays *Thank You Very Much, Elementary, My Dear Watson* and *Silver Wedding.* He has also written film and television versions of *One Way Pendulum.*

N.F. Simpson once commented: 'My plays are about life — life as I see it. Which is to say that they are all in their various ways about a man trying to get a partially inflated rubber lilo into a suitcase slightly too small to take it even when uninflated.'

Sinden, Donald (Alfred), CBE

Born in Plymouth, Devon, on 9 October 1932, he made his first appearance on the stage as Dudley in Gerald Savory's *George and Margaret*, with Charles F. Smith's company, Mobile Entertainments, Southern Area (MESA), in January 1941. He remained with the company and played one-night stands in comedies for the Forces. In 1944 he studied for the stage at the Webber-Douglas School of Dramatic Art and returned to MESA for tours of France, Belgium, Germany, India and Burma. After a short period with the Leicester Repertory Company he joined the **Shakespeare Memorial Theatre** Company at Stratford-upon-Avon (April 1946). For the 1946 season at Stratford his parts included Dumain in *Love's Labour's Lost* and Arviragus in *Cymbeline*. In the following season he was Paris in *Romeo and Juliet* and Adrian in *The Tempest*, among other parts.

He made his London début as Aumerle in *Richard II* (His Majesty's, October 1947) and came to particular notice when he was Arthur Townsend in Ruth and Augustus Goetz's *The Heiress* (Haymarket, January 1949), an adaptation of Henry James's novel, *Washington Square*. The production ran for 644 performances. After a period with the **Bristol Old Vic** Company he left the stage and worked in films for the Rank Organisation (1952-7). On returning to the stage he played parts which included Mervyn Browne in Claude Magnier's *Odd Man In* (St Martin's, July 1957), Frank in Mac-Gilbert Sauvajon's *All in the Family* (Strand, June 1959) and Edward Bromley in George Ross and Campbell Singer's *Guilty Party* (St Martin's, August 1961).

In April 1963 Donald Sinden joined the **Royal Shakespeare Company** at Stratford-upon-Avon. For that season his roles included Sebastian in *The Tempest* and he gave an outstanding performance as Richard Plantagenet in John **Barton**'s Shakespeare trilogy *The Wars of the Roses* (with Peggy **Ashcroft** as Queen Margaret). After another season in the latter production he played Mr Prince in Henry **Livings**'s *Eh?* (Aldwych, October 1964) and in 1965 was George Bernard Shaw in *Dear Liars* and Willie in Samuel **Beckett**'s *Happy Days* (British Council tour, South America).

He continued playing in both classics and modern comedy, his roles including Robert in Terence **Frisby**'s *There's a Girl in My Soup* (Globe, June 1966), Lord Foppington in Vanbrugh's *The Relapse* (RSC, Aldwych, August 1967), Gilbert in Ray **Cooney** and John Chapman's *Not Now Darling* (Strand, June 1968), Malvolio in *Twelfth Night* (RSC, Stratford-upon-Avon, August 1969, tour of Japan and Australia, January 1970, Aldwych, 1970-1 season), the title-role in *Henry VIII* (RSC, Stratford-upon-Avon, August 1969, Aldwych 1970-1 season), Sir William Harcourt in Boucicault's *London Assurance* (Aldwych 1970-1 season, New Theatre, April 1972) and Baron Scarpia and Sebastian in Terence **Rattigan**'s double-bill *In Praise of Love* (Duchess, September 1973).

At the **Chichester Festival** he played Doctor Stockmann in Ibsen's *An Enemy of the People* (May 1975) and in New York he was seen as Arthur Wicksteed in Alan **Bennett**'s *Habeus Corpus* (Martin Beck Theatre, November 1975). Returning to the Royal Shakespeare Company for the 1976 Stratford season he was Benedick in *Much Ado About Nothing* and took the title-role in *King Lear* (both also at the Aldwych, 1977). In November 1977 he was Arthur in John Chapman and Anthony Marriott's farce *Shut Your Eyes and Think of England* (Apollo), and in August 1979 he played the title-role in *Othello* (RSC, Stratford-upon-Avon). He subsequently appeared in Noël **Coward**'s

Present Laughter (Greenwich, January 1981, Vaudeville, March 1981), played Vanya in Chekhov's *Uncle Vanya* (Haymarket, August 1982) and Sir Peter Teazle in Sheridan's *The School for Scandal* (Haymarket, January 1983, Duke of York's, December 1983). In October 1984 he was in **Ray Cooney**'s *Two Into One* (**Theatre of Comedy**, Shaftesbury Theatre) and in July 1985 was Percy Blakeney in *The Scarlet Pimpernel* (Chichester Festival, transferred Her Majesty's, December 1985.)

Films include *The Cruel Sea*, *Mogambo*, *Doctor in the House*, *Decline and Fall*, *Villain*, *The National Health*, *The Day of the Jackal*, and *The Island at the Top of the World*. Television work includes *Our Man from St Marks*, *Two's Company*, his own documentary series, *Discovering English Churches*, and the popular comedy series *Never the Twain*.

Donald Sinden is a virtuoso performer of immense range (from farce to tragedy) who possesses a mellow and powerful voice which at times can deliver lines at an extraordinarily fast pace without destroying sense and timing. In an interview in 1973 (*Plays and Players*) he expressed something of a preference for comedy acting in his comments that 'comedy simply has to have a far greater truth than any other style of drama ... I've always based my thinking about acting on that extraordinary remark of David Garrick's, that any fool can play Hamlet but comedy is a very serious business. It really does require the ultimate in technique.'

Further Reading

Donald Sinden, Patricia Routledge and W. Stephen Gilbert, 'Funny Old Business', *Plays and Players*, November 1973, pp. 16-18.

Donald Sinden, *A Touch of the Memoirs*, Hodder and Stoughton, London, 1982.

Smith, 'Maggie' (Margaret Natalie), CBE

Born in Ilford, Essex, on 28 December 1934, she was educated at Oxford High School for Girls and trained for the stage at the Oxford Playhouse Theatre School. She did various jobs with the repertory company at Oxford Playhouse and made her début on the stage as Viola in *Twelfth Night* (OUDS, June 1952). Her early career was as a comedy actress and revue artist and she played in revues at Riddle's Court, the **Edinburgh Festival** and Watergate Theatre and was in *Faces of 1956* (Ethel Barrymore Theatre, New York, June 1956) and *Share My Lettuce* (Lyric, Hammersmith, August 1957, Comedy, September 1957).

A change of direction occurred when she did a season with the **Old Vic** Company (1959-60). Appearances during this season included Lady Plyant in Congreve's *The Double Dealer*, Celia in *As You Like It*, the Queen in *Richard II* and Mistress Ford in *The Merry Wives of Windsor*. At the Strand she replaced Joan **Plowright** in Ionesco's *Rhinoceros* (June 1960). Subsequently her major appearances were Lucile in Anouilh's *The Rehearsal* (Theatre Royal, Bristol, March 1961, Globe, London, April 1961, Queen's, May 1961, Globe, July 1961, Apollo, December 1961), Doreen and Belinda in Peter **Shaffer**'s double-bill *The Private Ear* and *The Public Eye* (Globe, May 1962) and Mary in Jean Kerr's *Mary, Mary* (Queen's, February 1963).

A further development in her career came about when she joined Laurence **Olivier**'s first **National Theatre** Company at the Old Vic in December 1963. Her chief roles with the company were Silvia in Bill **Gaskill**'s production of Farquhar's *The Recruiting Officer* (December 1963) in which Robert **Stephens** (to whom she was married in 1967) played Captain Plume, Desdemona in *Othello* (April 1964, and **Chichester Festival**, 1964) which she played to Laurence Olivier's Othello, Hilde Wangel in Ibsen's

The Master Builder (June 1964) to Olivier's Solness, Myra in Noël **Coward**'s *Hay Fever* (October 1964) to Robert Stephens's Sandy Tyrell (the play being directed by Coward himself), Beatrice in *Much Ado About Nothing* (February 1965) to Stephens's Benedick, Clea in Shaffer's *Black Comedy* (Chichester, July 1965), the title-role in Strindberg's *Miss Julie* (Chichester July 1965, Old Vic, March 1966), Mrs Sullen in Bill Gaskill's production of Farquhar's *The Beaux' Strategem* (National Theatre at Los Angeles, January 1970) with Stephens as Francis Archer, Hedda in Ibsen's *Hedda Gabler* with Stephens as Loëvborg and directed by Ingmar Bergman, and Amanda in John **Gielgud**'s production of Coward's *Private Lives* (Queen's, September 1972, Colosseum, December 1973, Los Angeles 1974, New York, February 1975) with Stephens as Elyot Chase. Her marriage to Robert Stephens broke up in 1975 and she married the dramatist Beverley Cross.

The next phase of her work took her to Canada for several seasons at the Stratford Festival Theatre, Ontario. In an interview with Mary Harron (*Observer*, 18 November 1984) Maggie Smith said 'In Canada I felt I could have a damned good try at a lot of things that I probably would never be cast in here [in England].' These included, in the 1976 season, Cleopatra in *Antony and Cleopatra*, Millamant in Congreve's *The Way of the World* and Masha in *Three Sisters*; in the 1977 season she was Titania and Hippolyta in *A Midsummer Night's Dream*, Queen Elizabeth in *Richard III*, Judith Bliss in *Hay Fever* and Rosalind in *As You Like It*; in the 1978 season she was Lady Macbeth in *Macbeth* and Amanda in *Private Lives*.

On her return to London she took over the part of Ruth Carson from Diana **Rigg** in Tom **Stoppard**'s *Night and Day* (Phoenix, 1979, subsequently Washington and New York, 1979). She again played at Stratford, Ontario, this time as Virginia Woolf in Edna O'Brien's *Virginia*, Beatrice in *Much Ado About Nothing* and Masha in *Three Sisters* (all for the 1980 season). She also appeared as Virginia Woolf when *Virginia* was put on in London (Haymarket, January 1981). At the Chichester Festival in July 1984 she played Millamant in Congreve's *The Way of the World* which transferred to the Haymarket in November 1984.

Film work includes *The Pumpkin Eater, Young Cassidy, Othello, The Prime of Miss Jean Brodie, Oh! What A Lovely War, Travels with my Aunt, California Suite, Death on the Nile, Quartet, The Missionary,* and *A Private Function.* Television work includes *Much Ado About Nothing, Man and Superman, On Approval* and *Home and Beauty.* Maggie Smith said in an interview with Ronald Hayman that acting is 'complicated' because 'there are so many facets to absolutely anything. You have to show every single possible bit and ... you have to learn to live with yourself in repose.'

Further Reading

Ronald Hayman, 'Maggie Smith and Robert Stephens', *Playback 2*, Davis-Poynter, London, 1973, pp. 108-21.

Spill

Used in lighting to refer to stray or scattered light outside the main beam. The light 'spills' over into areas not intended to be lit. Can be corrected by altering the **Barn Doors** of the lamps.

Spot

Spotlight. *See* **Follow**, **Fresnel** and **Profile**.

Spriggs, Elizabeth

Born in Buxton, Derbyshire, in 1926, she attended schools in Buxton and Coventry, trained for opera and the stage at the Royal

School of Music and taught speech and drama at Coventry Technical College and privately. In 1953 she appeared in repertory at the **Bristol Old Vic** and then Birmingham Reportory Theatre (under Barry **Jackson**), taking the parts of Cleopatra in *Antony and Cleopatra* and Madame Ranevsky in Chekhov's *The Cherry Orchard* (1958).

In 1962 she joined the **Royal Shakespeare Company** (she said, in a Stratford 'Profile' of 1966, 'this company is what I've worked towards since the age of eleven') and in the 1963-4 season at the Aldwych Theatre her parts included Mrs Vixen in John Gay's *The Beggar's Opera* and Rossignol in Peter **Brook**'s celebrated production of Weiss's *Marat/Sade.* Among her subsequent roles with the RSC have been Phrynia in *Timon of Athens* (Stratford, 1965), Gertrude in *Hamlet* (Stratford, 1965), the Locksmith's Wife in Gogol's *The Government Inspector* (Aldwych, 1965-6), Gertrude in *Hamlet* (continuing at the Aldwych and then returning to Stratford, 1966), Mistress Quickly in *Henry IV Parts 1 and 2* (Stratford, 1966), Hostess in *Henry V* (Stratford, 1966), a Witch in *Macbeth* and the Nurse in *Romeo and Juliet* (both these latter at Stratford, 1966, then on tour to Helsinki, Leningrad and Moscow, 1967, and then at the Aldwych, January 1968).

For the 1968 Stratford season she played Portia in *Julius Caesar* and Mistress Ford in *The Merry Wives of Windsor.* In the following year, at the Aldwych, she played Claire in Edward Albee's *A Delicate Balance* and at Stratford-upon-Avon repeated the part of Mistress Ford which she also played on tour to Japan and Australia (1969). In addition, on this tour, she played Paulina in *The Winter's Tale* and Maria in *Twelfth Night.* Further parts have included Lady Britomart in Shaw's *Major Barbara* (Aldwych, October 1970), Emilia in *Othello* (Stratford, 1971), Duchess of York in *Richard II* (for the RSC's 'Theatregoround' touring company, 1971), and Beatrice in *Much Ado About Nothing* (Stratford, 1971 and Aldwych, December 1971), Eleanor in David **Mercer**'s *Duck Song* (Aldwych, February 1974) and Lady Spanker in *London Assurance* (Palace, New York, December 1974).

Elizabeth Spriggs joined the **National Theatre** Company in 1976 and has played Madame Arcati in Noël **Coward**'s *Blithe Spirit* (Lyttleton, June 1976), Valerie in Christopher **Hampton**'s version of Von Horvath's *Tales from the Vienna Woods* (Olivier, January 1977), Lady Wouldbe in Jonson's *Volpone* (Olivier, 1977), Lady Fidget in Wycherley's *The Country Wife* (Olivier, 1977), Sonia Marsden in Arnold **Wesker**'s *Love Letters on Blue Paper* (Cottesloe, February 1978) and a Witch in *Macbeth* (Olivier, June 1978). She has appeared in numerous television plays, including *The Glittering Prizes, Victorian Scandals, Wings of a Dove, 'Fox'* and *Shine on Harvey Moon.*

She has said of acting, 'You have to be open to new ideas, but it's painful, a little like an open wound, never healing, never damaged too much. It's vital to be constantly stretched ... I hated most of my disciplining, but it taught me more than technique, it developed my instinct for life and became the backbone of all my work.'

Further Reading

Gordon Gow, 'Vive la différence!', interview with Elizabeth Spriggs, *Plays and Players,* March 1974, pp. 18-21.

Squire, William

Born in Neath, Wales on 29 April 1920, he was educated in Wales and became a bell founder. He studied for the stage at the Royal Academy of Dramatic Art and made his first appearances with the **Old Vic** Company (1945-7). In 1948 he joined the **Shakespeare Memorial Theatre** Company at Stratford-upon-Avon, subsequently playing, among other parts, Laertes in *Hamlet*

(1948), Ulysses in *Troilus and Cressida* (1948), the Duke in *Othello* (1948), Oberon in *A Midsummer Night's Dream* and the Lord Chamberlain in *Henry VIII*.

At the Birmingham Repertory Theatre in 1950 he played Dawlish in *Summer Day's Dream* and at Stratford-upon-Avon parts included Exton in *Richard II*, Rumour and Silence in *Henry IV Part 2*, Sebastian in *The Tempest*, and Ratty in *Toad of Toad Hall* (all 1951).

Joining the **Bristol Old Vic** Company in 1952, his chief roles were the Duke in *The Two Gentlemen of Verona* and Banquo in *Macbeth*, after which he appeared at the Old Vic (September 1952-4) in a number of parts, including Benvolio in *Romeo and Juliet*, Gratiano in *The Merchant of Venice*, the First Tempter in T.S. **Eliot**'s *Murder in the Cathedral*, Horatio in *Hamlet*, the King of France in *King John* and Aguecheek in *Twelfth Night*.

At the Criterion Theatre in September 1955 he took over the role of Vladimir in Samuel **Beckett**'s *Waiting for Godot* in the original production transferred from the Arts Theatre. Subsequent work included Captain Cat in Dylan Thomas's *Under Milk Wood* (New Theatre, September 1956), Gomez in Eliot's *The Elder Statesman* (**Edinburgh Festival** and Cambridge Theatre, 1958) and Arthur in *Camelot* (Majestic, New York, 1961).

In the 1964 season William Squire joined the **Royal Shakespeare Company** and played Mowbray in *Richard II*, Glendower in *Henry IV Part 1*, Charles VI in *Henry V*, Suffolk and Buckingham in John **Barton**'s history cycle *The Wars of the Roses* and the Player King in *Hamlet* (1965 season). In May 1966 he played Teddy Lloyd in Jay Allen's *The Prime of Miss Jean Brodie* (Wyndham's).

Joining the **National Theatre** Company at the Old Vic in 1974 his parts included Sebastian in *The Tempest* and the Headmaster in Edward **Bond**'s adaptation of Wedekind's *Spring Awakening*. At the Criterion Theatre in 1976 he appeared as the Player in Tom **Stoppard**'s *Rosencrantz and Guildenstern are Dead*. In April 1976 he played Sir Toby Belch in *Twelfth Night* (St George's, Islington) and in September 1979, Rear Admiral Knatchbull-Folliatt in *The Case of Oily Levantine*.

Film work has included *The Battle of the River Plate*, *Where Eagles Dare*, *Anne of the Thousand Days*, *Les Misérables* and *The Thirty-Nine Steps*. His best known television role is Hunter in the series *Callan*.

Stafford-Clarke, Max

See **Alternative Theatre**; **Gaskill, William** and **Hare, David**.

Stage Manager (SM)

Person in charge of the backstage **Crew**, all technicians and the management of a performance.

Stephens, Robert

Born in Bristol on 14 July 1931, he went to schools in Bristol and trained for the stage at Bradford Civic Theatre School. He started his acting career with the Caryl Jenner Mobile Theatre Company in the early 1950s and then joined George Devine's **English Stage Company** at the **Royal Court** Theatre where his parts included Judge Haythorne in Arthur Miller's *The Crucible* (April 1956) with Joan **Plowright** starring as Mary Warren, Mr Dorilant in Wycherley's *The Country Wife* (December 1956, transferred Adelphi, May 1957 when he played Quack), Jim in Michael **Hastings**'s *Yes — And After* (June 1957), and Krank in John **Arden**'s *The Waters of Babylon* (October 1957). At the Palace Theatre (September 1957) he appeared as Graham in John **Osborne**'s *The Entertainer* and on his return to the Royal

Court was the original George Dillon in John Osborne and Anthony Creighton's *Epitaph for George Dillon* (February 1958, Comedy, May 1958, Golden Theatre, New York, November 1958, Henry Miller Theatre, January 1959). Further parts at the Royal Court included Peter in Arnold **Wesker**'s *The Kitchen* (September 1959 and again in June 1961) and at the **Edinburgh Festival** in 1963 (September) he was the Dauphin in Shaw's *Saint Joan.*

In October 1963 Robert Stephens joined the **National Theatre** at the **Old Vic** where he played numerous parts (many opposite Maggie **Smith** to whom he was married from 1967 until 1975) including Horatio in *Hamlet* (October 1963) which was the National's inaugural production, Captain Plume in Farquhar's *The Recruiting Officer* (December 1963), and his highly-acclaimed Atahuallpa in Peter **Shaffer**'s *The Royal Hunt of the Sun* (**Chichester Festival**, July, Old Vic, December 1964). This latter part demanded considerable gymnastic movement, ritual mime and chanted speech. (In an interview for *Playback 2*, he told Ronald Hayman: 'With a gymnast I worked very hard on making my figure look slightly different ... the Incas used to speak hitting consonants terribly hard and sighing away on some diphthongs ... they were very influenced by birds, and made a lot of bird sounds ... It was a very gruelling thing to do.'!) Other major parts with the National Theatre were Man in Samuel **Beckett**'s *Play* (1964), Benedick in *Much Ado About Nothing* (February 1965), Sir David Lindsay in John Arden's *Armstrong's Last Goodnight* (October 1965), a performance in connection with which (in *Drama in the Sixties*, 1966) Laurence Kitchin described Stephens as 'unfailingly intelligent and in this part unexpectedly courtly ... brittle, finely drawn dignity, like that of a greyhound'. Some of his other roles with the National were Harold Gorringe in Shaffer's *Black Comedy* (Chichester, July 1965), Kurt in Strindberg's *The Dance of Death*, Vershinin in Chekhov's *Three Sisters*, Jacques in *As You Like It* and the title-role in Molière's *Tartuffe* (all 1967). In April 1970 he was Francis Archer in Farquhar's *The Beaux' Stratagem* (also at Los Angeles) and Eilert Loevborg in Ibsen's *Hedda Gabler.*

He became an Associate Director of the National Theatre in 1969 and subsequently appeared in a number of roles elsewhere in London productions, including Appollon in *Apropos of Falling Sleet* which he also directed (**Open Space**, November 1973), Pastor Mandors in Ibsen's *Ghosts*, Trigorin in Chekhov's *The Seagull* and Claudius in *Hamlet* (all at Greenwich, January-March 1974). He created a splendid characterisation of Sherlock Holmes in *Sherlock Holmes* (Broadhurst, New York, August 1975) and he played the title-role in *Othello* for the 1976 and 1977 seasons at the Open Air Theatre, Regent's Park. More recently he has appeared at the National Theatre as Gayev in Chekhov's *The Cherry Orchard* (Olivier, February 1978), the Mayor in Ibsen's *Brand* (Olivier, February 1978), Maskwell in Congreve's *The Double Dealer* (Olivier, September 1978), Sir Flute Parsons in Charles **Wood**'s *Has 'Washington' Legs?* (Cottesloe, November 1978), Oberon in *A Midsummer Night's Dream* (Lyttleton, April 1983) and Pasquale in N.F. **Simpson**'s English version of Eduardo de Filippo's *Inner Voices*, with a cast which included Sir Ralph **Richardson** and Michael **Bryant**. In January 1985 he played Pontius Pilate in *The Mysteries* at the Cottesloe Theatre.

Robert Stephens has appeared in numerous films including *A Taste of Honey*, *Cleopatra*, *The Prime of Miss Jean Brodie*, *The Private Life of Sherlock Holmes*, *Travels with my Aunt*, *The Asphyx*, *Luther* and *Alexander the Great.* Television work includes the six-part series *Vienna 1900*, *Kean*, *The Voyage of Charles Darwin*, *Office Story*, *Friends in Space*, *Suez*, *The Executioner*, the series *Adelaide Bartlett*, *The Winter's Tale*, *The Double Dealer*, *Holocaust*, *Eden End*, *The Year of the*

French, The Box of Delights, Puccini and *By the Sword Divided.*

Further Reading

Ronald Hayman, 'Maggie Smith and Robert Stephens', *Playback 2*, Davis-Poynter, London, 1973, pp. 108-21.

Stewart, Patrick

Born in Mirfield, Yorkshire, on 13 July 1940, he was educated at Mirfield Secondary School and worked as a journalist before training for the stage at the **Bristol Old Vic** Theatre School. He began his acting career in repertory, first appearing as Morgan in *Treasure Island* (Theatre Royal, Lincoln, August 1959), and continued in repertory at Sheffield, Manchester (Library Theatre), and Liverpool. Parts included the title-role in *Henry V* and Aston in Harold **Pinter**'s *The Caretaker.* In 1965 he joined the Bristol Old Vic Company and appeared in a number of parts, including Goldberg in Pinter's *The Birthday Party,* the title-role in Bertholt **Brecht**'s *Galileo* and Shylock in *The Merchant of Venice.*

He joined the **Royal Shakespeare Company** in February 1966, playing Witness Two in *The Investigation* (Aldwych). In 1967 he became an Associate Artist of the RSC and has remained one of the company's finest supporting actors ever since. His appearances at Stratford and the Aldwych have been extensive and include the First Player in *Hamlet* (1966), Hippolito in Tourneur's *The Revenger's Tragedy,* and Worthy in Vanbrugh's *The Relapse* (1967), Cornwall in *King Lear* (1968), Touchstone in *As You Like It* (1968), Foran in O'Casey's *The Silver Tassie* (1969), Edward IV in *Richard III* (1970), the title-role in *King John* (1970), Snout in Peter **Brook**'s production of *A Midsummer Night's Dream* (Billy Rose Theatre, New York, January 1971 and Aldwych, June 1971), Cassius in *Julius Caesar* (1972), Enobarbus in *Anthony and Cleopatra* (1972) and Astrov in *Uncle Vanya* (1974).

In February 1975 Patrick Stewart toured with the RSC in America and Australia, playing Eilert Löevborg in Ibsen's *Hedda Gabler* (later transferred to the Aldwych, July 1975). Subsequent parts have included Oberon in *A Midsummer Night's Dream* (1977), the Doctor in Tom **Stoppard**'s *Every Good Boy Deserves Favour* (Royal Festival Hall, 1977) and Shakespeare in Edward **Bond**'s *Bingo* (1977). For the 1978 and 1979 seasons he repeated the roles of Enobarbus and Shylock and also played Viktor in *The White Guard* (Aldwych, 1979).

For the opening of the Barbican Theatre in June 1982 he played Prince Hal and the King in *Henry IV Parts I and II* and in July 1982 was Leontes in *The Winter's Tale.*

Patrick Stewart is an actor and administrator of 'Actors in Residence', a group (based at the University of California) which teaches and performs Shakespeare and other playwrights in American colleges and universities. He has compiled an anthology of Shakespearean pieces called *The Loving Voyage.*

Film work has included *Hennessy* and *Hedda Gabler*; television work includes *When the Actors Come, Oedipus Rex, Omnibus* (in which Stewart played Joseph Conrad in a dramatised documentary about Conrad), *Tinker, Tailor, Soldier, Spy* and the drama series about a hospital psychiatrist, *Maybury.*

Stock, Nigel

Born in Malta on 21 September 1919, he was educated at St Paul's School, London. At the age of eleven he appeared at the Grafton Theatre, Warren Street, and made many other appearances as a boy-actor including the boy Dan in *The Traveller in the Dark* (Savoy, December 1931), Mamilius in *The Winter's Tale* (**Old Vic** and Sadler's Wells, April 1932) and Young Macduff in *Macbeth* (Old Vic, April 1934). He was an Assistant

Stage Manager at the Lyric Theatre in 1936. He trained for the stage at RADA where he gained the Principal's Medal and subsequently took roles in a number of productions at London theatres. He served in the army for seven years (London Irish Rifles, 1939-41, and the Indian Army, Assam Regiment, 1941-5, serving in Burma, China and Kohima) and achieved the rank of Major.

After the war he appeared at London theatres again and in March 1948 was Philip in George Bernard Shaw's *You Never Can Tell* in New York (Martin Beck Theatre). After a period with the **Bristol Old Vic** Company (1948-9) he joined the Old Vic Company at the New Theatre (October–November 1949) where his roles included Dumaine in *Love's Labour's Lost*, Tony Lumpkin in Goldsmith's *She Stoops to Conquer* and Belyayev in Turgenev's *A Month in the Country.* Since then his major roles in the post-war period have included Starkwedder in Agatha Christie's *The Unexpected Guest* (Duchess, August 1958), Werner in Jean-Paul Sartre's *Altona* (**Royal Court**, April 1961, Saville, June 1961), the Doctor in Strindberg's *The Father* (Piccadilly, January 1964), four parts in the entertainment *We Who Are About To...* (Hampstead Theatre Club, February 1969, Comedy, April 1969, renamed *Mixed Doubles*) written by a number of writers including Alan **Ayckbourn**, Harold **Pinter** and James **Saunders**, Roebuck Ramsden in Shaw's *Man and Superman* (Gaiety, Dublin, October 1969), Serebryakov in Chekhov's *Uncle Vanya* and the Prime Minister in Shaw's *The Apple Cart* (both at Theatre Royal, Bristol, September 1973–February 1974), Sir Winston Churchill in Guy Bolton's *A Man and his Wife* (tour, April 1974), Andrew Crocker-Harris in Terence **Rattigan**'s *The Browning Version* (King's Head, Islington, January 1976), Major Petkoff in Shaw's *Arms and the Man* (Oxford Festival, August 1976 and tour, Hong Kong Arts Festival, 1977), Proteus in Shaw's *The Apple Cart* (**Chichester Festival**, 1977, Phoenix, November 1977), van Putzeboum and the Inspector in *Look After Lulu* (Chichester, 1978, Haymarket, October 1978), and Widdecome in Simon **Gray**'s *Stage Struck* (Vaudeville, November 1979). In 1980 he was in Peter Jenkins's *Illuminations* and in 1982 at the Chichester Festival he played in Keith Baxter's *Cavell* (July) with Joan **Plowright**, Shaw's *On the Rocks* (May) and Roland Starke's *Goodbye, Mr Chips* (August) with Sir John **Mills**.

His many appearances in films include *Brighton Rock, The Dam Busters, Eye Witness, HMS Defiant, The Lost Continent, The Lion in Winter, Cromwell, Seven Men at Daybreak* and *Russian Roulette.* On television he became familiar to millions in the title-role of *Owen MD* and as Dr Watson in *Sherlock Holmes.* In 1985 he played Mr Pickwick in the television serialisation of Dickens's *Pickwick Papers.*

Stoppard, Tom

Born in Zlin, Czechoslovakia on 3 July 1937, he emigrated to Singapore in 1938 and to England in 1946. He was educated abroad and at the Dolphin School, Nottinghamshire and Pocklington School, Yorkshire. In 1965 he married José Ingle and 1972 Miriam Moore-Robinson. He has four children.

Stoppard worked initially as a journalist with the *Western Daily Press*, Bristol, 1954-8 and then the *Bristol Evening World*, 1958-60. From 1960 to 1963 he was a free-lance journalist.

His first plays were for television and radio and he gained major acclaim with the theatre play *Rosencrantz and Guildenstern Are Dead*, produced at the **Edinburgh Festival** by the Oxford Theatre Group in August 1966 and later at the **Old Vic** in April 1967. The play takes the minor characters of Shakespeare's *Hamlet* and makes them the centre of the action and has been recognised as having many similarities with **Beckett**'s *Waiting for Godot* in that Rosencrantz and

Guildenstern have time to kill in waiting for instructions as to what they are to do and what their purpose is — they are waiting for 'meaning' just as Vladimir and Estragon wait for 'Godot'. They fill the time with logic-games and word-play in an attempt to make sense of their lives and their roles in the actual play *Hamlet* (which is taking place 'offstage' as it were, simultaneously with Stoppard's play). The interest the play shows in philosophical gaming is a feature of some of Stoppard's later plays, notably *Albert's Bridge* (broadcast by BBC Television, July 1967) which concerns the Sisyphean problems of painting a bridge from end to end, and *Jumpers* (presented by the **National Theatre** Company at the Old Vic, April 1972) which has a professor of logic as its central figure. In these plays it is the rigorous exploration of logical problems which produces a sense of irrationality, absurdity and sheer comedy. It is clear that Stoppard's themes arise most strongly from his cultural and intellectual pursuits prior to writing: *After Magritte* (presented by Inter-Action, April 1970) attempts to explore in dramatic terms, the kind of surreal situation depicted in a Magritte painting and *Travesties* (**RSC** at the Aldwych Theatre, June 1974) is based firmly upon Stoppard's interest in the Dada movement, his reading of Richard Ellmann's biography of James Joyce and his studies of the structure of Wilde's *The Importance of Being Earnest.* The plays do not, however, suffer unduly from such direct influences but possess a wit and playfulness revealed particularly in Stoppard's deft handling of dialogue and wordplay which at times is reminiscent of Wilde and Coward.

Stoppard has worked on a number of occasions with Ed Berman, the American director of Inter-Action (Berman's nickname being Professor Dogg, the company took the name 'Dogg's Troupe'). *Dogg's Our Pet* (an anagram of 'Dogg's Troupe'), presented by Inter-Action at the Almost Free Theatre in London, 1971, concerns a Wittgensteinian language game of building a platform out of slabs of wood, blocks, bricks and cubes. Another work specially written for Berman's group was *Dogg's Hamlet, Cahoot's Macbeth* (1980).

As well as his literary, philosophical and artistic interests Stoppard has explored (satirically) political morality in *Dirty Linen* (presented by Inter-Action at the Almost Free Theatre, April 1976) and political dissidence in *Every Good Boy Deserves Favour* (presented by the London Symphony Orchestra and RSC, July 1977).

Perhaps our only true 'University Wit', Stoppard seems to have distilled the best qualities of the **Absurdists** while extending comedy beyond the 'humours', 'manners' and 'social satire' traditions of English Comedy to a new kind of philosophical comedy, bringing to it a fresh level of verbal energy and metaphysical wit.

Recently Stoppard has shown interest in translation and adaptation (some recent works are an English version of Arthur Schnitzler's *Undiscovered Country* (1980) and *On the Razzle* (September 1981), an adaptation of a mid-nineteenth-century comedy by Johann Nestroy). One of his latest original plays is *The Real Thing* (November 1982, Strand) which uses what appears to be a gauze safety-curtain, sections of which slide up and down in various combinations which alter the **proscenium** frame. This constant questioning of theatrical convention relates to the tensions in the play between 'fictionality' and 'reality' which face a creative writer. In May 1984 Stoppard's television film, about Lech Walesa and the rise and fall of the Polish trade union 'Solidarity', was broadcast on Channel Four. The title, *Squaring the Circle,* is taken from a speech in the play which likens the geometric impossibility of squaring a circle to the impossible hope of a free trade union existing in a totalitarian Marxist state. Of the play Stoppard has said (in a television interview, 1984): 'I don't know what kind of animal *Squaring the Circle* is. It's not a filmed play, it's not a straight movie, it's not a documentary reconstruction. It's a bit of all these things. I think the thing which attracted me about it first was that one could tell the story using imagination, metaphor and speculation, and have various levels of truth.'

Further Reading

C.W.E. Bigsby, *Tom Stoppard*, 'Writers and their Work', No. 250, Longman for the British Council, London, 1979.

Ronald Hayman, *Tom Stoppard* (4th edn), Heinemann Educational Books, London, 1982.

Storey, David (Malcolm)

Born in Wakefield, Yorkshire, on 13 July 1933, the son of a miner, he was educated at Queen Elizabeth Grammar School, Wakefield, and (1951-3) studied art at Wakefield School of Art (which David **Mercer** also attended) and the Slade School of Fine Art, London (1953-6). In 1956 he was married to Barbara Hamilton. He had numerous jobs, including bus conductor, marquee erector, farm worker, professional Rugby League footballer (for Leeds) and teacher (in Islington). His plays and novels draw on most of these practical experiences although his skilful detachment from his work prevents them from being too directly personal and autobiographical.

Storey's first play was *The Restoration of Arnold Middleton* (Traverse Theatre, Edinburgh, 1966, English Stage Company, **Royal Court**, July 1967), orginally written in 1958 and called *To Die With the Philistines.* It is about a teacher who undergoes something like a mental breakdown as a result of his alienation from his wife, mother-in-law (to whom he is strongly attracted) and society in general. Arnold's fantasies about his revolutionary-flavoured school production of *Robin Hood* lead him to use his house as a museum for sundry items including a suit of armour. At the time of the original London production (starring Jack **Shepherd**), Harold Hobson wrote that it was the 'best first play produced by the English Stage Company since *Look Back in Anger*'. Storey's next play, *In Celebration* (Royal Court Theatre, April 1969), which starred Alan **Bates**, was directed by Lindsay **Anderson** who had made the film of Storey's novel, *This Sporting Life* (1960), and who subsequently directed most of his other plays. *In Celebration* portrays the tensions of a family reunion on the fortieth wedding anniversary of a coalminer and his wife. Less naturalistic a play was *The Contractor* (Royal Court Theatre, October 1969) about the erection and taking down of a marquee for a wedding breakfast. The celebratory meals of both these plays occur off-stage during the intervals and we follow the less formal moments of the surrounding events and relationships. *The Contractor* draws partly on Storey's novel *Radcliffe* (1963).

Further moves away from realism came with *Home* (Royal Court Theatre, June 1970), which starred Sir John **Gielgud** and Sir Ralph **Richardson** as two elderly men (Harry and Jack). Storey's superbly-conceived dialogues and silences constantly avoid confrontation or any close communication between the characters. It is the Chekhovian-like sub-text of human desolation and loneliness which is the play's real exploration. Storey stated, in an interview with Ronald Hayman (*Playback*, 1973): 'They're all plays of understatement in a way and if you don't get what they're understating, then you've really had it, because there's nothing great going on on the surface. It's all got to be going on in the audience's mind, particularly with *Home.*' Harry and Jack's identities are diffused and there are ambiguous suggestions that they may either be in a hotel or a mental home. As Benedict Nightingale put it in 1977, '*Home* evokes a more total dislocation than any Storey play to date. Indeed, alienation has gone so far that the old men cannot even approximately say what they mean.' The play was also performed in New York in 1970.

Subsequent plays have been *The Changing Room* (Royal Court Theatre, November 1971), about a professional Rugby Football club, *Cromwell* (London, 1973) about an increasingly lonely and isolated Oliver Cromwell, *The Farm* (Royal Court Theatre, September 1973), about the insecurities and grumbling conflicts of life on a farm, *Life Class* (Royal Court Theatre, April 1974, which starred Alan Bates), set in an art class, *Mother's Day* (Royal Court Theatre, September 1976) and *Sisters* (Royal Exchange, Manchester, September 1978) both of which explore the complexities of sexual morality. *Early Days* (**National Theatre**, Cottesloe, April 1980) portrays Kitchen, an elderly, isolated politician (originally played by Sir Ralph Richardson) who looks back over his past. Like many of Storey's plays, *Early Days* sees man, one critic (Benedict Nightingale) argues, as 'alienated from his family, his roots, his class, his work, his language, and even from himself'. Nevertheless, Storey's plays are not pessimistic. Humanity is shown ultimately to be resilient, stoically accepting, and not without hope and dignity. *Phoenix* (Questors Theatre, April 1984), set in a North of England theatre on the day of its closure, portrays an Artistic Director who faces not only the collapse of his dreams for the future but also the failure of his personal relationships.

Storey's novels include *This Sporting Life, Flight into Camden, Radcliffe, Pasmore, A Temporary Life, Edward, Saville* and *A Prodigal Child.* In his interview with Ronald Hayman he said that he still saw life 'in working-class terms, as competition, like a runner trying to get some impossible record; or a boxer fighting for a championship: I write every day — in one sense — in order to keep "fit"'.

Further Reading

David Storey, 'A Discussion on Contemporary Theatre', *New Theatre,* Vol. VII, No. 2, 1967.

John Russell Taylor, *David Storey,* 'Writers and Their Work', Longman for the British Council, London, 1974.

Ronald Hayman, 'David Storey', *Playback,* Davis-Poynter, London, 1973, pp. 7-20.

Stott, Mike

Born in Rochdale on 2 January 1944, he was educated locally and at Manchester University. He began his career in the theatre as **Stage Manager** at the Library Theatre, Scarborough (the **'theatre-in-the-round'** first established by Stephen **Joseph** and subsequently directed by Alan **Ayckbourn**).

His first play for the stage, a comedy called *Mata Hari,* was produced at the Library Theatre, Scarborough in 1965. His next play, *Erogenous Zones* (**Royal Court**, Theatre Upstairs, 1969), was a series of sketches about sex and manslaughter and began an exploration of permissive sex comedy which has subsequently preoccupied Stott. His most successful play has been *Funny Peculiar* (Germany, 1973, Everyman Theatre, Liverpool, 1974, **Mermaid Theatre**, January 1976), notable for its inclusion of fellatio on the stage. It is a witty play about a Northern grocer who is hospitalised after falling into his cellar during a chase with a sex-mad but puritan woman. His confinement only heightens his sexual frustration and gives fuel to his obsessive creed of sexual freedom, a creed to which he attempts to convert his sexually unadventurous wife. *Lenz* (Almost Free Theatre, 1974, Hampstead Theatre Club, 1976) was an adaptation, developed in rehearsals, of a story by Georg Büchner about an intellectual from Strasbourg who believes he can resurrect a dead girl. The character is a type of 'looney' — as Stott has remarked, 'I write (hopefully) funny plays about loonies and sex' (*New Playwrights Directory,* Theatre Quarterly Publications, 1976, p. 50).

Stott's other work has included *Other People* (Hampstead Theatre Club, 1974), *Ghosts* (**Edinburgh Festival**, 1974, an adaptation of a play by Wolfgang Bauer), *Lorenzaccio* (Northcott, Exeter, 1976, an adaptation of a play by Alfred de Musset), *Comings and Goings* (Everyman, Liverpool, 1978) and *Ducking Out* (Greenwich Theatre and Duke of York's, November and December 1982, an adaptation of a play by de Filippo).

Mike Stott has written numerous radio plays, including *Lucky, Early Morning Glory, Lincoln,* and *The Bringer of Bad News.* Television plays include *The Flaxton Boys, Susan* and *Thwum.*

He has also been a play-reader for the **Royal Shakespeare Company**, a Script Editor for BBC Radio and Thames Television, and Resident Writer at the Hampstead Theatre Club.

'Strike The Set'

Take down the complete set after the last performance of a play.

Suzman, Janet

Born in Johannesburg, South Africa, on 9 February 1939, she was educated at Kingsmead College and the University of Witwatersrand, Johannesburg, and then trained for the stage at the London Academy of Music and Dramatic Art. Her first professional appearance on the stage was as Liz in Keith **Waterhouse** and Willis **Hall**'s *Billy Liar* (Tower Theatre, Ipswich, April 1962).

She joined the **Royal Shakespeare Company** in December 1962 and made her first London appearance as Luciana in *The Comedy of Errors* (Aldwych). Her performance of Joan la Pucelle in *Henry VI* and Lady Anne in *Richard III* gave her wide recognition (Stratford-upon-Avon, 1963) and in the following year she played Lady Percy in *Henry IV Parts 1 and 2* (Stratford, 1964 season). At the Aldwych, also in 1964, she played Lulu in Harold **Pinter**'s *The Birthday Party.*

Since this highly successful start to her acting career she has played many leading roles for the RSC and other companies, the chief of which are Portia in *The Merchant of Venice* (Stratford, 1965 season), Ophelia in *Hamlet* (Aldwych, 1965, to David **Warner**'s Hamlet), Kate Hardcastle in Oliver Goldsmith's *She Stoops to Conquer* (Oxford Playhouse, 1966), Carmen in Jean Genet's *The Balcony* (Oxford Playhouse, 1967), Katherina in *The Taming of the Shrew* and Celia in *As You Like It* (Stratford 1967, Aldwych and tour of USA, 1968), Berinthia in Vanbrugh's *The Relapse* (Aldwych, 1968), Rosalind in *As You Like It* and Beatrice in *Much Ado About Nothing* (Stratford 1968, *Much Ado* transferring to the Aldwych and forming part of a USA tour, 1969).

In 1972 at Stratford-upon-Avon she gave one of her finest performances as Cleopatra in *Antony and Cleopatra,* playing it again in the following year at the Aldwych. Other greatly successful parts which followed include Hester in Athol Fugard's *Hello and Goodbye* (King's Head, Islington, March 1973, and the Place, October 1973), Masha in Chekhov's *Three Sisters* (Cambridge Theatre, June 1976), Hedda in *Hedda Gabler* (Duke of York's and **Edinburgh Festival,** 1977), Shen Te in Bertolt **Brecht**'s *The Good Woman of Setzuan* (**Royal Court**, October 1977), Clytemnestra and Helen in John **Barton**'s adaptations of Euripides and Aeschylus, *The Greeks* (Aldwych, January 1980). In July 1981 she took part in revivals of John Barton's *The Hollow Crown* and Terry **Hands**'s *Pleasure and Repentance* at the Fortune Theatre and in the following year she was seen in Joanna Glass's *Artichoke* (Tricycle, October 1982). In 1983 she was in Sean Mathias's *Cowardice* (Ambassadors) and the film *The Draughtsman's Contract.*

Her work in films includes *A Day in the Death of Joe Egg* and *Nicholas and Alexandra.* For television she has appeared in many productions of classic drama including *Three Sisters, Hedda Gabler, Twelfth Night,*

Julius Caesar, a television play called *Miss Nightingale*, and an adaptation of Arnold Bennett's novel *Clayhanger*, and she took part in *Let's Parlez Franglais.*

Janet Suzman was married to the director Trevor **Nunn** in 1969 and since 1983 she has been Visiting Professor of Drama Studies at Westfield College, London University.

T

Tabs

Originally the front curtain in a **Proscenium** theatre ('tableaux curtain') but now generally used to refer to almost any stage curtaining.

Terson, Peter (*pseudonym for* Peter Patterson)

Born in Newcastle-upon-Tyne on 24 February 1932, he went to school at Heaton Grammar School, left at the age of 15 to work in a drawing office whilst also attending Newcastle-upon-Tyne Technical College, and did National Service as a wireless mechanic in the RAF (1950-2). He trained as a schoolteacher at Bristol Training College (1952-4) and subsequently taught games and PE for ten years, during which time he also began to write plays.

Terson's work can be broadly divided between his plays set mostly in the Vale of Evesham and written for Peter Cheeseman's Victoria Theatre, Stoke-on-Trent, and his plays written for large casts of young people for Michael Croft's **National Youth Theatre**. Known to write prolifically and at great speed Terson has often collaborated, in different ways, in the reworking of his plays, either with Peter Cheeseman at Stoke, or with the whole cast of the National Youth Theatre. These two different ways of working on a final script, the one with an individual and the other through collective exploration, have occasionally been confused when describing Terson's plays — the corrective being supplied by Peter Cheeseman in *Plays and Players*, March 1972, when he wrote: 'I must correct that repetitive programme-note writer for the National Youth Theatre and the new Shaw Theatre. Terson didn't "develop the habit of writing a loose script and extensively reworking it in rehearsal at Stoke". This is another quite separate creative process he has developed with the National Youth Theatre for their large-cast Tersons.'

His first play to be performed was *A Night to Make the Angels Weep* (Victoria, Stoke-on-Trent, June 1964) produced during his 18-month period as resident dramatist at the Victoria Theatre. The play explores the growing delusions of a Midlands village community about returning to a feudal way of life. *The Mighty Reservoy* (Victoria, Stoke, September 1964) also explored the problems of change, this time through an allegory about the possible psychological and social effects of a new reservoir (in the Cotswolds) upon the lives of two men who have markedly different personalities. *All Honour Mr Todd* (Victoria, Stoke, 1966), similarly, examined the disruption of rural life by the digging of a sewer, and in *I'm in Charge of These Ruins* (Victoria, Stoke, 1966) the opposing forces of tradition and modern progress are a ruined medieval castle and a new power-station. *Mooney and his Caravans* (Victoria, Stoke, 1967, Hampstead Theatre Club, May 1968), originally a television play, was a dialogue between a husband and wife from a town, who attempt to 'return to nature' by living on a rural caravan site, only to find the site is run by a dictator of a landlord (Mooney) who exploits his tenants.

In 1967 Terson also began to write for the National Youth Theatre, his first play (and still one of the greatest successes) being *Zigger-Zagger* (Jeannetta Cochrane Theatre, London, August 1967), about a football fan and a football crowd (led by Zigger) anticipating a match. The play was particularly remarkable for its scenes of crowd ritual. Similar effects were produced with *The*

Apprentices (Jeannetta Cochrane Theatre, 1968), set in a factory yard. Other plays of note have included *Fuzz!* (Jeannetta Cochrane Theatre, 1969), *The Last Train through the Harecastle Tunnel* (Jeannetta Cochrane, 1969), *Spring-heeled Jack* (Jeannetta Cochrane, 1970), *The 1861 Whitby Lifeboat Disaster* (Victoria, Stoke, 1971), *But Fred, Freud is Dead* (Victoria, Stoke, 1972), an adaptation of Melville's *Moby Dick* (Victoria, Stoke, 1972), *The Bread and Butter Trade* (NYT, Shaw, 1976, revived Shaw, August 1982), *England, My Own* (NYT, Shaw, August 1978), and *Strippers* (Newcastle Playhouse, March 1984, Phoenix, May 1985). Many of Terson's plays for the National Youth Theatre have been seen abroad and gained him international fame, but, as John Russell Taylor states in *The Second Wave* (1978): 'Terson feels that fundamentally they are much less him, less reflective of his own private personality and preoccupations, than the Stoke plays.'

Further Reading

'ohn Russell Taylor, 'Peter Terson', *The Second Wave*, Eyre Methuen, London, 1978.

Texturing

Giving texture to scenery by various means such as flicking paint of different colours, using Artex, Gesso or newspaper screwed up and sprayed, etc., depending on the effect required under stage lights.

Theatre-in-the-Round

Form of **Open Stage** which has an audience completely surrounding it. Often the acting area (subdivided into six areas) is at ground level and the audience seating **raked**. It was an idea promoted successfully by Stephen Joseph (1921-67), an actor and director who was the son of Hermione Gingold. He set up such a theatre at the Library Theatre, Scarborough, in the summer of 1956 for his company Studio Theatre Limited. In 1962 he set up a permanent 'theatre-in-the-round', the Victoria Theatre, Stoke-on-Trent. Stephen Joseph died in 1967 but Alan **Ayckbourn**, many of whose plays had been premièred at the Library Theatre, became Director of Productions when the Scarborough theatre moved to new premises in 1970 and was renamed the Stephen Joseph Theatre-in-the-Round.

Further Reading

Stephen Joseph, *Planning for New Forms of Theatre*, Strand Electric and Engineering Co. Ltd, London, 1966.

Stephen Joseph, *Theatre-in-the-Round*, Barrie and Rockliffe, London, 1967.

'Theatre Of Comedy'

See **Cooney, Ray.**

Theatre Workshop

See **Littlewood, Joan.**

Thorndike, Dame (Agnes) Sybil

Born in Gainsborough on 24 October 1888 and educated at Rochester High School (her father was a Canon of Rochester Cathedral), she trained as a pianist but began an acting career with Ben Greet's Pastoral Players, making her first appearance in the role of Palmis in W.S. Gilbert's *The Palace of Truth* and the Green Fairy in scenes from *The Merry Wives of Windsor* (Downing College, Cambridge, June 1904). After touring for four years in the USA in many classic roles, chiefly Shakespearean, she joined Miss Horniman's Company in 1908 (Gaiety Theatre, Manchester, and London venues). In 1909 she married Lewis Casson, actor and director with whom she was later frequently to appear in jointly-managed productions.

During the First World War Dame Sybil was with Lilian Baylis's company at the **Old Vic** playing roles which, owing to the shortage of male actors through enlistment, included a number of male parts such as Prince Hal in *Henry IV*, the Fool in *King Lear*, Ferdinand in *The Tempest*, Puck in *A Midsummer Night's Dream* and Lancelot Gobbo in *The Merchant of Venice*. After the war she played many of the great tragic roles for women, such as Hecuba in Euripides' *The Trojan Women* (Alhambra and Old Vic, October 1919) which was translated by Gilbert Murray, and Medea in Euripides' *The Medea* (Holborn Empire, Spring 1920). As J.C. Trewin has written of Dame Sybil at this time: 'The English theatre has known relatively few major tragediennes, but she was herself an army with banners.'

Dame Sybil also distinguished herself in the seasons of 'Grand Guignol' (melodramatic cabaret shows which have their origins in eighteenth-century French puppetry and sixteenth-century *Italian Commedia del'Arte*) at the Little Theatre, London (1920-2). She also took the title-role in the first English production of Shaw's *Saint Joan* (New Theatre, March 1924) and subsequently played it in many revivals. It was one of her great performances and was a role which she felt was close to her own nature and beliefs — Elizabeth Sprigge (in her biography of Dame Sybil) quotes her as saying of Joan: 'I simply lived in that part ... It confirmed my faith, it confirmed something in my life that I've always known intuitively from my father's saintliness and my mother's ridiculousness, and all the things I had to say were things I wanted to say.' In January 1929 at Wyndham's Theatre she played another great Shavian heroine, Barbara in *Major Barbara*.

Sybil Thorndike was at the Old Vic in Spring 1932 playing the Citizen's Wife in Beaumont and Fletcher's *The Knight of the Burning Pestle*. Ralph **Richardson**, who appeared in the same production, said of her, 'She can make an actor act. Any actor. I've seen her do it. She could act with a tailor's dummy and bring it to life. Anything she touches comes to life — just as it does with Chaplin.' Other noteworthy performances before the Second World War were as Mrs Conway in J.B. Priestley's *Time and the Conway*'s (Ritz Theatre, New York, 1938), Volumnia in *Coriolanus* (Old Vic, 1938), in which the title-role was played by Laurence **Olivier**, and Miss Moffat in Emlyn Williams's *The Corn is Green* (Duchess, September 1938). During the war she toured for ENSA with Olivier's Old Vic Company, her roles including Mistress Quickly in *Henry IV*, the title-role in Shaw's *Candida*, Lady Macbeth in *Macbeth* and Medea in Euripides' *The Medea*. In 1945 she was Jocasta in W.B. Yeats's translation of Sophocles' *Oedipus the King* (Old Vic Company, New Theatre) and in 1946 was Clytemnestra in *Electra* (King's Theatre, Hammersmith).

Dame Sybil once said 'I want to be lots of different people. Isn't that what acting's meant to be?' and it certainly was the case that in the post-war years she extended her range and style more than in previous years. She was Mrs Linden in Priestley's *The Linden Tree* (London Mask Theatre at Westminster Theatre, 1947-8), Aunt Anna Rose in M.J. Farrell and John Perry's comedy *Treasure Hunt* (Apollo, 1949), Mrs Whyte in N.C. Hunter's *Waters of the Moon* (Haymarket 1951-3) and Laura Anson in the same author's *A Day By The Sea* (Haymarket, 1953-4). After these long runs she gave recitals in Australia, Africa, Turkey, New Zealand, the Far East and Israel (British Council Tour, 1954-6), returned to England to play Amy in a revival of T.S. **Eliot**'s *The Family Renunion* (Phoenix, June, 1956) and then went to New York to play Mrs Callifer in Graham **Greene**'s *The Potting Shed* (Bijou Theatre and Golden Theatre, 1957). She toured Australia (1957-8) as Mrs St Maugham in Enid Bagnold's *The Chalk*

Garden and in London (January 1959) appeared at the Globe Theatre in *Eighty in the Shade*, written by Clemence Dane for Sybil and Lewis's golden wedding. On a Canadian tour in Autumn she was Mrs Kittridge in Jess Gregg's *The Seashell* and in 1960 was on tour and at the Duke of York's theatre as Lotta Bainbridge in Noël **Coward**'s *Waiting in the Wings.*

At the Dublin Festival in September 1961 Dame Sybil played the name part in Hugh Ross Williamson's *Teresa of Avila* (also Vaudeville Theatre, London, October 1961). In January 1962 Lewis and Sybil again gave recitals on tour in Australia and afterwards both played with Sir Laurence Olivier in Chekhov's *Uncle Vanya* for the opening of Olivier's first **Chichester Festival** (July 1962). Dame Sybil played Marina. Her subsequent appearances included Miss Crawley in Julian Slade and Robin Miller's version of Thackeray's *Vanity Fair* (Queen's, November 1964) which she also directed, and the Dowager Countess of Lister in William Douglas **Home**'s *The Reluctant Peer* (Duchess, January 1964). Her last London appearance was in a revival of Joseph Kesselring's *Arsenic and Old Lace* (Vaudeville February 1966) after which she was in Marguerite Duras's *The Viaduct* (Yvonne Arnaud, Guildford, 1967) and played Mrs Basil in Enid Bagnold's *Call Me Jacky* (Playhouse, Oxford, February 1968). Her last appearance was as the leading lady in John Graham's *There Was An Old Woman* (1969) for the opening of the theatre named after her in Leatherhead.

Filmwork included appearances in *Hindle Wakes, Tudor Rose, Major Barbara, Nicholas Nickleby, Stage Fright, The Magic Box, Alive and Kicking, Big Gamble, Hand in Hand, The Prince and the Showgirl* and *Smiley Gets a Gun.*

Dame Sybil Thorndike died on 9 June 1976. In his obituary (*Plays and Players*, July 1976) J.C. Trewin wrote that she possessed 'the power any great player must have: an utter command; the power, from the first word, of holding listeners so that they can neither look at anyone else nor think of anything else'.

Further Reading

Elizabeth Sprigge, *Sybil Thorndike Casson*, Victor Gollancz Ltd, London, 1971.
Sheridan Morley, *Sybil Thorndike: A Life in the Theatre*, Weidenfeld and Nicolson, London, 1977.
John Casson, *Lewis and Sybil: A Memoir*, Collins, London, 1972.

Thrust Stage

See **Open Stage.**

'Total' Theatre

See **Theatre of Cruelty.**

de la Tour, Frances

Born at Bovington, Hertfordshire, on 30 July 1944, she was educated at the Lycée Français de Londres and trained for the theatre at the Drama Centre, London. She went straight from drama school to the **Royal Shakespeare Company** to play a beggar in *Timon of Athens* (Stratford-upon-Avon, July 1965). She subsequently played many other roles for the RSC at Stratford-upon-Avon and the Aldwych Theatre, including Helena in Peter **Brook**'s production of *A Midsummer Night's Dream* (Stratford, 1970 season, Billy Rose, New York, January 1971, Aldwych, June 1971).

Since leaving the RSC in 1972 her major successes have been as Miss Jones in Eric Chappell's *The Banana Box* (Hampstead, May 1973, Apollo, June 1973) which also starred Leonard **Rossiter**, Rosalind in *As You Like It* (Oxford Playhouse, April 1975), Isabella in Webster's *The White Devil* (**Old Vic**, July 1976) and the title-role in *Hamlet* (New Half Moon, October 1979). In February

1980 she starred in *Duet for One* (Bush, February 1980), a play written specially for her by her husband Tom Kempinski. Since then she has played Jean in Catherine Hayes's *Skirmishes* (Hampstead, February 1982), Sonya in Chekhov's *Uncle Vanya* (Haymarket, August 1982) and Josie in Eugene O'Neill's *A Moon for the Misbegotten* (Riverside, June 1983, **Mermaid**, September 1983). At the **National Theatre** she played the title-role in Shaw's *Saint Joan* (Olivier, February 1984).

On television she became well known as Leonard Rossiter's partner in *Rising Damp.* Other television work includes *All Good Men, Housewives Choice, A Cottage to Let, Flickers* and *Murder With Mirrors* (USA). Film appearances include *Our Miss Fred, Wombling Free, To the Devil a Daughter* and *Rising Damp.*

Tower

Building over the stage large enough to accommodate the **Flies** and **Fly Gallery**, sometimes called the 'fly tower'. The term 'tower' is also used to refer to a wheeled scaffolding tower built in sections which is used for altering the position of lamps and any other jobs requiring a high platform.

Townsend, Sue

On leaving school at the age of 15 she worked in various jobs and then trained as a community worker. Her plays include *Woomberang* (Soho Poly, October 1979), about the comic and frustrating tensions of a gynaecology waiting-room, *Dayroom* (Croydon Warehouse, 1981), *The Ghost of Daniel Lambert* (Phoenix Arts Company, Leicester, 1981) and Leicester Haymarket, 1981), *Bazaar and Rummage* (**Royal Court**, Theatre Upstairs, May 1982 and BBC TV, 1983) which depicts three agoraphobics, a trainee social worker and a volunteer helper who attempt to run a jumble sale. *Groping for Words* (Croydon Warehouse, March 1983) explores the fears of social embarrassment felt by the working-class members of an adult literacy class. *The Great Celestial Cow* (**Joint Stock** Company on tour, and Royal Court, March 1984) is about the tensions in an Asian immigrant family attempting to adapt to life in Leicester.

Committed to portraying the problems faced by women in society, Sue Townsend blends the seriousness of her themes with sharply-written dialogue and a great sense of comedy. She also achieved enormous success with her witty and best-selling novels *The Secret Diary of Adrian Mole aged 13¾* (Methuen, 1982) and *The Growing Pains of Adrian Mole* (Methuen, 1984). The former was dramatised by Sue Townsend for the theatre (Wyndham's, December 1984) and television.

Trap

Trapdoor opening in the stage floor leading to and from a space beneath.

Traverse (Curtain)

Pair of curtains which can be drawn across the stage roughly half-way between the front curtain and **Blackcloth**.

Truck

Rostrum on castors or wheels.

Tutin, Dorothy, CBE

Born in London on 8 April 1930, and educated at St Catherine's School, Bramley, Surrey, she left school at the age of 15 to train for a career in music but then studied for the stage at RADA. Her first professional role was as Princess Margaret of England in William Douglas **Home**'s *The Thistle and the Rose* (the Boltons, September 1949). She was with the **Bristol Old Vic** Company in 1950 and the **Old Vic** (1950-1 season), one of her roles for the latter being Princess Katherine in *Henry V.* She played Hero in the London run of John **Gielgud**'s **Shakespeare Memorial Theatre** Company's production of *Much Ado About Nothing* (Phoenix, January 1952) and came to prominence with her superb performance as Rose Pemberton in Graham **Greene**'s first original play for the theatre, *The Living Room* (Wyndham's, April 1953).

Following her success in the latter production her chief roles included Sally Bowles in John Van Druten's *I am a Camera* (New, March 1954), Hedvig in Ibsen's *The Wild Duck* (Saville, December 1955) and Jean Rice in the original production of John **Osborne**'s *The Entertainer* at the **Royal Court** Theatre (April, 1957). In April 1958 she joined the Shakespeare Memorial Theatre Company at Stratford-upon-Avon and appeared as Juliet, Viola and Ophelia (also at Leningrad and Moscow, December 1958). For the 1960 season she was Portia, Viola and Cressida, and at the Aldwych Theatre again played Viola (December 1960) and also Sister Jeanne in John **Whiting**'s *The Devils* (February 1961). She remained with the company (renamed the **Royal Shakespeare Company**) and played further roles including Desdemona (Stratford, October 1961), Varya in Chekhov's *The Cherry Orchard* (Aldwych, December 1961), Sister Jeanne and Cressida again (**Edinburgh Festival**, September 1962, Aldwych, October 1962).

In January 1963 she took part in John **Barton**'s *The Hollow Crown* (Henry Miller, New York) and left the RSC for a short time to play Queen Victoria in William Francis's *Portrait of a Queen* (Bristol Old Vic, March 1965, Vaudeville, May 1965, later at Henry Miller, New York, February 1968). For the RSC at Stratford-upon-Avon and the Aldwych she was Rosalind (1967 season, Ahmanson Theatre, Los Angeles, January 1968), and was later Alice in *Arden of Faversham* (RSC Theatregoround Festival, Round House, November 1970) and Kate in Harold **Pinter**'s *Old Times* (Aldwych, June 1971). Having subsequently left the RSC she played Natalya in Turgenev's *A Month in the Country* at the **Chichester Festival** and gave an award-winning performance of the part again when she joined the **Prospect Theatre** Company (Albery, November 1975). Also for the Prospect Theatre Company she was Cleopatra in *Antony and Cleopatra* at the 1977 Edinburgh Festival (transferred to Old Vic, November 1977).

In February 1978 Dorothy Tutin joined the **National Theatre** to play Madame Ranevsky in Chekhov's *The Cherry Orchard* (Olivier). Also with the National she was Lady Macbeth in Peter **Hall** and John Russell Brown's production of *Macbeth* (June 1978), Lady Plyant in Congreve's *The Double Dealer* (September 1978), Genia Hofreiter in Tom **Stoppard**'s version of Arthur Schnitzler's *Undiscovered Country* (June 1979) and Lady Fanciful in Vanbrugh's *The Provok'd Wife* (June 1980). Leaving the National Theatre she played Hester in **Rattigan**'s *The Deep Blue Sea* (Greenwich, September 1981) and also appeared as Sarah Bernhardt in Ronald Harwood's *After the Lions* (Royal Exchange, Manchester, November 1982).

In an interview with Gordon Gow (*Plays and Players*, August 1978) she said: 'One of the necessities of acting is to be released from yourself. Obviously you are still there, unmistakably … but the desire in oneself is to be a transformed person … but I have no idea what makes an imagination develop. Perhaps it's that mankind cannot bear too much reality.'

Filmwork includes *The Importance of Being Earnest, The Beggar's Opera, A Tale of Two Cities, Cromwell* and *Savage Messiah.* Television appearances include *The Six*

Wives of Henry VIII, *South Riding* and *Willow Cabins.*

Further Reading

Dorothy Tutin and Gordon Gow, 'First Lady at the National', *Plays and Players*, August 1978.

Tynan, Kenneth (Peacock), FRSL

Born on 2 April 1927, in Birmingham and educated at King Edward's School, Birmingham, and Magdalen College, Oxford, he began his career as the director of Lichfield Repertory Company in 1949. He subsequently directed a number of plays including *Man of the World* (Lyric, Hammersmith, February 1950) and *Othello* (Arts Council tour, 1950). In May 1951 he appeared in the role of the First Player in *Hamlet* (New Theatre) with Alec **Guinness** playing the lead.

From 1951 onwards he spent most of his career as a drama critic, rapidly becoming one of the leading critics of the post-war period. He was often witty, abrasive and contentious in his reviews, yet had an eye for acting talent and good play-writing and was never prepared to accept mediocrity, a fact which caused him to be scorned and admired alike. As Charles **Marowitz** put it in 'Tynan and After' (*Plays and Players*, August 1983) Tynan possessed, 'a voice which demanded excellence of an art-form which, when it lagged behind the other arts or the best of which it was capable, deserved to be ferociously savaged'. It was Tynan who, in a now legendary review, championed John **Osborne**'s *Look Back in Anger* (**Royal Court**, May 1956) in the *Observer* when he stated 'I doubt if I could love anyone who did not wish to see *Look Back in Anger.* It is the best young play of its decade.' He had a gift for turning a phrase in a manner capable of both humour and criticism (memorable examples are his description of Ralph **Richardson** as Macbeth in 1952: 'Sir Ralph, who seems to me to have become the glass eye in the forehead of English acting, has now bumped into something quite immovable'; Charles Laughton as Bottom in 1959: 'a rapscallion uncle dressed up to entertain the children at a Christmas party', Michael **Redgrave** in *Hobson's Choice*, 1964: 'the difficulty about judging this actor is that I have to abandon all my standards of great acting'; and Alec **Guinness**, as described in Tynan's biography: 'you might easily take him for a slightly tipsy curate on the verge of being unfrocked'.

Tynan was drama critic of the *Spectator* (1951-2), the *Evening Standard* (1952-3), the *Daily Sketch* (1953-4), the *Observer* (1954-8), the *New Yorker* (1958-60) and the *Observer* (1960-3). He was also a script editor for Ealing Films (1956-8), editor of the television programme *Tempo* (1961-2) and film critic of the *Observer* (1964). He co-produced Hochhuth's *The Soldiers* (New, 1968) after fighting against its censorship for a **National Theatre** production and he devised the erotic revue *Oh! Calcutta!* (Eden, New York, June 1969, London, 1970).

From 1963 until 1969 Tynan was Literary Manager of the National Theatre and from 1969 until 1973 Literary Consultant. He wrote a number of books including *He That Plays the King* (1950), *Persona Grata* (1953), *Curtains* (1961), *Tynan Right and Left* (1967), *A View of the English Stage* (1975), *The Sound of Two Hands Clapping* (1975) and *Show People* (1980).

Kenneth Tynan died on 26 July 1980.

Further Reading

Kenneth Tynan, *A View of the English Stage*, Methuen, London, 1975.

U

Understudy

An actor who, in addition to his own part in a play, learns somebody else's part and performance in order to take over from him if he is ill or cannot continue in the role. Leading roles are usually understudied by actors in minor roles.

United British Artists

See **Rigg, Diana**, and **Johnson, Richard**.

V

Verse Drama

A term used to refer, in its most restricted sense, to plays written in verse form, but often more generally used as a term synonymous with 'poetic drama' referring to plays which have poetic and non-naturalistic qualities and may not necessarily be written in verse (examples of which are particularly found in plays such as Dylan Thomas's *Under Milk Wood* and in the works of the '**Theatre of the Absurd**').

Although the genre can be seen as a modernist experiment beginning perhaps with W.B. Yeats's plays early in the twentieth century, it has a long and distinguished pedigree in the theatre stretching back as far as Greek tragedy, Italian and English Renaissance and Jacobean drama, English seventeenth-century dramatic poetry, Restoration comedy, Romantic and Victorian dramatic poetry, and some of the plays of Ibsen. Yeats's plays were in the mode of symbolic '**total theatre**' based on ancient Irish myth, the Japanese Noh Play tradition, and traditions of dance and mime. In the 1920s and 1930s the American-born poet T.S. Eliot (1888-1965) created the theoretical space for a revival of interest in seventeenth-century 'poetic drama' (as he also did for a revival of interest in Metaphysical poetry) in his essays '"Rhetoric" and Poetic Drama' (1920), 'The Possibility of a Poetic Drama' (1920) and 'A Dialogue on Dramatic Poetry' (1932). Eliot's unfinished musical drama *Sweeney Agonistes* (1926) and the religious verse pageant *The Rock* (1934) were highly innovative and led him to write the successful verse plays for the theatre *Murder in the Cathedral* (Canterbury Festival, Canterbury Cathedral, 1935) and *The Family Reunion* (Westminster Theatre, March 1939).

In 1933 the Group Theatre, a private theatre society dedicated to low-budget experimental drama, was formed. Its base was initially at the Westminster Theatre where the company presented plays, chiefly directed by Rupert Doone, whose productions employed minimal scenery and props. In October 1935 the company performed Eliot's *Sweeney Agonistes* at the Westminster Theatre and the following year W.H. Auden and Christopher Isherwood's satire *The Dog Beneath the Skin* (Westminster, January 1936). Later the Group Theatre produced Auden and Isherwood's *The Ascent of F6* (Little Theatre, April 1937) with music by Benjamin Britten, and *On the Frontier* (Globe, 1939). During the war the company closed but reformed in 1950 until 1953, its productions including Sartre's *Les Mouches.*

In the post-war period T.S. Eliot continued to write verse plays. *The Family Reunion* (1939) had, like *Murder in the Cathedral* (1935), concerned itself with an individual struggling towards some transcendent moment, some spiritual illumination or divine salvation, as is similarly inferred in Eliot's poem *Four Quartets* (1943) which is strongly related to his plays. Eliot's later plays, first performed at the **Edinburgh Festival**, *The Cocktail Party* (1949), *The Confidential Clerk* (1953) and *The Elder Statesman* (1958) continued the exploration, even through comedy (as in parts of *The Confidential Clerk*).

Closely rivalling Eliot in verse drama was Christopher Fry (born in Bristol on 18 December 1907) whose plays in the 1930s included *The Boy with a Cart* (Coleman's Hatch, Sussex, 1938) about St Cuthbert, *The Tower* (Tewkesbury, 1939) which was a pageant, and another pageant *Thursday's Child* (GFS production, 1939). He came to recognition with *A Phoenix Too Frequent*

(Mercury Theatre, April 1946) and further plays included *The Firstborn* (Edinburgh Festival, 1948), *The Lady's Not For Burning* (Globe, May 1949) which was set in the medieval period and explored the tensions between a man with a death-wish (Thomas Mendip) and a woman condemned to be executed but who desires to live (Jennet Jourdemayne), *A Sleep of Prisoners* (St Thomas's Church, Regent Street, May 1951) which depicted prisoners of war who dream they are characters from the Bible, and his plays celebrating the seasons: the 'autumn' play *Venus Observed* (St James's, January 1950) which starred Laurence **Olivier**, the 'winter' play *The Dark is Light Enough* (Aldwych, April 1954) starring Edith **Evans**, and the 'summer' play *A Yard of Sun* (Nottingham Playhouse, 1970, **National Theatre, Old Vic**, 1970). Fry has also written verse translations of Ibsen's *Peer Gynt* (**Chichester Festival**, 1970) and Rostand's *Cyrano de Bergerac* (Chichester Festival, 1975).

The rise of neo-naturalistic drama in the late 1950s and its continuations into political drama in the 1970s has tended to force fashions away from verse drama although Peter Dale has written *Cell* and *Sephe* in recent years. Far more successful have been the 'poetic dramas' of Samuel **Beckett**, Harold **Pinter**, Tom **Stoppard** and Edward **Bond**.

Further Reading

Arnold P. Hinchliffe, *Modern Verse Drama*, 'The Critical Idiom', No. 32, Methuen, London, 1977.
Agenda, 'Verse Drama Double Issue', Vol. 18, No. 4, 1984.
Raymond Williams, *Drama from Ibsen to Brecht*, revised second edn, Pelican Books, Harmondsworth, 1983, Part 3, Chapters 3 and 4, pp. 193-238.
Michael Sidnell, *Dances of Death*, Faber and Faber, London, 1985.

Vomitory

Originally a large door in a Roman amphitheatre, now referring to the gangway entrances which emerge from beneath the **auditorium** of an **Open Stage** theatre.

W

Wall, Max (Maxwell George Lorimer)

Born in Brixton, London, on 12 March 1908 and educated privately, he first appeared in the theatre at the age of 14 when he played Jack in *Mother Goose* with a touring pantomime company (Devon and Cornwall tour, December 1922). Before the Second World War he was a speciality dancer and variety artist but also appeared in a number of musical comedies. In 1932 he was with Earl Carroll's Vanities in New York and on his subsequent return to England again played in variety and comedies.

In May 1940 he played Tom Carroway in Rodgers and Hart's musical *Present Arms* (Prince of Wales) and the following year toured in the leading part of Stanley Lupino's *Funny Side Up*. After serving in the Royal Air Force from 1941 until 1943 he appeared in a number of shows including *Make It a Date* (Duchess, March 1946) and from 1948 until 1950 was in variety and broadcasting. It was in the 1950s he developed his act as 'Professor Walloffski' (partly a parody of Liszt) characteristically wearing a wig of long hair, black tights, white socks and flat, long-toed boots. Wall perfected superb pianistic jokes, body antics and a famous 'eccentric walk' routine. In October 1955 he was Hines in the musical *The Pyjama Game* (Coliseum) and in 1958 he toured Australia in variety.

From the early 1960s Max Wall began to play in 'legitimate' theatre as well as keeping up his work in variety. He was Père Ubu in Alfred Jarry's *Ubu Roi* at the **Royal Court** Theatre (July 1966), Emmanuel in Arnold **Wesker**'s *The Old Ones* (Royal Court, August 1972) and Archie Rice in John **Osborne**'s *The Entertainer* (Greenwich, December 1974). He developed a one-man show *Aspects of Max Wall* which was first seen at the Greenwich Theatre in January 1974 (transferred to Garrick Theatre, February 1975) subsequently performed, with variations, on a number of occasions. Lyall Wilkes, in his short lyric poem 'Max Wall at Sunderland' (*Stand*, Vol. 23, No. 1, 1983) wrote of Wall's one-man shows: 'His act is the debris of a life/dredged up from disaster ... it is a Gothic extravaganza of incoherence/but each layer of nonsense is as carefully laid/as a dry stone wall ... It is two hours without a single stage-worn cliché.'

He later took the title-role in Samuel **Beckett**'s *Krapp's Last Tape* (Greenwich, December, 1976), played Malvolio in *Twelfth Night* (Greenwich, March 1977), Davies in Harold **Pinter**'s *The Caretaker* (Greenwich, October 1977), Vladimir in Beckett's *Waiting for Godot* (Manchester Royal Exchange, May 1981, Round House, June 1981) and Bludgeon in John **Arden**'s *Sergeant Musgrave's Dance* (**Old Vic**, May 1984) with Albert **Finney** in the name-part. For the Samuel Beckett celebration at the 1984 **Edinburgh Festival** he performed readings and played Malone in John Elsom's dramatisation of Beckett's novel *Malone Dies* (Church Hill, Edinburgh, August 1984). Wall continues the tradition of actors (such as Jack MacGowran and Patrick Magee) particularly associated with the work of Samuel Beckett.

On television he has played in *Waiting for Godot, Emmerdale Farm, Born and Bred, An Evening with Max Wall* and *Jane in the Desert*. Films include *Jabberwocky* and *Hound of the Baskervilles*.

Walter Plinge

The name sometimes given to an actor who plays more than one role in a play, that is, who 'doubles'. It derives from an incident at the turn of the century when an actor from Frank Benson's Shakespearean company refused to allow his 'doubling' to be revealed in the programme cast list. Instead the name of a publican, Walter Plinge (whose premises were opposite the stage door of the theatre), was used for the fictitious 'actor' playing the second role.

Warner, David

Born in Manchester on 29 July 1941, he was educated at Feldon School, Leamington Spa (where he played Lady Macbeth), and after working as a bookseller he trained at the Royal Academy of Dramatic Art. His first professional stage part was Snout in *A Midsummer Night's Dream* (**Royal Court**, January 1962), having previously played a walk-on part as a Nubian slave in *Aida* at Covent Garden. He then played Conrade in *Much Ado About Nothing* (Belgrade, Coventry, March 1962), Jim in David **Rudkin**'s *Afore Night Come* (New Arts, June 1962).

In April 1963 he joined the **Royal Shakespeare Company** in Stratford-upon-Avon. His parts that season included a much-acclaimed King Henry in adaptations of *Henry VI Parts 1, 2 and 3* for John **Barton**'s trilogy *The Wars of the Roses* (July 1963). It was a sensitive portrayal and emphasised the character's weakness, isolation and personal suffering, finding a great deal in Henry which had previously never been seen in the theatre. Other parts followed, including the title-role in *Richard II* (Stratford-upon-Avon, April 1964), Valentine Brose in Henry **Livings**'s *Eh?* (Aldwych, October 1964), and, perhaps his finest performance to date, the title-role in Peter **Hall**'s production of *Hamlet* (Stratford-upon-Avon, August 1965, Aldwych, December 1965). He was 24 when he played the part and was, and still is, considered the 'Hamlet of the Sixties'. As Stanley Wells put it, this was 'no princely, romantic embodiment of the role. Mr Warner was, frankly, a gangling, spotty young man with traces of a Midlands accent ... [who] did much to emphasize Hamlet's nonconformity, his inner rebellion against the Establishment by which he was surrounded.'

Subsequent parts have included the Postmaster in Gogol's *The Government Inspector* (Aldwych, January 1966), Sir Andrew Aguecheek in *Twelfth Night* and a repeat of his role as Hamlet (Stratford-upon-Avon, 1966 season), Julian in Albee's *Tiny Alice* (Aldwych, January 1970), Hammett in David **Hare**'s *The Great Exhibition* (Hampstead, February 1972), Claudius in John **Mortimer**'s adaptation of Graves's novel *I, Claudius* (Queen's, July 1972). Since the mid-1970s Warner has been mainly involved in theatre management and acting in film and television.

His film appearances since 1962 include *Tom Jones, Morgan, The Fixer, A Midsummer Night's Dream, The Thirty-Nine Steps, The Seagull* and *Airport '79*. Television work has included *Pushover, Clouds of Glory, Holocaust,* and in 1984 he played a private detective in the title-role of Nigel William's *Charlie*.

Further Reading

Stanley Wells, *Royal Shakespeare*, Manchester University Press, Manchester, 1976, pp. 23-42.
David Addenbrooke, *The Royal Shakespeare Company: The Peter Hall Years*, Kimber Press, London, 1974.

Waterhouse, Keith

See **Hall, Willis.**

Weights

See **Braces.**

Wesker, Arnold

'A Socialist of Communist East End parentage

and Russo-Hungarian ancestry' (as Laurence Kitchin described him), Wesker was born in Stepney, London, on 24 May 1932, the son of Jewish emigré parents. He attended the Jewish infant school in Hackney, various local schools and Upton House Central School, Hackney. In 1948 he became a furniture-maker's apprentice and carpenter's mate and a year later a bookseller's assistant. After National Service with the Royal Air Force (1950-2) he had a variety of jobs including plumber's mate, farm labourer, seed sorter, kitchen porter and for four years he was a pastry cook (until 1958). In 1956 he attended a short course at the London School of Film Technique, wrote film scripts and began writing for the stage. A number of his various occupations appear in Wesker's plays (which John **Arden**, in 1960, described as 'autobiography treated in documentary style').

Wesker is often seen as a central figure, with John **Osborne**, of the so-called '**Angries**' drama of the second half of the 1950s which opened up new possibilities for drama as social and political criticism and the inclusion of the rights and problems of the working classes in stage plays. Wesker commented in 1958: 'We are in the midst of a new movement, ideas are stirring and the artist is beginning to realise that the man in the street affects his life so he must affect theirs.'

The **Royal Court** Theatre staged Wesker's first play *Chicken Soup With Barley* in July 1958 after it had been performed (on George **Devine**'s recommendation) at the Belgrade Theatre, Coventry. It was directed by John **Dexter** who directed all Wesker's early plays (and in rehearsals contributed much to their writing, in collaboration with Wesker). *Chicken Soup With Barley* forms the first play in a trilogy comprising, in addition, *Roots* (Belgrade, Coventry and Royal Court, London, June 1959) and *I'm Talking About Jerusalem* (Belgrade and Royal Court, July 1960). The three plays were first performed as a trilogy (directed by Dexter) at the Royal Court Theatre in June and July 1960. The trilogy documents the experiences of a Jewish East End family, the Kahns, and *Chicken Soup* spans the period 1936 to 1956. We see the gradual disillusionment of the family ('all, except the mother', Wesker has written, 'lose faith in an ideal'). From the political confrontation between Mosley's Fascists and the East Enders in 1936, to Harry (the father) becoming an invalid, Ronnie Kahn (the son) taking work in a kitchen and through to a disillusionment with the working classes of the 1950s, the play is an examination of the social and political origins of what Wesker called 'a general malaise'. In a 'note' to actors and producers Wesker emphasised the three plays' social realism when he stated: 'My people are not caricatures. They are real (though fiction), and if they are portrayed as caricatures the point of all these plays will be lost.' It seems that Wesker had a didactic purpose too: as he suggested in his essay of 1958 called 'Let Battle Commence': 'I want to teach ... it is the bus driver, the housewife, the miner and the Teddy Boy to whom I should like to address myself', and (again in the 'note' to the trilogy) he takes a stance of protest at the absence of a more vital and fulfilling life for the underprivileged classes when he observes, 'I am at one with these people: it is only that I am annoyed, with them and myself.'

In contrast to *Chicken Soup* the middle play of the trilogy, *Roots*, is set in the Norfolk cottage of a family of farm labourers (the Bryants). The young daughter, Beatie, is a student and her return home after exposure to higher education and the radical views of Ronnie Kahn creates friction in the family and some personal anguish in herself. Ronnie never appears in this play but is the all-pervading presence in the household as Beatie mouths his views on culture, the arts, education and politics. The alienation of Beatie from the family is particularly brought out in her relationship with her mother (whom she tries, for example, to convert to an appreciation of classical music). Beatie's liberation is second-hand, however, and it is only at the end of the play (when Ronnie fails to appear for his visit) that Beatie achieves a leap of comprehension and begins to find herself: 'The writers don't write thinkin' we can understand, nor the painters don't paint expecting us to be interested ... We want the third-rate — we got it! We got it! We ... D'you hear that? ... I'm not quoting no more ... It does work, it's happening to me, I can feel it's happened, I'm beginning on my own two feet — I'm beginning.' Regarded as one of Wesker's finest plays, *Roots*, has continued to be performed frequently. It stands up well as a single play in its own right and possesses its own unique qualities outside the trilogy — an assured handling of dialect, a sensitivity and good-humoured warmth towards farm-labouring people and a superb evocation of rural domestic life reminiscent of some of D.H. Lawrence's writing.

The last play in the trilogy, *I'm Talking About Jerusalem*, spans ten years and is again set in the East End with the Kahn family but looks towards the ideal of a 'new Jerusalem' in the midst of disenchantment: Ada and her husband, Dave, move to Norfolk as a kind of 'rural experiment' but Dave's jobs all fail and they have to return to London. Harry, the father, dies. To Dave's retort that 'visions' do not work Ronnie replies, 'They *do* work! And even if they don't work then for God's sake let's try and behave as though they do — or else nothing will work.' Alone at the close of the whole trilogy Ronnie yells bitterly to the sky: 'We — must — be — bloody — mad — to cry!'

Simultaneously with the trilogy Wesker had *The Kitchen* presented as a Sunday evening performance at the Royal Court (September 1959). Set in a kitchen which increasingly becomes full of activity it generates a claustrophobic and oppressive image of the working classes and is something of a critique of the capitalist system.

In 1961 Wesker was briefly imprisoned for anti-nuclear activities and in the same year set out to establish a centre for working-class theatre and the improvement of the popular arts. It was a practical expression of Wesker's Socialist ideals and his own conviction that underprivileged working people should be given the opportunity to enjoy life and art more fully. The support of trades unions (who were circulated with a pamphlet by Wesker entitled 'The Modern Playwright or Mother Is It Worth It?') and of the Labour movement were sought and the centre was known as Centre 42 (after the 42nd resolution of the 1960 Trades Union Congress which recognised the importance of the arts and pledged support for promotion schemes). In 1966 Wesker acquired the Round House (a disused railway shed), Chalk Farm, and Centre 42 was based there. In spite of some support from unions and from the Wilson government the venture was not successful (either culturally or financially) and it closed down in 1970. Nevertheless it could be argued that the growth in the 1970s of a large number of left-wing community theatre groups and 'people's theatre' movements was partly made possible by such experiments.

After the trilogy and *The Kitchen* Wesker's next play was *Chips with Everything* (Royal Court, April 1962) which uses the divisions of the Royal Air Force between the officer-class and the ordinary ranks as a microcosm of class division in British society. Pip, a middle-class educated young man joins ranks with the ordinary servicemen and he rebels against his own officer-class (the climax being a superb piece of stage action as the men steal some coke from a compound). Wesker stated the play was 'the beginning of a break-out in terms of form' and certainly there are differences from his first plays: a tight control over the language differences between characters and social groups, the use of folk-song ('The Lyke Wake Dirge' and the revolutionary song 'The Cutty Wren' are employed as a political and cultural protest at a Christmas party given by the officers) and the sympathetic exploration of a weak and defenseless, near-tragic figure (Ginger) who is victimised by the whole system. Pip's attempt to integrate with the lower ranks and to rebel against his own class fail and he finally dons an officer's uniform and joins the officers.

The changes of form evident in *Chips* were extended in his next play *The Nottingham Captain: A Moral for Narrator, Voices and Orchestra* (with music by Wilfred Josephs and Dave Lee, Wellingborough Festival, 1962) and *The Four Seasons* (Belgrade and Saville, September 1965, directed by Wesker). This latter play explores a destructive love relationship between (the significantly named) Adam and Beatrice whose past failures come to the surface. Their relationship is set within the framework of the seasonal cycle and this gives it a poetic dimension which enriches the excursion into personal suffering and the pain of failure — less public themes than in previous plays (Glenda Leeming, for example, suggests that 'the message is one of psychological fatalism'). *Their Very Own and Golden City* (Brussels 1965, Royal Court, May 1966) was described by Wesker as 'in terms of technique, an attempt to break out'. The play covers the period 1926 to 1990 and involves chronological time-shifts. It concerns an architect who envisages a 'golden city' (symbolic of a new Socialist society) but, as Hinchliffe has remarked, the struggle involves 'the necessity of compromising with the Establishment'.

The Friends (Stockholm 1969, Centre 42 at the Round House 1970, directed by Wesker) marks an even greater turning point in Wesker's plays. Here the private suffering of individuals leads to a greater centralisation of the inner psychology of his characters than in any plays previously. It is an exploration of what has been described as 'private pain': one of the characters (Esther) is dying of leukaemia and this condition forces the other characters into a confrontation with their own mortality and what Wesker has described as 'a sense of one's mistakes'. In *The Old Ones* (Royal Court 1972, directed by John Dexter) Wesker returned to a Jewish East End locale and makes his characters elderly (Sarah is 70 years old). The central conflict between Sarah and her two brothers, Manny and Boomy, is enriched by their use of allusions to great writers' statements about the human condition (in the form of a kind of quotation-contest) and the quasi-ritualistic elements of the play (such as the Jewish feast of Succoth). Wesker has said it is a play partly concerned with 'growing old without faith' and it is the first of his plays to take an interest in Judaism and religious faith. *The Journalists* (written 1971), a play about a group of Sunday newspaper journalists was worked on by the RSC in 1974 but abandoned. It was eventually put on as an amateur production in Coventry in 1977.

Wesker adapted a story by Dostoevsky (called *An Unpleasant Predicament*) which he titled *The Wedding Feast* (Stockholm 1974, Leeds 1977). The play is set in Norfolk where a rich Jewish shoe-manufacturer (Louis Litvanov) has an idealistic desire for equality with his employees. He attends, as an uninvited guest, the wedding reception of one of his employees and the embarrassment only serves to emphasise class differences and barriers. Again the ceremonial aspect of the play is an important dimension. There followed *The Merchant* (Stockholm 1976, Broadway 1977, Birmingham Repertory, 1979) based on Shakespeare's *The Merchant of Venice, Love Letters on Blue Paper* (**National Theatre**, Cottesloe, February 1978, Oslo 1980) an adaptation of one of Wesker's own short stories concerning, like Esther in *The Friends*, a character dying from leukaemia whose attempts to accept death are strengthened by letters from his wife which express his past achievements. It was originally a television adaptation.

Recent plays have been *Fatlips* (1978), a play for young people, *Caritas* (Scandinavian Project, 1980, National Theatre, Cottesloe, October 1981) based on the life of Christine

Carpenter, a fourteenth-century 'anchoress' (a female anchorite, a religious recluse, who in this extreme and fanatical case of self-denial is walled up in her cell and not seen until half-way through the action of the play). The location is Norfolk instead of Surrey (the real historical location) and the period altered to include the Peasants' Revolt. Wesker's latest plays have been *One More Ride on the Merry-Go-Round* (1981), *Sullied Hands* (1982), *Four Portraits* (1982) and *Annie Wobbler* (New End, 1983, Fordre, November 1984 directed by Wesker) which is a play comprising three monologues for the actress Nichola McAuliffe who collaborated in the writing. In the first monologue she is an old woman who feels a failure, in the second a modern university-educated girl who is narcissistically contemplating a date, and in the third a successful writer who answers questions put by two (male and female) voices. This latest move towards monologue-drama to a certain extent places Wesker alongside **Beckett** and **Pinter**, both of whom have explored the form. Wesker has also written short stories, television plays and criticism.

He once affirmed that the art he must practise is one that 'struggles to rouse interest in the world and persuade one to have faith in life'. Even though some have not been successful in the theatre, that positive attitude rings true in the majority of his plays.

Further Reading

Glenda Leeming, *Wesker the Playwright*, Methuen, London, 1983.

Arnold Wesker, *Fears of Fragmentation*, Cape, London, 1970.

West, Timothy (Lancaster)

Born in Bradford on 30 October, 1934, the son of parents who were actors and a grandson of an actor (who appeared in the 1939 film verson of *Goodbye Mr Chips*, with Robert Donat), he was educated at the John Lyon School, Harrow and Regent Street Polytechnic. He began his career first as a furniture salesman, then as a recording engineer, and in 1956 worked in the theatre at Wimbledon as an assistant stage manager. His first appearance was at this same theatre, where he played the Farmer in Ugo Betti's *Summertime* (March, 1956). He married his first wife Jacqueline Boyer in 1956 and worked in repertory in Salisbury, Hull, Wimbledon and Northampton. His first **West End** appearance was as Talky in *Caught Napping* (Piccadilly, May 1959). Subsequent parts included the Informer in Bertholt **Brecht**'s *The Life of Galileo* (**Mermaid**, June 1960) and in 1964 he joined the **Royal Shakespeare Company** and in that year, at the Aldwych, some of his parts were Ginger in David **Rudkin**'s *Afore Night Come*, the Doctor in Roger Victrac's *Victor*, the schoolmaster in Peter Weiss's *Marat/Sade* and Pilia-Borza in Marlowe's *The Jew of Malta*. His second marriage was in 1963, to Prunella **Scales**.

Remaining with the RSC for the 1965 Stratford season his roles included Sir Nathaniel in *Love's Labour's Lost*, Tubal in *The Merchant of Venice* and Aegeon in *The Comedy of Errors*. The following year he played Korobkin in Gorgol's *The Government Inspector* (Aldwych, 1966).

In 1966 he joined the **Prospect Theatre Company** and remained with them until 1972. His chief performances in this period were as Samuel Johnson in *Madam, Said Doctor Johnson* and Prospero in *The Tempest* (tour, autumn 1966), Emerson in *A Room with a View* (**Edinburgh Festival**, 1967), Bolingbroke in *Richard II* and Mortimer in Marlowe's *Edward II* (tour, 1969, later at Edinburgh, Mermaid, Piccadilly, and European tour), Lear in *King Lear* (Edinburgh Festival and Venice Festival, 1971), Holofernes in *Love's Labour's Lost* and Lear again (tour of Australia, Britain and then a run at the Aldwych Theatre, 1972).

In 1972 West played Falstaff in *Henry IV Parts 1 and 2* (**Bristol Old Vic**, October) and a year later was appointed Artistic Director of the Forum Theatre, Billingham, for a season, during which he directed a number of plays including Peter **Nichols**'s *The National Health* and played Undershaft in Shaw's *Major Barbara.* After this, parts included the title-role in *Macbeth* and George in Tom **Stoppard**'s *Jumpers* (Gardner Centre, Brighton, 1974), Judge Brack in Ibsen's *Hedda Gabler* (RSC tour of Australia, USA and Canada) and for the Prospect Theatre Company, of which he became co-director in 1975, he appeared in *A Room with a View* on tour and at the Albery Theatre. He went on further tours abroad and in Britain, with Prospect Theatre, playing, among other roles, Claudius in *Hamlet* (May 1977), Enobarbus in *Antony and Cleopatra* (May 1977), Max in Harold **Pinter**'s *The Homecoming* (Garrick, May 1978) and parts in *Great English Eccentrics* (**Old Vic**, June 1978). In December 1979 he became Artistic Controller of the Old Vic Theatre Company.

Timothy West has become well-known for his roles as national figures, particularly on television (playing Churchill in *Churchill and the Generals* and the title-roles in *Edward VII* and *Henry VIII*). He played Sir Thomas Beecham in Caryl **Brahms**'s *Beecham* (Salisbury, July 1979, Apollo, January 1980) and Stalin in David Pownall's *Master Class* (Leicester Haymarket and Old Vic, January 1984), of which latter performance Ned Sherrin wrote (*Plays and Players,* March 1984), 'Timothy West's fine realisation is a fully rounded monster, by turns brutal and sentimental, broad and subtle, philistine and musicianly ... formidable and unpredictable.' Interviewed by Ken Roche (*TV Times,* 7-13 May 1983) West commented on such roles: 'People assume that because you've played one national figure you can play them all. Thank goodness I'm too large for Hitler ... but I must admit I do love playing awful people.'

He has appeared frequently on television, his best-known role being Bradley Hardacre in *Brass.*

West End

Originally referring to the theatres in London in and around Shaftesbury Avenue and the West End, it now refers much more widely to the whole of London's commercial theatre.

'Whitehall Farce'

See **Rix, Brian.**

Whitelaw, Billie

Born on 6 June 1932, in Coventry, she was educated at Thornton Grammar School, Bradford and began her career as an assistant stage manager in repertory. She first appeared on the stage in *Pink String* and *Sealing Wax* (Princes Theatre, Bradford, 1950) and made her London début as Victoire in Feydeau's *Hotel Paradiso* (Winter Garden, 1954, Oxford Playhouse, 1956). She appeared with Joan **Littlewood**'s **Theatre Workshop** as Mag Keenan in Alun Owen's *Progress to the Park* (Stratford East, August 1960, and Saville, May 1961). In May 1962 she starred in the revue *England, Our England* (Prince's Theatre) and from September to October 1962 played Sarah in *A Touch of the Poet* (Dublin and Venice Festivals).

Billie Whitelaw joined the **National Theatre** Company in 1963 for three years, during which she played in *Othello* (**Old Vic** and Moscow tour), Samuel **Beckett's** *Play* (Old Vic, April 1964), *The Dutch Courtesan* (**Chichester Festival**, July 1964, Old Vic, October 1964), *Hobson's Choice* (Old Vic, March 1965) and *Trelawney of the 'Wells'* (Chichester Festival, July 1965). Appearing as Desdemona in *Othello* and Maggie Hobson in *Hobson's Choice,* she went to Moscow and Berlin with the National Theatre in September 1965.

Later she joined the **Royal Shakespeare Company** and played Clare in David

Mercer's *After Haggerty* (Criterion, February, 1971) and a further part in a Samuel Beckett play, Mouth in *Not I* (**Royal Court**, January 1973 and January 1975). In March 1975 she took the role of Lucy in Michael **Frayn**'s *Alphabetical Order* (Hampstead) and then May in Beckett's *Footfalls* (Royal Court, May 1976), which was written specially for her. Although she has said in an interview with Peter Roberts (*Plays and Players*, September 1983) that she 'never really wanted to go into straight theatre at all' and that what she 'really wanted was to be a song and dance person', Billie Whitelaw has become thought of, as Roberts puts it, 'the leading exponent of Beckett in this country'. She said in this same interview that she finds it 'very embarrassing when I read in print that when Samuel Beckett was writing this or that passage he had Billie Whitelaw's voice in mind'. She took the title-role in Beckett's *Molly* at the Comedy Theatre (October 1978) and the following year played Winnie in his *Happy Days* (Royal Court, June 1979). In a television interview (*Pebble Mill at One*, 6 January, 1983) she commented on the playing of Beckett: 'I do wish people who go to see Beckett would go as if they were listening to a piece of music ... he puts the emotion into musical terms.' Interesting in this connection was her comment to Roberts, 'I only know I've got a part right when the music I hear in my head when I first read a part is what I get out of my mouth.'

She played Andromache, Athene and the Chorus Woman in John **Barton**'s adaptation *The Greeks* (RSC, Aldwych, January 1980), appeared in Peter **Nichols**'s *Passion Play* (RSC, Aldwych, January 1981) and Beckett's *Rockabye* and *Enough* (National Theatre, Cottesloe, December 1982). In September 1983 she took the part of Nelly Mann in Christopher **Hampton**'s *Tales From Hollywood* (National Theatre, Olivier), described by Martin Esslin as 'magical — poignant, funny and profound ... a performance to be treasured'.

Film work includes *No Love for Johnny, Charlie Bubbles, Twisted Nerve, The Adding Machine, Eagle in a Cage, Gumshoe, Frenzy, The Omen, An Unsuitable Job for a Woman* and *Tangier*. She has made numerous appearances on television including *Resurrection, The Skin Game, Beyond the Horizon, Lady of the Camelias, Love on the Dole, Sextet, Napoleon and Love, The Withered Arm, Not I, Eustace and Hilda, The Serpent Son, Happy Days, Private Schulz, A Tale of Two Cities*, and *Jamaica Inn*.

She has said of her work in the theatre, 'I never stop being afraid of being on stage. I have to conquer the fear of it ... and I think if ever I did overcome that fear I'd never want to appear on stage again.'

Further Reading

Peter Roberts, interview with Billie Whitelaw, 'Conquering Fear', *Plays and Players*, September 1983.

Whiting, John (Robert)

Born on 15 November 1917, in Salisbury, Wiltshire, he was the son of an army captain (who, on leaving the army, set up in legal practice). John was educated at Taunton School, Somerset, and in 1934 trained as an actor at the Royal Academy of Dramatic Art. On leaving, he had a number of small acting roles at the New Garden Theatre, Bideford, and with Croydon Repertory Company. During the Second World War he served in the Royal Artillery (and was commissioned in 1942). He married the actress Jackie Mawson in 1940 and after the war returned to acting, at theatres in Peterborough, Harrogate, Hammersmith (Lyric), York and Scarborough. He wrote some short stories (*Stairway* and *Valediction*) and a radio play (*Eye Witness*) which were broadcast in 1949.

He joined John **Gielgud**'s company in 1951 and played in *The Winter's Tale* (Phoenix Theatre), *Much Ado About Nothing* (Phoenix Theatre) and *Richard II* (Lyric,

Hammersmith). In the same year his first stage play, a comedy set in the period of the Napoleonic wars, called *A Penny for a Song,* was performed (Haymarket, March 1951). It was directed by Peter **Brook**. This was followed in the same year by another play, *Saint's Day* (Arts Theatre Club, September 1951), which was directed by Stephen Murray with a cast which included Michael **Hordern** and Donald **Pleasence**. It ran for only three weeks and received bad notices from most of the press, yet much praise from Kenneth **Tynan**, Sir John Gielgud and a number of prominent people in the theatre. It is a play about an 83-year-old poet who is celebrating his birthday, the date being the 25th January (in the Bible the day of St Paul's conversion to Christianity and his redemption after persecuting Christians). The poet, Paul Southam, keeps himself and his family isolated from the local village community and wages a private war against it. He is visited by Robert Procathren who tries to persuade him to come to London to celebrate his long-awaited recognition by the literary world. Frictions compound the tensions in the household: Stella, Paul's granddaughter, is shot by accident, some deserters arrive, hang Paul and Stella's husband and fire the village. Yet, in the course of these melodramatic events Paul has learned compassion. The play ends with a young girl dancing, perhaps an image of regeneration, sensitivity and cosmic order. It is a bleak play in which the protagonist, like others in Whiting's work, seems self-destructive. Simon Trussler has suggested that 'Whiting's best plays are most readily understood as parables and paradigms of human behaviour'. It is the case with *Saint's Day* that the 'parable' contains many levels of preoccupation (parallelism with St Paul's conversion, the dropping of the nuclear bomb on Hiroshima, to name but two). It is a poetic and metaphysical statement in a dramatic form ahead of its time, a play which influenced the new generation of dramatists in the second half of the 1950's, in particular John **Arden** and Harold **Pinter**. It was revived in May 1965 (Theatre Royal, Stratford East, transferring St Martin's Theatre, June 1965), again with Michael Hordern as Paul.

Whiting's next play, *Marching Song* (St Martin's Theatre, April 1954), again centred round an individual under psychological pressure, in this case a General Rupert Forster who is guilty of war crimes involving the slaughter of innocent children. His relationships with a mistress and young girl add to the complex states of feeling which ultimately lead him to commit suicide. It is a symbolic play with little dramatic action but great emotional force and intellectual weightiness (Whiting once said it suffered from 'intellectual elephantisis'), a dark and nihilistic vision of the power of moral conscience over an individual. Like *Saint's Day* it is a play which makes its statement, as Whiting puts it (*Encore,* 1961), 'by a method of revelation. It does not do it by a method of direct teaching . . . it can't be done by direct statement . . . An artist should be non-engaged.' Apart from the one-act play *No Why* (which was not performed until July 1964) Whiting wrote no more original plays for the theatre until 1960 but wrote translations and film scripts.

In 1960 Peter **Hall** invited John Whiting to write *The Devils,* an adaptation of Aldous Huxley's novel *The Devils of Loudun.* It was performed with great success at the Aldwych Theatre by the **Royal Shakespeare Company** (February 1961), directed by Peter **Wood** with a cast which included Richard **Johnson** (Grandier), Dianna **Rigg** (Phillipe) and Dorothy **Tutin** (Sister Jeanne). The play's subject is the diabolic possession of a group of nuns through, it is suspected, the influence of a permissive priest, Grandier. Yet the sexual frustration of Sister Jeanne could be regarded as much the cause as the effect of the demonic force and she provides much of the moral ambiguity of the play. Grandier is another powerful, self-destructive and near-tragic central figure, another example of what one critic (Benedict Nightingale) has called Whiting's 'fascination with the man of more than usual honesty, insight and spiritual ambition'. Peter McEnery, who played Grandier in the RSC's revival of *The Devils* (Barbican, Pit, August 1984), said in the *Observer* (19 August 1984), 'Grandier is a fascinating man seeking confrontation and danger, trying to find a real way through to God.' Grandier undergoes hideous torture (his legs are smashed) and is eventually burned. Whiting has so balanced the moral complexity of the play that condemnation of Grandier is as open a possibility as martyrdom. *The Devils* is perhaps the closest any post-war dramatist has come to writing a tragedy with epic proportions and it remains a remarkable play.

Whiting's death through cancer on 16 June 1963 was one of the theatre's greatest losses this century. His three major plays are unique and influential.

Other plays by Whiting, some discovered among his papers and performed posthumously, include *The Gates of Summer* (1956 tour, Tower Theatre, London, 1970), *A Walk in the Desert* (BBC Television, September 1960), *Conditions of Agreement* (**Bristol Old Vic**, October 1965, New York 1972) and *No More A-Roving* (published 1975). In an interview for *Encore* magazine in 1961 John Whiting told Tom Milne and Clive Goodwin, 'I am of that disappearing species, a private individual. As an artist I mean. They are becoming very rare.'

Further Reading

Simon Trussler, *The Plays of John Whiting*, Gollancz, London, 1972.

Ronald Hayman, *John Whiting*, Heinemann, London, 1969.

Tom Milne and Clive Goodwin, interview with John Whiting (from *Encore*, 1961), in Charles Marowitz and Simon Trussler (eds), *Theatre at Work*, Methuen, London, 1967.

Williams, Clifford

Born in Cardiff on 30 December 1926, he was educated at Highbury County Grammar School in London and started his career as a dancer, worked in a coalmine, served in the army and appeared as an actor in repertory and London productions including *Larissa* and *More Than Science* (Chanticleer Theatre, London, 1945) and *These Mortals* (People's Palace, November 1948) in which he played Julius Caesar. In 1950 he founded the Mime Theatre Company for which he wrote and directed numerous plays in its three years of existence. He subsequently became a director and was Director of Productions at the Marlowe Theatre, Canterbury (1956) and the Queen's Theatre, Hornchurch (1957). From 1957 until 1960 he directed plays at the Arts Theatre in London and in October 1961 he began his long association with the **Royal Shakespeare Company**. He became an Associate Director of the RSC in 1963.

His major productions for the RSC have included David **Rudkin**'s *Afore Night Come* (New Arts Theatre, June 1962), Rolf Hochhuth's *The Representative* (Aldwych, September 1963), *Richard II* and *Henry IV Parts 1 and 2* (Stratford-upon-Avon, 1964 season) which he co-directed, *The Merchant of Venice* and Marlowe's *The Jew of Malta* (Stratford-upon-Avon, 1965 season) starring Eric **Porter** as Shylock and Barabas, Friedrich Dürrenmatt's *The Meteor* (Aldwych, July 1966), Marlowe's *Doctor Faustus* (Stratford-upon-Avon, 1968 season) with Porter in the title-role, and Shaw's *Major Barbara* (Aldwych, 1970). In February 1970 he also directed Anthony Shaffer's highly successful thriller *Sleuth* (St Martin's) which ran for 2,359 performances and starred Anthony **Quayle**.

Other productions for the RSC, The **National Theatre**, and others include an all-male *As You Like It* (National Theatre, **Old Vic**, October 1967), Shaw's *Back To Methuselah* (National Theatre, Old Vic, July

1969), Kenneth **Tynan**'s *Oh! Calcutta!* (the Round House, July 1970), Webster's *The Duchess of Malfi* (RSC, Stratford-upon-Avon, March 1971) with Judi **Dench** in the title-role, *The Taming of the Shrew* (RSC, Stratford, May 1973), John Wiles's *A Lesson in Blood and Roses* (RSC, The Place, November 1973), James Barrie's *What Every Woman Knows* (Albery, November 1974) starring Dorothy **Tutin**, Shaw's *Too True To Be Good* (RSC, Aldwych, January 1975), Alan **Bennett**'s *The Old Country* (Queen's, September 1977) starring Alec **Guinness**, Ibsen's *Rosmersholm* (Haymarket, October 1977) starring Claire **Bloom** and Daniel **Massey**, *The Tempest* (RSC, Stratford-upon-Avon, April 1978) with Michael **Hordern** as Prospero, Alexander Solzhenitsyn's *The Love-Girl and the Innocent* (RSC, Aldwych, September 1981), Hugh Whitemore's *Pack of Lies* (Lyric, October 1983) starring Judi Dench, John Dighton's *The Happiest Days of Your Life* (RSC, Barbican, July 1984) and Shaw's *Saint Joan* for Anthony Quayle's Compass Company (tour, October 1985) with Jane **Lapotaire** in the title-role.

In an interview with John Miles-Brown (*Directing Drama*, 1980) Clifford Williams said a director must be 'interested in what makes people tick and also you've got to have the capacity to be awed and amused by human behaviour ... to find human behaviour and actions extraordinary and sometimes horrifying and sometimes incredibly funny'.

Further Reading

John Miles-Brown, 'Clifford Williams', *Directing Drama*, Peter Owen, London, 1980, pp. 155-66.
Gordon Gow, interview with Clifford Williams, *Plays and Players*, May 1973.

Williams, Michael (Leonard)

Born in Manchester on 19 July 1935 and educated at St Edward's College, Liverpool, he began his career as an insurance clerk but then went to RADA and trained for the stage. He made his début as Auguste in J.B. Priestley's *Take the Fool Away* (Nottingham Playhouse, September 1959) and first London appearance as Bernard Fuller in Willis **Hall** and Keith **Waterhouse**'s *Celebration* (Duchess, June 1961, transferred from Nottingham Playhouse).

In 1963 Michael Williams became a member of the **Royal Shakespeare Company** and appeared in several productions at the Aldwych Theatre including *A Midsummer Night's Dream* (1963 season) in which he was Puck, and *King Lear* (Aldwych and world tour, 1964) in which he played Oswald. He was Pinch in *The Comedy of Errors*, Kokel in Peter Weiss's *The Marat/Sade* and Lodowick in Marlowe's *The Jew of Malta* (Aldwych, 1964 season). For the 1965 season at Stratford-upon-Avon his roles included Dromio of Syracuse in *The Comedy of Errors* and Guildenstern in *Hamlet*. He was the Herald in *The Marat/Sade* (Aldwych, November 1965, Martin Beck, New York, December 1965) and then for the Stratford 1967 season played Petruchio in *The Taming of the Shrew*, Orlando in *As You Like It*, the Fool in *King Lear* and Troilus in *Troilus and Cressida* (also Aldwych, 1969 season). For the 1971 Stratford season his parts included the title-role in *Henry V*.

In April 1972 he played Charles Courtly in Boucicault's *London Assurance* at the New Theatre. Other parts have included Ian in Charles **Wood**'s *Jingo* (Aldwych, August 1975), Private Meek in Shaw's *Too True to Be Good* (Globe, December 1975), the title-role in **Brecht**'s *Schwek in the Second World War* (Stratford, the Other Place, 1976 season, Warehouse, August 1977), Autolycus in *The Winter's Tale* (Stratford 1976), the title-role in Simon **Gray**'s *Quartermaine's Terms* (1982 tour), Bob in Hugh Whitemore's *Pack of Lies* (Lyric, October 1983) and George Pidgen in Ray **Cooney**'s *Two Into One* (Shaftesbury, October 1984) for the '**Theatre of Comedy**' Company.

His film appearances include *The Marat/Sade, Eagle In a Cage, Dead Cert, Enigma* and *Educating Rita.* Television work includes *Elizabeth R, A Raging Calm, The Hanged Man, Turtle's Progress, Love in a Cold Climate, Amnesty* and the series *A Fine Romance* in which he appeared with Judi **Dench** to whom he was married in 1971.

Williamson, Nicol

Born in Hamilton, Scotland, on 14 September 1938, and educated at the Central Grammar School, Birmingham, he began his acting career with the Dundee Repertory Theatre Company (1960-1) and appeared as I-ti in Henry Chapman's *That's Us* (Arts, Cambridge, October 1961, **Royal Court**, November 1961). A year later he appeared again at the Royal Court Theatre, as Flute in *A Midsummer Night's Dream* (January 1962) and Malvolio in *Twelfth Night* ('Production without Décor', February 1962). With the **Royal Shakespeare Company** at the New Arts Theatre he played Meakin in Henry **Livings**'s *Nil Carborundum* (April 1962), Satin in Gorky's *The Lower Depths* (May 1962) and Leantio in Middleton's *Women Beware Women* (July 1962).

He subsequently played roles in many productions at the Royal Court including the Man at the End in Wedekind's *Spring Awakening* ('Production without Décor', April 1962), Sebastian Dangerfield in J.P. Donleavy's *The Ginger Man* (November 1963, transferred from Ashcroft, Croydon), Bill Maitland in John **Osborne**'s *Inadmissible Evidence* (September 1964), Peter in Ben Travers's *A Cuckoo in the Nest* (October 1964), Vladimir in Samuel **Beckett**'s *Waiting for Godot* (December 1964) and Joe Johnson in David Cregan's *Miniatures* ('Production without Décor', April 1965). In December 1965 he appeared in New York as Bill Maitland in Osborne's *Inadmissible Evidence* (Belasco Theatre) and in March 1967 he gave the solo performance as Alexei in Gogol's *The Diary of a Madman* (Duchess Theatre).

At the Round House in March 1969 he gave an award-winning performance of the title-role in *Hamlet* and also played the role in New York (Lunt-Fontanne, May 1969) and on a tour of the United States (1969). Other major roles have included the title-role in Chekhov's *Uncle Vanya* (Circle in the Square, New York, June 1973), the title-role in *Coriolanus* (RSC, Aldwych, October 1973), the title-role in *Macbeth* (RSC, Stratford-upon-Avon, October 1974, Aldwych, March 1975) and Henry VIII in *Rex* (Lunt-Fontanne, New York, April 1976). He again played Bill Maitland in September 1978 at the Royal Court Theatre and in 1981 he played the role in New York. In New York he also recently played the title-role in *Macbeth* (1982) and Archie Rice in Osborne's *The Entertainer* (1983).

Nicol Williamson has devised and appeared in his own off-Broadway show *Nicol Williamson's Late Show* (New York, June 1973) which was a compilation of music, songs and readings. In an interview in 1973 (with Gordon Gow) Williamson said of acting that it 'is not an art — it's a craft. I care very much about what is on the written page, which is why I don't work every week ... I have to believe very passionately in what I'm doing ... In any case, I have to have a director ... I don't believe that an actor should bring his problems of self to the stage. The character has to be built up in the way it was written and was meant to be played.'

His work for films has included *Inadmissible Evidence, The Bofors Gun, Laughter in the Dark, Hamlet, The Jerusalem File, The Goodbye Girl, The Human Factor, Excalibur* and *I'm Dancing as Fast as I Can.* Television appearances include *Terrible Jim Fitch, The Resistible Rise of Arturo Ui, I Know What I Meant, The Word, Macbeth* and *Sakharov.*

Wilson, Snoo (Andrew)

Born in Reading, Berkshire, on 2 August 1948, he went to school at Bradford College, Berkshire (where his father was a teacher), and studied English and American Studies at the University of East Anglia (1966-9). Whilst at university he wrote and directed a revue called *Girl Mad As Pigs* (1968). Some of his most successful plays have surrealistically explored the inner fantasy-lives, destructive sexual impulses and unconscious dream imagery of characters who nevertheless have to live in civilised society in some way. As Wilson said in an interview with Simon Trussler and others in 1980: 'You have the "interior" and the "exterior" world ... we exist with a foot in each camp, as cultural beings ... But you can invent a situation where you *can* make a free ethical choice.' The presentation of such subjects on the stage has led Wilson's work, on a number of occasions, to be visually spectacular and arresting, and also be to innovative in narrative structure. His early interests in the '**Theatre of the Absurd**' (his student play *Ella Daybelle Fesse's Machine* was strongly influenced by **Beckett**), his reading of Freud and Jung, and his fascination with the unconscious, the occult and magic, have all influenced his plays and often been blended with history and political ideology.

Wilson's association with the group of young playwrights (Tony Bicat, David **Hare** and Howard **Brenton** in particular) working with the Portable Theatre touring company in the late 1960s and early 1970s, gave him the opportunities for the performance of some of his plays at the **Edinburgh Festival** and elsewhere. His major successes have been *Blowjob* (Portable Theatre, Edinburgh Festival, 1971) about an unsuccessful raid, by two skinheads, on an ageing homosexual recluse in Liverpool, *Vampire* (Portable Theatre, 1973, revived Bush Theatre, March 1977) which took a surrealistic look at the repressive effects of Victorian moral values (and included the return, in astral form, of a dead character, the bizarre images of Freud and Jung on stilts, the appearance of a rampant talking ox and Enoch Powell delivering his 'Rivers of Blood' speech as he rises from a coffin), and *The Pleasure Principle* (**Royal Court**, Theatre Upstairs, December 1973). This latter play was a comedy which investigated two characters, Robert, a businessman and advocate of capitalism (originally played by Dinsdale **Landen**) and Gale, a psychology graduate who lives in her own dreamworld, as they both search for 'pleasure' (the title of the play referring to Freud's concept). The search takes the form of an Irish holiday, sexual seduction in a flat, and entertainment at a circus. Robert's nervous breakdown in Act 1 is foreshadowed by the stage manifestation of dancing gorillas and there are seduction scenes which take place in a swan, the appearance of a masked and phallused spirit of pleasure, and spectacular circus décor — a visual atmosphere reminiscent of the Jacobean masques and Metaphysical imagery of the seventeenth century. In a review of the original production Peter Ansorge wrote that such spectacle is 'typical of Wilson's excursions into a highly theatrical version of the unconscious: vampires, animals, mysterious spirits, will suddenly take over a scene and completely transform the course of an apparently naturalistic scene or conversation'.

The Beast (Palace Theatre, November 1974) was commissioned by the **Royal Shakespeare Company** for its experimental season in 1974. The play focused on aspects of the life of the occultist and self-styled magus Aleister Crowley (played by Richard **Pasco** in the first production). It was revised in 1982 as *The Number of the Beast* (Bush, February 1972). Other plays have included *The Everest Hotel* (Scarab Theatre at the Bush, 1975, Traverse, Edinburgh, February 1976) about three girls from a remand home who form a singing group and perform from the top of Mt Everest in order to stop the world from becoming a huge communist state, *England-England* (Jeanetta Cochrane

Theatre, 1977) a musical about the Kray twins, *The Glad Hand* (Royal Court, May 1978) which explored fantasies about fascism on board an oil tanker, *A Greenish Man* (Bush Theatre, November 1979) involving ghostly events in the world of Irish industry and finance, and *Flaming Bodies* (Institute of Contemporary Art, 1979) about a woman gradually going mad in a Los Angeles film company (a play which requires the spectacle of a car crashing through a window).

Recent plays have included *Loving Reno* (Bush, July 1983, also New York Theatre Studio) about a magician who has an intimate relationship with his daughter, and *The Grass Widow* (Royal Court, Theatre Upstairs, November 1983) which explores disagreements over land ownership on a Californian marijuana farm. Wilson also directed Portable Theatre's *Lay-by* (Edinburgh Festival, 1971) which he co-wrote with Howard **Brenton**, David **Hare** and Trevor **Griffiths**.

His television plays include *Swamp Music, The Trip to Jerusalem, The Barium Meal, A Greenish Man* and, with Trevor Griffiths, *Don't Make Waves.* In an interview with Peter Ansorge in 1974 Wilson stated 'a play should always be new — the exciting plays always are. They create solutions for ideas to be moved around and be discussed in new ways. If that stops happening it can be a real disaster.'

Further Reading

Simon Trussler, 'Snoo Wilson', *New Theatre Voices of the Seventies: Sixteen Interviews from 'Theatre Quarterly' 1970-1980*, S. Trussler (ed.), Eyre Methuen, London, 1981, pp. 172-83.

Wings

In **Proscenium** theatre the stage space to the left and right of the **Acting Area**. It is where actors mostly enter from and so is concealed from the audience's view by **Legs**, **Masking** curtains or wing **Flats**.

Wolfit, Sir Donald, CBE

Born on 20 April 1902, in Balderton, Newark, he was educated at Magnus School, Newark, and became a schoolmaster. In 1920 he joined Charles Doran's company and toured in small parts and stage management for many productions of the classics. On leaving Doran in 1923 he joined Fred Terry's touring company and played Armand St Just in *The Scarlet Pimpernel.* His first appearance in London was as Phirous in *The Wandering Jew* (1924) by Temple Thurston and, after further years on tour, he was in the company led by John **Gielgud** and Harcourt Williams at the **Old Vic** (1929-30) where his parts included Claudius in *Hamlet,* Cassius in *Julius Caesar* and Touchstone in *As You Like It.* From 1930 to 1935 he was in a number of **West End** productions and on tour (including a tour of Canada for Sir Barry **Jackson** in 1931-2), parts including Browning in Besier's *The Barretts of Wimpole Street* (Canada tour) and Thomas Mowbray in Gordon Daviot's *Richard of Bordeaux* (New Theatre, 1932). John Gielgud played Richard in the latter production. Wolfit was at the **Shakespeare Memorial Theatre**, Stratford-upon-Avon, for the 1936 and 1937 seasons for which, among other roles, he played the title-role in *Hamlet,* Cassius in *Julius Caesar*, Ulysses in *Troilus and Cressida,* the Chorus in *Henry V* and Kent in *King Lear.*

In 1937 he became an actor-manager (one of the last of a tradition spanning a period from Sir Johnston Forbes-Robertson to Harley Granville-Barker) and toured Britain in many of the great Shakespearean roles including Shylock, Macbeth, Hamlet and Malvolio. In January 1938 he gave highly-acclaimed performances in the title-role of Jonson's *Volpone* and in the autumn of the same year he added the lead roles in *Othello, Romeo and Juliet* and *Much Ado About Nothing* to his repertoire.

When war was declared in 1939 Wolfit's company returned (from appearances in

Dublin) to Brighton and then played for a season at the Kingsway Theatre in the West End (1940). This was followed by a season of 'Scenes from Shakespeare' in the lunch hours at the Strand Theatre (where he and his company gave over 112 performances, many during the Battle of Britain air-raids). Wolfit was also a member of the Frensham Home Guard at this time. In 1941 he formed another touring company and added to his roles King Richard in *Richard III.* Later in the year Wolfit returned to the Strand and in January 1942 gave his first, now legendary, performances in the title-role of *King Lear* (St James's Theatre) which production he also directed. In a season at the Scala Theatre in the West End (February–April 1944) he directed his company in *Richard III, Othello, As You Like It, Hamlet, King Lear* and *Twelfth Night,* himself playing Richard, Othello, Touchstone, Hamlet, Lear and Malvolio. Rosalind Iden (daughter of the actor and director Ben Iden Payne), who became his third wife in 1948, also appeared with the company for this season. Wolfit's Lear won the admiration of critics, in particular James Agate who (according to J.C. Trewin's *Shakespeare on the English Stage,* 1964) said Wolfit was 'every inch King Lear' and T.C. Worsley who remarked that 'whereas other actors begin to tap our tears in the storm scene, Mr Wolfit has them pricking at our eyelids long before'. Enemy raids forced the company to return to touring, some of which included ENSA tours of Alexandria, Cairo, Paris and Brussels (1945).

Except for a season at the Winter Garden where he played Macbeth, Shylock and Benedick (February 1945) and Iago, Iachimo and Lear (February–April, 1946) and at the Savoy (April–May 1947) the immediate post-war years were spent touring the British Isles, and Canada, also making an appearance in New York (Century Theatre, 1947). At the Malvern Festival in 1950 Wolfit played Sir Giles Overreach in Massinger's *A New Way to Pay Old Debts* and in 1951 was invited by Tyrone **Guthrie** to play the title-role in Marlowe's *Tamburlaine the Great* (for the re-opening of the Old Vic, autumn 1951) and Lord Ogleby in Colman and Garrick's *The Clandestine Marriage.* It was during this run of the highly-praised and successful *Tamburlaine* that Wolfit's assertive personality took over his performance and he became notoriously difficult to act with, even sending notes to other members of the cast about their performances. During the run of the production at Stratford-upon-Avon Guthrie reprimanded Wolfit for his travesty of the production. After the run Wolfit claimed breach of contract with the governors and never played again at the Old Vic. Leo **McKern**, who once worked with Wolfit, said in an interview (*Desert Island Discs,* 1984) that Wolfit's 'behaviour was monstrous on the stage ... he honestly and truly believed that nothing of any possible interest to any person could be happening while he was not either speaking or acting on the stage ... yet, in a funny way, you could never feel anything but a sort of stunned amazement'.

At the King's Theatre, Hammersmith, between February and December 1953, he put on a season of classic plays including *Twelfth Night, The Merchant of Venice, Macbeth, The Taming of the Shrew, As You Like It, Henry IV Part 1* and *King Lear.* He gave 280 performances of all his chief roles including an exceptional performance as Oedipus in Sophocles' *Oedipus at Colonus.* At the Scala Theatre he was Sir Peter Teazle in Sheridan's *The School For Scandal* (1953-4 season) and later appeared in *The Strong are Lonely* (Piccadilly, Haymarket, **Edinburgh Festival**, 1955-6). In 1957 he was in Montherlant's *The Master of Santiago* and *Malatesta* (Lyric, Hammersmith) and in 1959 he was in Ibsen's *Ghosts* (Princes Theatre). Between 1959 and 1963 he toured Kenya, Ethiopia, Italy, South Africa and also appeared in New York. In Britain he was in *Cromwell at Drogheda* (Leatherhead, 1961), *Fit to Print* (Duke of

York's, 1962), *John Gabriel Borkman* (Duchess, 1963) and *Treasure Island* (**Mermaid**, 1965). His last performance was as Mr Barrett in Ronald Millar and Ron Grainer's musical *Robert and Elizabeth* (Lyric, 1966-7). He died on 17 February 1968.

Donald Wolfit's chief film roles were in *Pickwick Papers, Room at the Top, Lawrence of Arabia, Becket, Life at the Top* and *Decline and Fall.*

In an interview with Charles **Marowitz** (*Encore,* July 1963) Kenneth **Tynan** said that the 'romantic heroic actor of the old school ... is either temperamentally servile to them [the audience], coaxing and cajoling them in comedy, or he thunders them into submission in tragedy. And this can produce marvellous effects. Wolfit's *Lear* at its best, was a performance like that. It was shattering – it was like being run over by a train.' Laurence Kitchin (who wrote that 'none of our great actors conforms, perhaps, so well to the popular idea of one as Sir Donald Wolfit'), quotes Wolfit as stating 'you have to work on the audience for the first fifteen minutes or so. But they're digging in that stage music which is part of their inheritance. It slowly grows on them.'

The Dresser (Queen's, April 1980, Broadway, 1981), a play by Wolfit's biographer Ronald Harwood and starring Freddie **Jones**, was based on Wolfit's last years as an actor-manager with his touring company. It was made into a film starring Albert **Finney** and Tom **Courtenay**.

Further Reading

Ronald Harwood, *Sir Donald Wolfit, CBE: his Life and Work in the Unfashionable Theatre,* Secker and Warburg, London, 1971.

Donald Wolfit, *First Interval,* Odhams, London, 1954.

Wood, Charles (Gerald)

Born in St Peter Port, Guernsey, on 6 August 1932, the son of parents who were professional actors in his grandfather's touring repertory company, he was educated at Chesterfield Grammar School (1942-5) and King Charles I School, Kidderminster (1945-8). This latter town was where his parents (John and Catherine Wood) ran a theatre in the immediate post-war years. Charles Wood worked in the theatre as a boy actor and took great interest in stage design and lighting, an interest which led him to study art at Birmingham College of Art (1948-50). He then served five years as a trooper in the 17th and 21st Lancers (1950-5) and for two years worked in a factory (1955-7). He married the actress Valerie Newman in 1954.

Charles Wood began his career in the theatre as a **stage manager** and designer (1957-9), including work for Joan **Littlewood's Theatre Workshop** in 1957. His upbringing and experiences working in the theatre, his army service and his interests and involvement in the film industry, have together formed the basic sources for most of his plays, the first of which was the trilogy of one-act plays *Cockade* (New Arts, October 1963), which viewed the army as a near-fascist organisation. Of his subsequent plays the most important have been *Fill the Stage with Happy Hours* (Nottingham Playhouse, November 1966) set in a small provincial repertory theatre, and *Dingo* (Bristol Arts Centre, October 1967, **Royal Court**, November 1967) which was a parody of the heroic myths generated about Churchill, Montgomery and other heroes of the desert war during the Second World War. It was a play which approached the **'Theatre of the Absurd'** in its language and stylised form. *H: or Monologues at Front of Burning Cities* (**National Theatre, Old Vic**, 1969) employed spectacular and complicated backdrops, an inset stage based on Pollock's toy theatres, elements of Victorian pantomime and one scene with a completely bare stage. The play explored General Havelock's (H's) conflicts of loyalty to his Christian faith on the one hand and the Empire on the other, during the relief of Lucknow at the time of the Indian Mutiny.

Veterans (Royal Court, March 1972), partly based on Wood's experiences as a film script writer for *The Charge of the Light Brigade* (1968), starred John **Gielgud** and John **Mills** as two veteran actors (Sir Geoffrey Kendle and Laurence D'Orsay) on location in Turkey, who pass their time in boredom, waiting to be called to the film set. The play was written partly in verse and in some ways can be seen as a sensitive and poetic portrait of Gielgud himself. John Russell Brown (in *A Short Guide to Modern British Drama*, 1982) quotes Ronald Bryden as saying that 'the total impression is of a kind of saint of the theatre'. However, Wood has written that the play is about 'the failure of theatrical success' in that stardom, for all its glamour, can hide a deep sense of loneliness and isolation. Another play which centred round the making of a film was *Has 'Washington' Legs?* (National Theatre, Cottesloe, November 1978). The film being made is about the American Revolution but the play explores the tensions between the actors and film director (who was played by Albert **Finney** in the original production). As in Wood's other plays about film-making, the film director's dominance over everything is equated with tyrannical dictatorship.

In July 1984 the **Royal Shakespeare Company** presented Wood's *Red Star*, (Barbican, Pit) about Nikolai (played by Richard **Griffiths**) a Russian actor who, after playing Julius Caesar in a production by the 'Glorious Union of Soviet Agricultural Workers', is tempted into stardom and corruption by the offer of playing Stalin (whom he physically resembles) in an epic Soviet film. In terms of his plays, theatrical staging and narrative forms Wood has been described by one critic (Derek Weeks, *Plays and Players*, December 1984) as 'the most important epic dramatist since **Brecht**'. Further to this, his work possesses 'a fascinating visual imagination, supported by vividly poetic and evocative language, full of rich idiom and surprising juxtapositions, tempered by a cartoon-like sense of humour, and bearing a strong message of hope for the future'.

Charles Wood has written a number of filmscripts including those for *The Knack*, *Help!*, *How I Won the War*, *The Charge of the Light Brigade*, *The Long Day's Dying*, *Wagner* and *Vile Bodies*. His television plays include *Prisoner and Escort*, *Drill Pig*, *Do As I Say*, *Love Lies Bleeding*, *Don't Forget to Write* (series) and *Puccini*.

Recently Wood has worked on the writing of two plays with women as central characters, *Across the Garden of Allah* (written with Glenda **Jackson** in mind for the leading role) and *Ms Courage* based on *Landstörtzerin Courasche* (1670) the novel by Johann Grimmelhausen which was also the source of **Brecht**'s *Mother Courage* (1941).

Further Reading

John Russell Taylor, 'Charles Wood', *The Second Wave*, Methuen, London, 1978, pp. 59-76.

Working Lights

Ordinary domestic lights used during rehearsals and set construction.

Worth, Irene, CBE

Born in Nebraska, USA, on 23 June 1916, she trained as a teacher at the University of California, Los Angeles, and began her career in that job. Her first stage appearance was in 1942 as Fenella in Margaret Kennedy's *Escape Me Never* (tour) and she first appeared in New York (Booth Theatre) as Cecily in Martin Vale's *The Two Mrs Carrolls*. She came to London in 1944 and studied acting with Elsie Fogerty. Her first London appearance was as Elsie in Saroyan's *The Time of Your Life* (Lyric, Hammersmith,

February 1946) and she has since spent the majority of her career in the British theatre.

Her chief roles include Celia Copleston in the original production of T.S. **Eliot**'s *The Cocktail Party* (**Edinburgh Festival**, August 1949, Henry Miller, New York, January 1950, New Theatre, London, July 1950) and, for the **Old Vic** Company which she joined in 1951, Desdemona in *Othello* (Berlin Festival, October 1951, Old Vic, October 1951), Helena in *A Midsummer Night's Dream* and Catherine in *The Other Heart* (1951-2 and tour of South Africa, 1953). She also played Portia in *The Merchant of Venice* (Old Vic, January 1953), Helena in *All's Well That Ends Well* and Queen Margaret in *Richard III* (both at Shakespeare Festival Theatre, Stratford, Ontario, 1953), Argia in the original production in English of Ugo Betti's *The Queen and the Rebels* (Midland Theatre Company, Coventry, March 1955, Haymarket, London, October 1955), Sara Callifer in Graham **Greene**'s *The Potting Shed* (Globe, London, February 1958) the cast of which included John **Gielgud**, and the title-role in Schiller's *Mary Stuart* (Phoenix, New York, October 1957, Edinburgh Festival, September 1958, Old Vic, September 1958).

In 1962 Irene Worth joined the **Royal Shakespeare Company** with whom her work has included the Marquise de Merteuil in *The Art of Seduction* (Aldwych, March 1962), Lady Macbeth in *Macbeth* (Stratford-upon-Avon, June 1962) and Goneril in Peter **Brook**'s production of *King Lear* which starred Paul **Scofield** in the title-role (Stratford-upon-Avon, November 1962, Aldwych, December 1962, Aldwych, February 1964, British Council tour of Europe, Russia and Canada, 1964, New York State Theatre, May 1964). In January 1963 she was Doktor Mathilde in Dürrenmatt's *The Physicists* (Aldwych).

She gave award-winning performances in Noël Coward's double-bill *Suite in Three Keys* (Queen's, 1966) and at the 1967 **Chichester Festival** was Hesione Hushabye in Shaw's *Heartbreak House* (also Lyric, November 1967). In March 1968 she played Jocasta in Sophocles' *Oedipus* at the Old Vic and later was Miss Alice in Edward Albee's *Tiny Alice* (Aldwych, January 1970). Major roles in the 1970s included the title-role in Ibsen's *Hedda Gabler* (Stratford, Ontario, June 1970), Irina Arkadina in Chekhov's *The Seagull* (Chichester Festival, May 1973, Greenwich, January 1974), Mrs Alving in Ibsen's *Ghosts* (Greenwich, January 1974), Gertrude in *Hamlet* (Greenwich, March 1974), Madame Ranevskaya in Chekhov's *The Cherry Orchard* (Lincoln Center, New York, February 1977), Anna in Harold **Pinter**'s *Old Times* (Lake Forest, Illinois, 1977) and Winnie in Samuel **Beckett**'s *Happy Days* (Public Theatre, New York, June 1979). In December 1984 she was Volumnia in the **National Theatre**'s production of *Coriolanus* (Olivier Theatre) with Ian **McKellen** in the title-role.

Irene Worth's film appearances include *Orders to Kill*, *King Lear*, *Nicholas and Alexandra*, *Eye Witness*, *Forbidden* and *Fast Forward*. Television appearances include *The Lake*, *The Lady from the Sea*, *Candida*, *The Duchess of Malfi*, *Antigone*, *Prince Orestes*, *Variations on a Theme*, *The Way of the World*, *Separate Tables* and *Coriolanus*.

Title-Author Index

Original plays since 1945 referred to in the text. Dates are the years of first performances.

A-A-America (1976), Bond, Edward 42
Abide With Me (1977), Keeffe, Barrie 132
Abigail's Party (1977), Leigh, Mike 138
Absent Friends (1974), Ayckbourn, Alan 21
Absurd Person Singular (1972), Ayckbourn, Alan 21
Act Without Words (1957), Beckett, Samuel 29
Actors' Rehearsal Group (1958), Arden, John and McGrath, John 15
Afore Night Come (1962), Rudkin, David 218
After Haggerty (1970), Mercer, David 153
After Liverpool (1971), Saunders, James 220
After Lydia (1973), Rattigan, Terence 199
After Magritte (1970), Stoppard, Tom 236
After Mercer (1980), Hampton, Christopher 108
After the Ball is Over (1985), Home, William Douglas 117
Agamemnon (1973), Berkoff, Steven 35
All Fall Down (1955), Arden, John 15
All Honour Mr. Todd (1966), Terson, Peter 242
All Things Bright and Beautiful (1962), Hall, Willis and Waterhouse, Keith 107
Alpha Alpha (1971), Barker, Howard 24
Alphabetical Order (1975), Frayn, Michael 82
Amadeus (1979), Shaffer, Peter 225
American Days (1979), Poliakoff, Stephen 189
An Othello (1972), Marowitz, Charles 150
Annie Wobbler (1983), Wesker, Arnold 253
Apprentices, The (1968), Terson, Peter 242
Apricots (1971), Griffiths, Trevor 97
Are You Lonesome Tonight (1985) Bleasdale, Alan 38
Aristocrats (1979), Friel, Brian 84
Armstrong's Last Goodnight (1964), Arden, John 15
Ars Longa, Vita Brevis (1964), Arden, John and D'Arcy, Margaretta 15
Artaud at Rodez (1975), Marowitz, Charles 150
Ashes (1974), Rudkin, David 218

Babies Grow Old (1974), Leigh, Mike 138
Ballygombeen Bequest, The (1972), Arden, John and D'Arcy, Margaretta 15
Balmoral (1978), Frayn, Michael 82
Barbarians (1977), Keeffe, Barrie 132
Bargain, The (1979), Jellicoe, Ann 128
Bastard Angel (1980), Keeffe, Barrie 132
Battle of Shrivings, The (1970), Shaffer, Peter 225
Bazaar and Rummage (1982), Townsend, Sue 246
Beast, The (1974), Wilson, Snoo 264
Bedroom Farce (1975), Ayckbourn, Alan 21
Beecham (1980), Brahms, Caryl 44
Before Dawn (1973), Rattigan, Terence 199
Belcher's Luck (1966), Mercer, David 153
Bells of Hell, The (1977), Mortimer, John 160
Benefactors (1984), Frayn, Michael 82
Betrayal (1978), Pinter, Harold 182
Better Times (1984), Keeffe, Barrie 132
Bewitched (1974), Barnes, Peter 26
Beyond the Fringe (1960), see Bennett, Alan and Miller, Jonathan 34 and 156
Big House, The (1958), Behan, Brendan 32
Big Soft Nellie (1961), Livings, Henry 141
Billy Liar (1960), Hall, Willis and Waterhouse, Keith 107
Bingo (1973), Bond, Edward 42
Birthday Party, The (1958), Pinter, Harold 182
Black Comedy (1965), Shaffer, Peter 225
Black Lear (1980), Keeffe, Barrie 132
Black Mass (1970), Bond, Edward 42
Bleak Moments (1970), Leigh, Mike 138
Blood of the Bambergs, The (1962), Osborne, John 174
Blood Red Roses (1980), McGrath, John 146
Blood Sports (1976), Edgar, David 74
Bloody Poetry (1984), Brenton, Howard 46
Blowjob (1971), Wilson, Snoo 264
Bodies (1977), Saunders, James 220
Bond Honoured, A (1966), adaptation by Osborne, John 174
Borage Pigeon Affair, The (1969), Saunders, James 220
Born in the Gardens (1979), Nichols, Peter 165
Box Play, The (1966), Leigh, Mike 138
Brassneck (1973), Brenton, Howard and Hare, David 46 and 111
Bread and Butter Trade, The (1976), Terson, Peter 242
Breaking the Silence (1984), Poliakoff, Stephen 189
Breath (1970), Beckett, Samuel 29
Brimstone and Treacle (1977), Potter, Dennis 191
Browning Version, The (1948), Rattigan, Terence 199
Bundle, The (1977), Bond, Edward 42
Burglars (1968), Rudkin, David 218
Buried Man, The (1962), Mercer, David 153
Business of Good Government, The (1960), Arden, John 15

But Fred, Freud is Dead (1972), Terson, Peter 242
Butley (1971), Gray, Simon 93
Bye Bye Blues (1973), Saunders, James 220

Caretaker, The (1960), Pinter, Harold 182
Caritas (1980), Wesker, Arnold 253
Carnival War a Go Hot (1979), Hastings, Michael 113
Carving a Statue (1964), Greene, Graham 95
Castle, The (1985), Barker, Howard 24
Catastrophe (1982), Beckett, Samuel 29
Cause Célèbre (1977), Rattigan, Terence 199
Celebration (1961), Hall, Willis and Waterhouse, Keith 107
Changing Room, The (1971), Storey, David 238
Chase Me, Comrade (1964), Cooney, Ray 61
Cheek (1970), Barker, Howard 24
Cheviot, the Stag and the Black, Black Oil, The (1973), McGrath, John 146
Chez Nous (1974), Nichols, Peter 165
Chicken Soup with Barley (1958), Wesker, Arnold 253
Chiltern Hundreds, The (1947), Home, William Douglas 117
Chips with Everything (1962), Wesker, Arnold 253
Chorus Girls (1981), Keeffe, Barrie 132
Chorus of Disapproval, A (1985), Ayckbourn, Alan 21
Christie in Love (1969), Brenton, Howard 46
Churchill Play, The (1974), Brenton, Howard 46
'Cindy-Ella' or 'I Gotta Shoe' (1962), Brahms, Caryl 44
City Sugar (1975), Poliakoff, Stephen 189
Claw (1975), Barker, Howard 24
Clever Soldiers (1974), Poliakoff, Stephen 189
Close of Play (1979), Gray, Simon 93
Close the Coalhouse Door (1968), Plater, Alan and Glasgow, Alex 185
Cloud Nine (1976), Churchill, Caryl 59
Clouds (1976), Frayn, Michael 82
Cockade (1963), Wood, Charles 267
Cocktail Party, The (1949), Eliot, T.S. *see* Verse Drama 250
Collaborators (1973), Mortimer, John 160
Collection, The (1961), Pinter, Harold 182
Come As You Are (1970), Mortimer, John 160
Come Laughing Home (1964), Hall, Willis and Waterhouse, Keith 107
Comedians (1975), Griffiths, Trevor 97
Comic Pictures (1976), Lowe, Stephen 143
Comings and Goings (1978), Stott, Mike 239
Common Pursuit, The (1984), Gray, Simon 93
Complaisant Lover, The (1959), Greene, Graham 95
Conditions of Agreement (1965), Whiting, John 259
Confidential Clerk, The (1953), Eliot, T.S. *see* Verse Drama 250
Confusions (1974), Ayckbourn, Alan 21
Contractor, The (1969), Storey, David 238
Cousin Vladimir (1978), Mercer, David 153
Cresta Run, The (1965), Simpson, N.F. 228
Cries from Casement as His Bones Are Brought to Dublin (1973), Rudkin, David 218
Crimes in Hot Countries (1985), Barker, Howard 24
Crimes of Passion (1967), Orton, Joe 172
Critic and the Heart, The (1957), Bolt, Robert 40
Cromwell (1973), Storey, David 238
Crystal and Fox (1968), Friel, Brian 84

Dark is Light Enough, The (1954), Fry, Christopher *see* Verse Drama 250
Day in the Death of Joe Egg, A (1967), Nichols, Peter 165
Dayroom (1981), Townsend, Sue 246
Decadence (1981), Berkoff, Steven 35
Deeds (1978), Brenton, Howard, Griffiths, Trevor and Hare, David 46, 97 and 111
Deep Blue Sea, The (1952), Rattigan, Terence 199
Destiny (1976), Edgar, David 74
Devil Inside Him, The (1950), Osborne, John and Linden, Stella 174
Devils, The (1961), Whiting, John 259
Dick Deterred (1974), Edgar, David 74
Dingo (1967), Wood, Charles 267
Dirty Linen (1976), Stoppard, Tom 236
Dock Brief, The (1958), Mortimer, John 160
Dog Days (1977), Gray, Simon 93
Dogg's Hamlet, Cahoot's Macbeth (1980), Stoppard, Tom 236
Dogg's Our Pet (1971), Stoppard, Tom 236
Don Quixote (1980), Arden, John 15
Donkeys' Years (1976), Frayn, Michael 82
Don't Destroy Me (1956), Hastings, Michael 113
Down the Dock Road (1976), Bleasdale, Alan 38
Downchild (1985), Barker, Howard 24
Downstairs (1958), Churchill, Caryl 59
Duck Song (1974), Mercer, David 153
Ducking Out (1982), adaptation by Stott, Mike 239
Dumb Waiter, The (1960), Pinter, Harold 182
Dutch Uncle (1969), Gray, Simon 93

Early Days (1980), Storey, David 238
Early Morning (1968), Bond, Edward 42
East (1975), Berkoff, Steven 35
Easy Death (1962), Churchill, Caryl 59
Ecstasy (1979), Leigh, Mike 138
Education of Skinny Spew, The (1969), Brenton, Howard 46
Edward: the Final Days (1971), Barker, Howard 24
Eh? (1964), Livings, Henry 141

1861 Whitby Lifeboat Disaster, The (1971), Terson, Peter 242
Elder Statesman, The (1958), Eliot, T.S. *see* Verse Drama 250
Ella Daybelle Fesse's Machine (1968), Wilson, Snoo 264
End of Me Old Cigar, The (1975), Osborne, John 174
Endgame (1957), Beckett, Samuel 29
Enemy Within, The (1962), Friel, Brian 84
England – England (1977), Wilson, Snoo 264
England, My Own (1978), Terson, Peter 242
England, Our England (1962), Hall, Willis 107
England's Ireland (1972), Brenton, Howard 46
Enjoy (1980), Bennett, Alan 34
Enough (1982), Beckett, Samuel 29
Entertainer, The (1957), Osborne, John 174
Entertaining Mr. Sloane (1964), Orton, Joe 172
Epitaph for George Dillon (1958), Osborne, John and Creighton, Anthony 174
Epsom Downs (1977), Brenton, Howard 46
Equus (1973), Shaffer, Peter 225
Erogenous Zones (1969), Stott, Mike 239
Erpingham Camp, The (1967), Orton, Joe 172
Events While Guarding the Bofors Gun (1966), McGrath, John 146
Everest Hotel, The (1975), Wilson, Snoo 264
Every Good Boy Deserves Favour (1977), Stoppard, Tom 236

Fair Slaughter (1977), Barker, Howard 24
Faith Healer (1979), Friel, Brian 84
Fall (1984), Saunders, James 220
Fall of the House of Usher, The (1974), adaptation by Berkoff, Steven 35
Family Voices (1981), Pinter, Harold 182
Fanshen (1975), Hare, David 111
Farm, The (1973), Storey, David 238
Fart for Europe, A (1973), Edgar, David 74
Fat Harold and the Last Twenty Six (1975), Bleasdale, Alan 38
Fatlips (1978), Wesker, Arnold 253
Favorite Nights (1981), Poliakoff, Stephen 189
Fear of Heaven, The (1976), Mortimer, John 160
Fen (1983), Churchill, Caryl 59
Ffinest Ffamily in the Land, The (1970), Livings, Henry 141
Fill the Stage with Happy Hours (1966), Wood, Charles 267
Filth Hunt, The (1972), Rudkin, David 218
Firstborn, The (1948), Fry, Christopher *see* Verse Drama 250
Fish in the Sea (1973), McGrath, John 146
Fish Out of Water (1971), Brahms, Caryl 44
Five Finger Exercise (1958), Shaffer, Peter 225
Flaming Bodies (1979), Wilson, Snoo 264
Flea in Her Ear, A (1966), adaptation by Mortimer, John 160
Flint (1970), Mercer, David 153
Flowering Cherry, The (1957), Bolt, Robert 40
Fool, The (1975), Bond, Edward 42
Footfalls (1976), Beckett, Samuel 29
For All Those Who Get Despondent (1977), Barnes, Peter 26
Forget-Me-Not-Lane (1971), Nichols, Peter 165
Forty Years On (1968), Bennett, Alan 34
Fosdyke Saga, The (1976), Plater, Alan 185
Four Portraits (1982), Wesker, Arnold 253
Four Seasons, The (1965), Wesker, Arnold 253
Francophile, The (1960), Friel, Brian 84
Freedom of the City, The (1973), Friel, Brian 84
Freeway, The (1974), Nichols, Peter 165
Friday's Hiding (1966), Arden, John and D'Arcy, Margaretta 15
Friends, The (1969), Wesker, Arnold 253
Frozen Assets (1977), Keeffe, Barrie 132
Full Frontal (1979), Hastings, Michael 113
Funny Peculiar (1973), Stott, Mike 239
Fuzz! (1969), Terson, Peter 242

Games (1971), Saunders, James 220
Garden of England, The (1985), McGrath, John 146
Gates of Summer, The (1956), Whiting, John 259
Gem (1977), Keeffe, Barrie 132
Genius, The (1983), Brenton, Howard 46
Gentle Jack (1963), Bolt, Robert 40
Getaway (1977), Keeffe, Barrie 132
Getting On (1971), Bennett, Alan 34
Ghost of Daniel Lambert, The (1981), Townsend, Sue 246
Ghosts (1974), adaptation (of Bauer) Stott, Mike 239
Gimme Shelter (1977), Keeffe, Barrie 132
Girl in Melanie Klein, The (1980), Saunders, James 220
Giveaway, The (1969), Jellicoe, Ann 128
Glad Hand, The (1978), Wilson, Snoo 264
Glasshouses (1981), Lowe, Stephen 143
Gloo Joo (1978), Hastings, Michael 113
Goose-Pimples (1981), Leigh, Mike 138
Gotcha (1977), Keeffe, Barrie 132
Governor's Lady, The (1965), Mercer, David 153
Grass Widow, The (1983), Wilson, Snoo 264
Great Celestial Cow, The (1984), Townsend, Sue 246
Great Exhibition, The (1972), Hare, David 111
Great Jowett, The (1981), Greene, Graham 95
Greek (1979), Berkoff, Steven 35
Greenish Man, A (1979), Wilson, Snoo 264
Groping for Words (1983), Townsend, Sue 246
Gum and Goo (1969), Brenton, Howard 46

H: or Monologues at Front of Burning Cities (1969), Wood, Charles 267

Habeus Corpus (1973), Bennett, Alan 34
Hang of the Gaol, The (1978), Barker, Howard 24
Happy Haven, The (1960), Arden, John 15
Harding's Luck (1974), adaptation by Nichols, Peter 165
Harlequinade (1948), Rattigan, Terence 199
Harold Muggins is a Martyr (1969), Arden, John and D'Arcy, Margaretta 15
Has 'Washington' Legs? (1978), Wood, Charles 267
Having a Ball (1981), Bleasdale, Alan 38
Having a Wonderful Time (1960), Churchill, Caryl 59
Heads (1969), Brenton, Howard 46
Heart of the Matter, The (1950), Greene, Graham 95
Heaven and Hell (1976), Mortimer, John 160
Here Comes the Sun (1976), Keeffe, Barrie 132
Hero Rises Up, The (1968), Arden, John and D'Arcy, Margaretta 15
Hitler Dances (1972), Brenton, Howard 46
Hitting Town (1975), Poliakoff, Stephen 189
Hole, The (1958), Simpson, N.F. 228
Home (1973), Storey, David 238
Homecoming, The (1965), Pinter, Harold 182
Honour and Offer (1969), Livings, Henry 141
Hostage, The (1958), Behan, Brendan 32
Hotel in Amsterdam, The (1968), Osborne, John 174
House That Jack Built, The (1979), Delaney, Shelagh 67
How Beautiful With Badges (1972), Brenton, Howard 46
How the Other Half Loves (1969), Ayckbourn, Alan 21

I Spy (1959), Mortimer, John 160
I'm in Charge of These Ruins (1966), Terson, Peter 242
I'm Talking About Jerusalem (1960), Wesker, Arnold 253
In Celebration (1969), Storey, David 238
In Praise of Love (1973), Rattigan, Terence 199
In the City (1977), Keeffe, Barrie 132
Inadmissible Evidence (1964), Osborne, John 174
Intimate Exchanges (1982), Ayckbourn, Alan 21
Island of the Mighty, The (1972), Arden, John and D'Arcy, Margaretta 15
It Could Be Any One of Us (1983), Ayckbourn, Alan 21
It's a Madhouse (1976), Bleasdale, Alan 38
It's My Criminal (1966), Brenton, Howard 46

Jail Diary of Albie Sachs, The (1978), Edgar, David 74
Jaws of Death, The (1973), Leigh, Mike 138
Jill and Jack (1975), Osborne, John 174
Jockey Club Stakes, The (1970), Home, William Douglas 117
John Mortimer's Casebook (1982), Mortimer, John 160
Joking Apart (1976), Ayckbourn, Alan 21
Journalists, The (1971), Wesker, Arnold 253
Jug (1975), Livings, Henry 141
Judge, The (1967), Mortimer, John 160
Jumpers (1972), Stoppard, Tom 236
Just Between Ourselves (1973), Ayckbourn, Alan 21

Kayf Up West, A (1964), Littlewood, Joan 140
Keeping Body and Soul Together (1984), Lowe, Stephen 143
Kelly's Eye (1963), Livings, Henry 141
Killing Time (1977), Keeffe, Barrie 132
Kingfisher, The (1977), Home, William Douglas 117
Kitchen, The (1959), Wesker, Arnold 253
Knack, The (1961), Jellicoe, Ann 128
Knuckle (1974), Hare, David 111
Krapp's Last Tape (1958), Beckett, Samuel 29

Ladder of Fools (1965), Brenton, Howard 46
Landscape (1969), Pinter, Harold 182
Last Train Through the Harecastle Tunnel, The (1969), Terson, Peter 242
Laughter! (1978), Barnes, Peter 26
Lay-by (1971), Brenton, Howard, Griffiths, Trevor and Hare, David 97 and 111
Lear (1971), Bond, Edward 42
Left-handed Liberty (1965), Arden, John 15
Lenz (1974), Stott, Mike 239
Leonardo's Last Supper (1969), Barnes, Peter 26
Let's Murder Vivaldi (1972), Mercer, David 153
Liberty Hall (1979), Frayn, Michael 82
Liberty Ranch (1972), Brahms, Caryl 44
Life Class (1974), Storey, David 238
Light Shining in Buckinghamshire (1976), Churchill, Caryl 59
Lion in Love, The (1960), Delaney, Shelagh 67
Live Like Pigs (1958), Arden, John 15
Living Quarters (1977), Friel, Brian 84
Living Room, The (1953), Greene, Graham 95
Living Together (1973), Ayckbourn, Alan 24
Little Gray House in the West, The (1978), Arden, John and D'Arcy, Margaretta 15
Lloyd George Knew My Father (1972), Home, William Douglas 117
Londoners, The (1972), Littlewood, Joan 140
Long and the Short and the Tall, The (1958), Hall, Willis 107
Look Back in Anger (1956), Osborne, John 174
Loot (1966), Orton, Joe 172
Lorenzaccio (1976), adaptation by Stott, Mike 239

Lost Empires (1985), Hall, Willis and Waterhouse, Keith 107
Loud Boy's Life, The (1980), Barker, Howard 24
Love Letters on Blue Paper (1978), Wesker, Arnold 253
Love of a Good Man, The (1978), Barker, Howard 24
Lover, The (1963), Pinter, Harold 182
Loves of Cass McGuire, The (1966), Friel, Brian 84
Loving Reno (1983), Wilson, Snoo 264
Lunch Hour (1960), Mortimer, John 160
Luther (1961), Osborne, John 174

Macbird (1967), Littlewood, Joan 140
Mad World, My Masters, A (1977), Keeffe, Barrie 132
Magnificence (1973), Brenton, Howard 46
Make and Break (1980), Frayn, Michael 82
Making Tracks (1983), Ayckbourn, Alan 21
Man For All Seasons, A (1960), Bolt, Robert 40
Man Has Two Fathers, A (1958), McGrath, John 146
Map of the World, A (1983), Hare, David 111
Marching Song (1954), Whiting, John 259
Marie Lloyd Story, The (1967), Littlewood, Joan 140
Mata Hari (1965), Stott, Mike 239
Maydays (1983), Edgar, David 74
Meet My Father (1965), Ayckbourn, Alan 21
Merchant, The (1976), Wesker, Arnold 253
Metamorphosis (1969), adaptation by Berkoff, Steven 35
Midnite at the Starlite (1980), Hastings, Michael 38
Mighty Reservoy, The (1964), Terson, Peter 242
Mitford Girls, The (1981), Brahms, Caryl 44
Molly (1978), Gray, Simon 93
Mooney and his Caravans (1967), Terson, Peter 242
Mother's Day (1976), Storey, David 238
Move Over, Mrs. Markham (1969), Cooney, Ray 61
Mr. Whatnot (1963), Ayckbourn, Alan 21
Murder of Jesus Christ, The (1980), Berkoff, Steven 35
My Girl (1975), Keeffe, Barrie 132

Narrow Road to the Deep North, The (1968), Bond, Edward 42
National Health, The (1969), Nichols, Peter 165
National Interest, The (1972), Edgar, David 74
New House, The (1958), Behan, Brendan 32
Next Time I'll Sing to You (1962), Saunders, James 220
Nicholas Nickleby (1969), adaptation by Brahms, Caryl 44
Nicholas Nickleby (The Life and Times of) (1980), adaptation by Edgar, David 74
Nickleby and Me (1975), Brahms, Caryl 44
Night Out, A (1960), Pinter, Harold 182
Night to Make the Angels Weep, A (1964), Terson, Peter 242
Nil Carborundum (1962), Livings, Henry 141
No Bed for Bacon (1959), Brahms, Caryl 44
No End of Blame (1981), Barker, Howard 24
No Limits to Love (1980), Mercer, David 153
No Man's Land (1975), Pinter, Harold 182
No More A-Roving (1975), Whiting, John 259
No One Was Saved (1970), Barker, Howard 24
No Title (1974), Rudkin, David 218
No Why (1964), Whiting, John 259
Noises Off (1982), Frayn, Michael 82
Non-Stop Connolly Show, The (1975), Arden, John and D'Arcy, Margaretta 15
Noonday Demons (1969), Barnes, Peter 26
Norman Conquests, The (1973), Ayckbourn, Alan 21
Not Now, Darling (1967), Cooney, Ray 61
Nottingham Captain, The (1962), Wesker, Arnold 253
Now Barabbas (1947), Home, William Douglas 117
Number of the Beast, The (1972), Wilson, Snoo 264
Number One (1984), Frayn, Michael 82

Objections to Sex and Violence (1975), Churchill, Caryl 59
Occupations (1970), Griffiths, Trevor 97
Office Suite (1981), Bennett, Alan 34
Oh, Calcutta! (1969), Tynan, Kenneth 248
Oh What! (1975), Leigh, Mike 138
Oh, What a Lovely War! (1963), Littlewood, Joan 140
Ohio Impromptu (1981), Beckett, Samuel 29
Old Country, The (1977), Bennett, Alan 34
Old Ones, The (1972), Wesker, Arnold 253
Old Times (1971), Pinter, Harold 182
On the Razzle (1981), adaptation by Stoppard, Tom 236
On Your Way, Riley (1982), Plater, Alan 185
One For the Pot (1961), Cooney, Ray 61
One For the Road (1984), Pinter, Harold 182
One Man (1982), Berkoff, Steven 35
One More Ride on the Merry-Go-Round (1981), Wesker, Arnold 253
One Way Pendulum (1959), Simpson, N.F. 228
Only a Game (1973), Keeffe, Barrie 132
Only Make Believe (1974), Potter, Dennis 191
Operation Iskra (1977), Edgar, David 74
Other People (1974), Stott, Mike 239
Other Places (1982), Pinter, Harold 182
Otherwise Engaged (1975), Gray, Simon 93
Our Own People (1977), Edgar, David 74
Owners (1972), Churchill, Caryl 59

Party, The (1973), Griffiths, Trevor 97
Party's Over, The (1975), Bleasdale, Alan 38
Passion (1971), Bond, Edward 42
Passion Play (1981), Nichols, Peter 165
Patriot for Me, A (1965), Osborne, John 174
Penal Colony, The (1968), Berkoff, Steven 35
Penny for a Song, A (1951), Whiting, John 259
Personal Enemy (1955), Osborne, John and Creighton, Anthony 174
Philadelphia, Here I Come! (1964), Friel, Brian 84
Philanthropist, The (1970), Hampton, Christopher 108
Phoenix (1984), Storey, David 238
Phoenix Too Frequent, A (1946), Fry, Christopher *see* Verse Drama 250
Picture of Dorian Gray, The (1975), adaptation Osborne, John 174
Piece of Dialogue, A (1980), Beckett, Samuel 29
Place Calling Itself Rome, A (1973), adaptation Osborne, John 174
Playback 625 (1970), Simpson, N.F. 228
Playbill (1948), Rattigan, Terence 199
Plays for England (1962), Osborne, John 174
Pleasure Principle, The (1973), Wilson, Snoo 264
Plenty (1978), Hare, David 111
Plugged In (1972), McGrath, John 146
Pongo Plays (1970), Livings, Henry 141
Pope's Wedding, The (1962), Bond, Edward 42
Poppy (1982), Nichols, Peter 165
Portage to San Cristobal of A.H., The (1982), adaptation by Hampton, Christopher 108
Potting Shed, The (1957), Greene, Graham 95
Power of the Dog, The (1984), Barker, Howard 24
Prez (1984), Plater, Alan 185
Prince of Darkness, The (1976), Mortimer, John 160
Private Ear, The (1962), Shaffer, Peter 225
Private Parts (1972), Barker, Howard 24
Privates on Parade (1977), Nichols, Peter 165
Projector, The (1970), Littlewood, Joan 140
Public Eye, The (1962), Shaffer, Peter 225

Quare Fellow, The (1954), Behan, Brendan 32
Quartermaine's Terms (1981), Gray, Simon 93

Ragged Trousered Philanthropists, The (1978), adaptation by Lowe, Stephen 143
Random Happenings in the Hebrides (1970), McGrath, John 146
Random Moments in a May Garden (1980), Saunders, James 220
Real Thing, The (1982), Stoppard, Tom 236
Rear Column, The (1978), Gray, Simon 93
Reckoning, The (1979), Jellicoe, Ann 128
Red Noses (1985), Barnes, Peter 26
Red Star (1984), Wood, Charles 267
Referees, The (1963), Plater, Alan 185
Relative Values (1951), Coward, Noël 62
Relatively Speaking (1977), Ayckbourn, Alan 21
Reluctant Debutante, The (1955), Home, William Douglas 117
Reluctant Peer, The (1964), Home, William Douglas 117
Rent, or Caught in the Act (1972), Edgar, David 74
Resounding Tinkle, A (1957), Simpson, N.F. 228
Restoration (1981), Bond, Edward 42
Restoration of Arnold Middleton, The (1966), Storey, David 238
Return of A.J. Raffles, The (1975), Greene, Graham 95
Revenge (1969), Brenton, Howard 46
Richard's Cork Leg (1972), Behan, Brendan 32
Ride a Cock Horse (1965), Mercer, David 153
Rockaby (1982), Beckett, Samuel 29
Romans in Britain, The (1980), Brenton, Howard 46
Room, The (1957), Pinter, Harold 182
Roots (1959), Wesker, Arnold 253
Rosencrantz and Gildenstern Are Dead (1966), Stoppard, Tom 236
Ross: a Dramatic Portrait (1960), Rattigan, Terence 199
Round and Round the Garden (1973), Ayckbourn, Alan 21
Royal Hunt of the Sun, The (1964), Shaffer, Peter 225
Royal Pardon, The (1966), Arden, John and D'Arcy, Margaretta 15
Ruffian on the Stair, The (1967), Orton, Joe 172
Ruling Class, The (1968), Barnes, Peter 26
Run For Your Wife (1982), Cooney, Ray 61

Saint's Day (1951), Whiting, John 259
Sam, Sam (1972), Griffiths, Trevor 97
Sandboy, The (1971), Frayn, Michael 82
Saturday, Sunday, Monday (1973), Hall, Willis and Waterhouse, Keith 107
Savages (1973), Hampton, Christopher 108
Saved (1965), Bond, Edward 42
Say Who You Are (1965), Hall, Willis and Waterhouse, Keith 107
Scent of Flowers, A (1964), Saunders, James 220
Schreber's Nervous Illness (1972), Churchill, Caryl 59
Sclerosis (1965), Barnes, Peter 26
Scott of the Antarctic (1971), Brenton, Howard 46
Scribes (1975), Keeffe, Barrie 132
Sea, The (1973), Bond, Edward 42
Sea Change (1984), Lowe, Stephen 143
Seaside Postcard (1977), Frisby, Terence 85
Season's Greetings (1982), Ayckbourn, Alan 21

Secret Diary of Adrian Mole Aged 13¾, The (1984), Townsend, Sue 246
Secretary Bird, The (1968), Home, William Douglas 117
Sense of Detachment, A (1972), Osborne, John 174
Separate Tables (1954), Rattigan, Terence 199
Sergeant Musgrave's Dance (1959), Arden, John 15
Shelley: or, The Idealist (1965), Jellicoe, Ann 128
She's So Modern (1980), Keeffe, Barrie 132
Shooting, Fishing and Riding (1977), Lowe, Stephen 143
Short Sharp Shock!, A (1980), Brenton, Howard 46
Shout Across the River (1978), Poliakoff, Stephen 189
Sight of Glory, A (1975), Keeffe, Barrie 132
Signed and Sealed (1976), Hampton, Christopher 108
Silence (1960), Pinter, Harold 182
Silence of Lee Harvey Oswald, The (1966), Hastings, Michael 113
Simon Says! (1970), Plater, Alan and Glasgow, Alex 185
Sing a Rude Song (1970), Brahms, Caryl 44
Sisterly Feelings (1979), Ayckbourn, Alan 21
Sisters (1978), Storey, David 238
Sky-Blue Life, A (1966), Brenton, Howard 46
Slag (1970), Hare, David 111
Sleep of Prisoners, A (1951), Fry, Christopher *see* Verse Drama 250
Sleeping Policemen (1983), Brenton, Howard 46
Sleeping Prince, The (1953), Rattigan, Terence 199
Slight Ache, A (1961), Pinter, Harold 182
Smashing Day, A (1965), Plater, Alan 185
So You Want to Be in Pictures? (1973), Littlewood, Joan 140
Soft or a Girl (1971), McGrath, John 146
Softcops (1984), Churchill, Caryl 59
Son of Man (1969), Potter, Dennis 191
Sons of Light, The (1976), Rudkin, David 218
Sore Throats (1979), Brenton, Howard 46
Sovereignty Under Elizabeth (1978), Rudkin, David 218
Spoiled (1971), Gray, Simon 93
Spoils, The (1968), Brahms, Caryl 44
Sponge Room, The (1963), Hall, Willis 107
Sport of My Mad Mother, The (1958), Jellicoe, Ann 128
Spring-heeled Jack (1970), Terson, Peter 242
Squat Betty (1962), Hall, Willis 107
Stage-Struck (1979), Gray, Simon 93
State of Emergency (1972), Edgar, David 174
State of Revolution (1977), Bolt, Robert 40
Stone (1976), Bond, Edward 42
Stop It, Whoever You Are (1961), Livings, Henry 141
Strawberry Fields (1977), Poliakoff, Stephen 189
Strippers (1984), Terson, Peter 242
Stripwell (1975), Barker, Howard 24
Strive (1983), Lowe, Stephen 143
Subject of Scandal and Concern, A (1960), Osborne, John 174
Subtopians, The (1964), Frisby, Terence 85
Suburban Strains (1982), Ayckbourn, Alan 21
Sufficient Carbohydrate (1983), Potter, Dennis 191
Suite in Three Keys (1966), Coward, Noël 62
Sullied Hands (1982), Wesker, Arnold 253
Summer (1982), Bond, Edward 42
Summer Party, The (1979), Poliakoff, Stephen 189
Sus (1979), Keeffe, Barrie 132
Swallows on the Water (1973), Plater, Alan 185

Table Manners (1973), Ayckbourn, Alan 21
Taking Steps (1980), Ayckbourn, Alan 21
Tales from Hollywood (1982) Hampton, Christopher 108
Tales of Humberside (1975), Plater, Alan 185
Taste of Honey, A (1958), Delaney, Shelagh 67
Teendreams (1979), Edgar, David 74
Teeth 'n' Smiles (1975), Hare, David 111
Ten Times Table (1977), Ayckbourn, Alan 21
That Good Between Us (1976), Barker, Howard 24
That Time (1976), Beckett, Samuel 29
Their Very Own and Golden City (1965), Wesker, Arnold 253
Then and Now (1979), Mercer, David 153
There Goes the Bride (1974), Cooney, Ray 61
There is a Happy Land (1957), Hall, Willis 107
There's a Girl in My Soup (1966), Frisby, Terence 85
Thermidore (1971), Griffiths, Trevor 97
Thirteenth Night (1981), Brenton, Howard 46
Thistle and the Rose, The (1949), Home, William Douglas 117
Three More Sleepless Nights (1980), Churchill, Caryl 59
Thwarting of Baron Bolligrew, The (1965), Bolt, Robert 40
Tibetan Inroads (1981), Lowe, Stephen 143
Tide, The (1980), Jellicoe, Ann 128
Tiger and the Horse, The (1960), Bolt, Robert 40
Tigers are Coming, O.K., The (1973), Plater, Alan 185
Time and Time Again (1977), Ayckbourn, Alan 21
Time of the Barracudas, The (1963), Barnes, Peter 26
Time Present (1968), Osborne, John 174
Tom and Viv (1984), Hastings, Michael 113

Top Girls (1982), Churchill, Caryl 59
Total Eclipse (1968), Hampton, Christopher 108
Touched (1977), Lowe, Stephen 143
Translations (1981), Friel, Brian 84
Traps (1977), Churchill, Caryl 59
Travesties (1974), Stoppard, Tom 236
Treats (1976), Hampton, Christopher 108
Trees in the Wind (1971), McGrath, John 146
Trial, The (1970), adapted by Berkoff, Steven 35
Trinity Tales (1975), Plater, Alan 185
Truer Shade of Blue, A (1970), Edgar, David 74
Two Into One (1984), Cooney, Ray 61
Two Kinds of Angel (1970), Edgar, David 74
Two of Us, The (1970), Frayn, Michael 82
Two Stars for Comfort (1962), Mortimer, John 160

Under Plain Cover (1962), Osborne, John 174
Underneath (1972), McGrath, John 146
Up Your End (1970), Littlewood, Joan 140

Vampire (1973), Wilson, Snoo 264
Vandaleur's Folly (1978), Arden, John and D'Arcy, Margaretta 15
Variations on 'The Merchant of Venice' (1977), Marowitz, Charles 150
Venus Observed (1950), Fry, Christopher *see* Verse Drama 250
Veterans (1972), Wood, Charles 267
Victoria Station (1984), Pinter, Harold 182
Victory (1983), Barker, Howard 24
Vinegar Tom (1976), Churchill, Caryl 59
Vivat! Vivat! Regina! (1970), Bolt, Robert 40
Volunteers (1975), Friel, Brian 84
Vote, Vote, Vote for Nigel Barton (1968), Potter, Dennis 191
Voyage Round My Father, A (1970), Mortimer, John 160

Wages of Thin (1969), Griffiths, Trevor 97
Waiting for Godot (1955), Beckett, Samuel 29
Waiting in the Wings (1960), Coward, Noël 62
War Plays (1985), Bond, Edward 42
Was He Anyone? (1972), Simpson, N.F. 228
Watch It Come Down (1976), Osborne, John 174
Waters of Babylon, The (1957), Arden, John 15
Way Upstream, (1982), Ayckbourn, Alan 21
Wax (1976), Barker, Howard 24
Weapons of Happiness (1976), Brenton, Howard 46
Wedding Feast, The (1974), adaptation by Wesker, Arnold 253
Well ... Goodnight Then (1978), Plater, Alan 185
Wesley (1970), Brenton, Howard 46
West (1983), Berkoff, Steven 35
West of Suez (1971), Osborne, John 174
Western Women, The (1984), Jellicoe, Ann 128
What Shall We Tell Caroline? (1958), Mortimer, John 160
What the Butler Saw (1969), Orton, Joe 172
What Where (1983), Beckett, Samuel 29
When Did You Last See My Mother? (1964), Hampton, Christopher 108
White Liars, The (1968), Shaffer, Peter 225
Wholesome Glory (1973), Leigh, Mike 138
Why Not Stay For Breakfast? (1973), Cooney, Ray 61
Winslow Boy, The (1946), Rattigan, Terence 199
Winter, Daddykins (1966), Brenton, Howard 46
Wise Child (1967), Gray, Simon 93
Woman, The (1978), Bond, Edward 42
Woman in Mind (1985), Ayckbourn, Alan 21
Woomberang (1979), Townsend, Sue 246
Workhouse Donkey, The (1963), Arden, John 15
World of Paul Slickey, The (1959), Osborne, John 174
Wreckers (1977), Edgar, David 74
Wrong Side of the Park, The (1960), Mortimer, John 160

Yard of Sun, A (1970), Fry, Christopher *see* Verse Drama 250
Yes — And After (1957), Hastings, Michael 113
Yes and No (1980), Greene, Graham 95
Yobbo Nowt (1975), McGrath, John 146
Yonadab (1985), Shaffer, Peter 225

Zigger-Zagger (1967), Terson, Peter 242